A Da Capo Press Reprint Series

FRANKLIN D. ROOSEVELT AND THE ERA OF THE NEW DEAL

GENERAL EDITOR: FRANK FREIDEL
Harvard University

STATE PUBLIC WELFARE LEGISLATION

Division of Research
Work Projects Administration

Research Monographs

I. Six Rural Problem Areas, Relief—Resources—Rehabilitation

II. Comparative Study of Rural Relief and Non-Relief Households

III. The Transient Unemployed

IV. Urban Workers on Relief

V. Landlord and Tenant on the Cotton Plantation

VI. Chronology of the Federal Emergency Relief Administration May 12, 1933, to December 31, 1935

VII. The Migratory-Casual Worker

VIII. Farmers on Relief and Rehabilitation

IX. Part-Time Farming in the Southeast

X. Trends in Relief Expenditures, 1910-1935

XI. Rural Youth on Relief

XII. Intercity Differences in Costs of Living in March 1935, 59 Cities

XIII. Effects of the Works Program on Rural Relief

XIV. Changing Aspects of Rural Relief

XV. Rural Youth: Their Situation and Prospects

XVI. Farming Hazards in the Drought Area

XVII. Rural Families on Relief

XVIII. Migrant Families

XIX. Rural Migration in the United States

XX. State Public Welfare Legislation

XXI. Youth in Agricultural Villages

XXII. The Plantation South, 1934-1937

XXIII. Seven Stranded Coal Towns

XXIV. Federal Work, Security, and Relief Programs

XXV. Vocational Training and Employment of Youth

XXVI. Getting Started: Urban Youth in the Labor Market

Works Progress Administration
Division of Social Research
Research Monograph XX

STATE PUBLIC
WELFARE LEGISLATION

By Robert C. Lowe

DA CAPO PRESS • NEW YORK • 1971

A Da Capo Press Reprint Edition

This Da Capo Press edition of *State Public Welfare Legislation* is an unabridged republication of the first edition published in Washington, D.C., in 1939. It is reprinted by permission from a copy of the original edition owned by the Harvard College Library.

Library of Congress Catalog Card Number 75-165602

ISBN 0-306-70352-1

Published by Da Capo Press, Inc.
A Subsidiary of Plenum Publishing Corporation
227 West 17th Street, New York, N.Y. 10011
All Rights Reserved

Manufactured in the United States of America

STATE PUBLIC
WELFARE LEGISLATION

WORKS PROGRESS ADMINISTRATION
F. C. Harrington, *Administrator*
Corrington Gill, *Assistant Administrator*

DIVISION OF RESEARCH
Howard B. Myers, *Director*

STATE
PUBLIC WELFARE
LEGISLATION

By

Robert C. Lowe

•

RESEARCH MONOGRAPH XX

1939

UNITED STATES GOVERNMENT PRINTING OFFICE, WASHINGTON

Letter of Transmittal

WORKS PROGRESS ADMINISTRATION
Washington, D. C., March 20, 1939.

Sir: I have the honor to transmit an analysis of public welfare legislation in the 48 States, Alaska, Hawaii, and the District of Columbia as of January 1, 1939. This analysis brings together in one volume, for the first time, current information on the State legislative and constitutional provisions governing public welfare. The emphasis in this report is placed upon the laws providing for relief and public assistance, but appendix material is included to indicate the scope of public welfare legislation in each State.

Effective coordination of the Works Progress Administration with State and local relief programs has required complete information on the provisions for relief and public assistance in the States. State and local relief agencies have been called upon to assume important duties in relation to the Works Program, the most important of which has been to certify the need and employability of persons seeking employment on work projects.

State welfare provisions have also had a very important bearing upon the policy of the Works Progress Administration in connection with assistance to special groups like the aged and persons with dependent children. In order to determine whether individuals on projects are eligible for such special types of care, it has been necessary to digest and analyze the provisions made for them in State laws.

The analysis has spotlighted the great diversity among States in the financial provisions for the administration of relief and in the availability of funds for sponsors' contributions for WPA projects.

Prior to 1931 the majority of States relied principally upon the old poor laws to assist persons in need of relief. Less than one-half of the States had enacted blind pension laws, and only about one-fourth had provided for old age pensions. With the exception of laws providing for veterans' pensions and State institutions for veterans and children, the statutes effective before 1931 for the most part placed the administrative and financial responsibility upon local units of government. The principle of supplying employment instead of relief had not yet been accepted even though many of the poor laws required able-bodied recipients to work in return for aid.

The first State emergency relief administrations were established in 1931, and by 1933 the majority of States had established such administrations and had appropriated funds for relief of the unemployed. Many of the States took such action in response to the Federal Emergency Relief Act of 1933.

In 1933 States began to adopt categorical relief programs with increasing rapidity; this movement was greatly accelerated by the adoption of the Federal Social Security Act in 1935.

With the passage of the Social Security Act there began a definite trend toward the assumption by the States of both administrative and financial responsibility for permanent general relief and public assistance programs. The majority of States participate in all these programs at the present time, although fewer States assume responsibility for general relief than for categorical assistance.

Recognition of the necessity of coordinating measures designed to assist persons in need has caused a trend toward the integration of State relief and public assistance programs. By January 1, 1939, approximately one-third of the States had placed the administrative responsibility for all of their public welfare functions within a single agency, and most of the other States had accomplished some degree of integration.

The study was made in the Division of Research under the direction of Howard B. Myers, Director of Research. It was prepared by Robert C. Lowe under the supervision of A. Ross Eckler, Assistant Director. Tabular and other appendix materials were prepared by L. T. Bennett, Jr., Frances Engeman, William H. Garner, John A. Hanley, Alfred Noyes, and Mary P. Ragatz under the supervision of Mr. Lowe. Gertrude Bancroft and Theodore Savage assisted in the editing of this report.

Special acknowledgment is due the members of the staff of the Bureau of Public Assistance of the Social Security Board and Robert T. Lansdale, Professor of Public Welfare, New York School of Social Work, for their helpful suggestions.

Respectfully submitted.

CORRINGTON GILL,
Assistant Administrator.

COL. F. C. HARRINGTON,
Works Progress Administrator.

Contents

	Page
Introduction _	XIII
Section I. Development of public welfare in the United States _ _ _ _ _ _ _ _ _ _ _ _ _ _ _ _ _ _ _	1
Section II. Eligibility provisions and types of care granted recipients of relief and public assistance _ _ _ _ _ _ _ _ _ _ _ _ _ _ _ _ _	7
General relief _	7
Old age assistance _ _ _ _ _ _ _ _ _ _ _ _ _ _ _ _ _ _	9
Blind assistance _ _ _ _ _ _ _ _ _ _ _ _ _ _ _ _ _ _ _	11
Dependent children _ _ _ _ _ _ _ _ _ _ _ _ _ _ _ _ _ _	13
Aid to dependent children in their own homes _ _ _	13
Dependent and neglected children _ _ _ _ _ _ _ _	15
Veteran relief _	16
Section III. Administrative responsibility for relief and public assistance _ _ _ _ _ _ _ _ _ _ _ _	19
Incidence of administrative responsibility _ _ _ _ _ _	20
General relief _ _ _ _ _ _ _ _ _ _ _ _ _ _ _ _ _ _ _	20
Old age assistance _ _ _ _ _ _ _ _ _ _ _ _ _ _ _ _ _	20
Blind assistance _ _ _ _ _ _ _ _ _ _ _ _ _ _ _ _ _ _	20
Aid to dependent children in their own homes _ _ _	20
Dependent and neglected children _ _ _ _ _ _ _ _	21
Veteran relief _ _ _ _ _ _ _ _ _ _ _ _ _ _ _ _ _ _ _	22
Section IV. Provisions for administrative procedures for the determination of eligibility for relief and public assistance_ _ _ _ _ _ _ _ _ _ _	23
Final original determination _ _ _ _ _ _ _ _ _ _ _ _ _	23
Relief and public assistance other than care of dependent and neglected children by agencies and in institutions_ _ _ _ _ _ _ _ _ _ _ _ _ _ _ _	23
Dependent and neglected children _ _ _ _ _ _ _ _	25
Appeals and fair hearings_ _ _ _ _ _ _ _ _ _ _ _ _	26
Complaints _	27
Review on own motion and further investigation _ _	27
Section V. Provisions for the financing of relief and public assistance_ _ _ _ _ _ _ _ _ _ _ _ _ _	29
Provisions for the distribution of State funds _ _ _ _	30
Sources of funds for relief and public assistance_ _ _	31

Page

Section VI. Integration of public welfare functions within a single State agency _ _ _ _ _ _ _ _ _ _ _ _ 33
  Relief and public assistance _ _ _ _ _ _ _ _ _ _ _ _ _ _ 33
  General public welfare program _ _ _ _ _ _ _ _ _ _ _ _ 34
Section VII. Types of State and local agencies administering relief and public assistance _ _ _ 37
  State boards of public welfare _ _ _ _ _ _ _ _ _ _ _ _ _ 37
    Organization _ _ _ _ _ _ _ _ _ _ _ _ _ _ _ _ _ _ _ 37
    Qualifications _ _ _ _ _ _ _ _ _ _ _ _ _ _ _ _ _ _ 37
    Selection and appointment_ _ _ _ _ _ _ _ _ _ _ _ _ 38
    Terms of office_ _ _ _ _ _ _ _ _ _ _ _ _ _ _ _ _ _ 38
    Compensation _ _ _ _ _ _ _ _ _ _ _ _ _ _ _ _ _ _ _ 38
  Executive of State department of public welfare_ _ _ _ 38
    Selection and appointment_ _ _ _ _ _ _ _ _ _ _ _ _ 39
    Terms of office_ _ _ _ _ _ _ _ _ _ _ _ _ _ _ _ _ _ 39
    Qualifications _ _ _ _ _ _ _ _ _ _ _ _ _ _ _ _ _ _ 39
    Compensation _ _ _ _ _ _ _ _ _ _ _ _ _ _ _ _ _ _ _ 39
  Local departments of public welfare_ _ _ _ _ _ _ _ _ _ 39
    Organization _ _ _ _ _ _ _ _ _ _ _ _ _ _ _ _ _ _ _ 40
    Functions of local boards_ _ _ _ _ _ _ _ _ _ _ _ _ 40
    Qualifications of local boards _ _ _ _ _ _ _ _ _ _ 40
    Selection and appointment of local boards_ _ _ _ _ 41
    Terms of office of local boards_ _ _ _ _ _ _ _ _ _ 41
    Compensation of local boards _ _ _ _ _ _ _ _ _ _ _ 41
  Local executive_ 41
Appendix A. Basic tables _ _ _ _ _ _ _ _ _ _ _ _ _ _ _ _ _ 45

GENERAL RELIEF

Table
1. Provisions for the administration of general relief_ 48
2. Requirements for eligibility for general relief _ _ 54
3. Responsibility of relatives and provisions for recovery of cost of general relief from recipients and their estates _ _ _ _ _ _ _ _ _ _ _ _ _ _ _ _ 63
4. Provisions affecting status of recipients of general relief_ 68
5. Provisions for types of aid granted and for financing general relief_ _ _ _ _ _ _ _ _ _ _ _ _ _ _ _ 70

OLD AGE ASSISTANCE

6. Provisions for the administration of old age assistance_ 78
7. Personal qualifications for old age assistance_ _ _ 84
8. Need qualifications for old age assistance_ _ _ _ _ 87
9. Types of aid received or needed which disqualify applicants for old age assistance _ _ _ _ _ _ _ _ 90

Table   *Page*

10. Provisions for recovery of cost of old age assistance from recipients and their estates _ _ _ _ _   92
11. Provisions for granting and financing old age assistance _ _ _ _ _ _ _ _ _ _ _ _ _ _ _ _ _ _   96

BLIND ASSISTANCE

12. Provisions for the administration of blind assistance_   102
13. Personal qualifications for blind assistance _ _ _   109
14. Need qualifications for blind assistance _ _ _ _ _   113
15. Types of aid received or needed which disqualify applicants for blind assistance_ _ _ _ _ _ _ _ _   115
16. Provisions for recovery from recipients and their estates for blind assistance granted _ _ _ _ _ _   117
17. Provisions for granting and financing blind assistance _   119

AID TO DEPENDENT CHILDREN IN THEIR OWN HOMES

18. Provisions for the administration of aid to dependent children in their own homes_ _ _ _ _ _ _ _ _ _ _   126
19. Personal qualifications for aid to dependent children in their own homes _ _ _ _ _ _ _ _ _ _ _ _ _ _   132
20. Need qualifications for aid to dependent children in their own homes_ _ _ _ _ _ _ _ _ _ _ _ _ _ _ _   136
21. Provisions for granting and financing aid to dependent children in their own homes_ _ _ _ _ _ _ _ _   140

DEPENDENT AND NEGLECTED CHILDREN (INSTITUTIONS AND AGENCIES)

22. Characteristics of dependent and neglected children coming within jurisdiction of juvenile courts_ _   148
23. Provisions for instituting proceedings, investigations, and hearing of cases of dependent and neglected children by juvenile courts _ _ _ _ _ _ _   149
24. Types of homes and institutions to which dependent and neglected children may be committed by juvenile courts_ _ _ _ _ _ _ _ _ _ _ _ _ _ _ _ _ _   151
25. State institutions caring for dependent and neglected children _   152
26. Major powers and duties of principal public agencies in relation to care of dependent and neglected children outside of own homes or State institutions_   158
27. Governmental unit responsible for financing specified types of care for dependent and neglected children_   176

VETERAN RELIEF

28. Personal and other qualifications for eligibility for direct relief to veterans_ _ _ _ _ _ _ _ _ _   178

Table   *Page*

29. Provisions for the administration and financing of
    direct relief to veterans- - - - - - - - - - - - - -   182
30. Personal and other qualifications for eligibility
    for pensions to veterans - - - - - - - - - - - - -   187
31. Provisions for the administration and financing of
    pensions to veterans - - - - - - - - - - - - - - -   192
32. Personal and other qualifications for eligibility
    for institutional care for veterans- - - - - - - -   196
33. Provisions for the administration and financing of
    institutional care for veterans- - - - - - - - -   203

STATE BOARDS AND LOCAL BOARDS

34. Composition and appointment of State boards of pub-
    lic welfare-   210
35. Appointment and qualifications of executives of
    State boards or departments of public welfare- -   221
36. Composition and appointment of local boards of pub-
    lic welfare-   226
37. Appointment and qualifications of executives of
    local boards or departments of public welfare- -   234

CITATIONS TO STATUTORY PROVISIONS

38. Citations to statutory provisions contained in tables
    1—37-   241
**Appendix B. Supplementary tables (summary of provisions
            enacted from July I, 1938, to January I,
            1939)**- - - - - - - - - - - - - - - - - -   253
California (table 1, p. 254; table 5, p. 255).
Illinois (table 37, p. 266).
Louisiana (table 1, p. 254; table 6, p. 256; table 7, p. 257;
    table 9, p. 258; table 10, p. 258; table 11, p. 259; table
    12, p. 260; table 13, p. 261; table 14, p. 262; table 15,
    p. 262; table 16, p. 262; table 17, p. 263; table 18, p.
    264; table 21, p. 264; table 34, p. 265; table 36, p. 266;
    table 37, p. 266).
Massachusetts (table 5, p. 255).
New Jersey (table 6, p. 256; table 7, p. 257; table 8, p. 257;
    table 10, p. 258; table 11, p. 259).
Ohio (table 1, p. 254; table 2, p. 254; table 5, p. 255; table
    35, p. 265).
Rhode Island (table 12, p. 260; table 13, p. 261; table 14,
    p. 262; table 15, p. 262; table 16, p. 262; table 17, p. 263).
**Appendix C. Summaries of State provisions for public wel-
            fare and charts of State and local public
            welfare agencies** - - - - - - - - - - - - -   267
Alabama-   268
Arizona-   271

	Page
Arkansas	273
California	275
Colorado	278
Connecticut	280
Delaware	282
Florida	284
Georgia	286
Idaho	289
Illinois	291
Indiana	294
Iowa	297
Kansas	299
Kentucky	301
Louisiana	303
Maine	305
Maryland	308
Massachusetts	310
Michigan	313
Minnesota	316
Mississippi	319
Missouri	321
Montana	323
Nebraska	326
Nevada	329
New Hampshire	331
New Jersey	333
New Mexico	336
New York	338
North Carolina	341
North Dakota	344
Ohio	347
Oklahoma	350
Oregon	353
Pennsylvania	356
Rhode Island	359
South Carolina	362
South Dakota	365
Tennessee	368
Texas	371
Utah	374
Vermont	377
Virginia	380
Washington	382
West Virginia	385
Wisconsin	388
Wyoming	391
Alaska	393
District of Columbia	395
Hawaii	397

State Public Welfare Legislation

XI

INTRODUCTION

THIS STUDY of State public welfare legislation in the United States presents in tabular and digest form the basic laws which provide the foundation for public welfare programs of the States, Territories, and the District of Columbia, with particular emphasis on those statutes which provide for aid and relief to dependent persons. It also analyzes some of the major trends in relief and public assistance legislation occurring since 1930.

The study, current as of January 1, 1939, is based on an intensive analysis of constitutional provisions, statutes, opinions of attorneys general, and the case law of the several States and Territories. The operation of laws, of course, depends to some extent upon amplifications and interpretations by administrative rules and regulations, opinions of attorneys general, and court decisions, and to a greater extent upon the individuals responsible for their administration. Administrative rules and regulations have not been included, but correspondence has been carried on with attorneys general and various other State officials to secure interpretations and to clarify the laws of individual States where conflicts and ambiguities have appeared.

Details of the laws providing for the relief of dependency—i.e., general relief, old age assistance, aid to dependent children in their own homes, blind assistance, care of dependent and neglected children by agencies and institutions, and veteran relief—are presented in a series of tables. (The term *relief and public assistance* whenever used in the text is intended to include all of these functions.)[1] Tabulations of the laws providing for the composition and appointment of the governing

---

[1] Wide differences of opinion exist as to the definition of relief and public assistance. The above classification which has been adopted for the purpose of the present analysis is used with full knowledge that it may not be acceptable to all students of the field. An attempt has been made to include all statutes which provide for the expenditure of public funds for persons who are in need and who do not require specialized treatment because of physical handicaps, mental deficiencies, or moral delinquencies. It is recognized that overlapping exists in this classification: for example, blind assistance statutes which provide for money payments to needy blind

bodies and executives of the more important State and local agencies concerned with the administration of these programs are also presented.[2]

The headings on the tables are for the most part self-explanatory. In some cases the actual legal provision has been summarized and used as a caption. An attempt has been made to follow the same pattern in each series of tables. In general they indicate the following points: the nature of the law (mandatory or optional), location and type of administrative responsibility, qualifications and limitations imposed upon applicants and recipients, type and amount of aid, and financial responsibility.

The complete public welfare program in each State has been summarized in an appendix which also includes charts of the statutory and constitutional public welfare organization for each State. The functions, which in this study are uniformly considered to be of a public welfare nature, are those providing for dependent, handicapped, defective, and delinquent persons. The provisions for the relief of dependency are: general relief, old age assistance, aid to dependent children in their own homes, blind assistance, care of dependent and neglected children by agencies and institutions, and veteran relief. Functions performed for the welfare of handicapped and defective persons are: the care and treatment of the insane, the feeble-minded, and the epileptics; and services to the blind.

---

individuals also contain provision for supplementary services to prevent blindness or to remove the disability.

Questions may be raised as to the desirability of including the care of dependent and neglected children in foster homes and institutions as well as aid to dependent children in their own homes among relief and public assistance functions. Despite the fact that important factors other than need are involved in caring for dependent and neglected children, this function has been included for the following reasons: many children are placed in foster homes and institutions because they are in need and expenditures for their care are made from public funds; moreover, several of the State statutes do not distinguish between the types of care granted children, and make provision for money payments to foster homes and institutions caring for children in the same manner as for children who are cared for by relatives in their own homes; in addition, powers and duties relative to foster home and institutional care of children are vested in several of the State agencies established to administer or supervise relief and public assistance, exclusive of other public welfare functions.

Questions also may be raised as to the desirability of including statutes which provide for the care of veterans without prescribing need. The three types of statutes included under veteran relief in this study are those making special provision for direct relief, pensions, and institutional care. All of the statutes providing for direct relief to veterans prescribe need as a condition for eligibility. About one-half of the State statutes providing for veterans' pensions and most of the laws providing institutional care prescribe need. Complete coverage of statutes falling within these three groups has necessitated the inclusion of those statutes which do not specify need. Whether or not need is a condition to eligibility is indicated on tables 28, 30, and 32.

[2] Nearly one-third of the State agencies which have administrative or supervisory powers in relation to relief and public assistance also have the responsibility for the administration or supervision of the majority of public welfare functions performed by the State.

Provisions for delinquents include: care, confinement, and reformation of juvenile and adult delinquents; and the administration of parole and probation. Among the borderline functions, which are considered only in those States where the responsibility for their administration has been placed within a department of public welfare, are: care of crippled children; maternal and child health; education of the deaf, the dumb, and the blind; vocational rehabilitation; and care of persons afflicted with tuberculosis.[3]

[3]The above determination of functions to be covered by the present analysis was made by the following method. For the purpose of the original studies (Digest of Public Welfare Provisions Under the Laws of the Several States) upon which this part of the analysis is based, any function the administration of which was placed by law within a State department of public welfare or similar agency in any State was considered to be a public welfare function in every State, and all State laws providing for these functions were analyzed. Upon the completion of these studies a reappraisal was made to determine what functions should be consistently considered of a public welfare nature. Certain functions which were contained in these State studies but which are performed more frequently by departments of education and departments of public health and are considered by authorities to be more appropriately educational or health functions were thus eliminated from the scope of the present report. However, in States where the administration of these functions is placed within a public welfare department, they have been included in order to indicate the breadth of activity of the particular department.

Section I

DEVELOPMENT OF PUBLIC WELFARE IN THE UNITED STATES

THE PRINCIPLE of public responsibility for the dependent classes was recognized by the English poor laws. The English system of poor relief dates back to the fourteenth century, but it was not until the Poor Relief Act of 1601 that a unified system was established. This act which was incorporated into colonial statutes formed the basis for colonial poor relief systems.

The early colonial laws provided only custody for dependent, defective, and delinquent persons who received practically the same treatment. Prior to 1700 the boarding of paupers with local citizens was an established practice, since neither cash relief nor almshouse care was common. Jails housed delinquents of all ages. The insane, if homeless and indigent, received care as paupers, perhaps by the lowest bidder willing to assume charge of such persons; if the insane were considered to be dangerous to the community they were thrown into jail; if they were not paupers and were not destructive they were given no care.

In the New England colonies responsibility for poor relief devolved upon the towns. The Southern colonies adopted the county as the administrative unit. In the Middle colonies a combination of the two systems existed with responsibility in some instances placed upon counties and in other instances upon towns, townships, and other local governmental units. In Virginia and Maryland the care of indigents and the insane rested with the vestries of the established church until the Revolutionary War dissolved the relation of church and State. At this time county boards of overseers of the poor were created to assume the function of the church in the administration of relief. The colonial systems were carried over unchanged by the State governments after the revolution.

Specialized care of the dependent, defective, and delinquent groups developed slowly during the eighteenth century and the early part of the nineteenth century. It was not until the latter half of the nineteenth century that the need for differentiation in types of care given each group and for classification within the defective and delinquent groups began to be recognized. Classification of dependent persons, however, did not take place to any great extent until after 1900.

Specialized treatment first took the form of institutional care of insane and delinquent persons. The first attempt at institutional care of the insane as a specialized class was in 1752 in connection with the Pennsylvania Hospital at Philadelphia. The first State institution in the United States devoted exclusively to the care of the insane was opened at Williamsburg, Virginia, in 1773. A few other State institutions were opened early in the nineteenth century, and in 1843 the Utica State Hospital in New York, soon to become a model for other such institutions, was established. In the meantime a few sectarian, private, and semiprivate institutions for the insane had been established, some of which were later taken over by the State or were opened to public patients at State, county, or local expense.

The earliest institutions for the care of criminals and misdemeanants were local jails. The first significant change in our prison system came in 1790 when Pennsylvania inaugurated the classification of prisoners according to the offense committed. Later the Auburn State Prison in New York State, established in 1816, became a model prison for other States. New York established a parole system in 1876, and Massachusetts passed the first State probation law in 1878.

The first State institution for delinquent children was provided in Massachusetts in 1854. The first juvenile court was created in Illinois in 1899.

Special institutions, both custodial and educational, for the feeble-minded and the epileptic were established in New York, Massachusetts, and Ohio before 1900. Workshops for the adult blind and special hospitals for the crippled were also established in a few States before the turn of the century.

With the establishment of State institutions, there developed a need for a centralized State agency for the control or supervision of institutional care. Massachusetts created the first State board of charities in 1863. New York and Ohio established such boards in 1867, and other State boards of welfare, with varying scopes of activities, were later established in practically all of the States.

Since 1900 there has been much improvement in provisions for all groups requiring institutional care. With institutional control largely centralized in most States, emphasis has shifted from custody to care and treatment. The main objectives of institutions for delinquents and defectives are now education, reformation, rehabilitation, and restoration to useful citizenship.

Until relatively recently the only legislation in this country for the public care of needy individuals other than children and war veterans was contained in the State poor laws, which had undergone little change since colonial days. From the early part of the eighteenth century until the latter part of the nineteenth century, almshouse care was considered to be the best method of providing for the poor. Outdoor care under the poor laws was not provided for to any extent prior to the last third of the nineteenth century. Poor relief recipients were usually designated "paupers" and, in certain States, were deprived of some of the privileges of citizenship. Frequently, these statutes required "paupers' oaths" and excluded from military duty those requiring public aid. The posting of the names of such individuals in a public place was common. Many States disfranchised recipients of this relief, and a few refused them the right to marry.

Eventually with increased acceptance of social responsibilities, State legislatures recognized that there were certain classes of needy individuals who were entitled to public assistance without being subjected to the pauperizing aspects of the poor laws. This recognition resulted in special legislation providing for such types of needy individuals as dependent and neglected children and orphans, mothers with dependent children, the blind, and the aged.

Private institutions for the care of dependent and neglected children and orphans were first established late in the eighteenth century, but laws providing public care for these children by agencies and institutions were enacted mainly during the last third of the nineteenth century. Aid to dependent children in their own homes was a still later development. The first statute providing aid to dependent children in their own homes was not enacted until 1911,[1] but the adoption of this type of legislation was rapid, and by 1920 the majority of States had passed such statutes which were known as "mothers' aid" or "widows' pension" laws. There has been considerable revision in this legislation, however, since the enactment of the Federal Social Security Act in 1935.

The first blind assistance law was enacted in Indiana in 1840, but the development of legislation in this field was not rapid until after 1910.[2] The greatest development occurred within the 5-year period from 1933 through 1937.

---

[1]Missouri and Illinois were the first States to enact this type of legislation. The Missouri statute applied only to St. Louis City and Jackson County. The Illinois statute was the first State-wide law.

[2]The Indiana statute was a county optional law. The next State law providing blind assistance was passed in Ohio in 1898; however, such a statute was enacted for New York City in 1872.

Old age assistance has developed still more recently. The first State law was passed in Arizona in 1914 but was declared unconstitutional and it was not until 1923 that the next State statute was enacted.[3] There has been a tremendous increase in this type of legislation within the last 5 years, particularly since 1935 when Federal legislation providing for grants to States for assistance to the aged was adopted.

Special provisions for relief to war veterans have been included in State statutes since colonial days. The end of each war has brought forth additional statutes providing aid to needy individuals with honorable records of military service. In a number of States the poor laws contained separate provisions for the care of veterans which removed them from the pauperizing effect of the statutes.

In spite of these special types of legislation, probably the majority of needy persons who received public assistance were still provided for under the old poor laws until 1931. The diminishing importance of the old poor relief statutes has been one of the most important developments in the field of relief and public assistance within the last 7 or 8 years. By 1931 it had become evident that the provisions of the poor laws were not adequate to care for the rapidly mounting burden of unemployment resulting from the serious depression which had begun in 1929; and it was in 1931 that the first State legislation providing for emergency unemployment relief was enacted.[4] This legislation was adopted to supplement the existing relief provisions. In some States the emergency program was integrated with existing outdoor relief systems and in others separate programs were established. By 1933 nearly three-fourths of the States had enacted legislation to provide emergency unemployment relief.

In the latter part of 1932 the Federal Government began to loan funds to State and local governmental units for the relief of the unemployed. In May 1933 the Federal Emergency Relief Administration was authorized to allocate funds to the States for emergency unemployment relief purposes. This factor was largely responsible for the enactment of much of the State emergency relief legislation. The basic reason for both the Federal and State activity, of course, was the widespread economic reverses which had been caused by the depression. Federal Emergency Relief Administration grants to the States for emergency unemployment relief purposes were discontinued in December 1935, when the Works Program, provided for in the Federal Emergency

---

[3]Montana, Nevada, and Pennsylvania enacted old age assistance laws in 1923. The Nevada law was repealed the same year and the Pennsylvania statute was declared unconstitutional.

[4]New Jersey, New York, Oklahoma, Pennsylvania, and Rhode Island provided State funds for emergency unemployment relief during 1931.

Relief Appropriation Act of 1935, was furnishing employment to the bulk of the needy employable load.

From its inception in 1931, emergency unemployment relief tended to overshadow poor relief in the general relief field. During the years from 1931 to 1934 the bulk of the general relief load (i.e., needy persons who were not receiving old age assistance, blind assistance, aid to dependent children, and other special types of relief or assistance) was being assisted largely on an emergency basis. The need for a longer range program became recognized in 1935 when a transition began in the field of general relief which led to the superseding of both the emergency unemployment relief and poor relief systems in many States by permanent programs of general relief in which the States participate both financially and administratively. There has been a small decline since 1935 in the number of States which participate in general relief programs. This has been due to the expiration of emergency relief legislation in a few States which have not replaced it by permanent general relief legislation.[5]

Prior to 1933 the responsibility for the administration and financing of relief and public assistance was most frequently placed upon local units of government, although a majority of States had assumed responsibility for State institutions for children and veterans. In instances where the State participated in the administration of two or more programs, the tendency was to set up separate agencies to carry out the different functions. This same tendency also existed in local governmental units. By 1935 the prevailing practice had changed and from that year until the present the majority of laws which have been enacted in the relief and public assistance fields have provided for State responsibility and for the direct administration or supervision of all of these functions by a single State agency. This has been largely due to the enactment of the Federal Social Security Act which requires State administrative participation before the Federal Government may reimburse States for expenditures for old age and blind assistance, and aid to dependent children.

By January 1, 1939, very few States did not have legislation providing for all types of relief and assistance. Delaware has made no provision for blind assistance or for the special care

---

[5]No attempt has been made to distinguish among poor relief, emergency unemployment relief, and permanent general relief programs, except in individual States where two or more programs exist which are administered by different agencies and/or financed by different governmental units. The majority of States which have assumed some administrative responsibility for general relief have placed this responsibility within a permanent agency which administers the majority of the other relief and public assistance functions performed by the State. Other States are at present taking steps to achieve this same result and only a small number have programs which appear to be purely temporary or emergency in character (tables 1—5).

of veterans; Arizona, Nevada, New Mexico, and West Virginia have
made no special provision for veterans.[6] Detailed provisions
of the laws in effect in all States, and in Alaska, Hawaii, and
the District of Columbia as of January 1, 1939, are indicated
in the following sections and supporting tables.

[6]In order to completely cover all of the veteran legislation coming within
the scope of this study (see footnote 1), the States are considered to have
made special provision for veterans, even though need is not involved in
the consideration of eligibility. Specific information on these laws is
contained in tables 28—33, inclusive, and described in the text on pages
26—27.

Section II

ELIGIBILITY PROVISIONS AND TYPES OF CARE GRANTED RECIPIENTS OF RELIEF AND PUBLIC ASSISTANCE

ALL OF the State statutes providing for relief and public assistance define the class of persons eligible and the types of care which may be granted. The more recent enactments are much more general in their terminology than were the earlier statutes and allow considerably more administrative discretion in determining who shall receive relief and public assistance and in deciding the kind and amount of such aid.

GENERAL RELIEF

The general relief laws (tables 1—5) as they appear on the statute books of many States at the present time are an admixture of the old poor relief statutes and the recent laws drafted in the light of modern concepts; accordingly their interpretation raises many problems. The class of persons cared for under these statutes cannot be accurately defined. They consist of that residual group of needy persons who are either not eligible for special forms of State relief and public assistance or for Federal Works Program employment, or who because of lack of funds or some other reason cannot be cared for under these special programs.[1]

Eligibility requirements consist mainly of need and residence (table 2). The terms *poor, needy,* and *indigent* appear frequently, but none of the statutes contain an exact definition of *need*. Nearly two-thirds of the States have some provision relating to the liability of relatives to support applicants for general relief (table 3). In some of these States no relief may be given if the applicant has a legally responsible relative able to support him, and in a few others relief may be granted and reimbursement obtained from such relatives by voluntary or court action.

---

[1] *General relief* as used in this report includes all types of relief granted to recipients described above. It includes institutional care and services as well as direct relief (table 5). This definition is somewhat broader than the one generally used in statistical reporting. Delimitation of the field is necessary in statistical reporting because of the lack of information concerning the number of persons cared for in almshouses, by contract, etc.

7

State and local residence requirements are prescribed in nearly one-half of the States, while over an additional one-third of the State statutes specify periods of local residence only. Residence in the State satisfies the requirement in Delaware and Minnesota, and in five States there is no residence requirement prescribed by statute. State residence requirements range from 1 to 3 years, and in those States which prescribe both State and local residence the State residence period required is usually longer than the local period. This has the effect of restricting the entrance into the State of persons who are not self-supporting and of allowing some freedom for intrastate movement. Local residence periods range from 90 days to 5 years. In the New England States and New York the State assumes responsibility for "state poor"; i.e., persons for whom no governmental unit is responsible because they fail to meet local residence requirements. Indians on reservations also come within this class in New York. It is interesting that in more than three-fourths of the State laws some provision is made for the temporary relief of nonresidents (table 5).

The old poor relief statutes have not been repealed in many States but have been supplemented and broadened by the recent laws providing for general relief. Under the recent laws, relief is given to needy persons in their own homes by means of money payments rather than by placing them in almshouses or contracting for their care (table 5). There are, however, a few State laws which still specify only almshouse care, contract care, or some other method for the relief of the poor. Because of the current tendency to replace almshouse care with public assistance and direct relief in some States, it is probable that most of these institutions will eventually either fall into disuse or be converted into infirmaries. The letting out of the poor and contracting for their support are still provided for in approximately one-third of the States. The extent to which this practice is currently being followed is not known, but it has undoubtedly diminished greatly within the last 5 or 6 years. Public medical care and hospitalization are provided for indigent persons in nearly all of the States. These provisions are, for the most part, contained in the poor relief statutes; however, in a few of the States special provisions for the hospitalization of the indigent sick have been recently enacted while in others the general relief statutes though not specifically authorizing medical care and hospitalization are so worded as to appear to allow the granting of this type of aid.[2] The majority of State statutes provide for the burial of persons leaving insufficient resources for burial.

---

[2] Many States have made provisions for the care of poor persons in State hospitals which are frequently connected with the medical schools of State universities. These provisions do not appear in the general relief statutes.

Many of the early statutes granting poor relief deprived recipients of such citizenship rights as the exercise of franchise and the right to marry and excluded them from military duty (table 4). These provisions (both constitutional and statutory) do not assume the same importance today as they did prior to 1931, except in a few States, since many of them are directed at paupers and most of the recent State laws do not specify general relief recipients as "paupers." The provisions of this type which remain on the statute books of the States have been included in table 4 but are probably ineffective in many States.

OLD AGE ASSISTANCE

Old age assistance statutes (tables 6—11) provide for cash payments to needy individuals who have reached a specified age, usually 65 years. A few States have established an age limit of 70, while Colorado has lowered its limit to 60 but grants aid to persons under 65 only if they are registered voters and have resided in the State for 35 years preceding the application.

Citizenship, residence, and need are the most frequent qualifications to be met before an aged person becomes eligible for this assistance (tables 7 and 8). A few State laws contain requirements relating to the moral fitness of an applicant. Nearly two-thirds of the old age assistance statutes require that a recipient be a citizen of the United States, but a few of these State laws waive the citizenship requirement if the applicant has resided in the country for a specified period—usually 20 or 25 years. The residence requirement enacted in all but a few States is that the applicant must have resided within the State 5 of the 9 years immediately preceding his application and 1 year immediately preceding the application. The provision in the Federal Social Security Act which prevents the Social Security Board from approving a State plan which excludes persons who can fulfill this requirement from receiving benefits is responsible for the large number of States which have adopted this State residence requirement.

Residence within a local governmental unit is required by law in a small number of States, some of which prescribe that the total financial burden must be assumed by the State if the applicant has no local residence. Such provision is enacted only for the purpose of placing the financial responsibility when the local units contribute to the payment of assistance. A State which enforces local residence requirements so as to bar applicants not meeting such requirements is ineligible for Federal assistance to the aged under the Social Security Act.

The majority of the State old age assistance statutes define need in general rather than specific terms, leaving to administrative determination the actual need of an individual applicant (table 8). The terminology most frequently used is that the applicant must not have sufficient property or income to provide reasonable subsistence compatible with decency and health. Approximately one-third of the States have retained or adopted the limitations found frequently in the earlier statutes which defined need by placing limits upon the maximum amount of property and the maximum income a recipient could have and still be eligible. All but one State (Oregon) disqualify applicants who have disposed of property in order to qualify. In some jurisdictions the property must have been disposed of within a specified period (from 2 to 5 years) prior to the filing of the application.[3]

Applicants who have relatives legally liable and able to support them are ineligible for old age assistance in about one-half of the States. Many laws disqualify applicants who are receiving other types of public assistance or who are inmates of institutions. Because of the provision in the Federal act which forbids payments to States for grants to inmates of public institutions, such inmates are disqualified more frequently than those of private institutions. Some statutes disqualify only

---

[3]Approximately two-thirds of the States granting old age assistance provide for recovery by the State of the amount of assistance properly granted recipients (table 10). These provisions take three forms, all of which are found in some State laws. One type provides for an assignment or transfer of the recipient's property prior to the granting of assistance. Another type provides for the execution of an agreement by the recipient to reimburse the State and/or local unit for the amount of assistance received. These two types may be properly considered as a requirement to be met before the applicant becomes eligible to receive old age assistance. The third type does not so directly affect the applicant's eligibility as it provides for a statutory lien or a prior claim against the property of the recipient which does not take effect until his death or the death of both the recipient and his spouse. All of the State statutes which provide for the assignment or transfer of the property of a recipient also provide for liens or claims against the recipient's estate.

About one-third of the States provide for the assignment of the recipient's property to administrative agencies or require a transfer of such property to the State or local unit. These provisions are not often mandatory, and the advisability of requiring an assignment or transfer is generally left to administrative discretion. A few of the States providing for an assignment or transfer require the administrative agency to assume control of the property and administer it for the benefit of the recipient.

Provisions requiring the recipient to execute an agreement to reimburse the State or local unit for the amount of assistance granted are found in a few States and are supplementary to the other types of provisions for recovery.

Liens or claims against the recipient's estate for the total amount of aid granted are provided by statute in about two-thirds of the States, several of which charge interest on the amount of aid granted.

Approximately one-third of the States have some provision for immediate recovery in case of misrepresentation or concealment of income or property by the recipient. Some of the statutes, as a penalty, allow double recovery in such instances. Provisions allowing immediate recovery in cases where the recipient becomes possessed of property or income in excess of his need or in excess of the amount stated in the application are also found in approximately one-third of the State statutes.

Provisions for recovery are also found in approximately one-half of the general relief statutes (table 3) and in about one-third of the blind assistance statutes (table 16). These provisions usually take the form of a lien or a claim against the estate of a recipient.

inmates of penal institutions, reformatories, or insane asylums (table 7). The provision that an applicant in need of continuing institutional care is ineligible for old age assistance if such care is reasonably available appears frequently (table 9).

Provisions disqualifying applicants because of lack of moral fitness are contained in the laws of a few States (table 7). These provisions are based on the theory that old age assistance is granted for service the recipient has rendered the community by being a good citizen. The desertion of one's spouse or the commission of a felony within a specified period prior to application and the failure to support children (usually under 16 years of age) are among the most common acts which disqualify applicants for old age assistance. The laws of a few States also make an applicant ineligible for old age assistance if he has been a tramp or beggar within a period of 1 or 2 years prior to his application.

The maximum amount which an applicant may receive is specified in most States, with a few States also specifying minimum allowances (table 11). Also, a number of States have attempted to determine the standard of the grant by establishing an income which recipients of old age assistance are entitled to receive from all sources combined. These statutes provide that the grant shall be an amount which when added to the recipient's income from other sources will equal the established figure.

The amount of the maximum grants allowed by law ranges from $15 to $45 a month for an individual, with the majority of States adopting the $30 maximum. This maximum has probably been adopted because of the Federal Social Security Act which provides for matching State grants to individuals in an amount not exceeding $15 a month. The majority of statutes provide for burial allowances (ranging from $75 to $150) if the estate of the deceased is insufficient to cover burial expenses.

BLIND ASSISTANCE

Blind assistance statutes (tables 12—17) provide for cash payments to needy blind individuals. The more important qualifications for the receipt of this assistance are: age, citizenship, degree and incurability of blindness, and need (tables 13 and 14). The majority of States have specified a minimum age (ranging from 16 to 21 years) under which a person is ineligible for blind assistance. Since other provisions have been made for the education and training of young persons it has been considered that money payments should not be made to blind minors before they have had the opportunity through specialized training and education to become self-supporting. Two State laws render ineligible persons over 65 years old, with the intention of granting such persons old age assistance.

Citizenship in the United States is much less frequently a requirement for blind assistance than for old age assistance. Only one-fourth of the States demand citizenship as a prerequisite for aid to the blind, whereas approximately three-fourths require it for old age assistance.

A statutory period of State residence, however, is specified for blind assistance in all the States with the exception of New Mexico and Massachusetts, while local residence requirements exist in only a few States. The most frequent State residence requirement is that also found in old age assistance laws, namely: that the applicant must have resided in the State 5 of the 9 years immediately preceding the application and for at least 1 year immediately preceding the application. Many of the States have alternative provisions which waive the residence requirement if a person has become blind while a resident of the State. In other States periods of residence range from 1 year to 10 years immediately preceding the application. In some States in which the local units contribute to the payment of blind assistance a local residence requirement is prescribed for the purpose of determining financial liability. In these States if an applicant has no local residence, the State pays the total amount of assistance. As in the case of old age assistance laws, States whose statutes prescribe a local residence and deny aid if that requirement is not met are ineligible for Federal aid under the Social Security Act.

Blindness is usually defined in general terms which state that vision with correcting glasses must be so defective as to prevent the performance of ordinary activities for which eyesight is essential, leaving to administrative determination the technical degree of blindness necessary for eligibility of the applicant. However, a few States define blindness in technical optometric terms. In approximately one-fourth of the States the administering officials may require as a condition to receiving blind assistance that an applicant undergo treatment or an operation if there is a possibility of restoring his sight.

A blind person unable to support himself or having insufficient income or resources to provide reasonable subsistence compatible with decency and health is eligible for blind assistance in three-fourths of the States, provided he meets the additional requirements specified by law. Applicants for blind assistance are denied aid in approximately one-half of the States if there are persons legally liable and able to support them. Three States have no statutory need qualifications, and the remaining States place a specific limitation on the amount of property and income which an individual may have without becoming ineligible for blind assistance. The limitations on property range from $2,500 to $5,000, and the limit placed upon income (including assistance) ranges from $360 to $1,200 a year.

A provision disqualifying applicants who have disposed of property in order to qualify is contained in the majority of blind assistance statutes. As in old age assistance statutes this provision usually specifies that the property must have been disposed of within periods ranging from 2 to 5 years prior to the application.

Blind assistance recipients are disqualified from receiving any other type of public assistance in approximately one-third of the States, and in an additional one-half of the States they are specifically disqualified from receiving old age assistance (table 15).

Inmates of institutions are frequently barred from the receipt of blind assistance. A provision disqualifying applicants who are in need of continuing institutional care is found in several of the statutes. The solicitation of alms also disqualifies recipients in about one-half of the States.

The maximum amount which an applicant may receive is specified in most States, with a few States also specifying minimum allowances (table 17). The maximum which may be granted ranges from $15 to $50 a month. The majority of States have adopted a maximum of $30 a month. As in the case of old age assistance, the Federal Social Security Act provides for matching State grants to blind assistance recipients in an amount not to exceed $15 a month. Additional assistance or supplementary services for the purpose of removing a disability may be given in many States. In several of these States supplementary services may be granted to blind individuals who would not be otherwise entitled to monthly allowances. This provision has been included as a preventive measure in the hope that a person's eyesight may be so improved as to enable him to become self-supporting before he actually needs blind assistance. Approximately one-third of the States provide burial allowances ($50 to $150) for recipients of blind assistance.

DEPENDENT CHILDREN

There are two types of provisions for dependent children. One type provides for those children who may be cared for in their own homes and the homes of relatives or specified persons by means of cash payments to the person responsible for the care of the child (tables 18—21). The other type relates to orphans or children who are neglected and hence are dependent upon the public for support (tables 22—27). These latter children frequently come within the jurisdiction of the juvenile courts and are placed and maintained in foster homes or institutions.

Aid to Dependent Children in Their Own Homes

Eligibility requirements for aid to dependent children in their own homes relate principally to age, residence, the persons eligible to care for the child, and need (tables 19 and 20).

In the majority of States a child must be under 16 years of age in order for his relatives to be eligible to receive aid in his behalf. There are, however, two States which place the age at 14, and a few have placed the age at 18 years.

Citizenship on the part of the applicant is required infrequently and in the majority of these States a declaration by the applicant of his or her intention to become a citizen satisfies the requirement. Only one State statute requires that the child must be a citizen.

The residence requirement adopted by the majority of States is that the child must have resided in the State for 1 year immediately preceding the application or have been born in the State within 1 year immediately preceding the application if its mother resided in the State 1 year immediately preceding its birth. This provision is the most stringent State residence requirement which a State may enact and still be eligible for grants under the Federal Social Security Act. A few States require that the applicant have a local residence of 1 or 2 years. As in the two other social security categories, a requirement of local residence which prohibits the granting of aid to cases not meeting the requirement disqualifies the State for reimbursement under the Social Security Act.

Any of the following relatives, if caring for the child, are eligible to receive aid under most State statutes: father, mother, grandfather, grandmother, brother, sister, stepfather, stepmother, stepbrother, stepsister, uncle, or aunt. These are the persons who are specified as eligible by the Federal Social Security Act. A few States specify that only mothers may receive aid, while a few others have broadened the class so as to include any person standing in loco parentis to the child.

Less than one-third of the State laws contain provisions relating to the fitness of the person caring for the child. These provisions usually state that the person must be morally, mentally, and physically fit to care for the child; interpretation of this phrase is left to administrative discretion. Nearly one-half of the State laws specify that the home must be suitable for the purposes of raising the child.

Need is not expressed in definite terms in the majority of statutes, but it must arise from certain conditions or circumstances. Financial inability of applicant is not sufficient to meet the need qualification. The prevailing requirement, enacted in three-quarters of the States, is very broad and specifies that the applicant must be unable to support the child and that such inability must be caused by the death, continued absence from the home, or the physical or mental incapacity of a parent. A few statutes, much narrower in their provisions, allow aid only if the father is dead or mentally incapacitated.

However, in some of the States with narrow statutory provisions, aid may be granted to a mother who is divorced or unmarried, or whose husband is an inmate of an institution. Only a few States place any specific limitation upon the amount of property which an applicant may own.

Allowances for aid to dependent children are based upon the number of children being cared for by the applicant (table 21). They are usually expressed in maximum terms, and the sum allowed for the first child is generally greater than for each additional child. The Federal Social Security Board makes grants to States for one-third of their expenditures for aid to dependent children up to a maximum grant of $6 a month for the first child and $4 for each additional child. The maximum grant of $18 a month for the first child and $12 for each additional child has been adopted in less than 10 States. Other grants range from $2.50 a week for each child up to $25 a month for the first child, with a limit of $75 for an entire family. About one-half of the States do not specify maximum allowances but state that aid must be granted in the amount necessary for the support of the child in a manner compatible with decency and health. Burial allowances (ranging from $50 to $150) are provided for in seven States.

Dependent and Neglected Children

Dependent and neglected children are those children who are dependent upon the public for support because they have no persons responsible for their care or because the persons responsible for their care have neglected this responsibility. Since these children have no suitable homes of their own and their relatives are not willing to make homes for them, it is necessary to care for them by other means (table 22). They are usually, though not always, brought within the jurisdiction of the juvenile court for the purpose of deciding questions of guardianship and liability for their care. Where these questions are not involved, many public and private agencies have the power and authority to care and provide for children, but in all jurisdictions it is necessary to obtain a court order to remove children from the custody of parents who are neglecting them. Children must be under specified ages (ranging from 10 to 21 years depending upon the State, with the majority of States placing the age for boys at 16 and girls at 18) to come within the jurisdiction of the juvenile court. In all States any child under the statutory age who is destitute, homeless, abandoned, and dependent upon the public for support or who is living in an unfit environment with improper parental care may be placed in a foster home, a public institution, or with a private association or agency willing to care for it (table 24). The majority of statutes express a preference for foster home care

and provide in most instances that children maintained in institutions shall be placed in private homes as soon as possible.
Thirty-one States and the District of Columbia maintain institutions for the care of dependent and neglected children, and
many States provide for the establishment of county and local
detention homes and institutions (tables 25 and 26).

In several States dependent and neglected children may be committed to industrial schools and similar institutions designated
by law as primarily for the care of delinquent children. Some
State statutes specifically prohibit the maintaining of children
in almshouses; but in jurisdictions which have no such expressed
prohibition, children may be cared for in these institutions.
There has been, however, a decided trend away from this type of
care.

VETERAN RELIEF

Special statutory provisions for the care and support of veterans exist in practically all States (tables 28—33).[4] These
provisions are of three types: direct relief (26 States), pensions (21 States), and care in State institutions (38 States).

The majority of statutes providing for direct relief include
the wives, widows, and dependent children of veterans in the
class of eligibles; over one-half of the statutes also include
other dependent relatives. Pensions are granted only to the
veteran or his widow under the majority of State pension acts;
a few provide for pensions to other dependent relatives. Care
in State institutions is generally restricted to veterans and
their wives or widows; only about one-half of the States provide
for institutional care of other dependent relatives. Nurses who
served in time of war are frequently designated as eligible for
relief, pensions, and institutional care. Servants of soldiers
are granted pensions under the laws of a few of the Southern
States.

Eligibility requirements for all three types of veteran assistance relate principally to residence, the war in which service was rendered, and need. Disability is a condition for
receipt of such aid in a few States, some of whose statutes provide that the disability must have resulted from military service.

---

[4] Veterans are usually eligible for any type of relief and assistance provided they meet the qualifications imposed. However, special provisions
for veterans have been made in many States and it is these special provisions
which are referred to in the discussion of veteran relief. Some of the
statutes providing for pensions or institutional care for veterans do not
prescribe need as a qualification for eligibility. These statutes have
been included in the tabulations and text only for the purpose of providing
a complete coverage of legislation providing relief, pensions, or institutional aid to veterans.

The majority of State statutes providing for all three types of aid prescribe residence requirements. The periods of residence required for eligibility for direct veteran relief range from 3 months to 5 years. Periods necessary for receipt of pensions vary from 1 to 31 years. The residence requirements for institutional care vary even more widely. In some instances these requirements are waived if the veteran enlisted from the State and in other instances enlistment from the State is the only qualification imposed in the nature of a residence requirement.

Veterans of all wars are eligible for direct relief in the majority of States making provisions for direct relief to veterans. However, legal provisions granting pensions to veterans of all wars exist in only three States (Massachusetts, New Jersey, and New York). Approximately three-fourths of the States providing for pensions grant them only to veterans of the Civil War, and most of these are Southern States which grant pensions to Confederate veterans. Minnesota does not provide pensions to any veterans except those of the Indian Wars. World War and Spanish-American War veterans receive pensions under the laws of Maine.

Nearly one-half of the States providing institutional care do not require service in any specific war but grant aid to all veterans of the armed forces of the United States. Approximately one-fourth of the States provide institutional care for Civil War veterans only, and these institutions are principally for the care of Confederate veterans. The statutes of the remaining States specify that the veteran must have been engaged in a particular war.

The statutes providing direct relief do not define need by specific terms but use such descriptive words as "dependent," "needy," and "poor." Ten of the twenty-one States granting pensions prescribe need as a qualification; seven State laws make disability a condition for receiving a pension without prescribing need; and the remaining four State laws authorize pensions on the basis of veteran status alone. Approximately one-half of the States which prescribe need as a condition for eligibility for a pension define need in terms of specific limitations on property and income, while those remaining use the same type of descriptive language as that found in the statutes providing direct relief to veterans. The statutes in two-thirds of the States providing institutional care state in general terms that an applicant for admittance must be in need.

The type and amount of aid granted veterans varies widely. Relief in cash or in kind is provided for frequently under veteran direct relief statutes. Many of these laws use the term *relief* without definition. A few of the statutes provide that a veteran may not be removed to an almshouse without his consent and must receive relief in his own home. Pensions generally take the form of fixed cash sums paid periodically and may amount to as much as $500 a year. All of the States, whether or not they have provision for the relief of veterans, make some provision for their burial.

Section III

ADMINISTRATIVE RESPONSIBILITY FOR RELIEF AND PUBLIC ASSISTANCE

TWO FACTORS in the early development of relief and public assistance programs greatly influenced their administration. The first of these was the placement of administrative responsibility upon local units. The doctrine of local responsibility so firmly established within the earliest systems was carried over to the special types of programs which developed much later. The second factor was the establishment in many States of separate agencies to administer each function. Such agencies were either State or local, depending upon the incidence of administrative responsibility. Experience showed, however, that there was often an absence of uniform administration throughout the State when the responsibility was entirely local and a lack of coordination and a duplication of effort when similar functions were administered by separate agencies. Consequently, new principles of centralization and integration have gradually been adopted.

Until as late as 1932 administrative responsibility for relief and public assistance was usually placed exclusively upon local units of government, except in those instances where State institutions had been established for the care of children and veterans. In addition, the State usually assumed the administrative responsibility for veterans' pensions. With the establishment of State emergency relief agencies between 1931 and 1933, there began a definite shift away from placing full responsibility for general relief upon local units. During the period since January 1, 1930, there has been also a rapid increase in the number of States enacting old age assistance and blind assistance laws, and there has been considerable revision in the laws providing for aid to dependent children in their own homes. Practically all of this new legislation has provided for State administrative participation; by the end of 1938 the majority of States had established State agencies to administer directly, or to supervise, relief and public assistance. Federal participation in the field—through the Federal Emergency Relief Administration (established in 1933) and later through the Social Security Board (established in 1935)—gave impetus to the movement toward centralization. This movement has not excluded local participation, since the majority of States have established local agencies either to administer relief and public assistance under the supervision of a State agency or to assist the State agency in the administration of these programs.

INCIDENCE OF ADMINISTRATIVE RESPONSIBILITY
General Relief

State administrative participation in general relief programs exists in less than two-thirds of the States (table 1). This participation usually consists of the supervision by State agencies of local units having direct administrative responsibility. Only 10 States[1] have assumed direct administrative responsibility for general relief, and in 8 of these the local units are also authorized to administer a general relief program based on the old poor laws.

Old Age Assistance

All States have enacted old age assistance laws and have placed some administrative responsibility upon a State agency (table 6). This is due directly to the provisions of the Federal Social Security Act which require that a State agency have either direct or supervisory responsibility for the administration of old age assistance. Twenty-six States make the State agency directly responsible, and the remaining twenty-two have placed supervisory responsibility upon the State agency.

Blind Assistance

Because of the influence of the Federal Social Security Act, State administrative participation in blind assistance programs is similar to that of old age assistance programs (table 12). State agencies participate in all but 1 State, with State agencies supervising local administrative units in 23 States and having direct responsibility in 21 States. Under the laws of New Jersey both the State and county agencies participate in making final original determinations of blind assistance applications. In Florida each of the State and local units have direct administrative responsibility for separate programs of blind assistance.

Aid to Dependent Children in Their Own Homes

State programs for aid to dependent children in their own homes must include provision for State supervision or direct

---

[1]Texas is included in these 10 States; however, no State funds have been appropriated for the State administered general relief program as of January 1, 1939.

administration if the States are to receive Federal benefits under the Social Security Act. As a result only 3 States out of 48 have made no provision for such State administrative participation (table 18). State agencies are vested with supervisory responsibility in 24 States and with direct administrative responsibility in the remaining States. Three States which have enacted legislation to conform to the Federal Social Security Act have retained the older "mothers' aid" statutes which are locally administered.

Dependent and Neglected Children

State laws providing for the care of dependent and neglected children by agencies and in institutions are much more complex than other relief and public assistance statutes. Because of the part played by juvenile courts, these programs are quasi-judicial as well as administrative. Since diversified types of care are given by both public and private agencies, it is difficult to establish criteria for determining direct administrative or supervisory responsibility, and it is impossible to employ the criteria used to place administrative responsibility in systems which grant cash payments to individuals.

There are three steps in the administration of the care of dependent and neglected children. The first involves the commitment or placement of the child with a person, association, or institution if it is impossible for it to remain in its own home. The second step concerns the administration of the actual care of the child and the third the supervision of both placement and care.

Commitments of dependent and neglected children are made by local juvenile courts, or other courts exercising juvenile jurisdiction, in all the States and Territories and in the District of Columbia. Placements of such children are made by both State and local welfare agencies in most States and by private child-caring agencies and public and private institutions in some States. Whenever questions of guardianship or legal custody are involved, it is necessary to bring the child within the jurisdiction of the juvenile court. Welfare agencies receive children for placement by either court commitment or by voluntary surrender of the child by its parents or guardian.

In most States the administration of the actual care of these children is divided among State, local, and private agencies and institutions. Thirty-one States and the District of Columbia have established institutions to care for dependent and neglected children. A number of States have provided for the establishment of such institutions by counties or other local governmental units.

Supervision of the care of dependent and neglected children is exercised by juvenile courts, local agencies, and State agencies. The supervisory power of the juvenile courts is derived from the provision in the statutes of the majority of States granting such courts continuing jurisdiction over children who have appeared before them until they reach the age of 21 years or are legally adopted. This supervision is usually performed by probation officers or local boards of visitors appointed by the courts who visit children cared for by both public and private agencies and institutions.

In nearly all of the States there is a State agency charged with the supervision of local public institutions and private agencies and institutions. This supervision consists of the establishment of standards of care and their enforcement. Approximately three-fourths of the States give this agency the power to license all child-caring agencies. In about one-half of the States the State agency may delegate power of supervision to local agencies. Frequently, local institutions are placed by law under the supervision of county agencies which may be courts, boards of visitors, or county welfare departments.

Veteran Relief

In the determination of the administrative responsibility for veteran relief, it is necessary to consider the three types of care (direct relief, pensions, and institutional care) separately. Ten of the twenty-six States providing for direct relief place the administrative responsibility exclusively upon local units. In three States private veteran organizations administer these programs. Rhode Island and Connecticut have dual programs, one administered by the State and the other by local units. Seven additional States have assumed complete administrative responsibility while Georgia, Kansas, Massachusetts, and Michigan provide for the supervision of local administration.

Veterans' pensions are directly administered by State agencies in the majority of States. Only 5 of the 21 States providing pensions place this responsibility upon local units, and 3 of these provide for State supervision.

The responsibility for the direct administration of institutional care of veterans is lodged with the State in all jurisdictions but California, which provides for the establishment of county or city veteran homes.

Section IV

PROVISIONS FOR ADMINISTRATIVE PROCEDURES FOR THE DETERMINATION OF ELIGIBILITY FOR RELIEF AND PUBLIC ASSISTANCE [1]

THE PROCEDURE adopted for the determination of the eligibility of an applicant is an important part of administration. The pattern of this procedure has been set by law and depends considerably upon the location of administrative responsibility and upon the relationship between State and local administrative units (tables 1, 6, 12, 18, 29, 31, and 33).

The various types of procedure may be divided into two general groups: (1) the procedures for making the final original determination; [2] and (2) those providing for further consideration of an application if the parties involved are not satisfied with the final original determination. The latter procedures consist of appeals by the applicant, complaints by citizens, reviews by the State agency either on its own motion or on appeal or complaint, and periodic reconsideration by State or local agencies.

FINAL ORIGINAL DETERMINATION

Relief and Public Assistance Other Than Care of Dependent and Neglected Children by Agencies and in Institutions [3]

The following nine methods have been provided by law for making the final original determination: (1) exclusive investigation and determination by a State agency; (2) final original

---

[1] It is emphasized that this analysis is based entirely upon legal provisions and that actual practice may vary from the administrative procedures outlined in this section.

[2] The seemingly contradictory words *final original* have been used because under many State statutes the original determination is not final but must be approved by another administrative agency before becoming effective. The term *final original responsibility* means the responsibility for determining whether or not an applicant shall receive relief or assistance in the absence of an appeal or review.

[3] Because procedures for determining the eligibility of dependent and neglected children differ considerably from other types of relief they will be considered separately.

23

determination by the central State office upon the advice of its local office[4] which makes the investigation; (3) final original determination by the State agency upon the advice of a local agency[5] which makes the investigation; (4) investigation and final original determination by a local office of a State agency which establishes rules and regulations and supervises its local office; (5) investigation and final original determination by a local agency under supervision of a State agency; (6) investigation by a State agency which advises a local agency which makes the final original determination; (7) investigation by a State agency which makes the final original determination jointly with a local agency; (8) exclusive investigation and determination by a local agency; and (9) investigation by one local agency which advises a second local agency which makes the final original determination.

These procedures have not been adopted uniformly for all types of relief and public assistance. In fact, varying procedures for different types of relief or public assistance are found within statutes of individual States. The procedures most commonly enacted into law are those listed as (4) and (5) above, in which the investigation and final original determination are made by a local office or local agency under the supervision of a State department. Legislation providing for advisory procedures [(2) and (3) above] has been adopted with some frequency as also has the provision for exclusive investigation and final original determination by a State agency [procedure (1)]. This latter procedure may easily be varied in practice, however, by the delegation of part of the function of the State agency to either its local offices or to local agencies. Such a delegation may result in making the State agency supervisory in character or in placing it in the position of receiving advice from local offices or agencies to which investigatory powers have been delegated.

The procedures in which one agency makes the investigation and advises a second agency [(2) and (3) above] may also vary in practice depending upon the consideration given the recommendations of the investigating agency. In some States this procedure may amount to nothing more than a clerical check of all applications by the agency authorized to make the final original determination in order to ascertain whether or not matters of form have been complied with. In other jurisdictions the powers may result in a real weighing of the merits of each individual application by the agency with the final authority.

---

[4]The term *local office* used here refers to a local authority which is an agent of the State department.

[5]The term *local agency* refers to an authority which is an agent of the local governmental unit.

In the majority of States where the law has placed no administrative responsibility on the State, the investigation and final original determination is made by a single local agency. This type of procedure (8) is found most frequently in the laws providing for general relief and direct relief to veterans.

The remaining procedures [(6), (7), and (9)] have been adopted in only a few instances.[6]

Dependent and Neglected Children

Because children without parents or proper guardianship cannot be relied upon to provide for themselves adequately, legal procedures have been established which insure that dependent and neglected children shall receive care and training. Of course, in practically all of the States parents or guardians may for good cause voluntarily surrender their children or wards to agencies or institutions authorized to care for them. However, in several of these States even this voluntary surrender can be consummated only with the approval of a court having juvenile jurisdiction.

The procedure provided in statutes establishing juvenile courts is fairly uniform (table 23). In all States there exist county and city courts vested with jurisdiction over dependent and neglected children. Usually any resident of the community having knowledge that a child is dependent or neglected may file a petition to that effect with such a court. Welfare officials are specifically authorized frequently to file these petitions and in some States are required to do so.

The next step, the investigation of the petition, is provided for in all States. This investigation is usually made by probation officers attached to the juvenile court or by welfare agencies designated by the court to act in this capacity. Children are generally placed in the care of these officers or agencies until their final disposition has been determined by the court.

A private hearing is usually provided for. Many State laws specify that no jury be impaneled, though several State statutes do provide for a jury if desired by the interested parties. The laws generally require the investigating officer to be present to represent the interests of the child.

All of the statutes grant the presiding judge discretionary power, within limitations, to make final disposition of the child in a manner which will best serve its interests.

---

[6]**Reinvestigations and reconsiderations.**—Provisions for reinvestigations and reconsiderations of the grant of assistance are found principally in the statutes providing for the categories included in the Social Security Act. Only a few general relief and none of the veteran relief statutes contain such provisions. Most States provide that reinvestigations and reconsiderations must be made when required by the State board or department, but in some States periodic reinvestigation and reconsideration of the eligibility of all recipients are required.

APPEALS AND FAIR HEARINGS

The Federal Social Security Act stipulates that a State is ineligible to receive Federal grants for old age assistance, blind assistance, and aid to dependent children, unless it allows an applicant for any of these three types of assistance an opportunity for a fair hearing before the State agency if his or her claim for assistance is denied. Provisions allowing fair hearings under such circumstances are found in the majority of State laws providing for these three special types of aid. Frequently fair hearings are also allowed if the applicant is dissatisfied with the final original decision. Provisions allowing appeals and fair hearings are found in relatively few State statutes providing for general and veteran relief.

In States in which the final original decision is made by a local administrative unit, the law generally provides for an appeal to a State agency which makes the final decision. In States in which the final original decision is made by the State agency, the hearing is usually conducted by the State board or other designated officials within the State agency. Technically, there is no appeal in these instances since the final original decision is reviewed by officials of the agency which made that decision. A few States, in which the law is directly administered by a State agency, have felt the need for a further appeal and have made provision for an appeal to a court of law from the decision of the officials conducting the fair hearing.

Provisions for appeals to courts of law are found in several State statutes even though in some instances an appeal to a State agency is allowed from the decision of a local agency. Judicial review of administrative decisions has been seriously opposed on the ground that the administration of relief and public assistance is not a judicial function but one to be performed only by trained administrators. However, whenever an applicant is denied relief or assistance under a mandatory statute, he may sue for a writ of mandamus against the administering official, which in effect is an appeal of the original decision to a court of law. Some of the recent statutes, with the specific intent of barring court action, make the decision of the State agency final. Such provision tends to prevent the issuance of writs of mandamus except in those cases which have been arbitrarily and unfairly decided against an applicant.

Approximately one-half of the State juvenile court statutes allow appeals to higher courts. Denial of appeal, because it seems arbitrary and may be held to abridge a constitutional right, may result in the use of another legal method (habeas corpus proceedings) to achieve the same result. The exercise of the right of appeal from juvenile court decisions may be easily abused since an appeal, barring statutory provision to the contrary, has the legal effect of suspending the operation of the decree until the appeal is decided. In such cases the child is often returned to the situation which led to the juvenile court proceedings. A few States providing for appeals from juvenile court decisions have taken steps to prevent such occurrences by requiring continued care by the court pending the outcome of the appeal.

COMPLAINTS

Specific provisions are made in a few States for complaints from citizens or taxpayers who believe that aid has been improperly granted. Less than one-fourth of the old age assistance statutes contain such a provision; while in laws providing for other types of relief and assistance, complaints are specifically authorized only in isolated instances. They do not appear at all in veteran relief statutes. In the majority of States authorizing complaints, it is mandatory upon the State agency to make investigation.

REVIEW ON OWN MOTION AND FURTHER INVESTIGATION

The majority of State agencies which supervise direct administration of the public assistance provisions contained in the Social Security Act are granted the authority to review applications on their own motion. Generally coupled with this authority is the power to make further investigations of applications. Such additional investigation may be necessary in cases where complaints have been made or appeals taken.

Section V

PROVISIONS FOR THE FINANCING OF RELIEF AND PUBLIC ASSISTANCE

THE TREND toward an increasing centralization in financial responsibility for relief and public assistance is similar to the trend in administrative responsibility. Financial responsibility was placed entirely upon local units in the majority of early laws except those providing for State institutions for children and veterans and pensions for veterans. Prior to 1930 no State had assumed any responsibility for the total general relief load, although New York and the New England States reimbursed local units of government for the funds expended on the "State poor" (persons without legal settlement in a local governmental unit and for whom no local unit of government was financially responsible).[1] Only 2 of the 10 States which had old age assistance programs contributed State funds to the care of the aged. Approximately one-third of the statutes establishing programs for aid to dependent children in their own homes and less than one-half of blind assistance systems provided for State contributions. An increase in the proportion of States participating in the financing of these programs began in 1933, and by January 1, 1939, most of the States had assumed some financial responsibility for all these programs.

Some State funds for general relief are currently provided in approximately two-thirds of the States (table 5). State participation is found much more widely in the three categories (old age, blind assistance, and aid to dependent children) included in the Federal Social Security Act, which requires that the State assume some financial responsibility in order to qualify for Federal reimbursement. State funds are granted for old age assistance in all States, over one-half of which share financial responsibility with local units (table 11). Approximately the

---

[1] In New York the State also assumed responsibility for needy Indians on reservations.

same situation exists in the statutes granting blind assistance except that two States have not as yet assumed any financial responsibility (table 17). All but four States have made funds available for aid to dependent children programs, but less than one-third of them have assumed the entire responsibility (table 21).

The care of dependent and neglected children is at least partially financed by a majority of States, which maintain either State institutions or appropriate funds for the care of children in foster homes or private institutions. Local units of government are also given some financial responsibility for the care of such children in practically all of the States (table 27).

Institutional care of veterans and veterans' pensions are financed from State funds in all States. However, approximately two-thirds of the States granting direct relief to veterans place the financial responsibility upon local units (tables 29, 31, and 33).

PROVISION FOR THE DISTRIBUTION OF STATE FUNDS

Several methods have been provided for the distribution of State funds (tables 5, 11, 17, and 21). States assuming the full responsibility may either distribute funds directly to individuals or may transfer such funds to local units of government for distribution. In States which share the financial responsibility with local units, the funds may be allotted to local governmental units for distribution or the State may make payments and obtain reimbursements from the local units.

The majority of States that have assumed the total financial responsibility provide for the distribution of funds directly to individual applicants. In most instances where the financial responsibility is shared, State funds are allocated to local units for distribution to individuals. A few States, however, provide for the distribution of funds by the State which is reimbursed by local units for their proportionate share.

The method of distribution most frequently found in instances where the responsibility is divided consists of a rigid statutory formula in which the percentage contributions of the State and local units are specified. The extent of State contributions ranges from 25 percent to 90 percent of the total. Another type of rigid statutory formula has been adopted in a few States which provide for the distribution of funds on the basis of population.

Several State statutes have been drafted so as to allow administrative officials to consider the financial capacity of local units. The majority of these State laws do not establish definite legal formulae for the allocation of funds but have left to administrative discretion the determination of the need of the various local units. A few States, however, have established criteria for administrative guidance. Among them are: (1) the number of cases and the cost of living within each local unit; (2) the number of cases and ability of the local unit to meet costs; and (3) population, need, and financial condition of the local unit.

The Louisiana statutes provide for a flat percentage reimbursement but authorize the State Department of Public Welfare to assume the total burden if a parish is unable to contribute its share because of financial inability or legal prohibition. Several other States which have provided for a flat percentage contribution have also taken into consideration the possible financial incapacity of local units and have provided for this contingency by authorizing loans or additional grants.

SOURCES OF FUNDS FOR RELIEF AND PUBLIC ASSISTANCE

An examination of the types of funds used for relief and public assistance shows that practically all States at present are financing these programs out of current revenue rather than from borrowed funds. This is in sharp contrast to the general use of borrowed funds for emergency unemployment relief prior to 1935.

Relief and public assistance are financed more frequently from general revenue than from any other source. However, the receipts of certain taxes are specifically appropriated to these activities in many States, but no one type is used consistently throughout the States.[2] Liquor and beverage taxes are applied in about one-fourth of the States to finance general relief, old age assistance, blind assistance, or aid to dependent children. Sales taxes serve the same purpose in about 10 States. Since, for the majority of local governmental units, property taxes are the only source of revenue this type of tax is generally used where the law requires local contribution.

---

[2]Only the legal sources of funds have been studied. In order to make a complete analysis of the sources of funds for these activities, it would be necessary to go beyond the acts appropriating relief money from general revenue to discover when specified taxes had been levied to reimburse the general fund depleted by such appropriations. Such instances cannot be traced by examination of the statutes alone.

Section VI

THE INTEGRATION OF PUBLIC WELFARE FUNCTIONS WITHIN A SINGLE STATE AGENCY

RELIEF AND PUBLIC ASSISTANCE

IN 1934, following the assumption of some administrative responsibility (either direct or supervisory) by the States for relief and public assistance, there began a trend toward the centralization of administrative responsibility within a single State agency. The degree of integration which has occurred varies among the several States. Strictly speaking, complete integration exists only in those States where all types of relief or public assistance for which the State has some administrative responsibility are administered by a single State agency. However, for the purpose of this analysis it is considered that a significant degree of integration exists when at least three types of relief or public assistance are administered by a single State agency. Integration to this extent indicates a fairly clear intention to centralize the administration of relief and assistance within a single agency. On the other hand, the administration of only two types of relief by a State agency does not necessarily show an intention on the part of the legislature to set up an integrated system. Some States which formerly had only two types of relief, both of which were administered by the same agency, had at a later date adopted new types of relief for which the administrative responsibility rested in separate independent agencies.

The types of assistance included in the Federal Social Security Act were the first to be included in partially or completely integrated systems. The Federal act requires State administrative participation, and many of the States were placing some administrative responsibility for these public assistance functions upon State agencies for the first time where integration first occurred.

On January 1, 1939, 45 States had State agencies administering or supervising at least 3 types of relief and public assistance. Approximately one-half of those State agencies participated administratively in five relief or assistance functions, while several States had a completely integrated system.[1] Only Delaware, Michigan, and Mississippi administered the bulk of their relief and assistance programs through independent agencies.

Those functions which are included in the Federal Social Security Act are more frequently administered or supervised through integrated systems than either general or veteran relief. Old age assistance is administered or supervised through an integrated system in 44 States, blind assistance in 41 States, and aid to dependent children in 44 States. Some administrative function relating to dependent and neglected children is carried out through an integrated system in 43 States. There are, however, several States which have in addition independent agencies administering or supervising care of dependent and neglected children.

The majority (24) of the States which have assumed some administrative responsibility for general relief have placed this responsibility within an integrated system. As many as 18 States, however, have not assumed any administrative responsibility.

Veteran relief has been included within integrated systems less frequently than any other type. In only 13 States do agencies which administer 3 or more other types of relief or public assistance also administer some phase of veteran relief, and in only a very few of these does such agency administer or supervise the complete veteran relief program.

GENERAL PUBLIC WELFARE PROGRAM

The discussion of integration up to this point has been concerned with relief and public assistance. Inasmuch as there is a close relationship among dependency, deficiency, and delinquency, it is important that close cooperation exists among agencies concerned with these various phases of a complete welfare program. Necessary cooperation may exist between independent agencies handling these problems, but the difficulty of effective cooperation increases with every increase in the number of independent agencies.

An analysis of the statutes providing for the public welfare systems of the several States indicates that, generally speaking, they fall into one of five types:[2] (1) Complete or almost complete integration of all public welfare functions within one

---

[1] See organizational charts and summaries in appendix C.

[2] This classification is based upon the legal and constitutional provisions of the several States. It does not take into consideration such qualitative factors as the relative importance of various State agencies or the fact that integration may exist by informal or extra-legal methods. For the

agency.[3] Thirteen States[4] and the District of Columbia fall within this group, while New Hampshire and Virginia are on the borderline between this group and group 3. (2) Complete or almost complete integration of relief and public assistance functions within one agency and complete or almost complete integration of other public welfare functions (usually institutional) within a second agency. Seventeen States[5] come within this class. (3) Complete or almost complete integration of relief and public assistance functions within a single agency with other public welfare functions administered by independent agencies. Thirteen States,[6] Alaska, and Hawaii come within this group. (4) Complete or almost complete integration of functions other than relief or public assistance with relief and public assistance being administered by independent agencies. Mississippi is the only State coming within this class. (5) All public welfare functions administered by independent agencies. Delaware and Michigan come within this class. It is interesting that types 4 and 5, which, except in a few of the larger industrial States, were the prevailing types of public welfare systems prior to 1933, exist now in only a negligible number of States.

purpose of this classification integration is considered to have occurred where several agencies are, under the law, finally responsible to a single agency; in fact, such integration may be of little significance since the separate agencies act quite independently of one another. It is to be noted, moreover, that a number of States have shown a definite preference for establishing certain functions under the control of a completely independent agency. For example, Maryland, Massachusetts, and New York have established separate departments of correction or mental hygiene.

[3]The term *complete or almost complete integration* means that the agency administers or supervises at least three relief or public assistance functions and a majority of the other public welfare functions performed by the State.

[4]Georgia, Illinois, Indiana, Kentucky, Maine, Minnesota, Nebraska, New Jersey, Ohio, Rhode Island, Tennessee, Texas, and Vermont. For complete welfare statutory organization see charts and summaries in appendix C.

[5]Arizona, California, Colorado, Florida, Idaho, Iowa, Kansas, Missouri, North Dakota, Oklahoma, Oregon, Pennsylvania, South Dakota, Washington, West Virginia, Wyoming, and Wisconsin.

[6]Alabama, Arkansas, Connecticut, Louisiana, Maryland, Massachusetts, Montana, Nevada, New Mexico, New York, North Carolina, South Carolina, and Utah.

Section VII

TYPES OF STATE AND LOCAL AGENCIES ADMINISTERING RELIEF AND PUBLIC ASSISTANCE [1]

STATE BOARDS of public welfare or public welfare commissions have been established by law in more than three-fourths of the States, while agencies administered by a single administrator, executive director, or commissioner are found in only six States.

STATE BOARDS OF PUBLIC WELFARE

The part which the board or commission plays in the administration of public welfare varies greatly among the States. Their function ranges from being purely advisory, as with the Massachusetts Board of Public Welfare, to being executive in character, as with the Minnesota Board of Control. The powers and duties of these boards and commissions, as distinguished from the powers and duties of the executive or department, are usually statutory; but classification of these boards and commissions on the basis of law alone is meaningless without consideration of their actual operation which is not within the scope of this study.

Organization

The composition of public welfare boards varies somewhat among the several States (table 34). The number of members provided for ranges from 3 to 15, with approximately one-third of the State laws providing for boards with 5 members and about an additional one-third for public welfare boards of 7 members.

Qualifications

The qualifications for membership on a State public welfare board are usually stated in general terms and require that the

---

[1] Only those State agencies which administer any three relief and public assistance functions or general relief or old age assistance are analyzed in detail. This analysis is concerned principally with the types of governing bodies of State departments and does not include internal organization which is usually established by rules and regulations rather than statute.

appointee have a recognized interest in and knowledge of public welfare problems. A few State laws specify that members must be citizens or residents of the State.

Selection and Appointment

Most of the State statutes place limitations upon the appointment of members of public welfare boards (table 34). The provision that the appointment must be made without regard to political affiliation is found frequently as is the requirement for definite representation of different political parties. Some laws prevent the appointment of any political officeholder or public employee, and a few statutes even prohibit a member of the board from holding office for a specified period after retirement from the board. Several State statutes provide for the selection of members from different geographical sections of the State. The laws frequently provide for the appointment of at least one or two women to serve on the board. In a few States members are precluded from serving more than two consecutive terms.

In almost all States public welfare boards are appointed by the Governor. In about half of these the Governor has the sole authority for making appointments, and in the other half appointments must be confirmed or approved by the State Senate or General Assembly or the Governor's council. The remaining State laws provide that existing State officers serve on the board in an ex officio capacity. In several States the Governor is an ex officio member of the board.

Terms of Office

In almost all States appointees serve rotating or overlapping terms in order to assure continuity of policy. Terms range from 3 to 9 years, but 4- or 6-year terms have been most frequently adopted.

Compensation

Members of public welfare boards in most of the States serve gratuitously except for actual expenses. Few States pay fixed salaries to members. Approximately one-fourth of the State laws specify per diem allowances and the majority of these place a limit on the amount which any member may receive in a year. Service on a public welfare board is considered a full-time job only in those States which place administrative or executive duties upon the board. In these instances fixed salaries are paid to the members.

EXECUTIVE OF STATE DEPARTMENT OF PUBLIC WELFARE

In most States provisions are made for an administrator, executive director, or commissioner who usually functions with the assistance of a board and who carries out or directs the execution of the duties and policies of the board or department (table 35). He may also determine policies or assist a board in determining policies.

Selection and Appointment

Several methods of selecting the executive have been adopted. Selection and appointment by the board is the method provided for in nearly one-half of the States. In a few States this selection and appointment must be in conformity with the State civil service laws. In the remaining States the Governor is given some share in the selection and appointment. Selection or appointment by the Governor with the advice of his council or the consent of the State legislative body is the method that has been adopted in about one-fourth of the States. The remaining State statutes either grant the Governor the sole authority to make the appointment or the authority to approve or disapprove the selection of the board.

Terms of Office

In over one-half of the States the executive serves at the pleasure of the board, while in an additional one-fourth a term of office ranging from 2 to 6 years is stated in the law. In the remaining States the executive is either a civil service employee with tenure of office or else serves at the pleasure of the Governor.

Qualifications

The qualifications of the executive are included in the statutes providing for his appointment in about one-half of the States. The most common provision is that he must be a trained administrator of public welfare. A number of State statutes provide that only citizens or residents of the State are eligible and the length of residence required is usually 5 years. The New Jersey statute specifically states that the appointment need not be limited to residents. In some States civil service statutes specify qualifications for the executive of the welfare board.

Compensation

The salary of the executive is usually fixed by law or a maximum is placed upon the amount which may be paid. The board is given the power to fix the salary without limitation in only a few States.

LOCAL DEPARTMENTS OF PUBLIC WELFARE

In local governmental units there are several types of organizations which have been provided to administer public welfare functions (table 36). The local public welfare administrative unit may be a township, town, city, county, or district. In the majority of States the county has been designated as the local unit, but frequently large cities are constituted separate administrative units. Many State statutes authorize two or more counties or cities and counties to unite to form a district public welfare administrative unit, usually with the consent of the State department.

Organization

The board and executive form of local organization has been adopted in the majority of States (table 36). Agencies with responsibility placed in a single executive without the assistance of a board have been provided for in less than a half dozen States. Less than one-fourth of the States have made no provision for local public welfare organization. In these States the functions are performed entirely by the State department, or the administrative duties are placed upon the governing bodies of local governmental units acting in their official capacity. The latter situation differs somewhat from that in which a local public welfare board is established by law and the local governing body (boards of county commissioners, city councils, etc.) ex officio constitutes such board. This type of organization has been provided for in a few States.

Functions of Local Boards

The functions performed by local boards range from executive to purely advisory. In some instances these boards meet periodically and pass upon all applications. In other instances the boards' work is confined to advising the local director and acting in a liaison capacity between local officials and the community.

Qualifications of Local Boards

In those States which have provided for the appointment of local boards of public welfare, residence within the governmental unit to be served is the qualification most frequently required of appointees. Often this is the only requirement, though several State statutes provide that members must be selected on the basis of their interest in and knowledge of public welfare. The size of local boards varies considerably among the States. The number of members provided for ranges from 3 to 11. Boards consisting of five or seven members are most frequently provided.

Provisions assuring the service of women on local boards appear with some frequency, and a few statutes bar public officials and relatives of members of local governing bodies. The Arkansas statute bars retail merchants, presumably because of the influence they might have over the expenditure of a relief recipient's funds.

Selection and Appointment of Local Boards

State departments of public welfare have been granted some authority in relation to the appointment of local boards of welfare in approximately one-half of the States which provide for the appointment of local boards (table 36). Various methods have been provided by statutes: selection and appointment of total membership by the State department; selection and appointment of part of membership by the State department; appointment by the State department from lists submitted by local officials; selection and appointment by local officials from lists submitted by the State department; and selection and appointment by local officials with the advice or approval of the State department. In the majority of the remaining States the membership is selected and appointed by local officials without the assistance of the State department. Local boards are appointed by the Governors of a few States, and in one State, Massachusetts, they are elected.

Terms of Office of Local Boards

Rotating or overlapping terms are usually established for periods ranging from 1 to 6 years. Three-year or four-year terms have been adopted in approximately one-half of the States providing for the appointment of local boards. In three States the length of term is fixed by the State department.

Compensation of Local Boards

Some provision for remuneration of members of local boards is contained in the laws of about one-half of the States providing for their appointment. Compensation is usually restricted to expenses incurred in the performance of their duties; however, a few of these States also grant a per diem allowance.

LOCAL EXECUTIVE

Specific provisions for local directors or administrators have been made in about two-thirds of the States (table 37). Where local boards or departments have been established with the power to appoint a staff, an executive could probably be appointed under such provision even though the appointment is not specifically authorized.

In about one-third of the States which make specific provision for a local executive, the State department participates in the selection and appointment. The types of participation by the State department are similar to those providing for the appointment of local boards. Local boards are authorized to appoint an executive in an additional one-third of these States. In the remaining States the executive is elected or appointed by either the local governing body or the Governor.

Generally the executive holds office during the pleasure of the appointing body. Specific qualifications for the local director are not usually established by law, although many statutes provide that he must meet the qualifications imposed by the State department of public welfare. The provision that the appointee must be a resident of the county is found in a few States.

Appendixes

Appendix A

BASIC TABLES

EXPLANATIONS OF TERMS USED IN TABLES

Rapid expansion and recent developments in the field of public welfare have made it necessary to set up various terms and definitions for the purposes of this study. They are indicated and explained in the following paragraphs.

M or **O** indicate the mandatory or optional nature of the law (tables 1, 6, 12, 18, 29, 31, and 33). A law is considered to be mandatory when it is phrased in such a way that it requires the administering official to grant aid if the applicant meets all of the qualifications imposed by law. If the granting of aid to a specific individual when he meets the qualifications is discretionary with the official, the law is considered optional.

Direct responsibility as used in tables 1, 6, 12, 18, 29, and 31 under the caption "administrative responsibility" means the final original responsibility[1] for determining whether relief or assistance shall be given an applicant. If the final original decision is made by the State department or its agent, the direct responsibility is considered to be upon that department. On the other hand, if the final original decision is made by an agent of the local unit of government, then the direct responsibility is considered to be upon that unit.[2]

Assisted by as used in the text of tables 1, 6, 12, and 18 under the caption "direct responsibility" indicates that the administrative agency assisting is not an agent of the administrative agency having direct responsibility but is serving in an advisory capacity to such administrative agency.

Through as used in the text of tables 1, 6, 12, and 18 indicates that the local administrative agency is an agent of the administrative agency having direct responsibility and makes the final original determinations for that administrative agency.

Supervisory responsibility wherever used means that the administrative agency does not have direct responsibility but has substantial control of policy and has the power to adopt rules and regulations which are binding on the administrative agency with direct responsibility.

Final and **advisory** column heads as· used in tables 1, 6, 12, and 18 under the caption "original determination" and tables 29, 31, and 33 under the caption "determination of eligibility" indicate the administrative agency making the final original determination or serving in an advisory capacity without considering the effect of the presence of an agency relationship. An administrative agency is considered to be acting in an advisory capacity when its duties consist of making investigations and forwarding its findings and recommendations to another administrative agency which makes the final original determination.

Administrative responsibility as used in table 33 is restricted to the responsibility for the management or control of an institution and does not necessarily involve the determination of eligibility for admission to the institution.

Financial responsibility means the responsibility for supplying funds for relief and public assistance, either for grants to individuals or for administrative expenses. No consideration has been given to Federal financial participation unless such participation is specifically mentioned in the State statute.

Administered by as used in the summary statements in the appendix means that the agency concerned has the direct responsibility as defined above.

---

[1] The seemingly contradictory words "final original" have been used because under many State statutes the original determination is not final but must be approved by another administrative agency before becoming effective. The term *final original responsibility* means the responsibility for determining whether or not an applicant shall receive relief or assistance in the absence of an appeal, review, or reconsideration.

[2] The administrative agency making the final original determination is considered to be an agent of the State department if the power of appointment and removal of such administrative agency is vested within the department. If the power of appointment and removal of the administrative agency is vested in the political heads of the local units or in some body other than the State department, or if such administrative agency is an elected local official, then the administrative agency is considered to be an agent of the local unit of government.

General Relief

Table 1.—Provisions for the Administration of General Relief

State	Nature of law	Administrative responsibility		Determination of eligibility		
		Direct	Supervisory	Original determination		Appeal by applicant
				Final	Advisory	
Alabama	M	County department of public welfare	State Department of Public Welfare.	County board of public welfare		
Arizona	M'	County board of social security and public welfare.[1]	State Department of Social Security and Welfare.	County board of social security and public welfare.[1]		
Arkansas:[2] State	M	State Department of Public Welfare through county or district department of public welfare.		County or district department of public welfare.		
Local	M	County court		County court		To circuit court.
California:[2] (See appendix B.) State	O	State Emergency Relief Administration		State Emergency Relief Administration	[3]	[5].
Local	M	County board of supervisors[4]		County board of supervisors		
Colorado	M	County or district department of public welfare.	State Department of Public Welfare.	County or district department of public welfare.		
Connecticut	M	Town overseer of the poor[6]		Town overseer of the poor[6]		
Delaware	M[8]	State Old Age Welfare Commission[7]		State Old Age Welfare Commission[7]		
Florida	M[8]	Board of county commissioners. City council. Town council. County welfare board.[8] County board of charity.[9]		Board of county commissioners. City council. Town council. County welfare board.[8] County board of charity.[9]	[10]	
Georgia	O	County or district department of public welfare.	State Department of Public Welfare.	County or district department of public welfare.		
Idaho	M	Board of county commissioners. County welfare commission.[11]	State Department of Public Assistance.	Board of county commissioners. County welfare commission.[11]	Probate judge, clerk of board of county commissioners, or justice of the peace.[12]	To State Department of Public Assistance.[13]
Illinois	M	Overseer of the poor or designated official.[14] County bureau of public welfare.[15]	[16]	Overseer of the poor or designated official.[14] County bureau of public welfare.[15]		
Indiana	M	Township overseer of the poor		Township overseer of the poor		To board of county commissioners.
Iowa	M	County board of supervisors. Township trustees as overseers of the poor.[17]	[18]	County board of supervisors. Township trustees as overseers of the poor.[17]		To county board of supervisors from decision of township trustees.

Kansas	M	County board of social welfare	State Board of Social Welfare.	County board of social welfare		To State Board of Social Welfare.[19]
Kentucky	M	County court	State Department of Welfare.	County court		
Louisiana (See appendix B.)	M	Parish department of public welfare	State Department of Public Welfare.	Parish department of public welfare		
Maine	M	City, town, or plantation overseers of the poor.	(20)	City, town, or plantation overseers of the poor.		
Maryland	M[21]	County welfare board. Baltimore Department of Welfare.[22]	Board of State Aid and Charities.	County welfare board. Baltimore Department of Welfare.[22]		
Massachusetts	M	Local board of public welfare		Local board of public welfare		
Michigan:[2] State	M	State Emergency Welfare Relief Commission		State Emergency Welfare Relief Commission		
Local	M	County superintendents of the poor. Local supervisors and directors of the poor.		County superintendents of the poor. Local supervisors and directors of the poor.	County welfare relief commission.[23]	
Minnesota	M	County or city welfare board. Local supervisors of the poor.[24]	State Executive Council.[25]	County or city welfare board. Local supervisors of the poor.		
Mississippi	M	County board of supervisors		County board of supervisors		
Missouri:[2] State	M	State Social Security Commission		State Social Security Commission	County social security commission.[26]	(27).
Local	M	County court. City board of social welfare[28]	(29)	County court. City board of social welfare[28]		
Montana	M	County department of public welfare	State Department of Public Welfare.	County department of public welfare		To either county or State Board of Public Welfare, or to both.
Nebraska	M	County assistance committee[30]		County assistance committee[30]		
Nevada	M	Board of county commissioners	State Welfare Department.	Board of county commissioners		
New Hampshire	M	Town overseers of the poor. Board of county commissioners.[31]		Town overseers of the poor. Board of county commissioners.[31]		
New Jersey	M	Local overseer of the poor. County welfare board. Local assistance board.[32]	(33)	Local overseer of the poor. County welfare board. Local director of welfare.[32]		(33).
New Mexico:[2] State	M	State Department of Public Welfare[34]		State Department of Public Welfare.[34]	(34)	(35).
Local	O	Board of county commissioners. City council or other governing board of cities, towns, or villages.		Board of county commissioners. City council or other governing board of cities, towns, or villages.		
New York[2]	M	Local public welfare official[36]	State Department of Social Welfare.	Local public welfare official[36]		State Board of Public Welfare.[35]

[1] See footnotes at end of table.

Table 1.—Provisions for the Administration of General Relief—Continued

State	Nature of law	Administrative responsibility		Determination of eligibility		
				Original determination		
		Direct	Supervisory	Final	Advisory	Appeal by applicant
North Carolina	O	Board of county commissioners through county superintendent of public welfare. City public welfare officer.[37]		County superintendent of public welfare. City public welfare officer.[37]		
North Dakota	M	County welfare board	State Public Welfare Board.	County welfare board		
Ohio (See appendix B.)	M	Township trustees. City director of public safety. Board of county commissioners.	[38]	Township trustees. City director of public safety. Board of county commissioners.		
Oklahoma:[2]						
State	O	State Board of Public Welfare[39]	State Board of Public Welfare[39]	State Board of Public Welfare[39]		
State—county	M	County overseers of the poor.[40] County welfare board.[41]	State Board of Public Welfare.[40]	County overseers of the poor.[40] County welfare board.[41]		(40).
Oregon:[2]						
State	M	County relief committee	State Relief Committee.	County relief committee		
Local	M	County court or board of county commissioners.		County court or board of county commissioners.		
Pennsylvania	M	County board of assistance	State Department of Public Assistance.	County board of assistance		State Board of Public Assistance.
Rhode Island	M	Local director of public welfare or local work relief bureau.	State Unemployment Relief Commission.[42]	Local director of public welfare or local work relief bureau.		(42)
South Carolina:[2]						
State	M	State Department of Public Welfare through county department of public welfare.[43]		County department of public welfare[43]		To State Department of Public Welfare.[44]
Local	M	Board of county commissioners[45]	(46)	Board of county commissioners[45]		
South Dakota	M	Board of county commissioners		Board of county commissioners	Township board or governing body of town or city.	To judge of circuit court of the county.
Tennessee	M	County court		County court		Decisions of commissioners of poor on admissions to poorhouse may be appealed to county court.
Texas:[2]						
State[47]	M	State Board of Control, division of public welfare, through local agency designated by it.		Local agency designated by State Board of Control, division of public welfare.		
Local	M	County commissioners' court		County commissioners' court		

Utah	M	County or district department of public welfare.[48]	State Department of Public Welfare.	To State Department of Public Welfare, from county department.[44]
Vermont	M	Town overseers of the poor. Supervisors of unorganized towns and gores.[49]		
Virginia	M	County or city board of public welfare.[48]	State Board of Public Welfare.	To circuit court of county or corporation court of city.
Washington	M	County administrator of public assistance.	State Department of Social Security.	To the board of county commissioners, then to the State Department of Social Security,[50] and then to the county superior court.
West Virginia	M	County public assistance council[51]	State Department of Public Assistance.	To advisory board of State Department of Public Assistance.[52]
Wisconsin	M	Town boards, village trustees, city common councils, county departments of trustees, managers of county institutions, or such persons as the county council may designate.[53]	(53)	
Wyoming	O	County department of public welfare.	State Department of Public Welfare.	To State Board of Public Welfare.[54]
Alaska:				
Temporary Pioneers' Home	O	Territorial Department of Public Welfare		
	M	Board of trustees of Pioneers' Home		
District of Columbia	M	Board of Public Welfare		
Hawaii	M	County public welfare commission	Territorial Board of Public Welfare.	To Territorial Board of Public Welfare.[55]

M indicates mandatory provision.
O indicates optional provision.

[1] County boards of supervisors administer provisions for hospitalization and care of the indigent sick.
[2] systems of general relief provided for by law.
[3] The State Emergency Relief Administration may appoint city and county citizens' relief committees to assist in the administration of relief.
[4] County board of public welfare may be established by county board of supervisors on petition of electorate.
[5] Any citizen is entitled to demand and receive a statement of the amount, character, and value of the relief received by any person.
[6] State commissioner of welfare is responsible for State paupers.
[7] Levy courts of Kent and Sussex Counties grant and approve hospitalization benefits.

[8] Law mandatory only in counties of 155,000 population. County welfare boards are provided for in these counties.
[9] established in counties of 9,700 to 10,500 population.
[10] The State Welfare Board may accept such duties as may be delegated to it by the counties or by municipal agencies.
[11] County welfare commissions are authorized, if cooperative agreements are executed between the State Department of Public Assistance and the board of county commissioners, to assume administrative responsibility for general or poor relief financed by county funds. State funds for general relief are administered by county welfare commissions whose activities are supervised by the State Department of Public Assistance.
[12] Above mentioned officials act in an advisory capacity to board of county commissioners if administrative responsibility for general or poor relief has not been delegated to the county welfare commission.

Table 1.—Footnotes Continued

13 No appeal allowed in instances where the board of county commissioners has delegated its powers in relation to local poor relief to the county welfare commission.

14 Established in each city, village, precinct, or incorporated town with a population of more than 500,000. Does not apply in counties of 500,000 population or more.

15 Established in counties of 500,000 or more (Cook County).

16 The State Department of Public Welfare inspects and investigates outdoor relief and almshouses. The State Emergency Relief Commission determines and certifies amounts to be allocated from the emergency relief fund to the counties.

17 Application may be made to county board of supervisors or township trustees. Township trustees may grant temporary relief subject to the approval of county board of supervisors who may continue or deny relief.

18 The State Emergency Relief Administration must allocate funds to the several counties.

19 Complaint may be made by interested person or taxpayer.

20 The State Department of Health and Welfare investigates and inspects all systems of public charity and public institutions.

21 Except in Baltimore, Garrett, and Wicomico Counties.

22 Welfare activities supported in whole or in part by State funds are administered by the county welfare activities supported in whole or in part by State funds are administered by the county welfare boards where established, the department of welfare of Baltimore City, or other agency designated by the Board of State Aid and Charities. In the absence of State funds, general relief is administered by the boards of county commissioners or agents designated by them, trustees of the poor, or justices of the peace, depending upon the law applicable in a particular county.

23 The county welfare relief commission certifies eligibility of applicants and has such powers and duties as may be prescribed by the State Emergency Welfare Relief Commission.

24 See summary of public-welfare provisions for Minnesota for more nearly complete information (pp. 316—318).

25 Supervises expenditure of State funds.

26 The county commission is an agent of the State commission.

27 All benefits granted may be reconsidered by the State administrator as frequently as he may deem necessary.

28 Established in counties containing first class cities.

29 City boards must report on request to the mayor, common council, and county court.

30 Consists of a board of county commissioners or supervisor, county treasurer, and the county board of public welfare, if in existence.

31 County commissioner administers relief to persons for whose support no person or town in the State is chargeable.

32 In counties operating under the local system whereby the poor are chargeable to the township, towns, boroughs, and cities, general relief is administered by the overseers of the poor of the respective political subdivision. In counties operating under the county system whereby the poor are chargeable to the county, general relief is administered by county welfare boards. Municipal governing bodies must appoint a local assistance board for each municipality. The local director of welfare, who may be the overseer of the poor of the municipality, is the executive officer of the local assistance board. The State Department of Institutions and Agencies approves plans for county welfare houses and has power of inspection over all institutions for the poor. The State Financial Assistance Commission

38 State funds are allocated to counties by the State treasurer on voucher and warrant of the State auditor.

39 The State Board of Public Welfare may establish necessary agencies to administer relief.

40 The board of county commissioners, as ex officio overseers of the poor, administers indoor relief from county funds without State supervision. Decisions of the overseers of the poor may be allowed to the county district court.

41 The board of county commissioners and the county health officer, serving as the county welfare board, administer relief, other than indoor relief, from State and county funds. The State Board of Public Welfare may appoint a representative to act in place of the county welfare board.

42 Poor law provides for care in a poorhouse, a workhouse, or with some private family, and is administered locally without State supervision. Poor law also provides for appeals to the superior court. The State supervised and State financed program of home relief and work relief ends with the emergency period on June 30, 1939.

43 In Charleston County a county welfare board is created to administer in the county all matters of direct welfare and relief under the supervision of the State Department of Public Welfare.

44 State Department of Public Welfare may review awards on own motion and make further investigations. Grants must be reconsidered by local departments as frequently as may be required by the State department.

45 In Columbia the city authorities are authorized to administer local poor relief. In Aiken County a committee appointed by the Governor has charge of the poorhouse and farm. In Darlington County the county commission of public welfare is created to administer all poor relief on the part of the county.

46 The State Department of Public Welfare is authorized to make investigations into the administration and affairs of any public or private agency or institution in the State concerned with the problems of dependency, defectiveness, or delinquency.

47 No State funds have been made available as of January 1, 1939.

48 No person may be received into any hospital or infirmary maintained by a county without an order of the board of county commissioners or commissioner of the poor.

49 Unorganized towns and gores have the same rights as towns and are subject to the same duties and liabilities in regard to poor and indigent persons.

50 The State department may make such further investigation as it deems necessary.

51 The management and operation of county infirmaries or institutions providing relief is vested in the respective county courts. Such management and operation may, by written agreement, be transferred to the county public assistance council.

52 Advisory board may review local decision on petition of county council, county court, or any interested person.

53 Every town, village, and city is charged with the relief and support of all poor and indigent persons having settlement therein. Counties are responsible for those persons not having settlement. The county board of supervisors may abolish this distinction between town, village, city, and county poor, in which case the county must relieve and support all poor and indigent persons. The board of supervisors may also return the support of such persons to the towns, villages, and cities. In counties having established a county home or hospital the following provisions apply: if population is fewer than

is empowered to allocate funds to municipalities and to establish rules and regulations governing the expenditures of these funds.

[33] The overseer must determine who are to be relieved by him subject to appeal by any person to the juvenile and domestic relations court.

[34] Application must be made to local office which investigates and makes report of findings and recommendations to the State department. The State department must decide eligibility and amount of assistance. The State department may allow its local office to determine whether assistance may be granted and the amount and manner thereof.

[35] State board may review awards on own motion, and make further investigation. Grants must be reconsidered by local office as frequently as may be required by the State board.

[36] "Public welfare official" means county commissioner of public welfare, city commissioner of public welfare, town public welfare officer, or city public welfare officer.

[37] City of Rocky Mount may be constituted a local welfare district with a city public welfare officer who must perform all duties and functions within the city limits of Rocky Mount as are conferred by law on county superintendents of public welfare.

250,000 the county board of trustees has charge of all indoor and outdoor relief, or the county board of supervisors may employ some competent person to have charge of outdoor relief; if the population is 250,000 or more the manager of county institutions has charge of all relief. In all counties which have not established a county home or hospital, county boards of trustees have charge of all relief, or the county boards of supervisors may otherwise provide for the support and maintenance of the poor. State relief funds are administered in accordance with rules and regulations adopted by the State Industrial Commission or other agency designated by the Governor to administer relief, except that standards of eligibility shall be determined by individual local units. The State Board of Control has supervision over all county and municipal institutions.

[54] The State board may make such additional investigation as it deems necessary, and grants must be reviewed as frequently as may be required by the State department.

[55] The Territorial board may review awards on own motion and make further investigation. Grants must be reconsidered by local office as frequently as may be required by board.

Table 2.—Requirements for Eligibility for General Relief

State	Description of class	Residence provisions			Provisions for removal of needy nonresidents
		Acquisition of residence		Loss	
		State	Local		
Alabama	Persons in need of assistance		6 months in county immediately preceding application.		Pauper may be removed to county of residence.
Arizona	Indigent, sick, and disabled persons	3 years immediately preceding application.[1]	6 months in county immediately preceding application; 12 months immediately preceding application to receive hospitalization or medical care from county board of supervisors.[2]		
Arkansas:[3] State	Any needy person or family with insufficient income or resources to provide a reasonable subsistence.[4]				([5]).
Local	Lame, blind, sick, and aged and infirm persons who are unable to support themselves.				
California:[3] State	Destitute and unemployed persons	3 years continuously[7]	---	1 year uninterrupted absence from State except when called elsewhere for labor or other temporary purposes.	County may remove person to State or county of residence.
Local	All incompetent and indigent persons, and those incapacitated by age, disease, or accident, who are without means of self-support, not supported by friends or relatives, and not confined in State hospitals or State or private institutions.[6]		1 year in county immediately preceding application.[8]		
Colorado	Poor persons unable to earn a livelihood because of bodily infirmity, idiocy, lunacy, or other unavoidable cause; destitute unemployed and unemployables.	1 year immediately preceding application and actual physical presence of 350 days or 3 years immediately preceding application with actual physical presence of 30 months.	6 months in county immediately preceding becoming chargeable.		May be removed to county of residence.[5]
Connecticut	Persons with insufficient estate for support and no relatives able and liable by law for support.		4 years in town or 1 year if applicant owns $500 worth of realty.[9]		May be removed to place of residence.
Delaware	Any person unable to obtain work and who has no permanent abode or friends or relatives to maintain him, any indigent sick person, and any person with insufficient resources and income for necessities.	Legal residence			([5]).

State	Classes of persons eligible	Residence required	Acquisition of new residence	Removal
Florida	Indigent, infirm, and insane persons; in a county with a population of 155,000 or more, persons who because of age, infirmity, or misfortune have claims upon the aid and sympathy of society; in a county with a population 50,000 to 55,000, persons unable to support or maintain themselves because of delinquency, indigency, or other causes.	No general provision; county with population of 9,700 to 10,500, 2 years. County with population of 9,700 to 10,500, 1 year. County with population of 155,000 or more, 1 year.	------	------
Georgia	Persons without means of support and unable to maintain themselves by labor.	------	------	(5).
Idaho	Persons who are sick, indigent, or unable to work because of physical infirmities and would suffer if not aided by the county.	1 year immediately preceding application. 6 months in county immediately preceding application.	------	------
Illinois	Destitute persons and persons unable to earn a livelihood because of bodily infirmity, idiocy, lunacy, or other unavoidable causes.	1 year in county immediately preceding application.	------	May be removed to place of residence.
Indiana	Indigent persons or families who require aid and any person in a township who is sick or in distress without friends or funds.[10]	Uninterrupted residence of 1 year in township.[11]	Acquisition of new residence; wilful and uninterrupted absence for 1 year from township.	May be returned to place of residence on order of justice of the peace.
Iowa	Poor persons with no property who, because of physical disabilities, are unable to earn a living; needy persons with some means of support may be given aid if conducive to their welfare and to the best interests of the public.	1 year continuously in county[12]	Acquisition of new residence or absence for 1 year from State.	May be removed to State or county of residence on order of district or superior court.
Kansas	Persons in need of aid or service and unable to care for themselves.	1 year in county	Acquisition of new residence in State; wilful absence of 1 year from county of legal residence.	Provided for by rules and regulations of State board.[5]
Kentucky	Persons helpless and so destitute of property as to require public assistance.	------	------	------
Louisiana	Needy persons who are infirm and sick and disabled paupers. Entire support given only to those who are destitute and helpless.	------	------	------
Maine	Persons in need of relief because of poverty.	5 successive years in a town without receiving supplies as a pauper.	Acquisition of new residence or by 5 years' absence from town.[13]	Upon request of overseer where found, person may be removed to town of residence, unless overseer of latter town files written objection.[5]
Maryland	County welfare board designates poor relief recipients.[14]	(15).	------	------

See footnotes at end of table.

Table 2.—Requirements for Eligibility for General Relief—Continued

State	Description of class	Residence provisions			Provisions for removal of needy nonresidents
		Acquisition of residence		Loss	
		State	Local		
Massachusetts	Indigent persons needing support and destitute and extremely neglected children.[16]	----------	5 consecutive years in town[17]	Failure to reside in town for 5 consecutive years.	Board of public welfare may remove person to town of residence. Persons for whom no town is liable may be removed to State infirmary or to State or place where person belongs.
Michigan:[3]					
State	Destitute and unemployed persons	----------	----------	----------	May be removed to place of residence or transported out of the State.
Local	Poor persons unable to earn a living because of physical or mental disability. Aid given must be conducive to welfare of person and in the best interests of the public.	----------	1 year in township, city, or county.[18]		
Minnesota	Every poor person who is unable to earn a livelihood	1 year[19]	----------	Acquisition of new residence; voluntary uninterrupted absence for 1 year from State with intent to abandon residence.	May be removed to place of residence.
Mississippi	Paupers	----------	6 months in county	----------	Board of supervisors may direct constable to remove pauper to county of residence.
Missouri:[3]					
State	Persons needing aid or relief in cases of public calamity.[20]	----------	----------		
Local	In counties with first-class cities: indigent, sick dependent persons (except insane), and those suffering from a contagious disease. In all counties: aged, infirm, lame, blind, or sick persons unable to support themselves.	----------	12 months in county immediately preceding date of order for relief.[21]		
Montana	Destitute unemployed and unemployable persons and those in need of public assistance, who are not eligible for or are not receiving old age assistance, blind assistance, or aid to dependent children in their own homes, are eligible for direct relief. Persons must not be in need of continued care in	1 year[22]	6 months in county[23]	----------	Nonresidents may be removed to county of residence.

		State residence	County residence	Loss or acquisition of residence	Removal of nonresidents
Nebraska	public institution because of mental or physical condition. Persons without means of support because of infirmity, idiocy, lunacy, or other causes are eligible for poorhouse or workhouse care, medical aid, or hospitalization. Poor persons unable to earn livelihoods because of unavoidable causes.	1 year.[24]	6 months in county.[24]	Acquisition of new residence or uninterrupted absence for 1 year from State with intent to abandon residence.	By county of residence at request of county where found. Transportation afforded to nonresidents of State.
Nevada	Poor persons unable to earn livelihoods because of bodily infirmity, idiocy, lunacy, or other causes.	3 years	6 months in county		Upon request of county where found, person must be removed by county of residence.
New Hampshire	Poor persons unable to support themselves		5 consecutive years in town.[25]	Acquisition of new residence, abandonment of domicile for 5 consecutive years, or receipt of assistance as pauper for 5 consecutive years.	Overseers of town may cause applicant to be returned to his home. County commissioners or superior court may remove person to the county which gave relief to applicant within 1 year, or to the county in which applicant lived 1 year in last 5 if he seeks relief before having resided in county 3 months.[5]
New Jersey	Persons unable to maintain themselves or dependents. Needy persons not otherwise provided for under State laws who are willing to work but are unemployed or unemployable because of physical disability.	1 year without interruption immediately preceding May 4, 1936. 5 years without interruption for persons not qualifying under the preceding provision.[26]	1 year in municipality or if legal resident of State, residence is in municipality in which applicant spent major part of preceding year.[26]	Continuous absence for 1 year from State or municipality.	Applicant may be removed to place of residence. If applicant has no place of residence he may be removed to place from which he came.[5]
New Mexico:[3] State	Needy persons without reasonable subsistence who are not receiving other relief or assistance except medical or surgical care.				
Local	Deserving indigent persons who are objects of charity	1 year	90 days in county		
New York	Persons in need of relief and care who are unable to provide for themselves. Sick and dependent Indians who reside on any reservation within State.		1 year continuous residence in town or city.[27]	Acquisition of new residence or continuous absence for 1 year from State.	May be removed to place of residence in or out of the State.

See footnotes at end of table.

Table 2.—Requirements for Eligibility for General Relief—Continued

State	Description of class	Residence provisions			
		Acquisition of residence		Loss	Provisions for removal of needy nonresidents
		State	Local		
North Carolina	Indigent persons	3 years[28]	1 year continuously in county	Acquisition of new residence.	Upon complaint of county commissioners to justice of peace. County of residence must pay expense of removal.
North Dakota	Destitute and necessitous persons	1 year continuously[29]	1 year in county or if legal resident of State, residence is in county in which applicant spent major part of preceding year.[29]	Acquisition of new residence or voluntary absence for 1 year or more from county.	Overseers of poor may apply to district court for order to remove person to county of legal residence.
Ohio (See appendix B.)	Persons requiring public support or relief		County, 12 consecutive months. Town or city, 12 consecutive months in county, 3 consecutive months in town or city.[18]		May be removed to place of residence; upon refusal, court order may be obtained.
Oklahoma:[3] State	Destitute able-bodied persons and unemployables[30] not otherwise cared for by Government, State, or county relief agencies or by public or private charity.				
State—county	Indigent and destitute unemployables[30]	1 year for State funds	6 months for county funds		May be removed to county or State of residence.
Oregon:[3] State	Needy persons and their dependents				
Local	Any poor person unable to earn a living because of bodily infirmity, idiocy, lunacy, or other cause.	1 year[31]	6 months in county	1 year continuous residence in another State.	Paupers may be removed by county court to State of residence. Paupers who have resided in another county in the State 1 year prior to becoming a public charge may be removed thereto.
Pennsylvania	Persons who need assistance in order to maintain themselves and their dependents.	1 year immediately preceding application.			Any person with a quasi settlement in the State may receive assistance until removed to place of legal residence.

Rhode Island	Needy persons who are unemployed or whose employment is inadequate to provide the necessities of life.[32]	2 years[32]	6 months in town,[32] 5 years in town,[18] or possession of estate of inheritance or freehold in town and yearly income of $20 clear for 3 years.[33]	5 years continuous absence from town or acquisition of a new residence.[33]	May be removed to place of residence.[33]
South Carolina:[3] State					
Local	Persons in need who are unable to support themselves because of physical or mental infirmity and who are ineligible for other forms or public assistance. Inhabitants who by reason of age, infirmities, or misfortune have claim on sympathy and aid of society.		3 successive years in county or city.[34]		Overseers may remove person to place of residence.
South Dakota	Indigent persons	1 year	90 days in county	By acquiring new residence in the State or by wilful absence for 30 days from the State.	Upon complaint of any county commissioner, the justice of peace may cause any nonresident to be sent to his place of residence at the expense of the county.
Tennessee	Poor persons who may become chargeable as paupers and indigent sick or injured.		1 year in county[35]		
Texas:[3] State	All persons or families in dependent and needy circumstances who are ineligible for aid and are not concurrently receiving aid under other types of assistance.[36]				
Local	Paupers, indigent sick, and indigent public charges afflicted with tuberculosis.	1 year	6 months in county		
Utah	Persons who are indigent, sick, or otherwise dependent. Persons in destitute circumstances.	1 year	4 months in county (minors, 1 year).[37]	By acquisition of new residence or by 4 months' absence from county.	
Vermont	Poor and indigent persons in need of assistance for themselves or families.	([38])	3 years in town or gore		Nonresidents of State may be transported out of State. Nonresidents of towns may be transported to place of residence.[5]
Virginia	Vagrants and persons physically incapable of supporting themselves or providing maintenance. Destitute persons in need of public relief who are not, at time of receiving assistance, inmates of any county, municipal, State, or national institution.	Interstate migrants must reside in State 3 years unless at time of migration person was able to support self.[39]	12 consecutive months in county, town, or city.[40]		
Washington	In need because of unemployment because of physical disability or any other cause.				May be removed to place of residence in or out of the State.

See footnotes at end of table.

Table 2.—Requirements for Eligibility for General Relief—Continued

State	Description of class	Residence provisions			
		Acquisition of residence		Loss	Provisions for removal of needy nonresidents
		State	Local		
West Virginia	Indigent persons who are or will become public charges, who are in need of institutional care because of physical or mental condition, or are in need of medical or surgical care.	1 year[41]	Actually residing in county		
Wisconsin	Indigents and paupers who by reason of sickness, infirmity, decrepitude, old age, drunkenness, or pregnancy are likely to become public charges. Indigent persons afflicted with disease, malady, deformity, or ailment which can probably be remedied or advantageously treated.		1 year in town, city, or village.[48]	Absence from place of residence for 1 year or more or acquisition of new residence.	May be ordered to return to place of residence.
Wyoming	Indigent persons lacking sufficient income and resources for subsistence.	1 year[43]	1 year in county[4L]		County departments of public welfare must request authority from proper officials of county and State of residence to return nonresident and must provide transportation and expenses en route.
Alaska: Temporary	Persons without means who are unable to earn livelihoods because of immaturity, sickness, or physical infirmity and the unfortunate and needy in the Territory who are not entitled to the benefits of the Pioneers' Home or to old age pensions.				
Pioneers' Home	Worthy persons who are destitute and in need of aid because of physical disability or other reason.	5 years in Territory immediately preceding application.			
District of Columbia	All aged, infirm, or needy persons	Legal residence			May be removed to place of residence.
Hawaii	Needy persons or families who for any reason satisfactory to the county public welfare commission are unable to procure or provide sufficient support for themselves. Applicants must not have made an assignment or transfer of property to qualify for assistance. Applicants must not be inmates of any public institution while receiving aid.[44]				

[1]Temporary absence for periods amounting to 1 year does not affect the right to relief.

[2]Requirement waived in emergency cases.

[3]2 systems of general relief provided for by law.

[4]To qualify, applicant must not have disposed of property within 2 years prior to application.

[5]Reciprocal agreements are authorized with other States relating to transportation of indigents.

[6]Board of supervisors may specify the amount of property an applicant may possess while receiving aid.

[7]Without receiving relief. Time spent in public institution or on parole not counted in computing residence period.

[8]If no county residence, then county where applicant last resided 1 year within 3 years preceding application is liable. If applicant does not have 1 year's residence, the county in which applicant spent longest period is liable.

[9]Aliens and inhabitants of other towns in the State entitled to relief only by vote of inhabitants or by majority vote of selectmen, justices of the peace, and inhabitants. All applicants must have been self-supporting for 4 years. State assumes responsibility for "State poor"; i.e., persons in need of relief for whom no town is responsible because of lack of residence.

[10]Aid must not be refused any healthy person until the overseer of the poor is satisfied that the applicant is trying to find work for himself. No aid may be furnished to any person who refuses work at reasonable compensation.

[11]Married women abandoned by their husbands are eligible if they were residents of the township 6 months prior to abandonment. If applicant was supported by governmental agency during first 6 months, such time is eliminated in computing residence.

[12]Without receiving support from public funds, or care in any charitable institution, and without being warned to depart. If person warned to depart files an affidavit that he is not a pauper, he becomes eligible for relief 1 year after filing affidavit.

[13]Receipt of relief during absence prevents loss of settlement in town of original settlement.

[14]Provision is made for reception in almshouses of vagrants, beggars, dissolute persons who have no occupation and no visible means of support, and disorderly persons likely to become county charges. Baltimore City also cares for sick, disabled, destitute, and homeless persons. Baltimore County authorized to provide for unemployed, destitute, and indigent persons. State funds when available may be used for the relief of unemployed and unemployables.

[15]In Prince Georges County recipient of out-pension must be a citizen of the county; in Anne Arundel County recipient of out-pension must be a citizen of the United States and a resident of the county for 1 year immediately preceding application; in Baltimore County a recipient of relief must be a resident of the county.

[16]Ownership of insurance policies not in excess of $300 does not disqualify applicant.

[17]Without receiving any public relief except soldiers' and sailors' relief unless within 2 years after receiving relief recipient tenders the cost thereof to the commonwealth or town furnishing it.

[18]Without receiving public relief.

[19]County in which person resided longest within the year is liable, if relief is administered under county system. Town in which person resided longest within the year is liable if relief is administered under the town system. Time spent in public institutions, under commitment to guardianship of State Board of Control, or while receiving relief is excluded in determining residence.

[20]To qualify, applicant must not possess cash or negotiable securities in the sum of $500 or more, or interest in property of any kind in excess of $1,500 ($2,000 if owned by husband and wife living together).

[21]County court may, in its discretion, grant relief to any person without regard to residence.

[22]Aliens illegally in United States are not eligible.

[23]1-year county residence required for care in poor farm or workhouse.

[24]Excluding any period during which person was an inmate of any charitable or penal institution or received relief.

[25]Counties must support any person for whose support no person or town in State is chargeable.

[26]Time spent in charitable, custodial, or correctional institution excluded. Provided that the period beginning January 31, 1935, during which a resident of the State has received dependency or poor relief from State or local agency, must not be counted in determining residence, in order that a person's residence shall remain the same during the emergency period. This provision becomes inoperative on January 1, 1940.

[27]Without receiving public relief. Time spent while patient in hospital or inmate of any public institution or while on parole from such institution may not be counted as residence in order to gain settlement. Exceptions.—The following persons must reside in town 5 years to be eligible: tuberculous residents of Franklin, Greene, Ulster, Essex, Orange, Livingston, Otsego, Tompkins, Rockland, or Sullivan Counties, or a patient of a State district tuberculosis hospital and his family; residents of towns in Steuben County who have become members of the National Soldiers' Home at Bath; and members, inmates, and employees of the Veterans' Administration Facility in Ontario County.

[28]Unless at time of entering State person was able to support himself. Time spent in any institution or on parole therefrom is not counted.

[29]Without receiving public relief. Time spent in charitable, custodial, or correctional institution excluded.

[30]An "unemployable" is defined as a person who is destitute and unable to secure employment because of age, physical or mental disability, infirmity, temporary illness, or other disability; because of the rules of the Federal relief administration relating to age requirements on work relief programs; because of ineligibility for workmen's compensation insurance; because of inability to leave home to secure employment; or because of illness requiring supervision or attention.

[31]Under this act a resident of the State is a person who has lived continuously in the State for 3 years without receiving relief and with intent to make it his or her home. Time spent in a public institution or on parole therefrom, in a private charitable institution, or while child is dependent on public or private relief is not counted in determining residence.

[32]Requirement for home relief or work relief under State financed and State supervised program ending June 30, 1939. State Unemployment Relief Commission may waive residence requirements in special cases.

[33]Applies only to county financed and administered permanent poor relief program.

Table 2.—Footnotes Continued

[34]Person must be a citizen of this or some other State and must have maintained self and family during 3-year period.

[35]Applies to poorhouse care only.

[36]The types include aid to dependent and destitute children in their own homes or those of relatives, assistance to needy blind, or other types of assistance provided by the Social Security Act.

[37]No settlement can be acquired while a person is a recipient of charity.

[38]State provides for nonresidents of towns who have resided in State 1 year or more.

[39]Does not apply to outdoor relief to which State contributes.

[40]Without receiving public or private relief. Does not apply to outdoor relief to which State contributes.

[41]When funds are specifically available for that purpose, relief may be granted to those who have not been residents of the State 1 year.

[42]Time spent as follows shall not give a person legal residence: (1) while supported as a pauper; (2) while employed on a Works Progress Administration project or on any of the State or Federal work relief programs; (3) while a member of the Civilian Conservation Corps; (4) while residing in any public or private institution; (5) while residing in a transient camp; and (6) while residing or employed on any Indian reservation not under State jurisdiction.

[43]Provided that applicant has not been physically absent from State or county for a period of more than 1 year immediately preceding application; absence for service of the State or United States is excepted. Person must not have received public relief during this period.

[44]Inmate of an institution may apply for assistance to begin after his discharge from such institution.

Table 3.—Responsibility of Relatives and Provisions for Recovery of Cost of General Relief From Recipients and Their Estates

State	Relatives responsible for support of applicant	Recovery from recipients and their estates	
		Type and extent of recovery	Limitations on recovery
Alabama	Father, grandfather, brother, mother, grandmother, child, or grandchild.[1]		
Arizona:[2]			
Arkansas:[2]			
State			
Local			
California:[2]			
State			
Local	Spouse, parent, or adult child[1]	County has claim against recipient's property for total amount of aid. May require lien conditional to grant or continuance of aid.[3]	Liens held subject to preferred claims of counties for reimbursement.
Colorado	Children, parents, brothers, sisters, grandchildren, or grandparents.[4]	If recipient or person liable for support acquires property, money, or credit he or she must reimburse the county for any relief granted and may be sued on failure to do so.	
Connecticut	Husband, wife, father, mother, grandfather, grandmother, children, or grandchildren.[1]	Town has claim against recipient's estate	
Delaware	Parents, grandparents, children, and grandchildren[1]	If inmate of home is found to own property such property is liable for the expense incurred.[5]	
Florida	Children[1]		
Georgia	Father, mother, or child[1]	Any assistance granted after recipient comes into possession of property or income in excess of need is recoverable as a debt.	
Idaho		Total cost of relief or assistance must be allowed as preferred claim against estate, in favor of the State.	Funeral expenses not to exceed $100 and expense of administering estate exempted from lien. No claim enforced against realty occupied by surviving spouse or dependent. Statute of limitations does not run against claim while so occupied.
Illinois	Child, parents, brothers, sisters, grandchildren, or grandparents, except married female without independent property.[1] If person becomes a pauper from intemperance or bad conduct, parent or child liable.		
Indiana	Relatives in township[1]	Upon death of recipient, township may recover from estate total amount of aid granted for a period of 3 years prior to his death.	No recovery if spouse or minor children survive.
Iowa	Father, mother, children, male grandchildren, and grandparents.[6]	Total amount of aid may be recovered from estate of relative, from the recipient, or his estate.	Homestead liable at death of recipient unless husband, wife, or minor children survive.

See footnotes at end of table.

Table 3.—Responsibility of Relatives and Provisions for Recovery of Cost of General Relief From Recipients and Their Estates—Continued

State	Relatives responsible for support of applicant	Recovery from recipients and their estates	
		Type and extent of recovery	Limitations on recovery
Kansas		Amount spent for medical service and treatment may be recovered from recipient having property.	
Kentucky	Adult children[1]		
Louisiana			
Maine	Father, mother, grandfather, grandmother, children, and grandchildren living in State.[1]	Cost of relief may be recovered from the recipient, relative, or estate of recipient.	Relative liable for cost of relief incurred 6 months prior to filing action for recovery and any future relief costs incurred.
Maryland			
Massachusetts	Father, grandfather, mother, grandmother, children, and grandchildren by consanguinity and living in the State.[1]	Recipient or his executor or administrator is liable in contract to any town for expenses incurred for support.[7]	
Michigan:[2]			
State			
Local	Husband, wife, father, grandfather, mother, grandmother, and children.[1]	Total cost may be recovered from recipient or his estate.	
Minnesota	Children, parents, brothers, sisters, grandchildren, and grandparents.[8]	Claim allowed against recipient or estate for reasonable value of aid given by local subdivision.	
Mississippi	Father, grandfather, mother, grandmother, brothers, sisters, or descendents.[9]		
Missouri:[2]			
State			
Local			
Montana	Father, grandfather, mother, grandmother, children, grandchildren, brothers, or sisters.[1] If indigence is due to vice or intemperance, parent or child must support.		
Nebraska	Father, grandfather, mother, grandmother, children, grandchildren, brothers, or sisters.[8]	Reasonable cost of aid may be recovered from recipient or his estate.	
Nevada	Father, grandfather, mother, grandmother, children, grandchildren, brothers, or sisters.[8]		
New Hampshire	Father, mother, son, daughter, or person in relationship of parent to a minor stepchild.	County furnishing assistance to any person within 6 years preceding his death may recover cost of assistance from his estate.	Funeral expenses, expenses of last illness, and administration costs exempt from claim. No claim exists if widow or minor child survives.
New Jersey	Father, mother, grandfather, grandmother, children, grandchildren, husband, or wife.[1]	Total cost of assistance may be recovered from recipient or his estate.	No recovery permitted if estate is needed to prevent surviving widow or minor child from becoming dependent.

	Relatives legally responsible	Property/recovery provisions	Claim provisions
New Mexico:[2]			
State-------	-----	-----	No claim enforced against realty while occupied by surviving spouse or dependent.
Local-------	-----	Any assistance granted after recipient comes into possession of property or income in excess of his need may be recovered by the State department. Total amount of assistance may be recovered from estate.	
New York-------	Husband, wife, father, mother, grandparent, child, grandchild, or stepparents.[1]	Total cost of assistance may be recovered from recipient or his estate. Public welfare official has preferred claim against insurance policy.[10]	Action must be brought for recovery within 10 years after receipt of relief. If recipient leaves a widow or minor children who are or are liable to become public charges, claim against insurance policy may be waived.[11]
North Carolina--		Real property may be sold or rented to reimburse county for maintaining recipient.	
North Dakota----	Father, mother, or children[1]	-----	
Ohio-----------	([12])	All property of indigent is chargeable for support ----	Commissioners must petition probate court for sale of property.
Oklahoma:[2]			
State--------	-----	-----	
State—county-	-----	-----	
Oregon:[2]			
State--------	-----	-----	
Local-------	Children, parents, brothers, or sisters[13]	County may recover from estate of deceased pauper ----	
Pennsylvania---	Husband, wife, child, father, mother, grandparent, or grandchild.[14],	All property of an indigent is liable for the expense of support, maintenance, aid, and burial. Judgments recovered against indigents are liens on the property as in the case of other judgments. The property of a man deserting his wife or children without cause may be attached.	Authorities may apply for appointment as trustees of recipient's property; may lease it and receive income.
Rhode Island---	Father, grandfather, mother, grandmother, children, or grandchildren by consanguinity, or children by adoption living within the State.[1]	-----	
South Carolina:[2]			
State-------	Relatives or other persons legally responsible or willing to provide maintenance.[1]	Total amount of assistance may be recovered from recipient's estate.	No claim enforced against realty while occupied by surviving spouse. Funeral expenses may not exceed $100. ([16]).
Local-------		([15])	
South Dakota---	Father, mother, or children[1]	County has lien on all nonexempt property of recipient and spouse for all sums expended.	Lien effective upon payment of assistance to recipient.
Tennessee-----		-----	
Texas:[2]			
State--------	Parents, children, or spouse[1]	-----	
Local-------		-----	

See footnotes at end of table.

Table 3.—Responsibility of Relatives and Provisions for Recovery of Cost of General Relief From Recipients and Their Estates—Continued

State	Recovery from recipients and their estates		
	Relatives responsible for support of applicant	Type and extent of recovery	Limitations on recovery
Utah	Children, parents, brothers, sisters, grandchildren, or grandparents.[16]	Amount of assistance paid after recipient has come into property or income in excess of his need is recoverable by the State and county in proportion to the respective amounts paid by each.	
Vermont	Father, mother, or children[1]	Amount of assistance may be recovered from recipient or his estate.	Statutory exemptions apply.
Virginia			
Washington			
West Virginia	Children, father, brother, sister, or mother[1]		
Wisconsin	Husband, wife, father, child, or mother in order named.[1]	Property of indigent is chargeable for support[17]	If a parent, wife, or child is dependent on property for future support, the court may refuse to enter judgment or allow claim.
Wyoming		Total amount of assistance must be deducted as a preferred claim out of proceeds of property not included in any exemptions allowed by law.[18]	Property valued at less than $100 administered by county board.[18] Property valued at more than $100 administered by court action.
Alaska: Temporary	Father, mother, grandmother, grandfather, grandchildren, children, brothers, or sisters.[1] Parents or children responsible if cause of dependency is intemperance or vice.	Total amount of expense incurred, plus interest at 8 percent per annum, may be recovered from recipient or from his estate.	Preferred claim against estate after claims have been met for food, clothing, fuel, shelter, medical aid, or burial.
Pioneers' Home	Father, mother, grandfather, grandmother, grandchildren, children, brothers, or sisters.[1] Parents and children responsible if cause of dependency is intemperance or vice.	Total amount of expense incurred may be recovered from recipient or from his estate. The home has a lien on any money or clothing left by deceased inmate.	Preferred claim against estate after claims have been met for food, clothing, fuel, shelter, medical aid, or burial.
District of Columbia			
Hawaii	Spouse, child, or parent[1]	Total amount of assistance may be recovered from recipient's estate.	May be exercised in the discretion of the county public welfare commission.

[1] Relatives liable for support to extent of their ability.
[2] Systems of general relief provided for by law.
[3] Conditional to granting or continuing aid, an applicant may be required to transfer or grant to the board of supervisors such property or interest in property which he may have.
[4] Relatives who fail to support must forfeit $20 per month to the county and they may be sued for the same.
[5] Property of husband, brother, or mother who deserted person admitted to home is also liable.

[10] A public welfare official may accept a deed of real property or a mortgage thereon in behalf of the public welfare district for the care and maintenance of a person at public expense.
[11] Before the expiration of 1 year from date of transfer, the property or mortgage may be redeemed by the payment of any expense incurred.
[12] Every reasonable effort must be made to secure aid from relatives and interested organizations.
[13] Only parents or child liable if indigency is due to intemperance or other bad conduct. If relatives refuse to support, they must forfeit the sum of $30 per month to the county.

[6]Grandparents liable if able to support without personal labor. Property of deserting spouse or parent may be used to support abandoned spouse or child.

[7]Board of Public Welfare may take possession of real and personal property to reimburse itself for expenses incurred for recipient.

[8]Relatives liable for support to extent of their ability. Only parent or child responsible if indigency is caused by bad conduct or intemperance.

[9]The above relatives are responsible for any pauper unable to work as directed by the board of supervisors, and such relatives must relieve and maintain such pauper. In case of refusal to do so, they must pay to the county or other person caring for such pauper the sum of $10 per month.

[14]Relatives must financially assist indigent person at such rate as the court of the county orders or directs.

[15]Boards of county commissioners may demand, sue for, and receive all gifts, legacies, fines, forfeitures, and all other money or things which may be given for the use of the poor.

[16]Only parent or child responsible if indigency is due to intemperance or other bad conduct. Relatives liable to the extent of their ability, not to exceed $20 per month.

[17]No applicant may be required to assign an equity in a home or in an insurance policy of cash or loan value in excess of $300 as a condition for receiving relief.

[18]Transient or nonresident owning property other than personal effects necessary for decency and health must dispose of property and apply proceeds toward payment of transportation and other expenses.

Table 4.—Provisions Affecting Status of Recipients of General Relief

| State | Provisions relating to paupers[1] | | Miscellaneous provisions |
	Disfranchisement	Exemption from military duty	
Alabama			
Arizona		Paupers	Voting residence neither gained nor lost because of residence in any almshouse or other asylum at public expense.
Arkansas:			
State			
Local		Paupers	
California:			
State			
Local			Voting residents neither gained nor lost because of residence in any almshouse or other asylum at public expense.
Colorado			Voting residence neither gained nor lost because of residence in any poorhouse or asylum at public expense.
Connecticut			
Delaware	Paupers		Paupers who marry are discharged from State welfare home.
Florida			
Georgia		Paupers	
Idaho			Voting residence neither gained nor lost because of residence in almshouse at public expense.
Illinois			Voting residence not gained by virtue of residence in poorhouse, asylum, or hospital.
Indiana			
Iowa			
Kansas			Voting residence neither gained nor lost because of residence in almshouse.
Kentucky			
Louisiana	(²)		Inmates of poorhouses may not hold office.
Maine	Paupers	Paupers	No certificate of intention to marry may be issued to a pauper.
Maryland		Paupers	
Massachusetts	Paupers		
Michigan:			
State			
Local			Voting residence neither gained nor lost because of residence in any almshouse or other asylum at public expense.
Minnesota			Voting residence neither gained nor lost because of residence in any almshouse or other asylum.
Mississippi			
Missouri:			
State			
Local	(³)		Voting residence neither gained nor lost because of residence in any almshouse or other asylum at public expense.
Montana			
Nebraska		Paupers	
Nevada			Voting residence neither gained nor lost because of residence in any almshouse or other asylum at public expense.
New Hampshire	(⁴)		While Federal funds are available, receipt of unemployment relief or other temporary aid does not affect civil or political status of recipient or members of his family.
New Jersey	Paupers		
New Mexico:			
State			
Local			
New York			Voting residence neither gained nor lost because of residence in any almshouse or institution supported in whole or in part by public funds.
North Carolina		Paupers	
North Dakota			
Ohio			

See footnotes at end of table.

Table 4.—Provisions Affecting Status of Recipients of General Relief—Continued

| State | Provisions relating to paupers[1] | | Miscellaneous provisions |
	Disfran-chisement	Exemption from military duty	
Oklahoma:			
State			
State—county	([5])		
Oregon:			
State			
Local			Voting residence neither gained nor lost because of residence in any almshouse or other asylum at public expense.
Pennsylvania		Paupers	Voting residence neither gained nor lost because of residence in any almshouse or other asylum at public expense.
Rhode Island	Paupers		
South Carolina:			
State			
Local	Paupers		
South Dakota			
Tennessee		Paupers	
Texas:			
State			
Local	Paupers		Voting residence neither gained nor lost because of residence in a public asylum or eleemosynary institution.
Utah			
Vermont			Marriage license may be issued to a pauper only upon written consent of selectmen. The commissioner of motor vehicles may, upon written notice from any overseer of the poor, suspend for 1 year the motor vehicle operator's license of any person who has received assistance during the preceding 2 years.
Virginia	Paupers		Voting residence neither gained nor lost because of residence in any charitable institution.
Washington			Voting residence neither gained nor lost because of residence in any almshouse or other asylum.
West Virginia	Paupers[6]		
Wisconsin			
Wyoming			
Alaska:			
Temporary			
Pioneers' Home			
District of Columbia			
Hawaii			

[1]The term *pauper* refers to recipients of "poor relief." Many States which have adopted recent laws providing for general relief do not designate recipients as "paupers." Therefore, the provisions indicated may be ineffective even though they have not been specifically repealed.

[2]Inmates of charitable institutions may not vote.

[3]Person kept in any poorhouse or other asylum at public expense, except the Soldiers' Home at St. James and the Confederate Home at Higginsville, may not vote.

[4]Paupers receiving relief within a period of 90 days prior to town meeting may not vote.

[5]Inmates of poorhouses or asylums (except Federal and Confederate soldiers) may not vote.

[6]Person not deemed a pauper because of receipt of general relief.

Table 5.—Provisions for Types of Aid Granted and for Financing General Relief

State	Institutional care (poorhouse, poor farm, etc.)	Direct relief	Contract care	Medical care	Hospitalization	Burial	Miscellaneous	Specific provisions for types of relief to nonresident persons	Incidence — State	Incidence — Local	Basis for distribution of State funds
Alabama	X	X		X	X	X	Work may be required	Temporary relief and burial. Sick and disabled person must be provided for until removed.		X	Population, extent of need, and financial condition of county.
Arizona	X	X	X	X	X	X		Relief or aid in emergency cases.	X		State Board of Social Security and Welfare administers State funds for relief of dependent persons.
Arkansas: State		X[1]			X[2]			[3]	X		Allocations governed by rules of State department.
Local	X[4]		X[5]	X[4]		X	Work may be required[6]	Temporary relief, medical care, and burial.		X	
California: State (See appendix B.)		X		X	X		Work relief. No person is entitled to relief who unjustifiably refuses employment.		X	[7]	State relief administrator directs expenditure of funds. Funds may be paid directly to individuals or through such governmental agencies as the administrator may select.
Local	X	X		X	X	X	Work may be required	Emergency relief		X	
Colorado	X	X		X	X	X		Temporary care, medical and surgical assistance, and burial.	[8]	X	Allocated to counties on basis of need or paid directly to recipient by State department.
Connecticut	X			X	X	X	Temporary outdoor aid may be given.	Necessary aid		X	
Delaware	X[9]	[10]		[10]	X[11]	X	Work must be assigned to able-bodied persons.	In extreme emergency, persons without legal residence may be admitted to State welfare home.	50 per-cent[12]	50 per-cent[12]	One-half of local expense for outside relief. Counties reimburse State for care in State welfare home.
Florida	X	[13]		[13]	X[13]	[15]				X	
Georgia	X	X		X		X	Work may be required			X	

State	1	2	3	4	5	Work requirement	Relief provided	8	9	10	Remarks
Idaho	X	X	X	X	X	Employment must be provided for able-bodied persons.	Temporary relief[3]	X	X	X	State department fixes allocations to counties which may vary with ability of county to meet obligations if an emergency arises or if maximum county levy is insufficient.
Illinois	X[14]	X	X[5]	X	X	Recipients must be suitably employed.[16]	Temporary relief	X	X		Need determined by formula prescribed by law.
Indiana	X	X	X	X		Able-bodied persons required to labor.[16]	Temporary relief, surgical and medical aid, and burial. Almshouse care. Work relief for able-bodied males.	X[17]	X		
Iowa	X	X	X	X	X	Able-bodied persons may be required to work.	Temporary relief	X[18]	X		To counties on basis of need.
Kansas	X	X	X	X	X	Persons in county homes and those receiving relief may be required to work.	Such relief as is deemed necessary.	X	X		Counties reimbursed uniformly by State for 30 percent of their welfare service costs, contingent, however, upon availability of State funds.
Kentucky			X	X	X	Able-bodied inmates may be coerced to labor.		X			
Louisiana	X	X	X	X				X	X		Percent of reimbursement to parishes fixed by State department based upon amount of State and local funds available. State may pay all expense if parish is unable because of lack of funds or if funds are legally barred.
Maine	X	X	X	X	X	Able-bodied persons may be employed in workhouses.	Temporary relief[19]	(8)	X		
Maryland	X[20]	(20)	(20)	(20)	(20)	(20)	Temporary relief	X	X		Balance remaining in State fund for aid to needy, after allocations for old age assistance, dependent children, aid to blind, and administration, is allocated on basis of 60 percent to Baltimore City and 40 percent to counties to be used for needy persons or for ordinary governmental expense.
Massachusetts	X	X	X	X	X	Work may be required[21]	Temporary relief	(8)	X		(See appendix B.)
Michigan: State	X	X	X			Relief of destitution and unemployment.		X			
Local	X	X	X				Temporary relief	X			State Emergency Welfare Relief Commission controls distribution of relief funds.

See footnotes at end of table.

Table 5.—Provisions for Types of Aid Granted and for Financing General Relief—Continued

State	Types of relief — Institutional care (poorhouse, poor farm, etc.)	Direct relief	Contract care	Medical care	Hospitalization	Burial	Miscellaneous	Specific provisions for types of relief to nonresident persons	Incidence of financial responsibility — State	Incidence of financial responsibility — Local	Basis for distribution of State funds
Minnesota	X	X		X	X	X	Employment provided on poor farm and in workhouses. Employable recipients of direct relief must accept suitable employment in lieu thereof.	Temporary care	X[18]	X	At discretion of State Executive Council; financial and economic conditions and relief load of local unit seeking aid to be taken into consideration.
Mississippi	X	(22)	X[25]	X		X	Work may be required of inmates of county homes.	Relief, support, employment, and burial.		X	
Missouri: State	X[24]	X[24]	X	(24)			Work may be required in return for relief.	Temporary relief	X[24]		State pays individual applicants.
Local	X	X	X	X		X		Temporary relief		X	
Montana	X	X	X	X	X		Able-bodied male paupers may be required to work out relief.	Temporary care and burial	X[25]	X	Financial inability of county.
Nebraska	X[26]	X	X	X	X	X	Able-bodied person may be required to labor in order to receive relief.	Temporary relief and burial	(27)	X	
Nevada	X	X	X	X		X	Minors may be apprenticed with respectable householders. Work may be required of inmates of poor farms and workhouses.	Temporary board, nursing, medical care, and burial.		X	
New Hampshire	X	X				X		Temporary relief and burial. May be required to work as reimbursement for transportation.		X	
New Jersey	X	X	X[28]	X	X	X	Work may be provided in welfare houses.	Temporary outdoor relief, or almshouse care, hospitalization, and burial.	X[29]	X	On basis of need, to counties and municipalities which apply.[30]
New Mexico: State	X	X				X	Such support as the local authorities deem proper.		X		State pays individual applicants.
Local										X	

State						Labor or work provision		Nature of relief		State participation in costs
New York	X	X		X	X	Inmates of institutions must be suitably employed if physically able.	X	Care in own home when practicable, or ip publicly maintained camp, shelter, or institution, and burial. Non-resident may be employed.	X	State reimburses city or county 40 percent of amount expended for home relief and its administration, and 100 percent of cost of care for State poor. Additional State grants may be made in exceptional cases or when the district is unable to provide adequate care.[31]
North Carolina	X		(32)	X	X		X	Sick and disabled maintained if unable to be removed to county of settlement; burial.		
North Dakota	X	X		X	X	Applicant must work if given opportunity and may be compelled to labor upon poor farms or in asylum. Applicant refusing to work may be prosecuted as a vagrant.	X	Temporary care for indigent sick; burial. Able-bodied persons must be employed.	X	To counties on basis of number of relief cases and availability to meet costs.
Ohio (See appendix B.)	X		X	X	X	Recipients may be required to perform labor to value of relief afforded, on public park, road, highway, or other public contract. Reasonable and moderate labor required in county infirmary suited to age and bodily strength.	X	Temporary relief pending removal.	X	Sums allocated to each county in the ratio which the average of the real, public utility, and tangible personal property tax duplicate of the county during the previous 5 years bears to the average of all such duplicates of all the counties during the same period. As a condition precedent to receiving State grants, each county or subdivision must agree to match grants in an amount equal to 50 percent of the total allocations.[33]
Oklahoma: State	X			X	X		X		X	State pays individual applicants.
Oklahoma: State-county	X	X[34]	X	X	X	Temporary employment relief to able-bodied destitute persons. Inmates of asylum may be required to work.	X	May be provided for in same manner as residents.	X (35)	Amount sufficient to supplement county funds. Discretion of State Department of Public Welfare.
Oregon: State	X		X	X		Aid of any character may be given to extent of need and availability of funds.	Not less than 50 percent.[35]		(35)	State pays individual applicants.[35]
Oregon: Local	X[37]	X	X	X			X	Temporary relief	X	
Pennsylvania	X		X	X	X	Assistance means money, goods, shelter, services, or burial.[38]	X	Temporary relief until removed to place of legal settlement.	X	Extent of need in the county.

See footnotes at end of table.

Table 5.—Provisions for Types of Aid Granted and for Financing General Relief—Continued

State	Types of relief						Miscellaneous	Specific provisions for types of relief to nonresident persons	Incidence of financial responsibility		Basis for distribution of State funds
	Institutional care (poorhouse, poor farm, etc.)	Direct relief	Contract care	Medical care	Hospitalization	Burial			State	Local	
Rhode Island	X	X[39]		X[39]		X	Work relief[39]	Persons may be sent to State institutions caring for indigents. Towns may furnish temporary relief and burial.	X[39]	X	State pays $2.50 from State unemployment relief fund for every $3 made available by town.
South Carolina: State		X							X	X	State may match county funds in an amount not to exceed $120 per case per year.
Local	X					X	Persons in poorhouses or on poor farms may be employed.	Temporary relief pending removal or burial.		X	
South Dakota	X	X	X[40]	X	X	X	Labor or other services may be required of able-bodied persons.	May be placed temporarily in poorhouse; where there is no poorhouse, may be given the same care as persons possessing settlement and may be given medical care and burial.	X	X	Funds from nonintoxicating liquor tax placed in "poor relief fund," which is allocated as follows: 50 percent is transferred to the general fund subject to appropriation for poor relief and welfare; the remaining 50 percent is proportioned to the counties on the basis of population for poor relief.
Tennessee	X	X	X	X	X	X	Surplus coal from State mines distributed annually from December to March to needy unemployed persons. This service will end April 1, 1939.			X	
Texas: State							Federal surplus commodities and other Federal resources may be distributed.		(41)		
Local	X			X	X	X	Support.			X	
Utah	X	X		X	X	X	Temporary relief and burial.		X	X	State pays 85 percent of direct relief payments.

State							General relief [1]	Other provisions		Basis / remarks
Vermont	X	X			X	(43)	Towns or gores must relieve and support persons found therein.[42]		X	
Virginia	X	X	X		X	X[44]	Temporary care, medical aid, and burial.	If able, person must work at place of general reception for the poor.	X	City or county must provide funds equal to 60 percent of amount to be received from State. Not more than 10 percent of State funds may be used for administration.
Washington	X	X			X	X	Board, nursing, medical aid, or burial expenses.	Work relief. Assistance may be given in cash or in any other form of materials or services.	X	Quarterly budgets submitted by county commissioners.
West Virginia	X	X	X		X	X	Temporary relief as exigencies of the case require.		X	Relative number of known eligible cases, relative costs, and such factors as may be appropriate to assure reasonable distribution.
Wisconsin	X	X			X	X	Board, maintenance, medical and nursing aid, and burial.	Interest on mortgage on homestead may be paid to prevent payment of larger sum as shelter allowance should homestead be lost by default.	X	State emergency board makes allotments to State Industrial Commission or other agency designated by Governor in such amounts as emergency board deems necessary; including not less than 5 percent for all counties or other local units.
Wyoming	X	X			X	Y[45]	Temporary relief	Relief may be given in any other manner deemed advisable by the county department of public welfare.	X	To the extent that county revenues are insufficient.
Alaska:										
Temporary		X			X	X				Territory pays individual applicants.
Pioneers' Home	X					X				Cost of maintenance of home.
District of Columbia	X		X		X	X	Transportation to legal residence.			District pays individual applicants.
Hawaii		X			X	X				Funds allocated to the respective counties for cost of relief and administration.

X indicates that the provision applies without limitation in a given State.

[1] "General relief" is defined as material aid or service, other than money payments, given to persons under the Federal Social Security Act.
[2] Hospitalization granted to persons not suffering from contagious, venereal, mental, or tuberculous disease and with income less than $30 per month. Total care may not exceed 21 days per year.
[3] Reciprocal agreements with other States regarding relief to transients and nonresidents are authorized.

[4] Counties not liable for support of pauper who neglects or refuses to accept aid in the manner provided.
[5] Contract care is permissible in the absence of a poorhouse.
[6] If pauper protests against working, he cannot be employed without doctor's certificate stating that required labor is not injurious to health.
[7] State relief administrator may require communities which have received unemployment relief loans to contribute an equal or stipulated amount.
[8] State reimburses town for expenses of State paupers.
[9] Insane, criminal, or vicious persons are not admitted to the State welfare home.

Table 5.—Footnotes Continued

10 Outside relief given only to persons who cannot be removed to State welfare home.

11 In Sussex and Kent Counties.

12 Hospitalization provided by county funds only.

13 Provided in counties of more than 155,000 population. A county with a population of 50,000 to 55,000 and with an assessed valuation of more than $32,500,000 may issue bonds to build a poor farm, may maintain a county hospital, care for indigent sick, and bury paupers. A county with a population of 9,700 to 10,500 may create a "physicians' fund" for indigent sick and a county charity fund to grant cash allowances up to an aggregate of $5,000 annually.

14 No feeble-minded girl or woman between ages of 14 and 45, and no male child under 17 or female under 18 may be committed to any poorhouse or poor farm.

15 No relief may be furnished to any employable person who refuses to accept employment from any highway or street officer.

16 Assistance given when applicant is unable to provide household supplies and necessities of life.

17 Counties advance funds to townships for relief purposes. Townships must reimburse counties for all such sums advanced.

18 State funds used for direct relief only.

19 Consent of town of residence must be obtained in order to obtain reimbursement from such town for temporary relief granted resident of such town. State assumes financial responsibility for persons for whom no town is liable.

20 Almshouse care is provided by all counties and Baltimore City. 15 counties provide out-pensions. Medical aid and hospitalization are provided by 5 counties and Baltimore City. Burial is provided for by Anne Arundel and Montgomery Counties and Baltimore City. State funds are allocated to all the counties and to Baltimore City for relief of the unemployed, unemployable, and for other governmental purposes. In the majority of counties the almshouse may be let out for operation.

21 Burial expenses must not exceed $40 if deceased is over 12 years of age and $20 if deceased is under such age.

22 Temporary direct relief pending removal to county home.

23 Pauper children may be apprenticed by agreements made by the county boards of supervisors.

24 Expenditure of State funds restricted to money payments to individuals, sufficient food, clothing, shelter, medicine, and other necessary supplies or services compatible with decency and health.

25 State does not contribute to care in poor farms or workhouses.

26 Children under 16 and pregnant women may not be admitted to poorhouse.

27 Not more than 8 percent of balance of State assistance fund, after deductions for administration and child welfare services, may be used for surplus commodities distribution and certification for Federal assistance and service projects. Any portion of the 8 percent not used for such purpose within any 6-month period reverts to fund to be distributed to counties in ratio the county population bears to total population of the State.

28 Authorities may contract with relatives not legally liable for support or contract for care in welfare house of another county.

29 State funds expended for public assistance which is defined to mean "assistance rendered to needy persons not otherwise provided for under the laws of this State where such persons are willing to work but are unable to secure employment due either to physical disability or inability to find employment, and includes what is commonly called 'emergency relief.'"

30 No allotments made to municipalities which do not levy a tax of at least 3 mills for general relief.

31 State assumes total support of nonresidents and Indian poor (State poor).

32 Poor persons must be maintained in such place or places as the board of county commissioners select.

33 The sum of $1,500,000 was appropriated on June 10, 1936, to be distributed to the several subdivisions in accordance with their relief load, based upon comparative need as evidenced by the records for the first 5 months of 1938 on file in the State auditor's office.

34 Applicable in a county with a population of 115,000 or more.

35 County expenditures for care of indigent persons in poor farms and county hospitals and for relief of indigent veterans and their dependents shall be taken into account and offset against the county's contribution for relief purposes in allocating State funds for direct relief.

36 County reimburses State for not more than 50 percent of expenditures.

37 Provisions apply to those counties which have established workhouses, poor farms, or hospitals.

38 The State Board of Public Assistance by its rules and regulations establishes the nature and extent of assistance.

39 State financed and supervised home relief and work relief programs end June 30, 1939.

40 Applies only in counties without poorhouses.

41 No funds have been made available as of January 1, 1939.

42 If person has not resided in State 1 year supporting himself and family, transportation to place from which he came into the State may be provided. If such person again applies for support, he may be fined or imprisoned. Transients suddenly taken sick or lame or otherwise disabled and confined to a house or committed to a jail may be given support including hospitalization and, in the case of death, burial.

43 State reimburses towns for support of poor persons not a charge upon the town who are committed to jail while residing in the town or injured while traveling on State highways.

44 State funds expended only for destitute persons who are not inmates of county, municipal, State, or national institutions.

45 State grants may not be used for hospitalization, medical and dental services, drugs, or burials. State department is authorized to make grants-in-aid for general health purposes.

Old Age Assistance

Table 6.—Provisions for the Administration of Old Age Assistance

State	Nature of law	Administrative responsibility		Determination of eligibility							
				Original determination		Reconsideration		Appeal and review			
		Direct	Supervisory	Final	Advisory	Periodic	At request of State board or department	Appeal of applicant to State department[1]	Review by State department on own motion[1]	Upon complaint by person other than applicant	Further investigation by State department[1]
Alabama	M	County department of public welfare.	State Department of Public Welfare.	County board of public welfare.[2]	---	Annually	---	X	X[3]	---	On appeal.
Arizona	M	State Department of Social Security and Welfare assisted by county board of social security and public welfare.	---	State Department of Social Security and Welfare.	County board of social security and public welfare.	---	X	State board	State board	---	State board.
Arkansas	M	State Department of Public Welfare.	---	State Department of Public Welfare.	County or district board of public welfare.	---	X	X[4]	---	---	---
California	M	County board of supervisors[5]	State Department of Social Welfare.	County board of supervisors.[5]	---	Annually	---	State board	X	---	X
Colorado	M	County or district department of public welfare.	State Department of Public Welfare.	County or district department of public welfare.	---	---	X	X	X	---	---
Connecticut	M	Commissioner of Welfare through Bureau of Old Age Assistance assisted by chief executive authority of town.	---	Bureau of Old Age Assistance.	Chief executive authority of town.	---	---	(6)	---	---	---
Delaware	M	State Old Age Welfare Commission.	---	State Old Age Welfare Commission.	---	Annually	X	(7)	---	---	---
Florida	M	State Welfare Board through district board of social welfare.	---	District board of social welfare.	---	---	---	State board	State board	---	State board.
Georgia	M	County or district department of public welfare.	State Department of Public Welfare.	County or district department of public welfare.	---	---	X[8]	X	X	Tax payer	X
Idaho	M	County welfare commission	State Department of Public Assistance.	County welfare commission.	---	---	X	X	X	---	X

State		Administration	State agency	Local agency	Local detail					
Illinois	M --	County department of public welfare. County bureau of public welfare.[9]	State Department of Public Welfare.	County department of public welfare. County bureau of public welfare.[9]			X	X[10]	X	X.
Indiana	M --	County or district department of public welfare.	State Department of Public Welfare.	County or district department of public welfare.			X	X	X	X.
Iowa	M --	State Board of Social Welfare assisted by the county board of social welfare.	State Board of Social Welfare.	County board of social welfare.	County board of social welfare.	Biennially		(11)	(12)	X.
Kansas	M --	County board of social welfare.	State Board of Social Welfare.	County board of social welfare.			X	(13)		(14)
Kentucky	M --	State Department of Welfare.[15]	State Department of Welfare.	State Department of Welfare, division of public assistance.[15]			X	(16)	X	X.
Louisiana (See appendix B.)	M --	Parish department of public welfare.	State Department of Public Welfare.	Parish department of public welfare.			X	X	X	X.
Maine	M --	Old age assistance commission in State Department of Health and Welfare.		Old age assistance commission in State Department of Health and Welfare.				Old age assistance commission.		
Maryland	M --	County welfare board. Baltimore Department of Welfare.	Board of State Aid and Charities.	County welfare board. Baltimore Department of Welfare.			X	X	X	X.
Massachusetts	M --	Local board of public welfare.	State Department of Public Welfare.	Local board of public welfare.			X	(17)	Y[18]	Appeal board.
Michigan	M --	State Old Age Assistance Bureau assisted by the county old age assistance board and the county welfare agent.	State Department of Public Welfare.	State Old Age Assistance Bureau.	County old age assistance board and the county welfare agent.		X	(19)	Y[19]	Director of State Welfare Department.
Minnesota	M --	County welfare board	State Board of Control.	County welfare board.			(20)	State board	Tax payer	State board.
Mississippi	M --	County agent and county board of public welfare.	State Department of Public Welfare.	County agent and county board of public welfare.			X	X	X	X.
Missouri	M --	State Social Security Commission.	State Social Security Commission.	State Social Security Commission.	County social security commission.[21]		X	(22)	X	State administrator.

See footnotes at end of table.

Table 6.—Provisions for the Administration of Old Age Assistance—Continued

State	Administrative responsibility			Determination of eligibility							
	Na-ture of law	Direct	Supervisory	Original determination		Reconsideration		Appeal and review			
				Final	Advisory	Periodic	At request of State board or department	Appeal of applicant to State department[1]	Review by State department on own motion[1]	Upon complaint by person other than applicant	Further investigation by State department[1]
Montana	M	County department of public welfare.	State Department of Public Welfare.	County department of public welfare.		Quarterly	X	X	X		State board.
Nebraska	M	State Board of Control.		State Board of Control, director of assistance.	County assistance committee.	Annually	X	(23)		Tax payer	Director of assistance.
Nevada	M	Board of county commissioners.	State Welfare Department.	Board of county commissioners.	State Welfare Department.		X	X	X		X.
New Hampshire	M	State Department of Public Welfare.	State Commissioner of Public Welfare.	State Commissioner of Public Welfare.	(24)			State board			
New Jersey (See appendix B.)	M	County welfare board	State Department of Institutions and Agencies, division of old age assistance.	County welfare board			X	Division of old age assistance.	Division of old age assistance.		Division of old age assistance.
New Mexico	M	State Department of Public Welfare.		State Department of Public Welfare.[25]	Local office of State Department of Public Welfare.		X	State board	State board		State board.
New York	M	Local public welfare official.[26]	State Department of Social Welfare.	Local public welfare official.[26]			X	X	X	Any person	X.
North Carolina	M	County board of charities and public welfare.[27] City public welfare officer.	State Board of Charities and Public Welfare.	County board of charities and public welfare.[27] City public welfare officer.			(28)	(29)	(29)		(29).
North Dakota	M	State Public Welfare Board assisted by county welfare board.		State Public Welfare Board.	County welfare board.		X	State board	State board		State board.
Ohio	M	State Department of Public Welfare, division of aid for the aged.	State Department of Public Welfare, division of old age assistance.[21]	State Department of Public Welfare, division of aid for the aged.	County subdivision of State department.[21]		X	Division of aid for the aged.	Division of aid for the aged.		Division of aid for the aged.

State		Agency administering assistance	State agency	Local agency			Citizen		
Oklahoma	M--	State Public Welfare Commission assisted by county assistance board.	State Public Welfare Commission.	County assistance board.	X	State commission.		State commission.	State commission.
Oregon	M--	State Relief Committee assisted by county relief committee.	State Relief Committee.	County relief committee.	X	State Relief Committee.		State Relief Committee.	State Relief Committee.
Pennsylvania	M--	State Department of Public Assistance.	County board of assistance.		X	X			
Rhode Island	M--	State Department of Public Welfare.	State Department of Public Welfare.	(30)	X	X			
South Carolina	M--	State Department of Public Welfare through county department of public welfare[31]	County department of public welfare.[31]		X	X		X.	X.
South Dakota	M--	State Department of Social Security.	County or district office of the State Department of Social Security.		X	X		X.	X.
Tennessee	M--	State Department of Institutions and Public Welfare.	Regional director of State Department of Institutions and Public Welfare jointly with county judge or chairman of county court.[32]		X	X		X.	X.
Texas	M--	State Old Age Assistance Commission through local agency designated by it.	Local agency designated by State Old Age Assistance Commission.			X		State commission.	State commission.
Utah	M--	County or district department of public welfare.	County or district department of public welfare.		X	X		X.	X.
Vermont	M--	State Old Age Assistance Commission assisted by locally designated official.	State Old Age Assistance Commission.	Locally designated official.	X	X		State commission.	State commission.
Virginia	M--	State Board of Public Welfare.	County or city board of public welfare.		X	State board.		State board.	State board.
Washington	M--	State Department of Social Security assisted by board of county commissioners.	State Department of Social Security.	Board of county commissioners.	X[35]	X		X.	X.

See footnotes at end of table.

Table 6.—Provisions for the Administration of Old Age Assistance—Continued

State	Nature of law	Administrative responsibility		Determination of eligibility							
		Direct	Supervisory	Original determination		Reconsideration		Appeal and review			
				Final	Advisory	Periodic	At request of State board or department	Appeal of applicant to State department[1]	Review by State department on own motion[1]	Upon complaint by person other than applicant	Further investigation by State department[1]
West Virginia	M	State Department of Public Assistance assisted by county public assistance council.		State Department of Public Assistance.	County public assistance council.	Semiannually	X	Board of review of State department.	X	Citizen	X.[34]
Wisconsin	M	County department of public welfare.[35] County pension department.[36] County judge.	Pension department of the Industrial Commission.	County department of public welfare.[35] County pension department.[36] County judge.		([8])		X	X		X.
Wyoming	M	State Department of Public Welfare assisted by county department of public welfare.		State Department of Public Welfare.	County department of public welfare.		X	State board			State board.
Alaska	M	Territorial Department of Public Welfare.		Territorial Department of Public Welfare.			X	Territorial board.			Territorial board.
District of Columbia	O	Board of commissioners through designated agency.[37]		Board of commissioners through designated agency.[37]		Semiannually	X	X	X		X.[38]
Hawaii	M	County public welfare commission.	Territorial Board of Public Welfare.	County public welfare commission.				Territorial board.	Territorial board.		Territorial board.

X indicates that the provision applies without limitation in a given State.
M indicates mandatory provisions.
O indicates optional provisions.

[1] If authority to hear appeals, to review decisions, and to make further investigations is placed by law with a specific agency within the department, the specific agency is named either in the body of the table or in a footnote.
[2] State department must review all awards, disallowances of applications, and modifications of awards made by the county board.
[3] State department cannot increase or decrease amount of assistance on own motion.
[4] Law forbids action in any court with the object of changing rule of State Department of Public Welfare as to the merits of any application.

[20] Appeal allowed to the State Board of Control whose decision may be appealed to the district court of the county of residence.
[21] Advisory authority is agent of State department.
[22] Appeal allowed to State department.
[23] Appeal allowed to State director of assistance who must report findings to the State Board of Control whose decision is final.
[24] Commissioner of public welfare must determine the eligibility of all applicants and the amount of assistance, but must in all cases first consult the proper officials of the counties or towns required to contribute to the cost of such assistance.
[25] State department may allow its local office to determine whether assistance may be granted and the amount and manner thereof.

[5] County boards of public welfare may be established by county board of supervisors or by petition of electorate.

[6] Appeal allowed to Bureau of Old Age Assistance whose decision may be appealed by the superior court of the county in which the applicant resides.

[7] Appeal allowed to president of State Old Age Welfare Commission.

[8] Reconsideration also provided for when local agency deems it necessary.

[9] A county bureau is established in Cook County.

[10] Applicant may appeal from decision of State department to circuit court of county in which the applicant resides.

[11] Appeal allowed to State Board of Social Welfare whose decision may be appealed to the district court of the county in which the applicant resides.

[12] Amount of assistance granted is subject to review at any time by the State Board of Social Welfare and may be increased, decreased, or discontinued.

[13] Appeal allowed to State appeal committee. State Board of Social Welfare may affirm, modify, or set aside any decision of the State appeal committee.

[14] The State director of social welfare is authorized to order an investigation of the activities of any county board or private agency whenever he deems necessary or whenever the State board recommends such an investigation.

[15] State Department of Welfare may organize local welfare departments to exercise delegated powers.

[16] Appeals allowed to division of public assistance. Awards of the division are subject at all times to review by the State Department of Welfare.

[17] Appeal allowed to appeal board within the State Department of Public Welfare.

[18] Both State department and appeal board authorized to review decisions of local board of public welfare.

[19] At the request of the applicant, or upon his own investigation, the director of the State Welfare Department may direct a hearing before the county old age assistance board. A further hearing may be had before the State director whose decision may be appealed to the circuit court of the county of residence.

[26] "Public welfare official" means county commissioner of public welfare, city commissioner of public welfare, town public welfare officer, or city public welfare officer.

[27] City of Rocky Mount is constituted a separate administrative district. Board of county commissioners may change decision of county board of charities and public welfare.

[28] County board of charities and public welfare is empowered to reconsider and make changes in amount of assistance. The State Board of Charities and Public Welfare and the board of county commissioners must be notified of such changes. Such action is subject to review by the State Board of Charities and Public Welfare, and a recipient may appeal the decision to the State Board of Allotments and Appeals.

[29] Powers relative to appeal, review, and reconsideration vested in the State Board of Allotments and Appeals, an agency created within the State Board of Charities and Public Welfare.

[30] Local directors of public welfare may be designated to assist in making investigations.

[31] In Charleston County the county welfare board has direct administrative responsibility for old age assistance under the supervision of the State Department of Public Welfare.

[32] In case of disagreement the State department makes decision.

[33] Applicant may appeal to the director of the Department of Social Security and from his decision to the county superior court.

[34] State department may also remand application to county for further investigation.

[35] Establishment is optional in counties of 500,000 or more population.

[36] Establishment is optional in counties of less than 500,000 population.

[37] Board of public welfare is vested with the power and duty of providing for the aged.

[38] When agency believes that aid has been improperly granted, it may conduct further investigation.

Table 7.—Personal Qualifications for Old Age Assistance

State	Age in years	U.S. citizenship	Residence		Reasons for disqualification					
			State	Local	Desertion for specified period within 10 years prior to application		Applicant failed to support children under specified age	Applicant convicted of felony within period specified prior to application	Applicant was tramp or beggar within period specified prior to application	Miscellaneous
					By husband	By wife				
Alabama	65	X	(1)	1 year[2]	6 months	6 months	16 years	10 years	----	Inmate of any penal, insane, or correctional institution for past year.
Arizona	65	X	(1)	----	----	----	----	----	----	Inmate of any institution except Home for the Aged and Infirm Arizona Pioneers.[3]
Arkansas	65	----	1 year continuously	----	----	----	----	----	----	
California	65	X	(4)	1 year[2]	----	----	----	----	----	
Colorado	60	X	(5)	----	----	----	----	----	----	
Connecticut	65	X	(1)	----	----	----	----	----	----	Failure to pay old age assistance tax. Inmate of jail or penal institution or out on bond or probation.
Delaware	65	X	(1)	----	----	----	----	----	1 year	Inmate of public reform, insane, or correctional institution.
Florida	65	----	(1)	----	----	----	----	----	----	
Georgia	65	----	1 year	1 year	----	----	----	----	----	Actual confinement upon final conviction of crime.
Idaho	65	X	(1)	----	----	----	----	----	----	
Illinois	65	X	(6)	----	----	----	----	----	----	
Indiana	65	----	(7)	1 year[8]	----	----	----	----	----	
Iowa	65	X[9]	(1)	----	X	----	15 years	----	2 years	Inmate of any insane asylum or public reform or correctional institution.
Kansas	65	----	1 year continuously	----	----	----	----	----	----	
Kentucky (See appendix B.)	65	X	(1)	----	----	----	----	----	----	
Louisiana (See appendix B.)	65	----	(1)	----	----	----	----	----	----	
Maine	65	----	(1)	----	----	----	----	----	----	
Maryland	65	X	(1)	----	----	----	----	----	----	
Massachusetts	65	X	(1)	----	----	----	----	----	----	Applicant is not deserving.
Michigan	65	----	(1)	----	6 months	X	16 years	5 years	1 year	Able to earn $1 per day regularly.

State	Age	Citizenship	Residence	Residence (add'l)	Other residence	Other provisions
Minnesota	65	X[10]	(11)	(12)		Inmate of any public charitable, custodial, or correctional institution (temporary medical or surgical care in hospital excepted).[14]
Mississippi	65		(13)	Resident		Intoxication or drug handling.
Missouri	70		(1)			Ability to earn livelihood.
Montana	65		(1)	(2)		
Nebraska	65		(16)			
Nevada	65	X	(1)	—	6 months — 16 years	10 years — 1 year · Inmate of any prison, jail, State insane asylum, or State institution for the blind.
New Hampshire (See appendix B.)	70	X	—	—		
New Jersey	65	X	(1)	Resident		
New Mexico	65	X	(1)			
New York	65[16]	X	(1)			
North Carolina	65	X	(1)			
North Dakota	65	X	(1)	X	15 years	
Ohio	65	X	(1)	1 year[17] — 6 months · X		1 year
Oklahoma	65	X	(1)			
Oregon	70[19]	X[18]	(1)			
Pennsylvania	65	X[20]	(7)			
Rhode Island	65	X[20]	5 within 10 years[21]			
South Carolina	65	X	(1)			
South Dakota	65	Citizen or has applied	(22)			
Tennessee	65	X	(1)			Habitual criminal or drunkard.
Texas	65	X	(1)		10 years	
Utah	65	X	5 within 10 years			
Vermont	65	X	(1)			
Virginia	65	X	5 within 10 years			
Washington	65	X	(1)			
West Virginia	65	X	(1)	(24) — (24)	10 years	1 year
Wisconsin	65[23]	X	(7)			
Wyoming	65	X[25]	(1)	5 within 9 years		
Alaska	65	X	(1)		Habitual	Inmate of any insane asylum or public reform or correctional institution.
District of Columbia	65	X	(1)			
Hawaii	65		5 within 9 years			

See footnotes on following page.

Table 7.—Footnotes

X indicates that the provision applies without limitation in a given State.

1 Applicant must have been resident for 5 years within last 9 years, 1 year immediately preceding application.

2 Pension paid entirely by State until legal residence is gained in county.

3 Inmate of any institution other than penal may make application for assistance, but such assistance, if granted, may not begin until after the applicant ceases to be an inmate.

4 Applicant must have been resident for 5 years within last 9 years; if Federal aid is not granted, applicant must have resided in State 15 years immediately preceding application or for 40 years, of which 5 years must have immediately preceded application. Periods of absence not exceeding a total of 3 years do not interrupt continuous residence.

5 If 65 years and over applicant must have resided in the State 5 years within 9 years immediately preceding application with 1 year immediately preceding application. At 60 to 65 years he must have been a resident for 35 years preceding the application and a registered voter at the general elections held next preceding the application.

6 Applicant must have been resident for 5 years within 9 years, 1 year immediately preceding application; absences not exceeding 90 days allowed (absence in service of State or United States does not interrupt residence if residence is not acquired elsewhere.

7 Applicant must have been resident for 5 years within 9 years, 1 year immediately preceding application; absence in service of State or United States does not interrupt residence.

8 Application must be filed in county in which applicant has resided 1 full year during the 9 years next preceding the application. If no such residence exists, the application must be filed in county of residence at the time of application.

9 Applicant is eligible if he has resided in the United States for 25 years and has thought himself to be a citizen.

10 Applicant is eligible if he has been a resident of the United States for 25 years.

11 Applicant must have been resident for 5 years within 9 years, 1 year immediately preceding application; when a resident for 2 years immediately preceding application and has not met the statutory residence requirement, he may be given credit for his previous residence in the State to enable him to meet the requirement.

12 Application must be filed in county in which applicant has legal settlement (1 year continuous residence). If applicant otherwise qualified has no settlement, legal settlement for purpose of making application is county in which he has resided longest within the year immediately preceding application.

13 Applicant must have been resident for 5 years within 9 years, 1 year immediately preceding application, and such residence must not have been established for the purpose of enabling applicant to receive assistance.

14 Applicant also disqualified if he contributes to support of able-bodied person over 18 years of age other than spouse.

15 Applicant must have been resident 5 years within 9 years immediately preceding application, or 25 consecutive years at any period and 1 year immediately preceding application.

16 In event Federal aid is discontinued, the age limit must be raised to 70 years after 1st day of February following such discontinuance.

17 May be waived if necessary to secure Federal aid.

18 Any native born American woman who lost her American citizenship because of marriage to an alien prior to September 22, 1933, and who is otherwise qualified, is eligible for assistance.

19 After December 31, 1939, age requirement is 65 years.

20 Applicant must be a citizen of the United States or have been a resident of the United States continuously for 20 years.

21 1 year's residence prior to time of application required. Regardless of State law rules and regulations necessary to conform to Federal old age legislation may be made by the chief of the Division of Social Security with the approval of the State Director of Public Welfare.

22 Applicant must have been resident 2 years within 9 years, 1 year immediately preceding application.

23 May be reduced to 60 years whenever Federal age limit is so reduced.

24 Applicant must not have failed to support wife or child under 15 years of age, for 6 months or more during 15 years preceding application.

25 Applicant must be a citizen of the United States or have been a resident of the United States for 15 years.

Table 8.—Need Qualifications for Old Age Assistance

| State | Limitations on property | | | Limitations on income | | Applicant must not have disposed of property to qualify | Applicant has no person legally liable and able to support him |
	General limitations	Limits on real property	Limits on personal property	Maximum income allowed	Income rate applied to nonrevenue producing property		
Alabama	(1)	---	(1)	$360 per year including assistance		X	Contributions from legally responsible relatives inadequate.
Arizona	(1)	Realty used as residence.	$1,000	$360 per year[2]		Within 5 years	
Arkansas	(1)	---	(1)	(1)		Within 2 years	
California	(1)	$3,000	$500[3]	$35 per month including assistance[4]		X	X.
Colorado	(1)	Realty used as residence.	Property exempt from execution or attachment.	$45 per month including assistance[5]		X	
Connecticut	(1)	---	(1)	(1)		X	X.
Delaware	(1)	---	(1)	$300 per year including assistance		X	X.
Florida	(1)	(1)	(1)	(1)		Within 2 years	
Georgia	(1)	(1)	(1)	(1)		Within 2 years	
Idaho	(1)	(1)	(1)	(1)		X	
Illinois	(1)	(1)	(1)	$30 per month including assistance	2 percent	Within 5 years[6]	Child.[7]
Indiana	(1)	(1)	(1)	(1)		Within 5 years	
Iowa	(1)	$2,000 ($3,000 if married).	$300 ($450 if married)	$25 per month including assistance	5 percent[8]	X	([9]).
Kansas	(1)	(1)	(1)	(1)		Within 2 years	
Kentucky	(1)	(1)	(1)	(1)		X	
Louisiana	(1)	(1)	(1)	(1)		Within 5 years	Relative.
Maine	(1)	(1)	(1)	(1)		X	Spouse or child.
Maryland	(1)	(1)	(1)	$1 per day including assistance		Within 2 years	X.
Massachusetts	(1)	(10)	(10)	$30 per month including assistance[11]		Within 5 years	
Michigan	(1)	$3,500[12]	$1,000 ($500 exemption for household goods).[12]	$30 per month including assistance	3 percent	X	
Minnesota	$3,500[15]	---	---	$30 per month including assistance[14]		Within 2 years	Spouse or child.
Mississippi	(1)	(1)	(1)	(1)		Within 5 years[15]	Brothers, sisters, sons, or daughters.

See footnotes at end of table.

Table 8.—Need Qualifications for Old Age Assistance—Continued

State	Limitations on property			Limitations on income		Applicant must not have disposed of property to qualify	Applicant has no person liable and able to support him
	General limitations	Limits on real property	Limits on personal property	Maximum income allowed	Income rate applied to nonrevenue producing property		
Missouri	$1,500 ($2,000 if married).		$500 in negotiable papers or cash.	$30 per month including assistance[16]		X	
Montana	(1)	(1)		(1)		Within 2 years	
Nebraska				$360 per year including assistance	5 percent	X	X.
Nevada	(1)	(1)	(1)	$30 per month including assistance		Within 3 years	
New Hampshire	(1)	(1)	(1)	(1)		Within 5 years	(17).
New Jersey (See ap. B.)	$3,000[18]					X	X.
New Mexico	(1)	(1)	(1)	(1)		Within 2 years	
New York	(19)	(19)	(19)	(19)		X	X
North Carolina	(1)	(1)	(1)	(1)		Within 2 years	
North Dakota	(1)	(1)	(1)	(1)		X	X.
Ohio	$3,000 ($4,000 if married).	(1)	(1)	$360 per year including assistance	5 percent	X	X.
Oklahoma	(1)	(1)	(1)	$30 per month including assistance		Within 5 years	
Oregon							X.[20]
Pennsylvania						Within 2 years[21]	Spouse, child, father, mother, grandparent, grandchild.
Rhode Island		$5,000[18]		$30 per month including assistance. May be more in exceptional cases.	5 percent	X	(22).
South Carolina	(1)	(1)	(1)	$240 per year		X	X.
South Dakota	(1)	(1)	(1)	(1)		X	
Tennessee	(1)	(1)	(1)	(1)		Within 2 years	
Texas				$30 per month including assistance		X	Spouse.
Utah				Must not exceed yearly average of $30 per month including assistance.[23]		Within 5 years	
Vermont	$2,500 ($4,000 if married), $1,000 homestead exemption.			$360 per year ($500 if married)[24]		X	X.
Virginia				$20 per month including assistance		Within 5 years	(25).

Washington				$360 per year[26]	X
West Virginia	(1)				X
Wisconsin	$5,000[13]				X
Wyoming	(1)	$1 per day including assistance	5 percent	(27)	X
Alaska	(1)				X[28]
District of Columbia	(1)				X (29).
Hawaii	(1)				X (30). Spouse, child, or parent.

X indicates that the provision applies without limitation in a given State.

[1] Applicant has property or income in excess of amount needed for reasonable subsistence compatible with decency and health.

[2] Contributions and assistance from public or private charities are not included as income.

[3] Personal property does not include insurance policies which have been in effect at least 5 years and the maturity value of which does not exceed $1,000.

[4] Income less than $15 per month is not considered if derived from personal services, value of foodstuff produced for use of family, rent from premises owned and occupied by applicant, value of firewood or water produced on premises or given to applicant, or gifts other than regular contributions from legally responsible relatives.

[5] The amount of net income from any source either in cash or in kind received by a person eligible for assistance is deducted from the amount of assistance which such person would otherwise receive.

[6] Applicant has not made a voluntary assignment to increase need for assistance.

[7] Assistance granted may be recovered from child liable for support.

[8] Value of household goods and heirlooms exempt to the amount of $500 in making computation.

[9] Applicant has no spouse, child, or other person, municipality, association, society, or corporation legally or contractually responsible and able to support him.

[10] Applicant is not disqualified by reason of ownership of equity in real estate upon which he actually resides (except that if such equity is in excess of $3,000 in each of the 5 years immediately preceding application, penal bond in amount of excess is required). The ownership of a policy of insurance not exceeding $3,000 and with a cash surrender value not in excess of $300 if in effect not less than 15 years does not disqualify applicant. The ownership of a policy of group insurance not in excess of $1,000 and with a weekly premium not exceeding 50 cents does not disqualify applicant if it has been in effect at least 5 years.

[11] $50 for married couples both eligible, $50 for sister and brother living together, and $15 for each additional eligible brother or sister. Maximum income allowed includes assistance.

[12] Property of husband or husband and wife jointly if they are not separated. In calculating income, earnings or gifts not exceeding $50 in any calendar year are not considered.

[13] Property of pensioner and spouse must not exceed limit. Does not include value of household goods, personal effects, and a lot in burial ground.

[14] Excludes irregular or casual gifts or earnings not over $100 a year.

[15] Applicant must not maintain or contribute to support of any able-bodied person over 18 years of age other than husband or wife.

[16] Earnings not exceeding $150 per year are not considered.

[17] Cost of assistance recoverable in action of debt by State Department of Public Welfare from father, mother, stepfather, stepmother, son, or daughter, jointly or severally, if able to provide.

[18] Not an exemption limit but merely a guide to administration. Applicant must be poor, deserving, and unable to support himself.

[19] Applicant must not have sufficient property or income to provide reasonable subsistence. If applicant has no funds, ownership of personal or real property or life insurance by applicant or spouse shall not preclude assistance.

[20] Action may be brought against person or persons liable for support of recipient to recover cost of assistance.

[21] Applicant has not disposed of property of $500 value or more unless fair consideration was received.

[22] If other persons are able to support, applicant's pension decreased accordingly.

[23] Rental value of home, if owned or being purchased and actually occupied by applicant, is not to be construed as income. Combined income of husband and wife must be considered in determining the need of either person.

[24] The law also provides that the amount of allowance can be no greater than an amount which when added to income from other sources will equal $30 per month for a single person and $45 per month for man and wife living together. Earnings or gifts which do not exceed $100 in any calendar year are not considered as income.

[25] Local board may proceed against any person legally liable and financially able and cause him to support applicant or recipient.

[26] Amount of assistance together with applicant's own resources and income must not be less than $30 per month.

[27] Income including assistance, which as nearly approximates $30 per month as circumstances in each case shall warrant.

[28] Applicant or spouse must not have deprived himself of any property, income, or resources in order to qualify for assistance.

[29] Territorial Department of Public Welfare may bring suit for recovery of assistance against persons liable and able to support recipient.

[30] Spouse, father, child, or grandchild living in the District of Columbia.

Table 9.—Types of Aid Received or Needed Which Disqualify Applicants for Old Age Assistance

State	Other public assistance	Institutional aid		In need of continuing institutional care
		Public or private institution	Public institution	
Alabama			X	
Arizona	X[1]	X[2]		X.[3]
Arkansas			X	
California		X[4]		
Colorado		X		X.
Connecticut		X		
Delaware			X	
Florida			X	
Georgia	(5)		X	
Idaho			X	X.
Illinois			X[6]	
Indiana	X[7]		X	
Iowa	X[8]			X.[3]
Kansas			X	
Kentucky	X[7]	X		X.
Louisiana (See appendix B.)	X[7]	X		
Maine			X[9]	
Maryland			X[9]	
Massachusetts			X[10]	
Michigan			X[7]	X.
Minnesota			X[7]	X.[3]
Mississippi	X[7]	X[9]		
Missouri			X	
Montana			X[7]	X.
Nebraska	X[11]			
Nevada			X	
New Hampshire	X[7]	X[12]		X.
New Jersey	X[7]			X.
New Mexico	X[7]		X[7]	
New York		X[9]		X.
North Carolina			X[9]	
North Dakota	X[7]		X[9]	
Ohio				
Oklahoma		X[9]		
Oregon	X[7]	X[13]		
Pennsylvania			X	
Rhode Island		X[14]		
South Carolina			X	
South Dakota	X[7]	X		
Tennessee		X[15]		
Texas		X[16]		
Utah		X		X.
Vermont	X[7]			
Virginia	X[7]		X[9]	
Washington	X[7]		X	X.
West Virginia	X[17]	X[9]		X.
Wisconsin	X[7]	X[18]		
Wyoming			X	
Alaska			X[9]	
District of Columbia	X[7]			
Hawaii	X[7]		X[9]	

See footnotes on following page.

Table 9.—Footnotes

X indicates that the provision applies without limitation in a given State.

[1] Recipient may not receive any other public assistance except temporary medical or surgical aid unless authorized by the State board.

[2] Assistance may be granted to inmates of the Home for the Aged and Infirm Arizona Pioneers at Prescott and to persons temporarily confined in institutions for medical or surgical care.

[3] Such care must be reasonably available.

[4] Temporary medical or surgical assistance does not disqualify applicant. Inmates of a boarding home or other institution not supported in whole or in part by public funds must be granted aid, except if such persons are cared for under a contract exceeding the period of 1 month or requiring payment of any sum other than for room or board.

[5] Blind assistance only.

[6] Assistance granted while maintained in private institution in which applicant has not purchased care and maintenance or where the amount paid for care and maintenance has been wholly consumed.

[7] Temporary medical or surgical assistance does not disqualify applicant.

[8] Receipt of fuel, dental, nursing, osteopathic, chiropractic, medical, or surgical assistance, or hospitalization does not disqualify applicant.

[9] An inmate may make application for assistance but, if granted, assistance must not begin until after he ceases to be an inmate.

[10] Applicant is also disqualified if cared for under contract by institution not supported in whole or part by public funds.

[11] Also State institution for the blind. Temporary hospitalization does not disqualify applicant.

[12] Inmate of public institution may make application for assistance but, if granted, assistance must not begin until he ceases to be an inmate.

[13] Any person qualified to receive assistance may live at a privately operated home for the aged.

[14] Hospitalization does not disqualify applicant; any applicant not an inmate of a private institution for the aged at the time of the passage of the act and who was not an inmate thereof during the period of 1 year just prior to the passage of the act may upon entering a private home continue to receive aid if such home is approved by the director of public welfare.

[15] Inmates of private institutions approved by State department are not disqualified.

[16] Hospitalization does not disqualify applicant.

[17] Applicant may not receive other public assistance (except temporary medical or surgical assistance) without approval of county council.

[18] Inmate of county home may apply for assistance but, if granted, assistance must not begin until after he ceases to be an inmate.

Table 10.—Provisions for Recovery of Cost of Old Age Assistance From Recipients and Their Estates

State	Liens	Requirement for execution of agreement by recipient to reimburse governmental unit	Requirement for assignment or transfer of property	Recovery in cases where recipient becomes possessed of property or income in excess of need or amount stated in application	Recovery from estate upon death of recipient	Limitations on recovery from estate	Recovery in cases of misrepresentation or concealment of income or property	Rate of interest charged on sums granted and recovered	Portion of sums recovered paid to Federal Government
Alabama							X[1]		Proportionate share.
Arizona				X					
Arkansas				X			X[3]		Not to exceed 50 percent.
California	(2)								
Colorado		Prohibited	(5)				X[1]		
Connecticut		M[4]				Surviving spouse may be allowed to occupy property.	X[1]	4 percent.	50 percent.
Delaware									
Florida					X	Claim must be waived if recipient leaves widow or minor children liable to become public charges.			Not to exceed 50 percent.
Georgia				X					
Idaho				X	X	No claim enforceable while property is occupied by surviving spouse or dependent children. $100 funeral expenses and costs of administration allowed as preferred claim.			Proportionate share.
Illinois					X	No claim enforceable if property is occupied by surviving spouse.[6]	X[7]		50 percent.
Indiana	X	M[8]	O	X	X	No claim enforceable while property is occupied by surviving spouse.	X[5]	3 percent.	50 percent.
Iowa	X		O[9]	X	X	No claim enforceable while property is occupied by surviving spouse.[10]	X[5]		Amount required by Federal law.
Kansas	X				X	No claim enforceable against property while occupied by surviving spouse. $100 funeral expenses and costs of administration allowed as preferred claims.			Not to exceed 50 percent.
Kentucky	X				X[11]			X[12]	50 percent.
Louisiana (See appendix B.)	X	M[8]	O		X	No claim enforceable against real property while occupied by surviving spouse, child, or children.	X[3]		50 percent.
Maine					X	No claim enforceable against real property while occupied by surviving spouse.[13] Expenses of last illness, burial, and administration are allowed as preferred claims.			50 percent.

State						Amount
Maryland		O	X	No claim enforceable against real property while occupied by surviving spouse. Claim for funeral expenses allowed.		50 percent.
Massachusetts		[14]				
Michigan		Prohibited	X			
Minnesota			X		X	Amount required by Federal law.
Mississippi			X	No claim enforceable against homestead while occupied as such by surviving spouse or dependent minor children.	Y[3]	50 percent.
Missouri			X			
Montana			X	No claim enforceable while real property is occupied by surviving spouse or dependent. $100 funeral expenses and costs of administration allowed as preferred claims.		Not to exceed 50 percent.
Nebraska			X	No claim enforceable against real property while occupied by surviving spouse or child of recipient or spouse.		50 percent.
Nevada			X	No claim enforceable against real property of the recipient while occupied by surviving spouse or dependent. Funeral expenses, expenses of last illness, and costs of administration allowed as preferred claims.		50 percent.
New Hampshire	X	O	X	No claim enforceable against real property while occupied as a home by surviving spouse. $100 personal property, funeral expenses, and costs of administration allowed as claims.		Not to exceed 50 percent.
New Jersey (See appendix B.)	X	M	X	No levy may be made on real property while occupied by surviving spouse.[15] $150 funeral expenses allowed as preferred claim.		Proportionate share.
New Mexico			X	No claim enforceable against real property while occupied by surviving spouse or dependent.		Not to exceed 50 percent.
New York	X	O[16]	X[17]	Claim may be waived if a widow or minor children survive who are liable to become public charges.		Proportionate share.
North Carolina						
North Dakota		M	X	No claim enforceable against real property while occupied by surviving spouse or dependent, or against personal property not exceeding $200 in value necessary for support, maintenance, and comfort of surviving spouse. $125 funeral expenses and administration expenses allowed as preferred claims.		50 percent.

See footnotes at end of table.

Table 10.—Provisions for Recovery of Cost of Old Age Assistance From Recipients and Their Estates—Continued

State	Liens	Requirement for execution of agreement by recipient to reimburse governmental unit	Requirement for assignment or transfer of property	Recovery in cases where recipient becomes possessed of property or income in excess of need or amount stated in application	Recovery from estate upon death of recipient	Limitations on recovery from estate	Recovery in cases of misrepresentation or concealment of income or property	Rate of interest charged on sums granted and recovered	Portion of sums recovered paid to Federal Government
Ohio			Ō[18]		X		X[19]		Proportionate share.
Oklahoma					X		X		Amount required by Federal law.
Oregon	X		O		X				
Pennsylvania					X		X		(21),
Rhode Island	X		O[20]	X	X	(21)	X[3]		50 percent.
South Carolina	(22)			X	X	No claim enforceable against real property while occupied by surviving spouse. $100 funeral expenses allowed.			50 percent.
South Dakota	X			X	X				Proportionate share.
Tennessee				X	X	No claim enforceable against real property while occupied by surviving spouse or dependent children. $100 funeral expenses and costs of administration allowed as preferred claims.			Not to exceed 50 percent.
Texas	(23)				(24)		X[3]	6 percent	50 percent.
Utah	(23)	(23)		(25)		(24)	(23)		Not to exceed 50 percent.
Vermont	X				X	No lien enforceable against real property while occupied by surviving spouse.[25] Funeral expenses, probate fees, and taxes allowed as preferred claims.	X[3]		50 percent.
Virginia				X	X	No claim enforceable against property while occupied by surviving unmarried spouse or dependent children. $100 funeral expenses and $150 doctor and hospital expenses allowed.			50 percent.
Washington	X[26]		O[26]	X	X[26]	No levy or lien enforceable against real property while occupied by surviving spouse.[10]	X[26]		
West Virginia	X		(27)		X	Lien not enforceable against real property occupied by surviving spouse.[28] $100 funeral expenses allowed as preferred claim.			50 percent.
Wisconsin	X[29]		O		X	No lien enforceable against homestead while occupied by surviving spouse or surviving minor children.[29]		3 percent	50 percent.

					No claim enforceable against property exempted by law.	Proportionate share.
Wyoming	X					
Alaska	X	O		X[1]		50 percent.
District of Columbia		O			Claim enforceable at death of recipient or survivor of a recipient married couple.	50 percent. — 3 percent.
Hawaii			X			50 percent.

X indicates that the provision applies without limitation in a given State.

M indicates that it is mandatory upon welfare officials to require applicant or recipient to execute agreement to reimburse or for recipient to transfer property or interest in property.

O indicates that it is discretionary with welfare officials whether agreement to reimburse shall be executed or whether recipient shall transfer property or interest in property.

[1] Recovery permitted for amount of assistance paid in excess of amount to which recipient would have been otherwise entitled.

[2] Total aid constitutes a debt to State and county but shall not constitute a lien upon any property of recipient.

[3] Recovery permitted for double the amount of assistance paid in excess of amount to which recipient would have been otherwise entitled.

[4] Agreement must be executed and acknowledged in the form and manner required for the transfer of an interest in real property, and constitutes a lien which may at any time during which the amount remains unpaid be foreclosed in behalf of the State. Commissioner of welfare may allow beneficiary to occupy such real property.

[5] Recipient must, if required by the commissioner of welfare, assign life insurance policy, bank account, or other personal property to the commissioner.

[6] If spouse is not more than 15 years younger than recipient and has not remarried, and if no creditors have filed claims against the estate.

[7] Amount of assistance obtained by false statement, wilful misrepresentation, or other voluntary device constitutes a lien upon all personal property of recipient.

[8] Applicant must assign as collateral security for reimbursement such part of his personal property as the local department requires.

[9] State board may require an absolute conveyance of property of an applicant. The deed making such conveyance must reserve to the grantor and his spouse a life estate in said property and an option to the grantor and his heirs to repurchase the property by repayment of the total amount of assistance paid to the recipient.

[10] If spouse is not more than 15 years younger than recipient and has not remarried.

[11] Recoverable on death of recipient or survivor of married couple. $100 must be allowed for burial expenses.

[12] Rate not specified.

[13] Provided spouse is eligible for old age assistance or will reach age of eligibility within 5 years from death of recipient and has not remarried.

[14] Applicant required to execute penal bond for excess of equity over $3,000 owned in real estate upon which he actually resides.

[15] Provided spouse is not more than 10 years younger than recipient.

[16] Public welfare official may accept a deed of real property and/or a mortgage thereon. Property may be redeemed 1 year from date of conveyance of mortgage by repayment of assistance.

[17] Public welfare district granted a preferred claim against any insurance held by applicant.

[18] Right to use property for life reserved to recipient. Upon reimbursement for assistance property must be transferred to recipient or surviving spouse. Personal property may be reassigned or transferred to recipient or surviving spouse without reimbursement for assistance granted if for the best interests of recipient or surviving spouse. All insurance held by a recipient in excess of $250 must be placed under the trusteeship of the State as a guarantee for repayment of assistance.

[19] In case of concealment or misrepresentation the amount of assistance gained by such misrepresentation must be collected at the death of the recipient in addition to the total amount of aid paid.

[20] The chief of the Division of Social Security may require an applicant to give a mortgage on his real property to the general treasurer or a power of attorney to such chief to manage said applicant's property.

[21] Upon death all sums paid constitute a lien on estate of recipient enforceable for the benefit of the State and the United States. No such lien shall be enforced while real property is occupied by surviving spouse, who is not more than 15 years younger than recipient and not remarried.

[22] The State Department of Public Welfare shall, under no circumstances, require the applicant for benefits to sign a lien agreement, acknowledgment of claim, or mortgage in any form.

[23] Provided the estate has a combined assessed valuation of less than $3,000, no recipient may be required to reimburse State for any assistance, except for assistance obtained fraudulently or contrary to law, and no lien or mortgage shall be taken on the estate of the recipient.

[24] Upon death of recipient, where there is no descendant of first or second degree in direct line and where combined value of home and furniture is $3,000, a claim for the total amount of assistance must be filed and allowed as other claims are.

[25] If marriage did not take place after April 11, 1935, and spouse has not remarried.

[26] Effective only if essential to obtain Federal participation.

[27] Applicant must assign any insurance policy granting death benefits.

[28] Unless such person is a widow who has remarried or there is a threatened or actual sale or transfer of the property. Real property to value of $1,500 and personal property to value of $200 exempt from exercise of any lien.

[29] Lien may be released by court if found necessary to provide for maintenance of spouse or surviving children.

Table 11.—Provisions for Granting and Financing Old Age Assistance

State	Maximum allowance (per month unless otherwise specified)	Minimum allowance (per month unless otherwise specified)	Burial allowance	Governmental unit determining amount of individual grant		Incidence of financial responsibility			Basis for distribution of State funds	Procedure in case of insufficiency of State funds
				Final	Advisory	State	County	Other local unit		
Alabama	$30[1]			County		50 percent.	50 percent.		State allocates to counties 50 percent of estimated expenditure for ensuing 3 months.	Funds prorated among the counties.
Arizona	$30	(2)	$75. If insufficient, $100.	State	County	X			Individuals paid by State Department of Social Security and Welfare by warrant drawn upon State auditor.	
Arkansas	(2)	(2)		State	(3)	X			State disburses funds to individuals	
California	$35[4]			County		50 percent.[5]	50 percent.		State reimburses county for 50 percent of amount expended.[5]	
Colorado	$45[6]		$100	County		100 percent.[7]	(7)		State apportions funds to counties upon request	
Connecticut	$7 per week		$125	State	Town	X			State disburses funds to individuals	
Delaware	$25		$100	State		X			State disburses funds to individuals	
Florida	$30			State[8]		X			State disburses funds to individuals	
Georgia	$30		$75	County		90 percent.	10 percent.		State reimburses county for 90 percent of amount expended for assistance and administration.[9]	
Idaho	(10)	(10)		County		$66\frac{2}{3}$ percent.[14]	$33\frac{1}{3}$ percent.[11]		County reimburses State for $33\frac{1}{3}$ percent of amount expended. State disburses funds to individuals.[11]	
Illinois	$30[12]		$100	County		X			State disburses funds to individuals	Funds prorated among approved applicants.
Indiana	$30		$75[13]	County		60 percent.	40 percent.		State reimburses county for 60 percent of amount expended.[14]	
Iowa	$25		$100	State	County	X			State disburses funds to individuals	
Kansas	(2)		$100	County		30 percent.	70 percent.		State reimburses county for 30 percent of expenditure less cost of administration.	
Kentucky	$15			State		X			State disburses funds to individuals	
Louisiana (See appendix B.)	(2)	(2)	$100	Parish		75 percent.[15]		25 percent (parish).	State reimburses parishes for 75 percent of expenditure for assistance and 50 percent of expenditure for administration.[15]	
Maine	$30	(2)	$100	State		X			State disburses funds to individuals	

State				Administered by		State share	Local share	Local share (special)	Remarks
Maryland	$30	---	$125	County	---	66⅔ per-cent.	33⅓ per-cent.	33⅓ per-cent (city of Balti-more).	State pays 66⅔ percent of local expense ------
Massachusetts	$30[16]	---	---	Town	---	33⅓ per-cent.		16⅔ per-cent (town).	State reimburses towns for ⅔ of total amount expended from town funds after allocating Federal grants.
Michigan	$30	---	$150	State	---	X			State disburses funds to individuals according to rules and regulations of State old age assistance bureau.
Minnesota	$30[17]	---	$100	County	---	66⅔ per-cent.[18]	33⅓ per-cent.		State reimburses county for 66⅔ percent of the amount expended.[18]
Mississippi	$15[19]	---	---	County	---	X			State disburses funds to individuals ------ Total amount of assistance must not exceed appropriations.
Missouri	$30[20]	---	---	State	---	X			State disburses funds to individuals ------
Montana	(2)	---	$100	County	---	83⅓ per-cent.	16⅔ per-cent.		County reimburses State for 16⅔ percent of amount expended.
Nebraska	$30	---	$75	County	---	X	X		State disburses funds to counties in the ratio of the population of each county to the total population of the State. Funds prorated among applicants.
Nevada	$30[21]	---	---	County	State	25 per-cent.[22]	25 per-cent.[22]		State and county funds paid into combined old age assistance fund and disbursed to individuals upon warrant of State comptroller.
New Hampshire	(2)	---	---	State[23]	Town or county,[23]	75 per-cent.	X	25 per-cent (county or town).	State disburses funds to individuals. County or town reimburses State 25 percent of amount expended for persons for whom the county or towns are liable.[24]
New Jersey (See appendix B.)	$30	---	$100	County	---	87½ per-cent.[25]	12½ per-cent.[26]		State reimburses county for 87½ percent of amount expended, but if no Federal aid is available, the State reimburses the county for 75 percent of amount expended.
New Mexico	(2)	---	$50	State[27]	---	X			State disburses funds to individuals ------
New York	(28)	---	(29)	City or county public welfare districts.	---	50 per-cent.[30]	50 per-cent.[30]		State reimburses city or county public welfare district for 50 percent of aid granted to persons for whose support State is not responsible and entire cost of assistance granted Indians and persons without legal settlement.[30]
North Carolina	$30	---	---	County[31]	---	25 per-cent.[32]	25 per-cent.[32]		State reimburses county for 25 percent of the amount expended.[32]

See footnotes at end of table.

Table 11.—Provisions for Granting and Financing Old Age Assistance—Continued

State	Maximum allowance (per month unless otherwise specified)	Minimum allowance (per month unless otherwise specified)	Burial allowance	Governmental unit determining amount of individual grant		Incidence of financial responsibility			Basis for distribution of State funds	Procedure in case of insufficiency of State funds
				Final	Advisory	State	County	Other local unit		
North Dakota	(2)	$40[33]	$75	State	County	85 per-cent.[34]	15 per-cent.[34]	----	County reimburses State for 15 percent of the amount expended in excess of the amount provided by the Federal Government. The State may provide, as a grant or loan, the county's share if the county cannot provide it.	State must levy tax sufficient to make up deficiency in State public welfare fund but not in excess of sum appropriated and chargeable to such fund.
Ohio	$30[35]	----	$100	State	----	X	----	----	State disburses funds to individuals	----
Oklahoma	$30	----	(36)	State	County	X	----	----	Individual applications paid by State through the county assistance board.	Total amount of State funds available considered when passing upon individual applications.
Oregon	$30	(2)	----	County[37]	----	25 per-cent.[37]	25 per-cent.[38]	----	State disburses funds to individuals. County reimburses State for 25 percent of the amount expended.	----
Pennsylvania	(39)	(39)	----	County	----	X	----	----	County board submits budget to State department as the basis of allocation of State funds for assistance and administrative cost.	----
Rhode Island	$30[40]	(2)	----	State	----	X	----	X	State reimburses city and town for entire amount expended for assistance but city and town must pay local administrative expenses.	----
South Carolina	$240 per year	----	----	State[8]	----	X	----	----	State disburses funds to individuals	Funds prorated among applicants.
South Dakota	$30	(2)	----	State[41]	----	X	----	----	State disburses funds to individuals	----
Tennessee	$25	----	$100	State	----	37½ per-cent.[42]	12½ per-cent.[42]	----	County contributes to State 12½ percent of amount expended for assistance.	Ordinary operating expenses of State must be paid, and in case of deficiency appropriations for old age assistance must be reduced or discontinued.
Texas	$30[43]	----	----	(44)	----	X	----	----	Individuals paid by State through local agency.	----
Utah	$30[45]	----	$150	County or district.	----	85 per-cent.	15 per-cent.	----	County reimburses State for 15 percent of amount of assistance and administrative costs. State disburses funds to individuals.	Funds prorated among applicants.

State								
Vermont	$30. Family, $45.	$150	State	Town	X	37½ per-cent.	State disburses funds to individuals	Most needy recipients accepted.
Virginia	$20[46]		County or city.		62½ per-cent.	37½ per-cent.	State reimburses county 62½ percent of the amount expended during the preceding month for cost of assistance and administration from 62½ percent of Federal grant for assistance and State funds. 37½ percent of Federal grant for assistance paid to the several counties and cities on the basis of the total amounts disbursed for old age assistance by such counties and cities during the period for which such grants are made.[47]	
Washington	$30[21]	$100	State		X	X	Percent of contribution by State not specified. State disburses funds to individuals.	
West Virginia	$30		State	County	X		State funds allocated in counties in proportion to number of cases and cost of living.	
Wisconsin	$1 per day	$100	County		80 per-cent.	20 per-cent.	State reimburses county for 80 percent of the amount expended.	Funds prorated among counties according to amounts paid by them.
Wyoming	$30[48]	(2)	State	County	50 per-cent.	50 per-cent.	State matches county funds by grants-in-aid[49]	
Alaska	$45	(2)	Territory.		Territorial general fund.		Territory disburses funds to individuals	
District of Columbia.	(50)		District of Columbia.		District of Columbia.		District of Columbia disburses funds to individuals.	
Hawaii	$30		County		Territory.		All expenses incurred by the several county welfare commissions are paid from funds made available to them by the Territorial Board of Public Welfare.	

X indicates that the provision applies without limitation in a given State.

[1] Civil War veterans allowed $50. County is authorized to secure hospitalization for physically incapacitated applicants even though the amount expended exceeds maximum allowance. In such cases State reimbursement must not exceed $15 per month.

[2] Allowance is an amount which, when added to income, is sufficient for reasonable subsistence.

[3] County or district board of public welfare; final approval by State department.

[4] Allowance may be increased to $40 per month if Federal contribution is increased.

[5] If applicant has no county residence, State pays total amount. For the fiscal year 1938—1939 the sum of $500,000 per month is appropriated by the State in addition to all other moneys appropriated for old age assistance. This appropriation is allocated to each county in a sum which bears such proportion to the sum of $500,000 as the amount expended by that county for old age assistance during the second month preceding the month for which the allocation is made bears to the total amount expended by all counties for old age assistance during the same month.

[6] There must be no variation among recipients in the amount of income they receive from all sources, including assistance.

[7] Counties must contribute 50 percent of administrative costs.

[8] Through county or district welfare boards which act as agents of the State department.

[9] State may use equalization fund if county is unable to furnish support.

[10] Amount which when added to income is sufficient for reasonable subsistence. Amount paid by the State and county must not exceed the amount of Federal contribution.

[11] Amount of county contribution may be varied if the State department determines that the county is unable to meet its obligations.

[12] In the absence of Federal grants for old age assistance, allowance must not exceed $15 per month.

Table 11.—Footnotes Continued

13 $25 maximum allowed for burial plot if deceased or persons legally responsible do not possess one.

14 State may, when necessary, pay all or any part of cost of local administration or assistance.

15 State may assume total expense if State department finds that parish or district is unable to pay its share.

16 Allowance must not be less than $50 per month for husband and wife living together and both eligible for assistance, for 2 brothers or 2 sisters, or for brother and sister living together and both eligible, and not less than $15 for each additional eligible brother or sister.

17 In event Federal funds are not available or are inadequate to pay % of all grants contemplated, county agency may reduce each old age assistance grant by an amount equal to such deficiency.

18 State reimburses county 50 percent of burial expenses.

19 In the event Federal grants-in-aid are substantially reduced below 50 percent, this act becomes ipso facto null and void upon public proclamation of the Governor.

20 $45 maximum allowed for husband and wife if living together.

21 Amount granted plus other income must not be less than $30 per month.

22 Law takes into consideration Federal contribution of 50 percent.

23 State commissioner of public welfare determines eligibility of applicant and amount of assistance upon consultation with proper officials of counties or towns required to contribute to the cost.

24 If county or town finds it impossible to pay the amounts required, it may file a petition with the State department requesting financial aid. The department may with the approval of the Governor and council loan or grant to such town or county such amount as may be necessary.

25 If applicant has no county residence, the State pays total amount.

26 In case of insufficiency of county funds temporary loans, notes, certificates of indebtedness, or temporary bonds must be issued.

27 Application must be made to local office which investigates and makes report of findings and recommendations to the State department. The State department decides questions of eligibility and the amount of assistance, but it may allow its local offices to determine these questions.

28 Amount and nature of allowance determined by public welfare official. Amount of assistance fixed with due regard to conditions existing in each case.

29 If recipient's estate is insufficient and if there are no relatives or friends able and willing to pay, the district furnishing assistance at time of recipient's death must pay full or partial cost of burial.

30 During such time as Federal funds are received by the State the above provisions are modified as follows: old age assistance districts (county or city public welfare districts or any city forming part of a county welfare district electing to administer old age assistance) are responsible for 25 percent of the assistance provided to persons for whose support the State is not responsible and the remaining cost is borne by the State and Federal Governments.

31 City welfare officer in the city of Rocky Mount if such city is designated a local welfare unit.

38 State pays 50 percent of county administrative expenses and 50 percent of assistance for recipients with no county residence. The act provides for 50 percent contribution from the Federal Government and further provides that upon failure of Federal funds the act shall become null and void. An equalization fund is established to be distributed to the counties according to their needs. No county is entitled to share in such fund unless a 10-mill levy has been made to pay old age assistance and aid to dependent children. The amount which may be allocated to any county from the equalization fund may not exceed % of the cost to the county in excess of the amount produced by the 10-mill levy.

33 Minimum amount of allowance must not be less than $30 per month for each recipient. If there is more than 1 recipient in the family. If the amount of Federal contribution exceeds $15 per month, the State agency has the authority to increase the minimum allowance in an amount corresponding to the increase of the Federal contribution.

34 The State pays 85 percent of the cost of assistance in excess of the amount of Federal contribution.

35 $60 maximum allowance for recipient and spouse.

36 Assistance paid on or after death of recipient must be applied to funeral expenses and debts of deceased unless estate less homestead is of $200 value or more.

37 County makes award which stands until modified or withdrawn. The State Relief Committee approves each application in an amount consistent with evidence of need and available funds.

38 Law takes into consideration 50 percent contribution of the Federal Government. State reimbursement includes both cost of assistance and cost of county administrative expenses.

39 State Board of Public Assistance establishes by rule and regulation the nature and extent of assistance.

40 Allowance may be more in exceptional cases.

41 State regional director acts jointly with county official; if disagreement, State department makes final decision.

42 State contributions supplemented by Federal contributions to extent of 50 percent of cost of assistance. Entire cost of administration is paid from State funds and such Federal funds as may be made available.

43 State contribution may not exceed $15.

44 Local administrative agency designated by the State Old Age Assistance Commission.

45 One-twelfth of average yearly income is deducted from amount allowed. Additional aid may be given for hospitalization, special diet, or medical assistance.

46 Allowance must not exceed $20 per month when added to income from all other sources. Recipient who is eligible for Confederate pension may receive old age assistance in an amount equal to such pension even though such amount is in excess of old age assistance maximum.

47 Not more than 10 percent of the funds allocated to the counties and cities may be used for local administrative expenses. If a county or city fails or refuses to provide funds the State board must require the local authorities to make funds available. During the period of refusal or failure the State must make payments and deduct the amounts so paid from future State reimbursements.

48 Allowance with other income and support must approximate $30 per month. If Congress provides larger grants-in-aid before March 31, 1939, the State Department of Public Welfare may provide larger grants.

49 State may pay larger amount if county tax is insufficient.

50 Reasonable funeral expenses.

Blind Assistance

Table 12.—Provisions for the Administration of Blind Assistance

State	Nature of law	Administrative responsibility		Original determination		Determination of blindness			Reconsideration		Appeal and review		
		Direct	Supervisory	Final	Advisory	Certificate of physician — Officially designated physician	Certificate of physician — Any physician	Periodic re-examination of applicant's eyesight	Periodic	At request of State board or department	Appeal of applicant to State department[1]	Review by State department on own motion[1]	Further investigation by State department[1]
Alabama	M	State Department of Public Welfare.[2]	(²)	State Department of Public Welfare.[2]	(²)		X[3]			X	X		X.
Arizona	M	State Department of Social Security and Welfare assisted by county board of social security and public welfare.		State Department of Social Security and Welfare.	County board of social security and public welfare.	X[4]		3 years		X	State board.	State board[5]	State board.[5]
Arkansas	M	State Department of Public Welfare.		State Department of Public Welfare.	County or district board of public welfare.	X				X	X		
California	;	County board of supervisors.[6]	State Department of Social welfare.	County board of supervisors.[6]			X[3]		Annually.		State board.		
Colorado	M	County or district department of public welfare.	State Department of Public Welfare.	County or district department of public welfare.		X		3 years		X	X	X	
Connecticut	M	State Commissioner of Welfare through State bureau of old age assistance assisted by chief executive authority of town.		State bureau of old age assistance.	Chief executive authority of town.						Bureau of old age assistance.[7]		
Delaware													
Florida: State	M	State Welfare Board through district board of social welfare.		District board of social welfare.							State board.	State board.	State board.
Local	M	Board of county commissioners.		Board of county commissioners.		(8) X			Annually.				

State		Administering agency	State agency	Local unit						
Georgia	M	County or district department of public welfare.	State Department of Public Welfare.	County or district department of public welfare.		X	(⁹)	X	X	X.
Idaho	M	County welfare commission.	State Department of Public Assistance.	County welfare commission.		X	(⁹)	X	X	X.
Illinois	M	Board of county commissioners or board of county supervisors. County bureau of public welfare.[10]		Board of county commissioners or board of county supervisors. County bureau of public welfare.[10]		X				
Indiana	M	State Department of Public Welfare assisted by county or district department of public welfare.	State Department of Public Welfare.	County or district department of public welfare.	X[11]	3 years		X	State board.	State board.
Iowa	M	State Board of Social Welfare assisted by the county board of social welfare.		State Board of Social Welfare.	County board of social welfare.	X	(⁹)	X	State board.	State board.
Kansas	M	County board of social welfare.	State Board of Social Welfare.	County board of social welfare.					State appeal committee.[12]	(¹³).
Kentucky	O	County court.	State Department of Welfare.	County court.		X				
Louisiana (See appendix B.)	M	Parish department of public welfare.	State Department of Public Welfare.	Parish department of public welfare.		X	3 years	X	X.	
Maine	M	State Department of Health and Welfare.		State Department of Health and Welfare.				X	Commissioner of health and welfare.	
Maryland	M	County welfare board. Baltimore Department of Welfare.	Board of State Aid and Charities.	County welfare board. Baltimore Department of Welfare.				X	State board.	State board.
Massachusetts	O	Director of division of the blind, Department of Education.		Director of division of the blind, Department of Education.						
Michigan		(¹⁴)		(¹⁴)						
Minnesota		State Board of Control.[15]		State Board of Control.		X	3 years[16]	X	State board[17]	State board.

See footnotes at end of table.

Table 12.—Provisions for the Administration of Blind Assistance—Continued

State	Administrative responsibility			Original determination		Determination of eligibility								
						Determination of blindness			Reconsideration		Appeal and review			
						Certificate of physician		Periodic re-examination of applicant's eyesight						
	Nature of law	Direct	Supervisory	Final	Advisory	Officially designated physician	Any physician		Periodic	At request of State board or department	Appeal of applicant to State department[1]	Review by State department on own motion[1]	Further investigation by State department[1]
Mississippi	M	County board of public welfare and county agent.[18]	State Department of Public Welfare.	County board of public welfare and county agent.[18]		X				X	X	X	X.
Missouri	M	State Commission for the Blind.		State Commission for the Blind.	County or city probate judge.		X[19]				([20])		
Montana	M	County department of public welfare.	State Department of Public Welfare.	County department of public welfare.		X		([21])		X	X[22]	X	X
Nebraska	M	State Board of Control		State Board of Control, director of assistance.	County assistance committee.				Annually	X	State board		Director of assistance.
Nevada	O	Board of county commissioners.	State Welfare Department.	Board of county commissioners.			X[23]						
New Hampshire	M	State Department of Public Welfare.		State commissioner of public welfare.	([24])		X		Annually		State board		
New Jersey	M	County welfare board and commissioner of State Department of Institutions and Agencies jointly.		County welfare board and commissioner of State Department of Institutions and Agencies jointly.	State Commission for the Amelioration of the Condition of the Blind.[25]				Annually[26]		([27])		([28]).
New Mexico	M	State Department of Public Welfare.[29]		State Department of Public Welfare.[29]	Local office of State Department of Public Welfare.	X		([21])		X	State board	State board	State board.
New York	M	Local public welfare official.[30]	State Department of Social Welfare.	Local public welfare official.[30]						([31])	X	X	X.

State												
North Carolina	M --	Board of county commissioners.[32]	State Commission for the Blind.	Board of county commissioners.[32]		(35)__	X[34] --	Biannually.[35]	(36)__	State commission.[36]		
North Dakota	M --	State Public Welfare Board assisted by county welfare board.		State Public Welfare Board.	County welfare board.	X --	(21)__		X	State board.	State board.	State board.
Ohio	M --	Board of county commissioners.	State Department of Public Welfare, commission for the blind.	Board of county commissioners.		(37)__ X	X	Annually.	X	State commission.	State commission.	
Oklahoma	M --	State Public Welfare Commission assisted by county assistance board.		State Public Welfare Commission.	County assistance board.				X	State commission.	State commission.	State commission.
Oregon	M --	County relief committee.	State Relief Committee.	County relief committee.	--	X --			X	State Relief Committee.		
Pennsylvania	M --	County board of assistance.	State Department of Public Assistance.	County board of assistance.						X		
Rhode Island (See appendix B.)	O --	State Department of Education.[38]		State Department of Education.[38]						Director of department of education.[39]		
South Carolina	M --	State Department of Public Welfare through county department of public welfare.[40]		County department of public welfare.[40]		X --	(21)__		X	X	X	
South Dakota	M --	State Department of Social Security.		County or district offices of State Department of Social Security.		X --	(21)__		X	X		
Tennessee	M --	Department of Institutions and Public Welfare.		Regional director of Department of Institutions and Public Welfare concurrently with county judge or chairman of county court.[41]		X --	(21)__		X	X	X	

See footnotes at end of table.

Table 12.—Provisions for the Administration of Blind Assistance—Continued

State	Administrative responsibility			Original determination		Determination of eligibility							
	Nature of law	Direct	Supervisory	Final	Advisory	Determination of blindness			Reconsideration		Appeal and review		
						Certificate of physician		Periodic re-examination of appli- cant's eyesight	Periodic	At request of State board or depart- ment	Appeal of applicant to State department[1]	Review by State depart- ment on own motion[1]	Further investi- gation by State department[1]
						Offi- cially desig- nated physi- cian	Any physi- cian						
Texas	M	State Board of Control, division of public wel- fare, through local agency designated by it.[42]		Local agency designated by State Board of Con- trol, division of pub- lic welfare.			X	2 years[43]		X	(44)		
Utah	M	County or district de- partment of public welfare.	State Depart- ment of Pub- lic Welfare.	County or district de- partment of public welfare.						X	X	X	X.
Vermont	M	State Department of Public Welfare.		State Department of Public Welfare.						X	X		
Virginia	M	County or city board of public welfare.	State Commis- sion for the Blind.	County or city board of public welfare.					(45)	X	State com- mission.	State com- mission.	State com- mission.
Washington	M	Board of county commis- sioners.	State Depart- ment of Social Security.	Board of county commis- sioners.			X		Annual- ly.[46]		Director of social se- curity.		X.
West Virginia	M	State Department of Public Assistance as- sisted by county pub- lic assistance council.		State Department of Public Assistance.	County public assistance council.	X		(21)	Semian- nually.	X	Board of re- view of State de- partment.[47]	X	(48).
Wisconsin	M	County department of public welfare.[49] Coun- ty pension department.[50] County judge.	State Pension Department.	County department of public welfare.[49] Coun- ty pension department.[50] County judge.		X		(51)			X	X	X.
Wyoming	M	State Department of Public Welfare assist- ed by county depart- ment of public welfare.		State Department of Public Welfare.	County depart- ment of pub- lic welfare.	X		(9)		X	State board.		State board.
Alaska													

		Board of commissioners through designated agency.[52]		Annually	X[19]	Board of commission- ers.[52]		
District of Co- lumbia.	M --	County public welfare commission.	Board of commissioners through designated agency.[52] County public welfare commission.			Territorial board.	Territorial board.	Territorial board.
Hawaii	M --	Territorial Board of Pub- lic Welfare.			X	Territorial board.	Territorial board.	Territorial board.

X indicates that the provision applies without limitation in a given State.

M indicates mandatory provisions.

O indicates optional provisions.

[1] If authority to hear appeals, to review decisions, and to make further investigations is placed by law with a specific agency within the department, the specific agency is named either in the body of the table or in a footnote.

[2] Law authorizes State Department of Public Welfare to administer or supervise the program for blind assistance. Law does not specify whether final original determination is made by the State department or the county departments of public welfare.

[3] Certification must be by licensed ophthalmologist or physician skilled in the diseases of the eye.

[4] If originally examined by doctor, re-examination must be made by an ophthalmologist within a year unless applicant is over 65 years of age or doctor certifies that restoration or improvement of vision is impossible.

[5] When application is not approved by county board, State board may review decision and make further investigation.

[6] County boards of public welfare may be established by county board of supervisors or by petition of electorate.

[7] Appeal allowed to State bureau of old age assistance whose decision may be appealed to the superior court of the county in which the applicant resides.

[8] Board of county commissioners may employ physician in addition to one subscribing to application.

[9] Re-examination as required by county or Cook County.

[10] A county bureau is established in Cook County.

[11] If no ophthalmologist or eye, ear, nose, and throat specialist available, certificate may be signed by licensed optometrist.

[12] Recipient, taxpayer, or local agency may appeal to State appeal committee.

[13] The State director of social welfare is authorized to order an investigation of the activities of any county board or private agency whenever he deems necessary or whenever the State board recommends such an investigation.

[14] A State financed program for blind assistance is administered by the State Emergency Welfare Relief Commission through county welfare relief commissions under rules and regulations of the State commission. Specific provisions relating to eligibility, etc., are not set forth by statute and therefore have not been included in these tables.

[15] County boards of welfare must render the State board such services, in connection with the administration of blind assistance, as the State board may find necessary.

[16] Re-examination also when required by State board.

[17] Decision of State board may be appealed to the district court of the county in which the application was filed.

[18] The county board of public welfare and the county agent, who is appointed by the State commissioner of welfare, constitute the county department of public welfare.

[19] Competent oculist and certification by 2 citizens.

[20] Decision of commission may be appealed to circuit court.

[21] Re-examination as required by State agency.

[22] Appeal may be had by recipient or taxpayer.

[23] Certification by 1 citizen.

[24] Commissioner of public welfare must determine the eligibility of all applicants and the amount of assistance, but must, in all cases, first consult with the public officials of the counties or towns required to contribute to the cost of such assistance.

[25] The board of control of State Department of Institutions and Agencies may designate another agency to act in an advisory capacity.

[26] The State commission may, at its discretion, examine any and all recipients of blind relief and must make an annual examination of all such recipients.

[27] Appeal allowed to board of control of State Department of Institutions and Agencies or its designated representative.

[28] County welfare board may order the State commission to make such further investigation as the county board deems necessary.

[29] State department may allow its local office to determine whether assistance may be granted and the amount and manner thereof.

[30] "Public welfare official" means county commissioner of public welfare, city commissioner of public welfare, town public welfare officer, or city public welfare officer.

[31] State department must investigate complaints by persons stating that assistance is being improperly granted or administered.

[32] The State Commission for the Amelioration of the Condition of the Blind must examine awards or decisions and in its discretion approve, increase, allow, or disallow any awards made. If residence requirements are met, but applicant does not have legal settlement in any county, application is made to and awards paid directly by the commission.

[33] Further examination by officially designated ophthalmologist may be required.

[34] Physician must be actively engaged in the treatment of eyes.

[35] State commission or board of county commissioners must make reinvestigations biannually or as often as may be found necessary.

[36] Applicant may appeal decision to the State commission. If, in the absence of an appeal, the State commission makes an order changing an award of the board of county commissioners, such board or the applicant is entitled to a review.

[37] Local agency may require further examination by designated ophthalmologist and certification by 2 citizens.

[38] Bureau for the blind in the division of rehabilitation of the crippled and blind in the State Department of Education.

[39] Hearing held before director in the presence of the advisory council.

[40] In Charleston County the county welfare board has direct administrative responsibility for blind assistance under the supervision of the State Department of Public Welfare.
[41] In case of disagreement the State department makes decision.
[42] Program not operative until State funds are provided; none were available January 1, 1939.
[43] Recipient must submit to re-examination unless excused therefrom by the division of public welfare.
[44] Applicants or recipients must be granted a fair hearing before the State board or its responsible agent. All decisions on such hearings must be made by the board.
[45] Assistance granted for 1 year or less.

[46] Reconsideration may be more frequent if deemed necessary.
[47] Citizen may object to a grant or continuance of assistance and may appeal to the board of review of the State department.
[48] State department may also remand application to county for further investigation.
[49] Establishment is optional in counties of 500,000 or more.
[50] Establishment is optional in counties of less than 500,000.
[51] When requested to do so, recipients must submit to a re-examination and furnish such other information to the county board as it may require.
[52] The board of commissioners has designated the Department of Public Welfare as the agency to administer blind assistance.

Table 13.—Personal Qualifications for Blind Assistance

State	Minimum age in years	U.S. citizenship	Residence		Definition of blindness	Applicant must not solicit alms	Applicant may be required to undergo operation or treatment	Miscellaneous qualifications
			State	Local				
Alabama	16		(1)	Legal settlement or 1 year immediately preceding application.[2]	Established by rules and regulations	X	X	Need due primarily to blindness.
Arizona	16		(1)		(3)		X	
Arkansas	16		1 year[4]		(5)			
California	16		(6)	(7)	Loss or impairment of eyesight to the extent that applicant is unable to provide himself with necessities of life.	X		
Colorado	18	X	(1)		(8)	X	X	
Connecticut	18	X	(9)		Total or permanent loss of sight in both eyes, or the reduction to 1/10 or less of normal vision with glasses.			Applicant has paid old age assistance tax, is not serving penal sentence, or out on bond or probation.
Delaware								
Florida: State		X	5 years[10]		Loss of eyesight precludes following usual vocations.	X		Must be deserving in opinion of board of county commissioners.
Local				2 years[10]				
Georgia	21		1 year		(3)	X		Assistance suspended during confinement in public penal institution, after final conviction of crime.
Idaho			(1)		(3)			
Illinois	Males, 21; females, 18.	X	10 consecutive years immediately preceding application.	3 years immediately preceding application.[11]	(3)			Must not be physically or mentally incapacitated by age prior to loss of sight.
Indiana	Males, 21; females, 18.	X	(1)	(12)	(8)	X		
Iowa	18	X[13]	(14)		(3)			
Kansas	16		1 year		(3)	X		
Kentucky	Adult		10 years immediately preceding application.	5 years immediately preceding application.	Destitute of useful vision	X		Must not be a professional beggar.

See footnotes at end of table.

Table 13.—Personal Qualifications for Blind Assistance—Continued

State	Minimum age in years	U.S. citizenship	Residence State	Residence Local	Definition of blindness	Applicant must not solicit alms	Applicant may be required to undergo operation or treatment	Miscellaneous qualifications
Louisiana (See appendix B.)	16 (maximum, 64).		(1)		(8)	X	X[15]	
Maine	16		(9)		(3)			
Maryland			(1)			X		
Massachusetts								
Michigan						X	X	
Minnesota	21		(1)		(3)			
Mississippi					Applicant has no vision, or vision with correcting glasses is so defective as to prevent performance of ordinary activities for which eyesight is essential.			
Missouri	21		10 consecutive years immediately preceding application.[16]		Vision with or without glasses sufficient only to distinguish light from darkness and to recognize motion but not form of hand at a distance 1 foot away.	X	Under 75 years	Must be of good moral character and must not refuse vocational or educational training.
Montana			(17)	1 year immediately preceding application.[18]	(3)			
Nebraska	16		(9)		(3)		X[15]	
Nevada			Resident since February 25, 1925.[4]	2 years immediately preceding application.				
New Hampshire					Established by rules and regulations			
New Jersey	21		(19)	1 year continuously[2]		X		Must not, if physically able, refuse to make return in service as required by commission. Must avail himself of any educational facilities.
New Mexico					(3)			
New York		X	(9)		Disqualifying visual field defect or 20/200 or less in better eye which cannot be improved.[20]	X	X	Must not decline reasonable employment, training, medical care, or other assistance which might improve his condition.

State	Age	Residence requirement	Legal settlement	Definition of blindness			Remarks
North Carolina		(9)		20/200 or less in better eye with correcting glasses, or eyesight insufficient for use in ordinary occupations.	X		
North Dakota	18	X — 1 year immediately preceding application.		(3)		X	
Ohio	18 (maximum, 65).	(1)					
Oklahoma		X — Legal settlement or 1 year immediately preceding application.[2]			X		
Oregon	16	X — (1)		(8)	X	X	
Pennsylvania	21	(9)		3/60 or 10/200 or less normal vision	X	X	
Rhode Island (See appendix B.)		X — 1 year immediately preceding application.					
South Carolina		(21)		(3)	X		
South Dakota	18	2 within 9 years, 1 year immediately preceding application.[4]		(3)	X		
Tennessee	16	(9)		(3)	X	X	Must not refuse educational or vocational training.
Texas	21	X — (22)		(3)	X	X	
Utah	21	(9)		Prescribed by State department	X	X	
Vermont	21	X — (1)					
Virginia		(9)		20/200 vision or less in better eye with correcting glasses.			
Washington	21[23]	(24)		(3)	X		
West Virginia	21	X — (9)		(8)	X		
Wisconsin	18	(1)			X		
Wyoming	17	(9)		Maximum amount of visual acuity must not be less than 3/60 or 10/200 central visual acuity in better eye with correcting glasses.			
Alaska					X		
District of Columbia	16[25]	(24)			X		No assistance granted if loss of eyesight intentional or due to vice or crime, or if applicant is between the ages of 16—55 and who, though capable, refuses to engage in occupation or re—

See footnotes at end of table.

Table 13.—Personal Qualifications for Blind Assistance—Continued

State	Minimum age in years	U.S. citizenship	Residence		Definition of blindness	Applicant must not solicit alms	Applicant may be required to undergo operation or treatment	Miscellaneous qualifications
			State	Local				
District of Columbia—Contd.								ceive training. Applicant must be incapable of rehabilitation for self-support.
Hawaii			5 years during 9 years immediately preceding application.		Vision in better eye with correcting glasses of less than 20/200 or a disqualifying field defect sufficient to incapacitate for self-support.			

X indicates that the provision applies without limitation in a given State.

[1] Applicant must have been a resident 5 years within last 9 years, 1 year immediately preceding application, or must have become blind while resident.

[2] If applicant has no local residence, State pays total amount of assistance.

[3] Vision so defective with correcting glasses as to prevent performance of ordinary duties.

[4] Alternative: or applicant became blind while resident.

[5] Vision so defective with correcting glasses as to prevent performance of ordinary duties. State department specifies the amount of visual acuity an applicant may have.

[6] If applicant became blind while a nonresident of the State, his State residence requirement is 5 years within last 9 years, 1 year immediately preceding application; or if there are no Federal funds, 10 years immediately preceding application. If applicant became blind while a resident of the State, he does not have to satisfy State residence requirements. Certification must be made by 2 citizens that applicant has met residence requirements.

[7] If applicant became blind while a resident of the State, his county residence requirement is 6 months. If applicant became blind while a nonresident of the State, his county residence requirement is 1 year. In either case, if State residence requirement is satisfied, the State will pay the total amount of assistance. Certification that applicant has met residence requirements must be made by 2 citizens.

[8] Disqualifying visual field defect or vision 20/200 or less in better eye with glasses.

[9] Applicant must have been a resident 5 years within last 9 years, 1 year immediately preceding application.

[10] Board of county commissioners must obtain evidence of at least 2 reputable citizens of the county that the applicant is blind and has met residence requirements.

[11] Certification must be made by 2 citizens that applicant has met residence requirements.

[12] Unless for good cause and otherwise ordered by the State department, applicant must apply in county in which he last resided continuously for 1 year during the last 9 years. If no such residence, application must be filed in county or residence at time of application.

[13] Alternative: or applicant has made application to become citizen.

[14] Applicant must have been a resident 5 years within last 9 years, 1 year immediately preceding application, or must have become blind while resident, or must have been blind and a resident of the State on May 7, 1937.

[15] Blind assistance granted only if eyesight cannot be restored.

[16] Alternative: or applicant became blind while resident and has since resided continuously in State.

[17] Applicant must have been a resident 5 years within last 9 years, 1 year immediately preceding application. If no county residence, State pays total amount of assistance.

[18] If applicant has no county residence, State pays total amount of assistance.

[19] Applicant must have been a resident 5 years within last 9 years, 1 year immediately preceding application. Certification must be made by 2 residents of the county that applicant has met residence requirements and is in need of assistance.

[20] Public welfare officials must aid and grant emergency relief pending investigation of application of any wholly or partially blind destitute person.

[21] Applicant must have been a resident 5 years within last 9 years, 1 year immediately preceding application, or must have become blind while resident. Blind applicant must have been a resident of State on date of passage of blind assistance law on April 16, 1937.

[22] Applicant must have been a resident 5 years within last 9 years, 1 year immediately preceding application; must have been a resident at date of passage of blind assistance law on June 3, 1937, and resided continuously in State for 1 year immediately preceding application; or must have become blind while resident and since resided continuously in State.

[23] Age requirement is 16 years if applicant is not acceptable for education at State School for Blind.

[24] Applicant must have been a resident 5 years within last 9 years, 1 year immediately preceding application, or must have become blind while resident and resided for 1 year immediately preceding application.

[25] Applicant must be 21 years or older if blindness originated outside of the District of Columbia.

Table 14.—Need Qualifications for Blind Assistance

State	Limitations on property	Limitations on income	Applicant must not have disposed of property to qualify	Applicant has no person liable and able to support him
Alabama	(^{1})	(^{1})	X	Relatives.
Arizona	(^{1})	(^{1})	Within 5 years	
Arkansas	(^{1})	(^{1})	Within 2 years	
California	$3,000	$50 per month including assistance.^{2}		(^{3}).
Colorado	(^{1})	$45 per month including assistance.^{4}	Within 5 years	
Connecticut	(^{1})	(^{1})	X	X.
Delaware				
Florida:				
State	(^{1})	(^{1})	Within 2 years	
Local				
Georgia	(^{1})	(^{1})	Within 2 years	
Idaho	(^{1})	(^{1})	X	
Illinois	$2,500	$465 per year^5		
Indiana	(^{1})	(^{1})	Within 5 years	
Iowa	(^{1})	(^{1})	X	
Kansas	(^{1})	(^{1})	Within 2 years	
Kentucky	$2,500	$400 per year^6		
Louisiana	(^{1})	(^{1})	Within 5 years	(See appendix B.)
Maine	(^{1})	$30 per month including assistance.	X	Relatives.
Maryland	(^{1})	(^{1})	Within 5 years	X.
Massachusetts				
Michigan				
Minnesota	(^{1})	(^{1})	Within 2 years	
Mississippi	(^{1})	(^{1})	Within 2 years	
Missouri	$5,000^7	$600 per year^8		Parents residing in the State.
Montana	(^{1})	(^{1})	Within 2 years	
Nebraska		$360 per year including assistance.^{9}	X	Relatives.^{10}
Nevada	(^{1})	(^{1})		
New Hampshire	(^{1})	(^{1})	Within 5 years	(^{11}).
New Jersey		(^{12})		X.
New Mexico	(^{1})	(^{1})	Within 2 years	
New York	(^{1})	(^{1})	X	Children or other person.^{13}
North Carolina	(^{1})	(^{1})		X.
North Dakota	(^{1})	(^{1})	X	Child or other relatives.
Ohio	(^{1})	(^{1})		(^{14}).
Oklahoma		$30 per month including assistance.	Within 5 years	Relatives if applicant is under 21 years of age.
Oregon				
Pennsylvania	Real property $5,000.	$1,200 per year including assistance.		Husband, wife, child, father, mother, grandparent, or grandchild.
Rhode Island	(^{15})	(^{15})		(See appendix B.)
South Carolina	(^{1})	(^{1})		X.
South Dakota	(^{1})	(^{1})	Within 2 years	
Tennessee	(^{1})	(^{1})	Within 2 years	
Texas	(^{1})	$30 per month including assistance.		Spouse, parent, or child.
Utah	(^{1})	(^{1})	X	
Vermont	(^{1})	(^{1})	X	
Virginia	(^{1})	$30 per month including assistance.	Within 5 years	(^{16}).
Washington		$900 per year		

See footnotes at end of table.

Table 14.—Need Qualifications for Blind Assistance—Continued

State	Limitations on property	Limitations on income	Applicant must not have disposed of property to qualify	Applicant has no person liable and able to support him
West Virginia	(¹)	(¹)	X	X.
Wisconsin		$780 per year including assistance.		Relatives.
Wyoming	(¹)	(¹)	X	
Alaska				
District of Columbia.	(¹)	(¹)		Spouse, father, child, or grandchild.
Hawaii	(¹)	(¹)	X	Spouse, child, or parent.

X indicates that the provision applies without limitation in a given State.

[1]Applicant is ineligible if he has property or income in excess of amount needed for reasonable subsistence compatible with decency and health.

[2]Income from the following sources not exceeding an annual average of $33.33 per month is not considered: income from applicant's labor; the value of foodstuffs produced by the applicant or his family for his use or for that of his family; the value of firewood and/or water produced on the premises of the applicant or given to him by another for the applicant's use; the value of gifts other than regular contributions by relatives legally responsible; the value of the use and occupancy of premises owned and occupied by the applicant; the net income of real and personal property owned by the applicant.

[3]Applicant is ineligible if he has spouse, parent, or adult child residing within the State.

[4]$60 per month including assistance if recipient has dependents.

[5]$1,000 per year for recipient and spouse.

[6]Applicant unable to earn more than $400 per year.

[7]Applicant is ineligible if living with sighted spouse who has an interest in property in the value of $5,000 or more.

[8]Applicant is ineligible if living with sighted spouse who receives $600 per annum or more from any source.

[9]Income from nonrevenue producing property computed at 5 percent of net value. No deduction may be made because property is a homestead or otherwise exempt from legal processes, but contributions and assistance from public or private charities are not included in the computation.

[10]Father, mother, or child of any recipient must reimburse the board if they have sufficient financial ability.

[11]Cost of assistance recoverable in action of debt by State Department of Public Welfare from father, mother, stepfather, stepmother, son, or daughter, jointly or severally, if able to provide.

[12]Applicant is unable to earn sufficient money to provide for the necessities of life and, if not relieved, would become a public charge.

[13]Public welfare officials must aid and grant emergency relief pending investigation of application of any wholly or partially blind destitute person.

[14]Applicant, unless relieved, would become a public charge or a charge upon those not required by law to support him.

[15]Applicant must be needy.

[16]The local board may proceed against any person legally liable and financially able and cause him to support applicant or recipient.

Table 15.—Types of Aid Received or Needed Which Disqualify Applicants for Blind Assistance

State	Assistance[1]		Institutional aid		
	Other public assistance	Old age assistance	Public or private institution	Public institution	In need of continuing institutional care
Alabama		X		X[2]	X.[3]
Arizona		X	X		X.
Arkansas		X		X[4]	
California		X		X[5]	
Colorado	X[6]			X	X.
Connecticut			X		
Delaware					
Florida:					
State		X		X	
Local	(7)				
Georgia		X		X	
Idaho				X	
Illinois				X	
Indiana	X			X	
Iowa		X		X	
Kansas		X		X	
Kentucky	(8)		X		
Louisiana (See appendix B.)	X[6]		X		
Maine		X		X[9]	
Maryland		X		X	
Massachusetts					
Michigan					
Minnesota	X[6]		X		X.
Mississippi		X		X[9]	
Missouri				X	
Montana		X[10]		X[6]	X.
Nebraska	X[6]			X[11]	X.
Nevada	X				
New Hampshire	X				
New Jersey	X				(12).
New Mexico		X		X[9]	
New York		X[10]		X[13]	X.[14]
North Carolina		X[10]		X	X.
North Dakota	X[15]			X[9]	
Ohio	X				
Oklahoma			X		
Oregon	X[6]			X[6]	X.
Pennsylvania		X		(16)	
Rhode Island (See appendix B.)		X[17]			
South Carolina					
South Dakota		X		X	
Tennessee		X	(18)	X[2]	
Texas		X		X	
Utah		X		X[9]	
Vermont		X	X[9]		
Virginia	X[6]			X[9]	
Washington		X		X	X.
West Virginia	(19)	X	X[9]		
Wisconsin	(20)	X		X	
Wyoming		X		X	
Alaska					
District of Columbia	(21)	X		X[22]	
Hawaii	X[6]	X		X[9]	

See footnotes on following page.

X indicates that the provision applies without limitation in a given State.

[1]Many State laws render ineligible for blind assistance persons who are receiving any other type of public assistance, while many other State laws specifically disqualify only recipients of old age assistance. The latter type of provision has been enacted because of the provision in the Federal Social Security Act which prevents the granting of Federal aid to blind persons who are receiving old age assistance under a State plan approved by the Social Security Board and for which Federal grants are being made.

[2]Applicant is disqualified if he is an inmate of a private institution not approved by the State board.

[3]Such care must be reasonably available.

[4]Institution supported in whole or in part by public funds.

[5]Except 30 days in a public hospital or employment (without board and room) in a shop maintained by the State.

[6]Except temporary medical and surgical assistance.

[7]Relief is granted in place of all other relief of a public nature to which a husband and wife or either of them might be entitled as a blind person.

[8]Applicant's earnings, together with any pension received from the United States, State, or foreign government, must not exceed $400.

[9]An inmate may make application for assistance; but, if granted, assistance must not begin until after he ceases to be an inmate.

[10]Applicant must not be receiving old age assistance or aid to dependent children.

[11]Applicant is disqualified if he is an inmate of any prison, jail, or State institution for the blind or the insane.

[12]Applicant was physically or mentally incapacitated prior to loss of sight.

[13]Applicant is disqualified if he is an inmate of a private institution to which an admission fee has been paid or a transfer of property has been made.

[14]Other than care in a private home for the blind to which payment of board is required.

[15]Temporary medical aid, surgical assistance, or vocational training are excepted.

[16]Applicant is disqualified if he is an inmate of any public reform or correctional institution.

[17]Blind assistance is not granted if person is eligible for old age assistance.

[18]Applicant is disqualified if he is an inmate of any public or private institution, except private institution approved by the Department of Institutions and Public Welfare. An inmate may make application for assistance; but, if granted, assistance must not begin until after he ceases to be an inmate.

[19]No other public aid, except temporary medical or surgical care, is granted without approval of the county council.

[20]The State summer school for the blind is excepted.

[21]Applicant is disqualified if he is receiving educational aid.

[22]Institution supported in whole or in part by public funds. An inmate may make application for assistance; but if granted, assistance must not begin until after he ceases to be an inmate.

Table 16.—Provisions for Recovery From Recipients and Their Estates for Blind Assistance Granted

State	For total amount of assistance	Exemptions
Alabama		
Arizona	(^{1})	
Arkansas	(^{2})	
California		
Colorado	X^2	Realty of recipient while occupied by surviving spouse.
Connecticut	X^3	Administration expenses, including probate fees and taxes, and $100 for expense of last illness and funeral.
Delaware		
Florida:		
State	X	Claim waived if, upon death of recipient, widow or minor children are likely to become public charges.
Local		
Georgia	X	Funeral expenses of $75, administration expenses, and realty of recipient while occupied by surviving spouse or dependent. No claim for recovery may be enforced against any property of Confederate veterans or their widows who are receiving or are entitled to receive a pension.
Idaho	X	Funeral expenses of $100, administration expenses, and realty while occupied by surviving spouse or dependent.
Illinois		
Indiana	X^4	Realty of recipient while occupied by surviving spouse, or real or personal property if recipient has a dependent child or children surviving.
Iowa	X^2	Expense of burial and last illness.
Kansas		
Kentucky		
Louisiana		(See appendix B.)
Maine		
Maryland	X^5	Funeral expenses and realty occupied by surviving spouse or dependents.
Massachusetts		
Michigan		
Minnesota	X^2	
Mississippi	(^{2})	
Missouri	(^{2})	
Montana	(^{2})	
Nebraska	X	Realty of recipient while occupied by a surviving spouse or by a child of the recipient or surviving spouse who has been dependent upon recipient or surviving spouse for more than 1 year prior to death. Personal effects or household goods owned by recipient or spouse. Real estate owned by Indian tribe residing in the State.
Nevada		
New Hampshire	(^{6})	
New Jersey		
New Mexico	X^2	Realty of recipient while occupied by surviving spouse or dependent.
New York	X	Funeral expenses and realty of recipient while occupied by surviving spouse or dependent.
North Carolina		
North Dakota	(^{2})	
Ohio		
Oklahoma	(^{7})	
Oregon	X^2	Realty of recipient while occupied by surviving spouse.
Pennsylvania	(^{8})	
Rhode Island		(See appendix B.)
South Carolina	X^9	Funeral expenses not to exceed $100 and realty of recipient while occupied by surviving spouse.
South Dakota	(^{2})	
Tennessee	X^2	Funeral expenses not to exceed $100, administration expenses, and realty of recipient while occupied by surviving spouse or dependent child.
Texas		

See footnotes at end of table.

Table 16.—Provisions for Recovery From Recipients and Their Estates for Blind Assistance Granted—Continued

State	For total amount of assistance	Exemptions
Utah	X^2	
Vermont	X	Realty of surviving spouse if such spouse is not 15 years younger than recipient and does not remarry, household furniture, and wearing apparel.
Virginia		
Washington	$(^2)$	
West Virginia	X	Real property $1,500, personal property $200. Real property of surviving spouse except real property of widow who remarries.
Wisconsin		
Wyoming		
Alaska		
District of Columbia	X^{10}	All property until death of surviving spouse.
Hawaii	X	

X indicates that the provision applies without limitation in a given State.

[1] Amount of assistance granted is recoverable as a debt if applicant failed to disclose possession of property or income which would have affected amount of assistance or made recipient ineligible.

[2] Assistance paid after recipient has come into possession of property or income in excess of his need is recoverable as a debt due the State.

[3] An agreement constituting a lien on any interest in real property must be made transferring it to the Commissioner of Welfare. Transfer of life insurance or bank account may be required before assistance is granted. Recipient or surviving spouse may be permitted to occupy realty transferred. Interest at 4 percent per annum is charged on amount of assistance granted and recovered. Double amount of assistance is recoverable for misrepresentation.

[4] Applicant must execute agreement to reimburse State. Applicant must assign as collateral security for reimbursement such part of his personal property as the county department requires. Interest at 3 percent per annum is charged on amount of assistance granted and recovered. Double amount of assistance is recoverable for misrepresentation. County department may, with the consent of the State Department of Public Welfare, require applicant to dispose of property or transfer it to them.

[5] Applies only to assistance granted after recipient reaches the age of 65 years.

[6] Cost of assistance recoverable in action of debt by the State Department of Public Welfare from father, mother, stepfather, stepmother, son, or daughter, jointly or severally, if able to provide.

[7] Any assistance received in excess of the amount to which the recipient is entitled by reason of misrepresentation or concealment of facts is recoverable as a debt due the State which has a first and paramount lien upon all the assets and effects of the recipient to secure repayment.

[8] Real and personal property of any indigent person shall be liable for the expenses of his support, maintenance, assistance, and burial. Any judgment shall be a lien upon the realty.

[9] Any assistance improperly granted is recoverable as a debt due the State.

[10] Interest at 3 percent per annum is charged on amount of assistance granted and recovered. Upon sufficient cause, the board may demand assignment of recipient's property after first grant of aid.

Table 17.—Provisions for Granting and Financing Blind Assistance

State	Maximum allowance (per month unless otherwise specified)	Minimum allowance (per month unless otherwise specified)	Burial allowance	Provision for removal of disability	Governmental unit determining amount of individual grant		Incidence of financial responsibility			Basis for distribution of State funds	Procedure in case of insufficiency of State funds
					Final	Advisory	State	County	Other local unit		
Alabama	$30	---	---	---	County	---	50 per-cent.	50 per-cent.	---	State allocates to counties 50 percent of estimated expenditure for ensuing 3 months.[1]	Funds prorated among the counties.
Arizona	$30	---	$100	Additional assistance.[2]	State	County	X	---	---	Individuals paid by State Board of Social Security and Welfare by warrant drawn upon State auditor.	
Arkansas	([3])	([3])	---	Supplementary services.[2]	State	County	X	---	---	State disburses funds to individuals.	
California	$50	---	---	---	County	---	50 per-cent.	50 per-cent.	---	State reimburses county for 50 percent of amount expended.[1]	
Colorado	$30	---	$100[4]	Necessary expenses.	County	---	75 per-cent.	25 per-cent.	---	State apportions funds to counties upon request.	
Connecticut	$7 per week	---	$125	---	State	Town	X	---	---	State disburses funds to individuals.	
Delaware											
Florida:											
State	$30	---	---	---	District	---	X	---	---		
Local	$180 per year.[5]	---	---	1 year's assistance.	County	---	---	X	---	State disburses funds to individuals.	
Georgia	([3])	---	$75[4]	Supplementary services.[2]	County	---	90 per-cent.	10 per-cent.	---	State reimburses county for 90 percent of amount expended for assistance and administration.[6]	
Idaho	([7])	---	---	Additional assistance.[2]	County	---	66⅔ per-cent.	33⅓ per-cent.	---	County reimburses State for 33⅓ percent of amount expended. State disburses funds to individuals.	
Illinois	$365 per year.	$365 per year.	---	---	County	---	50 per-cent.	50 per-cent.	---	State reimburses county for 50 percent of amount expended.	
Indiana	$30	---	$75[8]	Additional assistance.[2]	State	County	X[9]	---	---	State disburses funds to individuals.	
Iowa	$30	---	$100[4]	Supplementary services.[2]	State	County	75 per-cent.	25 per-cent.	---	County reimburses State for 25 percent of cost of assistance and administration. State disburses funds to individuals.	

See footnotes at end of table.

Table 17.—Provisions for Granting and Financing Blind Assistance—Continued

State	Maximum allowance (per month unless otherwise specified)	Minimum allowance (per month unless otherwise specified)	Burial allowance	Provision for removal of disability	Governmental unit determining amount of individual grant		Incidence of financial responsibility			Basis for distribution of State funds	Procedure in case of insufficiency of State funds
					Final	Advisory	State	County	Other local unit		
Kansas	(¹⁰)			(¹⁰)	County		30 per-cent.	70 per-cent.		State reimburses county for 30 percent of expenditure less cost of administration.	
Kentucky	$250 per year.				County			X			
Louisiana (See appendix B.)	$30			Temporary assistance.²	Parish		75 per-cent.¹¹		25 percent (parish).	State reimburses parish for 75 percent of cost of assistance and 50 percent of administrative costs.¹¹	State contribution based on amount of funds available.
Maine	$30		$100	Supplementary services.²	State		X			State disburses funds to individuals.	
Maryland	$30				County¹²		50 per-cent.	50 per-cent.	50 percent (city of Baltimore).	State pays 50 percent of local expenses.	
Massachusetts					State		X			State disburses funds to individuals.	
Michigan	(³)						(¹³)				
Minnesota	(³)				State		X			State disburses funds to individuals.	
Mississippi	(¹⁴)	(¹⁴)			County		X			State disburses funds to individuals.	
Missouri	$300 per year.	$300 per year.		Operation to restore vision.	State	County	X			State disburses funds to individuals.	
Montana	$30			Supplementary services.²	County		83⅓ per-cent.	16⅔ per-cent.		County reimburses State for 16⅔ percent of amount expended. State disburses funds to individuals.	
Nebraska	$30	$15	$75⁴	Temporary assistance.	State	County	X			State disburses funds to counties in the ratio of the population of each county to the total population of the State.	Funds prorated among the counties.
Nevada	$600 per year.				County			X			
New Hampshire	(³)				State¹⁵		X	X	X (town).	State disburses funds to individuals¹⁶	
New Jersey	$480 per year.			1 year's assistance.	County	State		X		State reimburses county for total amount of aid granted to persons not having settlement in county.	

State	Maximum grant	Additional amount	Other provisions	Administering agency	State participation	Local participation	Remarks
New Mexico	(3)	$50[4]	Temporary assistance or supplementary services.[2]	State[17]	X		State disburses funds to individuals.
New York	(18)	Unspecified amount.[4]	Such special aid as may be necessary.	City or county public welfare district.	50 per-cent.	50 per-cent.	State reimburses county or city public welfare district for 50 percent of aid granted to persons for whose support State is not responsible and entire cost of assistance granted to Indians and persons without local settlement.
North Carolina	$30			State; County[19]	25 per-cent.[1]	25 per-cent.[1]	County reimburses State for 25 percent of the amount of aid given from State and Federal funds.[20] State disburses funds to individuals.
North Dakota	$40 (3)	$75[4]	Supplementary services.[2]	State	X		State disburses funds to individuals. ([21]).
Ohio	$400 per year.[22]		1 year's assistance.	County	66⅔ per-cent.[23]	33⅓ per-cent.[1]	State reimburses county for % of aid.[23] % is maximum, but not absolute amount of reimbursement.
Oklahoma	$30			State	X		State disburses funds to individuals. Amount expected to be available considered when approving application.
Oregon	$30		Temporary or additional assistance.[2]	County	25 per-cent.	25 per-cent.	County reimburses State for 25 percent of amount expended. State disburses funds to individuals.[24]
Pennsylvania	$30	$30	Additional assistance not to exceed $100.	County	X		Upon the submission of budgets by the county boards, the State department allocates State funds for assistance and administrative costs on the basis of need.
Rhode Island (See appendix B.)	$30			State	X		State disburses funds to individuals.
South Carolina	$300 per year.		1 year's assistance.	State[25]	X		State disburses funds to individuals.
South Dakota	$30			State	X		State disburses funds to individuals.
Tennessee	$25			State[26]	37½ per-cent.[27]	12½ per-cent.[27]	County reimburses State for 12½ percent of the amount expended.[27] State disburses funds to individuals. Pro rata reduction of assistance.
Texas	$15[28]		1 year's assistance.	State[29]	X		Individual applications paid by State through county agency.

See footnotes at end of table.

Table 17.—Provisions for Granting and Financing Blind Assistance—Continued

State	Maximum allowance (per month unless otherwise specified)	Minimum allowance (per month unless otherwise specified)	Burial allowance	Provision for removal of disability	Governmental unit determining amount of individual grant		Incidence of financial responsibility			Basis for distribution of State funds	Procedure in case of insufficiency of State funds
					Final	Advisory	State	County	Other local unit		
Utah	($3)[4]	(3)	$150[4]	---	County or district.	---	85 percent.	15 percent.	---	State reimburses county for 85 percent of amount expended.	
Vermont	$30	---	$150	---	State	---	X	---	---	State disburses funds to individuals.	
Virginia	$30[30]	---	---	---	County or city.	---	62½ percent.	37½ percent.	City 37½ percent.	State reimburses county 62½ percent of the amount expended during the preceding month for the cost of assistance and administration from 62½ percent of Federal grant for assistance and State funds. 37½ percent of Federal grant for assistance paid to the several counties and cities on the basis of the total amount disbursed for blind assistance by such counties and cities during the period for which such grants are made.[31]	
Washington	---	$40[32]	$100	---	County	---	X	---	---	Percentage of contribution by State not specified. State disburses funds to individuals.	
West Virginia	$30	---	---	---	State	County	X	---	---	State funds allocated to counties in proportion to number of cases and cost of living.	
Wisconsin	$360 per year.[33]	---	---	---	County	---	80 percent.	20 percent.	---	State reimburses county for 80 percent of the amount expended.	Funds prorated among the counties.
Wyoming	$30[34]	---	---	---	State	County	X	---	---	State makes grants to counties which disburse funds to individuals.	
Alaska											
District of Columbia.	($35)	---	---	---	District of Columbia.	---	District of Columbia.	---	---	District of Columbia disburses funds to individuals.	
Hawaii	$30	---	---	---	County	---	Territory	---	---	Territory reimburses counties for cost of assistance and administration.	

X indicates that the provision applies without limitation in a given State.

[1] If applicant has no county residence, State assumes total cost.

[8] Assistance may also be granted to prevent blindness, including necessary traveling and other expenses to receive treatment at a hospital or clinic.

[19] If applicant does not have county settlement, application is made directly to State commission.

[20] Act takes into consideration Federal contribution, and further provides that upon failure of Federal funds the act shall become null and void.

Table 17.—Footnotes Continued

[3] Allowance must be an amount which is sufficient, when added to other income, to provide recipient with reasonable subsistence compatible with decency and health.

[4] Allowance granted only if persons legally responsible are unable to pay.

[5] $300 per year may be granted in cases where husband and wife are both blind.

[6] State may use equalization fund if county is unable to furnish support.

[7] Allowance must be an amount which is sufficient, when added to other income, to provide recipient with reasonable subsistence compatible with decency and health. Total amount of State and county contribution must not exceed Federal contribution.

[8] $25 maximum allowed for burial plot if deceased or persons legally responsible do not possess one.

[9] The State department must, when necessary in the opinion of the State Board of Public Welfare, provide all or any part of local administrative costs.

[10] "Assistance" includes money, food, clothing, shelter, medicine, other materials, and the giving of any service which may be necessary or helpful for providing the recipient with the necessities of life for himself and dependents.

[11] State may assume total financial responsibility if parish lacks funds.

[12] City of Baltimore also has final determination.

[13] A State financed program for blind assistance is administered by the State Emergency Relief Commission through county welfare relief commissions under rules and regulations of the State commission. Specific provisions relating to eligibility, etc., are not set forth by statute and therefore have not been included in these tables.

[14] The amount of assistance when added to all other income and support must be sufficient to provide a reasonable subsistence compatible with decency and health. The amount paid to each applicant must be on the same basis as the amount paid to other applicants similarly situated.

[15] Commissioner of public welfare required in all cases to first consult with the proper official of the county or town required to contribute to the cost of assistance.

[16] Counties and towns required to contribute to the cost of assistance. In the event a county or town cannot pay the amounts required, it may file a petition requesting financial aid and the State may, after investigation, grant or loan such funds as may be necessary.

[17] State department may allow its local office to determine the manner and amount of assistance.

[18] Amount of assistance fixed with due regard to conditions existing in each case.

[21] State must make a levy of a sum sufficient to make up any deficiency in the State public welfare fund not in excess of the sum appropriated and chargeable to the fund.

[22] $600 if both husband and wife are blind and both have applied for assistance.

[23] 75 percent of State reimbursement for county charges and 50 percent of the cost of State charges must be paid from funds made available by the Federal Government. Excludes any amount exceeding $30 a month paid to an individual and also excludes payment for surgical or medical treatment.

[24] Law takes into consideration 50 percent contribution of Federal Government, and act is not operative unless funds are made available by the Federal Government.

[25] Through county welfare boards as agents of the State department.

[26] State regional director jointly with county official. If disagreement, State department makes final decision.

[27] Act takes into consideration 50 percent contribution by Federal Government. The entire cost of administration is paid by the State with the exception of such Federal funds as may be available.

[28] Recipient may receive, in addition, such funds as are made available by the Federal Government, but in no case may assistance be an amount which, when added to the income of the recipient from all sources and from the Federal Government, exceeds $30 per month.

[29] Through district or county agencies designated by division of public welfare of State Board of Control.

[30] Blind person also eligible for Confederate pension may receive blind assistance in amount equal to that which he might receive as a Confederate pensioner, even though in excess of maximum allowance for blind assistance.

[31] Not more than 10 percent of the funds allocated to the counties and cities may be used for local administrative expenses. If the county or city fails or refuses to provide funds, the State board must require the local authorities to make funds available. During the period of refusal or failure, the State must make payments and deduct the amounts so paid from future State reimbursements.

[32] The total income of recipient including assistance must not be less than $40 per month.

[33] If applicant is blind and deaf, allowance is $480 per year.

[34] $50 is allowed for head of family.

[35] Maximum not specified, except that aid is not to exceed $30 per month when dependent blind child is living with parents.

Aid to Dependent Children in Their Own Homes

Table 18.—Provisions for the Administration of Aid to Dependent Children in Their Own Homes

State	Administrative responsibility			Determination of eligibility							
	Nature of law	Direct	Supervisory	Original determination		Reconsideration		Appeal and review			
				Final	Advisory	Periodic	At request of State board or department	Appeal of applicant to State department[1]	Review by State department on own motion[1]	Upon complaint by person other than applicant	Further investigation by State department[1]
Alabama	M	County department of public welfare.	State Department of Public Welfare.	County board of public welfare.	---	---	---	X	---	---	---
Arizona	M	State Department of Social Security and Welfare assisted by county board of social security and public welfare.	---	State Department of Social Security and Welfare.	County board of social security and public welfare.	X (No period stated.)	---	State board.	State board.	---	State board.
Arkansas	M	State Department of Public Welfare.	State Department of Public Welfare.	State Department of Public Welfare.	County or district board of public welfare.	---	X	X	---	---	---
California	M	County board of supervisors.[2]	State Department of Social Welfare.	County board of supervisors.[2]	---	---	---	State board.	---	---	---
Colorado	M	County or district department of public welfare.	State Department of Public Welfare.	County or district department of public welfare.	---	---	X	X	X	---	X
Connecticut	O	Commissioner of Welfare assisted by chief executive authority of town and board of county commissioners.	---	Commissioner of Welfare	Chief executive authority of town and board of county commissioners.	---	---	---	---	---	---
Delaware	M	State Mothers' Pension Commission.	---	State Mothers' Pension Commission.	---	---	X	State commission.	X	---	---
Florida:											
State	O	State Welfare Board through district board of social welfare.	---	District board of social welfare.	---	---	---	State board.	State board.	---	State board.
Local	O	Board of county commissioners.	---	Board of county commissioners.	---	---	---	---	---	---	---
Georgia	M	County or district department of public welfare.	State Department of Public Welfare.	County or district department of public welfare.	---	---	X	X	X	---	X
Idaho	M	County welfare commission.	State Department of Public Assistance.	County welfare commission.	---	---	X	X	X	---	X

State		Agency administering	State agency	Agency (determining)	Appeal / supervisory body	Frequency	Marks
Illinois	M	Juvenile court	State Department of Public Welfare.	Juvenile court			(8); X.
Indiana	M	County or district department of public welfare.	State Department of Public Welfare.	County or district department of public welfare.		Biennially	X — X — X — X.
Iowa	O	Juvenile court		Juvenile court			(5); (6).
Kansas	M	County board of social welfare.	State Board of Social Welfare.	County board of social welfare.	State appeal committee.[4]		(5); (6).
Kentucky	O	County children's bureau.[7]	State Department of Public Welfare.	County children's bureau.[7]			(8); X
Louisiana (See appendix B.)	M	Parish department of public welfare.	State Department of Public Welfare.	Parish department of public welfare.			X
Maine	M	State Department of Health and Welfare assisted by municipal board of child welfare.		Municipal board of child welfare.	Commissioner of health and welfare.		
Maryland	M	County welfare board. Baltimore Department of Welfare.	Board of State Aid and Charities.	County welfare board. Baltimore Department of Welfare.	State board — State board — State board.		X
Massachusetts	M	Local board of public welfare.	State Department of Public Welfare.	Local board of public welfare.	Appeal board.	Annually	
Michigan	M	County probate court, juvenile division.[9]		County probate court, juvenile division.	County welfare agent or probation officer.		
Minnesota	M	County welfare board	State Board of Control.	County welfare board	State board[10] — State board — State board.		X
Mississippi	O	Chancery court[11]		Chancery court		Semiannually	
Missouri	M	State Social Security Commission.[12]	State Social Security Commission.[12]	State Social Security Commission.	State commission.[13]		X
Montana	M	County department of public welfare.	State Department of Public Welfare.	County department of public welfare.			X — X.
Nebraska: Original	M	Juvenile court		Juvenile court			
Supplementary	M	County assistance committee.	State Board of Control.	County assistance committee.	State board — State board	Relief renewed semiannually. Annually	(15); (16)
Nevada	M	Board of county commissioners.	State Welfare Department.	Board of county commissioners.			(16); (17)

See footnotes at end of table.

Table 18.—Provisions for the Administration of Aid to Dependent Children in Their Own Homes—Continued

State	Nature of law	Administrative responsibility		Determination of eligibility							
		Direct	Supervisory	Original determination		Reconsideration		Appeal and review			
				Final	Advisory	Periodic	At request of State board or department	Appeal of applicant to State department[1]	Review by State department on own motion[1]	Upon complaint by person other than applicant	Further investigation by State department[1]
New Hampshire	M	State Department of Public Welfare.		State commissioner of public welfare.	(18)			State board			
New Jersey	M	County welfare board assisted by State Board of Children's Guardians.		County welfare board	State Board of Children's Guardians.	Family visited at least 4 times a year.		(19)	State Board of Children's Guardians.		State Board of Children's Guardians.
New Mexico	M	State Department of Public Welfare.		State Department of Public Welfare.[20]	Local office of State Department of Public Welfare.		X	State board	State board		State board.
New York	M	County or city board of child welfare.[21]	State Department of Social Welfare.	County or city board of child welfare.[21]		Allowances granted for 6-month periods, subject to renewal.		X		(22)	X.
North Carolina	M	County board of charities and public welfare. City public welfare officer.[23]	State Board of Charities and Public Welfare.[24]	County board of charities and public welfare. City public welfare officer.[23]			X	State Board of Allotments and Appeal.[25]	State Board of Allotments and Appeal.[25]		State Board of Allotments and Appeal.
North Dakota	M	State Public Welfare Board assisted by county welfare board.		State Public Welfare Board.	County welfare board.		X	State board	State board		State board.
Ohio	M	Juvenile judge or other board or agency designated by charter or law.	State Department of Public Welfare, division of charities.	Juvenile judge or other board or agency designated by charter or law.		At least 4 times a year.	X	X			X.
Oklahoma	M	State Public Welfare Commission assisted by county assistance board.		State Public Welfare Commission.	County assistance board.		X	State Public Welfare Commission.		(22)	X.
Oregon	M	County relief committee	State Relief Committee	County relief committee				State Relief Committee.			

State		Local administering agency	State administering or supervising agency	Administering agency	Local board	Frequency				
Pennsylvania---	M--	County board of assistance.	State Department of Public Assistance.				X			
Rhode Island---	M--	State Department of Public Welfare assisted by local director of public welfare or local board of aid to dependent children.		Bureau of Aid to Dependent Children, Division of Social Security, State Department of Public Welfare.	Local director of public welfare or local board of aid to dependent children.	Annually	X	State director of public welfare.[26]		
South Carolina--	M--	State Department of Public Welfare through county department of public welfare.[27]		County department of public welfare.[27]			X		X	X.
South Dakota---	M--	State Department of Social Security.		State Department of Social Security.			X		X	
Tennessee---	M--	Department of Institutions and Public Welfare.		Regional director of Department of Institutions and Public Welfare jointly with county judge or chairman of county court or juvenile judge.[28]			X		X	X.
Texas: State---	M[29]--	State Board of Control, division of public welfare through local agency designated by it.		Local agency designated by State Board of Control, division of public welfare.				State Board of Control.		
Local---	O--	County commissioners' court.		County commissioners' court.						
Utah---	M--	County or district department of public welfare.	State Department of Public Welfare.	County or district department of public welfare.			X		X	X.
Vermont---	M--	State Department of Public Welfare.		State Department of Public Welfare.			X			
Virginia---	M--	County or city board of public welfare.	State Board of Public Welfare.	County or city board of public welfare.			X	State board	State board	State board.
Washington---	M--	Board of county commissioners.	State Department of Social Security.	Board of county commissioners.			(30)			X.
West Virginia---	M--	State Department of Public Assistance assisted by county public assistance council.		State Department of Public Assistance.	County public assistance council.	Semiannually	X	Board of review of State department.	X	Citizen-(31).

See footnotes at end of table.

Table 18.—Provisions for the Administration of Aid to Dependent Children in Their Own Homes—Continued

State	Administrative responsibility			Determination of eligibility							
				Original determination		Reconsideration		Appeal and review			
	Nature of law	Direct	Supervisory	Final	Advisory	Periodic	At request of State board or department	Appeal of applicant to State department[1]	Review by State department on own motion[1]	Upon complaint by person other than applicant	Further investigation by State department[1]
Wisconsin	M	County department of public welfare.[32] County pension department.[33] Juvenile or county judge.	State pension department.	County department of public welfare.[32] County pension department.[33] Juvenile or county judge.		Annually		X	X		X.
Wyoming	M	State Department of Public Welfare assisted by county department of public welfare.		State Department of Public Welfare.	County department of public welfare.		X	State board			State board.
Alaska	O	Territorial Department of Public Welfare.		Territorial Department of Public Welfare.							
District of Columbia	M	Board of Public Welfare		Board of Public Welfare.		Semiannually					
Hawaii	M	County public welfare commission.	Territorial Board of Public Welfare.	County public welfare commission.				Territorial board.	Territorial board.		Territorial board.

X indicates that the provision applies without limitation in a given State.
M indicates mandatory provision.
O indicates optional provision.

[1] If authority to hear appeals, to review decisions, and to make further investigations is placed by law with a specific agency within the department, the specific agency is named either in the body of the table or in a footnote.

[2] County boards of public welfare may be established by county board of supervisors or by petition of electorate.

[3] In Cook County the bureau of public welfare investigates for and cooperates with the juvenile court.

[4] State Board of Social Welfare may affirm, modify, or set aside any decision of the appeal committee.

[5] Applicant, client, interested person, taxpayer, any county board, or private agency may appeal, setting forth particulars of violation.

[6] The State director of social welfare is authorized to order an investigation of the activities of any county board or private agency whenever he deems necessary, or whenever the State board recommends such an investigation.

[14] Nebraska has enacted an "aid to dependent children" statute in which it is specifically stated that the statute is supplementary to the original "mothers' aid" law. The terms original and supplementary are used to distinguish the 2 statutes.

[15] Appeal may be taken by taxpayer or any relative of the child.

[16] Appeal allowed to district court of county.

[17] Any taxpaying citizen or a member of the board of county commissioners may file a motion any time to set aside or modify the amount of assistance.

[18] Commissioner of public welfare must determine the eligibility of all applicants and the amount of assistance, but must in all cases first consult the proper officials in the counties or towns required to contribute to the cost of such assistance.

[19] Appeal allowed to State Department of Institutions and Agencies or to its duly authorized representative.

[20] State department may allow its local office to determine whether assistance may be granted and the amount and manner thereof.

[21] If an appropriation is not made to the board of child welfare, powers and duties devolve upon the county or city commissioner of public welfare.

[22] Any person having knowledge that relief is granted in violation of law may file a complaint.

[7] State Department of Welfare may organize local welfare departments.

[8] State board authorized to take necessary action to secure Federal benefits.

[9] A State financed program for aid to dependent children is administered by the State Emergency Welfare Relief Commission through county welfare relief commissions under rules and regulations of the State commission. Specific provisions relating to eligibility, etc., are not set forth by statute and therefore have not been included in these tables.

[10] Appeal from decision of the State board allowed to district court of county where application was filed. Applicant, recipient, or State board may appeal decision of district court to State Supreme Court.

[11] County departments of public welfare are authorized to grant aid to dependent children in their own homes from public funds made available for welfare services.

[12] The city of St. Louis is authorized to establish a board of children's guardians. Such board may administer local and private funds for aid to dependent children in their own homes and other child welfare activities.

[13] Further appeal allowed to the circuit court whose decision may be appealed as in civil cases.

[23] City of Rocky Mount may be constituted a separate administrative district.

[24] Board of county commissioners may also review award.

[25] Board of county commissioners may also review decision.

[26] State director of public welfare may designate persons to hear appeals.

[27] In Charleston County the county welfare board has direct administrative responsibility for aid to dependent children in their own homes under the supervision of the State Department of Public Welfare.

[28] In case of disagreement the Department of Institutions and Public Welfare makes decision.

[29] No State funds were available as of January 1, 1939.

[30] Applicant may appeal to the director of the State Department of Social Security and from his decision to the county superior court.

[31] State department may also remand application to county for further investigation.

[32] Establishment optional in counties of 500,000 population or more.

[33] Establishment optional in counties of less than 500,000 population.

Table 19.—Personal Qualifications for Aid to Dependent Children in Their Own Homes

State	Age in years[1]	Relationship of applicant to child	U. S. citizenship	Residence State	Residence Local	Other qualifications for aid: Personal fitness of applicant	Other qualifications for aid: Provision of suit-able home	Other qualifications for aid: Miscellaneous
Alabama	16 --	(2) --		(3) --				
Arizona	16 --	(2) --		(3) --			(4) --	
Arkansas	16 --	(2) --		Child must have 1 year's residence, or if child was born in State within year preceding application, mother must have resided in State 1 year.			(4) --	
California	18 --	Any person caring for child		Child or parents, 1 year immediately preceding application or child born in State.	(5) --			
Colorado	16 --	(2) --		(3) --			X	
Connecticut	16 --	Widowed mother --	Mother is citizen, has declared intention, or is a widow of United States veteran.	Child, 1 year, or born in State within year.[6]	(6) --			
Delaware	16 --	(7) --		Applicant, 1 year --				
Florida: State	16 --	Parents, relatives, or guardians.		(3) --				
Florida: Local	16[8]	Mother, female relative within 2d degree, or guardian.		Applicant, 2 years --	Applicant, 1 year	Mentally, morally, and physically fit.	(4) --	Child must attend school regularly.
Georgia	16 --	(9) --		(3) --			(4) --	
Idaho	16 --	(2) --		Mother, 1 year				
Illinois	16[10]	Mother --	Mother is citizen or has filed declaration of intention.	Mother, 1 year	Mother, 1 year	Mentally, morally, and physically fit.		
Indiana	16 --	(11) --		(3) --			(4) --	
Iowa	16 --	Mother --		Mother, 1 year	Mother, 1 year	Proper guardian		Aid is discontinued if mother remarries.
Kansas	16 --	(2) --		(3) --				
Kentucky	14[12]	Mother or female standing in loco parentis.		Mother, 2 years		Mentally, morally, and physically fit.	(13) --	
Louisiana	16 --	(2) --		(3) --				

State	Age	Relationship of applicant	Citizenship / requirement	Residence	Fitness	Notes	Conditions
Maine	16	(2)	(3)			(4)	(4) Child's religious faith is being fostered and protected.
Maryland	16	(2)	(14)			(4)	
Massachusetts	16	(2)	(3)		Fit to bring up children		
Michigan	17	Mother		Mother, 1 year	Proper guardian	(13)	To child's advantage to remain with mother. (15).
Minnesota	18	Mother, stepmother, grandmother, sister, stepsister, or aunt.	Mother is citizen or has declared intention.			(4)	
Mississippi	16	Parent, guardian, or other person having legal custody.	Applicant must be citizen or must have made application.	Parent, guardian, or other person having legal custody, 1 year.			
Missouri	16	(2)	(3)				Child must not, because of a physical or mental condition, be in need of continued care in a public institution.
Montana	16	(2)	(3)	(16)		(4)	
Nebraska:[17] Original	16	Mother		Mother, 2 years			Will be to child's advantage to remain at home with mother.
Supplementary	16	(2)	(3)		Mentally, morally, and physically fit.		
Nevada	16[18]	Mother		Mother, 2 years	Mentally, morally, and physically fit.		
New Hampshire	16	(2)					Child not inmate of public institution.
New Jersey	16	Mother or female standing in loco parentis.	Child, 1 year or born of mother who has resided in State 1 year.[19]	(20)		(13)	Need must not be due to willful neglect.
New Mexico	16	(2)	(3)		Mentally, morally, and physically fit.	(4)	
New York	16	(2)	(3)		Mentally, morally, and physically fit.		
North Carolina	16	(2)	(3)		Mentally, morally, and physically fit.	(21)	
North Dakota	18	(22)	(3)			(4)	
Ohio	16[23]	(2)	(3)		Mentally, morally, and physically fit.	(24)	
Oklahoma	16	(2)	Child must be citizen	(3)			

See footnotes at end of table.

Table 19.—Personal Qualifications for Aid to Dependent Children in Their Own Homes—Continued

State	Age in years[1]	Relationship of applicant to child	U. S. citizenship	Residence		Other qualifications for aid		
				State	Local	Personal fitness of applicant	Provision of suitable home	Miscellaneous
Oregon	16 --	([2])		([3])			([4])	
Pennsylvania	16 --	Mother		([3])				
Rhode Island	16 --	([2])		([3])		Suitability determined by rules of State department.		
South Carolina	16 --	([2])		([3])			([4])	
South Dakota	16 --	([2])		([3])			([4])	
Tennessee	16 --	([2])		([3])				
Texas: State	14 --	([2])	Child must be citizen	([3])				
Local	16 --	Mother			Mother, 2 years --			
Utah	16 --	([2])		([3])				
Vermont	16 --	([2])				Must be proper person to care for child.		
Virginia	16 --	([2])		([3])		Mentally, morally, and physically fit.		
Washington	16 --	([2])		Parent, 1 year[3]				
West Virginia	16 --	([2])		([3])			([4])	
Wisconsin	16[25] --	([2])			Child has legal settlement in county; may be waived by State department if child resided in State 1 year.	Fit and proper person for care and custody of child.		
Wyoming	16 --	([2])		([3])			([4])	
Alaska	16[26] --	Mother or female standing in loco parentis.		Mother must be resident for 1 year immediately preceding filing of petition.		Must be a fit and proper person to have care, control, and custody of the child.		
District of Columbia	16 --	Mother or guardian	Applicant is citizen or has made declaration of intention.	Applicant, 1 year --		Proper person to care for child.		
Hawaii	18 --	([27])		([3])			([4])	

X indicates that the provision applies without limitation in a given State.

1 Only children under the specified ages are eligible for aid.

2 Parents, grandparents, brother, sister, stepparents, stepsister, uncle, or aunt.

3 Child must have resided in State for 1 year immediately preceding application or must have been born in the State within 1 year immediately preceding application if mother resided in State 1 year immediately preceding birth of child.

4 Suitable family home meeting standards of care and health fixed by law and the rules of the State and/or a State agency.

5 Child must have resided in county for 1 year immediately preceding application to receive county aid.

6 If Federal grants are not available, mother must have a settlement or have resided in State 4 years.

7 Parents, grandparents, brother, sister, stepparents, stepbrother, stepsister, uncle, aunt, or any person standing in loco parentis to the child.

8 Aid may be continued beyond the age of 16 years if it appears to the board of county commissioners that it is for the best interest of the child.

9 Parents, grandparents, brother, sister, stepparents, stepbrother, stepsister, uncle, aunt, any person in loco parentis, or any person caring for children in private home by juvenile court order.

10 Child must be under 14 years of age and born in United States if mother is not a citizen but has declared her intention of becoming a citizen. County may order relief continued until child attains majority if the child is incapacitated for work.

11 Parents, grandparents, brother, sister, stepparents, stepbrother, stepsister, uncle, or aunt. Aid provided to children who are not public wards and who are living with persons not in the proper degree of relationship to make them eligible for aid to dependent children. Such child must be living in a suitable foster home or institution conforming to the standards of care and health fixed by law and the rules and regulations of the State Department of Public Welfare.

12 If school record is satisfactory or child is disabled for employment, aid may be continued until child is 16 years old.

13 Home satisfactory for training and rearing children.

14 Child must have resided in the State for 1 year immediately preceding application, must have been born in the State within 1 year immediately preceding application if the mother resided in the State 1 year immediately preceding the birth of the child, or if the mother has resided in the State for 1 year immediately preceding the date of application.

15 Child must attend school regularly unless incapacitated or over school age and unemployed through no fault of its own. If practicable home must be of same religious faith as child's family.

16 County contributes only if child has been resident of county for 6 months or if child is less than 6 months old and its mother has resided in county 6 months prior to application.

17 Nebraska has enacted an "aid to dependent children" statute in which it is specifically stated that the statute is supplementary to the original "mothers' aid" law. The terms original and supplementary are used to distinguish the 2 statutes.

18 Age limit extended if child is incapable of self-support because of physical disability.

19 If Federal aid is withdrawn residence in State 5 years immediately preceding the grant of assistance shall be required.

20 Residence of 1 year in county is required to establish liability of a county for the support of a child.

21 Person in whose home child resides must maintain a safe and proper home for himself and such child.

22 Parents, grandparents, brother, sister, stepparents, stepbrother, stepsister, uncle, or aunt. Aid is also granted if child is living in a foster home other than that of a relative, in a home maintained or provided by any child-caring or child-placing agency duly authorized under the laws of North Dakota, or in any foster home other than that of a relative approved and selected by such an agency and approved by the State board.

23 If child is more than 16 and less than 18 years of age, aid may be granted at discretion of county administration.

24 Conditions in home in which child is living must be such that it would be to his benefit to continue to live there.

25 Aid may be granted to minor child over 16 years of age, but in such cases the county is not entitled to Federal aid.

26 Except native children who are provided for by the Department of the Interior.

27 Parents, grandparents, brother, sister, stepparents, stepbrother, stepsister, uncle, or aunt. Aid also granted to child living in suitable family home or institution conforming to standards fixed by the Territorial board.

Table 20.—Need Qualifications for Aid to Dependent Children in Their Own Homes

State	Limitations on property	Limitations on income	Applicant must not have disposed of property to qualify	Aid necessary to preserve home	No relatives legally liable and able to support child	Death, continued absence from home, or physical or mental incapacity of a parent	Father deceased	Mother divorced	Continued absence of father	Mother unmarried	Physical or mental incapacity of father	Father confined in institution — Any type of institution	Father confined in institution — Penal	Father confined in institution — Mental
Alabama						X								
Arizona			Within 2 years.		X	X								
Arkansas		Sufficient income or resources for reasonable subsistence.				X								
California		Child receives support of $25 per month or more.					Father, mother, or both.		Child abandoned.		X	State or Federal hospital.[1]	X[1]	
Colorado						X	X							
Connecticut	Not more than $500 real and personal property or equity of over $2,000 in real estate on which family resides.	(2)			X	X								
Delaware						X								
Florida: State		Sufficient income					X[5]	X[3]	(4)		X	State institution.		
Florida: Local														
Georgia		(5)			X	X								
Idaho					X	X								
Illinois	$1,000 exclusive of household goods.			(6)	X		X		X[7]		X			
Indiana					X	X								
Iowa						X	X[8]					X[8]		
Kansas	Within 2 years.	Sufficient income or resources to provide reasonable subsistence.				X								
Kentucky				(9)										

State										
Louisiana										
Maine		X								
Maryland		X	X							
Massachusetts	X	X								X.
Michigan	(11)	X	X	X	X	X	X			
Minnesota: $300 exclusive of clothing, furniture, tools, and domestic animals.[12]	X	X	X	X	X	X				
Mississippi										
Missouri: $500 cash or negotiable security; $1,500 of any kind of property.	(13)	X	X	X						
Montana: Relatives within 2d degree.		X	X	X	X	X	X			
Nebraska:[14] Original: Real or personal property of $2,000 value owned by mother, household goods excepted.	X	X								
Supplementary										
Nevada: Mother has sufficient income to properly care for offspring.	X	X								
New Hampshire: Sufficient income or resources for reasonable subsistence.	(16)	X	X	X						
New Jersey: Mother has sufficient means to support child and maintain home. / Relatives of the mother.[18]		X	1 year[17]	X[18]	X[19]	X.				
New Mexico: Sufficient income or other resources for reasonable subsistence.	X	X		X	X					
New York: Sufficient income or other resources for reasonable subsistence.	(21)	X	X	X	X	X[1]				X.[1]
North Carolina: Adequate means of support		X								
North Dakota	X	X								
Ohio	X	X								
Oklahoma: Sufficient income or other resources.		X								
Oregon	(5)	X								

See footnotes at end of table.

Table 20.—Need Qualifications for Aid to Dependent Children in Their Own Homes—Continued

State	Limitations on property	Limitations on income	Applicant must not have disposed of property to qualify	Aid necessary to preserve home	No relatives legally liable and able to support child	Need due to following causes of inability of parents to support child — Death, continued absence from home, or physical or mental incapacity of a parent	Father deceased	Mother divorced	Continued absence of father	Mother unmarried	Physical or mental incapacity of father	Father confined in institution — Any type of institution	Penal	Mental
Pennsylvania					[23]	X	X		X		X			
Rhode Island						X								
South Carolina				X	X	X								
South Dakota					X	X								
Tennessee						X								
Texas: State		[5]												
Local					X	X	X	X	2 years				X	X.
Utah					X[24]	X								
Vermont				X		X								
Virginia		[25]		X	[26]	X								
Washington	Sufficient resources to provide reasonable subsistence.[27]													
West Virginia					X	X								
Wisconsin	Homestead excepted if maintenance is less than rent.	[28]				X	X	1 year	1 year[29]	X	Likely to continue for 1 year.		For 1 year.	
Wyoming		[5]	X		X	X								
Alaska		[30]												
District of Columbia	Sufficient for reasonable income.										X		X	
Hawaii	Sufficient income or resources to provide care and support.		X		X	X[31]								

X indicates that the provision applies without limitation in a given State.

[1] Provision applies to either parent.

[2] Applicant is not receiving aid from any other State.

[3] Allowance ceases if mother remarries.

[4] Wife is eligible if husband has been prosecuted for desertion and nonsupport and judged by court to be wholly unable to support wife and child.

[5] Child's relatives unable to provide adequately for child without public assistance.

[6] Aid granted if absence of relief would require mother to work away from home and child would benefit by remaining with mother.

[7] Father has abandoned wife and child within State and refuses or neglects to support them.

[8] Father deceased or an inmate of any institution under the State Board of Control of State Institutions. Because of indigency, mother is unable to care for child who would benefit by remaining in own home.

[9] Applicant desires and needs help.

[10] Person caring for child is not reasonably able to support it.

[11] Board must take all lawful means to compel support of such children and parents by persons able to do so.

[12] Ownership of real property with no gross income and with an unreasonable market price no bar to relief. Receipt or possession of sums from United States War Risk Insurance is no bar to relief if insufficient to maintain children at home.

[13] There must be no organization legally liable or able to support the child, or a person upon whom rests a moral obligation to assist in its support.

[14] Nebraska has enacted an "aid to dependent children" statute in which it is specifically stated that the statute is supplementary to the original "mothers' aid" law. The terms *original* and *supplementary* are used to distinguish the 2 statutes.

[15] The father, mother, stepfather, or stepmother are liable for assistance in an action of debt if their weekly income is more than sufficient to provide for reasonable subsistence.

[16] The word *mother* includes any female standing in loco parentis to any child.

[17] Father is unable to support child because he is under indictment for desertion of wife and child or has been deported as an alien.

[18] If father is physically or mentally incapacitated he must be under proper and reasonable treatment for possible removal of defect.

[19] Father is unable to support child because he is confined in a jail, prison, or penitentiary for a term extending 6 months beyond date of decision upon application for aid.

[20] Aid must be necessary to enable mother or relative to bring up the child.

[21] No allowance may be granted to a relative financially able to support the child; in making allowance consideration must be given to ability of all relatives to support.

[22] Father or mother is unable to support child because they are confined under a sentence of 2 years or more in an institution under the jurisdiction of the State Department of Correction or any Federal penal or correctional institution.

[23] General support law states that the husband, wife, father, mother, grandparent, and grandchild of every indigent person shall, if of sufficient ability, care for, maintain, or financially assist such indigent person at such rate as the court of the county where such indigent person resides shall order or direct.

[24] Relative could provide support without depriving himself or other members of his family of the necessities or conveniences that should be included in the ordinary standard of living in the community.

[25] Child is needy and in need of public assistance.

[26] Local board may proceed against any person legally liable for the support of any dependent child and cause such person to support such child.

[27] Receipt of public aid other than temporary medical and surgical is a bar to aid unless approved by county court.

[28] Receipt of other aid except medical and dental care is a bar to aid.

[29] If husband is legally charged with abandonment.

[30] Mother is unable to support child except by her own labor.

[31] Cruelty, neglect, or depravity on the part of a parent also basis for granting aid.

Table 21.—Provisions for Granting and Financing Aid to Dependent Children in Their Own Homes

State	Maximum allowance (per month unless otherwise specified)			Burial allowance	Governmental unit determining amount of individual grant		Incidence of financial responsibility			Basis for distribution of State funds	Procedure in case of insufficiency of State funds
	First child	Each additional child	Family		Final	Advisory	State	County	Other local unit		
Alabama	([1])	([1])			County		50 percent.	50 percent.		State reimburses counties 50 percent of amount expended.[2]	
Arizona	$18	$12			State	County	X			Individual recipients paid by State Board of Social Security and Welfare by warrant drawn upon State auditor.	
Arkansas	([1])	([1])			State	([3])	X			([4])	
California	$240 per year[5]	$240 per year[5]			County		50 percent.[6]	50 percent.		State reimburses county 50 percent of amount expended.	
Colorado	$18	$12			County		66⅔ percent.	33⅓ percent.		State reimburses county 66⅔ percent of the cost of assistance and administration.	
Connecticut	([7])	([7])		$100	State	Municipality and county.	33⅓ percent.	33⅓ percent.	33⅓ percent (municipality).	Municipality and county reimburse the State for the amount expended in proportion to their share. State disburses funds to individuals.	
Delaware	([1])	([1])			State		50 percent.	50 percent.		State reimburses county 50 percent of amount expended.	
Florida:											
State					District		X			State disburses funds to individuals	
Local	$25	$8			County			X			
Georgia	([1])	([1])			County		90 percent.	10 percent.		State reimburses county for 90 percent of assistance and administrative costs.[2]	
Idaho	([8])	([8])			County		⅔ to ⅘	⅕ to ⅓		County reimburses State not less than ⅕ or more than ⅓ of amount expended. State disburses funds to individuals.	
Illinois	$15[9]	$10[9]			County		X	X		State reimbursement not to exceed 50 percent of total county expenditure from 80 percent of funds available on basis of population. 20 percent of funds available allotted to counties on basis of ability to meet need.	Assistance granted to applicants in order of urgency of needs.
Indiana	$20[10]	$18 for 2d, $12 for others.			County		60 percent.	40 percent.		State reimburses county for 60 percent of amount expended.[11]	

State	Amount of grant (one child)	Amount (each additional child)	Maximum per month	Agency administering	Local subdivision	State share	County / local share	City or town share	Remarks
Iowa	$2.50 per week								Funds prorated among the applicants.
Kansas	$2.50 per week	$2.50 per week		County		30 per cent	70 per cent		State reimburses county 30 percent of expenditure less cost of administration.
Kentucky	Sufficient to insure proper maintenance.			County		X	X		
Louisiana (See appendix B.)	(12)			Parish		66⅔ per cent[13]		33⅓ per cent (parish).	State reimburses parish 66⅔ percent of cost of assistance and 50 percent of administrative costs.[13]
Maine	(1)			State	City, town, or plantation.	50 per cent		50 per cent (municipality).	Municipalities reimburse State 50 percent of expenditure to each child. State disburses funds to individuals.
Maryland	Maximum provided under any Federal law for reimbursement.			County (and city of Baltimore).		X	X	X (Baltimore City).	Allocation of amounts prescribed by Board of State Aid and Charities.
Massachusetts	Sufficient to bring up child properly.			Town or city.		33⅓ per cent		66⅔ per cent (town).[14]	State reimburses town for 33⅓ percent of amount expended.
Michigan	$10 per week[15]	$2 per week	$50	County					
Minnesota	$15	$20	$60	County		(16)	33⅓ per cent	66⅔ per cent	State reimburses county for 66⅔ percent of total expenditures.
Mississippi	Sufficient for proper care, maintenance, and support of child.			County[17]		66⅔ per cent	X[17]		
Missouri	$18	$12		State	(3)	X			State disburses funds to individuals.
Montana	(1)			County		50 per cent	50 per cent		County reimburses State for 50 percent of amount expended for aid after share of Federal Government is deducted. State disburses funds to individuals.
Nebraska:[18] Original	$18[19]			County		X			
Supplementary	$12[19]			County		X			State disburses funds to counties in the ratio of the population of each county to the total population of the State.

See footnotes at end of table.

Table 21.—Provisions for Granting and Financing Aid to Dependent Children in Their Own Homes—Continued

| State | Maximum allowance (per month unless otherwise specified) | | | Burial allowance | Governmental unit determining amount of individual grant | | Incidence of financial responsibility | | | Basis for distribution of State funds | Procedure in case of insufficiency of State funds |
	First child	Each additional child	Family		Final	Advisory	State	County	Other local unit		
Nevada	$25	$40 for 2 children; $55 for 3 children.	$75		County			X		State disburses funds to individuals.[22]	
New Hampshire	(1)	(1)		(20)	State[21]		X	X	X (town)		
New Jersey	Not to exceed cost of care in approved child-caring institution.	Not to exceed cost of care in approved child-caring institution.		$100	County	State	66⅔ per-cent.[23]	33⅓ per-cent.		State reimburses county for 66⅔ percent of amount expended, but, if no Federal aid is available or child is cared for by person other than a relative, the State must reimburse county to extent of 50 percent of amount expended.[23]	
New Mexico	(1)	(1)		$50	State[24]		X			State disburses funds to individuals.	
New York	(25)	(25)			County or city.		50 per-cent.	50 per-cent.		State reimburses county for 50 percent of total expenditures approved by State Department of Social Welfare.[26]	
North Carolina	$18	$12	$65[27]		County		(28)	(28)		(28)	
North Dakota	$18[29]	$12[29]			State	County	50 per-cent.[30]	50 per-cent.[30]		(30)	
Ohio	(1)	(1)			County		X	X		State funds apportioned to county in the proportion the number of children under 16 years of age in county bears to the total number in State.	
Oklahoma	$18	$12			State	County	X			Individuals paid by State through the county assistance boards.	
Oregon	(1)	(1)			County		50 per-cent.[31]	50 per-cent.[31]		(31)	
Pennsylvania	Extent of aid fixed by State Board of Public Assistance.	Extent of aid fixed by State Board of Public Assistance.		Amount not specified.	County		X			Upon the submission of budgets by the county boards, the State department allocates to the counties State funds for assistance and administrative costs on the basis of need.	
Rhode Island	(1)	(1)			State		66⅔ per-cent.[32]		33⅓ per-cent.	State reimburses city or town for 66⅔ percent of the amount expended for aid and cost of administration.[32]	

State				Administration	State	County	City	Method of disbursement of funds	Additional provisions
South Carolina	$15	$10		State[35]	X	X		State disburses funds to individuals.	
South Dakota	(1)	(1)		State	X	X		State disburses funds to individuals.	
Tennessee	$12	$8		State and county[35]	50 per cent	16⅔ per cent[36]	50 per cent[36]	County reimburses State for 16⅔ per cent of amount expended. State disburses funds to individuals.[36]	
Texas: State	$16[37]		$24[37]	State[37]	(3)	X		State disburses funds to individuals.	
Texas: Local	$15	$6		County	85 per cent	15 per cent		County reimburses State for 15 per cent of the amount expended. State disburses funds to individuals.	
Utah	(1)		$150	County or district.	85 per cent	15 per cent			State may advance county's share which is to be repaid.
Vermont	$4 per week		$4 per week	State	50 per cent	50 per cent		Town reimburses State for amount expended. State disburses funds to individuals.	
Virginia	$18		$12	County or city.	62½ per cent	37½ per cent	37½ per cent (city)	State reimburses county 62½ percent of the amount expended during the preceding month for the cost of assistance and administration from 62½ percent of Federal grant for assistance and State funds. 37½ percent of Federal grant for assistance paid to the several counties and cities on the basis of the total amounts disbursed for aid to dependent children by such counties and cities during the period for which such grants were made.[38]	
Washington	(1)	(1)		County	X	X		Percentage not specified[39]	
West Virginia	$12[40]	$8[40]		State	County	X		State funds allocated in counties in proportion to the number of cases and cost of living.	
Wisconsin	Aid sufficient to care for child properly.[41]		$100	County	33⅓ per cent	66⅔ per cent		State reimburses county for 33⅓ per cent of amount expended.[6]	State funds prorated among counties.
Wyoming	(42)	(42)		State	County	X		State matches county funds by grants-in-aid.	State may provide additional funds if county tax is insufficient.

See footnotes at end of table.

Table 21.—Provisions for Granting and Financing Aid to Dependent Children in Their Own Homes—Continued

| State | Maximum allowance (per month unless otherwise specified) | | | Burial allowance | Governmental unit determining amount of individual grant | | Incidence of financial responsibility | | | Basis for distribution of State funds | Procedure in case of insufficiency of State funds |
	First child	Each additional child	Family		Final	Advisory	State	County	Other local unit		
Alaska	$25	$15			Territory		Territory general fund.			Territory disburses funds to individuals.	
District of Columbia.	[43]	[43]			District of Columbia.		District of Columbia.			District of Columbia disburses funds to individuals.	
Hawaii	[1]	[1]			County		Territory.			Territory disburses funds to individuals.	

X indicates that the provision applies without limitation in a given State.

1 Aid must be an amount which is sufficient, when added to all other income and support available to the child, to provide child with a reasonable subsistence compatible with decency and health.

2 One-fifth of State funds may be used as an equalization fund to assist counties unable to bear their proportionate share.

3 County or district board of public welfare with final approval by State Department of Public Welfare.

4 State Department of Public Welfare authorized to allocate funds to county departments which are authorized to receive and disburse such funds.

5 County pays $120 per year, or as much thereof as is necessary. County may also pay additional sum.

6 State pays $120 per year for recipients with county residence. If recipient has no county residence, State pays all.

7 Maximum weekly allowance: food for widow, $2; food for each child over 14 years of age, $1.75; food for each child between 5 and 14 years of age, $1.25; food for each child under 5 years of age, $1.00; fuel, $1.00; clothing for each member of family, 50¢; allowance for tenement, $5.00; reasonable allowance for medical attention, treatment, or hospital care. No hospital receiving State aid may charge or receive more than $10.00 per week for care except in special cases approved by the commissioner of welfare, executive officer of the municipality, and the county commissioner.

8 Allowance must be an amount which when added to income is sufficient for reasonable subsistence, but the amount paid by State and county must not exceed the amount of Federal contribution.

9 Maximum allowance $25 for 1st child and $15 for each additional child in counties having over 300,000 population.

10 Maximum allowance of $23 per month for each child cared for in foster home or institution.

11 State may, when necessary, pay all or any part of local administration or cost of assistance.

25 Allowance must not exceed the difference between amount necessary for maintenance of mother or father and dependent child and the income of such mother and father of child from earnings or other sources. Allowance must be adequate to bring up child properly, having regard for the physical, mental, and moral well-being of the child. Allowance may also be made for the maintenance of a female relative caring for a dependent child if she is without means of support; and if the other parent of a person receiving aid for benefit of a child is at home because of physical disability, allowance may be made for the maintenance of such other parent.

26 State reimbursement ceases in case of discontinuance of Federal grants or failure to appropriate State funds.

27 Amount may be increased if State Board of Charities and Public Welfare is satisfied sum is insufficient.

28 State reimburses county for 66⅔ percent of cost of assistance from State and Federal funds and 50 percent of administrative costs from State funds. The State Board of Allotments and Appeal is authorized and directed to establish an equalization fund to be distributed to the counties according to their needs. No county is entitled to share in such fund unless a 10-mill property tax has been levied to pay aid to dependent children and old age assistance. The amount which may be allocated to any county from the equalization fund may not exceed ⅚ of the cost to the county in excess of the amount produced by the 10-mill levy. This act becomes null and void upon the failure of Federal funds.

29 State may increase maximum if Federal aid is increased.

30 County reimburses State 50 percent of money expended in excess of the amount provided by the Federal Government. State disburses funds to individuals. If the State Public Welfare Board finds upon investigation that the financial condition of any county is such that it cannot raise necessary funds, the State board may provide, either as a grant or a loan, that county's share or as much thereof as may be necessary.

31 Exclusive of all sums contributed by the Federal Government for aid to dependent children and the expenses of administration, the State and counties must each contribute ⅔ of all sums required. State disburses funds to individuals.

38 The amount of reimbursement by the State includes the funds received by the State from the Federal Government.

[33] Through county departments of public welfare which act as agents of the State Department of Public Welfare.

[34] Act becomes effective upon the approval of the Social Security Board of a State plan for aid to dependent children under the Federal statute authorizing payment to the State of ½ of the assistance furnished under the act.

[35] Amount of award must not exceed the amount approved by county judge or chairman and juvenile judge. In case of disagreement, the matter is referred to the State Department of Public Welfare for final decision.

[36] State and county contributions to be supplemented by Federal funds to the extent of 33⅓ percent of the cost of aid. The entire cost of administration is paid by the State with the exception of such Federal funds as may be made available.

[37] Maximum allowance which may be paid from State and Federal funds. Maximum of $8 per month for 1 child and $12 per month for all dependent children in the same home may be paid from State funds.

[38] Not more than 10 percent of the funds allocated to the counties or cities may be used for local administrative expenses. If a county or city fails or refuses to provide funds, the State Board of Public Welfare must require the local authorities to make funds available. During the period of refusal or failure, the State must make payments and deduct the amounts so paid from future State reimbursements.

[39] Board of county commissioners is authorized to expend funds for any category of public assistance and it also has the power to reimburse the State for expenditures made for public assistance within their county from State or Federal funds.

[40] Maximum allowances are amounts which may be granted from all sources including funds received from the Federal Government.

[41] Prenatal and postnatal aid is granted for 6 months.

[42] Aid not to exceed amount of Federal participation is given to support child in manner compatible with decency and health.

[43] Allowance must be sufficient to insure the proper maintenance of the child in the home.

[12] Aid necessary to support child in manner compatible with decency and health. Determined in accordance with standard budgets adopted by the State Department of Public Welfare.

[13] State may assume total financial responsibility if parish lacks funds or if funds are legally barred.

[14] Includes Federal funds which are allocated to cities and towns by the State Department of Public Welfare. Upon repeal of the Social Security Act, this act becomes null and void and the act in effect prior to its enactment becomes operative.

[15] Allowance must not be less than $2 per week if mother has 1 child.

[16] A State financed program for aid to dependent children is administered by the State Emergency Welfare Relief Commission through county welfare relief commissions under rules and regulations of the State commission. Specific provisions relating to eligibility, etc., are not set forth by statute and therefore have not been included in these tables.

[17] County departments of public welfare are authorized to grant dependent children aid in their own homes from public funds made available for welfare services.

[18] Nebraska has enacted an "aid to dependent children" statute in which it is specifically stated that the statute is supplementary to the original "mothers' aid" law. The terms *original* and *supplementary* are used to distinguish the 2 statutes.

[19] Allowance must not be less than $5 per month for any child.

[20] Reasonable funeral expenses may be paid if the estate of the deceased is insufficient.

[21] Commissioner of public welfare required in all cases to first consult proper official of the county or town required to contribute to the cost of assistance.

[22] Counties and towns required to contribute to the cost of assistance. In the event a county or town cannot pay the amounts required, it may file a petition requesting financial aid, and the State may, after investigation, grant or loan such funds as may be necessary.

[23] If no county residence, State pays all.

[24] The State Department of Public Welfare may allow its local offices to determine whether assistance may be granted and the amount and manner thereof.

Dependent and Neglected Children

Table 22.—Characteristics of Dependent and Neglected Children Coming Within Jurisdiction of Juvenile Courts

State	Age under which court has jurisdiction (in years)		Child destitute, homeless, or dependent upon the public for support	Child abandoned or with improper parental care or guardianship or unfit environment or occupation
	Boys	Girls		
Alabama	16	16	X	X.
Arizona	18	18	X	X.
Arkansas	21	21	X	X.
California	21	21	X	X.
Colorado	18	18	X	X.
Connecticut	16[1]	16[1]	X	X.
Delaware	18	19	X	X.
Florida	17	17	X	X.
Georgia	16	16	X[2]	X.[2]
Idaho	18	18	X	X.
Illinois	17	18	X	X.
Indiana	16	17	X	X.
Iowa	18	18	X	X.
Kansas	16	16	X	X.
Kentucky	17	18	X	X.
Louisiana	18	18	X	X.
Maine	([3])	([3])	X	X.
Maryland	20	18	X	X.
Massachusetts	16	16	X	X.
Michigan	17	17	X	X.
Minnesota	18	18	X	X.
Mississippi	17	17	X	X.
Missouri	17	17	X	X.
Montana	16	16	X	X.
Nebraska	18	18	X	X.
Nevada	18	18	X	X.
New Hampshire	18	18		X.
New Jersey	16	16		X.
New Mexico	16	16	X	X.
New York	16	16	X	X.
North Carolina	16	16	X	X.
North Dakota	18	18	X	X.
Ohio	18	18	X	X.
Oklahoma	16	18	X	X.
Oregon	18	18	X	X.
Pennsylvania	16	16	X	X.
Rhode Island	18	18	X	X.
South Carolina	16	16	X	X.
South Dakota	21	21	X	X.
Tennessee	17	17	X	X.
Texas	16	16	X	X.
Utah	18	18	X	X.
Vermont	16	16	X	X.
Virginia	18	18	X	X.
Washington	18	18	X	X.
West Virginia	16	18	X	X.
Wisconsin	([4])	([4])	X	X.
Wyoming	16	16	X	X.
Alaska	16	16	X	X.
District of Columbia	([5])	([5])	X	X.[6]
Hawaii	18[7]	18[7]	X	X.

X indicates that the provision applies without limitation in a given State.

[1] Juvenile court also has jurisdiction of persons 16—18 years of age transferred to it from the jurisdiction of a town, city, or police or borough court.
[2] In addition to these classes, children under 16 years of age confined in any penal institution or common jail may be given more suitable treatment.
[3] The statute provides for aid to "any child" without setting age limits, except that dependent children (without relatives able to support them) must be under 16 years of age.
[4] Neglected children under 18 years of age and dependent children under 16 years of age are also included.
[5] The law does not specify any age limit but refers to "any child destitute or homeless."
[6] Includes children under 8 years of age found peddling.
[7] Also includes children under 12 years of age who might otherwise be adjudged delinquents.

Note: Dependent and neglected children are those children under the specified ages who are destitute, homeless, dependent upon the public for support, abandoned, with improper parental care or guardianship, or with unfit environment or occupation.

Table 23.—Provisions for Instituting Proceedings, Investigations, and Hearings of Cases of Dependent and Neglected Children by Juvenile Courts

State	Persons authorized to institute proceedings in cases of dependency or neglect	Investigation By probation officer or other court agent	Investigation By other agencies[1]	Hearing Before court	Hearing Before referee or court commissioner[2]	Representation of child's interests at hearing By probation officer or other court agent	Representation of child's interests at hearing By other public agency[1]
Alabama	Any person having knowledge of a dependent or neglected child.	X	X	X	X		
Arizona	Any citizen who is a resident of the county.	X		X	X	X	
Arkansas	Any reputable resident of the county	X		X	X	X	
California	Any person within the county	X	X	X	X	(³)	X.
Colorado	Any county resident, officer of the Bureau of Child and Animal Protection or other bureau, or the juvenile court.	X		X			
Connecticut	Parent, guardian, selectman, any official charged with the care of the poor, any prosecuting or probation officer, the State Humane Society, or the Commissioner of Welfare.[4]	X	X	X		X	X.
Delaware	Any reputable resident of the county	X		X		X	
Florida	Any resident of the county, not under legal disability, or any probation officer.[5]	X		X		X	
Georgia	Any policeman or other officer	X		X	X	X	
Idaho	Any person	X	X	X		X	X.
Illinois	Any reputable resident of the county	X		X		X	
Indiana	Any person or county or district department of public welfare.	X		X	X		
Iowa	Any reputable citizen of the county	X		X		X	
Kansas	Any reputable resident of the county	X		X		X	
Kentucky	Board of Louisville and Jefferson County Children's Home or any reputable resident of the county.	X	X	X		X	X.
Louisiana	Any reputable person	X	X	X		X	X.
Maine	An agent of the State Department of Health and Welfare, a sheriff, county probation officer, police officer, member of a municipal board of child welfare, or 3 or more citizens of any town or city.			X			
Maryland	Any resident of a county, probation officer, or agent of a private society.	X	X	X		X	X.
Massachusetts	Any person	X	X	X			X.
Michigan	Any interested person	X	X	X			X.
Minnesota	Agent of State Board of Control or State Department of Labor and Industries, or any reputable resident of the county.	X	X	X			X.
Mississippi	Any resident of the county	X		X		X	
Missouri	Any 2 citizens of the county[6]	X		X		X	
Montana	Any resident of the county	X		X		X	
Nebraska	Any reputable resident of the county		X	X			X.
Nevada	Any reputable resident of the county	X		X		X	
New Hampshire	Any reputable person	X		X			
New Jersey	Any person or any corporation or association having as one of its objects the prevention of cruelty to children.	X	X	X	X		X.
New Mexico	District attorney for the county			X	X	X	
New York	Any person, authorized agency, or local welfare official.	X	X	X			X.
North Carolina	Any person	X		X		X	

See footnotes at end of table.

Table 23.—Provisions for Instituting Proceedings, Investigations, and Hearings of Cases of Dependent and Neglected Children by Juvenile Courts—Continued

State	Persons authorized to institute proceedings in cases of dependency or neglect	Investigation		Hearing		Representation of child's interests at hearing	
		By probation officer or other court agent	By other agencies[1]	Before court	Before referee or court commissioner[2]	By probation officer or other court agent	By other public agency[1]
North Dakota	Any person	X	X	X		X	X.
Ohio	Any person	X		X	X		
Oklahoma	Any reputable resident of the county	X		X		X	
Oregon	District attorney	X		X		X	
Pennsylvania	Any citizen who is a resident of the county.	X		X		X	
Rhode Island	Any person		X	X			X.
South Carolina	Any person	X		X			
South Dakota	Any resident of the State			X		X	
Tennessee	Any reputable resident of the county	X		X		X	
Texas	Any resident of the county	X		X		X	
Utah	Any person or peace officer		X	X	X		
Vermont	The commissioner of public welfare or any person having knowledge of a dependent or neglected child.		X	X		(3)	
Virginia	Any reputable person	X	X	X		X	X.
Washington	Any person	X		X			
West Virginia	The State Department of Public Assistance or any reputable person.	X	X	X		X	X.
Wisconsin	Any person		X	X	X		X.
Wyoming	Any interested person			X			
Alaska	Any parent, guardian, school teacher, member of the school board, truant officer, or any other reliable person.			X			
District of Columbia	Any person may file complaint with the corporation counsel or his assistant.			X			
Hawaii	Any person	X		X			

X indicates that the provision applies without limitation in a given State.

[1] For names of agencies and their powers see table 26.
[2] Findings of the referee are subject to court approval.
[3] The court may appoint some suitable person to act in behalf of the child.
[4] The Commissioner of Welfare must present cases to the court when other authorities fail to do so.
[5] The sheriff institutes proceedings where there is no probation officer.
[6] Any reputable citizen of the county may file a verified petition in the interests of a neglected child.

Table 24.—Types of Homes and Institutions to Which Dependent and Neglected Children May Be Committed by Juvenile Courts

State	Child's own home	Foster home	Public institution or agency	Private institution or agency
Alabama	X	X	X	X.
Arizona	X	X	X	X.
Arkansas	X	X	X[1]	X.
California	X	X	X	X.
Colorado	X	X	X	X.
Connecticut	X	X	X	X.
Delaware	X	X		X.
Florida		X	X	X.
Georgia	X	X	X	X.
Idaho	X	X	X	X.
Illinois	X	X	X	X.
Indiana		X	X	X.
Iowa	X	X	X	X.
Kansas	X	X	X	X.
Kentucky	X	X	X[2]	X.
Louisiana	X	X	X	X.
Maine	X	X	X	X.
Maryland	X		X	X.
Massachusetts	X	X	X	X.
Michigan	X	X	X	X.
Minnesota	X	X	X	X.
Mississippi	X	X		X.
Missouri	X	X	X	X.
Montana	X	X	X	X.
Nebraska	X	X	X	X.
Nevada	X	X	X	X.
New Hampshire	X	X	X	X.
New Jersey	X	X	X	X.
New Mexico		X		X.
New York	X	X	X	X.
North Carolina	X	X	X	X.
North Dakota	X	X	X	X.
Ohio	X	X	X	X.
Oklahoma		X	X	X.
Oregon		X	X	X.
Pennsylvania	X	X	X	X.
Rhode Island	X		X	X.
South Carolina	X	X	X	X.
South Dakota	X	X	X	X.
Tennessee		X	X	X.
Texas	X	X	X	X.
Utah	X	X	X	X.
Vermont		X	X	X.
Virginia	X	X	X	X.
Washington	X	X	X	X.
West Virginia	X	X	X	X.
Wisconsin	X	X	X	X.
Wyoming	X	X	X	X.
Alaska			X	X.
District of Columbia			X	
Hawaii	X	X		X.

X indicates that the provision applies without limitation in a given State.

[1] The courts may not commit any dependent or neglected child to any institution or home used for the care, imprisonment, or reformation of delinquent children or adult criminals.

[2] Children may be committed only for hospitalization and special care.

Table 25.—State Institutions Caring for Dependent and Neglected Children

State	Name of institution[1]	Age in years	Other characteristics	Name of agency	Extent of control or supervision
			Description of class admitted	Administrative and supervisory agencies	
Alabama	Boys' State Industrial School	6-13	White boys who because of conduct or surroundings are likely to become base, criminal, or hurtful to the State or to the best interest of society.[2]	Board of directors of the institution. State Department of Public Welfare (bureau of child welfare).	Has full management and control of school and inmates. Ex officio members of board must visit and inspect annually. Determines source of income and cost of maintenance, supervises placement of children out of the school, and visits and inspects the school.
Arizona					
Arkansas	State Industrial School for White Boys; State Industrial School for Negro Boys; State Training School for Girls.		Dependent children as defined in table 22.	Honorary boards of management and operation.	Must exercise such powers of supervision and control as are not specifically reserved to the respective superintendents. Must provide competent teachers to teach useful trades or vocations.
California[3]	Whittier State School	Over 8 and under 16.	Boys who are in need of education, training, supervision, and moral development.[2]	State Department of Institutions.	Has full control and supervision through the superintendent of the institution.
Colorado	State Home for Dependent and Neglected Children.	Under 16[4]	Children with sound minds and bodies who are dependent upon the public for support.[5]	Board of control of institution. Division of Public Welfare of the Executive Department.	Establishes system of government, makes all necessary rules and regulations for support, training, and placement of inmates. Board is the legal guardian of inmates. Supervises and controls, may inspect and make recommendations to the Governor, and requires reports from board of control.
Connecticut					
Delaware	Detention Home for Juveniles.		Dependent or neglected children as defined in table 22.	Board of managers of the institution. State Board of Charities.	Makes rules for government, regulation, and administration. Must visit, inspect, and report condition annually to Governor.
Florida					
Georgia					
Idaho					
Illinois	State Soldiers' and Sailors' Children's School.	Under 14.	Dependent or neglected children, residents in State for 1 year, whose parent served in United States forces.	State Department of Public Welfare.	Has full supervision and administrative control. Must obtain employment or make suitable placement plans for children in the school.
Indiana	State Boys' School	7-18	Dependent or neglected children as defined in table 22.[6]	Board of control of the school. Children's division of State Department of Public Welfare.	Responsible for government of the school. Has supervision of the school.
	State Soldiers' and Sailors' Children's Home.	Under 16.	Orphans or half-orphans, destitute of support and education, who are children	Board of trustees of the home.	Has immediate charge and management and may place children in homes.

State	Institution	Age	Eligible children	Administering agency	Powers
Iowa	State Soldiers' Orphans' Home; State Juvenile Home.	Under 18.	of veterans or nurses who served in United States wars.	Children's division of State Department of Public Welfare.	Has immediate supervision.
			Dependent or neglected children who are residents of the State. Preference must be given to children of soldiers, sailors, and marines. Other dependent or neglected children may also be admitted.[7]	State Board of Control of State Institutions.[8]	Has full management, control, and government. Superintendent, upon approval of the board, may place children in homes.
Kansas	State Orphans' Home	Under 14.	Dependent or neglected children with sound minds and bodies.	State Board of Administration.[9]	Has full control of the property, effects, and management. The board is the legal guardian of all inmates and places children in homes.
Kentucky					
Louisiana	State Industrial School for Girls.	12—19	White children legally adjudged dependent or neglected as defined in table 22.[2]	Board of commissioners of the school. State Board of Charities and Corrections.	Makes necessary rules and regulations for classification, discipline, and education of the inmates. Supervises the care given in the institution but may not exercise any administrative or executive power.
Maine	State Military and Naval Children's Home.	11 and over.	Poor and neglected children with preference given to children of soldiers and sailors of Maine who have served in United States wars.	State Department of Health and Welfare.	Has general supervision, management, and control of the home and inmates.
Maryland	Training School for Boys; Montrose School for Girls.	Under 21.	White neglected children, street beggars, and vagrants.[2]	Board of managers of the respective institutions.	Has full management and control and places inmates in homes.
				Board of State Aid and Charities.	Investigates, inspects, studies, and reports biennially to the Legislature.
Massachusetts					
Michigan	State Children's Institute	Under 14.	Dependent or neglected children who are sound in mind and body.	State Welfare Commission.	Has full jurisdiction and control. Makes all necessary regulations for the health, instruction, training, placement, and supervision of inmates. May place children in licensed boarding homes.
Minnesota	State Public School for Dependent Children.	Under 15.	Dependent or neglected children who are sound in mind and body.	State Board of Control	Has exclusive management and places children in homes.
Mississippi	State Industrial and Training School.	7—18	Destitute or abandoned children[2]	Board of trustees of State eleemosynary institutions.	Governs and makes necessary rules and regulations.
				State Board of Public Welfare.	Must supervise the operation of the institution.
Missouri	State Home for Children	Under 17.	Dependent or neglected children with sound minds; crippled children and those with contagious diseases may also be admitted.	State Social Security Commission.[10]	Has full management and control and places inmates in homes. Children diseased or of unsound mind may be committed to suitable institutions.

See footnotes at end of table.

Table 25.—State Institutions Caring for Dependent and Neglected Children—Continued

State	Description of class admitted			Administrative and supervisory agencies	
	Name of institution[1]	Age in years	Other characteristics	Name of agency	Extent of control or supervision
Montana	State Orphans' Home	Under 12[11]	Orphans, foundlings, or destitute children who are sound in mind and body.[11]	State Board of Education (executive board of the institution).[12]	Has general control and supervision.
	State Vocational School for Girls.	8—18	Girls who for lack of proper parental care are growing up as mendicants or vagrants.[13]	----do----	Do.
Nebraska	State School (Home) for Dependent Children.	Under 16.	Dependent or neglected children with normal and sound minds.	State Board of Control	Has general control, is the legal guardian of inmates, and places inmates in homes.
Nevada	State Orphans' Home		Dependent or neglected children as defined in table 22.	Board of directors of the home.	Manages, governs, and administers, makes rules and regulations, appoints superintendents, supervises appointment of other personnel, and may discharge inmates.
	State School of Industry		--do--	Board of government of the school.	Do.
New Hampshire					
New Jersey					
New Mexico					
New York	Thomas Indian School		Orphan, destitute, or neglected Indian children.	State Department of Social Welfare.	Prescribes rules governing admission, care, education, training, and discharge of inmates.
North Carolina					
North Dakota					
Ohio	State Soldiers' and Sailors' Orphans' Home.		Children of deceased or permanently disabled members of State National Guard, Naval Militia, Organized Reserves, or Officers Reserve Corps (such death or disability occurring in the course of active duty in the service of the State or United States), if without proper support.[14]	Board of trustees of the home.	Governs, controls, and manages home and inmates, appoints necessary personnel, establishes schools for education of inmates, and places children in homes.
				State Department of Public Welfare.	Must visit, inspect, and report upon condition of home.
Oklahoma	Whitaker State Orphan Home; West Oklahoma Home for White Children.		White dependent or neglected children as defined in table 22.	Board of managers for children's institutions[15]	Has complete charge over institutions and inmates.[16] May introduce and carry on industrial education, appoint personnel, and place children in homes.
				State Commissioner of Charities and Corrections.	Must visit, inspect, and inquire into conditions in all institutions at least once a year; may institute prosecutions for violations of the law in connection with an institution and report to Governor.
	Institute for Colored Deaf, Blind, and Orphans.		Colored dependent or neglected children as defined in table 22.	----do----	Do.

State	Institution		Supervising authority	Powers and duties
Oregon				
Pennsylvania	State Soldiers' Orphans' School.	Under 14	Children of soldiers who served in the Spanish-American War, the Philippine War, or the War with Germany and Austria are admitted in the following preference: (1) full orphans; (2) father deceased, mother living; (3) father or mother permanently disabled.[17]	Board of trustees of the school.	Has general direction and control of the property and management of the institution.[18]
				State Department of Welfare.	Has powers of supervision, visitation, examination, and inspection; may order that unsatisfactory conditions be remedied.
	Thaddeus Stevens Industrial School.	Under 14	Orphan boys or other deserving boys	do	Do.
Rhode Island	State Home and School		Dependent or neglected children as defined in table 22 who are not recognized as vicious or criminal.	State Department of Public Welfare.	Has control and management of the institution. Must establish a system of government and make all necessary rules and regulations for the training and education of the inmates; appoints necessary officers, teachers, and employees.
				Deputy in charge of the Bureau of Children's Care in the Division of Social Security.	Has supervision over the institution and the placing of children.
South Carolina	John De La Howe Industrial School.		Dependent or neglected children	Board of trustees	Has control of the business, property, and affairs. Makes all necessary rules and regulations for the government and management of the school.
South Dakota					
Tennessee	Tennessee Industrial School	([19])	Dependent or neglected children as defined in table 22.	State Department of Education.	Supervises management, determines rules and regulations, and appoints superintendent. Superintendent must report monthly to department.
Texas[20]	Waco State Home		Dependent or neglected children as defined in table 22.[21]	State Board of Control (Division of Public Welfare).	Has general control, management, and direction of the affairs, property, and business of the institutions. Makes all necessary rules and regulations, visits and inspects institutions, and approves all commitments to institutions made by juvenile courts.
	State Orphans' Home		Children under 14 years of age may be admitted subject to such restrictions as the State Board of Control may deem requisite.	do	Do.
	State Deaf, Dumb, and Blind Asylum for Colored Youths and Colored Orphans;[22] State Colored Orphans' Home.		Colored orphans	do	Do.
Utah					
Vermont	Kinstead Home		Dependent or neglected children as defined in table 22.[2]	Department of Public Welfare.	Has supervision and control.

See footnotes at end of table.

Table 25.—State Institutions Caring for Dependent and Neglected Children—Continued

State	Name of institution[1]	Description of class admitted		Administrative and supervisory agencies	
		Age in years	Other characteristics	Name of agency	Extent of control or supervision
Virginia					
Washington					
West Virginia	State Children's Home; State Colored Children's Home.		Dependent or neglected children as defined in table 22.	State Board of Control	Has full management, direction, control, and government and employs superintendents of the homes.
Wisconsin	State Public School	Under 16	Dependent and neglected children who are not feeble-minded, insane, or epileptic. Crippled or deformed children may be admitted if their conditions are amenable to treatment.	State Board of Control	Has full management and control. The board is the legal guardian of inmates and places children in homes.
				State Department of Public Instruction	Must inspect the educational work of the school and assist the State Board of Control in developing training activities.
Wyoming	State Children's Home		Dependent or neglected children as defined in table 22.	State Board of Charities and Reform.	Has general control and supervision.
Alaska					
District of Columbia.	National Training School for Boys.	Under 17	White and colored boys who are destitute of a suitable home and adequate means of obtaining an honest living.[2]	Board of trustees of the school.	Has full control and management; makes by-laws, rules, and regulations for government of the school; may direct studies; and appoints superintendent, necessary teachers, and assistants.
	National Training School for Girls.	do	White and colored girls who are destitute of a suitable home and adequate means of obtaining an honest living.[2]	Board of Public Welfare	Has complete and exclusive control and management of these schools.
	Industrial Home School		White boys and girls who are dependent or neglected.[2]	do	Do.
	Industrial Home School for Colored Children.		Colored boys who are dependent or neglected.[2]	do	Do.
Hawaii					

[1]Only those institutions which under the law are specifically established for the care of dependent and neglected children are included here. However, it should be noted that under juvenile court laws, which in some States provide that the courts may commit dependent and neglected children to institutions without any clear definition of what is meant, such children could possibly be committed to institutions established primarily for the care of delinquents.

[2]Delinquents are also admitted to the institution.

[3]According to the report of the State Department of Social Welfare to the Governor's Council (1935) commitments of dependent children were made to the Ventura State School for Girls and the Preston State School of Industry; these institutions were established for the care and training of delinquents.

[4]The board may admit any child dependent upon the public for support.

[12]The executive board has only such authority relative to the immediate control and management as may be conferred upon it by the State Board of Education.

[13]Girls must possess a degree of mental and bodily health which renders them fit subjects for training.

[14]Child and parents or guardian must have been residents of the State for not less than 1 year prior to date of application.

[15]No board has been appointed and no appropriation made for its operation for several years. The work of this department is carried on by the department of charities and corrections and the State Board of Public Affairs.

[16]The financial and fiscal affairs are under the control of the State Board of Public Affairs.

[17]Parents must have resided in the State at least 5 years preceding the date of application.

[5] The board may return to the county of commitment incorrigibles or children with unsound minds or bodies who, because of such conditions, cannot be placed or retained in a family home.

[6] Incorrigible children or children with vicious habits may also be admitted.

[7] Delinquents under 10 years of age and those over 10, if not seriously delinquent, may be admitted to the juvenile home.

[8] The State Board of Social Welfare must cooperate with the board in its management and control of State institutions and their inmates.

[9] The board constitutes the board of trustees of the home.

[10] The director of the children's bureau of the commission is ex officio superintendent of the home.

[11] Children over 12 years of age and under 16 and children with slight physical defects may be admitted at the discretion of the board of trustees.

[18] By-laws, rules, and regulations made by the board are subject to the approval of the superintendent of the State Department of Public Instruction.

[19] Males 8—18 years of age and females 8—16 years of age are admitted to the school.

[20] In addition to the institutions herein included there is provision in the law for the establishment of a colored girls' training school to care for dependent and delinquent children. No funds have been provided as of January 1, 1939, for the establishment of this school.

[21] Feeble-minded, epileptic, or insane children or those children afflicted with any communicable disease may not be admitted to this institution.

[22] This institution was primarily established for deaf, dumb, and blind children. The State Board of Control is authorized to transfer colored orphans to this institution from the State Colored Orphans' Home.

Table 26.—Major Powers and Duties of Principal Public Agencies in Relation to Care of Dependent and Neglected Children Outside of Own Homes or State Institutions

State	Agencies exercising control or supervision	Relationship to juvenile court	Power to license private agencies and institutions	Power to cooperate with Federal child welfare agencies	Miscellaneous powers and duties relating to dependent and neglected children
Alabama	State Department of Public Welfare (bureau of child welfare).	Advises with judges and probation officers. Requires reports from courts.	X	X	Must visit, inspect, and require reports from all public and private institutions to determine adequacy of facilities. Must establish, maintain, or provide homes or other agencies and receive children committed to the bureau.
	County departments of public welfare.	On appointment by court must perform the functions of a probation officer or agent and investigate commitments to, and discharge of children from, institutions under court's supervision.			Must cooperate with all child-caring agencies and investigate at their own discretion or as directed by the State department the conditions of any child. Carry on such child welfare activities as are delegated to them by the State department.
Arizona	State Department of Social Security and Welfare.		X	X	Supervises private and local public agencies and institutions and the care of children in foster homes and institutions.
	County boards of social security and public welfare.				Perform duties as prescribed by State department and cooperate with other local agencies.
Arkansas	State Department of Public Welfare.	Must supervise juvenile court department.	X	X	Must administer or supervise all child welfare activities and must supervise all public or private child-caring agencies, boarding homes, and institutions.
	County or district departments of public welfare.				Such powers and duties as may be prescribed by State department.
	County boards of visitation.				Must visit at least annually all institutions, societies, and associations receiving children and may make recommendations to the juvenile courts.
California	State Department of Social Welfare.	Must investigate, examine, and report on juvenile probation matters.	X	X	Must make rules and regulations for the proper maintenance and care of needy children and for the administration of aid to needy children. Must inquire at any time into the management of any institution receiving State aid or into the management by any county of aid to needy children.
	County boards of supervisors.				Appoint matrons and superintendents of county detention homes, subject to approval of juvenile courts.
	County boards of public welfare.				Must visit quarterly all institutions receiving county funds.
	County probation committees.	Must investigate the case of any ward and report to the court upon request of the juvenile court.			Control and manage internal affairs of county detention homes; must upon request of county supervisors or juvenile court judge examine qualifications and management of any institution other than a State institution caring for juvenile court wards.

State	Agency		X	Powers and duties
Colorado	State Department of Public Welfare.		X	Must administer or supervise all child welfare activities and provide services to county governments relative to county welfare departments and functions.
	Division of public welfare of the executive department.		X	May inspect the institutions under its supervision and control. Must receive complaints against and make investigations of private eleemosynary institutions and report to the Governor concerning such investigations.
	State Bureau of Child and Animal Protection.	May be appointed by the county court as guardian of any dependent, neglected, abandoned, or cruelly treated child under 14 years of age.		No private institution, society, or agency may receive any dependent children until such action has been approved by the bureau. Such institutions are subject to the visitation of the bureau which reports annually to the division of public welfare.
	County or district departments of public welfare.			Administer care and treatment to dependent and handicapped children under rules and regulations of the State department. Must investigate and pass upon all applications for admission to, or discharge from, county institutions caring for indigents.
	County boards of visitors.			Must visit and keep advised of conditions and management of all local, public, or private homes for children or institutions supported in whole or in part by county or municipal taxation; must recommend necessary changes and report annually to the State department.
Connecticut	Commissioner of Welfare.	Must cooperate with juvenile courts and with the approval of the attorney general establish rules for the investigation and keeping of juvenile court records. May represent interests of children in court, and as chief juvenile court probation officer may instruct and direct all probation officers.	X	Has general supervision over the welfare of dependent and neglected children. Supervises the placement of children in foster homes and must correct abuses in all child welfare institutions and agencies. Must cooperate with county commissioners as members of county detention home boards of management and may serve as a member of such boards.
	Public Welfare Council.		X	Must cooperate with, advise, and assist the Commissioner of Welfare in carrying out his duties and may inspect homes and institutions for dependent or neglected children.
	Boards of county commissioners.			As boards of managers they may have supervision of all children committed to county detention homes, and of all children transferred from such homes to a foster home or institution. They may visit such children and remove them for cause.
	Town selectmen[1]	May file petitions with juvenile court alleging children to be uncared for, dependent, or neglected.		As overseers of the poor they must cause all children in almshouses to be removed to a detention home.[2] Must visit and inspect monthly all private foster homes, reporting the reception, death, or removal of any child. Must report monthly to Public Welfare Council.[5]
Delaware	State Board of Charities.		X	Exercises such duties as are necessary, proper, and expedient for the supervision, care, custody, board, and placement of dependent or neglected children. May establish homes and other agencies, contract with approved agencies, and may place children committed to its care in family homes or institutions. Must establish standards of care in boarding homes, supervise and investigate all child-caring agencies and institutions supported in whole or in part by public funds.

See footnotes at end of table.

Table 26.—Major Powers * * * Public Agencies * * * Care of Dependent and Neglected Children Outside of Own Homes or State Institutions—Con.

State	Agencies exercising control or supervision	Relationship to juvenile court	Power to license private agencies and institutions	Power to cooperate with Federal child welfare agencies	Miscellaneous powers and duties relating to dependent and neglected children
Delaware—Contd	Children's Bureau of Delaware.				The objects of the bureau are: to provide effective means for the prevention of cruelty to children; to provide for enforcement of all laws enacted for the protection of children; to provide for children in need of special care; to initiate and execute plans for the general welfare of children; to cooperate with any other charitable organization, commission, or agency engaged in child welfare work; and accept the care and custody of children by direction or commitment of any competent court, judge, or officer.
Florida	State Welfare Board	Juvenile courts and judges must cooperate with the State board.	X		May establish and operate necessary public homes, farms, and schools. Prescribes standards for all child welfare institutions or agencies and may place children in public or private homes and institutions.[4]
	District boards of social welfare.			X	Must carry on activities delegated to it by the State board and is under the supervision and control of the State board.
	County boards of visitors.	Appointed by juvenile court			Control and manage detention homes and visit all institutions, societies, and associations receiving delinquents.
Georgia	State Department of Public Welfare.	Must cooperate with juvenile courts in arranging proper care for dependent or neglected children or those in danger of becoming so, and with parole, supervision, and probation services.	X[5]	X	Supervises all local public and private child-caring agencies and institutions. Has authority to investigate all children in almshouses and arrange for more suitable care. May contract with private institutions for the care of children. Authorized to appoint county or city boards of visitors, to inspect all institutions and agencies, and to report to the State department.
	Boards of county commissioners.				May establish, equip, and maintain temporary detention homes.[6]
	County or district departments of public welfare.				Must pass upon all applications for admission to, and discharge from, county institutions and perform such other welfare activities as may be delegated to them by the State department or the county commissioners.
	Advisory boards.	May be appointed by juvenile courts to advise and cooperate with the courts in matters concerning the welfare of children.			Visit institutions, societies, or associations receiving children, and report annually to the courts relative to the children committed.
Idaho	State Department of Public Assistance.			X	Empowered to administer children's aid programs in which the State or Federal Government participate and to supervise all other forms of charity administered by counties.
	County welfare commissions.	Authorized to cooperate with juvenile courts. County welfare supervisor, if designated by the court, may perform the functions			Administer child welfare services authorized under the supervision of the State department and may cooperate with all public or private agencies or organizations providing services for the protection and care of children.

State	Agency			Powers and duties
Illinois	State Department of Public Welfare.	of a probation officer or agency under the court's supervision.	X[5]	Must inspect and investigate children's homes, finding societies, orphanages, and lying-in-hospitals. Must visit children placed in family homes and pass upon all associations caring for poor children. May, upon complaint, visit and inspect charitable societies, institutions, or associations which appeal for public aid or are supported by trust funds.
	Overseers of the poor[7]			Have care and oversight of all needy persons and must see that they are suitably relieved and supported, subject to such regulations as may be prescribed by the governing board of the county, township, or city.
	Boards of county supervisors or commissioners.			Maintain and manage county poorhouses and poor farms and must pay the tuition of children living in such institutions and attending any district school. They may establish, support, and maintain homes for the temporary care and custody of dependent and delinquent children.
	County bureaus of public welfare.[8]			Carry out such powers, duties, and functions as may be prescribed by the board of county commissioners.
	County departments of public welfare.[9]			Under supervision of the State department, investigate and study problems of assistance, correction, and general welfare within the county. Serve as the agent and executive officer of the State department.
	Boards of visitation	May be appointed by county juvenile court.		The boards must visit annually all institutions to which children are committed and must report their findings to the court and to the State Board of Public Welfare.
Indiana	State Department of Public Welfare.[10]		X[5]	Must supervise and inspect all local public and private child-caring institutions and boarding homes and must supervise care of children in foster family homes or in institutions.
	County or district departments of public welfare.			Under rules and regulations of the State department are responsible for care and treatment of dependent, neglected, and handicapped children. May assume control of dependent or neglected children and with consent of juvenile court commit such children to orphan asylums or otherwise as the court directs. May determine sums to be paid for institutional or foster home care.
Iowa	State Department of Social Welfare.	Must cooperate with all juvenile courts in the State.	X	Plans, supervises, and regulates all child welfare agencies within the State. Designates, inspects, and approves all institutions for the commitment of children. Cooperates with all county welfare agencies, county boards of supervisors, and all other agencies in order to establish and strengthen public and private child welfare services and activities.
	County boards of supervisors.			Must appoint suitable persons to care for destitute orphans who are neglected and without guardians. May establish, supervise, and govern county homes to which children are admitted.[11]
Kansas	State Board of Social Welfare.		X	Must develop, administer, or supervise child welfare activities and services including the care and protection of dependent, neglected, defective, and illegitimate children. Must supervise private agencies and all activities of the county boards of social welfare.
	State Board of Administration.			All private institutions of a charitable nature receiving State aid are subject to visitation, inspection, and supervision by the board which must pass upon

See footnotes at end of table.

Table 26.—Major Powers * * * Public Agencies * * * Care of Dependent and Neglected Children Outside of Own Homes or State Institutions—Con.

State	Agencies exercising control or supervision	Relationship to juvenile court	Power to license private agencies and institutions	Power to cooperate with Federal child welfare agencies	Miscellaneous powers and duties relating to dependent and neglected children
Kansas—Contd	State Board of Administration—Continued.				their fitness annually. All associations of the State which receive dependent and neglected children are subject to the visitation, inspection, and supervision of the board and must file an annual report with the board.
	County boards of social welfare.12				Must provide aid, assistance, and service on the basis of need under rules and regulations of the State board. May place and supervise children in homes.
	Boards of county commissioners.				In counties with population of 53,000 or more, may establish county parental homes for dependent children. In counties of 20,000 or more, may establish with approval of electors, county detention homes or juvenile farms for the care of children who are in the custody of the juvenile court.
	Juvenile courts				Supervise county detention homes and juvenile farms.
Kentucky	State Department of Welfare (division of child welfare).	Must discover dependent and neglected children and secure the benefits of the law for them.	X	X	Empowered to administer and supervise all child welfare activities including the inspection of all public and private child-caring agencies; must supervise the work and methods of all institutions, associations, or societies receiving State aid; may provide care for children committed to it.
	County children's bureau	Serves as probation or parole officer if appointed by juvenile court or county judge.			Makes such investigations and performs such services pertaining to children as may be requested by the fiscal court of county. Assists the child welfare division of the State department and performs such services as may be required by it.
	Board of Louisville and Jefferson County Children's Home.	Must file petition in the county court whenever it has probable cause to believe that a boy under 17 years of age or a girl under 18 is delinquent, dependent, or neglected.			Charged with custody, care, training, and education of children committed to home. Must maintain schools and may bind out and apprentice children or place them in homes.
	County fiscal courts.--				May establish and maintain county detention schools in second class counties.
	Advisory board of the county court, juvenile session.				These boards may be appointed by the county judge of each county and must visit at least annually all institutions or societies receiving children committed by order of the juvenile court. The board must advise and cooperate with the court and recommend needful measures.
Louisiana	State Department of Public Welfare (bureau of child welfare).			X	Supervises parish welfare departments.
	Parish or district boards of public welfare.13	If appointed by court must perform function of probation officer or agent of the court in any welfare matters.			Charged with care and treatment of dependent, neglected, delinquent, and handicapped children, and such other welfare activities as may be delegated to them by the State department.

State	Agency			
Maine	State Board of Charities and Corrections.	Must investigate petitions filed for adoption of children and report findings to juvenile court.		Supervises State, parochial, and municipal charitable institutions. Has visitorial powers over private orphan asylums, hospitals, and charitable institutions. Does not exercise executive or administrative power.
	Parish police juries.			May contract for the care of children (held pending juvenile court proceedings) with any person, association, or institution possessing proper facilities.
	State Department of Health and Welfare.		X[5]	Must investigate and inspect the condition and management of all institutions and agencies of a charitable or correctional nature which derive any support from public funds. May provide care for children.
	Municipal boards of child welfare (ex officio overseers of the poor).	May make complaints concerning dependent and neglected children.		Must investigate all cases of cruel or injurious treatment of children. Overseers may place children in almshouses.
Maryland	Board of State Aid and Charities.		X	Must investigate, study, and consider the whole system of public and private institutions, organizations, and agencies of charitable nature. Must establish rules and regulations covering institutions, agencies, and societies having the care of 1 or more minors. May establish county welfare boards or designate existing agencies or organizations as its agents.[14]
	County welfare boards[14] and Department of Welfare of Baltimore City.	Render probation services to courts exercising jurisdiction over minors.		Charged with the care of dependent, neglected, and delinquent children. Under the supervision of the State board.
Massachusetts	State Department of Public Welfare.	Department must be advised by the court of all complaints filed alleging dependency or neglect of children.	X	Must receive and care for illegitimate children under 2 years of age surrendered by mother for adoption. Receives children committed to it by juvenile court and may provide for maintenance of dependent children under 21 years of age on application of parent, guardian, friend, or local board of public welfare. Must visit annually all minor children, all public lodging houses, and all charitable corporations which report annually to the department with the consent or at the request of such corporations. Passes upon fitness of child-caring agencies to serve as guardians of children.
	Town boards of public welfare.[15]			Must place children over 2 years of age in their charge in family homes or asylums to be supported by town until otherwise cared for. May commit any indigent or neglected infant without settlement to the custody of the State department. Must visit all children placed at least once every 3 months.
Michigan	State Welfare Commission.		X	Has general supervision of pauper and reformatory institutions of the State and counties. Empowered to make all necessary rules and regulations to promote the best interests of children. May visit and examine all licensed child-caring agencies.
	County welfare agents.	Must investigate cases involving children when referred to them by the probate court (juvenile division).		Are appointed for the care of juvenile offenders and dependent children. Must visit such children at least annually and report to the State Welfare Commission.
	County boards of supervisors (superintendents of the poor).			A county board may enter into an agreement, for a period not to exceed 1 year, with agencies and institutions approved by the State Welfare Commission for the care of poor, sick, distressed, abandoned, needy, or crippled children of the county. May also appropriate money to subsidize private charitable institutions or agencies.

See footnotes at end of table.

Table 26.—Major Powers * * * Public Agencies * * * Care of Dependent and Neglected Children Outside of Own Homes or State Institutions—Con.

State	Agencies exercising control or supervision	Relationship to juvenile court	Power to license private agencies and institutions	Power to cooperate with Federal child welfare agencies	Miscellaneous powers and duties relating to dependent and neglected children
Minnesota	State Board of Control	Must cooperate with juvenile courts in promoting enforcement of all laws for the protection of defective, illegitimate, dependent, and neglected children.	X	X	Must cooperate with public or private child-helping and child-placing agencies and is empowered to take initiative when adequate provision has not been made for defective, illegitimate, dependent, and neglected children. Receives children committed to it by courts and has powers of legal guardianship over such children and over children committed to institutions under its control. Prescribes rules and regulations for management of infants' homes and may visit and investigate conditions of all children for whom homes have been found by an institution.
	County or city welfare boards.				Charged with the administration of all forms of public assistance and welfare. Perform such duties as may be required by law or by the State Board of Control with regard to the enforcement of all laws for the protection of children.
	Boards of county commissioners or city councils.				Must secure admission to the State Public School or provide homes for minors who become public charges.
Mississippi	State Department of Public Welfare.		X		Must administer or supervise all public child welfare services; the inspection of all private child-caring agencies, institutions, and boarding homes; supervise the care of dependent and neglected children in foster homes or in institutions, especially children placed for adoption or those of illegitimate birth. The board must supervise the importation of children.
	County departments of public welfare.				May assume responsibility for the care and support of dependent children needing public care away from their homes, and may place such children in proper institutions or private homes, and may cooperate with public or private authorities in the placing of such children in proper institutions or suitable private homes. The necessary maintenance is to be provided for children in need of care in foster homes, under circumstances which do not require that such children become wards of the court, from public funds made available for welfare services.
	County boards of supervisors.				May bind out poor orphans and children of parents too poor to support them, may apprentice children, or commit them to an orphan asylum or any organization engaged in caring for poor and dependent children.
Missouri	State Social Security Commission.[16]	Supervises juvenile probation under the direction of but not in derogation of juvenile courts' orders.	X	X	Empowered to administer or supervise all child welfare activities. Supervises child-caring agencies and institutions except those conducted by well-known religious orders. Must establish local offices and may contract with local subdivisions.
	City boards of social welfare.[17]				Have exclusive power to make provisions for relief, maintenance, and support of all indigent persons within the county and city or cities.
	St. Louis Board of Children's Guardians.				May receive upon commitment by competent court defective or dependent children for such care and treatment as board may determine. May place children in any

State	Agency			
	County boards of visitors.			public institution in the State or with a suitable family. Empowered to manage any public institution established by the city for the care and maintenance of children.
Montana	State Department of Public Welfare.	X		Must visit and inspect at least once every 3 months all corrective institutions supported in whole or in part by county or municipal taxation or institutions which are under county or municipal control. Report to county courts and must annually report to State Social Security Commission.
	County departments of public welfare.			Must administer or supervise all child welfare activities except those administered by State Board of Health; supervises agencies and institutions caring for dependent, delinquent, or handicapped children, and supervises the care of such children in foster family homes.
	Boards of county commissioners.[18]			Charged with local administration of all child protection and welfare activities, subject to rules and regulations of the State department.
	County juvenile improvement committees.		Must be appointed by judge of juvenile court in every county.	Must provide and maintain county detention homes for dependent, neglected, or delinquent children.
Nebraska	State Board of Control.	X		Perform such duties as the court may designate and supervise county detention homes where established. Designated as sole State agency to supervise child welfare activities. Must co-operate with and coordinate all activities of the State institutions, department of health, the courts, county boards, charities, and all other organizations, societies, and agencies promoting child welfare and health. Vested with sole and exclusive custody of all minors under 18 years of age committed to it by the juvenile courts. May place such children in family homes or institutions.
	County child welfare boards.		Must investigate alleged neglected or abandoned children, and if necessary, bring cases before juvenile courts.	Under supervision of the State board. Must assume charge of and provide for any destitute child who cannot be properly cared for in its home. Must care for any child discharged to its care by the juvenile court, or pending action by the court. Must cooperate with all local, public, and private organizations, agencies, and institutions concerned with the general welfare of children in the county.
Nevada	State Welfare Department.	X		Charged with the supervision of all child welfare services. Must provide supervisory or advisory services to county governments.
	Boards of county commissioners.			Must apprentice minors who become county charges because of death of parents or the inability or refusal of parents to provide for them. May establish county detention homes.
	County probation committees.		May be required by the court to examine into the qualifications and management of any societies, associations, and corporations other than a State institution receiving or applying for any child.	Control and manage the county detention homes.
New Hampshire	State Department of Public Welfare.	X		Must develop and administer State responsibilities for child welfare and supervise the administration of same by county and town officials, or administer such child

See footnotes at end of table.

Table 26.—Major Powers * * * Public Agencies * * * Care of Dependent and Neglected Children Outside of Own Homes or State Institutions—Con.

State	Agencies exercising control or supervision	Relationship to juvenile court	Power to license private agencies and institutions	Power to cooperate with Federal child welfare agencies	Miscellaneous powers and duties relating to dependent and neglected children
New Hampshire—Con.	State Department of Public Welfare—Continued.				welfare activities directly.[19] Must supervise all private institutions and boarding homes providing services or care to neglected, delinquent, defective, or dependent children.
	Boards of county commissioners and town overseers of the poor.				Must procure the support of dependent and neglected children at orphan asylums, homes, or with private families. Must find permanent homes and make contracts for their education and support during minority.
New Jersey	Board of Control of State Department of Institutions and Agencies.			X	Has powers of visitation and inspection of all county and city places of detention, workhouses, hospitals, poor farms, almshouses, privately maintained institutions, and noninstitutional agencies conducted for the benefit of defective, dependent, or convalescent children. Has supervision over all county, municipal, public, or private institutions receiving State funds. May apply for court order to rectify unsatisfactory conditions. Must cooperate with county welfare boards in extending and strengthening public service for the protection and care of homeless, dependent, and neglected children.
	Board of Control of State Department of Institutions and Agencies (State Board of Children's Guardians).	Juvenile court serves a copy of any petition filed with it concerning a dependent or neglected child to the State Board of Children's Guardians.			Has care and supervision of all dependent and neglected children who are public charges. Assumes full guardianship of children committed to it by the courts.
	County boards of chosen freeholders.	Juvenile court serves a copy of any petition filed with it concerning a dependent or neglected child to the county board of chosen freeholders.			May establish and maintain almshouses, welfare houses, and county detention homes for dependent and neglected children, or with the consent of the juvenile court may negotiate with a society or institution to care for such children. May also bind out children to learn a trade or business.[20]
	County welfare boards, municipal assistance boards, or overseers of the poor.				Responsible for relief of the poor in respective subdivisions. County director of welfare may apply to the juvenile and domestic relations court for an order committing a child to an incorporated child-caring agency in the county.[20]
New Mexico	State Department of Public Welfare.			X	Must administer and supervise all child welfare activities. Must inspect and require reports from all private institutions, boarding homes, and agencies providing assistance, care, or other direct services to children.
	County or district offices of State Department of Public Welfare.				Must be established by the department to serve as its agents with powers and duties as may be prescribed by the State department.
New York	State Department of Social Welfare.	Must cooperate with all children's courts and bring cases involving child welfare before such courts.	(5)	X	Must visit, inspect, and supervise city and county boards of child welfare and/or commissioners of public welfare. May visit, inspect, and supervise all public and private institutions of a charitable, eleemosynary, reformatory, or correctional character and may order that unsatisfactory conditions be remedied.[21]

State	Administrative agency			Functions
North Carolina	Local public welfare officials.[22]	Must render assistance and cooperation to children's courts. May bring cases before the courts involving neglected children.		Must assist and cooperate with public and private welfare agencies. Are responsible for the welfare of children who are in need of public care, support, and protection in so far as consistent with the jurisdiction of children's courts and exclusive of children under the care of local boards of child welfare, within whose jurisdiction come dependent children living in their own homes or in the homes of specified relatives. These welfare officials must attempt to maintain family units but may provide relief and care in boarding homes, public or private homes, institutions, or hospitals.[23] Children born out of wedlock must be placed in institutions or in family boarding homes.
	State Board of Charities and Public Welfare.		X	Must investigate and supervise the whole system of charitable institutions in the State. Must study and promote the welfare of or provide for the placing and supervision of dependent and defective children. Must inspect and make reports on private orphanages, institutions, maternity homes, and persons or organizations receiving and placing children, and must require annual reports from such organizations.
	County boards of charities and public welfare. Boards of county commissioners.			Oversee children in the county and those placed in the county by the State board. Superintendent of public welfare reports to the State board. May provide for the establishment and maintenance of homes for indigent children with the approval of the State board. May establish public hospitals and homes for indigent orphans. Exercise general supervision over county charitable institutions.
North Dakota	State Public Welfare Board.[24]		X	Has the power and duty to provide for the welfare of dependent and neglected children and to provide for the placing and supervision of such children subject to the control of any court having jurisdiction.
	County welfare boards.	Must cooperate with juvenile courts.[25]		Must supervise and direct all relief and welfare activities conducted by the counties and those financed by State board funds. Must cooperate with all licensed private agencies and coordinate all public and private activities in behalf of children.
	Board of county commissioners.			May bind out poor children, see that they are properly treated, and take means of redress in case of maltreatment.
	County boards of visitors and children's guardians.	Must present cases involving children to the courts when other agencies have failed to do so.		Must annually visit all institutions, societies, associations, and persons receiving children. Must investigate into the conditions of dependent and neglected children within the county. Must investigate all applications for release of children from guardianship or apprenticeship.
Ohio	State Department of Public Welfare (division of public assistance).		X[5]	Must investigate public and private State benevolent and correctional institutions, county and municipal children's homes and infirmaries, and all institutions which receive and care for children. Must annually pass upon the fitness of all institutions or associations receiving or placing children. Must receive and exercise exclusive guardianship over wards committed to it by juvenile courts or by children's homes or institutions with the consent of the court, and must find suitable homes for such children, visit them semiannually, and provide them with needed clothing and personal necessities.
	Boards of county commissioners.	Must cooperate with juvenile courts.		Empowered, with the approval of the director of the State Department of Public Welfare, to establish county children's homes and provide for their upkeep and

See footnotes at end of table.

Table 26.—Major Powers * * * Public Agencies * * * Care of Dependent and Neglected Children Outside of Own Homes or State Institutions—Con.

State	Agencies exercising control or supervision	Relationship to juvenile court	Power to license private agencies and institutions	Power to cooperate with Federal child welfare agencies	Miscellaneous powers and duties relating to dependent and neglected children
Ohio—Continued	Boards of county commissioners—Continued.				the care of their inmates. May contract for care with other counties, institutions, or agencies. Upon the advice and recommendation of the county juvenile court judge, the county commissioners must provide a detention home for children.
	Boards of trustees of county children's homes.26	Must cooperate with juvenile courts.			Must receive for care and treatment children who are committed by juvenile courts, residents of the county, or children committed under contract from other counties because of orphanage, neglect, or inability of parents to provide for them. Must place eligible children with private families and for this purpose appoint a visiting agent or work through the agency of the division of public assistance in the State Department of Public Welfare. These boards report to the county commissioners.
	Boards of county visitors.				Must visit and inspect at least quarterly all charitable and correctional institutions supported in whole or in part by county or municipal taxation. Must recommend to the county commissioners necessary changes and additional provisions.
	Probation department of the juvenile court.				Supervises children placed in private homes.
Oklahoma	State Public Welfare Commission.			X	May establish a division for the protection and care of homeless, dependent, and neglected children, and provide an adequate child welfare service.
	State Board of Public Affairs.				May contract for the care of orphans and destitute and delinquent minors in institutions, not State owned or operated, devoted to the care of such children. May appoint placement officers who must cooperate with all public and private agencies caring for children, find homes for children in institutions, and visit and supervise such homes.
	State Commissioner of Charities and Corrections.		X		Empowered to investigate the entire system of public charities. Must inspect and examine all orphanages, home-finding societies, children's aid agencies, and all other similar organizations. The commissioner must inspect all city and county institutions and make written recommendations to the mayor, city council, and board of county commissioners.
	Boards of county commissioners.27				May establish county homes for the care of dependent and neglected children.28
Oregon	State Child Welfare Commission.	May require information regarding the commitment of any child. Approves appointment of all probation officers.	X		Must inspect and supervise all public or private child-caring agencies or societies. Must report and have corrected any unsatisfactory conditions and advise officers of agencies and institutions relative to the approved methods of child-care, records, etc. Requires annual reports from all public or private child-caring agencies and institutions.
	State Relief Committee.			X	Empowered to make all necessary rules and regulations for administering child welfare services. Must cooperate with the counties in furnishing relief and pay

State	Agency		Duties
	County relief committees		not less than % of the total cost of relief including institutional care of needy persons; must supervise the expenditure of all such funds (except State funds made available for the care of children in State institutions under the supervision of the State Board of Control). May cooperate with all agencies providing for the protection and care of homeless, dependent, or neglected children.
	County boards of visitors. May be appointed by county judge to constitute a board of visitation.		Charged with the administration of all assistance and relief to children in the county under the control and supervision of the State Relief Committee. Must report to the court the condition of children received by or in charge of associations and institutions.
Pennsylvania	State Department of Welfare.		Has supervision over all children's institutions, boarding homes licensed by the State, and all maternity homes and hospitals. Must make and enforce rules and regulations for the visitation, inspection, and examination of all such institutions. May appoint local boards of visitors for such institutions. Must supervise the importation and deportation of children. May issue requisitions to pay for the care of dependent and defective children in homes or institutions, and for the placement of dependent children through child-caring agencies. Incorporation of any institution to maintain indigents subject to approval of department.
	County institution districts (county commissioners) and city institutions districts (city departments of public welfare).		Local authorities of any such district, under rules, regulations, and standards established by State Department of Welfare must care for any dependent having settlement in the county or city who is not otherwise cared for; must place in foster homes, institutions, or homes for children, all dependent children who are in or committed to their charge, and whose placement and care are not otherwise provided for; and must contract with other local authorities for the care of dependents. County commissioners may establish and maintain homes and schools for the care, training, and education of children from 2 to 16 years of age.
Rhode Island	State Department of Public Welfare. Must cooperate with the juvenile courts in the enforcement of laws for the protection of children.	X	Must promote the enforcement of all laws for the protection of defective, dependent, and neglected children and children born out of wedlock. Must cooperate with all public and private child-helping and child-placing agencies and must take the initiative in matters involving their interests where adequate legal provision has not been made. Any person placing a child in a foster home must notify the department, which must investigate and place the child elsewhere if necessary. Receives annual reports from all organizations admitting, caring for, or placing children in homes.
	Bureau of Children's Care, Division of Social Security of the State Department of Public Welfare.	X	In accordance with rules of the State department may receive such children of sound mind as may be declared vagrant, truant, neglected, or dependent on the public for support. May place children in family homes on condition that they be properly educated and may pay an agreed amount for their support. May also place children in public or private institutions. Must supervise all children so placed and may remove them for cause.
	Town councils		May send minors to the State Home and School upon such terms as may be prescribed by the State department.

See footnotes at end of table.

Table 26.—Major Powers * * * Public Agencies * * * Care of Dependent and Neglected Children Outside of Own Homes or State Institutions—Con.

State	Agencies exercising control or supervision	Relationship to juvenile court	Power to license private agencies and institutions	Power to cooperate with Federal child welfare agencies	Miscellaneous powers and duties relating to dependent and neglected children
South Carolina	State Department of Public Welfare.		(5)	X	Must promote the unified development of welfare activities and agencies of the State and local governments so that each agency and governmental institution may function as an integral part of a general system. Empowered to investigate the administration and affairs of any institution or agency, public or private.
	County departments of public welfare.			X	Must serve as agents of the State department in performance of such functions as may be delegated to them, provide for the enforcement of all laws for the protection and welfare of minors, and promote their health, education, and general welfare.
	State Children's Bureau.				Designated guardian of all destitute, dependent, or neglected children committed to its care, and must place them in private homes and supervise them until they reach 18 years of age or until legally adopted. Must act as a bureau of investigation and may be used by State institutions to investigate all applications for admission or dismissal of children.
	Boards of county commissioners.				Have general supervision of paupers, must supply necessary buildings for county poor, and may bind out children.
	County advisory boards to juvenile courts.	Must advise and cooperate with the court and probation officer in all matters concerning the welfare of children.			Must visit all private and public institutions in which children are placed or committed, report to the judge and make such recommendations as are deemed necessary, and control and manage the county detention homes.
South Dakota	State Department of Social Security (division of child welfare).				Must develop satisfactory standards of care in public agencies and private organizations caring for dependent, neglected, or handicapped children, and must further the development of local public service for children through consultation and demonstration services. Must assist in the enforcement of all laws relative to the welfare of children, and take the initiative in securing the enforcement of all such laws where adequate provision has not been made.
	County child welfare boards.			X	Must act in a general advisory capacity to county and municipal authorities in dealing with questions of dependency and social conditions. Must perform such duties as may be required by State Department of Social Security through the division of child welfare.
	State Board of Charities and Corrections.				All institutions receiving children are subject to the visitation, inspection, and supervision of the board, which must also visit and inspect all private hospitals, reformatory homes, houses of detention, orphan homes, and boarding schools. The board must hear and receive complaints from inmates regarding their health and treatment.
Tennessee	Department of Institutions and Public Welfare.		X	X	Must administer or supervise all public child welfare services, including inspection of all private child-caring agencies and the supervision and inspection of all local public child-caring agencies, institutions, and boarding homes.

State	Agency		Functions
Texas	County courts[29]		Juvenile court commitments to State institutions must be approved by the division of public welfare, which may recommend type of care to be given children adjudged dependent and neglected.
	State Board of Control (division of public welfare).[30]	X	Must supervise the care of dependent and neglected children in foster family homes or institutions, especially children placed for adoption or those of illegitimate birth. May bind out as apprentices suitable orphans or children of any person unable to provide for their support. May establish institutions for neglected children. Must promote the enforcement of all laws for the protection of children. Must visit and inspect all agencies which receive State funds and care for children.[31] Supervises county child welfare boards.
	County commissioners' courts.		Responsible for the support of the poor, and may appoint child welfare boards to perform such duties as may be required by the commissioners or the State Board of Control. May establish detention homes and parental schools for dependent and delinquent juveniles.
	County child welfare boards.[30]		Must work jointly with county commissioners and State Board of Control for the care and protection of dependent and neglected children in the several counties.
Utah	State Department of Public Welfare.	X	Must promote the enforcement of all laws for the protection of children and cooperate with all licensed public or private child welfare agencies and institutions. Must take the initiative in the interests of children where adequate provision has not been made. All children's aid societies, except the State Industrial School, must file annual reports with the commission.
	Juvenile court and probation commission.		Must cooperate with juvenile courts in enforcement of laws for the protection of children. Has general control and supervision over the juvenile courts and probation officers.
	County or district departments of public welfare. Boards of county commissioners.		Must administer under the supervision of the State Department of Public Welfare all forms of public assistance, including the care of dependent, neglected, and handicapped children. Have visitation and inspection power over all children's aid societies or institutions except the State Industrial School. May erect and maintain such institutions as may be necessary to provide for the dependent poor. Authorized to cooperate with State, county, and district boards of public welfare in all State and local welfare activities.
Vermont	State Department of Public Welfare.	X	Has power of visitation over all institutions which are chartered by the State for the care of dependent children and which solicit public support. Supervises and controls such dependent and neglected children as it may take under its care or as may be committed to it by juvenile courts. May provide medical or surgical care for such children and must place them in foster homes. If such homes cannot be found, such children may be placed in institutions incorporated to receive them. Must visit such children at least semimonthly and may remove them from improper surroundings.
	Local overseers or supervisors of the poor.		Responsible for the relief of poor persons and must report all cases of dependent and neglected children to the commissioner of public welfare.

See footnotes at end of table.

Table 26.—Major Powers * * * Public Agencies * * * Care of Dependent and Neglected Children Outside of Own Homes or State Institutions—Con.

State	Agencies exercising control or supervision	Relationship to juvenile court	Power to license private agencies and institutions	Power to cooperate with Federal child welfare agencies	Miscellaneous powers and duties relating to dependent and neglected children
Virginia	State Board of Public Welfare (children's bureau).		X	X	Must visit and inspect annually (or more often) all State, county, municipal, and private institutions and agencies caring for children. Has general supervision of the interests and welfare of children. Must recommend measures to these agencies for improving the conditions and welfare of children. May receive children committed to it by the courts. May establish homes for them or make arrangements for their care with persons, institutions, or agencies.
	County or city boards of public welfare.	Must cooperate with juvenile and domestic relations courts. Superintendent of public welfare must act as chief probation officer for the county or city.			The superintendent of the local board, under the direction of the State Board of Public Welfare, has supervision of dependent children placed in the county or city by the board. Must act as agent of the State board for any of its work in the county or city. Must keep advised of the conditions and management of all charitable institutions in the county or city and is empowered to inspect them.
Washington	State Department of Social Security (division for children).		X[32]	X	Empowered to fix State-wide uniform standards for all types of public assistance[33] and to effect uniform observance of these standards. Must inspect, supervise, and provide rules and regulations for the operation and government of all child-caring agencies whether or not incorporated.[34]
	Boards of county commissioners.				Must act as the single administrative agency of the county through which all the categories of public assistance[33] must be administered; empowered to act in such capacity as the agent of the State Department of Social Security. Must in cooperation with the State department appoint an advisory committee experienced in child welfare.
West Virginia	State Department of Public Assistance.	May present petition to juvenile court in any county where it believes a child is neglected.	X[35]	X	The department, with the assistance of the county public assistance councils, administers the child welfare services of the State. Must supervise and annually visit and inspect children's institutions and organizations receiving children for the purpose of caring, training, or placing. Must recommend measures to correct unsatisfactory conditions to such institutions or organizations.
	County public assistance councils.	County directors are ex officio probation officers of the juvenile court.			Designated as the agency to administer public assistance[35] activities in the county. Must cooperate with private charitable organizations in the county.
	County courts.				May establish, equip, and maintain county detention homes for neglected children. These homes are to be known as children's shelters and are to be inspected frequently.
Wisconsin	State Board of Control (juvenile department).	Must cooperate with juvenile courts in the enforcement of all laws which protect children.	X		Must promote the enforcement of all laws for the protection of defective, illegitimate, dependent, or delinquent children except laws whose administration is vested in some other State agency). Must cooperate with all public and private licensed child welfare agencies and institutions and, upon the designation of the court, act as trustee of funds paid for the support of any child. Must

Jurisdiction	Agency		Functions
	County boards of supervisors.		supervise all county and municipal charitable and reformatory institutions, all child welfare agencies, and the placement of children in foster homes.
	County boards of visitation.	May be appointed by juvenile court judge.	May establish such agencies and employ such personnel as necessary for the social welfare and protection of dependent, neglected, and defective children. Must make provision for the temporary detention of children in a detention home conducted as an agency of the juvenile court. Must regularly visit all institutions, societies, and associations receiving children and report to the court. Must annually report on condition of same to State Board of Control.
Wyoming	State Department of Public Welfare.	X	Must provide organization, supervision, and other services to the county departments for the efficient administration of welfare functions. Must make rules, regulations, and orders necessary to carry out these functions, which are binding upon the counties.
	County departments of public welfare.		Perform such welfare functions as may be imposed by law or designated by the State Department of Public Welfare. Must provide care for needy children in private homes when proper care cannot be provided in their own homes, and render such assistance as is needed to enable children of the respective counties to take full advantage of the laws in behalf of dependent, neglected, and defective children. Must initiate, promote, and assist in enforcement of all laws designated for the protection of children.
	State Board of Charities and Reform.		Receives annual reports from each public or private child-caring agency or institution in the State. Has jurisdiction of all orphan and dependent children not otherwise provided for. Must apply to the courts for appointment as guardian of all children coming into its care and custody, and may consent to the adoption of such children.
Alaska	Territorial Department of Public Welfare.	X	Has jurisdiction of juveniles and provides for the keeping of records of all juveniles and for the payment of bills for their care or in connection with commitments.
	Boards of children's guardians.[36]		The boards are legal guardians of all children committed to their control. May provide for the care, maintenance, and education of such children and may commit them to the care and custody of some person, association, or institution and pay a sum not exceeding $25 per month for their care and maintenance. May bind out children, apprentice them, or give them in adoption to foster parents. All persons, institutions, or associations receiving children are subject to the supervision of the boards. A record of each commitment must be furnished the Territorial Department of Public Welfare and a semimonthly report must be made to the Governor and the department.
District of Columbia.	Commissioners		Must visit and investigate the management of all charitable institutions for which appropriations are made; must, by police force, aid the Washington Humane Society in the enforcement of all laws relating to or affecting the protection of children. Appoint the Board of Public Welfare.
	Board of Public Welfare..	Receives children committed to it by juvenile court.	Must have the legal guardianship, care, and supervision of children committed to it by the juvenile court.[37] May bind out or apprentice such children, give them in adoption to foster parents, make provision for their care and treatment in

See footnotes at end of table.

Table 26.—Major Powers * * * Public Agencies * * * Care of Dependent and Neglected Children Outside of Own Homes or State Institutions—Con.

State	Agencies exercising control or supervision	Relationship to juvenile court	Power to license private agencies and institutions	Power to cooperate with Federal child welfare agencies	Miscellaneous powers and duties relating to dependent and neglected children
District of Columbia—Cond.	Board of Public Welfare—Continued.	Receives children committed to it by juvenile court—Continued.			private homes or in public or private institutions at rates approved by the Commissioners. May accept voluntary aid in the placement and supervision of children. Maintains general supervision over all charitable, eleemosynary, correctional, or reformatory institutions supported by appropriation.
Hawaii	Territorial Board of Public Welfare.		X		Must administer child welfare activities, and must cooperate with public or private authorities in placing dependent children in suitable institutions or private homes. Must set standards of conditions, management, and competence necessary for an organization or institution having care and custody of dependent children. May review any decision of the county public welfare commissions.
	County public welfare commissions.			X	Must cooperate with the Territorial Board of Public Welfare in carrying out the program of child welfare service, subject to the rules, regulations, and administrative supervision of the board.

X indicates that the provision applies without limitation in a given State.

1 Powers and duties of selectmen are performed by a board of public welfare commissioners in the town of Manchester.

2 No child from 4 to 18 years of age may be placed in an almshouse.

3 Persons caring for more than 2 children under 10 years of age must report to the town selectmen within 3 days from the time of reception, death, or removal of child.

4 Unless committed to the board by a court, the consent of the child's parents is necessary before a child may be taken from its parents or guardians.

5 State department also has the power to approve proposed incorporations of charitable agencies.

6 When suitable arrangements with any society or association cannot be made by the judge of the juvenile court.

7 A bureau of public welfare has been created in Cook County to consolidate "all social welfare functions." It would appear that the functions of the overseers in Cook County might be transferred to such bureau although the law does not so specifically provide.

8 Purpose of the act creating this bureau is stated as follows: "* * * to consolidate in a single department or bureau of a county all branches of investigation, powers, functions, and duties, included in the term 'Social Service Functions,' i.e., dependent children in cases of pure dependency where the action of a court of record is not invoked; in * * * feeble-minded persons; deaf and blind children; paupers; adoption of children; insane persons; illegitimate children; minors' wards and guardians; cases involving 'social, economic, and home conditions, nonsupport, desertion and abandonment, where the aid of a county or jurisdiction of a court of record is invoked; aid, food, clothing and medical attention or other relief of all persons in the county applying for or in need of it."

22 For the purpose of administration of public relief and care, the State is divided into city and county public welfare districts. The term local public welfare officials includes county commissioners of public welfare, city commissioners of public welfare, town public welfare officers, and city public welfare officers.

23 No public welfare official may send a child under the age of 16 years to a public home, except that children under 2 years of age may be cared for with their mothers in a public home but must be removed when the children reach the age of 2.

24 Since powers and duties of the State Public Welfare Board might conflict with those vested by law in the State Board of Administration, the child welfare duties of both agencies have been consolidated and are administered by 1 supervisor. The State Board of Administration supervises and regulates maternity hospitals and lying-in institutions caring for or placing children. It also investigates homes for the placement of children, withdraws children from undesirable homes, and accepts guardianship of children committed to it by courts of competent jurisdiction. The board of administration also cooperates with the juvenile courts; investigates petitions for adoption, and secures the enforcement of all laws relating to children.

25 This provision does not give county boards the authority to make child placements.

26 Boards of county commissioners, with the approval of the division of public assistance of the State Department of Public Welfare, may appoint county child welfare boards. The boards, where existing, have the same powers and duties relative to dependent and neglected children as are given the trustees of the county children's home.

27 County boards of commissioners are ex officio county assistance boards operating under the supervision of the State Department of Public Welfare.

28 Applies only in counties with a population from 24,800 to 25,100 and/or 75,000 or more.

[9] Established in counties with a population less than 500,000.

[10] Department acts through children's division.

[11] Children in county homes must attend the district schools. In counties having 40,000 population or more, county boards must provide and maintain county detention homes and schools for dependent, neglected, and delinquent children.

[12] Composed of boards of county commissioners.

[13] In New Orleans Parish welfare functions are administered through the department of public safety, subdivision of charity and relief.

[14] The county trustees of the poor or commissioners (where no county welfare board exists) must place all poor children in their charge in some educational institution or home for children. These children must be visited semiannually. No child from 3 to 16 years of age may be retained in any county home for a period longer than 90 days.

[15] In Boston the institutions department has the powers and duties conferred upon the local boards of public welfare concerning aid to children.

[16] Establishes county offices and advisory county commissions.

[17] Created in all counties containing cities with a population from 75,000 to 150,000. In other counties county courts perform these welfare functions.

[18] County boards of public welfare consists of boards of county commissioners, ex officio.

[19] Child welfare activities must include the protection and care of homeless, dependent, and neglected children, and children in danger of becoming delinquent; cooperation with State and other institutions for children, including investigation and follow-up services; services and care of children in foster homes; and all other child welfare activities authorized by law.

[20] In the case of a commitment or admission of an infant to any almshouse or welfare house, a record of this action must be filed with the State Board of Children's Guardians.

[21] Order must be approved by a justice of the Supreme Court. The law provides that the powers and duties of the State Board of Social Welfare shall be regulatory and advisory and not administrative or executive. However, the State department is charged with the administration of all forms of public welfare work for which the State is responsible, the supervision of all public welfare work administered by any local unit of government, and the regulation of financial assistance granted by the State in connection with such work.

[29] The governing bodies of cities and towns may also establish such institutions.

[30] The State board may establish local units of administration to serve as its agents. Local boards of public welfare may be established to serve in an advisory capacity with these units. As soon as such boards are appointed, county child welfare boards are dissolved and cease to function.

[31] By statute all children in State or local public institutions not wards of any court are made wards of the State and their exclusive possession and custody is vested in the State Board of Control.

[32] Through the division for children in the department, the director must examine and approve all articles of incorporation for agencies, societies, associations, or institutions organized for the care of dependent children.

[33] The term *public assistance* includes care of dependent children away from their own homes.

[34] It is unlawful for any firm, society, association or corporation, or any person (except the parents) to assume the permanent care, custody, or control of any child under the age of majority unless authorized to do so by the Superior Court. It is unlawful without the written approval of the Superior Court for any person in any way to relinquish or transfer to another person, firm, society, or corporation, the permanent care, custody, or control of any child under the age of majority and any such relinquishment or transfer is void.

[35] The department must examine and approve the proposed articles of incorporation for a children's institution or organization.

[36] Established in each judicial division in the Territory.

[37] The following classes of children are designated by the juvenile court of the District as being under the care and supervision of the board: children committed by a court because of subjection to cruel treatment; children wilfully abused or neglected; any child under 17 years of age found in a house of ill-fame; all children who are destitute of suitable homes and adequate means of earning an honest living; all children abandoned by their parents; all children of habitually drunken, vicious, or unfit parents; all children habitually begging on the streets or from door to door; all children kept in vicious or immoral associations; and all children known by their language or life to be vicious or incorrigible.

Table 27.—Governmental Unit Responsible for Financing Specified Types of Care for Dependent and Neglected Children

State	Care in State institution		Care in local institution		Care by private agency or institution	
	State	Local	State	Local	State	Local
Alabama	X	X			X	X.
Arizona				X	X	X.
Arkansas					X	
California	X	X	X	X	X	X.
Colorado	X			X	X	X.
Connecticut				X		X.
Delaware	X	X			X	
Florida			X	X	X	X.
Georgia				X	X	X.
Idaho					X	X.
Illinois	X			X	X	X.
Indiana	X	X	X	X	X	X.
Iowa	X			X		X.
Kansas	X		X	X	X	X.
Kentucky				X	X	X.
Louisiana	X					X.
Maine	X			X	X	X.
Maryland	X			X	X	X.
Massachusetts					X	X.
Michigan	X	X				X.
Minnesota	X				X	X.
Mississippi	X	X			X	X.
Missouri	X			X		X.
Montana	X			X		X.
Nebraska	X				X	X.
Nevada	X	X		X	X	X.
New Hampshire					X	X.
New Jersey				X	X	X.
New Mexico					X	X.
New York	X			X	X	X.
North Carolina				X	X	X.
North Dakota					X	X.
Ohio	X			X	X	X.
Oklahoma	X		X	X	X	X.
Oregon					X	X.
Pennsylvania	X		X		X	X.
Rhode Island	X	X			X	X.
South Carolina	X			X	X	X.
South Dakota				X		X.
Tennessee	X			X		X.
Texas	X			X		X.
Utah				X	X	X.
Vermont	X	X			X	X.
Virginia				X	X	X.
Washington					X	X.
West Virginia	X			X		X.
Wisconsin	X	X		X		X.
Wyoming	X					X.
Alaska					Territory	
District of Columbia	District[1]				District[1]	
Hawaii					Territory	X.

X indicates that the provision applies without limitation in a given State.

[1]Supplemented by Federal funds.

Veteran Relief

Table 28.—Personal and Other Qualifications for Eligibility for Direct Relief to Veterans

State	Residence	Class of persons eligible[1]	War in which service was rendered	Branch of service	Provisions relating to receipt of other aid which disqualify applicants	Miscellaneous qualifications
Alabama		Veteran	Civil War (Confederate forces)[2]	Army or Navy		Veteran must be indigent and disabled because of loss of sight or other physical infirmity.
Arizona		Veteran and dependents[3]	Ex-service men	Army, Navy, or Marine Corps.		Indigent ex-service men.
Arkansas						
California		Veteran[4]	Any war	Army, Navy, or Marine Corps.		Veteran must be indigent.
Colorado						
Connecticut: Temporary assistance.	(5)	Veteran, wife or widow, dependent children, and dependent relative.[6]	War with Spain, Philippine Insurrection, China Relief Expedition, or World War.[7]	Army, Navy, or Marine Corps.		Indigence and need due to service-connected disability of veteran.
Care outside of home.	State, resident at time of enlistment or for 2 years continuously.	Veteran,[8] wife, dependent children, widowed mother, or husband.[6]	Any war	do		Dependents of veteran entitled to care in home or outside of home must be without adequate means of support.
Aid from the State Soldiers', Sailors', and Marines' Fund.	State, citizen or resident at time of enlistment.	Veteran and dependents[9]	World War[7]	do	Recipient of aid from Soldiers', Sailors', and Marines' Fund may not receive other assistance.	Wife must be living with veteran. Widow must have lived with veteran before his death. Children must be under 16 years of age and in need.
Delaware						
Florida						
Georgia		Veteran	Civil War (Confederate forces).	Army		Veteran must have become chargeable upon poor fund.
Idaho	State, resident.	Veteran and dependents[10]	World War[7]	Army, Navy, or Marine Corps.		Veteran must be disabled and destitute.
Illinois	State, 1 year.	Veteran and family	Civil War, War with Spain, Philippine Insurrection, China Relief Expedition, or World War.	Army, Navy, or Marine Corps.	Recipient may not be sent to an almshouse without consent of the commander and relief committee of the veteran's post, camp, or chapter of which he is a member.	Veteran must be indigent and suffering. Family must be in need of assistance.
Indiana						

State	Residence	Beneficiaries	War	Branch		Conditions
Iowa	County, 1 year continuously without being warned to depart.	Veteran, wife or widow, or children.[9]	Any war	Army, Navy, or Marine Corps.		Veteran, wife or widow, or children must be indigent.
Kansas		Veteran, wife or widow, or dependent children under 14 years of age.	Civil War (Union forces), War with Spain, or World War.	Army or Navy		Veteran and family must be destitute or in need.
Kentucky						
Louisiana						
Maine	Town, 5 years continuously.	Veteran and dependents	Civil War, War with Spain, or World War.	Army, Navy, or Marine Corps.		Veteran and dependents must, by reason of poverty, be in need of relief.
Maryland		Veteran, widow, or infant children.[11]	Any war	Army, Navy, or Marine Corps.		Veteran or dependents must be disabled, indigent, or sick.
Massachusetts	[12]	Veteran,[13] wife or widow, dependent minors, and father or mother.	[14]	Army, Navy, or Marine Corps.	Recipient of 1st and 3d class military aid may not receive other assistance.	*Military aid:* Veteran must, because of sickness or disability, be in such need as would entitle him to poor relief. *Soldiers' relief:* Veteran must be poor and unable to provide maintenance for self and dependents.
Michigan		Veteran, wife or widow,[9] children, or mother.[9]	Any war or military expedition of the United States.	Army, Navy, or Marine Corps.		Veteran or dependent must be indigent.
Minnesota	State, resident for 3 years or served in State regiment.[16]	Veteran, wife or widow, parents, or minor children.[16]	[14]	Army, Navy, or Marine Corps.		Veteran, wife or widow, or mother must, by reason of wounds, disease, old age, or infirmities, as the case may be, be unable to earn a living and without adequate means of support. Parents must be dependent. Wife or widow, or mother must be over 55 years of age. Wife, if deserted, must be worthy. Child must be under 14 years of age.[18]
Supplementary program	State, resident	Veterans and families	Any war			Veteran must be disabled.
Mississippi						
Missouri						
Montana						
Nebraska		Veteran	War of 1812, Mexican War, or Civil War.	Army, Navy, or Marine Corps.		County soldiers' relief commission determines need.
Nevada						
New Hampshire	State, 3 years	Veteran, wife or widow, or dependent children.	Any war	Army, Navy, or Marine Corps.	Federal pension must be used for support of self and dependents.	Veteran must be poor and unable to maintain self or family.

See footnotes at end of table.

Table 28.—Personal and Other Qualifications for Eligibility for Direct Relief to Veterans—Continued

State	Residence	Class of persons eligible[1]	War in which service was rendered	Branch of service	Provisions relating to receipt of other aid which disqualify applicants	Miscellaneous qualifications
New Jersey						
New Mexico						
New York	State, 1 year immediately preceding application. New York City, residence.	Veteran, wife or widow, dependent children, or dependent relative.[13]	Served in naval or military service of the United States.		Recipient may not be committed to an almshouse.	Veteran, nurse, or dependents must be in need of public relief or care.
North Carolina[17]						
North Dakota						
Ohio	State, 1 year; county, 6 months.	Veteran, parents, wife or widow, or minor children.	War with Spain or World War	Army, Navy, or Marine Corps.		Veteran and his dependents must be needy.
Oklahoma						
Oregon	State, 3 months	Veteran, widow, or dependent children.	Civil War (Union forces), Indian Campaign,[18] Philippine Insurrection, or World War.	Army, Navy, or Marine Corps.	Recipient may not be sent to an almshouse without consent of post commander of veterans' organization.	Veteran and his dependents must be indigent and without adequate means of procuring the necessities of life.[19]
Pennsylvania		Veteran, widow, or dependents.	Any war	Army, Navy, or Marine Corps.		Veteran must be sick, disabled, or indigent.
Rhode Island:						
State		Veteran or family and dependents.	Civil War (Union forces), War with Spain, Philippine Insurrection, China Relief Expedition, or World War.	Army, Navy, or Marine Corps.		Veteran and dependents must be worthy and dependent.
Local		Wife or widow or dependent children and family.	Any war			
South Carolina						
South Dakota	State, 3 years immediately preceding application.	Veteran, wife or widow	Civil War	Army or Navy		(20].
Tennessee						
Texas						
Utah						
Vermont	State, 1 year immediately preceding application.	Veteran and dependents		Army or Navy		Veteran or dependents must be disabled or indigent and unable to take advantage of the soldiers' home.

State	Residence	Who is eligible	War	Branch	Condition	Condition
Virginia		Veteran or widow	Civil War (Confederate forces)	Army, Navy, or Marine Corps.		Veteran must be maimed, afflicted, or disabled and indigent; widow, needy and indigent.
Washington	State, 1 year	Veteran or family	(21)	Army, Navy, or Marine Corps.	Recipient may not be sent to an almshouse without consent of commander of local veterans' post.	Indigent and suffering veterans and their families or the families of those deceased who need assistance are given relief.
West Virginia						
Wisconsin: Temporary aid	Town, city, or village, 1 year.	Veteran, wife or widow, or dependent children.[13]	Any war	Army, Navy, or Marine Corps.		Veteran or dependents must be indigent.
General relief.		Veteran, wife or widow, dependent children, or dependent parents.	Served in armed forces in time or war.	Army, Navy, or Marine Corps.		Veteran or dependents must be needy.
Wyoming						

[1]Veteran's dependents are eligible for direct relief if the veteran himself has or had the necessary qualifications. Wherever qualifications for dependents are specifically stipulated, the veteran himself must also have qualified. Direct relief for the widow of a veteran is provided if the veteran was eligible and she was living with him at the time of his death.

[2]The interest on funds remaining in the Spanish American War Relief Fund is appropriated to the quartermaster of the Alabama Spanish American War Veterans to be used for welfare work among needy comrades, their widows and children, and for the current needs of the organization.

[3]Naval nurses also eligible.

[4]Indigent persons who served in the Red Cross are also eligible.

[5]Applicant must be a citizen of the State.

[6]Nurses and yeomanettes also eligible.

[7]Any veteran is eligible who served in the army of any government associated with the United States in the World War and who was a resident of the State at the time of his enlistment.

[8]Aid may be given if veteran is eligible for care in Fitch's Soldiers' Home but cannot be removed to it.

[9]Nurses also eligible.

[10]Army nurses and yeomanettes also eligible.

[11]National guardsman if injured in line of duty is eligible.

[12]2 types of direct relief are granted to veterans: "soldiers' relief" and "military aid." Recipients of "soldiers' relief" must have legal settlement in the town aiding them. Recipients of "military aid" are divided into 4 classes. Similar qualifications have been set for 1st and 3d class recipients and for 2d and 4th class recipients, respectively, with the following exceptions: recipients of both 3d and 4th class aid must have been residents of the State for 3 years and must be residents of the town aiding them. All 4 classes of recipients must be disabled and, in the case of the 2d and 4th class, the disabilities must be service connected. Funds to recipients of all 4 classes are disbursed by towns and cities. The State reimburses the town and city for the total amount paid to 3d and 4th class recipients and $\frac{1}{2}$ of the amount paid to 1st and 2d class recipients.

[13]Civil War army nurses also eligible.

[14]Civil War, Indian Campaign, War with Spain, Philippine Insurrection, China Relief Expedition, Mexican Border Service, or World War.

[15]A wife or widow or parent must have 5 years residence in the State.

[16]Civil War (Union Army) nurses over 65 years of age with 1 year's service and members of the State National Guard disabled in line of duty also eligible.

[17]The directors of the Confederate Soldiers' Home may, at their discretion, discontinue the use of the home and furnish the inmates with accommodations elsewhere, and also such grants-in-aid as shall secure to them proper care and attention conducive to their health, welfare, and happiness. The directors of the Confederate Women's Home are empowered to solicit and receive donations for the purpose of aiding indigent Confederate women in their homes in the various counties.

[18]Veteran must have served not less than 10 days or have been permanently disabled in the Indian Campaign.

[19]Veteran is eligible if the value of home owned is not disproportionate to needs.

[20]Relief limited to veteran or wife or widow not in a condition to be taken to the soldiers' home.

[21]Civil War (Union forces), Indian Campaign, War with Spain, Philippine Insurrection, Mexican Border Service, World War or other foreign war, insurrection, or expedition.

Note: No program in Alaska, District of Columbia, or Hawaii.

Table 29.—Provisions for the Administration and Financing of Direct Relief to Veterans

State	Nature of law	Administrative responsibility		Determination of eligibility		Amount and type of relief	Financial provisions	
		Direct	Supervisory	Final	Advisory		Incidence of responsibility	Source of funds
Alabama	O	Court of county commissioners, county board of revenue, or other county governing body.		Court of county commissioners, county board of revenue, or other county governing body.		Not to exceed $40 per annum.	County	County general fund.
Arizona	M	State Veterans' Relief Commission.		State Veterans' Relief Commission.		Direct relief	State	State general fund.
Arkansas								
California	O	County board of supervisors.		County board of supervisors.	Military, marine, and naval organizations certify eligibles.	Financial assistance	County or municipality.	County or municipality general fund or special property tax.
Colorado								
Connecticut: Temporary assistance. Care outside of home.	O	State Veterans' Home commission.		State Veterans' Home commission.		Temporary financial assistance.	State	State general fund.
	M	do.		do.		Direct relief in amount not to exceed cost of care in State Veterans' Home.	do.	Do.
Aid from the State Soldiers', Sailors', and Marines' Fund.	O	Board of trustees of the American Legion.		Board of trustees of the American Legion.		Direct relief not to exceed cost of care in home and special treatment.	do.	State Soldiers', Sailors', and Marines' Fund and State general fund.
Delaware								
Florida								
Georgia	M	County director of public welfare.	State Department of Public Welfare.	County director of public welfare.		Food and clothing	County	County general fund.
Idaho	O	State Veterans' Welfare Commission.		State Veterans' Welfare Commission.		Financial relief and assistance.	State	State general fund.
Illinois	M	Commander, quartermaster, and relief committee of veterans' organization in conjunction with overseer of poor or county board of commissioners or supervisors.[1]	Annual report made to Governor by veterans' organization.	Commander, quartermaster, and relief committee of local veterans' organization.[1]		Such sum as may be necessary.	County	County general fund.

Indiana								
Iowa	M	County soldiers' relief commission.			Direct relief	County soldiers' relief commission.	County	County property tax.
Kansas	M	County board of social welfare.	State Board of Social Welfare.		Necessities of life	County board of social welfare.	Township, city, or county.	Township, city, or county general fund (county poor fund).
Kentucky								
Louisiana								
Maine	M	Town, city, or plantation overseer of the poor.			Direct relief or care in some place other than poorhouse.	Town, city, or plantation overseer of the poor.	Town, city, or plantation.	Town, city, or plantation general fund.
Maryland	O	State Veterans' Commission.	State Veterans' Commission.		Necessities of life and proper care.	State Veterans' Commission.	State	State Veterans' Relief Fund.
Massachusetts	M	Selectmen of town, aldermen of city, or Boston soldiers' relief commissioner.	Commissioner of State Aid and Pensions.		Military aid: Cash allowance sufficient to afford reasonable relief and support. Soldiers' relief: Care in applicant's home or other proper place or such support as may be necessary.	Selectmen of town, aldermen of city, or Boston soldiers' relief commissioner.	Town and city. State reimburses total of 1st and 2d class and % of 3d and 4th class military aid.	Town and city general fund. State general fund.
Michigan	M	County soldiers' and sailors' relief commission.	State Welfare Department.	Supervisors of each township and ward of county. Alderman of ward in incorporated cities where there is no ward supervisor.	Direct relief in such amount as is necessary. Emergency relief not to exceed $10 per month.	County soldiers'[4] and sailors' relief commission.[2]	County	County property tax.
Minnesota	O	State Soldiers' Home board.		County agents of board of soldiers' home.	Extent and character at discretion of board.[3]	State Soldiers' Home board.	State	State property tax.
Supplementary program	O	State Executive Council.	State Board of Control.		Necessary relief	State Board of Control.	do.	State general fund.
Mississippi								
Missouri								
Montana								
Nebraska	M	County soldiers' relief commission.			Such amount as may be determined by the commission.	County soldiers' relief commission.	County	County property tax.

See footnotes at end of table.

Table 29.—Provisions for the Administration and Financing of Direct Relief to Veterans—Continued

State	Nature of law	Administrative responsibility		Determination of eligibility		Amount and type of relief	Financial provisions	
		Direct	Supervisory	Final	Advisory		Incidence of responsibility	Source of funds
Nevada								
New Hampshire	M	Board of county commissioners or town overseer of the poor.		Board of county commissioners or town overseer of the poor.		Support in own home or such other place as overseers or commissioners may deem proper, almshouse excepted.	Town or county	Town or county general fund.
New Jersey								
New Mexico								
New York	M	Executive or relief committee of designated veterans' organization.[4]		Executive or relief committee of designated veterans' organization.[4]		Relief and care in own home or in a soldiers' home or other suitable State institution or hospital.[5]	City, town, or county.	City, town, or county general fund.
North Carolina[6]								
North Dakota								
Ohio	M	County soldiers' relief commission.		County soldiers' relief commission.	Township or ward soldiers' relief committee receives applications and submits list of eligible applicants.	Amount not specified	County	County property tax; bonds may be issued, to be financed by county's share of State tax on utilities.
Oklahoma								
Oregon	M	County court or in counties with a population of 100,000 or more an officer isappointed by the board of county commissioners.[7]		Relief committee of veterans' post or camp. In case there is no post or camp, a county judge.	Statement of relief extended by veterans' post or camp must be filed with the county court. Orders are drawn by the county court or judge in favor of such post or camp.	Provision must be made as far as practicable for care in homes of beneficiaries.	County	County property tax.
Pennsylvania	O	State adjutant general		State adjutant general	[8].	Not specified	State	State general fund.

State		Administering agency		Benefit	Unit	Source of funds
Rhode Island: State	M	State Department of Public Welfare, Division of Soldiers' and Sailors' Relief.		Not specified	State	State general fund.
Local	O	Person designated by town council or board of aldermen.		Not to exceed $4 per week per family.	City or town	City or town general fund.
South Carolina						
South Dakota	O	Board of managers of State Soldiers' Home.		Direct relief	State	State general fund.
Tennessee						
Texas						
Utah						
Vermont	M	State Board to Aid Indigent Veterans.[9]	Selectmen of town or city mayor investigates applicant and forwards report to board.	Direct relief (amount at discretion of board).	State	State general fund.
Virginia	M	County circuit court, city hustings, or corporation court in cooperation with county or city board of pension commissioners.	Report made of each case by committee appointed by camp of Confederate veterans, if in existence, or by county circuit court, city corporation, or hustings court.	Support and help	County	County property tax.
Washington	M	Veterans' organization of applicant's residence representing war in which veteran served.		Care in home of veteran.	County	County property tax.
West Virginia						
Wisconsin: Temporary aid	M	Village trustees, town board, or common council or county board of trustees if veteran has no legal residence in town, city, or village.		Not specified, but to continue not longer than 3 months out of year.	Town, city, or village.[10]	Town, city, or village general fund.

See footnotes at end of table.

Table 29.—Provisions for the Administration and Financing of Direct Relief to Veterans—Continued

State	Nature of law	Administrative responsibility		Determination of eligibility		Amount and type of relief	Financial provisions	
		Direct	Supervisory	Final	Advisory		Incidence of responsibility	Source of funds
Wisconsin—Contd. General relief -	M --	County soldiers' relief commission.		County soldiers' relief commission.	Chairman of town board, board of village trustees, or supervisors of each ward in city submits list of veterans entitled to relief.	Cash not to exceed $150 per person.	County -------	County special tax levy.
Wyoming								

M indicates mandatory provision.
O indicates optional provision.

[1] Where no such organization exists in a town, aid is administered by the overseer of the poor in conjunction with a local relief committee. If the overseer of the poor or board of county commissioners or supervisors fails or refuses to provide funds for indigent veterans, the commander or quartermaster must apply to the circuit court for a writ of mandamus.

[2] An appeal is allowed to circuit court of the county.

[3] State soldiers' welfare agent, appointed by State Board of Control, also grants assistance where other adequate aid is not available to the dependent family of a veteran who is receiving hospitalization.

[4] Nurses make application for aid to the State Department of Social Welfare or the local public welfare officials. Applications made to the local officials must be made through the National Association of Civil War Army Nurses.

[5] Upon written request of National Association of Civil War Army Nurses to the State Department of Social Welfare or to any public welfare official, cash allowances are given by the State to Civil War nurses.

[6] The directors of the Confederate Soldiers' Home may, at their discretion, discontinue the use of the home and furnish the inmates with accommodations elsewhere, and also such grants-in-aid as shall secure to them proper care and attention conducive to their health, welfare, and happiness. The directors of the Confederate Women's Home are empowered to solicit and receive donations for the purpose of aiding indigent Confederate women at their homes in the various counties.

[7] The county court consists of the county judge and the board of county commissioners.

[8] The State veterans' commission of the State Department of Military Affairs must advise the adjutant general upon such matters as he may bring before the commission.

[9] Board consists of 3 trustees of the soldiers' home.

[10] County must assume financial responsibility if veteran has no legal settlement in a town, city, or village.

Note: No program in Alaska, District of Columbia, or Hawaii.

Table 30.—Personal and Other Qualifications for Eligibility for Pensions to Veterans

State	Residence	Class of person eligible[1]	War in which service was rendered	Branch of service	Provisions relating to receipt of other aid which disqualify applicants	Miscellaneous qualifications
Alabama	State, veteran 5 years or widow 3 years. Applicant must be bona fide citizen of State.	Veteran or wife or widow.	Civil War (Confederate forces).	Army or Navy.		Limit of $5,000 on property and $1,200 on annual income.
Arizona						
Arkansas	State, 1 year immediately preceding application.	Veteran, widow, or mother.	Civil War (Confederate forces).	Army or Navy.	No inmate of the State Confederate Home is entitled to draw a pension but may be given an allowance not to exceed $5 per month.	Veteran must be indigent or incapacitated for performance of manual labor.[2] Indigent mother, now unmarried, also eligible. $500 limit on property (homestead exemption) and $250 limit on annual income.
California						
Colorado						
Connecticut						
Delaware						
Florida	State, citizen 8 years immediately preceding application.[3]	Veteran or widow.	Civil War (Confederate forces).	Army or Navy.	Recipient may not receive a pension from any other State or be confined in any institution except the home for Confederate veterans unless pensioner has wife or minor child dependent upon him for support.	Disabled veteran must have served at least 1 year or have been in active service at the close of the war.
Georgia	State, resident on January 1, 1920, or member of State regiment. Applicant must be resident citizen.	Veteran or widow.	Civil War (Confederate forces).	Army, Navy, or Marine Corps.		
Idaho						
Illinois						
Indiana						
Iowa						
Kansas						

See footnotes at end of table.

Table 30.—Personal and Other Qualifications for Eligibility for Pensions to Veterans—Continued

State	Residence	Class of person eligible[1]	War in which service was rendered	Branch of service	Provisions relating to receipt of other aid which disqualify applicants	Miscellaneous qualifications
Kentucky	State, since January 1, 1907	Veteran or widow	Civil War (Confederate forces).	Army or Navy	Recipient may not receive Federal or other State pension. Support of applicant must not be suitably provided for or secured by contract or agreement with a person able to provide such support.	Veteran must be indigent with inadequate support and unable to earn a living. Limit of $2,500 on property and $300 on annual income.
Louisiana	State, 5 years	Veteran or widow	Civil War (Confederate forces).			Widow must be over 65 years of age.
Maine: Pensions for veterans, their widows, and dependents.	State, 5 years	Veteran, widow, dependent children, or parents.	Civil War, War with Spain, or Philippine Insurrection.	Army or Navy		Veteran must be needy. Widow, children, or parent must have been dependent on veteran at time of his death.
Pensions for dependents of veterans.	State, veteran resident when enlisted or drafted.	Wife, dependent children, or parents.	World War	Army, Navy, or Marine Corps.		Dependents of deceased or disabled veterans must be needy; children must be under 16 years of age.
Maryland						
Massachusetts (State aid)	State, resident	Veteran, wife or widow, dependent children, or dependent relatives.[4]	[5]	Army or Navy	Recipient must not be in receipt of aid from any other town or State and must be in receipt of Federal disability compensation.	Veteran must be needy, have insufficient income or property for self-support, and must have service-connected disability.
Michigan						
Minnesota	State, citizen and resident or resident in State from September 15, 1862, to September 1, 1900.	Veteran or widow	Indian Campaign	Army	Recipient may not receive Federal or State pension.	Veteran must have service-connected disability.
Mississippi	State, 3 years immediately preceding application. Applicant must be citizen of State and United States.	Veteran or widow[6]	Civil War (Confederate forces).	Army or Navy		Widow must be over 60 years of age.
Missouri						
Montana						
Nebraska						
Nevada						

State	Residence requirement	Applicant	War	Branch	Conditions	Remarks
New Hampshire						
New Jersey	State, resident at time of enlistment.	Veteran[7]	Any war	Army, Navy, or Marine Corps.		Applicant must have suffered total loss of sight in service.
New Mexico						
New York: Cash allowance	State, resident as of May 2, 1923.	Veteran[8]	World War	Army, Navy, or Marine Corps.		Veteran must be suffering from sickness or disability of at least 10 percent incurred between April 6, 1917, and November 11, 1918, and be incapacitated from following regular employment for a period of at least 14 days preceding application, and be in need of relief.
Aid to blind veterans	State, resident at time of enlistment.	Veteran	Any war	Army, Navy, or Marine Corps.	Recipient may not receive or be entitled to receive benefit from any retirement system to which State contributes.	Veteran must be permanently and totally disabled by reason of loss of sight.
North Carolina	State, 1 year immediately preceding application.	Veteran or widow[6]	Civil War (Confederate forces).	Army or Navy	Applicant must not be inmate of the Confederate Soldiers' Home, asylum, or county home nor be receiving State aid for relief of blind or maimed soldiers.[9] "Class B" widows[10] and colored servants are ineligible if receiving old age assistance.	Veteran must be blind or have other physical disability.
North Dakota		Veteran, widow, or minor child.	State service			Veteran must have disability incurred in State service.
Ohio						
Oklahoma	State, 5 years	Veteran or widow	Civil War (Confederate forces).	Army or Navy		Limit of $2,000 on property and $500 on annual income.
Oregon						
Pennsylvania		Veteran[11]	Service of the State since March 4, 1861.	Army		
Rhode Island						
South Carolina	State, 2 years[12]	Veteran or widow[6]	Civil War (Confederate forces).	Army or Navy		Veteran must have service-connected disability.
South Dakota						

See footnotes at end of table.

Table 30.—Personal and Other Qualifications for Eligibility for Pensions to Veterans—Continued

State	Residence	Class of person eligible[1]	War in which service was rendered	Branch of service	Provisions relating to receipt of other aid which disqualify applicants	Miscellaneous qualifications
Tennessee	(13)	Veteran or widow[14]	Civil War (Confederate forces) or Mexican Border Service.	Army	Widow may not receive pension from any other source. Veteran must not be eligible for Federal pension or pension from any other State. Pensioner must apply for old age assistance and amount of pension must be reduced by amount of old age assistance granted.	Veteran must be disabled or deserving.[15]
Texas	(16)	Veteran or widow	Civil War (Confederate forces)or border service during such war.	Army or Navy	May not receive any other State pension nor be confined in an asylum or State penitentiary. ½ of pension paid if admitted to the State Confederate Home or State Confederate Women's Home.	Veteran or widow must be indigent.[17]
Utah	State, bona fide resident 2 years.	Veteran or widow[4]	Civil War	Army or Navy.	------	Veteran must be in need because of sickness or other disability.
Vermont	------	------	------	------	------	
Virginia	State, 2 years; county, 1 year. Applicant must be citizen.	Veteran or widow[8]	Civil War (Confederate forces).	Army, Navy, or Marine Corps.	Recipient may not be inmate of the Confederate Soldiers' Home.	Veteran must be disabled and in need because of age. Limit of $1,000 on property and $1,000 on annual income. Widow, if otherwise eligible, was deserted or not supported by husband.
Washington	------	------			------	
West Virginia	------	------			------	
Wisconsin	------	------			------	
Wyoming	------	------			------	

[1] Veteran's dependents are eligible for pensions if the veteran himself has or had the necessary qualifications. Wherever qualifications for dependents are specifically stipulated, the veteran himself must also have qualified. A pension for the widow of a veteran is provided if the veteran was eligible and she was living with him at the time of his death. In some States the widow must have married the veteran prior to a specified date.

[2] Disability because of age, accident, or disease.

[12] To receive additional pension provided for by Fairfield County, applicant must have 10 years' residence in State.

[13] Residents of State or former residents of State who have returned to State, 1 year State residence; veterans coming into State from other States, 3 years' State residence; widows of veterans, 3 years' State residence.

[14] Colored cooks and servants of veterans are also eligible for pensions.

[3]Requirement applies to Florida veterans. Members of militia of other Confederate States must have resided in Florida for 15 years.

[4]Nurses are also eligible for pensions.

[5]Civil War, Indian Campaign, War with Spain, Philippine Insurrection, China Relief Expedition, Mexican Border Service, or World War.

[6]Any servants who are indigent and disabled are eligible for pensions.

[7]Any person including nurses, regularly enlisted, commissioned, appointed, mustered, or inducted into the naval or military forces of the United States may receive pensions.

[8]A special appropriation is made by the State to meet needs of Civil War army nurses.

[9]Applicant must not hold a public office paying as much as $300 annually nor own property of tax value of $2,000 or more, but may be given aid if unable to earn a living.

[10]A "Class B" widow is one who was married prior to January 1, 1880, or one who is over 60 years of age and married prior to 1899.

[11]The widow, minor child, or dependent parent of a deceased member of the National Guard who died in line of duty may receive a pension not to exceed $25 a month.

[15]Deserving veteran is defined as a veteran over 75 years of age with 6 months or more of service. No pension may be paid to any person as a deserving veteran who owns property assessed at $10,000 or over.

[16]Pensions granted to veterans who came to Texas prior to January 1, 1928, and to widows of such veterans who have been bona fide residents of the State since January 1, 1928. Veterans of the militia of other Confederate States must have come to Texas 10 years prior to time of making application. Soldiers or widows, if over 88 years of age, are entitled to pensions if they have been bona fide citizens of Texas since January 1, 1938. All applicants for pensions must be certified as being bona fide residents of county for 6 months preceding application.

[17]Applicant, or applicant and wife together, may not own real or personal property (exclusive of homestead) of an assessed value in excess of $2,000 and personal effects in excess of $1,000 nor receive income in excess of $300 per annum.

Note: No program in Alaska, District of Columbia, or Hawaii.

Table 31.—Provisions for the Administration and Financing of Pensions to Veterans

State	Nature of law	Administrative responsibility		Determination of eligibility		Amount of pension	Financial provisions	
		Direct	Supervisory	Final	Advisory		Incidence of responsibility	Source of funds
Alabama	M.	State Pension Commission.		State Pension Commission.	Application filed with probate judge of county of residence who is the county pension commissioner. Application forwarded by probate judge to State agency.	Veterans, $150 quarterly; widows 80 years of age or over, $90 quarterly; widows under 80 years of age, $60 quarterly; widows totally blind, $90 quarterly; wife of insane veteran who received pension and is in insane hospital, $60 quarterly.	State	Confederate Pension Fund derived from State property tax.
Arizona								
Arkansas	M.	State Pension Board.	(1)	State Pension Board.	County board of pensions certifies application to State Pension Board.	Cash pension of $100 per annum.	State	Confederate Pension Fund derived from State property tax and 12 percent of beverage tax fund.
California								
Colorado								
Connecticut								
Delaware								State property tax.
Florida	M.	Board of county commissioners.	State Board of Pensions.[2]	Board of county commissioners.		$50 per month and $5 additional per month for pensioners who lost an eye, foot, or hand in actual Civil War service.	State	
Georgia	M.	State Department of Public Welfare.		State Department of Public Welfare.	Director of county board of public welfare certifies applicant's residence and service.	Veteran and widow, $30 per month.	State	State general fund, highway fund, property tax, and cigar and cigarette tax.
Idaho								
Illinois								
Indiana								
Iowa								
Kansas								
Kentucky	M.	Division of Confederate pensions in the State Military Department.		Division of Confederate pensions in the State Military Department.	Judge of county court, after hearing, forwards application to the division of Confederate pensions.	$50 per month.[3]	State	State general fund.

State		Administering agency (local)	Administering agency (State)	Amount	Source	Fund
Louisiana	M--	State Department of Public Welfare.	State Department of Public Welfare.	Not to exceed $60 per month[4]	State --	State property tax.
Maine:						
Pensions for veterans, their widows and dependents.	M--	State Department of Health and Welfare	State Department of Health and Welfare.	Not to exceed $12 per month	City, town, or plantation subject to reimbursement by State for total amount paid.	City, town, or plantation general fund. State general fund.
Pensions for dependents of veterans.	M--	State Department of Health and Welfare.	State Department of Health and Welfare.	Dependent wife, father, or mother, $7 per week. Dependent children, $3 per week.	City, town, or plantation subject to reimbursement by State for total amount paid.	City, town, or plantation general fund. State general fund.
Maryland	M--					
Massachusetts (State aid).	M--	Selectmen of town, aldermen of city, or Boston soldiers' relief commissioner; Commissioner of State Aid and Pensions administers aid to nurses.[5]	Commissioner of State Aid and Pensions.	1st class pensioner receives ¾ of Federal pension, not exceeding $10 per month; other 4 classes, $10 per month; no more than $20 may be paid in any 1 month for all dependent relatives of 1 pensioner.	Town or city subject to reimbursement by State for total amount paid.	Town, city, or State general fund.
Michigan						
Minnesota	M--	State adjutant general.	State adjutant general.	$12 per month for life	State --	State general fund.
Mississippi	M--	County board of inquiry.	State Pension Commissioner.	Veteran or widow of veteran if widow was married prior to January 1, 1866, $40 per month; widow of veteran married between January 1, 1866, and January 1, 1875, $25 per month; widow of veteran married between January 1, 1875, and January 1, 1900, $15 per month; blind widows of veterans if married subsequent to January 1, 1866, $30 per month; servants of veterans, $10 per month.	State --	State general fund.
Missouri						
Montana						
Nebraska						
Nevada						

See footnotes at end of table.

Table 31.—Provisions for the Administration and Financing of Pensions to Veterans—Continued

State	Nature of law	Administrative responsibility		Determination of eligibility		Amount of pension	Financial provisions	
		Direct	Supervisory	Final	Advisory		Incidence of responsibility	Source of funds
New Hampshire								
New Jersey	M	State adjutant general.		State adjutant general.		$500 annually	State	State general fund.
New Mexico								
New York: Cash allowance	M	Veteran relief commissioner in bureau for the relief of sick and disabled New York veterans in the division of military and naval affairs of the executive department.	State adjutant general.	Veteran relief commissioner in bureau for the relief of sick and disabled New York veterans in the division of military and naval affairs of the executive department.	Veterans' organization certifies applicant's eligibility.	$30 per month; $10 extra for dependent wife or widowed mother and $5 for each other dependent. Not to exceed $250 per year.	State	State general fund.
Aid to blind veterans.	M	State adjutant general.		State adjutant general.		$500 annually for life	State	State general fund.
North Carolina	M	State Board of Pensions.		State Board of Pensions.	The county pension board certifies applicant's eligibility.	$100 to $420 per year	State	State general fund.[6]
North Dakota	M	State adjutant general.	Governor	State adjutant general.		Pension in an amount which persons under similar circumstances would receive from the United States.	State	State general fund.
Ohio								
Oklahoma	M	State Commissioner of Pensions.		State Commissioner of Pensions.	County judge forwards application to commissioner.	Pensioners over 70 years of age, $27 per month; widows 60—70 years of age, $20 per month; widows under 60 years of age, $15 per month; and persons in soldiers' home, $5 per month.	State	State general fund.
Oregon								
Pennsylvania	M	State Department of Military Affairs.		State Department of Military Affairs.	State veterans' commission makes investigations and recommendations to the State department.	$8 per month, to continue only during disability or until Federal pension is received.[7]	State	State general fund.
Rhode Island								

South Carolina --	M --	County board of honor.	County board of honor -	Confederate veteran, $240 per annum;[8] widows over 55 years of age, $160 per annum; widows 45–55 years of age, $125 per annum; servants, $25 per annum; and pensioners in soldiers' home, $50 per annum.	State --	State general property tax and general fund.[8]
South Dakota -----						
Tennessee ---------	M --	State Board of Pension Examiners.	State Board of Pension Examiners.	Aid in home in lieu of pension. Veterans, $40 per month; widows, $20 per month; and servants, $10 per month.	State --	State general fund.
Texas -------------	M --	County judge ---------	County judge --------	Married veteran living with wife, $50 per month; unmarried veteran, widower, or widow, $25 per month.	State --	State property tax.
Utah --------------	M --	State attorney general.	Department commander of the Grand Army of the Republic presents written request in behalf of applicant.	Cash pension not to exceed $15 per month.	State --	State general fund.
Vermont -----------						
Virginia ----------	M --	State comptroller ---	Circuit court of counties and hustings or corporation court of cities with the county or city board of pension commissioners certify the application.	Maimed and disabled or blind or deaf veterans, $450 per year; veterans with infirmities of age, $360 per year; widows, married before January 1, 1890, or over 75 years of age, $120 per year; blind widows, $240 per year; Nurses (matrons), $120 per year; servants, $96 per year.	State --	State general fund.
Washington --------						
West Virginia -----						
Wisconsin ---------						
Wyoming -----------						

M indicates mandatory provision.

[1] The State Pension Claims Committee must investigate the pension rolls and cause the State Pension Board to remove all ineligibles.

[2] The State Board of Pensions, after a proper hearing, may have ineligibles removed from pension rolls.

[3] $50 per month for each eligible veteran; $50 per month for widow of such veteran if married prior to January 1, 1875; $40 per month for widow of such veteran if married prior to January 1, 1870; $30 per month for widow of such veteran if married prior to January 1, 1895, but subsequent to January 1, 1870; $30 per month for widow of such veteran if married prior to January 1, 1915, and subsequent to January 1, 1890.

[4] Applicant must apply for old age assistance, and the amount of Confederate pension must be reduced by the amount of old age assistance granted.

[5] Commissioner of State Aid and Pensions determines all controversies between pensioners and town and city authorities. Appeal may be taken from his determination to the Governor and council whose decision must be final.

[6] County commissioners may levy special poll and property taxes in order to increase the pensions if they deem it advisable.

[7] Pension not exceeding $25 may be paid to the widow, minor children, or dependent parent of any member of the National Guard or of the Naval forces who died from injuries received in service; administered by the State Department of Military Affairs (optional law).

[8] Additional pensions of $125 and $100 per year paid to veterans of Fairfield and Williamsburg Counties, respectively (mandatory); financed by property taxes.

Note: No program in Alaska, District of Columbia, or Hawaii.

Table 32.—Personal and Other Qualifications for Eligibility for Institutional Care for Veterans

State	Residence	Class of person eligible[1]	War in which service was rendered	Branch of service	Provisions relating to receipt of other aid which disqualify applicant	Miscellaneous qualifications
Alabama	State, 1 year immediately preceding application.	Veteran and wife	Civil War (Confederate forces).	Army or Navy	-----	Veteran must be indigent. Wife or widow must be 60 years of age.
Arizona	-----	-----	-----	-----	-----	-----
Arkansas: State Confederate Home.	-----	Veteran	Civil War	Army or Navy	-----	Veteran must be indigent.
Annex to State Confederate Home.	-----	Wife or widow, dependent daughter, or mother.	----do----	----do----	-----	Daughter has no child able to support her. Indigent dependents must be admitted.
California:[2] Veterans' Home of California.	State, bona fide resident for 6 years immediately preceding application.	Veteran	Service of the United States.	Army, Navy, or Marine Corps.	-----	Veteran must be aged and indigent.
Women's Relief Corps Home.	State, 1 year immediately preceding admission to home.	Wife or widow, unmarried daughter, mother, or sister.[3]	Civil War (Union forces).	Army or Navy	-----	
Colorado	State, 1 year immediately preceding application or service in State regiment.	Veteran, wife or widow	Any war	Army, Navy, or Marine Corps.	-----	Wife must be an invalid, over 50 years of age, or married to veteran prior to 1912. Wives may be admitted if veteran is invalid and care of the wife is required.
Connecticut	State, 2 years continuously if a nonresident, or resident of State when enlisted.	Veteran[4]	Any war	Army, Navy, or Marine Corps.	Invalid veterans and dependents may receive direct relief in lieu of institutional care.	Veteran must be indigent with inadequate support and in need of surgical care.
Delaware	-----	-----	-----	-----	-----	-----
Florida	-----	Veteran	Civil War (Confederate forces).	Army or Navy	Care in home does not cause forfeiture of pension.	-----
Georgia	State, 1 year's residence immediately preceding application.	Veteran	Civil War (Confederate forces).	Army, Navy, or Marine Corps.	Care in home in lieu of pension.	Veteran must be unable to maintain self because of age, infirmity, or poverty.
Idaho	State, resident when enlisted.[5]	Veteran[6]	(?)[7]	Army, Navy, or Marine Corps.	-----	-----
Illinois: State Soldiers' and Sailors' Home.	-----	Veteran and wife[8]	Civil War, War with Spain, Mexican Border Serv-	Army, Navy, or Marine Corps.	-----	Wife must be at least 50 years of age and be married to veteran at least 10 years; veteran unable to earn a livelihood because of physical disability.

	Residence	Eligible persons	War service	Branch	Personal qualifications
State Soldiers' Widows' Home.	State, 1 year	Veteran's mother, wife or widow, or daughter.	ice, or World War. Service of the United States.	Army or Navy	Dependent must be indigent and with inadequate support and because of mental or physical disability unable to earn a livelihood.
State Home for the Rehabilitation of World War Veterans.		Veteran[3]	World War	Army, Navy, or Marine Corps.	Veteran must be mentally incapacitated.
Indiana	State, 2 years immediately preceding application.	Veteran, wife or widow[3]	Any war	Army, Navy, or Marine Corps. [9]	Veteran must be destitute and disabled because of service-connected disabilities; wife must be over 45 years of age; wife or widow must have been married 2 years prior to application.[10]
Iowa	State, 2 years	Veteran, wife or widow	Service of the United States.	Army, Navy, or Marine Corps.	Veteran must be needy. Wife or widow must have been married at least 10 years prior to application.
Kansas: State Soldiers' Home	State, 2 years immediately preceding application.	Veteran and dependent family.	[11]	Army, Navy, or Marine Corps.	Veteran must be disabled because of wounds, disease, or old age, have no adequate means of support and likely to become a public charge. Wife must be at least 50 years of age or needed to care for veteran.[12]
Mother Bickerdyke Annex to State Soldiers' Home.		Widow, dependent children, or mother.[13]	[11]	--do--	Children must be under 16 years of age or incapable of supporting themselves by their own labor.
Kentucky					
Louisiana	State, 5 years prior to application.	Veteran, wife or widow.	Civil War (Confederate forces).	Army or Navy — Recipient may not receive any other State aid.	Veteran must be maimed or disabled because of service or infirm because of sickness or old age.
Maine					
Maryland					
Massachusetts					No personal qualifications prescribed by statute.
Michigan: State Soldiers' Home	State, 5 years immediately preceding application, service in State regiment, or service accredited to State.	Veteran	Any war	Army, Navy, or Marine Corps.	Veteran must be disabled by disease, wounds, or otherwise, without adequate means of support, and by reason of disability incapacitated from earning a living.
Dormitory for Ex-nurses and Veterans' Dependents.	State, 5 consecutive years preceding application.	Wife or widow or mother[13]	[14]	--do--	[15].

See footnotes at end of table.

Table 32.—Personal and Other Qualifications for Eligibility for Institutional Care for Veterans—Continued

State	Residence	Class of person eligible[1]	War in which service was rendered	Branch of service	Provisions relating to receipt of other aid which disqualify applicant	Miscellaneous qualifications
Minnesota	State, 3 years or served in State regiment.[16]	Veteran, wife or widow, parents, or minor children.[17]	(18)	Army, Navy, or Marine Corps.	(19)	Veteran, wife, widow, or mother must, by reason of wounds, disease, old age, or infirmity, as the case may be, be unable to earn a living and without adequate means of support. Wife, widow, or mother must be over 55 years of age. Wife maybe admitted with husband.
Mississippi	State, 3 years immediately preceding application.	Veteran, wife or widow	Civil War (Confederate forces).	Army or Navy		Veteran or widow must be eligible to draw State pension. Widow must be over 60 years of age.
Missouri: State Federal Soldiers' Home.	State, citizen.	Veteran, aged wife or widow.[20]	Service of the United States.	Army or Navy		Veteran must be indigent, disabled, and unable to support himself by manual labor.
Confederate Soldiers' Home.		Veteran, wife or widow, and orphans.	Civil War (Confederate forces).	do		Veteran must be infirm and dependent.
Montana	State, 1 year immediately preceding application; county, 3 months immediately preceding application.	Veteran, wife or widow	(18)	Army, Navy, or Marine Corps.		Veteran must be an invalid because of disease, wounds, or other disability. His wife or widow must be over 50 years of age.
Nebraska	State, 2 years immediately preceding application.	Veteran, wife or widow, or mother.[21]	Civil War, Indian Campaign, War with Spain, Philippine Insurrection, or World War.	Army, Navy, or Marine Corps.		(22).
Nevada		Veteran	Civil War, War with Spain, Mexican Border Service, or World War.	Army or Navy		Veteran who is or may become unable to earn a livelihood by reason of wounds, disease, old age, or other infirmity and without adequate means of support.
New Hampshire	State, 3 years immediately preceding application.	Veteran				Veteran must be indigent and disabled.
New Jersey: State Memorial Home for Disabled Soldiers.	State, 2 years prior to application.[23]	Veteran	Service of the United States.	Army, Navy, or Marine Corps.		Veteran must be indigent and disabled.
State Memorial Home for Disabled Soldiers, Sailors, Marines, and Their Wives and Widows.	State, resident at time of application and for 7 years preceding application.	Veteran, wife or widow	do	do		Veteran must be indigent and disabled. Wife must have been married at least 10 years and must be at least 50 years of age.[24]

State	Residence requirement	Applicant	War	Branch of service	Conditions
New Mexico	—	—	—	—	—
New York	State, 1 year immediately preceding application, or enlisted from State.	Veteran, wife or widow, daughter, or mother.[3]	Civil War, War with Spain, Philippine Insurrection, or World War.	Army, Navy, or Marine Corps.	Veteran must be aged and dependent.[25]
North Carolina: Confederate Soldiers' Home.	State, bona fide resident.	Veteran	Civil War (Confederate forces).	Army	Veteran must be deserving and needy.
Confederate Women's Home.	---do---	Wife or widow	---do---	---do---	
North Dakota	State, at least 1 year immediately preceding application.[26]	Veteran, wife or widow	Service of the United States.	Army, Navy, or Marine Corps.	Veteran must be disabled by disease, wounds, old age, or otherwise.
Ohio: State Soldiers' and Sailors' Home.	State, citizen for 1 year.	Veteran	([27])	Army, Navy, or Marine Corps.	Veteran must be disabled by disease or wounds and unable to earn a living.
Madison Home	State, citizen and resident.[28]	Veteran, wife or widow, or dependent mother.[28]	Any war[28]	---do---	Applicant must be unable to support self.
Oklahoma: Confederate Soldiers' Home.		Veteran, wife or widow	Civil War (Confederate forces) or World War.	Army or Navy	Veteran must be disabled and indigent; wives or widows must be aged.
Union Soldiers' Home		Veteran, wife or widow, or mother.[21]	([29])	Army, Navy, or Marine Corps.	Veteran must be indigent, aged, and dependent. Wife, widow, or mother must be dependent.
Oregon					
Pennsylvania	State, resident at time of enlistment or served in some Pennsylvania organization, or resident in State for 1 year immediately preceding time of application.	Veteran[30]	Any war	Army, Navy, Marine Corps, or U.S. Coast Guard.	Veteran must be indigent and disabled because of disease, wounds, or service-connected disability.
Rhode Island	State, 5 years immediately preceding application, resident of State when enlisted, or accredited to quota of State.	Veteran	Any war	Army, Navy, or Marine Corps.	Applicant must be, by reason of wounds, disease, old age, or other infirmity, unable to earn his living and without adequate means of support.
South Carolina	([31])	Veteran, wife or widow, sister, or daughter.	Civil War (Confederate forces).	Army or Navy	Veteran must be infirm or destitute; wife, widow, sister, or daughter must be indigent and have been born prior to 1865. All classes must be over 70 years of age.

See footnotes at end of table.

Table 32.—Personal and Other Qualifications for Eligibility for Institutional Care for Veterans—Continued

State	Residence	Class of person eligible[1]	War in which service was rendered	Branch of service	Provisions relating to receipt of other aid which disqualify applicant	Miscellaneous qualifications
South Dakota	State, 3 years immediately preceding application.	Veteran, wife or widow	Civil War, Indian Campaign, War with Spain, Philippine Insurrection, Mexican Border Service, or World War.	Army, Navy, or Marine Corps.		Veteran must be incapacitated from earning a livelihood, with income not in excess of $900 per annum. Wife must be 60 years of age and married to veteran not less than 5 years. Widow must be 60 years of age and with insufficient income to support herself.
Tennessee		Veteran, wife or widow, or orphan.	Civil War (Confederate forces).	Army or Navy		Home is for indigent and disabled veterans, widows, and orphan children.
Texas: Confederate Home	State, bona fide citizen. If not in Texas command, bona fide resident of State as of January 1, 1895.	Veteran and wife[32]	Civil War (Confederate forces).	Army or Navy	May not receive pension from any source.	Veteran must be disabled and indigent.
Confederate Women's Home.	([33])	([33])	...do...	...do...	If admitted to home, person may receive only ½ of pension to which otherwise entitled.	Indigent wives or widows of soldiers and sailors who were disabled in actual service of at least 3 months' duration.
Utah						
Vermont		Veteran and dependents[34]		Army or Navy		
Virginia		Veteran[35]	Civil War (Confederate forces).			
Washington: State Veterans' Home	State, bona fide resident for 3 years.	Veteran, wife or widow	Civil War (Union forces) or any war.	Army, Navy, or Marine Corps.		([36]).
State Soldiers' Home and Colony.	State, bona fide citizen for 3 years.	...do...	Any war	...do...		([36]).
West Virginia						
Wisconsin	State, 10 years immediately preceding application if enlisted from the State or 15 years immediately preceding application if service is not credited to the State.	Veteran, mother, wife or widow.[21]	([37])	Army, Navy, or Marine Corps.		Veteran must be 50 years of age or over and have had at least 70 days of service unless service was terminated as the result of physical disability in the line of duty.[38]

	State, bona fide resident for 1 year preceding application.	Veteran and dependents[39]	(39)	Army, Navy, or Marine Corps.	
Wyoming					Veteran must be unable to earn his living because of wounds, disease, old age, or other infirmity and without adequate means of support. Member of National Guard must have been disabled while on duty.

[1] Veteran's dependents are eligible for institutional care if the veteran himself has or had the necessary qualifications. Wherever qualifications for dependents are specifically stipulated, the veteran himself must also have qualified. Institutional care for the widow of a veteran is provided if the veteran was eligible and she was living with him at the time of his death.

[2] Additional institutional care is provided in city and county veteran homes.

[3] Nurses are also eligible for institutional care.

[4] Nurses are also eligible as are aliens who served in the forces of a government associated with the United States during the World War.

[5] Applicant must also have been a bona fide resident for 2 years and, prior to application, must have voted in 1 or more general elections.

[6] World War nurses are also eligible.

[7] Civil War (Union forces), Indian Campaign, War with Spain, Philippine Insurrection, Mexican Border Service, or World War. Members of the National Guard with service-connected disabilities are also eligible.

[8] War servants are also eligible.

[9] All unmarried soldiers, nurses, and widows may be required, as a condition for admission to the home, to pay to the board of trustees of the home any gratuity which they receive from the United States in excess of $16 per month. Married soldiers may be required to pay to the board amounts in excess of $25 per month.

[10] Deserving and destitute widows of Spanish-American and World War veterans under the age of 45 years may be admitted to the home.

[11] Civil War, War with Spain, Philippine Insurrection, China Relief Expedition, or World War. A member of the State Militia guarding Kansas border also eligible if a resident of State for 35 years.

[12] Wives of Civil War veterans are eligible for admission regardless of time of marriage or financial standing provided they have reached the age of 65 years. No girls may be admitted after they reach 14 years of age or retained after they reach the age of 16 years. Boys may not be admitted after they reach 12 years of age or retained after they reach 14 years. These provisions do not apply to children incapable of earning support by their own labor.

[13] Civil War nurses are also eligible for admission.

[14] Civil War, War with Spain, Philippine Insurrection, Mexican Border Service, War with Russia or Russian expeditionary forces, or World War.

[15] Wives or widows of veterans of Mexican or Civil Wars must be at least 55 years of age at time of application and married to the veteran before December 1, 1905. Wives or widows of veterans of War with Russia or Russian Expedition must beat least 50 years old at time of application and married to veteran before April 6, 1937. If applicant is wife or widow or Civil War nurse and unable to earn a livelihood, she must be admitted regardless of other qualifications if she has resided in the State 5 consecutive years preceding application.

[16] A wife or widow or parent must have 5 years residence in the State.

[17] Civil War (Union Army) nurses over 65 years of age with 1 year's service and members of the State National Guard disabled in line of duty are also eligible.

[18] Civil War, Indian Campaign, War with Spain, Philippine Insurrection, China Relief Expedition, Mexican Border Service, or World War.

[19] All inmates are required to make a will disposing of personal property as a condition precedent to admission. If pension received from any other source exceeds $4 a month, the applicant or inmate may be required to send half of such pension to wife or dependent child.

[20] Army nurses who served with the Army of the United States or indigent ex-members of the militia who served 90 days or more in the field during the Civil War are also eligible for admission.

[21] Army nurses are also eligible.

[22] Applicant must have become disabled because of war service, old age, or be otherwise incapacitated from earning a livelihood. Widows and mothers must be dependent, unable to earn a livelihood, and 50 years of age or over. Wives must be 50 years of age or over and have been married for at least 10 years before entering the home. Widows and mothers must have resided in the State for at least 2 years prior to admission to the home.

[23] Residence provisions do not prevent any applicant who actually served in a State military or naval organization, and who is otherwise qualified, from entering the home, but preference is given to a person who has been a resident 2 years prior to application.

[24] Veteran's widow required to prove the following: State residence for 10 years, marriage to veteran at time of service or prior to June 27, 1915, no remarriage since her husband's death, and eligibility of husband for admission if he were alive.

[25] Veteran may not be admitted unless accompanied by his wife but may remain after death of wife upon consent of superintendent, subject to approval of board of visitors of the home. Veteran must have been married for at least 10 years, except World War veterans who must have been married prior to January 1, 1930. World War veterans' wives or widows or mothers may be incapacitated. In case of veterans and wives admitted together, both must be incapacitated. Dependent daughter of any veteran over 55 years of age.

[26] Alternative: veteran who served in a State regiment or was accredited to the Dakota Territory.

[27] Civil War, Indian Campaign, War with Spain. Philippine Insurrection, China Relief Expedition, Mexican Border Service, or World War. Members of the National Guard and Naval Militia are also eligible.

[28] Preference for admission to the home must be given to Civil War veterans and their wives or widows or mothers, widows or mothers of veterans of the Spanish War, and nurses who served in the Spanish War. Subject to the above preferences, not more than 10 wives, widows, or mothers may be admitted. They must have resided in Ohio 1 year preceding their admission to the home, and veteran must have been citizen of Ohio at time of enlistment or induction into service.

Table 32.—Footnotes Continued

[29]Civil War, Indian Campaign, War with Spain, Philippine Insurrection, China Relief Expedition, Mexican Border Service, or World War. Members of the National Guard are also eligible.

[30]Persons who have served in some Pennsylvania organization or in the Pennsylvania National Guard are also admitted.

[31]Veteran must be on honor roll of county. Wife or widow, sister, or daughter must be State residents.

[32]Wife may be transferred from Confederate Women's Home to live with husband in Confederate Home.

[33]Wives and widows of veterans who entered the service from Texas or who came to the State prior to January 1, 1880, and women who aided the Confederacy.

[34]Home is maintained for veterans and such members of their families as the trustees of the home shall deem proper.

[35]Wife is admitted if husband is an inmate of the home.

[36]Veteran of the State Militia must have a service-connected disability. Widow must have become indigent after husband's death. Wife must have been married to veteran at least 3 years before application or have been otherwise eligible at time of application.

[37]Civil War, War with Spain, Philippine Insurrection, China Relief Expedition, World War, or any other war or military expedition of the United States.

[38]Disabled veterans under 50 years of age if unable to obtain adequate care from Federal Government also received. Wives of veterans must have lived continuously with their husbands not less than 10 years preceding application. Widows of veterans of the Civil War, Spanish American War, Philippine Insurrection, China Relief Expedition, and the World War (if married prior to November 11, 1918) must not have remarried and must be 50 years of age or over.

[39]Civil War (Confederate and Union Armies) and all wars in which the United States has been or may be engaged. Members of the National Guard are also eligible.

Note: No program in Alaska, District of Columbia, or Hawaii.

Table 33.—Provisions for the Administration and Financing of Institutional Care for Veterans

State	Nature of law	Name of institution	Administrative responsibility		Determination of eligibility		Source of funds
			Direct	Supervisory	Final	Advisory	
Alabama	M	State Soldiers' Home	Board of control of State Soldiers' Home.		Board of control of State Soldiers' Home.		State general fund.
Arizona							
Arkansas	M	State Confederate Home	Honorary board for the management and operation of the Confederate home.	(1)	Honorary board for the management and operation of the Confederate home.		State general fund.
	M	Annex to State Confederate Home.[2]	--do--	(1)	--do--		Do.
California	O	Veterans' Home of California.[3]	Board of directors of the Veterans' Home of California.	Division of veterans' home in the Department of Military and Veterans' Affairs.	Board of directors of the Veterans' Home of California.		State general fund; Veterans' Home of California Federal Fund.
	M	Women's Relief Corps Home.	Board of directors of Women's Relief Corps Home.	--do--	Board of directors of Women's Relief Corps Home.		State general fund.
Colorado	M	State Soldiers' and Sailors' Home.	State Soldiers' and Sailors' Home commission.	Division of Public Welfare of the Executive Department.	State Soldiers' and Sailors' Home commission.		State general fund.
Connecticut	M	Fitch's State Soldiers' Home.	State Veterans' Home commission.		State Veterans' Home commission.		State general fund.
Delaware							
Florida	M	Old Confederate Soldiers' and Sailors' Home.[4]	Board of managers	Board of Commissioners of State Institutions.	Board of Commissioners of State Institutions.		State general fund.
Georgia	M	Confederate Soldiers' Home.	State Department of Public Welfare.		State Department of Public Welfare.	County director of public welfare.	State general fund.
Idaho	M	State Soldiers' Home.	Commandant of State Soldiers' Home.	State Department of Public Welfare.	Commandant of State Soldiers' Home.		State general fund.[5]
Illinois	M	State Soldiers' and Sailors' Home.	State Department of Public Welfare.		State Department of Public Welfare.		State general fund.
	M	State Soldiers' Widows' Home.	--do--		--do--		Do.
	M	State Home for the Rehabilitation of World War Veterans.	--do--		Voluntary application to the managing officer; or commitment by court of record of county upon petition by relative or guardian.		Do.

See footnotes at end of table.

Table 33.—Provisions for the Administration and Financing of Institutional Care for Veterans—Continued

State	Nature of law	Name of institution	Administrative responsibility		Determination of eligibility		Source of funds
			Direct	Supervisory	Final	Advisory	
Indiana	M	State Soldiers' Home	Board of trustees of State Soldiers' Home.	State Department of Public Welfare.	Board of trustees of State Soldiers' Home.	------	State general fund.
Iowa	M	State Soldiers' Home	Commandant ------	State Board of Control of State Institutions.	State Board of Control of State Institutions.	Affidavit to commandant signed by county board of supervisors.	State general fund.
Kansas	M	State Soldiers' Home	Board of managers of State Soldiers' Home.	------	Board of managers of State Soldiers' Home.	Certification of need by board of county commissioners.	State general fund.
	M	Mother Bickerdyke Annex to the State Soldiers' Home.	------do	------	------do	------do	Do.
Kentucky							
Louisiana	M	State Soldiers' Home	Board of directors of State Soldiers' Home.	State Board of Charities and Corrections.	Board of directors of State Soldiers' Home.	------	State general fund.
Maine		(⁶) ------					
Maryland							
Massachusetts	M	State Soldiers' Home	Board of trustees of State Soldiers' Home.	Governor and council ------	Board of trustees of State Soldiers' Home.	------	State general fund.
Michigan	M	State Soldiers' Home	Board of managers of State Soldiers' Home and Dormitory for Ex-nurses and Veterans' Dependents.	------	Board of managers of State Soldiers' Home and Dormitory for Ex-nurses and Veterans' Dependents.	------	State general fund.
	M	Dormitory for Ex-nurses and Veterans' Dependents.	------do	------	------do	------	Do.
Minnesota	M	State Soldiers' Home	State Soldiers' Home board	------	State Soldiers' Home board	------	State general fund.
Mississippi	M	Jefferson Davis Beauvoir Soldiers' Home.	Board of directors of Jefferson Davis Beauvoir Soldiers' Home.	------	Board of directors of Jefferson Davis Beauvoir Soldiers' Home.	------	State general fund.
Missouri	M	State Federal Soldiers' Home.	Board of trustees of State Federal Soldiers' Home.	------	Board of trustees of State Federal Soldiers' Home.	------	State general fund.
	O	Confederate Soldiers' Home.	Board of trustees of Confederate Soldiers' Home.	------	Board of trustees of Confederate Soldiers' Home.	------	Do.
Montana	M⁷	State Soldiers' Home.	Board of managers of State Soldiers' Home.	------	Board of managers of State Soldiers' Home.	------	State general fund.

State		Name of home					
Nebraska	M	State Soldiers' and Sailors' Home at Grand Island and branch at Milford.	State Board of Control		State Board of Control	County board of commissioners or supervisors makes inquiry and forwards application and findings to State Board of Control.	State general fund.
Nevada							
New Hampshire	M	State Soldiers' Home.	Board of managers of State Soldiers' Home.	State Department of Public Welfare.[8]	Board of managers of State Soldiers' Home.	Board appointed by Governor and council investigates applicant.	State general fund.
New Jersey	O	State Memorial Home for Disabled Soldiers.	Board of managers of State Memorial Home for Disabled Soldiers.	Board of Control of the State Department of Institutions and Agencies.[9]	Board of managers of State Memorial Home for Disabled Soldiers.	Judge of court of common pleas certifies applicant's eligibility.	State general fund.
	O	State Memorial Home for Disabled Soldiers, Sailors, Marines, and Their Wives and Widows.	Board of managers of State Memorial Home for Disabled Soldiers, Sailors, Marines, and Widows.		Board of managers of State Memorial Home for Disabled Soldiers, Sailors, Marines, and Their Wives and Widows.	------do------	Do.
New Mexico							
New York	M	State Women's Relief Corps Home.	Superintendent of State Women's Relief Corps Home.	State Department of Social Welfare.	Board of visitors of State Women's Relief Corps Home.		State general fund.
North Carolina	O	Confederate Soldiers' Home.	Board of directors of Confederate Soldiers' Home.		Board of directors of Confederate Soldiers' Home.		State general fund.
	O	Confederate Women's Home.	Board of directors of Confederate Women's Home.		Board of directors of Confederate Women's Home.		Do.
North Dakota	O	State Soldiers' Home.	Board of trustees of State Soldiers' Home.		Board of trustees of State Soldiers' Home.		State general fund.
Ohio	M	State Soldiers' and Sailors' Home.	Superintendent of State Soldiers' and Sailors' Home.	State Department of Public Welfare.	State Department of Public Welfare.		State general fund.[10]
	M	Madison Home.	Superintendent of Madison Home.	------do------			State general fund.
Oklahoma	M	Confederate Soldiers' Home.	Board of trustees of Confederate Soldiers' Home.	State Commissioner of Charities and Corrections.	Board of trustees of Confederate Soldiers' Home.		State general fund
	O	Union Soldiers' Home.	Board of trustees of Union Soldiers' Home.	------do------	Board of trustees of Union Soldiers' Home.		Do.[11]
Oregon	O	State Soldiers' Home.[12]					
Pennsylvania	M	State Soldiers' and Sailors' Home.	Board of trustees of State Soldiers' and Sailors' Home.[13]	State Department of Military Affairs.[13]	Board of trustees of State Soldiers' and Sailors' Home.[13]		State general fund.
Rhode Island	M	State Soldiers' Home.	Commandant of State Soldiers' Home.	Director of public welfare of State Department of Public Welfare.	State Department of Public Welfare, Division of Soldiers' and Sailors' Relief.		State general fund.

See footnotes at end of table.

Table 33.—Provisions for the Administration and Financing of Institutional Care for Veterans—Continued

State	Nature of law	Name of institution	Administrative responsibility		Determination of eligibility		Source of funds
			Direct	Supervisory	Final	Advisory	
South Carolina	M	State Confederate Home.	Commission for State Confederate Home.	State Department of Public Welfare.	Commission for State Confederate Home.	Probate court of county certifies that applicant is on honor roll.	State general fund derived from general property tax.
South Dakota	M	State Soldiers' Home.	Board of managers of State Soldiers' Home.		County judge.		State general fund.
Tennessee	M	Confederate Soldiers' Home.	Superintendent of Confederate Soldiers' Home.	Department of Institutions and Public Welfare.	Commissioner of Department of Institutions and Public Welfare.[14]		State general fund.[15]
Texas	M	State Confederate Home.	Superintendent of State Confederate Home.	State Board of Control.	State Board of Control		State general fund.
	M	State Confederate Women's Home.	Superintendent of State Confederate Women's Home.	----do----	----do----		Do.
Utah							
Vermont	O	State Soldiers' Home.	Board of trustees of State Soldiers' Home.		Board of trustees of State Soldiers' Home.		State general fund.
Virginia	M[7]	Confederate Soldiers' Home (Robert B. Lee Camp No. 1 Confederate veterans).[16]	Board of visitors.		Board of visitors.		State general fund.
Washington	M	State Veterans' Home.	Superintendent of State Veterans' Home.	Director of State Department of Finance, Budget, and Business.	Superintendent of home.		State general fund.
	M	State Soldiers' Home and Colony.	Superintendent of State Soldiers' Home and Colony.	----do----	----do----		Do.
West Virginia	M						
Wisconsin	M	Grand Army Home for Veterans.	Adjutant general.	Board of managers.	Adjutant general.		State general fund.[17]
Wyoming	O	State Soldiers' and Sailors' Home.	Commandant of State Soldiers' and Sailors' Home.	State Board of Charities and Reform.	State Board of Charities and Reform.		State general fund.

M indicates mandatory provision.
O indicates optional provision.

[1] State Pension Claims Committee investigates residents of the State Confederate Home and causes State board to remove ineligible persons.
[2] The annex is located at the State Confederate Home and is under the control of the same board and superintendent.

[10] The county pays the cost of transportation to the home.
[11] All monies donated and all monies received from the sale or exchange of products of the home are placed in a revolving fund for the use of the home.
[12] State Soldiers' Home was transferred to the Federal Government.
[13] The board of trustees is a departmental administrative board within the State Department of Military Affairs.

[3] Additional institutional care is provided in city and county veteran homes.

[4] When necessity for home no longer exists, the home and its assets must be sold, and the proceeds thereof used for scholarship fund for the lineal descendants of the veterans.

[5] One-sixth of money accruing to charitable institutions endowment fund is appropriated to the home. Estate of any inmate, who dies without heirs, vests in the Department of Public Welfare, subject to claim within 5 years.

[6] No institutional care is provided for veterans, but the State Military and Naval Children's Home is maintained for poor and neglected children, preference being given to children of soldiers and sailors of Maine.

[7] The admission of the wife or widow of a veteran to the home is optional with the board of managers.

[8] The department must inspect the home and make necessary recommendations.

[9] The board of managers may grant relief in an amount not in excess of % of the average cost of each patient at the home to persons as outpatients who have some but not sufficient means for comfortable support in their private residence.

[14] An advisory committee of 5 members of the United Daughters of the Confederacy cooperates with the commissioner of Department of Institutions and Public Welfare in the management of the home.

[15] The home is practically self-sustaining, but is aided by the State general fund.

[16] This institution is incorporated under the laws of the State.

[17] Applicant must pay State 20 percent of income, or at option of commandant of home all income over $400, into a general fund for maintenance of the home. A wife is allowed to retain independent income of $100 per annum for personal use. Inmates must execute an agreement to the effect that all personal property at death will, if they leave no heirs or next of kin, vest in the home, subject to reclamation, however, by the heirs of legatees with 5 years.

Note: No program in Alaska, District of Columbia, or Hawaii.

State Boards and Local Boards

Table 34.—Composition and Appointment of State Boards of Public Welfare

| State | Name of State department | Name of governing or advisory board | Number of board members | Terms of office | | Method of selection | | | Remuneration | Qualifications | Limitation on appointment | Provision for removal | Provision for filling vacancies created by death, resignation, or removal |
				Rotating (number of years)	Other	By Governor	By Governor with consent of Senate	Other					
Alabama	State Department of Public Welfare.	State Board of Public Welfare.	7[1]	6[2]	---	X	---	---	Expenses --	Recognized interest in welfare work.	At least 2 members of the board must be women.[3]	---	By Governor for unexpired term.
Arizona	State Department of Social Security and Welfare.	State Board of Social Security and Welfare.	5	3	---	X	---	---	Expenses --	Recognized interest in or knowledge of public welfare problems.	(3)	Any member who becomes a candidate for public office is automatically disqualified for board membership.	By Governor for unexpired term.
Arkansas	State Department of Public Welfare.	State Board of Public Welfare.	7[4]	7[2]	---	X	---	---	Expenses --	Recognized interest in or knowledge of public welfare problems.	Members shall be appointed from each of the 7 congressional districts of the State and shall not serve for more than 2 consecutive terms.[3]	By Governor for malfeasance, misfeasance, or nonfeasance. Any member who becomes a candidate for public office automatically disqualified for board membership.	By Governor for unexpired term.
California	State Department of Social Welfare.	State Board of Social Welfare.	7	4	---	X	---	---	Traveling expenses.	Interest and leadership in social welfare activities.	No board member shall be a trustee, manager, director, or employee of an institution under the jurisdiction of the department, nor shall a board member hold any other office or employment in the department.[5]	Members who are absent from 3 consecutive regular meetings shall be deemed to have resigned from the board, but the board may for good cause grant leave of absence to its members.	By Governor for unexpired term. Vacancy must be filled within 60 days.
Colorado	State Department of Public Welfare.	State Board of Public Welfare.	7	3[2]	---	X	---	---	Traveling expenses.	---	---	By Governor at any time for cause.	By Governor for unexpired term.
Connecticut	Public Welfare Council.	Public Welfare Council.	5	4[2]	---	(6)	---	---	No compensation.	---	The council consists of 3 men and 2 women.	By Governor for cause.	By Governor for unexpired term.
Delaware	State Old Age Welfare Commission.	State Old Age Welfare Commission.	4	4	---	X	---	---	$5 per diem and expenses.	---	1 member from city of Wilmington, 1 from rural New Castle County, 1 from Kent County, and 1 from Sussex County.	If a majority of the commission requests the removal of a member, the Chief Justice for the un-	Vacancies shall be filled by the Chief Justice for the unexpired term.

State	Agency	No.	No.	No.	X	Compensation	Qualifications	Additional provisions	Removal
Florida	State Welfare Board.	7	4	---	X	Expenses; $1,200 per annum maximum.	Citizen and elector for at least 5 years prior to appointment.	Not more than 2 members shall be from the same social welfare district.	tice may, upon a full presentation of the facts, remove such member.
Georgia	State Department of Public Welfare. / State Board of Public Welfare.	7[7]	3	---	X	Expenses.	Recognized interest in and knowledge of public welfare problems.	1 of the members shall be a medical doctor and 1 a dentist, both in active practice. The members of the board must be selected from the 10 congressional districts and should represent the geographical sections of the State.	
Idaho	State Department of Public Assistance. / Commissioner of State Department of Public Assistance (see table 35).	---	---	---	---	---	---	---	---
Illinois	State Department of Public Welfare. / State Board of Public Welfare Commissioners.	5	---	2[2]	X	No compensation.	---	---	---
Indiana	State Department of Public Welfare. / State Board of Public Welfare.	5	4[2]	---	X	$300 per annum and expenses.	Recognized interest in and knowledge of public welfare problems.	Not more than 3 of the same political party.	By Governor for misconduct, incapacity, or neglect of duty.
Iowa	State Department of Social Welfare. / State Board of Social Welfare.	5	4[2]	---	X	$15 per diem and expenses. $1,200 per annum maximum.	---	At least 1 woman; not more than 1 member from any congressional district; and not more than 3 of the same political party.	Vacancies occurring while the General Assembly is in session are filled in same manner as full term appointments. Vacancies occurring while General Assembly is not in session are filled by Governor and approved / By Governor for unexpired term.

See footnotes at end of table.

Table 34.—Composition and Appointment of State Boards of Public Welfare—Continued

State	Name of State department	Name of governing or advisory board	Number of board members	Terms of office — Rotating (number of years)	Method of selection — Other	Method of selection — By Governor	Method of selection — By Governor with consent of Senate	Remuneration	Qualifications	Limitation on appointment	Provision for removal	Provision for filling vacancies created by death, resignation, or removal
Iowa—Contd												by executive council, but such appointments terminate 30 days after the convening of the next General Assembly.
Kansas	State Board of Social Welfare.	State Board of Social Welfare.	5	4			X	$10 per diem and expenses. $500 per annum maximum.	Recognized interest in and knowledge of public welfare problems.	A board member is ineligible for any public office during his term of appointment or for 2 years after retirement from the board.[5]	By Governor for good cause.	By Governor for unexpired term.
Kentucky	State Department of Welfare.	State Board of Welfare.	5[8]	4		X		$10 per diem and expenses.	Citizen of State, appointed from State at large on basis of interest in public affairs, good judgment, and knowledge and ability in the field.	During term of membership a board member is ineligible for any public office, but immediately upon retirement from the board he may stand as a candidate for public office.[5]		
Louisiana (See appendix B.)	State Department of Public Welfare.	State Board of Public Welfare.	5		(9)	X		Expenses	Recognized interest in and knowledge of public welfare problems.			
Maine	State Department of Health and Welfare.	Advisory Council of Health and Welfare.	7[10]	6		X[10]		Expenses		1 woman and 2 members of the minority party shall be named to the board.		
Maryland	Board of State Aid and Charities.	Board of State Aid and Charities.	8[11]	4			X	Expenses		Not more than 3 residents of any county or city shall be board members.		Filled for unexpired term in same manner as original appointment.

State	Department	Board or commission						Compensation	Qualifications	Other requirements	Removal	Filling of vacancies
Massachusetts	State Department of Public Welfare.	Advisory Board of State Department of Public Welfare.	7	3¹²		X¹²		Expenses	---	2 members of the board shall be women.	---	---
Michigan	State old age assistance bureau (in the State Welfare Department).	State old age assistance bureau (see Director of State Welfare Department, table 35).	---	---	---	---	---	---	---	---	---	---
		State Emergency Welfare Relief Commission.	3	---	---	X	---	Expenses	---	---	---	---
Minnesota	State Board of Control.	State Board of Control.	3	6²	X			Salary and expenses.	---	1 woman and not more than 2 of same political party. Members may not hold any other lucrative office.	By Governor for malfeasance, nonfeasance, or any other cause which renders member unfit for office. A member may be removed for exerting political influence to induce members or officers to change their affiliation.	For unexpired term in same manner as original appointment.
Mississippi	State Department of Public Welfare.	State Board of Public Welfare.	3	4	---	X	---	Expenses	---	At no time shall more than 1 member be a resident of any 1 of the 3 supreme court districts (as now constituted) of the State.	---	By Governor for unexpired term.
Missouri	State Social Security Commission.	State Social Security Commission.	5	4²	---	X	X	Expenses	Appointee must be a resident of the State, a taxpayer, and a qualified voter of the State for at least 10 years.	The commission must be nonpartisan.	By Governor, after notice and hearing, for gross inefficiency, neglect of duty, malfeasance, nonfeasance, or misfeasance in office.	By Governor for unexpired term.

See footnotes at end of table.

Table 34.—Composition and Appointment of State Boards of Public Welfare—Continued

State	Name of State department	Name of governing or advisory board	Number of board members	Terms of office — Rotating (number of years)	Terms of office — Other	Method of selection — By Governor	Method of selection — By Governor with consent of Senate	Method of selection — Other	Remuneration	Qualifications	Limitation on appointment	Provision for removal	Provision for filling vacancies created by death, resignation, or removal
Montana	State Department of Public Welfare.	State Board of Public Welfare.	5	3			X		$10 per diem and expenses. Per diem must not exceed $300 annually.	Appointee must have interest and experience in civic affairs and matters of public welfare and must be a citizen of State and resident for 5 years immediately preceding date of appointment.	No member of the State board shall have any direct financial interest in or profit by any of the operations of the State Department of Public Welfare or any of its agencies.[3]	By Governor for cause.	By Governor for unexpired term.
Nebraska	State Board of Control.	State Board of Control.	3	6[2]		X			$4,000 per annum and traveling expenses.	----	Not more than 2 board members shall be of the same political party or residents in the same congressional district. No board member may engage in any other occupation.	By Governor for malfeasance, nonfeasance, or any cause that makes a member ineligible or unfit for office. If the Legislature does not confirm the suspension during its first session after such action, the member suspended is to be reinstated and is entitled to draw full pay for the duration of his suspension.	Appointments to fill vacancies occurring during a legislative session must be made before the end of the session and within 5 days after any nomination shall have failed of confirmation.[15]
Nevada	State Welfare Department.	State Board of Relief, Work Planning, and Pension Control.	7	4				X	No compensation.	----	1 woman must be appointed to the board.	By Governor when in his discretion it seems advisable.	All appointments made by the Governor to fill any vacancy shall be made for a term of 4 years.

State	Agency	Board				Compensation	Qualifications	Special requirements	Removal	Vacancies
New Hampshire	State Department of Public Welfare.	State Board of Public Welfare.	3	3[2]	X[14]	$8 per diem and expenses.	Recognized interest in and knowledge of problems of public assistance and public welfare.	Not more than 2 of same political party may be members of the board.	By Governor and council at any time for cause.	For unexpired term.
New Jersey	State Financial Assistance Commission.[15]									
	State Department of Institutions and Agencies.	Board of Control of State Department of Institutions and Agencies.	10[16]	8	X	Necessary expenses.		1 member of the board must be a woman.[3]	By Governor at any time for good and sufficient cause.	By Governor for unexpired term only.
New Mexico	State Department of Public Welfare.	State Board of Public Welfare.	5[17]	6[2][17]	X	$10 per diem and expenses. Per diem may not exceed $500 annually.	Recognized interest in and knowledge of public welfare problems.	([3])		By Governor for unexpired term.
New York	State Department of Social Welfare.	State Board of Social Welfare.	15	5	X	$20 per diem and expenses. Per diem may not exceed $1,000 annually.		Members must be appointed from each of the 9 judicial districts of the State, and 6 from the State at large. No member shall serve more than 2 successive terms of 5 years, or for more than 10 successive years. No member shall serve on the board while he is a trustee, manager, director, officer, or member of the governing board of any institution subject to visitation or inspection by the State Board of Social Welfare.	By Governor for cause, after an opportunity for a hearing. A board member who is absent from 3 successive meetings, unless excused by formal vote of the board, shall be deemed to have vacated his position.	By Governor for unexpired term with advice and consent of Senate.
North Carolina	State Board of Charities and Public Welfare.	State Board of Charities and Public Welfare.	7	6	([18])	Expenses		1 woman must be named on the board.		By Governor for unexpired term.

See footnotes at end of table.

Table 34.—Composition and Appointment of State Boards of Public Welfare—Continued

State	Name of State department	Name of governing or advisory board	Number of board members	Terms of office: Rotating (number of years)	Terms of office: Other	Method of selection: By Governor	Method of selection: By Governor with consent of Senate	Remuneration	Qualifications	Limitation on appointment	Provision for removal	Provision for filling vacancies created by death, resignation, or removal
North Dakota	State Public Welfare Board.	State Public Welfare Board.	7	6[8]		(19)		Expenses		1 World War veteran must be named on the board.	By Governor for cause.	For unexpired term in same manner as original appointment.
Ohio	State Department of Public Welfare.	Director of public welfare (see table 35).										
Oklahoma	State Department of Public Welfare.	State Public Welfare Commission.	9	9[8]		X		Expenses	Appointee must have recognized interest in and knowledge of public welfare problems and must be at least 30 years of age, citizen of United States, and a qualified elector of State for at least 5 years preceding appointment.			By Governor for unexpired term.
	State Board of Public Welfare.	State Board of Public Welfare.	5[20]					No compensation.				
Oregon	State Relief Committee.	State Relief Committee.	7		[21]	X		Expenses				
Pennsylvania	State Department of Public Assistance.	State Board of Public Assistance.	9[22]	6[8]		Y[22]		Expenses	Citizens of the State.	No member shall serve more than 2 consecutive terms. Members may not hold office in any political party.		By Governor for unexpired term.
Rhode Island	State Department of Public Welfare.	Director of Public Welfare (see table 35).										

State	Agency	No.			Compensation	Qualifications	Restrictions	Removal
	State Unemployment Relief Commission.	7[23]	---	(23)	X	$10 per diem and expenses. Ex officio members receive no compensation.[23]		2 members from the Senate and 2 from the House; 1 member from each body to come from each major political party.	
South Carolina	State Department of Public Welfare.	7	4[2] [24]			$10 per diem and mileage. $200 per annum maximum.		After 1940 no member shall be eligible to succeed himself nor shall any citizen residing in the county from which the preceding commissioner came be eligible to succeed him. No member of the General Assembly shall be eligible for election as chairman or commissioner.	By Governor for unexpired term.
South Dakota	State Department of Social Security.	5	6		X	$10 per diem and expenses. Total compensation including expenses may not exceed $100 per month.		Not more than 3 commission members shall be of the same political party, nor shall a commissioner be a committee member or officer of any political party organization.	
Tennessee	Department of Institutions and Public Welfare (see table 35).								
Texas	State Board of Control.	3	6		X	$4,200 per annum.	Citizen of the State		By Governor for good cause, the reason to be specified and filed with the secretary of state.
	State Old Age Assistance Commission.	3	6[2] [25]		X	$10 per diem and expenses.[25]			By Governor for unexpired term with advice and consent of the Senate.

See footnotes at end of table.

Table 34.—Composition and Appointment of State Boards of Public Welfare—Continued

State	Name of State department	Name of governing or advisory board	Number of board members	Terms of office		Method of selection		Remuneration	Qualifications	Limitation on appointment	Provision for removal	Provision for filling vacancies created by death, resignation, or removal
				Rotating (number of years)	Other	By Governor	By Governor with consent of Senate					
Utah	State Department of Public Welfare.	State Board of Public Welfare.	7[28]	6[2]			X	Expenses		No more than 3 appointees shall be members of the same political party.	By Governor for cause	By Governor for unexpired term.
Vermont	State Department of Public Welfare.	Commissioner of public welfare (see table 35).										
	State Old Age Assistance Commission.	State Old Age Assistance Commission.	3	6			X	$10 per diem and expenses.	Citizen of the State	No more than 2 members shall be of same political party.		By Governor when Legislature is not in session.
Virginia	State Board of Public Welfare.	State Board of Public Welfare.	5	4[2]		(27)		$10 per diem and expenses. Per diem must not exceed $1,000 per annum.		No director, officer, or employee of any State institution may be appointed a member of the board.	At pleasure of Governor.	For unexpired term in same manner as original appointment.
Washington	State Department of Social Security.	State advisory committee to the State Department of Social Security.	(28)									
West Virginia	State Department of Public Assistance.	State Advisory Board.	5	6			X	$10 per diem and expenses.	Ability and fitness to establish a permanent system of public assistance and public welfare.	Not more than 3 board members shall be of the same political party. A board member must not be a candidate for or hold any public office or engage in any political activity other than voting.	At will and pleasure of Governor. Any violation by a member of the provisions concerning qualifications shall automatically vacate his membership on the board.	By Governor for unexpired term.

State	Agency	No.			Compensation	Qualifications	Removal	Appointment
Wisconsin	Pension department of the Industrial Commission. State Board of Control.	3[89]	6[2]	X	$5,000 and expenses.	1 member must be a woman. Members must devote entire time and attention to duties of office.	The Governor may remove any member for inefficiency, neglect of duty, or malfeasance in office. Before such removal he may give the member a public hearing.	By Governor for unexpired term subject to confirmation by Senate, and such appointment shall be in full force until acted upon by the Senate.
Wyoming	State Department of Public Welfare. State Board of Public Welfare.	5[90]			Expenses	1 member from each judicial division.		By Governor.
Alaska	Territorial Department of Public Welfare. Territorial Board of Public Welfare.	5[91]	4[2]	X[92]	$10 per diem and expenses. Per diem may not exceed $1,000 per annum.	Citizen of the United States and resident of the Territory and judicial division from which appointed for at least 5 years immediately preceding appointment.		By Commissioners for unexpired term.
District of Columbia	Board of Public Welfare. Board of Public Welfare.	9	6	(33)	No compensation.	Legal residents of the District of Columbia for at least 3 years. Appointment to the board made without regard to sex or color.[4]	By Commissioners for cause.	By Commissioners for unexpired term.
Hawaii	Territorial Board of Public Welfare. Territorial Board of Public Welfare.	7	4[2]	X	Expenses	1 member from Honolulu, Hawaii, Maui, and Kauai. 3 members from the Territory at large. Any person holding an elective or appointive salaried position with the Federal, Territorial, or county governments is ineligible for board membership. During term of office no board member shall be a candidate for public office or serve as an officer or committee member of any political party.		By Governor for unexpired term.

See footnotes on following page.

X indicates that the provision applies without limitation in a given State.

[1] The board consists of the Governor and 6 members appointed by him.

[2] Term continues until successor is appointed and qualified.

[3] Board members are to be appointed without regard to political affiliation.

[4] Commissioner is an ex officio member of the board and serves as secretary.

[5] Board members are to be appointed without regard to political or religious affiliation.

[6] With the advice and consent of the General Assembly.

[7] The board consists of the director and 6 members.

[8] The commissioner of welfare serves as chairman ex officio.

[9] Members serve during term of Governor or until their successors have been appointed by succeeding Governor.

[10] Council appointed by the Governor and his advisory council.

[11] Composed of 6 members with the Governor and the director of health ex officio members.

[12] 2 members appointed annually by the Governor with the advice and consent of the council. The commissioner of the State Department of Public Welfare is an ex officio member of the board.

[13] Appointments to fill vacancies occurring between sessions expire 30 days from the time of the convening of the session unless confirmed at the next session. No vacancy shall be deemed to have occurred between legislative sessions if there shall be a failure to nominate and confirm appointee.

[14] Board appointed by the Governor with the advice and consent of his council.

[15] The commission consists of the Governor, State treasurer, comptroller, chairman of committee on appropriations of the Senate, and chairman of committee on appropriations of the General Assembly. The commission selects a chairman.

[16] The board consists of 9 members and the Governor, ex officio.

[17] The Governor is an ex officio member of the board.

[18] The members of the board are elected by the General Assembly upon recommendation of the Governor.

[19] Appointed by the Governor, the attorney general, and the commissioner of agriculture and labor.

[20] The State board is composed of the Governor as chairman, the chairman of the State Board of Public Affairs, the State treasurer, the State commissioner of health, and the adjutant general.

[21] Members serve at pleasure of the Governor.

[22] Board consists of State treasurer, the auditor general, and 7 other citizens of the State.

[23] The commission consists of the Governor, the State budget director, and the comptroller, ex officio; 2 members appointed from the Senate and 2 from the House of Representatives. The terms of office expire June 30, 1939, but the members must remain in office until July 31, 1939, in order to prepare the commission's report to the Governor.

[24] 1 commissioner is elected from each congressional district by the General Assembly. Chairman of the State Board of Public Welfare is elected from the State at large by the General Assembly.

[25] Commission may not remain in session more than 120 days in any 1 year.

[26] The Governor is chairman of the board.

[27] Members selected with the consent of the General Assembly.

[28] The State advisory committee to the State Department of Social Security consists of the directors of the State Department of Health and the Department of Finance, Budget, and Business and the superintendent of public instruction, together with a representative of the superior court judges association and of the State association of county commissioners.

[29] The department consists of a member of the Industrial Commission, selected by such commission, the director of the budget, and the supervisor of pensions.

[30] The Governor, secretary of state, State auditor, State treasurer, and superintendent of public instruction constitute the State Board of Public Welfare.

[31] Governor and 4 members constitute the board.

[32] Selection of the board must be approved by the Senate and House of Representatives in joint session.

[33] Members appointed by the Commissioners of the District of Columbia.

Table 35.—Appointment and Qualifications of Executives of State Boards or Departments of Public Welfare

State	Title of executive	Term of office	By Governor	By Governor with consent of Senate	By commission or board	Remuneration	Qualifications	Provision for filling vacancy in office
			Method of selection					
Alabama	Commissioner of State Department of Public Welfare.	Pleasure of board.			X	Fixed by board[1]	Education, ability, and experience in field of public welfare without regard to residence or political affiliation.	
Arizona	Commissioner of State Department of Social Security and Welfare.	Pleasure of board.			X	Fixed by board[2]	Training, ability, and experience in field of public welfare.	
Arkansas	Commissioner of public welfare.	Pleasure of Governor.	X			Fixed by law	Training, ability, and experience in field of public welfare without regard to political affiliation.	
California	Director of State Department of Social Welfare.	Pleasure of board[3].			X[3]	Fixed by law	Training, demonstrated ability, leadership, and experience in organized social welfare administration.[4]	
Colorado	Director of State Department of Public Welfare.	Pleasure of Governor.			X	([5])		
Connecticut	Commissioner of welfare.	4 years beginning July 1, 1939.	X[6]					
Delaware								
Florida	State welfare commissioner.	4 years.	X			Fixed by board[2]	Citizen and elector for 5 years, with at least 2 years practical business experience and any qualifications set by the Governor.	
Georgia	Director of State Department of Public Welfare.	2-year term concurrent with Governor.	X			Fixed by law	Training, ability, and experience in public welfare administration.	
Idaho	Commissioner of State Department of Public Assistance.		X[7]					
Illinois	Director of public welfare for State Department of Public Welfare.	2 years[8]		X		Fixed by law		
Indiana	Administrator of State Department of Public Welfare.	Pleasure of board.			X[9]	Fixed by Governor.[2]		Governor may make temporary appointment until next meeting of Senate.

See footnotes at end of table.

Table 35.—Appointment and Qualifications of Executives of State Boards or Departments of Public Welfare—Continued

State	Title of executive	Term of office	Method of selection — By Governor	By Governor with consent of Senate	By commission or board	Remuneration	Qualifications	Provision for filling vacancy in office
Iowa	Secretary of State Board of Social Welfare.	Pleasure of board			X	Fixed by board[2]	Must have been a resident of the State for at least 2 years immediately preceding employment and must qualify in an examination covering general training, character, and experience given to State board employees.	
Kansas	Director of State Board of Social Welfare.	Pleasure of board			X	Fixed by board[2]	Recognized interest, knowledge, and executive ability in the field of social welfare.	
Kentucky	Commissioner of welfare	Pleasure of Governor but not more than 4 years.	X			Fixed by law	Merit and fitness to perform duties of office.	Governor may authorize the head of a division or other executive officer in the department to act as head of such department until the absence or disability of the commissioner is terminated or the vacancy is filled.
Louisiana	Commissioner of State Department of Public Welfare.	Pleasure of board			X	Fixed by board	Training, ability, and experience in public welfare administration.	
Maine	Commissioner of health and welfare.	3 years or during pleasure of Governor and council.	X[10]			Fixed by Governor and council.		Filled in same manner as original appointment.
Maryland	Executive secretary of Board of State Aid and Charities.				X	Fixed by board[2]	Training and practical experience in social welfare and relief work.	
Massachusetts	Commissioner of public welfare	5 years	X[10]			Fixed by Governor and council.[2]		
Michigan	Director of State Welfare Department.[11]	Until successor is appointed and qualified.		X		Fixed by legislative appropriation.	Must devote entire time to duties of office.	Filled by authority making original appointment.
	Chairman of State Emergency Welfare Relief Commission (see State Emergency Welfare Relief Commission, table 34).	do		X		do	do	Do.

State	Administrative officer	Tenure			Salary	Qualifications	Remarks
Minnesota							
Mississippi	State commissioner of public welfare.	Pleasure of board, but not to exceed 4 years. Reappointment possible.		X	Fixed by law	Must not engage in other business, vocation, or employment during term of office.	Filled by Governor pending confirmation by Legislature.
Missouri	State administrator	4 years	X		Fixed by law	Citizen and taxpayer for at least 10 years with education and experience in public welfare administration.	
Montana	State administrator of public welfare.	Determined by board.		X[12]	Fixed by board[2]	Resident of State for 5 years with education, training, and ability in public welfare administration.	
Nebraska	Director of assistance	2 years[8][13]	X[14]		Fixed by Governor.[2]		
Nevada	Secretary of State Board of Relief, Work Planning, and Pension Control.			X			
New Hampshire	State commissioner of public welfare.	Pleasure of board		X	Fixed by law	Citizen of the United States and of the State of New Hampshire.	
New Jersey	Commissioner of institutions and agencies.	Pleasure of board		X	Fixed by board[2]	Office must be in unclassified list of civil service. Not limited to residents of State.[15]	
	Director of financial assistance			X	Fixed by commission.		
New Mexico	Director of State Department of Public Welfare.	Pleasure of board		X	Fixed by board[2]	Resident of State for 1 year with training, experience, and ability in public welfare administration.	
New York	State commissioner of social welfare.	Pleasure of board		X	Fixed by law		
North Carolina	Commissioner of public welfare			X[16]		Trained social worker	
North Dakota	Executive director	Pleasure of board		X	Fixed by board	Resident of State for 5 years, with wide experience, education, and training in administration of public and/or private welfare institutions, agencies, and activities.[15]	
Ohio (See appendix B.)	Director of public welfare	Pleasure of Governor.	X		Fixed by law	May not hold another office or position for profit.	The assistant director acts as director of department until vacancy is filled.
Oklahoma	Director of public welfare of the State Department of Public Welfare.	Pleasure of commission.		X	Fixed by board	Ability, training, and experience in the field of public welfare. Director must not be a member of the commission.	

See footnotes at end of table.

Table 35.—Appointment and Qualifications of Executives of State Boards or Departments of Public Welfare—Continued

State	Title of executive	Term of office	Method of selection			Remuneration	Qualifications	Provision for filling vacancy in office
			By Governor	By Governor with consent of Senate	By commission or board			
Oregon	Administrator				X	Fixed by board		
Pennsylvania	Secretary of public assistance of the State Department of Public Assistance.	4-year term beginning 3d Tuesday in January next following election of Governor.[8]		X		Fixed by law		
Rhode Island	Director of Public Welfare	Appointed biennially and holds office at pleasure of Governor.[8]	X			Fixed by law		By Governor, in same manner as original appointment. Governor may make ad interim appointments.
South Carolina	State director of public welfare	Holds office until his successor has been appointed.			X	Fixed by board[2]		
South Dakota	Director of State Department of Social Security.	Pleasure of Governor.	X			Fixed by Governor.[2]	Standards fixed by State commission	
Tennessee	Commissioner of institutions and public welfare for the Department of Institutions and Public Welfare.	Pleasure of Governor.[8]	X			Fixed by law[17]	Appointed solely on basis of merit measured by education, ability, experience, and administration of public welfare activities without regard to residence or political affiliation.	
Texas	Executive director of division of public welfare of State Board of Control.	Pleasure of board			X	Fixed by board[2]	Executive ability and extensive experience in public welfare.	
	Executive director of State Old Age Assistance Commission.				X	Fixed by law	Citizen of State with residence in State for at least 10 years preceding date of appointment. Must be at least 35 years old at time of appointment.[18]	
Utah	Director of State Department of Public Welfare.	Pleasure of board			X	Fixed by board		
Vermont	Commissioner of public welfare	2 years. (Appointed biennially, during session of General Assembly.)	X			Fixed by law	(19)	

State	Officer (Director of old age assistance)	Term and removal	Appointment	Salary	Qualifications	Filling vacancies
Virginia			X[20] X[21]	Fixed by commission.[2]		In same manner as original appointment.
	State commissioner of public welfare.	At pleasure of Governor for term coincident with that of Governor making the appointment.[8]		Necessary expenses and such salary as may be appropriated for the purpose.		
Washington	State director of social security.	Pleasure of Governor.	X	Fixed by Governor.[2]		If a vacancy occurs while the Senate is not in session, the Governor shall make a temporary appointment until the next meeting of the Senate, when he shall present to the Senate his nomination for office.
West Virginia	State director of public assistance of the State Department of Public Assistance.	6 years, unless removed at pleasure of Governor.	X	Fixed by law.	Training, experience, capacity, and interest in public welfare activities.[22]	
Wisconsin	Supervisor of pensions		X[23]	(23)	(23)	
Wyoming	Director of State Department of Public Welfare.	Pleasure of board.	X	Fixed by board.	Training, ability, and experience in public welfare administration.	
Alaska	Welfare director	4 years. May be removed at pleasure of board.	X	Fixed by law.	Citizen of the United States and resident of the Territory at least 5 years immediately preceding his appointment.	
District of Columbia	Director of public welfare		(24)	Fixed by law.	Proper training and experience	
Hawaii	Director	Pleasure of board.	X	Fixed by board[25]		

X indicates that the provision applies without limitation in a given State.

[1] With the approval of the Governor, and within limit set by law.
[2] Within limit set by law.
[3] At least 4 members shall agree on appointment or removal of the director.
[4] May be affiliated in any way with an institution subject to examination, inspection, or supervision by the department.
[5] Fixed by executive council of the State.
[6] Appointed by and with advice and consent of the General Assembly.
[7] The Governor is a commissioner, ex officio.
[8] Term continues until successor is appointed and qualified.
[9] With advice and approval of the Governor.
[10] With consent of the council.
[11] The director is the executive of the State Department of Public Welfare.
[12] In cooperation with the Governor.
[13] May be removed by the Governor.
[14] With consent of the majority of the Legislature.
[15] Officer must devote entire time to performance of his duties.
[16] Subject to the approval of the Governor.
[17] Fixed by the General Assembly on the Governor's recommendation.
[18] Must not have occupied any elective State office 6 months prior to his appointment.
[19] Must not be the owner of, or in any way interested in any corporation or association subject to the supervision of his department, except as a policy holder in an insurance company or a depositor in a bank.
[20] Governor designates one of the members of the commission as chairman. Such person is known as the director of old age assistance.
[21] With the confirmation of the General Assembly.
[22] Must not be a candidate for or hold any political post during his term of office, or for 2 years after expiration of his term. Any violation of this provision automatically terminates appointment.
[23] By the Industrial Commission, in accordance with civil service requirement.
[24] By Commissioners of the District of Columbia on nomination of the board. Director may be removed by the Commissioners on the board's recommendation.
[25] Salary is fixed by board, subject to approval by the Governor.

Table 36.—Composition and Appointment of Local Boards of Public Welfare

State	Name of board	Number of members	Terms of office		Person or agency making appointments	Remuneration	Qualifications	Limitation on appointment	Provision for removal
			Rotating (number of years)	Other					
Alabama	County board of public welfare.	7	6		County board of commissioners, county board of revenue, or other county governing body.[1]	Expenses	Members must be citizens of the county with a recognized interest in public welfare.	2 board members must be women.	
Arizona	County board of social security and public welfare.	3	3[1]		County board of supervisors.	Traveling expenses	Board consists of 2 citizen members and 1 member of the board of supervisors.	The citizen members must be residents of different communities in the county.	
Arkansas	County board of public welfare.	5	5		(1)		Recognized interest in and knowledge of public welfare.	Members must be qualified voters and must be appointed without regard to political affiliation and must be so domiciled that they will be geographically distributed over the county. They may not hold any other elective or appointive position, nor may a member be a retail merchant. No member may serve more than 2 consecutive terms.	May be removed by State board for malfeasance, nonfeasance, or misfeasance.
California	County board of public welfare.[1]	7	4		County board of supervisors.[1]	Traveling expenses		Not more than 4 members may be of the same sex. Members may not be officially connected with any institution in the county supported by public funds.	Members shall be deemed to have resigned upon absence from 2 consecutive quarterly meetings.
Colorado	County board of public welfare.	(1)	(1)		(1)				
Connecticut									
Delaware									
Florida	County welfare board.[1]	9	4[2]		Governor	No compensation	Qualified electors of the county.	The board is composed of 5 men and 4 women.	Governor may remove any member for cause.

State	Name of agency	Number of members	Term of office	By whom appointed	Compensation	Qualifications	Restrictions on membership	Removal
	District board of social welfare.	([1])	4	----do----	Expenses	Citizen and elector of State for 5 or 9 years immediately preceding date of appointment.	No Federal, State, county, or municipal official is eligible for board membership.	Members serve at pleasure of Governor.
	County board of charity.	6[1]	3	Board of county commissioners.	No compensation	Board members must be tax payers and qualified voters over 30 years of age.	The board consists of 3 men and 3 women. No member shall be related by affinity or consanguinity within the 3d degree to a member of the board of county commissioners or any other county officer.	
Georgia	County board of public welfare.[1]	5	3	County commissioner or board of county commissioners, or the constituted fiscal agent of each county with the approval of the State department.[1]	Expenses		No elected officer of the State or any subdivision shall be eligible for appointment to the board.	
Idaho	County welfare commission.	5	3	([1])	Expenses			
Illinois	County department of public welfare.[1]							
	County bureau of public welfare.[1]							
Indiana	County board of public welfare.[1]	5	4[2]	Judge of the county circuit court.	Traveling expenses	Resident of county for at least 2 years prior to appointment. Must have recognized interest in and knowledge of problems of public welfare.	2 board members must be women and not more than 3 members shall be of the same political party.	The judge of the circuit court may, after a written notice, remove a board member for misconduct, incapacity, or neglect of duty.
Iowa	County board of social welfare.	([1])	1 year[2]	County board of supervisors.	$3 per diem and expenses.[1]	([1])	([1])	
Kansas	County board of social welfare.			([1])				
Kentucky								
Louisiana (See appendix B.)	Parish board of public welfare.[1]	5[1]	([1])	([1])	Expenses	Board members must be citizens of the parish.		
Maine								

See footnotes at end of table.

Table 36.—Composition and Appointment of Local Boards of Public Welfare—Continued

State	Name of board	Number of members	Terms of office: Rotating (number of years)	Terms of office: Other	Person or agency making appointments	Remuneration	Qualifications	Limitation on appointment	Provision for removal
Maryland	County welfare board.	7	3	—	Board of county commissioners.	No compensation	———	(1)	
	Advisory welfare committee, Baltimore City Department of Welfare.	7	6	—	Mayor of Baltimore.	—do—	Members must understand the problems of social welfare.		
Massachusetts	Local boards of public welfare.	(1)	3 or 5	—	(1)	———	Members must be residents of the county.	———	
Michigan	County old age assistance board.	(1)	—	(1)	(1)	Expenses[1]	(1)	———	
	County welfare relief commission.	3	—	—	State Emergency Welfare Relief Commission, with approval of Governor.	Expenses			By authority making original appointment.
Minnesota	County welfare board.	5[1]	2[1]	—	(1)	$3 per diem and expenses.	Members must be residents of the county.[1]	1 of the board members must be a woman. At least 1 but not more than 3 members of the county welfare board shall be members of the board of county commissioners.	
Mississippi	County board of public welfare.	3 to 5[1]	—	(1)	County board of supervisors.	(1)		———	
Missouri	County social security commission.	4	4	—	State Social Security Commission.[1]	Expenses	Qualifications for county commissioners are the same as those for State commissioners (see table 34).	No more than 2 commission members may be of the same political party. No elective officer shall be appointed to the commission.	Any member of the commission who becomes a candidate for an elective office forfeits his position on the commission.
Montana	County board of public welfare.[1]				(1)			———	
Nebraska	County assistance committee.[1]				(1)				
Nevada	County board of relief, work	5	—	(1)	State Board of Relief, Work Planning,	No compensation		At least 1 , member must be a woman.	

State	[planning, and pension control.[1]]			[...and Pension Control]				
New Hampshire ---								
New Jersey ------	County welfare board.	8[1]	5	County board of chosen freeholders.	Expenses ------	Member must be a citizen of the county.	At least 2 members of the board must be women.	
	Local assistance board.[1]	3 to 5	Fixed by local governing body.	Chief executive officer of local unit, upon approval of local governing body.	No compensation but necessary and actual expenses may be allowed.		1 member must be a woman -----	
New Mexico ------	Local boards of public welfare.[1]			State Department of Public Welfare.[1]				
New York -------	See table 37 ---							
North Carolina --	County board of charities and public welfare.	3	3	([1]) ---------	No compensation --		No member may serve more than 2 successive terms.	
North Dakota ----	County welfare board.	([1]) ---	3[2]	Board of county commissioners.[1]	Expenses[1]	Must be chosen on basis of fitness by reason of character, experience, and training.	Appointed without regard to political affiliation. Board must contain members of both sexes.	May be removed without cause by board of county commissioners and State Board of Public Welfare.
Ohio -----------		([1]) ---		([1]) ---------				
Oklahoma -------	County assistance board.	([1]) ---		([1]) ---------				
	County welfare board.	([1]) ---		([1]) ---------				
Oregon ---------	County relief committee.	7[1]	([1]) ----	Governor[1]				([1]).
Pennsylvania ---	County board of assistance.	7 or 11	3	Governor[1]	Expenses ------		No member may hold office in a political party and all members must not belong to same political party. No member may serve more than 2 consecutive terms.	
Rhode Island ---	See table 37 ---							
South Carolina --	County board of public welfare.	3	3[2]	([1]) ---------	([1]) ---------	Members must have resided in State 1 year immediately preceding appointment and at least 3 years out of the 5 preceding years.		

See footnotes at end of table.

Table 36.—Composition and Appointment of Local Boards of Public Welfare—Continued

State	Name of board	Number of members	Terms of office — Rotating (number of years)	Terms of office — Other	Person or agency making appointments	Remuneration	Qualifications	Limitation on appointment	Provision for removal
South Dakota									
Tennessee	See table 37								
Texas									
Utah	County board of public welfare.[1]	7[1]	6		Board of county commissioners.		Residents who have demonstrated their interest in social service and public welfare problems are eligible for board membership.	The board must include at least 1 woman. Not more than ¾ of the members, other than the county commissioners, may be members of the same political party.	May be removed by board of county commissioners for neglect or failure to perform and carry out the duties of their office properly.
Vermont									
Virginia	County or city board of public welfare.	([1])	2		([1])		Must be a resident of county or city.	([1])	May be removed by State Board of Public Welfare for cause by and with the approval of the court or judge making the appointment.
Washington	Advisory committee.[1]	5 or more.		2 years	Board of county commissioners.[1]	Expenses	Local citizens selected on basis of interest and experience in public welfare, child welfare, health, employment, and education.	May be reappointed regularly at pleasure of board of county commissioners.	
West Virginia	County public assistance council.	5	3		Governor[1]	No compensation	Citizens of county are appointed to council on basis of character, experience, and training.	Not more than 3 council members shall be of the same political party.	May be removed at pleasure of Governor. If a member of the council becomes a candidate for or is appointed to any other public office or political committee or serves as an election official, his office is automatically vacated.

State	Agency			Selecting authority		Notes
Wisconsin	County department of public welfare.[1]	5		County board of supervisors.		At least 3 members shall be members of county board.
	County pension department.[1]	(1)	(1)	do	(1)	May be removed by State board for failure to attend regular meetings for a period of 3 months or failure to meet other responsibilities delegated to the county board.
Wyoming	County board of public welfare.	5	3	Board of county commissioners.[1]	Expenses	County residents are eligible for appointment.
Alaska						
District of Columbia						
Hawaii	County public welfare commission.	6[1]	4[2]	Governor[1]	Expenses	

[1]See explanatory notes.

[2]Term continues until successor is appointed and qualified.

EXPLANATORY NOTES

Alabama.—In counties with cities of 60,000 population or more, the city commissioner or governing body of the city has equal authority with the county governing body in selecting the members of the county board of public welfare.

Arizona.—Term of office applies only to citizen members of the boards.

Arkansas.—The members of the board are selected by the State Board of Public Welfare from lists of 3 names submitted by each elected and commissioned county official except the county coroner and surveyor. No more than 1 name shall be selected by the State board from each list submitted. If the county officials fail, refuse, or neglect to nominate qualified persons within a reasonable time, then the State board shall have the power to name the county board members within and for such county.

California.—A county board of public welfare must be established in each county or city and county upon petition by 100 electors, except where county or city and county charter has established a board or officials to perform public welfare duties.

Colorado.—The county board of public welfare consists of the board of county commissioners in each county and the department of health and charities in the city and county of Denver. With the approval of the State department 2 or more counties may form a district department of public welfare, and 1 or more of the county commissioners of the counties in each district constitute the district board.

Florida.—A county welfare board is established in every county with a population of 155,000 or more. A district board of social welfare is created in each of the 12 social

welfare districts in the State. Each board consists of 1 member from each county in a social welfare district, which has a population of 25,000 or less, and 1 or more members from each county with a population of 25,000 or more, with 1 member for every 25,000 population. The county board of charities is appointed in counties having a population of 9,700 to 10,500. 1 member is appointed from each county commissioner's district and 1 from the county at large.

Georgia.—A district department may be formed by 2 or more counties with the approval of the State department. The combined boards of each county constitute the district board of public welfare. If the county board of public welfare is not named within a reasonable time, the director of the State department may name a temporary county board.

Idaho.—The county welfare commission is composed of the county welfare supervisor, 3 members designated jointly by the State Department of Public Assistance and the board of county commissioners, and an appointee of the board of county commissioners who may be a member of the board and who serves at the pleasure of the board.

Illinois.—A county department of public welfare must be established in each county with a population of 500,000 or less. A county bureau of public welfare must be established in Cook County.

Indiana.—2 or more county boards of public welfare may unite to form a district department of public welfare, subject to the approval of the State Department of Public Welfare.

Table 36.—Explanatory Notes—Continued

Iowa.—The county board of social welfare, in a county with a population of less than 33,000 is composed of 3 members, not more than 2 of whom may belong to the same political party, and whose remuneration must not exceed $90 per annum. In a county with a population of 33,000 or more, the board is composed of 5 members, not more than 3 of whom may belong to the same political party, and whose remuneration must not exceed $120 per annum. At least 1 woman must be appointed to each board.

Kansas.—The county board of social welfare is composed of the board of county commissioners of each county.

Louisiana.—The parish board of public welfare is composed of 5 members, selected by the police jury of each parish from a list of 10 names submitted by the State department. In the parish of Orleans, the parish board is composed of 5 to 15 members, selected by the commission council of the city of New Orleans from a list submitted by the State department. Members of the parish boards serve during term of office of police juries or council appointing them.

Maryland.—The county welfare board is composed of 7 members, 6 of whom are appointed by the board of county commissioners from a list of persons submitted by the Board of State Aid and Charities. The board of county commissioners designates 1 of its members to serve ex officio. Mayor and commissioner of health of Baltimore City are ex officio members of the advisory welfare committee, Baltimore City Department of Welfare.

Massachusetts.—The town board of public welfare is composed of the town selectmen in towns which have not authorized the election of a town board. The selectmen may act as the town board of public welfare if approved by a majority vote upon petition of 10 percent of the registered voters. Each town must, at its annual meeting, elect 3 or 5 members to the board for a term of 1 to 3 years. The salaries of the welfare board members are fixed by town vote. 2 or more towns may, upon recommendation of the commissioner of public welfare, or by vote of each such town and subject to the approval of said commissioner, form a public welfare district for the purpose of employing therein suitable persons to assist the board of public welfare, or the selectmen acting as such board, of each constituent town. In such cases a district welfare committee is provided for, to be composed of 1 member elected by and from each board of public welfare within the district.

Michigan.—An old age assistance board in each county is composed of the county welfare agent, the probate judge, and the chairman of the superintendents of the poor. In counties with more than 1 probate judge the probate judge of the juvenile division is also a member of the board. The county welfare agent is appointed in each county by the State Welfare Commission.

Minnesota.—The county welfare board is composed of 5 members, 3 appointed by the board of county commissioners, and 2 by the State Board of Control. The members appointed by the State Board of Control are selected from a list submitted by the State board of county commissioners. Exceptions: The board of county commissioners constitutes the county welfare board in any county containing a 1st class city (a city having a population of 50,000 or more) operating under a home rule charter, wherein a city board of public welfare is established. In a county with a 1st class city having an assessed valuation of more than 95 percent of the assessed valuation of the entire county, the board of public welfare acts as the county welfare board. In a county with a population of 200,000 or more, an assessed valuation of over $250,000,000, and an area of over 5,000 square miles, the board of poor commissioners acts as the county welfare board. In a county with a poor and hospital commission, this body acts as the county welfare board.

North Dakota.—The county welfare board consists of 5, 7, or 9 members. Not less than 1 nor more than 2 of the board members shall be county commissioners. The other members of the county welfare board are appointed by the board of county commissioners with the advice and consent of the State Public Welfare Board. Members serve without compensation except that they may, at the discretion of the board of county commissioners, receive expenses incurred.

Oklahoma.—The county assistance board is composed of members of the board of county commissioners. The county welfare board is composed of the county health officer and the board of county commissioners.

Oregon.—The county relief committee is composed of 7 members, 3 of whom are members of the board of county commissioners or of the county court, ex officio. The other 4 members are appointed by the Governor and are subject to removal by him.

Pennsylvania.—The county board of assistance is composed of 11 members in 1st and 2d class counties and 7 members in all other counties. Members are appointed by the Governor with the advice and consent of the Senate.

South Carolina.—The county board of public welfare is composed of 3 members appointed by the State board or the State director of public welfare upon recommendation of a majority (including the Senator) of the county legislative delegation. If 40 days elapse and the county delegation has not made its recommendations, the State board has the authority to appoint a county board. The members receive $3 per diem and a mileage allowance of 5¢ a mile. Maximum amount received per diem must not exceed $120 the 1st year and $75 in subsequent years. The Charleston County Welfare Board consisting of 3 members is elected by a majority, including the Senator, of the Charleston County legislative delegation. Members hold office for 3-year rotating terms and until the election or qualification of their successors. Any member may be removed for cause, after hearing, by the delegation. Per diem compensation is annually fixed by the Charleston County Supply Act. The local agency designated to administer poor relief in Darlington County consists of a commission of public welfare consisting of 5 members, 1 of whom must be a member of the county board of directors and serve ex officio as chairman of the commission. The other members are appointed by the county board of directors to serve for a term of 2 years. The commissioners receive no compensation except travel expenses. The county board of directors may abolish this commission and appoint a new commission if it deems such action necessary in order to meet the requirements of Federal or State legislation and to obtain Federal or State funds for relief work in the county.

Utah.—A district department of public welfare, which may include 2 or more counties, may be established by the State Board of Public Welfare. 1 member of the county or district board must be a county commissioner of 1 of the counties constituting the district. Each county in the district must be represented on the district board.

Virginia.—A local board of public welfare must be established in each county or city in the State. In cities of the 1st class (a city having a population of 10,000 or more) the officer in charge of the division or department of public welfare constitutes such local board. In each 2d class city (a city having a population of 5,000 or more) the local board is composed of 3 members appointed by the judge of the corporation court, or in the absence of such court, by the judge of the circuit court having jurisdiction within the city. In counties the board is composed of 3 members appointed by the judge of the local board circuit court. At the discretion of the appointing judge, 1 member of the local board

Mississippi.—The county board of public welfare consists of 3 to 5 members representing 3 to 5 supervisors' districts as the case may be. The terms of office and salaries of the board members are fixed by the State department.

Missouri.—The county social security commission is selected by the State Social Security Commission. If the county court does not submit a list of eligibles, the State commission makes the appointments. In the city of St. Louis the duties of the county court must be performed by the board of estimate and apportionment. Statute provides for the creation of city boards of social welfare in counties containing cities of the 1st class (cities having a population from 75,000 to 150,000). The board is composed of the mayor, members of the county court, and 6 other members, 3 of whom are appointed by the county court and 3 of whom are appointed by the mayor and city council. The members receive no compensation and hold office for 3-year rotating terms. They must be nonpartisan and nonsectarian, and may be removed by the appointive authority for misconduct.

Montana.—The county board of public welfare is composed of the county commissioners, ex officio, who receive no extra compensation for serving as a welfare board. 2 or more counties may combine into an administrative unit.

Nebraska.—The county assistance committee is composed of the board of county commissioners or supervisors, the county treasurer, and the county board of public welfare, if established. A county board of public welfare may be established in any county by resolution of the board of county commissioners or supervisors. Such board is composed of 5 members who serve without compensation. 2 such members must be women.

Nevada.—A county board of relief, work planning, and pension control is established in each county where deemed advisable by the State Board of Relief, Work Planning, and Pension Control.

New Jersey.—The county welfare board is composed of 5 members. 2 designated members of the board of chosen freeholders and the county adjuster (when not serving as director of welfare) are ex officio members. Local assistance boards must be appointed in each municipality. The word *municipality* shall include any county, city, borough, township, town, village, or municipality governed by an improvement commission.

New Mexico.—Local boards of public welfare, to serve as agents of the State department, may be established by the State Department of Public Welfare in counties or in districts which may include 2 or more counties.

North Carolina.—The county board of charities and public welfare is composed of 3 members: 1 member appointed by the board of county commissioners, 1 by the State Board of Charities and Public Welfare, and the 3d member is selected by the first 2. If the first 2 members cannot come to an agreement, the 3d member is appointed by the judge of the superior court. In Wake County the county board is composed of 3 members: 1 appointed by the board of county commissioners of Wake County, 1 by the board of commissioners of the city of Raleigh, and 1 by the State Board of Charities and Public Welfare.

may be a member of the county board of supervisors or a member of the city council or other governing body. Members of county and 2d class city boards receive necessary traveling and other expenses. In addition, at the discretion of the governing body of the county or 2d class city, such boards may be compensated in an amount not to exceed $100 per year. In any county which has adopted a county executive, county manager, or executive manager form of government, the members of the board of public welfare are appointed and their compensation is fixed by the board of county supervisors. However, in counties operating under the county manager form of government such boards may be appointed and their compensation fixed by the county manager, the board of county supervisors, or other governing body.

Washington.—The advisory committee is composed of 5 or more members appointed by the board of county commissioners in cooperation with the State Department of Social Security. The boards of county commissioners serve as local administrative boards through which all categories and activities of public assistance are administered.

West Virginia.—The county public assistance council is composed of 5 members, 4 of whom are appointed by the Governor upon the recommendation of the State Advisory Board. The president of the county court is an ex officio member, or he may appoint a member of the court to serve in his place.

Wisconsin.—A county department of public welfare may be created in each county with more than 500,000 population. The county board of supervisors may at any time return the powers of such county department to the court or other agency which administered relief and public assistance prior to the creation of the county department. A county pension department may be established by the county board of supervisors in each county with less than 500,000 population. The pension department may be discontinued at the discretion of the county board of supervisors, and the administration of relief and public assistance may be vested in those agencies which administered relief prior to the creation of the pension department.

Wyoming.—The county board of public welfare is composed of 5 members. The board of county commissioners appoints 2 members, 1 of whom may come from their own membership; 1 member is the superintendent of schools in the largest city or town in the county; 1 member is appointed by the district judge of the district in which the county is located; and 1 is appointed by the State Board of Public Welfare.

Hawaii.—The county public welfare commission is composed of 7 members in the county of Hawaii, and 6 members in each of the counties of Maui, Kauai, and the city and county of Honolulu. The Governor appoints 1 member of the county public welfare commission of each of the above counties to the Territorial Board of Public Welfare. This member is designated as chairman of the county public welfare commission. The judges of the juvenile courts in the 3d and 4th judicial circuits in the county of Hawaii and the judges of the juvenile courts in other counties are ex officio members of the county public welfare commission.

Table 37.—Appointment and Qualifications of Executives of Local Boards or Departments of Public Welfare

State	Title of executive	Term of office	Method of selection			Remuneration	Qualifications
			Appointed by State Department of Public Welfare	Appointed by local governing body	Appointed by local board of public welfare		
Alabama	County director of public welfare.	Pleasure of county board.			X	Fixed by county department.[1]	Must meet qualifications prescribed by State Board of Public Welfare.
Arizona	Secretary of county board of social security and public welfare.				X		
Arkansas	County director of public welfare.				X	Fixed by county department.	Must meet qualifications prescribed by State Department of Social Security and Welfare. Director must be appointed without regard to political affiliation.
California	(2)						
Colorado	County director of public welfare.	Pleasure of county board.			X[3]	Fixed by county department.[4]	Must meet qualifications prescribed by State Department of Public Welfare.
Connecticut							
Delaware							
Florida	Secretary of district board of social welfare.[3]				(3)		
Georgia	County director of public welfare.	Pleasure of county board.			X	Fixed by county department.[4]	Must meet qualifications prescribed by State Department of Public Welfare.
Idaho	County welfare supervisor.[3]		X				Must be legal resident of State and county.
Illinois (See appendix B.)	County superintendent of public welfare.	4 years[5]		X[3]			Selected in accordance with county civil service law.
	Director of the county bureau of public welfare.[3]			X			
Indiana	County director of public welfare.	At pleasure of appointing board.			X[3]	Fixed by county department.[4] Mileage also allowed.	Director is chosen from list of eligibles established by the State Department of Public Welfare. He must have resided in county at least 2 years prior to date of appointment, but this requirement is waived if qualified person cannot be found in the county.
Iowa	County director of social welfare.				X[3]	Fixed by county board.[3]	Must have resided in county 2 years. Must be fit, experienced, and trained for the position, but graduation from college may not be made a prerequisite.
Kansas	County director of social welfare.	Pleasure of county board.[3]			X	Fixed by county board.[3]	Must be qualified in social work field and meet standards set by State Board of Social Welfare.

State	Title	Term of office				Compensation	Qualifications
Kentucky							
Louisiana (See appendix B.)	Parish director of public welfare.	Pleasure of parish board.			X[3]	Fixed by parish department.[4]	Must meet qualifications prescribed by State Department of Public Welfare.
Maine	(2)						
Maryland	Director of welfare of Baltimore City.	6 years	X			Fixed by city board of estimates.	Must be trained and have had at least 5 years' experience in social welfare work as an executive in charge of important welfare activities.
Massachusetts	Public welfare agent		X[3]				Must devote entire time to duties of office.
Michigan	County welfare agent.[3]	Pleasure of State Welfare Commission.	X			Fixed by law	May be employee of State or county.
Minnesota	County emergency welfare relief administrator.[3] Executive secretary of county welfare board.				X[3]	Fixed by county board[3]	Must have experience, training, and general qualifications.
Mississippi	County welfare agent.[3]		X			Fixed by State board	Fixed by State Board of Public Welfare.
Missouri	Secretary of county social security commission.[3]		X			Fixed by State board	Must have resided in State 5 years.
Montana	(2)						
Nebraska	(2)						
Nevada	(2)						
New Hampshire							
New Jersey	Director of welfare[3] (county welfare board).	5 years[5]			X	Fixed by county board	Must be a citizen of the United States and of the State. Must read and write the English language and be capable of making and keeping such records and reports as are lawfully required. Must know the poor relief laws, and, in the judgment of the county welfare board, must be a technically trained and qualified expert and administrator in the field of welfare service. May not be a member of the county welfare board.
	Director of welfare (local assistance board).				(3)	(3)	
New Mexico	(2)						
New York	Local public welfare officials.[3]	3 years[5]		(3)		Fixed by county governing body.	A supervisor of a town or a county treasurer shall not be eligible for appointment.
North Carolina	County superintendent of public welfare.[3]	2 years[3]			(3)	Fixed by county governing body.	Must have character, fitness, and experience for the position, and must be approved by the State Board of Charities and Public Welfare.[3]
North Dakota	(2)						
Ohio							

See footnotes at end of table.

Table 37.—Appointment and Qualifications of Executives of Local Boards or Departments of Public Welfare—Continued

State	Title of executive	Term of office	Method of selection			Remuneration	Qualifications
			Appointed by State Department of Public Welfare	Appointed by local governing body	Appointed by local board of public welfare		
Oklahoma	(2) Chairman of county welfare board.[3]						
Oregon	County relief officer	(3)			X[3]	Fixed by State board	
Pennsylvania	Executive director of county board of assistance.	(3)			X[3]	Fixed by State board	
Rhode Island	Local director of public welfare.[3]						
South Carolina	County director of public welfare.				X[3]	Fixed by State board[3]	Must have resided in State 1 year immediately preceding appointment or at least 3 years in the preceding 5 years. Must meet standards fixed by State Department of Public Welfare as to education, training, fitness, and experience in social work.
South Dakota							
Tennessee	Regional director of the Department of Institutions and Public Welfare.[3]		X			(3)	Must have training, ability, and experience.
Texas	Director of county department of public welfare.				X		Must have training, experience, and general ability.
Vermont	(2)						
Virginia	County or city superintendent of public welfare.	Pleasure of board[5]			(3)	Fixed by local board of public welfare.[3]	Appointed from list of eligibles furnished by State commissioner of public welfare.[3]
Washington	County administrator of public assistance.[3]	Pleasure of board of county commissioners.		X			Certificate of eligibility for office of administrator is issued by the State Department of Social Security.
West Virginia	County director of public assistance.	Pleasure of county council.			X[3]	Fixed by county department.[4]	Must meet qualifications prescribed by the State advisory board and must devote entire time to duties of his office.
Wisconsin	Administrator of county department of public welfare.[3]				X	Fixed by county department of public welfare.	Employed in accordance with county civil service laws.

	County director of public welfare.			Fixed by county board[4]	X	Selected in accordance with standards established by the State Department of Public Welfare.
Wyoming					X	
Alaska						
District of Columbia						
Hawaii	(2)					

X indicates that the provision applies without limitation in a given State. See explanatory notes.

[1] In conformity with salary schedule fixed by State board.

[2] Only those statutes which specifically provide for the appointment of a local executive have been included. General provisions for the appointment of local staffs may be construed to authorize the appointment of an executive in those States which have provided for local boards or departments without making specific provision for the appointment of an executive.

[3] See explanatory notes.

[4] In conformity with salary schedule fixed by State board or department.

[5] Term continues until successor is appointed and qualified.

EXPLANATORY NOTES

Alabama.—The salary of the county director as recommended by the commissioner and approved by the State Board of Public Welfare may not exceed $125 per month and $50 per month for traveling expenses.

Colorado.—The county director of public welfare is selected from a list of eligibles submitted by or through the board of county commissioners and certified by the State Department of Public Welfare.

Florida.—The secretary of the district board of social welfare is appointed by the board with the consent and approval of the State Welfare Board. No provisions are made for the executives of the county welfare boards or county boards of charity.

Idaho.—A county welfare supervisor may be designated by the State Department of Public Assistance to act in more than 1 county.

Illinois.—The superintendent of the county department of public welfare, in counties with population of 500,000 or less, is selected by the county board of supervisors or commissioners from a list of 5 persons who have been certified by the State Department of Public Welfare after a competitive examination. The superintendent may be removed by the State department for inefficiency, misfeasance, or other good cause. The director of the county bureau and his subordinates are appointed in accordance with the civil service laws of Cook County.

Indiana.—The county director of public welfare, in counties with populations of 400,000 or more, is appointed by the State Board of Public Welfare. The county director may be removed by the State board for nonconformance with the rules of that body. If a successor is not appointed by the State board within 10 days, the office of the county director is declared vacant. If the county board fails or refuses to appoint a successor, or if a vacancy occurring for any other reason is not filled within 30 days, the State department shall appoint a county director.

Iowa.—The county director is appointed and his compensation fixed by the county board of social welfare with the approval of the State Board of Social Welfare. The county director may be removed for inefficiency or incapacity in office on order of the State board.

Kansas.—The county director of social welfare serves at the pleasure of the county board or until approval is withdrawn by the State Board of Social Welfare.

Louisiana.—The parish director is selected from a list of eligibles certified by the State Department of Public Welfare.

Massachusetts.—A public welfare agent may be appointed by the town selectmen when they are authorized to act as the town board of public welfare. In towns with populations of 3,000 or less, the selectmen may appoint the school physician to act as public welfare agent.

Michigan.—The county welfare agent is appointed in each county by the State Welfare Commission. He is the representative of the State Old Age Assistance Bureau in his county. County welfare relief commission may appoint county emergency welfare relief administrator.

Minnesota.—An executive secretary is appointed by the county welfare board in accordance with the rules of the State Board of Control. The salary of the executive secretary is fixed by the county welfare board, subject to the approval of the board of county commissioners, except that in counties containing a 1st class city (a city having a population of 50,000 or more) with an assessed valuation of more than 95 percent of the total assessed valuation of the county, the salary is approved by the board of county commissioners and the city council of such city.

Mississippi.—A county welfare agent in each county is appointed by the State commissioner of public welfare. The county welfare agent may be removed from office for active political participation.

Missouri.—City boards of social welfare, which may be established in counties containing cities of the 1st class (a city having a population between 75,000 and 150,000), employ and discharge all persons or officers necessary to carry out matters over which they have jurisdiction.

New Jersey.—A director of welfare may be appointed by the county welfare board, subject to the approval of the board of chosen freeholders, to the position of acting director of public welfare, for a 6 months' probationary period. Upon expiration of such period, if there is no adverse action by the county welfare board, said appointment becomes permanent. The county adjuster, when qualified, may be appointed as director of welfare. The director may be removed for misconduct, neglect, incompetence, or other cause by the county welfare board after due notice in writing and a hearing. Local assistance boards must appoint local directors of welfare. These directors are paid such salaries as may be fixed by

Table 37.—Explanatory Notes—Continued

the local boards subject to the approval of the governing body of the municipality. Nothing is to be construed so as to make overseers of the poor ineligible for appointment.

New York.—The territory of each county exclusive of the town and city of Newburgh and the cities of Oswego, Kingston, Poughkeepsie, New York, and Auburn, if it so elects, constitutes a county public welfare district. The territory of each of the above cities constitutes a city public welfare district. City board of social welfare is retained in Buffalo for administration of general and veteran relief. In each county or city public welfare district, there is elected a county or city commissioner of public welfare for a term of 3 years. The salary of the county commissioner is fixed by the county board of supervisors. Vacancies in this office are filled for the unexpired term by the county supervisors, if in session, otherwise by the county judge. In counties which have not abolished the distinction between county poor and town poor, town public welfare officers and city public welfare officers are created. A member of the town board may be authorized to act as the welfare officer or a town public welfare officer may be appointed by the town board of supervisors which also fixes the salary and term of office. The city public welfare officer is the city authority elected to administer public relief. In counties adopting an optional form of county government, a director of the public welfare department, known as the county commissioner of public welfare, is appointed by the county executive.

North Carolina.—The superintendent of public welfare is elected by the county board of charities and public welfare and the board of county commissioners in joint session, subject to the approval of the State Board of Charities and Public Welfare. In the case of a tie vote, the judge of the superior court has the final decision. A superintendent may be dismissed by joint action of above boards for proven unfitness or failure in the performance of duty. The superintendent of public welfare for Wake County is appointed by the board of charities and public welfare for Wake County to serve at its pleasure. He receives such salary as may be determined by the above board subject to the approval of the board of county commissioners of Wake County. The State Board of Charities and Public Welfare and the commissioner of public welfare are authorized, in their discretion, to designate the city of Rocky Mount as a local welfare unit. If the city of Rocky Mount is designated as a local welfare unit, a city welfare officer qualified by character, fitness, and experience may be appointed by the city manager, subject to the approval of the State board.

Oklahoma.—The chairman of the board of county commissioners is the ex officio chairman of the county welfare board.

Oregon.—A county relief officer may be employed by the county relief committee with the approval of the State Relief Committee, and may be removed at the pleasure of the county relief committee.

Pennsylvania.—The executive director of the county board of assistance is appointed, transferred, suspended, or removed in accordance with the employment regulations of the State Department of Public Assistance.

Rhode Island.—As many local directors of public welfare as are required may be elected by the electors of each town. Under the rules and regulations of the State Unemployment Relief Commission, the local director of public welfare, or the local work relief bureau must serve as agent of the commission in the administration of home relief or work relief. Local work relief bureaus, when established, consist of 3 persons, the public works or highway commissioner, the town treasurer, and 1 other qualified elector of the town. If both a local director of public welfare and a local work relief bureau are designated to administer relief, the local director must serve as an executive officer of the work relief bureau.

South Carolina.—The county director of public welfare is selected by the county board of public welfare, subject to the rules of the State Department of Public Welfare. The salary of the director, as fixed by the State board, may not exceed $1,200 but the county boards may increase the salary of a director with funds other than those supplied by the State department. In Charleston County the Charleston County Public Welfare Board is authorized to employ an executive secretary, who serves for a term of 1 year at such salary as the board may fix. In Darlington County a member of the county board of directors serves as chairman of the county commission of public welfare.

Tennessee.—The State must be divided into regions composed of 1 or more counties, with a maximum of 14 regions. A regional director for each region so created is appointed by the commissioner of institutions and public welfare. Compensation is recommended by the commissioner and is finally fixed by the division of personnel in the Department of Administration.

Virginia.—2 or more counties, or a county and a 1st class city (a city having a population of 10,000 or more) may unite to have 1 superintendent. The board of supervisors or other governing body of the county or the city board of public welfare must, upon request of the State Board of Public Welfare, consider the discharge and replacement of any county or city superintendent. In a county with an executive manager, such manager may be appointed or designated as superintendent of public welfare with the approval of the State commissioner of public welfare. In a county which has adopted the county executive form of local government, the board of county supervisors shall appoint and fix the compensation of the local superintendent who serves at the pleasure of such board; however, the board of county supervisors may authorize the county board of public welfare to exercise all powers in so far as they relate to the local superintendents.

Washington.—A county administrator of public welfare may be appointed by a joint board acting for 2 or more counties, subject to the approval of the State Department of Social Security.

West Virginia.—The county director of public assistance is appointed from a list certified by the State Advisory Board. Upon approval of the State director of public assistance, 2 or more county councils may jointly employ a single director. With the approval of the State Advisory Board, the State director may order 2 or more county councils to employ a single county director. The county council shall discharge any county director of public assistance who becomes a candidate for public office, is a member of any political committee, serves as an election official, or engages in any other political activity other than to vote.

Wisconsin.—Qualifications, duties, and compensation of personnel of county pension departments are determined by county boards of supervisors.

Table of Citations to Statutory Provisions
Contained in Tables 1–37

Table 38.—Citations to Statutory

State	General relief tables 1—5	Old age assistance tables 6—11	Blind assistance tables 12—17	Aid to dependent children in their own homes tables 18—21
		Provisions granting relief and public		
Alabama	Michies Code Ann. (1928), secs. 2787—2806(44). Michies Code Ann. (1936 Cum. Supp.), secs. 2806(31); 2806(45); 2931(10)—2931(27); 6755(13). Gen. and Local Acts (1935, 2d ex.), No. 170.	Michies Code Ann. (1936 Cum. Supp.), secs. 2723(1); 2723 (3); 2723(11)—2723(12); 2723(17); 2723(19)—2723 (20). Gen. and Local Acts (1935, 2d ex.), Nos. 143; 170.	Laws (1935, 2d ex.), Nos. 87; 170.	Michies Code Ann. (1936 Cum. Supp.), secs. 3566 (1)—3566(10). Gen. and Local Acts (1935, 2d ex.), No. 170.
Arizona	Const., Art. 7, sec. 3 Rev. Code Ann. (1928), secs. 813— 815; 2195. Rev. Code Ann. (1936 Cum. Supp.), secs. 774(5); 774(12); 774(28); 811. Acts (1937), chs. 18; 69. Acts (1937, 3d ex.), ch. 4.	Acts (1937), chs. 69—70 Acts (1937, 3d ex.), ch. 2	Acts (1937), chs. 69; 71.	Acts (1937), chs. 69; 72
Arkansas	State: Digest of Stat. (1937), secs. 10676—10693; 10708; 10715—10731. Local: Digest of Stat. (1937), secs. 2906; 2913; 9157; 10586—10594.	Digest of Stat. (1937), secs. 10676—10695; 10699— 10711; 10725—10731.	Digest of Stat. (1937), secs. 10676—10694; 10697—10711; 10725—10731.	Digest of Stat. (1937), secs. 10658—10669; 10676—10694; 10696; 10699—10700; 10702— 10711; 10725—10731.
California	Const., Art. II, sec. 4; Art. XVI, sec. 10. Gen. Laws (1937), Act. 8780e; 8780e-1. Welfare and Institutions Code (1937), secs. 200—208; 2500— 2615. Stat. (1937, 1st ex.), S. Const. Amend. No. 2.	Welfare and Institutions Code (1937), secs. 2000— 2228.	Welfare and Institutions Code (1937), secs. 3000—3091.	Welfare and Institutions Code (1937), secs. 1500— 1575.
Colorado	Const., Art. VII, sec. 4 Stat. Ann. (1935), chs. 59, sec. 15; 124; 141, secs. 1—12, 15, 20, 24. Laws (1937), chs. 216; 223—224; 262.	Const., Art. XXIV Stat. Ann. (1935), ch. 141, secs. 13—27. Laws (1937), chs. 200—201; 223.	Stat. Ann. (1935), chs. 22, secs. 37— 68; 141, secs. 13, 20. Laws (1937), ch. 106.	Stat. Ann. (1935), chs. 33, secs. 85—106; 141, secs. 19—20, 24. Laws (1937), ch. 223.
Connecticut	Gen. Stat. (1930), secs. 1684— 1685; 1687—1701; 1703—1707; 1710—1719. Gen. Stat. (1935 Cum. Supp.), secs. 661c—673c; 713c. Gen. Stat. (1937 Supp.), secs. 361d—365d; 384d.	Gen. Stat. (1935 Cum. Supp.), secs. 674c; 732c; 734c— 737c; 740c—756c; 758c— 759c; 761c—764c. Gen. Stat. (1937 Supp.), secs. 392d—405d.	Gen. Stat. (1937 Supp.), sec. 401d.	Gen. Stat. (1930), secs. 1925—1929, 1931. Gen. Stat. (1935 Cum. Supp.), secs. 672c; 728c. Gen. Stat. (1937 Supp.), secs. 384d—385d; 390d— 391d.
Delaware	Rev. Code (1935), secs. 1628— 1644. Const., Art. V, sec. 2. Laws (1937), ch. 96.	Rev. Code (1935), secs. 1604—1608; 1611—1627. Laws (1937), ch. 124.		Laws (1937), ch. 95
Florida	Comp. Gen. Laws (1927), secs. 2153(4); 2267; 2373; 2904—2907; 2985; 5873—5875. Comp. Gen. Laws (1935 Cum. Supp.), secs. 2276(1)—2276(45). Gen. Acts (1937), chs. 18061— 18062; 18285.	Comp. Gen. Laws (1935 Cum. Supp.), secs. 4151(365)— 4151(378). Gen. Acts (1937), chs. 18015; 18285.	Comp. Gen. Laws (1935 Cum. Supp.), secs. 4151(304)— 4151(308). Gen. Acts (1937), chs. 18015; 18285.	Comp. Gen. Laws (1935 Cum. Supp.), secs. 2276(15)— 2276(16); 3727(1)—3727 (12). Gen. Acts (1937), chs. 18015; 18285.

Provisions Contained in Tables 1—37

| assistance | | Agencies administering relief and public assistance | |
Dependent and neglected children (institutions and agencies) tables 22—27	Veteran relief tables 28—33	State departments of public welfare (boards and executives) tables 34—35	Local departments of public welfare (boards and executives) tables 36—37
Michies Code Ann. (1928), secs. 103; 108; 110—114; 116—152; 3533; 3535; 3538; 3541—3542. Michies Code Ann. (1936 Cum. Supp.), secs. 104; 115; 152(1); 3528—3540; 2931(10)—2931(27); 6755. Gen. and Local Acts (1935, 2d ex.), No. 170.	Michies Code Ann. (1928), secs. 2797; 2933—2992. Michies Code Ann. (1936 Cum. Supp.), secs. 2974(3)—2974(5). Gen. Acts (1931), No. 134. Gen. and Local Acts (1935, 2d ex.), Nos. 143, sec. 3; 13; 187.	Michies Code Ann. (1928), secs. 103; 105—114. Michies Code Ann. (1936 Cum. Supp.), secs. 104; 115; 2723 (1); 2931(10); 2931(14)—2931(27); 3566(1)—3566(10). Gen. and Local Acts (1935, 2d ex.), Nos. 143; 170.	Michies Code Ann. (1928), secs. 143—152. Michies Code Ann. (1936 Cum. Supp.), secs. 152(1); 2723 (1); 2931(10)—2931(27); 3566(1)—3566(10); 6755. Gen. and Local Acts (1935, 2d ex.), Nos. 87; 143.
Rev. Code Ann. (1928), secs. 1932; 1934. Rev. Code Ann. (1936 Cum. Supp.), secs. 1928—1931; 1942. Acts (1937), ch. 69.	Rev. Code Ann. (1928), secs. 3222—3225. Rev. Code Ann. (1936 Cum. Supp.), secs. 3225a—3225f.	Acts (1937), ch. 69 _____	Rev. Code Ann. (1928), sec. 814. Acts (1937), chs. 69—72. Acts (1937, 3d ex.), ch. 3.
Digest of Stat. (1937), secs. 6350; 7459—7460; 7462—7479; 7481—7483; 7490; 7494; 10713. Acts (1937), Act 232.	Digest of Stat. (1937), secs. 10618—10657; 10670—10675; 12779; 12795—12802; 12906—12916.	Digest of Stat. (1937), secs. 10676—10731. Acts (1937), Act 232, secs. 2—5.	Digest of Stat. (1937), secs. 2906; 2913; 10586; 10590; 10676; 10682; 10684—10731.
Welfare and Institutions Code (1937), secs. 550—580; 630—701; 720—750; 860—884; 900—911; 1020—1202; 1620—1630.	Military and Veterans Code (1937), secs. 690—700; 920—950; 1010—1121. Political Code (1937), sec. 4408a.	Const., Art. XVI, sec. 10 ___ Gen. Laws (1937), Acts 8780e, 8780e-1. Welfare and Institutions Code (1937), secs. 100—130; 1551; 1554; 1556; 1621; 2005; 2140; 3075. Military and Veterans Code (1937), sec. 921. Stat. (1937, 1st ex.), S. Const. Amend. No. 2.	Welfare and Institutions Code (1937), secs. 200—221; 1550; 2140; 2503; 3078.
Stat. Ann. (1935), chs. 3, sec. 10(9); 33, secs. 1—43, 69—75, 81—84. Laws (1937), ch. 223.	Stat. Ann. (1935), ch. 150, secs. 1—21. Laws (1937), ch. 242.	Stat. Ann. (1935), chs. 22, sec. 39; 33, secs. 85—86; 141, secs. 2—20, 27, 30. Laws (1937), chs. 201, secs. 1—2; 216, secs. 1, 6; 223, secs. 2—3; 224; 262, sec. 1.	Stat. Ann. (1935), chs. 22, sec. 40; 33, secs. 85, 88; 124, sec. 3; 141, secs. 13, 21—26. Laws (1937), chs. 201, secs. 1, 3; 216, secs. 1, 7; 223, secs. 1, 3.
Gen. Stat. (1930), secs. 1817—1819; 1854—1863; 1865—1872; 1874—1876; 1879; 1880—1883; 1885—1891; 1893—1906; 1912; 1914; 1916; 1921; 2680. Gen. Stat. (1935 Cum. Supp.), secs. 687c—688c; 692c—704c; 706c; 709c; 712c—717c; 721c—726c. Gen. Stat. (1937 Supp.), secs. 374d; 380d—389d.	Gen. Stat. (1930), secs. 1944—1950; 1952; 1954—1956; 1960; 1966—1967; 1970. Gen. Stat. (1935 Cum. Supp.), secs. 768c—774c; 776c; 779c—780c. Gen. Stat. (1937 Supp.), secs. 172d—175d; 407d—409d; 411d—413d; 416d—419d.	Gen. Stat. (1930), secs. 1710; 1723—1724; 1914; 1916; 1921; 1927. Gen. Stat. (1935 Cum. Supp.), secs. 667c—668c; 670c—674c; 710c—716c; 721c; 728c; 734c—735c. Gen. Stat. (1937 Supp.), secs. 126d; 363d—365d; 384d—389d; 391d; 395d; 401d. Sp. Laws (1937), pp. 396—397.	
Rev. Code (1935), secs. 1118—1119; 1127—1135; 2538—2547; 2621—2622; 4327—4353. Laws (1937), chs. 97—98.	Rev. Code (1935), secs. 325—327 __ Laws (1937), ch. 32.	Rev. Code (1935), secs. 1115—1124; 1130; 1604—1608; 1628—1629. Laws (1937), ch. 95, sec. 2.	
Comp. Gen. Laws (1927), secs. 3684—3704; 3709—3715. Comp. Gen. Laws (1935 Cum. Supp.), secs. 3691(1); 3700(1)—3700(9); 3715(1). Gen. Acts (1937), ch. 18285.	Comp. Gen. Laws (1927), secs. 2097—2129. Comp. Gen. Laws (1935 Cum. Supp.), secs. 2102(1); 2121(1); 2124. Gen. Acts (1937), chs. 18046—18047.	Gen. Acts (1937), ch. 18285 _	District Board; Gen. Acts (1937), ch. 18285. County Welfare Board: Comp. Gen. Laws (1932), secs. 2153; 2276(1)—2276(5); 2904—2907; 2909—2912; 2985. Comp. Gen. Laws (1935 Cum. Supp.), sec. 2903. Gen. Acts (1937), chs. 18062; 18409.

Table 38.—Citations to Statutory Provisions

State	General relief tables 1—5	Old age assistance tables 6—11	Blind assistance tables 12—17	Aid to dependent children in their own homes tables 18—21
			Provisions granting relief and public	
Georgia	Const., Art. II, secs. 2-603; 2-5402. Code (1933), secs. 23-2101—23-2310; 34-203; 86-209; 92-3715. Acts (1937), p. 355.	Acts (1937), pp. 311, 355. Acts (1937, 1st ex.), pp. 68—69; 292; 351.	Acts (1937), pp. 355; 568. Acts (1937, 1st ex.), pp. 68—69; 292.	Acts (1937), pp. 355; 630. Acts (1937, 1st ex.), pp. 68—69; 292.
Idaho	Const., Art. VI, sec. 5. Code Ann. (1932), secs. 30-601— 30-605; 30-706; 30-2802; 30-2901—30-2911; 30-3302—30-3303; 33-403. Laws (1935), chs. 15; 104. Laws (1935, 3d ex.), ch. 2. Laws (1937), chs. 81; 115; 216.	Laws (1937), chs. 216; 244	Laws (1937), chs. 216; 244.	Laws (1937), chs. 216; 244
Illinois	Smith-Hurd Rev. Stat. (1935), chs. 23, secs. 393—409; 46, sec. 69; 107, secs. 1—44. Smith-Hurd Rev. Stat. (1936 Cum. Pam.), ch. 107, secs. 2, 4a—4b, 6, 10, 12, 14—14a, 15.1, 16, 17a, 18a—18b, 19a—19b, 21—22, 24—27a, 30, 34, 45—46. Laws (1935, 2d ex.), H. Bs. 85, p. 94; 99, p. 78; 100, p. 88. Smith-Hurd Rev. Stat. (1938 Supp.), chs. 24, sec. 65.102, 102, 123; 34, sec. 25; 107, secs. 20, 36a.	Smith-Hurd Rev. Stat. (1935), ch. 23, sec. 28. Smith-Hurd Rev. Stat. (1936 Cum. Pam.), ch. 23, secs. 410—427. Laws (1937), H. B. 959, p. 265.	Smith-Hurd Rev. Stat. (1935), chs. 23, secs. 279—287a; 34, sec. 67. Smith-Hurd Rev. Stat. (1936 Cum. Pam.), ch. 34, secs. 67k, 67q.	Smith-Hurd Rev. Stat. (1935), chs. 23, secs. 322—340; 34, sec. 67b. Laws (1937), H. B. 86, p. 270.
Indiana	Baldwin's Stat. Ann. (1934), secs. 13321—13322; 13326; 13360; 13362—13391; 13395. Baldwin's Stat. Ann. (May 1935 Supp.), secs. 13320-1—13320-38; 13359-1—13359-12; 13364-1— 13364-3; 13370; 13392—13394; 13395-1. Laws (1937), chs. 41; 119, sec. 1; 208; 254.	Baldwin's Stat. Ann. (May 1936 Supp.), secs. 14078-1; 14078-32—14078-51; 14078-98—14078-130. Laws (1937), chs. 41; 47.	Baldwin's Stat. Ann. (May 1936 Supp.), secs. 14078-1; 14078-52— 14078-70; 14078-98—14078-130. Laws (1937), chs. 41; 47.	Baldwin's Stat. Ann. (May 1936 Supp.), secs. 14078-71—14078-82; 14078-90— 14078-130. Laws (1937), ch. 41.
Iowa	Code (1935), secs. 388; 4005—4030; 5130(12); 5297—5337; 5338—5347; 5362; 5771; 6742. Acts (1937), ch. 195.	Code (1935), secs. 5296-f9; 5296-f29; 5296-f37; 5296-f39—5296-f40. Acts (1937), chs. 137; 139; 151; 186; 195.	Acts (1937), chs. 144; 151.	Code (1935), secs. 3641; 3641-b1; 3642—3645. Acts (1937), chs. 118; 151.
Kansas	Const., Arts. 5, sec. 3; 7, sec. 4. Gen. Stat. Ann. (1935), secs 19-244; 39-101—39-102; 39-301—39-340; 39-342d—39-353; 39-359—39-362; 39-3a04—39-3a13; 39-401—39-414; 39-510—39-527. Laws (1937), chs. 242—244; 248; 327; 374. Laws (1937, 1st ex.), H. B. 80.	Const., Art. 7, secs. 4—5 Laws (1937), ch. 327.	Const., Art. 7, sec. 4. Laws (1937), ch. 327.	Const., Art. 7, sec. 4 Laws (1937), ch. 327.
Kentucky	Carroll's Stat. Ann. (1936), secs. 913-1; 1840; 1882; 3058-14; 3922—3933. Acts (1936, 1st ex.), ch. 1, Art. 13. Acts (1938), ch. 122.	Carroll's Stat. Ann. (1936), secs. 3766bb-1—3766bb-16. Acts (1936, 1st ex.), ch. 1, Art. 13. Acts (1938), chs. 20; 56—58.	Carroll's Stat. Ann. (1936), secs. 1893a-10—1893a-13. Acts (1936, 1st ex.), ch. 1, Art. 13. Acts (1938), ch. 20.	Carroll's Stat. Ann. (1936), secs. 331L-8; 331L-16—331L-29; 4618-35. Acts (1936, 1st ex.), ch. 1, Art. 13. Acts (1938), ch. 20.
Louisiana	Const. (1921), Arts. 6, sec. 10; 8, secs. 2—3, 6, 13. Gen. Stat. (1932), secs. 6470—6486. Gen. Stat. (1936 Cum. Supp.), secs. 6537.8; 6537.12.	Const. (1921), Art. 18, sec. 7. Gen. Stat. (1936 Cum. Supp.), secs. 6538.26—6538.49.	Const. (1921), Art. 18, sec. 7. Gen. Stat. (1936 Cum. Supp.), secs. 6538.1—6538.25.	Const. (1921), Art. 18, secs. 5; 7. Gen. Stat. (1936 Cum. Supp.), secs 6539.4—6539.12

Contained in Tables 1—37—Continued

assistance		Agencies administering relief and public assistance	
Dependent and neglected children (institutions and agencies) tables 22—27	Veteran relief tables 28—33	State departments of public welfare (boards and executives) tables 34—35	Local departments of public welfare (boards and executives) tables 36—37
Code (1933), secs. 24-2401—24-2442; 35-505—35-506. Acts (1935), pp. 398—399; 490. Acts (1937), p. 355. Code Ann. (1932), secs. 31-1201—31-1223; 31-1312. Laws (1937), ch. 216.	Code (1933), secs. 23-2401—23-2403; 78-201—78-230; 35-901—35-905; 92-3701. Acts (1937), p. 355. Acts (1937, 1st ex.), pp. 292; 304. Code Ann. (1932), secs. 30-2911; 63-201—63-202; 63-204—63-205; 64-701—64-706; 64-806. Laws (1935), ch. 130.	Code (1933), chs. 35; 77—78; 99. Acts (1937), pp. 311; 355; 370; 565; 579; 630. Laws (1935), ch. 104 _____ Laws (1937), chs. 204; 216; 244.	Code (1933), secs. 78-205—78-213; 23-2101; 23-2401. Acts (1937), pp. 364; 612. Laws (1937), ch. 216.
Smith-Hurd Rev. Stat. (1935), chs. 23, secs. 190—220, 304—311; 107, sec. 44. Smith-Hurd Rev. Stat. (1936 Cum. Pam.), ch. 34, sec. 67k. Smith-Hurd Rev. Stat. (1938 Supp.), ch. 34, secs. 25, 67.2.	Smith-Hurd Rev. Stat. (1935), chs. 23, secs. 3—5, 115—163; 34, secs. 131—141.	Smith-Hurd Rev. Stat. (1935), chs. 23, secs. 43, 136—138, 299a—299e, 393—409; 127, secs. 3—11, 53—54b. Laws (1937), H. B's. 565, p. 271; 958, p. 451. Laws (1937), S. B's. 195, p. 1155; 276. Smith-Hurd Rev. Stat. (1938 Supp.), chs. 23, sec. 394; 34, sec. 67.2.	Smith-Hurd Rev. Stat. (1935), ch. 34, secs. 67a—67i. Smith-Hurd Rev. Stat. (1936 Cum. Pam.), ch. 34, secs. 67j—67u. Laws (1937), H. B. 958, p. 451. Smith-Hurd Rev. Stat. (1938 Supp.), chs. 24, sec. 65.102; 34, sec. 67.2.
Baldwin's Stat. Ann. (1934), secs. 4400—4440; 5669—5684; 5696—5696; 5700—5705; 5712—5714; 5716—5717. Baldwin's Stat. Ann. (May 1935 Supp.), secs. 5694; 5706—5711; 5715. Baldwin's Stat. Ann. (May 1936 Supp.), secs. 14078-1; 14078-8—14078-9; 14078-11; 14078-21; 14078-26; 14078-83. Laws (1937), chs. 41; 298.	Baldwin's Stat. Ann. (1934), secs. 4084—4110. Baldwin's Stat. Ann. (May 1935 Supp.), secs. 4086; 4086-1—4086-3; 4095-1; 4441—4458; 11019. Baldwin's Stat. Ann. (May 1936 Supp.), secs. 14078-8—14078-9; 14078-11. Laws (1937), chs. 41; 112.	Baldwin's Stat. Ann. (May 1936 Supp.), secs. 14078-2—14078-4; 14078-6—14078-17; 14078-28—14078-31. Laws (1937), ch. 41, secs. 1, 6—7.	Baldwin's Stat. Ann. (1934), secs. 5684—5685. Baldwin's Stat. Ann. (May 1936 Supp.), secs. 14078-18; 14078-21; 14078-23; 14078-25—14078-26; 14078-28—14078-31. Laws (1937), ch. 41, secs. 1—7.
Code (1935), secs. 3605—3616b; 3617—3640; 3656—3657; 3661-a8—3661-a10; 3661-a43; 3661-a58—3661-a100; 3666—3683; 3698—3703; 3706—3720; 7173. Acts (1937), ch. 118.	Code (1935), secs. 3287—3384; 5325—5326; 5385—5396-a2; 6020.	Acts (1937), chs. 118; 137; 144; 151; 195.	Acts (1937), chs. 137; 144; 151.
Gen. Stat. Ann. (1935), secs. 38-301—38-318; 38-401—38-410; 38-412—38-415; 38-422—38-432; 38-501—38-515; 39-101—39-109; 76-1701—76-1712. Laws (1937), ch. 327.	Gen. Stat. Ann. (1935), secs. 39-101—39-109; 73-211—73-212; 73-301—73-307; 76-101—76-163; 76-1901; 76-1918; 76-1920—76-1926. Laws (1937), chs. 342—343.	Const., Art. 7, sec. 4 _____ Laws (1937), chs. 29; 327—328; 374.	Laws (1937), ch. 327.
Carroll's Stat. Ann. (1936), secs. 216a-3; 216a-22; 216aa-32; 331b-1; 331c-1; 331e-1—331e-15; 331e-19—331e-21; 331L-6—331L-19; 331m-1; 331m-2; 938b-1—938b-22; 4618-35. Acts (1936, 1st ex.), ch. 1, Art. 13.	Carroll's Stat. Ann. (1936), secs. 415a-1—415a-12; 415b—415b-24; 4618-25—4618-27; 4619-81. Acts (1936, 1st ex.), ch. 1, Arts. 2, 13, 26, 27. Acts (1938), ch. 39. Acts (1938, 1st ex.), ch. 33.	Carroll's Stat. Ann. (1936), secs. 216a-3—216a-4; 216aa-2—216aa-34; 216aa-102—216aa-107; 331L-2—331L-29; 3766bb-4; 4618-35. Acts (1936, 1st ex.), ch. 1, Arts. 2, 13, 26—27. Acts (1936, 4th ex.), ch. 15. Acts (1938), chs. 57—58. Acts (1938, 1st ex.), ch. 26.	
Const. (1921), Arts. 6, sec. 10; 7, sec. 96. Gen. Stat. (1932), secs. 1679—1718. Gen. Stat. (1936 Cum. Supp.), secs. 1709; 1718.1—1718.3; 6537.8; 6537.12.	Const. (1921), Arts. 6, sec. 10; 18, sec. 1—3, 7. Gen. Stat. (1932), secs. 8295; 9185—9187; 9194—9196; 9198—9221. Gen. Stat. (1936 Cum. Supp.), secs. 9193.1—9193.9; 9197.	Const. (1921), Arts. 6, sec. 10; 18, sec. 7. Gen. Stat. (1936 Cum. Supp.), secs. 6537.1—6537.8; 6537.15—6537.28; 9193.1—9193.9.	Gen. Stat. (1936 Cum. Supp.), secs. 6537.8—6537.15.

Table 38.—Citations to Statutory Provisions

State	Provisions granting relief and public			
	General relief tables 1—5	Old age assistance tables 6—11	Blind assistance tables 12—17	Aid to dependent children in their own homes tables 18—21
Maine	Const., Arts. 2, sec. 1; 44. Rev. Stat. (1930), chs. 6, sec. 2; 18, sec. 4; 33; 72, sec. 5; 153. Laws (1931), chs. 124; 216. Laws (1933), chs. 1, sec. 301; 23; 188; 223; 228. Laws (1935), chs. 1; 91. Laws (1937), ch. 191.	Laws (1937, 1st ex.), ch. 105.	Laws (1937), ch. 210.	Laws (1937), ch. 177.
Maryland	Bagby's Ann. Code (1924), Arts. 4; 25; 65, sec. 1. Ann. Code (1935 Supp.), Arts. 4, sec. 3; 88A, secs. 3, 7, 8B—8D, 9A—9G. Flack's Code of Public Local Laws (1930), Arts. 1—24. Baltimore City Charter (1927), secs. 103—114. Laws (1936, 1st ex.), chs. 10—11. Laws (1937), ch. 191.	Laws (1937, 1st ex.), ch. 12.	Laws (1935, 1st ex.), ch. 145. Laws (1937, 1st ex.), ch. 4.	Laws (1935, 1st ex.), ch. 148. Laws (1937), ch. 39. Laws (1937, 1st ex.), ch. 3.
Massachusetts	Ann. Laws (1932), chs. 47; 116—117. Ann. Laws (1936 Cum. Supp.), chs. 116, sec. 2; 117, secs. 1, 2A, 6, 18, 24. Acts (1937), chs. 86; 107; 113; 125; 277. Acts (1938), chs. 186, sec. 4; 425; 465; H. B. 981.	Ann. Laws (1936 Cum. Supp.), chs. 118A; 138, sec. 27. Acts (1937), chs.107; 165; 440. Acts (1938), chs. 186, sec. 4; 274; 285; 467.	Ann. Laws (1932), chs. 15, secs. 5, 13; 69, secs. 12—24. Ann.Laws (1936 Cum. Supp.), ch. 69, sec. 25. Acts (1937), ch. 107.	Ann.Laws (1936 Cum. Supp.), ch. 118. Acts (1937), ch. 107.
Michigan	Const., Art. 3, sec. 2. Stat. Ann. (1935), secs. 5.331; 14.1139; 14.1147; 16.31—16.46; 16.121—16.195; 16.251—16.306. Stat. Ann. (1938 Cum. Supp.), sec. 16.367.	Stat. Ann. (1935), secs. 16.201—16.239.	Stat. Ann. (1935), secs. 16.33—16.37. Stat. Ann. (1938 Cum. Supp.), secs. 16.367; 25.297.	Stat. Ann. (1935), secs. 25.297. Stat. Ann. (1938 Cum. Supp.), secs. 16.367; 25.297.
Minnesota	Mason's Minn. Stat. (1927), secs. 3157—3160; 3162—3164; 3166; 3168—3198; 3199-1; 3199-3. Mason's Minn. Stat. (1938 Supp.), secs. 1192-1—1192-5; 3159-3; 3161; 3164-1—3164-8; 3164-19—3164-21; 3165; 3167; 3171-1—3171-2; 3177-1—3177-6; 3195-1—3195-4; 3199.	Mason's Minn. Stat. (1938 Supp.), secs. 53-18a; 974-17; 3183-1; 3199-11—3199-47.	Mason's Minn. Stat. (1938 Supp.), secs. 53-18a; 974-17; 3199-42—3199-89.	Mason's Minn. Stat. (1938 Supp.), secs. 53-18a; 8688-3—8688-26.
Mississippi	Const. (1890), secs. 241; 243. Code Ann. (1930), secs. 214—215; 3127; 5694—5716. Laws (1932), ch. 101. Laws (1934), ch. 308. Laws (1936), ch. 319.	Laws (1936), ch. 175. Laws (1938), ch. 361.	Laws (1938), ch. 181.	Code Ann. (1930), secs. 4011—4020.
Missouri	Const., Art. VIII, sec. 2. Stat. Ann. (1932), secs. 10179; 12939; 12944; 12950—12967. Stat. Ann. (1938 Cum. Pocket Part), secs. 12967b-1; 12967b-11; 12967b-14—12967b-20.	Stat. Ann. (1938 Cum. Pocket Part), secs. 12967b-1; 12967b-3; 12967b-11; 12967b-12; 12967b-14—12967b-20.	Const., Art. IV, sec. 4. Stat. Ann. (1932), secs. 8893; 8895—8900; 8902—8905. Stat. Ann. (1938 Cum. Pocket Part), secs. 8894; 8901.	Stat. Ann. (1938 Cum. Pocket Part), secs. 12967b-1; 12967b-11; 12967b-13—12967b-20.
Montana	Rev. Code Ann. (1935), secs. 4521—4541. Laws (1937), ch. 82.	Laws (1937), ch. 82, pts. I, III, VIII.	Laws (1937), ch. 82, pts. I, V, VIII.	Laws (1937), ch. 82, pts. I, IV.
Nebraska	Comp. Stat. (1929), secs. 55-101; 68-102; 68-106—68-109; 68-117—68-120; 68-123; 77-1802. Comp. Stat. (1937 Cum. Supp.), secs. 27-748; 68-101; 68-103—68-105; 68-110—68-116; 68-121; 68-124—68-125; 68-324; 77-1801.	Comp. Stat. (1937 Cum. Supp.), secs. 68-257—68-286; 68-317—68-318; 68-324—68-325.	Comp. Stat. (1929), secs. 83-317. Comp. Stat. (1937 Cum. Supp.), secs. 68-317—68-318; 68-324—68-325; 68-401—68-433.	Comp. Stat. (1929), secs. 43-401—43-403; 43-405; 43-407; 43-414. Comp. Stat. (1937 Cum. Supp.), secs. 43-404; 43-406; 43-415; 43-501—43-523; 68-318; 68-325.

Contained in Tables 1—37—Continued

assistance		Agencies administering relief and public assistance	
Dependent and neglected children (institutions and agencies) tables 22—27	Veteran relief tables 28—33	State departments of public welfare (boards and executives) tables 34—35	Local departments of public welfare (boards and executives) tables 36—37
Acts (1933), chs. 1, secs. 203—209, 471; 118. Acts (1937), chs. 5; 177; 197.	Rev. Stat. (1930), chs. 5, secs. 70—71; 33, sec. 8. Laws (1931), ch. 216. Laws (1933), ch. 1, secs. 234—240. Laws (1935), ch. 116. Laws (1937), ch. 215.	Laws (1931), ch. 216 _____ Laws (1933), chs. 1, 188. Laws (1937), chs. 138—139; 141, 177, 210. Laws (1937, 1st ex.), chs. 105—106.	
Bagby's Ann. Code (1924), Art. 27, sec. 580. Ann. Code (1935 Supp.), Arts. 26, secs. 64, 72; 52, secs. 81—90; 88A, secs. 2, 6, 8B, 8D. Baltimore City Charter (1927), sec. 107. Laws (1937), ch. 490.	Ann. Code (1935 Supp.), Art. 65, secs. 57—60.	Ann. Code (1935 Supp.), Art. 88A, secs. 1—8D. Laws (1937), ch. 191. Laws (1937, 1st ex.), chs. 3—4; 12.	Ann. Code (1935 Supp.), Art. 88A, secs. 8A; 8D—8G. Laws (1935, 1st ex.), ch. 148. Laws (1937, 1st ex.), chs. 3—4; 12. Baltimore City Charter (1927), secs. 103—104.
Ann. Laws (1932), chs. 18, secs. 9, 11, 16; 47; 116, secs. 1(3)—1(4); 117, secs. 36—37; 119, secs. 1—51, 65—72; 121, secs. 7, 16; 276, secs. 83, 86. Acts (1937), ch. 332.	Ann. Laws (1932), chs. 6, secs. 40—41; 115; 116, secs. 1(5), 4—5. Ann. Laws (1936 Cum. Supp.), chs. 115, secs. 12A, 17—20; 118A. Acts (1937), chs. 107; 196; 273; 440.	Const., pt. II, ch. II, sec. III. Ann. Laws (1932), chs. 18; 119; 121, secs. 1—42. Ann. Laws (1936 Cum. Supp.), chs. 69, sec. 29; 18; 118; 118A; 121, secs. 8A, 9A; 138, sec. 27. Acts (1937), ch. 440. Acts (1938), ch. 476.	Ann. Laws (1932), chs. 40, secs. 4—5; 41, secs. 1, 20—22, 31, 34; 117; 119. Ann. Laws (1936 Cum. Supp.), chs. 117, sec. 1; 118, sec. 2; 118A, sec. 2. Acts (1937), chs. 113; 440. Acts (1938), ch. 476.
Stat. Ann. (1935), secs. 16.3—16.4; 16.271; 25.231—25.263; 25.291—25.304; 25.311—25.355; 25.361—25.371; 25.381—25.396.	Stat. Ann. (1935), secs. 4.871—4.894; 4.901—4.941; 4.1021—4.1041; 4.1051—4.1058; 4.1131—4.1151; 4.1321—4.1325.	Stat. Ann. (1935), secs. 16.1—16.46; 16.201—16.204.	Stat. Ann. (1935), secs. 16.36; 16.101; 16.113; 16.204—16.205.
Mason's Minn. Stat. (1927), secs. 4618—4627; 4454—4459; 4462—4469; 4560—4576; 4618—4627; 8636; 8639; 8642; 8645—8669; 8689-2—8689-5. Mason's Minn. Stat. (1938 Supp.), secs. 974-17a; 4460; 4467-1—4467-2; 4562—4563; 4569; 8637—8638; 8640—8641; 8642-1; 8643-1; 8644; 8644-1; 8664-1; 8664-3. Code Ann. (1930), secs. 4011; 5710; 7247—7268. Laws (1936), ch. 180. Laws (1938), ch. 172.	Mason's Minn. Stat. (1927), secs. 4346—4364; 4366; 4387—4390; 4599—4600. Mason's Minn. Stat. (1938 Supp.), secs. 1192-1—1192-5; 4344; 4365; 4370; 4372; 4397-3—4397-28; 4401-11—4401-12; 4601—4604. Code Ann. (1930), secs. 214; 290 (a); 3866—3874; 5807—5824. Laws (1936), ch. 316. Laws (1938), ch. 362.	Mason's Minn. Stat. (1927), secs. 4399—4433; 4437—4469; 4551; 4567; 4570; 4600. Mason's Minn. Stat. (1938 Supp.), secs. 53-18a; 3199-13; 3199-64; 4398; 4603; 8646-1; 8683-3—8683-4. Laws (1936), ch. 175 _____ Laws (1938), chs. 172; 181.	Mason's Minn. Stat. (1938 Supp.), secs. 974-11—974-21. Laws (1936), ch. 175. Laws (1938), chs. 172; 181.
Stat. Ann. (1932), secs. 7624—7630; 12939; 12948; 14095; 14097—14147; 14152—14158; 14164—14181. Stat. Ann. (1938 Cum. Pocket Part), secs. 12967b-1; 12967b-4; 14146.	Stat. Ann. (1932), secs. 13927; 13930—13940. Stat. Ann. (1938 Cum. Pocket Part), secs. 13928—13929.	Stat. Ann. (1938 Cum. Pocket Part), secs. 12967b-1—12967b-8; 12967b-20—12967b-25.	Stat. Ann. (1932), secs. 12938—12945. Stat. Ann. (1938 Cum. Pocket Part), secs. 12967b-2; 12967b-9—12967b-10.
Rev. Code Ann. (1935), secs. 1484—1510; 10465—10479.1. Laws (1937), ch. 82. Comp. Stat. (1929), secs. 28—934; 43-201—43-228; 76-2601—76-2607; 83-501—83-502; 83-505—83-508. Comp. Stat. (1937 Cum. Supp.), secs. 43-229; 68-318; 83-503—83-504.	Rev. Code Ann. (1935), secs. 1520; 1526—1546; 4537—4541. Laws (1937), ch. 163. Comp. Stat. (1929), secs. 80-104—80-109; 80-302—80-306. Comp. Stat. (1937 Cum. Supp.), secs. 38-415; 77-1801; 80-301—80-308; 83-109; 83-111; 83-135.	Laws (1937), ch. 82 _____ Const., Art. IV, sec. 19 ____ Comp. Stat. (1929), secs. 83-101—83-106. Comp. Stat. (1937 Cum. Supp.), secs. 43-503; 66-411; 68-317—68-325; 68-403; 77-2306; 83-107; 83-109; 83-503—83-504.	Laws (1937), ch. 82. Comp. Stat. (1937 Cum. Supp.), secs. 43-502; 68-258; 68-326—68-334; 68-401.

Table 38.—Citations to Statutory Provisions

| State | Provisions granting relief and public | | | |
	General relief tables 1—5	Old age assistance tables 6—11	Blind assistance tables 12—17	Aid to dependent children in their own homes tables 18—21
Nevada	Comp. Laws (1929), secs. 2361; 5137—5142; 5145—5150. Comp. Laws (1934 Pocket Part), secs. 5143—5144. Stat. (1935), ch. 138. Stat. (1937), ch. 127.	Stat. (1935), ch. 138. Stat. (1937), chs. 58; 67; 127—128.	Comp. Laws (1929), secs. 2313—2321. Stat. (1935), ch. 138. Stat. (1937), ch. 127.	Comp. Laws (1929), secs. 5100—5107. Comp. Laws (1934 Pocket Part), sec. 984.02. Stat. (1935), ch. 138. Stat. (1937), ch. 127.
New Hampshire	Pub. Laws (1926), chs. 23, sec. 2; 105; 106, secs. 1, 7—8, 22—31; 107. Laws (1933), chs. 65; 137; 142. Laws (1937), ch. 202.	Laws (1937), ch. 202	Laws (1937), ch. 202.	Laws (1937), ch. 202
New Jersey	Const., Art. 2, sec. 1 Rev. Stat. (1937), secs. 2:160-13; 19:4-1; 44:1-3—44;1-9; 44:1-24—44:1-37; 44:1-61—44:1-166; 44:2-1—44:2-9; 44:3-1—44:3-4; 44:4-1—44:4-19; 44:4-45—44:4-103; 44:4-118—44:4-135; 44:5-1—44:5-19; 44:8-1—44:8-31; A:2-1—A:2-7. Laws (1938), chs. 28; 123.	Rev. Stat. (1937), secs. 44:7-1—44:7-35.	Rev. Stat. (1937), secs. 30:6-1—30:6-16.	Rev. Stat. (1937), secs. 30:5-1—30:5-45. Laws (1938), chs. 161; 400.
New Mexico	Stat. Ann. (1929), secs. 101-101—101-103; 130-803. Stat. Ann. (1938 Supp.), secs. 134-2503—134-2504; 134-2511—134-2521; 134-2525; 134-2528—134-2533.	Stat. Ann. (1938 Supp.), secs. 134-2501; 134-2504; 134-2511—134-2521; 134-2527—134-2533.	Stat. Ann. (1938 Supp.), secs. 134-2501; 134-2504; 134-2511—134-2521; 134-2527—134-2533.	Stat. Ann. (1938 Supp.), secs. 134-2501; 134-2511—134-2521; 134-2524; 134-2528—134-2533.
New York	Cahill's Cons. Laws (1930), ch. 49½. Cahill's Cons. Laws (1931—35 Supp.), ch. 49½. Laws (1936), chs. 426; 873. Laws (1937), chs. 73; 358; 411; 492; 877. Laws (1938), chs. 346; 443—444; 447; 590. Charter of New York City (1936), ch. 24.	Laws (1936), ch. 693 Laws (1937), ch. 645.	Laws (1937), ch. 15	Laws (1937), ch. 15 Laws (1938), ch. 478.
North Carolina	Code Ann. (1935), secs. 1335—1343(P); 5942.	Pub. Laws (1937), ch. 288 Pub. Local Laws (1937), ch. 538.	Const., Art. XI, sec. 10. Pub. Laws (1937), ch. 124.	Pub. Laws (1937), ch. 288
North Dakota	Comp. Laws Ann. (1913), secs. 7; 2534—2544. Comp. Laws Ann. (1913—1925 Supp.), secs. 2529—2530. Laws (1933), chs. 97—98. Laws (1935), chs. 119—120; 123; 276. Laws (1937), ch. 214.	Laws (1937), chs. 86, 211	Laws (1937), chs. 86; 210.	Laws (1937), chs. 86; 209.
Ohio	Code Ann. (1936), secs. 2522—2557-4; 3138-1; 3148; 3476—3496-16; 4021—4035; 4089—4096; 6308-7. Throckmorton's Code Ann. (April 1938 Supp.), secs. 2555; 3477.	Throckmorton's Code Ann. (1936), secs. 1359-1—1359-30 as amended by (January 1938 Supp.), secs. 1359-2; 1359-7; 1359-12; 1359-14; 1359-15a; 1359-16; 1359-18—1359-21.	Throckmorton's Code Ann. (1936), secs. 2965—2970.	Throckmorton's Code Ann. (1936), secs. 1359-31—1359-42; 1656. (January 1938 Supp.), sec. 1359-33a.
Oklahoma	Stat. (1931), ch. 35, Art. 10 Stat. Ann. (1938 Supp.), ch. 24, Art. 15A.	Stat. Ann. (1938 Supp.), ch. 24, Art. 15b.	Stat. Ann. (1938 Supp.), ch. 24, Art. 15b.	Stat. Ann. (1938 Supp.), ch. 24, Art. 15b.

Contained in Tables 1—37—Continued

assistance		Agencies administering relief and public assistance	
Dependent and neglected children (institutions and agencies) tables 22—27	Veteran relief tables 28—33	State departments of public welfare (boards and executives) tables 34—35	Local departments of public welfare (boards and executives) tables 36—37
Comp. Laws (1929), secs. 491; 1010—1017; 1020—1022; 1039; 5141; 7580—7601. Stat. (1937), chs. 127; 173.	Comp. Laws (1929), secs. 3526; 6876.	Stat. (1935), ch. 138 _____ Stat. (1937), ch. 127.	Stat. (1935), ch. 138. Stat. (1937), ch. 127.
Pub. Laws (1926), chs. 107; 109; 113; 108, sec. 7. Laws (1933), ch. 147. Laws (1937), chs. 143; 152; 202.	Pub. Laws (1926), chs. 12; 106, secs. 9—21. Laws (1929), ch. 28. Laws (1931), chs. 94; 138. Laws (1933), ch. 78. Laws (1935), chs. 157—158. Laws (1937), ch. 202, sec. 27.	Laws (1937), ch. 202 _____	
Rev. Stat. (1937), secs. 9:4-1— 9:4-19; 9:6-1—9:6-12; 9:7-1— 9:7-5; 9:8-1; 9:10-1—9:10-6; 9:11-1—9:11-8; 9:18-1—9:18-37; 30:1-1—30:1-18; 30:5-1—30:5-7; 30:5-19—30:5-32; 44:4-87; 44:4-88; 44:8-2.	Rev. Stat. (1937), secs. 30:4-1— 30:4-22; 30:6A-1; 30:6A-18; 38: 17-1—38:17-5; 38:18-1—38:18-3; 43:8-5—43:8-7.	Rev. Stat. (1937), secs. 30: 1-1—30:1-18; 30:4-1—30:4-22; 44:7-6. Laws (1938), chs. 89; 123.	Rev. Stat. (1937), secs. 30:6-3; 44:1-1; 44:1-10— 44:1-23; 44:1-38—44:1-58; 44:4-20—44:4-44; 44:4-120; 44:7-7—44:7-11. Laws (1938), chs. 123; 194.
Stat. Ann. (1929), secs. 22-101— 22-106; 22-401—22-402; 22-504— 22-506; 62-301—62-304; 130-701— 130-706; 130-802. Stat. Ann. (1938 Supp.), secs. 134-2503—134-2504.	Stat. Ann. (1929), secs. 33-5301— 33-5304. Stat. Ann. (1938 Supp.), secs. 134-2503—134-2504.	Stat. Ann. (1929), secs. 126-107; 126-109. Stat. Ann. (1938 Supp.), secs. 32-1416; 134-2501—134-2510.	Stat. Ann. (1938 Supp.), sec. 134-2504(h).
Cahill's Cons. Laws (1930), chs. 49½; 56; 67. Cahill's Cons. Laws (1931—35 Supp.), chs. 49½; 56. Laws (1936), chs. 426; 873. Laws (1937), ch. 411.	Cahill's Cons. Laws (1930), chs. 37; 49½. Cahill's Cons. Laws (1931—35 Supp.), chs. 37; 49½; 56. Laws (1936), chs. 102; 318; 750. Laws (1937), ch. 492.	Const., Act V, sec. 4 _____ Cahill's Cons. Laws (1930), chs. 49½; 56; 67. Cahill's Cons. Laws (1931—35 Supp.), ch. 56. Laws (1936), chs. 693; 873; 875. Laws (1937), chs. 15; 544; 603. Laws (1938), chs. 48; 481—482.	Cahill's Cons. Laws (1930), ch. 49½. Cahill's Cons. Laws (1931—35 Supp.), chs. 11; 49½. Laws (1936), chs. 463; 571; 693; 822; 828; 873. Laws (1937), chs. 15; 358; 411; 514; 645. Laws (1938), chs. 28; 330; 443; 467; 481—482.
Const., Act VII, sec. 2 _____ Code Ann. (1935), secs. 1297(43); 5008; 5017; 5039; 5051. Pub. Laws (1937), ch. 135.	Code Ann. (1935), secs. 5127— 5135; 5168(a)—5168(y). Pub. Laws (1937), ch. 227.	Code Ann. (1935), secs. 5004— 5013. Pub. Laws (1937), chs. 135; 288; 319; 436.	Code Ann. (1935), secs. 5014—5018. Pub. Local Laws (1937), chs. 538; 598. Pub. Laws (1937), chs. 243; 288; 319.
Comp. Laws Ann. (1913), secs. 7; 243. Comp. Laws Ann. (1913—1925 Supp.), secs. 283b5—283b7; 5099b1— 5106a2; 5109—5110. Laws (1929), ch. 113. Laws (1931), ch. 265. Laws (1935), chs. 123; 221. Laws (1937), ch. 209.	Const., sec. 216 _____ Comp. Laws Ann. (1913), secs. 1775—1796; 2423—2425; 3181. Comp. Laws Ann. (1913—1925 Supp.), secs. 1779; 1782. Laws (1933), ch. 200.	Laws (1935), ch. 221 _____ Laws (1937), chs. 209—211; 214.	Laws (1935), ch. 123. Laws (1937), chs. 209—211.
Throckmorton's Code Ann. (1936), secs. 1352—1352-15; 1642-1. (January 1938 Supp.), secs. 1639-1; 1639-3—1639-37.	Throckmorton's Code Ann. (1936), secs. 1905—1909; 2931—2942; 2942-2—2949-4; 2950—2952.	Throckmorton's Code Ann. (1936), secs. 154-1—154-27; 154-57—154-58; 1349—1359-45; 1871-1—1871-2; 2250. (January 1938 Supp.), secs. 1890-1—1890-32; 1359-12—1359-16.	Throckmorton's Code Ann. (1936), secs. 1359-12—1359-15b; 1359-31—1359-45; 2967—2968-1.
Const., sec. 13545 _____ Stat. (1931), chs. 14, Art. 4; 20, Art. 7; 26, Art. 10; 35, Art. 9. Stat. Ann. (1938 Supp.), ch. 14, Art. 4.	Stat. (1931), ch. 64, Arts. 1—8 . Stat. (1938 Supp.), ch. 64, Art. 4.	Stat. Ann. (1938 Supp.), ch. 24, Art. 15A	Stat. (1931), ch. 35, secs. 7542—7543. Stat. Ann. (1938 Supp.), chs. 24, secs. 4715b, i, j, z3, z20; 34, secs. 7348a—7348b.

Table 38.—Citations to Statutory Provisions

State	Provisions granting relief and public			
	General relief tables 1—5	Old age assistance tables 6—11	Blind assistance tables 12—17	Aid to dependent children in their own homes tables 18—21
Oregon	Code Ann. (1930), title XXVII, secs. 27-1401—27-1409; 27-1501. Code Ann. (1935 Supp.), title XXVII, ch. XIV. Laws (1935 1st ex.), ch. 55. Laws (1937), ch. 287.	Code Ann. (1935 Supp.), title XXVII, ch. XXXVII. Laws (1937), chs. 287; 309.	Laws (1935 1st ex.), ch. 60. Laws (1937), chs. 258; 287; 334.	Laws (1937), ch. 288
Pennsylvania	Purdon's Stat. (1936), title 51, sec. 1. Laws (1937), chs. 396—397; 399.	Laws (1937), chs. 398—399	Laws (1937), ch. 399.	Laws (1937), chs. 397; 399
Rhode Island	Const., Art. II, sec. 4 Gen. Laws (1923); chs. 104—106; 292. Pub. Laws (1926), ch. 842. Pub. Laws (1930), ch. 1580. Pub. Laws (1931), ch. 1885. Pub. Laws (1933), chs. 2011; 2015. Pub. Laws (1934), ch. 2114. Pub. Laws (1936), ch. 2312. Pub. Laws (1936 1st ex.), ch. 2453. Pub. Laws (1937), chs. 2494; 2532.	Pub. Laws (1935), ch. 2191 Pub. Laws (1936 1st ex.), ch. 2437. Pub. Laws (1937), ch. 2514. Pub. Laws (1938), chs. 2620; 2623.	Pub. Laws (1936), ch. 2428.	Pub. Laws (1936 1st ex.), ch. 2437.
South Carolina	Const., Arts. 2, sec. 6; 3, sec. 32; 12, sec. 3. Code (1932), secs. 3848—3856; 4966—4977. Acts (1937), No. 319.	Const., Art. 3, sec. 32 Acts (1937), No. 319. Acts. (1938), Nos. 972, sec. 23; 1073.	Const., Art. 3, sec. 32. Acts (1937), No. 319.	Const., Art. 3, sec. 32 Acts (1937), Nos. 22; 319.
South Dakota	Comp. Laws Ann. (1929), secs. 191; 7694; 10035—10065. Laws (1931), ch. 251. Laws (1933), chs. 159; 181. Laws (1933 1st ex.), ch. 12. Laws (1935), chs. 80; 98. Laws (1937), ch. 85.	Laws (1937), ch. 220	Laws (1937), ch. 222.	Laws (1937), ch. 221
Tennessee	Code (1932), secs. 845; 4792—4830; 10242(3)—10242(4). Laws (1935), ch. 1. Laws (1937), ch. 47.	Code (1937 Cum. Supp.), secs. 4988(1)—4988(20). Laws (1937 2d ex.), ch. 9.	Code (1937 Cum. Supp.), secs. 4988(21)—4988(41).	Code (1937 Cum. Supp.), secs. 844(1)—844(15); 4746(1)—4746(15).
Texas	Vernon's Stat. (1936), Arts. 1626; 2351; 2954—2955; 4438; 4440. Gen. Laws (1937), ch. 435, sec. 28.	Vernon's Stat. (1936), Arts. 6243-1(1)—6243-1(20). Gen. Laws (1937), ch. 435, secs. 1, 4(d), 12, 36.	Gen. Laws (1937), ch. 435, secs. 1, 4, 11—22, 31—35, 40—48.	Vernon's Stat. (1936), sec. 6228. Gen. Laws (1937), ch. 435, secs. 1, 4, 23—27, 31—41.
Utah	Rev. Stat. Ann. (1933), secs. 15-8-74; 19 5 54—19-5-67, 91-0-1—91-0-2. Laws (1937), chs. 88; 90.	Laws (1937), chs. 88—90	Laws (1937), chs. 88; 90.	Laws (1937), chs. 88; 90
Vermont	Pub. Laws (1933), secs. 3918; 3920—3925; 3927; 3935—3949; 3951—3981; 3984—3995; 4088; 5423; 5427. Pub. Acts (1935), Nos. 68; 76; 77; 80; 81. Pub. Acts (1937), Nos. 9; 61—62; 120.	Pub. Acts (1935), No. 82 Pub. Acts (1935 1st ex.), No. 8. Pub. Acts (1937), Nos. 17; 38, pt. IV, sec. 1; 65.	Pub. Acts (1935 1st ex.), No. 12.	Pub. Laws (1933), secs. 5418; 5444; 5446—5447; 5454. Pub. Acts (1935), No. 131. Pub. Acts (1935 1st ex.), No. 11.
Virginia	Const., secs. 18; 20; 23 Code Ann. (1936), secs. 82; 82c; 2773(24)—2773(36); 2795—2813k. Code Ann. (1938 Supp.), secs. 1904(1); 1904(4); 1904(7); 1904 (53)—1904(56); 1904(59)—1904 (60).	Code Ann. (1938 Supp.), secs. 1904(1); 1904(10)—1904(22); 1904(57)—1904 (60); 1904(65); 1904(67).	Code Ann. (1938 Supp.), secs. 1904 (1); 1904(35)—1904(52); 1904 (57)—1904(60); 1904(62)—1904 (64); 1904(67).	Code Ann. (1938 Supp.), secs. 1904(1); 1904(4); 1904(7); 1904(25)—1904 (34); 1904(57)—1904(61); 1904(67).

Contained in Tables 1—37—Continued

assistance		Agencies administering relief and public assistance	
Dependent and neglected children (institutions and agencies) tables 22—27	Veteran relief tables 28—33	State departments of public welfare (boards and executives) tables 34—35	Local departments of public welfare (boards and executives) tables 36—37
Code Ann. (1930), title XXXIII, chs. VI—VII; IX. Laws (1935 1st ex.), ch. 55. Laws (1937), chs. 170; 236; 287.	Code Ann. (1930), title LXVI, chs. II—III. Code Ann. (1935 Supp.), secs. 27-1414—27-1419; 66-509; 67-1808; 68-2610; 69-107.	Code Ann. (1935 Supp.), ch. XXVI. Laws (1935 1st ex.), chs. 55; 60. Laws (1937), chs. 264—265; 287—288; 309; 334.	Code Ann. (1935 Supp.), ch. XXVI. Laws (1935 1st ex.), chs. 55; 60. Laws (1937), chs. 288; 309; 334.
Purdon's Stat. (1936), titles 11, chs. 2—7, 10; 16, secs. 611—613, 3621; 50, secs. 10321—10322; 71, secs. 593—595, 597, 600, 1473.	Purdon's Stat. (1936), titles 16, secs. 421—428; 35, secs. 257—258; 51, chs. 8—9; 53, sec. 15037; 62, sec. 1829; 71, secs. 389, 391.	Const., Art. VI _____ Laws (1937), No. 395.	Laws (1937), Nos. 396; 399.
Gen. Laws (1923), chs. 114; 404 Pub. Laws (1926), chs. 834—836; 842; 847; 860. Pub. Laws (1928), ch. 1226. Pub. Laws (1929), ch. 1417. Pub. Laws (1930), ch. 1574. Pub. Laws (1935), ch. 2250. Pub. Laws (1936 1st ex.), ch. 2437. Pub. Laws (1938), ch. 2566.	Gen. Laws (1923), chs. 116—117 Pub. Laws (1927), chs. 960; 1025; 1145; 1188; 1227. Pub. Laws (1930), chs. 1555; 1560. Pub. Laws (1931), chs. 1730; 1867. Pub. Laws (1933), ch. 2025. Pub. Laws (1935), ch. 2250.	Gen. Laws (1923), ch. 108; 413. Pub. Laws (1926), chs. 834—836; 842; 847; 862. Pub. Laws (1928), ch. 1151. Pub. Laws (1929), chs. 1412—1413; 1417. Pub. Laws (1932), ch. 1910. Pub. Laws (1933), ch. 2025. Pub. Laws (1935), ch. 2250. Pub. Laws (1936 1st ex.), ch. 2437. Pub. Laws (1937), ch. 2546,	Gen. Laws (1923), chs. 50; 105—106; 292. Pub. Laws (1926), ch. 842. Pub. Laws (1930), ch. 1580. Pub. Laws (1931), ch. 1855. Pub. Laws (1933), chs. 2011; 2015. Pub. Laws (1935), ch. 2250. Pub. Laws (1936), ch. 2312.
Code (1932), secs. 243; 247; 255; 4989—4996; 5676—5682. Acts (1937), No. 319.	Const., Art. 13, sec. 5 _____ Code (1932), secs. 2244—2245; 4978—4988; 5711; 8639—8658. Code (1936 Supp.), sec. 2244.	Acts (1937), No. 319 _____	Acts (1937), Nos. 240; 278; 319.
Comp. Laws Ann. (1929), secs. 5374; 9968—9971; 9976; 9981. Laws (1937), ch. 219.	Comp. Laws Ann. (1929), sec. 9948—9966. Laws (1931), chs. 226—227. Laws (1937), ch. 225.	Laws (1937), chs. 219—222 __	Laws (1937), ch. 220.
Code (1932), secs. 4585; 4587; 4599; 4647; 4712—4746; 4822; 10279; 10288.	Code (1932), secs. 4934—4988 ___ Code (1937 Cum. Supp.), secs. 2540(3)—2540(6); 4937; 4941; 4952; 4975(1); 4976(1).	Code (1937 Cum. Supp.), secs. 844(1)—844(15).	
Vernon's Stat. (1936), Arts. 603; 695a; 2329—2337; 3174; 3208—3212; 3255—3259a; 5132—5138a; 5139—5142a. Gen. Laws (1937), chs. 435, sec. 7a; 492.	Vernon's Stat. (1936), Arts. 603; 3174; 3176; 3213—3220; 6204; 6208—6227. Gen. Laws (1937), ch. 485.	Vernon's Stat. (1936), Arts. 601—606; 690—695a; 842d (12)—842d(38); 3174—3183a; 5119; 5126. Gen. Laws (1937), ch. 435, secs. 1—10.	Gen. Laws (1937), ch. 435, sec. 29.
Rev. Stat. Ann. (1933), secs. 14-7-1—14-7-61; 14-8-1—14-8-8; 15-8-75; 19-5-55; 35-6-1—35-6-15; 90-0-1—90-0-2. Laws (1937), chs. 16; 88.	Rev. Stat. Ann. (1933), secs. 98-2-1—98-2-5.	Laws (1935), ch. 69, secs. 1, 4—6. Laws (1937), ch. 88, secs. 1—3, 8, 13—15, 17.	Laws (1937), ch. 88, secs. 1, 7, 11—12, 15—16.
Pub. Laws (1933), secs. 471; 3442; 5415—5434; 5443—5444; 5446; 5448—5467; 5486; 5498. Pub. Acts (1937), Nos. 135—137.	Pub. Laws (1933), secs. 3931—3934; 5549—5551. Pub. Acts (1935), No. 79. Pub. Acts (1937), No. 63.	Pub. Laws (1933), secs. 454—464; 467; 471; 5415—5437; 5527—5551; 5562—5574; 8865—8872; 8875; 8915. Pub. Acts (1935 1st ex.), Nos. 11—12.	
Code Ann. (1936), secs. 1902f; 1902k; 1902L; 1905—1922 e; 1930a—1930c; 1935a—1935k1; 1945—1953m. Code Ann. (1938 Supp.), secs. 1902k; 1922b; 1953a.	Code Ann. (1936), secs. 19c; 60—61a; 2642—2672b; 5214. Code Ann. (1938 Supp.), secs. 1904(14); 1904(42).	Code Ann. (1936), secs. 585 (66); 585(67); 585(87)—585 (88); 1902a—1902j; 1903; 1930a; 1935a. Code Ann. (1938 Supp.), secs. 1904(2)—1904(5).	Code Ann. (1936), secs. 1902 (L)—1902(o). Code Ann. (1938 Supp.), secs. 1904(6)—1904(9).

Table 38.—Citations to Statutory Provisions

State	Provisions granting relief and public			
	General relief tables 1—5	Old age assistance tables 6—11	Blind assistance tables 12—17	Aid to dependent children in their own homes tables 18—21
Washington _____	Rem. Rev. Stat. Ann. (1932), sec. 9986. Laws (1937), chs. 111; 180.	Laws (1935), ch. 182 _____ Laws (1937), chs. 111; 156; 180.	Laws (1937), chs. 111; 132; 180.	Laws (1937), chs. 114; 180 _
West Virginia ___	Code (1931), ch. 9, Arts. VI—VII as enacted by Acts (1936 1st ex.), ch. 1 and Acts (1937), ch. 73.	Code (1931), ch. 9, Art. V as enacted by Acts (1936 1st ex.), ch. 1.	Code (1931), ch. 9, Art. V as enacted by Acts (1936 1st ex.), ch. 1 and Acts (1937), ch. 75.	Code (1931), ch. 9, Art. V as enacted by Acts (1936 1st ex.), ch. 1.
Wisconsin _____	Stat. (1937), secs. 49.01—49.21; 59.03; 59.08(17); 61.19—61.20; 61.34; 62.11. Laws (1937 1st ex.), ch. 14.	Stat. (1937), secs. 49.20—49.38; 49.50—49.51. Laws (1937 1st ex.), ch. 7.	Stat. (1937), secs. 47.08—47.09; 49.50—49.51.	Stat (1937), secs. 48.33; 49.51.
Wyoming _____	Laws (1937), ch. 88 _____	Laws (1937), ch. 88 _____	Laws (1937), ch. 88__	Laws (1937), ch. 88 _____
Alaska _____	Comp. Laws (1933), secs. 1771—1814. Laws (1937 1st ex.), chs. 3; 5.	Laws (1937 1st ex.), chs. 2—3; 8—9.	Laws (1937 1st ex.), ch. 3.	Comp. Laws (1933), secs. 1821—1822. Laws (1937 1st ex.), chs. 3; 6.
District of Columbia.	Code (1929), title 8, secs. 6, 10, 23, 231, 235.	Code (1937 Supp.), title 30, secs. 21—35.	Code (1937 Supp.), title 30, secs. 1—16.	Code (1929), title 8, secs. 91—100.
Hawaii _____	Laws (1937), ch. 259A, secs. 1, 12, 44—52.	Laws (1937), ch. 259A, secs. 1, 12—25, 28, 33—37, 49, 51—56.	Laws (1937), ch. 259A, secs. 1, 12—24, 26, 28, 32—37, 51, 52, 54—56.	Laws (1937), ch. 259A, secs. 1, 12, 14—24, 27—31, 35, 37, 51—54.

Contained in Tables 1—37—Continued

assistance		Agencies administering relief and public assistance	
Dependent and neglected children (institutions and agencies) tables 22—27	Veteran relief tables 28—33	State departments of public welfare (boards and executives) tables 34—35	Local departments of public welfare (boards and executives) tables 36—37
Rem. Rev. Stat. Ann. (1932), secs. 1987-1; 1987-3; 1987-8—1987-10; 11238. Rem. Rev. Stat. Ann. (1935 Supp.), secs. 1700-1; 10802-2. Rem. Rev. Stat. Ann. (1936 Supp.), secs. 1700-1—1700-6. Laws (1937), chs. 114; 180; 230.	Const., Art. X, sec. 3 _____ Rem. Rev. Stat. Ann. (1932), secs. 10727—10758. Rem. Rev. Stat. Ann. (1936 Supp.), secs. 10730; 10737-1. Laws (1937), ch. 203, secs. 1—3.	Rem. Rev. Stat. Ann. (1935 Supp.), secs. 1700-1—1700-4; 9992-45; 10786-5; 10786-7; 10802-2; 10802-5. Laws (1937), chs. 111; 114; 132; 156; 180; 224; 231.	Laws (1937), ch. 180, secs. 8, 11.
Code (1931), ch. 49, Arts. I—III, V—VI as enacted by Acts (1936 1st ex.), ch. 1. Code (1931), ch. 26, Arts. I—II. Acts (1937), ch. 73.	Code (1931), ch. 9, Art. VIII as enacted by Acts (1936 1st ex.), ch. 1.	Acts (1936 1st ex.), ch. 1 __	Acts (1936 1st ex.), ch.1.
Stat. (1937), secs. 46.01—46.04; 46.16; 46.18; 48.01—48.22; 48.28—48.32; 48.35—48.50; 59.08(9a).	Stat. (1937), secs. 45.07—45.277; 49.01; 60.17; 142.09—142.10.	Stat. (1937), secs. 47.09; 48.33; 49.38; 49.50.	Stat. (1937), secs. 49.37; 49.51.
Rev. Stat. Ann. (1931), chs. 20, Arts. 1—2, 4—5; 103, secs. 102, 105; 108, sec. 703. Rev. Stat. Ann. (1934 Supp.), ch. 108, sec. 703. Laws (1937), chs. 25; 88.	Rev. Stat. Ann. (1931), chs. 100, Art. 3; 108, Art. 13.	Laws (1937), ch. 88 _____	Laws (1937), ch. 88.
Comp. Laws (1933), secs. 1911—1921. Laws (1937 1st ex.), chs. 6; 12.	-------------------------------------	Laws (1937 1st ex.), chs. 3; 5—6.	
Code (1929) titles 8, secs. 8, 10—11, 14—24, 70, 111, 128—129, 185, 218; 18, secs. 251—288.	-------------------------------------	Code (1929), titles 6, sec. 409; 8, secs. 1—25, 42, 91, 258, 276. Code (1937 Supp.), titles 8, sec. 3; 20, secs. 1, 23.	
Rev. Laws (1935), secs. 4538; 4610—4613; 4615; 4621. Laws (1937), chs. 133; 259A, secs. 1, 7—9, 30, 53.	-------------------------------------	Laws (1937), ch. 259A, secs. 1—9, 24, 38—44, 48—56.	Laws (1937), ch. 259A, secs. 1, 10—14, 24, 44.

Appendix B

SUPPLEMENTARY TABLES

INTRODUCTORY NOTE

The following supplementary tables make current as of January 1, 1939, the information contained in the original tables in appendix A. In general, the legislation tabulated in the original tables is presented as of July 1, 1938. However, because copies of new laws were not obtained at an early enough date, legislation in New Jersey, Rhode Island, and Ohio which was in effect on July 1, 1938, was not included. The legislation in these States along with legislation enacted after July 1, 1938, in California, Illinois, Louisiana, and Massachusetts is included in the supplementary tables. The effective dates are indicated in footnotes.

The supplementary tables are duplicates of the original tables with respect to form and terminology. They have been numbered to conform with the numbering of the original tables, but only those tables which have been changed by new legislation are included. Changes have been indicated by citations to the laws effecting them.

The following table indicates the States and tables for which the original set of tables must be supplemented by the second set in order to show the provisions as of January 1, 1939.

State	General relief	Old age assistance	Blind assistance	Aid to dependent children in their own homes	State or local boards of public welfare
		Supplementary table numbers			
California	1, 5				
Illinois					37.
Lousiana	1	6, 7, 9, 10, 11.	12, 13, 14, 15, 16, 17.	18, 21	34, 36, 37.
Massachusetts	5				
New Jersey		6, 7, 8, 10, 11.			
Ohio	1, 2, 5				35.
Rhode Island			12, 13, 14, 15, 16.		

GENERAL RELIEF

Supplementary Table 1.—Provisions for the Administration of General Relief

| State | Nature of law | Administrative responsibility | | Determination of eligibility | | |
| | | Direct | Supervisory | Original determination | | Appeal by applicant |
				Final	Advisory	
California (State)	O	State Department of Social Welfare[1]		State Department of Social Welfare[1]		(2)
Louisiana	M	State Department of Public Welfare through parish department of public welfare.[3]		Parish department of public welfare		
Ohio (State)[4]	O	Board of county commissioners. Township trustees. City director of public safety.[5]	State relief director. State auditor.[5]	Board of county commissioners. Township trustees. City director of public safety.		

M indicates mandatory provision.
O indicates optional provision.

[1] Stat. (1938 1st ex.), S. Const. Amend. No. 2. (Effective Nov. 8, 1938.)
[2] The State Department of Social Welfare may appoint city and county citizens' relief committees to assist in the administration of relief.
[3] Acts (1938), No. 344. (Effective July 27, 1938.)
[4] This program is not considered to be of a permanent nature and supplements the general relief program as shown on tables 1—5 inclusive (pp. 48—76).
[5] The State relief director must examine the conduct and methods of local relief administration. He may order the local officials to appear and show cause why changes should not be put into effect. After a hearing the director may order them to make changes for the improvement of local relief administration or to comply with the relief statutes. The local officials may appeal from the findings of the director to the board of appeals, whose decisions are final. In addition to the above provisions, the State auditor is empowered to make outside investigations of relief clients. Ineligible persons must be removed from the relief rolls as soon as the State auditor's examiner informs the local relief authority of such ineligibility. Laws (1937 3d ex.), S. B. 465. (Effective July 11, 1938.)

Supplementary Table 2.—Requirements for Eligibility for General Relief

| State | Description of class | Residence provisions | | | |
| | | Acquisition of residence | | Loss | Provisions for removal of needy nonresidents |
		State	Local		
Ohio (State)[1]	Persons requiring support and relief	Resident of State for 3 years.[2]	Resided in the county for 90 days.[2]	Acquisition of legal settlement in another State or county; residence outside of State for a period of more than 4 years.[2]	

[1] This program is not considered to be of a permanent nature and supplements the general relief program as shown on tables 1—5 inclusive (pp. 48—76).
[2] Laws (1937 3d ex.), S. B. 465. (Effective July 11, 1938.)

Supplementary Table 5.—Provisions for Types of Aid Granted and for Financing General Relief

State	Types of relief							Specific provisions for types of relief to nonresident persons	Incidence of financial responsibility		Basis for distribution of State funds
	Institutional care (poorhouse, poor farm, etc.)	Direct relief	Contract care	Medical care	Hospitalization	Burial	Miscellaneous		State	Local	
California (State)		X		X	X		Work relief. No person is entitled to relief who unjustifiably refuses employment.		X	(1)	State Department of Social Welfare directs expenditure of funds. Funds may be paid directly to individuals or through such governmental agencies as the State Department of Social Welfare may select.[2]
Massachusetts[5]	X	X		X		X[3]	Work may be required	Temporary relief	(4)	X	
Ohio (State)[5]		X		X	X		Relief may take the form of either work or direct relief or both, and may be provided through the furnishing of commodities and services.[6]		X[7]	X[8]	Allocated to each county in the ratio which the average of the real, public utility, and tangible personal property tax duplicate of the county during the previous 5 years bears to the average of the aggregate real, public utility, and tangible personal property tax duplicates of all the counties in the State during the previous 5 years respectively.[9] Where relief is furnished by the subdivisions, the county commissioners apportion the funds among them in direct proportion to the number of relief cases handled by them.

X indicates that the provision applies without limitation in a given State.

[1] State Department of Social Welfare may require communities which have received unemployment relief loans to contribute an equal or stipulated amount. Stat. (1938 1st ex.), S. Const. Amend. No. 2. (Effective Nov. 8, 1938.)

[2] Stat. (1938 1st ex.), S. Const. Amend. No. 2. (Effective Nov. 8, 1938.)

[3] Burial expenses must not exceed $100 if deceased is over 12 years of age and not exceed $20 for each person under that age. Laws (1938), ch. 465 (effective Sept. 27, 1938); Laws Ann. (1932), ch. 117, sec. 17.

[4] State reimburses town for expenses of State paupers.

[5] This program is not considered to be of a permanent nature and supplements the general relief program as shown on tables 1—5 inclusive (pp. 48—76).

[6] Persons competent to perform labor requiring employment (except at a place where there is a labor dispute), if offered at prevailing wages and under reasonable conditions as determined by the local administrative officials, must be stricken from the relief roll. Laws (1937 3d ex.), S. B. 466. (Effective June 9, 1938.)

[7] Administrative, clerical, and other similar expense of local administration must not exceed 12 percent of the relief expenditures and must be computed monthly. Laws (1937 3d ex.), S. B. 465. (Effective July 11, 1938.)

[8] Each subdivision must match State allocations. This does not apply to the $1,500,000 appropriated from the 1939 sales tax revenue to provide relief in 1938. Laws (1937 3d ex.), S. B. 465. (Effective July 11, 1938.)

[9] These provisions do not apply to the $1,500,000 appropriated from the 1939 sales tax revenue. These funds are allocated and distributed to the subdivisions in accordance with their respective relief loads, based upon the comparative need as evidenced by the records on file in the office of the auditor of State for the first 5 months of 1938. Laws (1937 3d ex.), S. B. 465. (Effective July 11, 1938.)

OLD AGE ASSISTANCE

Supplementary Table 6.—Provisions for the Administration of Old Age Assistance

| State | Administrative responsibility | | | Determination of eligibility | | | | | | | |
| | Nature of law | Direct | Supervisory | Original determination | | Reconsideration | | Appeal and review | | | |
				Final	Advisory	Periodic	At request of State board or department[1]	Appeal of applicant to State department[1]	Review by State department on own motion[1]	Upon complaint by person other than applicant	Further investigation by State department
Louisiana	M	State Department of Public Welfare through parish department of public welfare.[2]	----	Parish department of public welfare.	----	----	X	X	X	----	X.
New Jersey	M	County welfare board	State Department of Institutions and Agencies, Division of Old Age Assistance.	County welfare board	----	----	X	Division of Old Age Assistance.	Division of Old Age Assistance.	Any person[3]	Division of Old Age Assistance.

X indicates that the provision applies without limitation in a given State.
M indicates mandatory provision.
O indicates optional provision.

[1] If authority to hear appeals, to review decisions, and to make further investigations is placed by law with a specific agency within the department, the specific agency is named either in the body of the table or in a footnote.

[2] Acts (1938), No. 359. (Effective July 27, 1938.)
[3] Laws (1938), ch. 361. (Effective July 1, 1938.)

Supplementary *Table 7.*—Personal Qualifications for Old Age Assistance

State	Age in years	Residence			Reasons for disqualification					
		U.S. citizenship	State	Local	Desertion for specified period within 10 years prior to application		Applicant failed to support children under specified age	Applicant convicted of felony within period specified prior to application	Applicant was tramp or beggar within period specified prior to application	Miscellaneous
					By husband	By wife				
Louisiana	65	---	(1)	(2)	---	---	---	---	---	---
New Jersey	65	X	(3)	Resident[4]	---	---	---	---	---	Applicant has adequate support and is able to support himself.

X indicates that the provision applies without limitation in a given State.

[1] Applicant must have been resident for 5 years within last 9 years, 1 year immediately preceding application.

[2] Applicant for assistance must be actually residing in the parish in which the application is made. Acts (1936), No. 359, sec. 2(d). (Effective July 27, 1936.)

[3] Applicant must have been a resident 5 years within the last 9 years, 1 year immediately preceding application. If Federal aid should not be available or it should be withdrawn, all persons whose applications are pending and persons thereafter applying must have resided and been domiciled in this State continuously for at least 5 years immediately preceding application. Laws (1936), ch. 361. (Effective July 1, 1936.)

[4] A person applying for assistance is deemed a resident of that county in which he maintains his customary place of abode. Laws (1936), ch. 361. (Effective July 1, 1936.)

Supplementary *Table 8.*—Need Qualifications for Old Age Assistance

State	Limitations on property			Limitations on income			Applicant has no person liable and able to support him
	General limitations	Limits on real property	Limits on personal property	Maximum income allowed	Income rate applied to nonrevenue producing property	Applicant must not have disposed of property to qualify	
New Jersey	$3,000[1]	---	---	---	---	Y[2]	Parents, spouse, children, grandchildren, or other person.[3]

X indicates that the provision applies without limitation in a given State.

[1] Not an exemption limit but merely a guide to administration. Applicant must be poor, deserving, and unable to support himself.

[2] Such disposition must not have been made for the purpose of evading the necessity of pledging of such property as a guaranty for reimbursement of the amount of assistance paid. Laws (1936), ch. 361. (Effective July 1, 1936.)

[3] Director of welfare must proceed against persons chargeable to support applicant and compel them to render such assistance as is provided by law in such cases, and he may contract, in writing, with persons not chargeable for the support of the applicant. Laws (1936), ch. 361. (Effective July 1, 1936.)

Supplementary Table 9.—Types of Aid Received or Needed Which Disqualify Applicants for Old Age Assistance

State	Other public assistance	Institutional aid		
		Public or private institution	Public institution	In need of continuing institutional care
Louisiana			X[1]	

X indicates that the provision applies without limitation in a given State.

[1] Acts (1938), No. 359, sec. 2(e). (Effective July 27, 1938.)

Supplementary Table 10.—Provisions for Recovery of Cost of Old Age Assistance From Recipients and Their Estates

State	Liens	Requirement for execution of agreement by recipient to reimburse governmental unit	Requirement for assignment or transfer of property	Recovery in cases where recipient becomes possessed of property or income in excess of need or amount stated in application	Recovery from estate upon death of recipient	Limitations on recovery from estate	Recovery in cases of misrepresentation or concealment of income or property	Rate of interest charged on sums granted and recovered	Portion of sums recovered paid to Federal Government
Louisiana				X	X	No claim enforceable against real property while occupied by surviving spouse, child, or children. $100 personal or real property, reasonable funeral expenses, and costs of administration of the estate allowed as preferred claim.[1]			50 percent.
New Jersey	X	M[2]	M		X	No levy may be made on real property while occupied by surviving spouse. $150 funeral expenses allowed as preferred claim.			Proportionate share.

X indicates that the provision applies without limitation in a given State.
M indicates that it is mandatory upon welfare officials to require applicant or recipient to execute agreement to reimburse or for recipient to transfer property or interest in property.
O indicates that it is discretionary with welfare officials whether agreement to reimburse shall be executed or whether recipient shall transfer property or interest in property.

[1] Acts (1938), No. 359, secs. 18, 20. (Effective July 27, 1938.)
[2] The agreement to reimburse must contain therein a release of dower or curtesy, as the case may be, of the spouse of the recipient, and such release shall be as valid and effectual as if the spouse had joined the recipient in a conveyance of property to a third person. Laws (1938), ch. 361. (Effective July 1, 1938.)

Supplementary Table 11.—Provisions for Granting and Financing Old Age Assistance

State	Maximum allowance (per month unless otherwise specified)	Minimum allowance (per month unless otherwise specified)	Burial allowance	Governmental unit determining amount of individual grant		Incidence of financial responsibility			Basis for distribution of State funds	Procedure in case of insufficiency of State funds
				Final	Advisory	State	County	Other local unit		
Louisiana	(1)	(1)	(2)	Parish		75 per-cent.[3]		25 per-cent (parish).	State reimburses parishes for 75 percent of expenditure for assistance and 50 percent of expenditure for administration.[3]	
New Jersey	$30[4]		$100	County		87½ per-cent.[5]	12½ per-cent.[5]		State reimburses county for 87½ percent of amount expended, but if no Federal aid is available, the State reimburses the county for 75 percent of amount expended.	

X indicates that the provision applies without limitation in a given State.

[1] Allowance is an amount which, when added to income, is sufficient for reasonable subsistence.

[2] Reasonable funeral expenses may be paid, if the estate is insufficient or if there are no responsible relatives able to pay such expenses. Acts (1938), No. 359, sec. 20. (Effective July 27, 1938.)

[3] State may assume total expense if State department finds that parish or district is unable to pay its share.

[4] Assistance provided aged person only while living in his own or some other suitable family home within the State; except upon special resolution by county welfare board and upon written approval of the division of old age assistance in the State Department of Institutions and Agencies; assistance may be granted outside of his own or some suitable family home and outside of the State if the State to which the individual has moved will provide supervision and reports required by the State division. Laws (1938), ch. 361. (Effective July 1, 1938.)

[5] If applicant has no county residence, State pays total amount.

[6] Additional appropriations must be made if funds are exhausted during year, or if no money is available county must issue temporary loan bonds or certificates of indebtedness in amounts necessary to pay assistance. Laws (1938), ch. 361. (Effective July 1, 1938.)

BLIND ASSISTANCE

Supplementary Table 12.—Provisions for the Administration of Blind Assistance

State	Nature of law	Administrative responsibility		Original determination		Determination of eligibility							
						Determination of blindness			Reconsideration		Appeal and review		
						Certificate of physician		Periodic re-examination of applicant's eyesight	Periodic	At request of State board or department	Appeal of applicant to State department[1]	Review by State department on own motion[1]	Further investigation by State department[1]
		Direct	Supervisory	Final	Advisory	Officially designated physician	Any physician						
Louisiana	M	State Department of Public Welfare through parish department of public welfare.[2]		Parish department of public welfare.		X		(3)		X[4]	X	X	X
Rhode Island[5]	M	State Department of Public Welfare.		State Department of Public Welfare.		X				X	X	X	X

X indicates that the provision applies without limitation in a given State.
M indicates mandatory provision.
O indicates optional provision.

[1] If authority to hear appeals, to review decisions, and to make further investigations is placed by law with a specific agency within the department, the specific agency is named either in the body of the table or in a footnote.

[2] Acts (1938), No. 359. (Effective July 27, 1938.)
[3] The provision contained in table 12, appendix A, relating to periodic re-examination of applicant's eyesight has been repealed. Acts (1938), No. 359. (Effective July 27, 1938.)
[4] Acts (1938), No. 359, sec. 15. (Effective July 27, 1938.)
[5] Pub. Laws (1938), ch. 2622. (Effective July 1, 1938.)

Supplementary Table 13.—Personal Qualifications for Blind Assistance

State	Minimum age in years	U. S. citizenship	Residence		Definition of blindness	Applicant must not solicit alms	Applicant may be required to undergo operation or treatment	Miscellaneous qualifications
			State	Local				
Louisiana	(1)	----	(2)	An applicant must actually reside in the parish in which the application is made.3	Applicant has no vision, or vision with correcting glasses is so defective as to prevent performance of ordinary activities for which eyesight is essential.4	X	(5)	
Rhode Island6	16 years and over.	----	(7)	----	No vision or vision with correcting glasses is 20/200 or less or has disqualifying visual field defect.	----	X	

X indicates that the provision applies without limitation in a given State.

1 The provision contained in table 13, appendix A, relating to minimum age has been repealed. Acts (1938), No. 359. (Effective July 27, 1938.)

2 Applicant must have been a resident 5 years within last 9 years, 1 year immediately preceding application, or must have become blind while resident.

3 Acts (1938), No. 359, sec. 4(b). (Effective July 27, 1938.)

4 Acts (1938), No. 359, sec. 4. (Effective July 27, 1938.)

5 The provision contained in table 13, appendix A, relating to the requirement to undergo operation or treatment has been repealed. Acts (1938). No. 359. (Effective July 27, 1938.)

6 Pub. Laws (1938), ch. 2622. (Effective July 1, 1938.)

7 Applicant must have been a resident 5 years within the 9 years immediately preceding the application, the last year having been continuous and immediately preceding application, or must have become blind while a resident of the State.

Supplementary Table 14.—Need Qualifications for Blind Assistance

State	Limitations on property	Limitations on income	Applicant must not have disposed of property to qualify	Applicant has no person liable and able to support him
Louisiana	(^{1})	(^{1})	Within 5 years .	
Rhode Island^2 ...	(^{3})	(^{3})	Within 5 years .	

X indicates that the provision applies without limitation in a given State.

^{1}The provisions contained in table 14, appendix A, relating to limitations on property and income have been repealed. Acts (1938), No. 359. (Effective July 27, 1938.)

^{2}Pub. Laws (1938), ch. 2622. (Effective July 1, 1938.)

^{3}Applicant is ineligible if he has property or income in excess of amount needed for reasonable subsistence compatible with decency and health.

Supplementary Table 15.—Types of Aid Received or Needed Which Disqualify Applicants for Blind Assistance

State	Assistance		Institutional aid		
	Other public assistance	Old age assistance	Public or private institution	Public institution	In need of continuing institutional care
Louisiana	X^1	....	....	X^2	
Rhode Island^3	....	(^{4})	....	(^{5})	(^{6}).

X indicates that the provision applies without limitation in a given State.

^{1}Except temporary medical and surgical assistance.

^{2}Acts (1938), No. 359, sec. 4(c). (Effective July 27, 1938.)

^{3}Pub. Laws (1938), ch. 2622. (Effective July 1, 1938.)

^{4}Applicant must not be receiving old age assistance.

^{5}Applicant must not be an inmate of any public institution at time of receiving assistance.

^{6}Applicant must not be in need of continuing institutional care or other kinds of aid and service which are reasonably available.

Supplementary Table 16.—Provisions for Recovery From Recipients and Their Estates for Blind Assistance Granted

State	For total amount of assistance	Exemptions
Louisiana	X^1	(^{2}).
Rhode Island^3	X^4	Realty of recipient while occupied by surviving spouse.

X indicates that the provision applies without limitation in a given State.

^{1}Acts (1938), No. 359, secs. 17, 18, 19, 20. (Effective July 27, 1938.)

^{2}Costs of administration of the estate and reasonable funeral expenses are allowed. No claim is enforceable against real estate of recipient while occupied as a home by the surviving spouse, a child, or children, nor against any personal or real property of less than $100 in value. The cost of assistance may be recovered from the relatives of a recipient if they are legally responsible for his support and able to furnish such support. Acts (1938), No. 359, secs. 17, 18, 19, 20. (Effective July 27, 1938.)

^{3}Pub. Laws (1938), ch. 2622. (Effective July 1, 1938.)

^{4}Any assistance paid after the recipient has come into possession of property or income in excess of amount stated in the application, and such property or income in excess of his need shall be recoverable by the State as a debt due the State. On the death of any recipient, the total amount of assistance paid shall be allowed as a claim against the estate of such person.

Supplementary Table 17.—Provisions for Granting and Financing Blind Assistance

State	Maximum allowance (per month unless otherwise specified)	Minimum allowance (per month unless otherwise specified)	Burial allowance	Provision for removal of disability	Governmental unit determining amount of individual grant		Incidence of financial responsibility			Basis for distribution of State funds	Procedure in case of insufficiency of State funds
					Final	Advisory	State	County	Other local unit		
Louisiana	(1)	------	(2) ------	Temporary assistance.[3]	Parish --	------	75 percent.[4]	------	25 percent (parish).	State reimburses parish for 75 percent of cost of assistance and 50 percent of administrative costs.[4]	State contribution based on amount of funds available.
Rhode Island[5]	$30[6]	------	------	(7) ------	State --	------	X	------	------	State disburses funds to individuals.------	

X indicates that the provision applies without limitation in a given State.

[1] Allowance must be an amount which is sufficient, when added to other income, to provide recipient with reasonable subsistence compatible with decency and health. Acts (1938), No. 359, sec. 6. (Effective July 27, 1938.)

[2] Reasonable funeral expenses may be paid, if the estate is insufficient and if there are no responsible relatives able to pay such expenses. Acts (1938), No. 359, sec. 20.

[3] Assistance may also be granted to prevent blindness, including necessary traveling and other expenses to receive treatment at a hospital or clinic.

[4] State may assume total financial responsibility if parish lacks funds.

[5] Pub. Laws (1938), ch. 2622. (Effective July 1, 1938.)

[6] Assistance in excess of this amount may be granted in exceptional cases with the approval of the director of public welfare.

[7] State Department of Public Welfare must cooperate with the Bureau of the Blind in the Department of Education and with other agencies in measures for the prevention of blindness and restoration of eyesight.

AID TO DEPENDENT CHILDREN IN THEIR OWN HOMES

Supplementary *Table 18.*—Provisions for the Administration of Aid to Dependent Children in Their Own Homes

State	Administrative responsibility			Determination of eligibility							
				Original determination		Reconsideration		Appeal and review			
	Nature of law	Direct	Supervisory	Final	Advisory	Periodic	At request of State board or department	Appeal of applicant to State department[1]	Review by State department on own motion[1]	Upon complaint by person other than applicant[1]	Further investigation by State department[1]
Louisiana	M	State Department of Public Welfare through parish department of public welfare.[2]		Parish department of public welfare.			(3) --- X	(4)	(4)		(4).

X indicates that the provision applies without limitation in a given State.
M indicates mandatory provision.
O indicates optional provision.

[1] If authority to hear appeals, to review decisions, and to make further investigations is placed by law with a specific agency within the department, the specific agency is named either in the body of the table or in a footnote.

[2] Acts (1938), No. 359. (Effective July 27, 1938.)
[3] All grants must be reconsidered as frequently as may be required by the rules of the State department. Acts (1938), No. 359, sec. 15. (Effective July 27, 1938.)
[4] The State department may, upon its own motion, review any decision of a parish department or consider any application upon which no decision has been made and make original or additional investigation as it may deem necessary. Acts (1938), No. 359, sec. 15. (Effective July 27, 1938.)

Supplementary *Table 21.*—Provisions for Granting and Financing Aid to Dependent Children in Their Own Homes

State	Maximum allowance (per month unless otherwise specified)			Burial allowance	Governmental unit determining amount of individual grant		Incidence of financial responsibility			Basis for distribution of State funds	Procedure in case of insufficiency of State funds
	First child	Each additional child	Family		Final	Advisory	State	County	Other local unit		
Louisiana	(1)	(1)		(2)	Parish		66% percent.[3]		33% percent (parish).	State reimburses parish 66% percent of cost of assistance and 50 percent of cost of administrative costs.[3]	

X indicates that the provision applies without limitation in a given State.

[1] Aid necessary to support child in manner compatible with decency and health.
[2] Reasonable funeral expenses may be paid, if the estate is insufficient or if there are no responsible relatives able to pay such expenses. Acts (1938), No. 359, sec. 20. (Effective July 27, 1938.)
[3] State may assume total financial responsibility if parish lacks funds, or funds are legally barred.

STATE BOARDS AND LOCAL BOARDS

Supplementary Table 34.—Composition and Appointment of State Boards of Public Welfare

State	Name of State department	Name of State governing or advisory board	Number of board members	Terms of office		Method of selection		Remuneration	Qualifications	Limitation on appointment	Provision for removal	Provision for filling vacancies created by death, resignation, or removal
				Rotating	Other (number of years)	By Governor	By Governor with consent of Senate					
Louisiana ------	State Department of Public Welfare.	State Board of Public Welfare.	5--		5[1]	X ---		Expenses --	Recognized interest in and knowledge of public welfare problems.			

X indicates that the provision applies without limitation in a given State.

[1] Acts (1938), No. 344, sec. 3. (Effective July 27, 1938.)

Supplementary Table 35.—Appointment and Qualifications of Executives of State Boards or Departments of Public Welfare

State	Title of executive	Term of office	Method of selection			Remuneration	Qualifications	Provision for filling vacancy in office
			By Governor	By Governor with consent of Senate	By commission or board			
Ohio (State)-----	State relief director[1]	9 months[2]		X -----		Fixed by law --	Must devote his entire time and attention to the performance of his official duties.	

X indicates that the provision applies without limitation in a given State.

[1] Laws (1937 3d ex.), S. B. 465. (Effective July 11, 1938.)

[2] The law provides for the appointment of a State relief director to serve for a term of 9 months. Apparently no provision has been made for succeeding appointments after the expiration of this appointment.

Supplementary Table 36.—Composition and Appointment of Local Boards of Public Welfare

State	Name of board	Number of members	Terms of office		Person or agency making appointments	Remuneration	Qualifications	Limitation on appointment	Provision for removal
			Rotating (number of years)	Other					
Louisiana	Parish board of public welfare.[1]	5[1]	5[1] [2]		(1)	Expenses	Board members must be citizens of the parish.		

[1] The parish boards consist of 5 members selected by the police jury of each parish, except in New Orleans where the parish board consists of 7 members selected by the commission council of the city. Appointments must be made from a list of citizens of the respective parish certified by the State department, containing twice as many names as there are vacancies to be filled. Vacancies are filled in the same manner as original appointment.

Acts (1938), No. 344, sec. 9. (Effective July 27, 1938.) The State department may unite 2 or more parishes and form a district department of public welfare. Ibid., sec. 8. (Effective July 27, 1938.)

[2] Term continues until successor is appointed and qualified.

Supplementary Table 37.—Appointment and Qualifications of Executives of Local Boards or Departments of Public Welfare

State	Title of executive	Term of office	Method of selection			Remuneration	Qualifications
			Appointed by State Department of Public Welfare	Appointed by local governing body	Appointed by local board of public welfare		
Illinois	County superintendent of public welfare.[1]	4 years[2]	X				Must be legal residents of the State and of their respective counties for at least 3 years prior to their appointment.
Louisiana	Parish director of public welfare.	Pleasure of State director.[3]			(4)	Fixed by State department.	Must meet qualifications prescribed by State department.

X indicates that the provision applies without limitation in a given State.

[1] Laws (1938 1st ex.), H. B. 4. (Effective July 8, 1938.)

[2] Term continues until successor is appointed and qualified.

[3] Acts (1938), No. 344.

[4] State director.

Appendix C

SUMMARIES OF STATE PROVISIONS FOR PUBLIC WELFARE AND CHARTS OF STATE AND LOCAL PUBLIC WELFARE AGENCIES

THE FOLLOWING charts of State agencies and institutions performing public welfare functions indicate briefly the public welfare structure within each State and the names of the agencies and institutions performing public welfare functions. The summaries of statutory provisions for public welfare which accompany each chart and which are to be read in conjunction with the chart indicate very briefly the functions performed by the agencies and institutions contained in the chart.

The organizational charts are restricted to the legal and constitutional structure within the State. They do not indicate the extent to which divisions and bureaus have been established within particular agencies unless such divisions and bureaus are created by law. The lines joining the boxes on the charts indicate mainly the legal lines of control over agencies and institutions performing public welfare functions on both the State and local levels.

Functions which are uniformly considered to be of a public welfare nature and consistently included in the charts and summaries are those which provide for dependent, handicapped, defective, and delinquent persons.

Provisions for the relief of dependency included in the charts and summaries are: general relief, old age assistance, aid to dependent children in their own homes, blind assistance, care of dependent and neglected children by agencies and institutions, and veteran relief.[1]

Functions performed for the welfare of handicapped and defective persons included in the charts and summaries are: care and treatment of the insane and feeble-minded and epileptic persons; and services to the blind.

The charts and summaries include the following provisions for delinquents: the care, confinement, and reformation of juvenile and adult delinquents; and the administration of paroles and probation.

All agencies concerned with the administration of any of the above functions have been uniformly included in the organizational charts. In some instances agencies and institutions which are performing one or more of the above functions are also responsible for the administration of functions which in most States have not been brought within the public welfare structure. For the purpose of this study, these functions have been included in the summaries only when their administration is placed within an agency or institution which is performing one or more of the functions consistently considered to be of a public welfare nature. These functions include the care of crippled children; maternal and child health; education of the deaf, dumb, and blind; vocational rehabilitation; and the care of tuberculars. The absence of these functions from a particular summary does not indicate that they are not being undertaken by some other State department, such as the Department of Health or Department of Education.

---

[1] In a few States assistance to veterans is not restricted to those actually in need.

SUMMARY OF STATUTORY PROVISIONS FOR PUBLIC WELFARE
ALABAMA

Relief and Public Assistance.—The State Department of Public Welfare in conjunction with the county departments of public welfare is authorized to administer or supervise general relief, old age assistance, aid to dependent children in their own homes, and blind assistance.[1]

Cases involving dependent and neglected children come within the jurisdiction of juvenile courts. The State Department of Public Welfare must, through the bureau of child welfare, advise with judges and probation officers of the juvenile courts and aid in the work of the courts; it must visit and inspect all institutions caring for dependent, neglected, or delinquent children and license those not under State ownership. The State department through the bureau of child welfare likewise must establish and maintain homes or other agencies for the care of such children and receive children committed to it. The county departments of public welfare must, if appointed by courts of competent jurisdiction, perform the functions of probation officers in cases of such children. County departments must cooperate with the State department and other agencies caring for children and direct the care of dependent, neglected, delinquent, or otherwise handicapped children and such other child welfare activities as are delegated to the county departments by the State department or its bureau of child welfare.

State pensions to veterans are administered by the State Pension Commission assisted by the probate judge acting as county pension commissioner. County relief to veterans is administered by the court of county commissioners, county board of revenue, or other county governing body. Care of veterans in the State Soldiers' Home is administered by the board of control of the home.

Juvenile Delinquents.—Juvenile courts have jurisdiction in cases involving delinquent children. The case of a delinquent child more than 14 years of age, not subject to reformation, may be transferred to any other court having jurisdiction of the offense with which the child is charged. Delinquent girls may be committed to the State Training School for Girls. The Boys' State Industrial School receives delinquent white boys committed to it by courts or by voluntary commitment. Delinquent Negro children, with the exception of criminals over 15 years of age, may be committed to the State Reform School for Juvenile Negro Law Breakers.[2]

Services to the Blind.—The State Board of Education[3] must maintain a bureau of information to aid blind persons, whose training is not otherwise provided for, in finding employment, in developing home industries, and in marketing their products. It may furnish materials, tools, books, and home instruction. The board is authorized to maintain a register of blind persons in the State, describing causes of blindness and capacity for education and industrial training of each blind person.

Insane and Mental Defectives.—Insane persons are committed by probate courts to the Bryce and Searcy State Hospitals for the Insane (for white and colored persons, respectively). Idiots, imbeciles, feeble-minded persons, or morons, any of whom may be epileptic but not violent or insane, are committed by juvenile courts, if minors, or by probate courts if adults to the Partlow State School for Mental Deficients. The State Epileptic Colony receives epileptic children and adults (exclusive of criminals, inebriates, or violently insane persons); they are admitted by voluntary agreement in the case of pay patients or committed by probate courts in the case of indigents. The State Department of Public Welfare must provide a mental hygiene program of noninstitutional care in the interest of preventive work and general mental hygiene activities.

---

[1] The State Department of Public Welfare must cooperate with, and act as the agent of, the Federal Government in public welfare matters of mutual concern.

[2] See discussion of care of dependent and neglected children, above, for powers of the State and county departments of public welfare in relation to children.

[3] The State Board of Education supervises educational work of all charitable, penal, reformatory, and child-caring institutions, maintained in whole or in part by the State, through the State superintendent of education who is a member of the governing boards of institutions which have charge of such work.

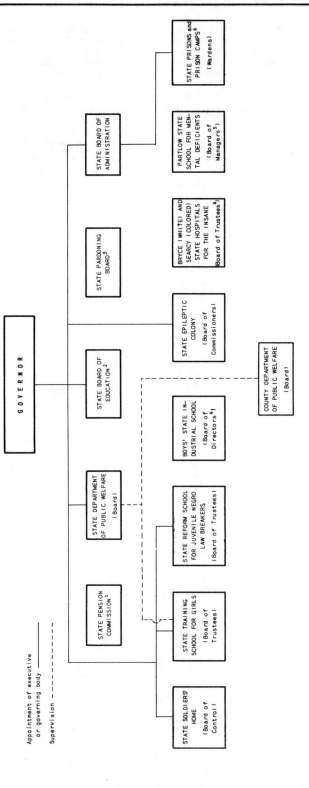

ALABAMA PUBLIC WELFARE AGENCIES
Statutory and Constitutional Organization

Appointment of executive
or governing body ─────────
Supervision ─ ─ ─ ─ ─ ─ ─ ─

GOVERNOR

STATE DEPARTMENT OF PUBLIC WELFARE (Board)

STATE BOARD OF EDUCATION [2]

STATE PARDONING BOARD [3]

STATE BOARD OF ADMINISTRATION

STATE PENSION COMMISSION [1]

STATE REFORM SCHOOL FOR JUVENILE NEGRO LAW BREAKERS (Board of Trustees)

BOYS' STATE INDUSTRIAL SCHOOL (Board of Directors [4])

STATE EPILEPTIC COLONY (Board of Commissioners)

BRYCE (WHITE) AND SEARCY (COLORED) STATE HOSPITALS FOR THE INSANE (Board of Trustees [4])

PARTLOW STATE SCHOOL FOR MENTAL DEFICIENTS (Board of Managers [5])

STATE PRISONS and PRISON CAMPS [6] (Wardens)

STATE SOLDIERS' HOME (Board of Control)

STATE TRAINING SCHOOL FOR GIRLS (Board of Trustees)

COUNTY DEPARTMENT OF PUBLIC WELFARE (Board)

[1] Composed of the State director of archives and history, the attorney general, and the State auditor.
[2] The State superintendent of education is a member of the governing board of each charitable, penal, reformatory, and child-caring agency maintained in whole or in part by the State.
[3] Composed of the attorney general, the secretary of state, and the State auditor.
[4] Self-perpetuating body of which the Governor is a member.
[5] Consists of the board of trustees of the State insane hospitals which elects additional members.
[6] Number is not specified in statutes.

Adult Delinquents.—The State Board of Administration has general supervision and control of the State and county convicts in State prisons and prison camps.[4] State convicts under 18 years of age are segregated from others and placed in a reformatory. The State Pardoning Board must examine applications made to the Governor for paroles, pardons, or commutations of sentences and must make recommendations thereon to the Governor.

Crippled Children.—The State Board of Education, through its division of vocational education, must administer State and Federal funds for services to crippled children.

---

[4]The State Board of Administration also has charge of the care, custody, equipment, repairing, insurance, and accounting of all property of the State, except the properties of educational, charitable, and eleemosynary institutions, which are under the management of their own boards of trustees.

SUMMARY OF STATUTORY PROVISIONS FOR PUBLIC WELFARE
ARIZONA

Relief and Public Assistance.—General relief is administered by county boards of social security and public welfare under the supervision of the State Department of Social Security and Welfare. Boards of county supervisors maintain homes, poor farms, and hospitals, and they are charged with the administration of provisions for hospitalization and care of the indigent sick, except provisions for care of such persons in the State Welfare Sanatorium.[1] Old age assistance, aid to dependent children in their own homes, and blind assistance are administered by the State Department of Social Security and Welfare assisted by county boards of social security and public welfare.[2] The State department must also supervise agencies and institutions (except those operated by the Board of Directors of State Institutions) caring for dependent or physically handicapped or aged adults, and it has authority to approve the incorporation of charitable agencies.

Cases involving dependent and neglected children come within the jurisdiction of the superior courts which control and supervise county detention homes receiving dependent and neglected children. The State Department of Social Security and Welfare with the assistance of county boards of social security and public welfare administers all child welfare activities including licensing and supervision of private and local public child-caring agencies and institutions.

Direct relief to veterans is administered by the Veterans' Relief Commission.

Juvenile Delinquents.—Superior courts have jurisdiction in cases involving delinquent children and may commit such children to their parents, to a reputable citizen, to an association or institution, to county detention homes, or to the State Industrial School for Juvenile Offenders. The State Department of Social Security and Welfare supervises the care and training of delinquent children. The Board of Directors of State Institutions may assign a delinquent girl to any institution with which it has made arrangements for the care of such children.

Services to the Blind.—The State Department of Social Security and Welfare must develop agencies or cooperate with agencies already established to provide services to the blind. These services include prevention of blindness, location of blind persons, medical services for eye conditions, vocational guidance and training of the blind, placement of blind persons in employment, and instruction of adult blind in their homes.

Insane and Mental Defectives.—The State Hospital for the Insane provides care and treatment for insane persons committed by superior courts. The superior courts commit to the Colony for Mentally Deficient Children those minors who are so mentally deficient that they are incapable of managing themselves and whose intelligence will not develop. The State Department of Social Security and Welfare must supervise all agencies and institutions caring for the mentally handicapped except State institutions operated by the Board of Directors of State Institutions.

Adult Delinquents.—The State Prison provides for confinement and training of adult delinquents. The State Board of Pardons and Paroles has power to pass upon and recommend to the Governor the granting of reprieves, commutations, pardons, and paroles.

Crippled Children.—The State Department of Social Security and Welfare is responsible for the administration of services for children who are crippled or suffering from conditions which lead to crippling. These services include locating such children and providing medical, surgical, corrective, and other care and facilities for diagnosis, hospitalization, and aftercare. The State department must supervise the administration of services included in the program that are not administered directly by the department. It must cooperate with medical, health, nursing, and welfare groups and organizations, and with any State agency administering laws providing for vocational rehabilitation of physically handicapped children.

---

[1] The State Welfare Sanatorium is operated by the State Board of Social Security and Welfare.

[2] The State Department of Social Security and Welfare must act as the agent of the Federal Government in furtherance of any functions of the State department and must also act as the official agency of the State in any welfare activity initiated by the Federal Government.

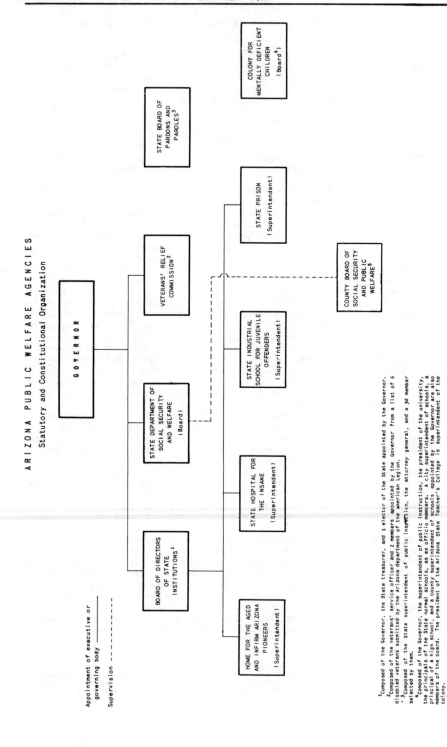

ARIZONA PUBLIC WELFARE AGENCIES
Statutory and Constitutional Organization

Appointment of executive or governing body —————————
Supervision - - - - - - - - - -

GOVERNOR

BOARD OF DIRECTORS OF STATE INSTITUTIONS[1]

STATE DEPARTMENT OF SOCIAL SECURITY AND WELFARE (Board)

VETERANS' RELIEF COMMISSION[2]

STATE BOARD OF PARDONS AND PAROLES[3]

COLONY FOR MENTALLY DEFICIENT CHILDREN (Board[4])

HOME FOR THE AGED AND INFIRM ARIZONA PIONEERS (Superintendent)

STATE HOSPITAL FOR THE INSANE (Superintendent)

STATE INDUSTRIAL SCHOOL FOR JUVENILE OFFENDERS (Superintendent)

STATE PRISON (Superintendent)

COUNTY BOARD OF SOCIAL SECURITY AND PUBLIC WELFARE[5]

[1] Composed of the Governor, the State treasurer, and 1 elector of the State appointed by the Governor.

[2] Composed of the veterans' service officer and 2 members appointed by the Governor from a list of 6 disabled veterans submitted by the Arizona department of the American Legion.

[3] Composed of the State superintendent of public inspection, the attorney general, and a 3d member selected by them.

[4] Composed of the Governor, the superintendent of public instruction, the president of the university, the principals of the State normal schools, as ex officio members. A city superintendent of schools, a principal of a high school, and a county superintendent of schools appointed by the Governor are also members of the board. The president of the Arizona State Teacher's College is superintendent of the colony.

[5] Composed of 1 member of the board of county supervisors and 2 citizens appointed by the board of county supervisors.

SUMMARY OF STATUTORY PROVISIONS FOR PUBLIC WELFARE
ARKANSAS

Relief and Public Assistance.—General relief is provided by two programs, one administered by the State Department of Public Welfare through county or district departments of public welfare and the other by county courts. Old age assistance, aid to dependent children in their own homes, and blind assistance are administered by the State Department of Public Welfare assisted by the county or district board of public welfare.[1] The State Department of Public Welfare must supervise and license private agencies and institutions providing assistance, care, or other direct services to the aged, the blind, and other dependent persons.

Cases involving dependent and neglected children come within the jurisdiction of juvenile courts. The State Department of Public Welfare is charged with the administration or supervision of all child welfare activities including the licensing and supervision of private and public child-caring agencies, institutions, and boarding homes for children.[2] The county or district departments of public welfare perform such duties as the State department may prescribe. The juvenile court department is placed within the Department of Public Welfare which supervises, directs, and controls its operation. County boards of visitation must visit all institutions, societies, and associations receiving children committed by juvenile courts.

Confederate veterans' pensions are administered by the State Pension Board assisted by county boards of pensions. Care of Confederate veterans in the State Confederate Home, and care of their mothers, widows, and daughters in the annex to the home is administered by the honorary board for the management and operation of the Confederate home.[3]

Juvenile Delinquents.—Juvenile courts have jurisdiction in cases involving delinquent children. The court may allow a child to remain in its own home, may designate a guardian and place the child in a home provided by the guardian, or it may commit the child to a public or private institution. The State Industrial School for White Boys, the State Industrial School for Negro Boys, and the State Training School for Girls have been established for the care and training of juvenile delinquents.[4]

Services to the Blind.—The State Department of Public Welfare must develop or cooperate with other agencies in developing measures for the prevention of blindness, restoration of sight, and the vocational adjustment of blind persons.

Insane and Mental Defectives.—The State Hospital and Hospital Dairy Farm provide care and treatment for insane, feeble-minded, or epileptic persons committed by county or probate judges. The State Department of Public Welfare must administer or supervise care of mentally handicapped children in foster family homes or institutions. The State department must supervise and license private agencies and institutions providing assistance, care, or other direct services to the feeble-minded. It must administer or supervise all mental hygiene work, including care of mentally ill or feeble-minded persons not in the State hospital.

Adult Delinquents.—The State Penitentiary, the Penitentiary Farms, and the State Farm for Women provide for confinement and training of adult delinquents. The State Board of Pardon and Parole has power to grant paroles and must consider all applications for executive clemency and make recommendations to the Governor. The State board also has visitorial power over all institutions to which persons may be committed upon criminal charges.

Crippled Children.—The State Department of Public Welfare must administer or supervise aid and services to crippled children, including services for locating crippled children and for providing medical, surgical, corrective, and other care and facilities for diagnosis, hospitalization, and aftercare for children who are crippled or who are suffering from conditions which lead to crippling. County or juvenile courts, at the request of parent, guardian, or interested person, may commit a crippled child to the State department for treatment or education.

---

[1] The State Department of Public Welfare must cooperate with the Federal Government in public welfare matters of mutual concern.

[2] The Arkansas Children's Home and Hospital, a State-aided institution, is recognized as an official agency of the State and of the several counties for the purpose of receiving, caring for, treating, and placing in homes dependent, neglected, and crippled children committed to it.

[3] The State Pension Claims Committee investigates persons on pension rolls and residents of the State Confederate Home and causes the State Pension Board to remove ineligibles.

[4] See discussion of care of dependent and neglected children, above, for powers of the State Department of Public Welfare and county boards of visitation in relation to children.

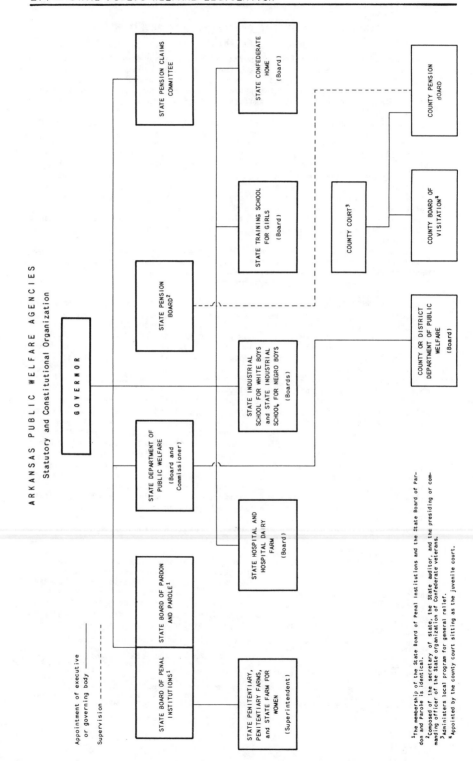

ARKANSAS PUBLIC WELFARE AGENCIES
Statutory and Constitutional Organization

Appointment of executive
or governing body ————————
Supervision ————————————

GOVERNOR

STATE BOARD OF PENAL INSTITUTIONS[1]

STATE BOARD OF PARDON AND PAROLE[1]

STATE DEPARTMENT OF PUBLIC WELFARE
(Board and Commissioner)

STATE PENSION BOARD[2]

STATE PENSION CLAIMS COMMITTEE

STATE PENITENTIARY, PENITENTIARY FARMS, and STATE FARM FOR WOMEN
(Superintendent)

STATE HOSPITAL AND HOSPITAL DAIRY FARM
(Board)

STATE INDUSTRIAL SCHOOL FOR WHITE BOYS and STATE INDUSTRIAL SCHOOL FOR NEGRO BOYS
(Boards)

STATE TRAINING SCHOOL FOR GIRLS
(Board)

STATE CONFEDERATE HOME
(Board)

COUNTY COURT[3]

COUNTY OR DISTRICT DEPARTMENT OF PUBLIC WELFARE
(Board)

COUNTY BOARD OF VISITATION[4]

COUNTY PENSION BOARD

[1] The membership of the State Board of Penal Institutions and the State Board of Pardon and Parole is identical.

[2] Composed of the secretary of state, the State auditor, and the presiding or commanding officer of the State organization of Confederate veterans.

[3] Administers local program for general relief.

[4] Appointed by the county court sitting as the juvenile court.

SUMMARY OF STATUTORY PROVISIONS FOR PUBLIC WELFARE
CALIFORNIA

Relief and Public Assistance.—General relief is provided by two programs, one administered by county boards of supervisors, or county boards of public welfare where established, and the other by the State Department of Social Welfare. Old age assistance, aid to dependent children in their own homes, and blind assistance are administered by county boards of supervisors, or the county boards of public welfare where established, under supervision of the State Department of Social Welfare.[1]

Cases involving dependent and neglected children come within the jurisdiction of juvenile courts. County probation committees appointed by the juvenile court must, upon request of the juvenile court judge or the county board of supervisors, investigate any society, association, or corporation other than a State institution receiving or applying for any ward. These county committees also control county detention homes. The State Department of Social Welfare must make rules and regulations for the proper maintenance and care of needy children and must inquire into the management of all institutions receiving State aid. It may also investigate the care of children in institutions not under the control of the State Department of Institutions and is empowered to license boarding homes, institutions, and other agencies caring for or finding homes for children under 16 years of age.[2]

The Whittier State School receives boys committed by the juvenile courts.

Direct relief to veterans is administered by county boards of supervisors with the assistance of military, naval, and marine organizations which certify to the eligibility of veterans. The Veterans' Home of California and the Women's Relief Corps Home provide for institutional care of veterans. Cities and counties may also establish veteran homes.

Juvenile Delinquents.—Cases involving delinquent children come within the jurisdiction of the juvenile courts. Provisions for care of dependent and neglected children also apply to delinquent children. The State Department of Social Welfare must investigate juvenile probation. The bureau of juvenile research must conduct research into the causes and consequences of delinquency and mental deficiency and inquire into social, educational, and psychological problems relating thereto. It has control of and directs all juvenile research and psychological work conducted in State schools, State homes for the feeble-minded, and other State institutions giving custodial care to minors. The Preston State School of Industry and the Ventura State School for Girls provide care and training for delinquent children.

Services to the Blind.—The State Industrial Home for the Adult Blind, the State Industrial Workshop for the Blind, and similar workshops which may be established by the State Department of Institutions with the approval of the department of finance provide training and employment of the blind. The State Department of Institutions may authorize work to be let out to the blind in their homes.

Insane and Mental Defectives.—The State Department of Institutions is charged with the execution of laws relating to the care, custody, and treatment of insane, feeble-minded, epileptic, idiotic, and other incompetent persons, and it must examine all public and private institutions receiving such persons.[3] The Mendocino, Stockton, Napa, Agnews, Patton, Norwalk, and Camarillo State Hospitals for the Insane provide care and treatment for insane persons committed by judges of superior courts. The Sonoma State Home for the Feeble-minded receives imbeciles, idiots, and epileptics who are not insane. The Pacific Colony and State Narcotic Hospital care for feeble-minded persons, epileptics, and drug addicts committed by judges of the superior courts.

---

[1] The State Department of Social Welfare must investigate charitable institutions other than those under jurisdiction of another State department. It may also act as the agent of or cooperate with the Federal Government on any matters within the scope of the functions of the department. County boards of public welfare, where established, must visit charitable institutions receiving county funds and report thereon to the State Department of Social Welfare.

[2] County boards of public welfare, where established, must visit and report to the State Board of Social Welfare concerning charitable and correctional institutions receiving support from county funds.

[3] See "Juvenile Delinquents," above, for powers of the bureau of juvenile research.

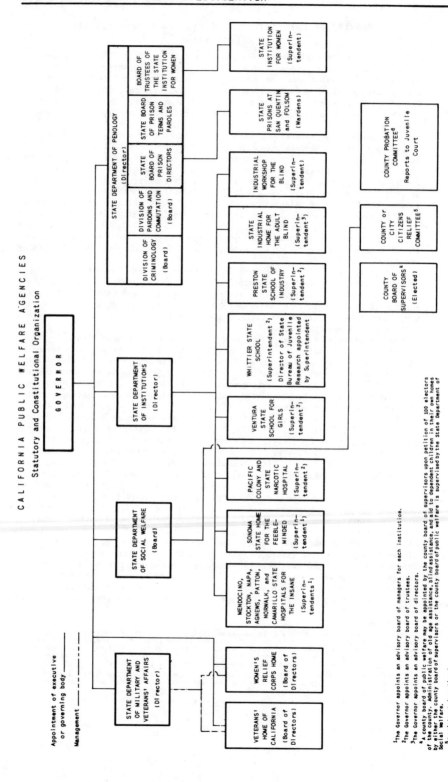

CALIFORNIA PUBLIC WELFARE AGENCIES

Statutory and Constitutional Organization

GOVERNOR

STATE DEPARTMENT OF MILITARY AND VETERANS' AFFAIRS (Director)

VETERANS' HOME OF CALIFORNIA (Board of Directors)

WOMEN'S RELIEF CORPS HOME (Board of Directors)

STATE DEPARTMENT OF SOCIAL WELFARE (Board)

MENDOCINO, STOCKTON, NAPA, AGNEWS, PATTON, NORWALK, and CAMARILLO STATE HOSPITALS FOR THE INSANE (Superintendents [1])

SONOMA STATE HOME FOR THE FEEBLE-MINDED (Superintendent [1])

PACIFIC COLONY AND STATE NARCOTIC HOSPITAL (Superintendent [2])

STATE DEPARTMENT OF INSTITUTIONS (Director)

VENTURA STATE SCHOOL FOR GIRLS (Superintendent [2])

WHITTIER STATE SCHOOL (Superintendent [2]) Director of State Bureau of Juvenile Research appointed by Superintendent

PRESTON STATE SCHOOL OF INDUSTRY (Superintendent [2])

STATE INDUSTRIAL HOME FOR THE ADULT BLIND (Superintendent [3])

INDUSTRIAL WORKSHOP FOR THE BLIND (Superintendent)

STATE DEPARTMENT OF PENOLOGY (Director)

DIVISION OF CRIMINOLOGY (Board)

DIVISION OF PARDONS AND COMMUTATION (Board)

STATE BOARD OF PRISON DIRECTORS

STATE BOARD OF PRISON TERMS AND PAROLES

BOARD OF TRUSTEES OF THE STATE INSTITUTION FOR WOMEN

STATE PRISONS AT SAN QUENTIN and FOLSOM (Wardens)

STATE INSTITUTION FOR WOMEN (Superintendent)

COUNTY BOARD OF SUPERVISORS [4] (Elected)

COUNTY or CITY CITIZENS RELIEF COMMITTEE [5]

COUNTY PROBATION COMMITTEE [6] Reports to Juvenile Court

Appointment of executive or governing body ————

Management ————————

[1] The Governor appoints an advisory board of managers for each institution.

[2] The Governor appoints an advisory board of trustees.

[3] The Governor appoints an advisory board of directors.

[4] A county board of public welfare may be appointed by the county board of supervisors upon petition of 100 electors of the county. Administration of old age assistance, blind assistance, and aid to dependent children in their own homes by either the county board of supervisors or the county board of public welfare is supervised by the State Department of Social Welfare.

[5] Appointment is optional.

[6] Appointed by judge of the juvenile court. Copies of reports to the courts are sent to county supervisors and to the State Department of Social Welfare.

Adult Delinquents.—The State Prison at Folsom, the State Prison at San Quentin, and the State Institution for Women provide for confinement and training of adult delinquents. The Governor has power to grant reprieves, pardons, and commutations for all offenses except treason and cases of impeachment. The State Board of Prison Terms and Paroles has general jurisdiction over the parole of prisoners and the determination of lengths of terms. The State Department of Social Welfare must investigate adult probation. County boards of public welfare, where established, must visit penal and correctional institutions receiving county funds and report thereon to the State Department of Social Welfare.

SUMMARY OF STATUTORY PROVISIONS FOR PUBLIC WELFARE
COLORADO

Relief and Public Assistance.—General relief, old age assistance, aid to dependent children in their own homes, and blind assistance are administered by the county or district departments of public welfare under the supervision of the State Department of Public Welfare.[1]

Cases involving dependent and neglected children come within the jurisdiction of juvenile courts. The State Department of Public Welfare is charged with the administration or supervision of all child welfare activities including the care of dependent and neglected children. County or district departments of public welfare must administer care and treatment to dependent and handicapped children under the rules and regulations of the State Department of Public Welfare, and they must investigate and pass upon all applications for admission to or discharge from county institutions. The county boards of visitors must keep advised of the conditions and management of all local public or private child-caring homes or institutions receiving county or municipal funds and make necessary recommendations. All private institutions, societies, and agencies receiving dependent children must be approved by the State Bureau of Child and Animal Protection which must cooperate with other agencies and secure the enforcement of laws for the protection of children. The bureau, if appointed by a competent court, may act as the guardian of any dependent, neglected, abandoned, or cruelly treated child under 14 years of age. The board of control of the State Home for Dependent and Neglected Children places in family homes children committed to the home and supervises the care of such children while they remain wards of the board.

Veteran relief is restricted to care in the State Soldiers' and Sailors' Home. Care in the home is administered by the soldiers' and sailors' home commission[2] and supervised by the Division of Public Welfare of the Executive Department.

Juvenile Delinquents.—Cases involving juvenile delinquents come within the jurisdiction of juvenile courts. The court may allow a child to remain in its own home, place it in a suitable home, or commit it to a county institution or to the State Industrial School for Girls or the State Industrial School for Boys. The county board of visitors[3] (appointed by county probate judge) must attend any proceedings involving the commitment of a boy to the State Industrial School in order to protect his interests.[4]

Services to the Blind.—The State Commission for the Blind is empowered to provide care, education, vocational training, employment, and treatment for any blind person, and to provide for the sale of products made by blind persons. It also has the power to investigate the causes and methods of preventing blindness, and it must cooperate with the State School for the Deaf and Blind, the State Department of Education, the State Department of Health, local school boards and health authorities, the United States Commissioner of Education, the Division of Vocational Rehabilitation, and other agencies for the prevention of blindness. The commission operates the Colorado Industrial Workshop for the Blind.

Insane and Mental Defectives.—Care and treatment of mentally defective and insane persons are provided by the State Home and Training School for Mental Defectives at Ridge, the State Home and Training School for Mental Defectives at Grand Junction, the State Hospital, and the State Psychopathic Hospital. These institutions receive voluntary patients and persons committed by county courts.

Adult Delinquents.—The State Penitentiary and the State Reformatory provide for the confinement and training of adult delinquents.

Tuberculars.—The director of the division of tuberculosis within the State Department of Public Welfare must, with the cooperation of local medical societies, conduct clinics in the diagnosis of tuberculosis throughout the State. The State Department of Public Welfare cooperates with the Federal Government in caring for indigent tuberculars.

---

[1] The State Department of Public Welfare must act as the agent of the Federal Government in welfare matters of mutual concern.

[2] *Need* is not specified as a condition of eligibility for care in the State Soldiers' and Sailors' Home.

[3] The county board of visitors must keep advised of the condition and management of all correctional institutions supported in whole or in part by county or municipal taxation.

[4] See discussion of care of dependent and neglected children, above, for powers of the State Department of Public Welfare in relation to children.

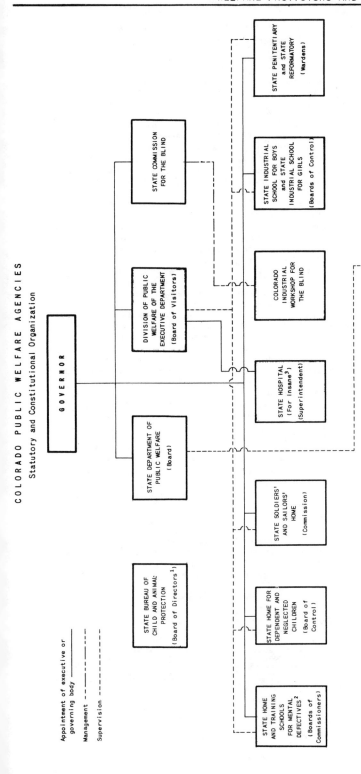

COLORADO PUBLIC WELFARE AGENCIES

Statutory and Constitutional Organization

Appointment of executive or
governing body ─────────
Management ── ── ── ──
Supervision ─ ─ ─ ─ ─ ─ ─

GOVERNOR

STATE BUREAU OF CHILD AND ANIMAL PROTECTION
(Board of Directors[1])

STATE DEPARTMENT OF PUBLIC WELFARE
(Board)

DIVISION OF PUBLIC WELFARE OF THE EXECUTIVE DEPARTMENT
(Board of Visitors)

STATE COMMISSION FOR THE BLIND

STATE PENITENTIARY and STATE REFORMATORY
(Wardens)

STATE INDUSTRIAL SCHOOL FOR BOYS and STATE INDUSTRIAL SCHOOL FOR GIRLS
(Boards of Control)

COLORADO INDUSTRIAL WORKSHOP FOR THE BLIND

COUNTY BOARD OF VISITORS[5]

STATE HOSPITAL
(For Insane[3])
(Superintendent)

COUNTY or DISTRICT DEPARTMENT OF PUBLIC WELFARE
(Board[4])

STATE HOME AND TRAINING SCHOOLS FOR MENTAL DEFECTIVES[2]
(Boards of Commissioners)

STATE HOME FOR DEPENDENT AND NEGLECTED CHILDREN
(Board of Control)

STATE SOLDIERS' AND SAILORS' HOME
(Commission)

[1] Composed of the Governor, the superintendent of public instruction, and the attorney general.

[2] 2 institutions have been established. 1 is situated at Ridge and the other at Grand Junction.

[3] In addition to the State Hospital, the State Psychopathic Hospital has been established, which is managed and controlled by the board of regents of the State university.

[4] Composed of the board of county commissioners.

[5] Appointed by the county probate judge. In counties where no board exists, the Division of Public Welfare of the State Executive Department must petition the county to appoint a board. If no action is taken on its petition, the Division of Public Welfare may appoint a board.

SUMMARY OF STATUTORY PROVISIONS FOR PUBLIC WELFARE
CONNECTICUT

Relief and Public Assistance.—General relief is administered by town overseers of the poor. Care for "State paupers" is administered by the Commissioner of Welfare.[1] Old age assistance and blind assistance are administered by the Commissioner of Welfare through the bureau of old age assistance assisted by the chief executive authorities of the towns. Aid to dependent children in their own homes is administered by the Commissioner of Welfare assisted by the chief executive authorities of the towns and boards of county commissioners.

Cases involving dependent and neglected children come within the jurisdiction of juvenile courts; except in matters of guardianship and adoption and all other matters affecting the property rights of any child, the probate courts have jurisdiction. The Commissioner of Welfare has general supervision over the welfare of dependent and neglected children and must cooperate with all juvenile courts. The Commissioner of Welfare licenses all child-caring agencies, supervises the placement of children in foster homes, and must cooperate with boards of county commissioners in the administration of temporary county detention homes which are under the control of the county commissioners. The county commissioners have supervision over children transferred from these homes to foster homes and institutions. The town selectmen must visit and inspect monthly all private foster homes. The public welfare council may inspect all child-caring agencies.

Direct relief to veterans and institutional care in the Fitch's State Soldiers' Home are administered by the veterans' home commission. The American Legion administers State funds allocated to it from the State Soldiers', Sailors', and Marines' Fund and the State general fund.

Juvenile Delinquents.—Juvenile courts have jurisdiction in cases involving delinquent children. The court may commit a child to any public or private institution or agency, to the care of some reputable person, or order the child to remain in its own home subject to the supervision of the probation officer. The Mansfield State Training School and Hospital, the State School for Boys, and the Long Lane Farm receive delinquents. The public welfare council must inspect all institutions where persons are detained by compulsion.[2]

Services to the Blind.—The State Board of Education for the Blind may prepare and maintain a register of the blind describing their condition, cause of blindness, and capacity for education and industrial training. It may register cases of persons whose eyesight is seriously defective and who are likely to become visually handicapped or blind; and it may take measures in cooperation with other authorities for the prevention of blindness or the conservation of eyesight. The board may contract with institutions, individuals, and mercantile and manufacturing establishments having facilities for the instruction of the blind, may provide for the instruction of adult blind in their homes, and may aid in securing employment and provide machinery, tools, and materials for the purpose of establishing blind persons in some useful occupation.

Insane and Mental Defectives.—The Mansfield State Training School and Hospital provides care, custody, treatment, education, and employment for feeble-minded and epileptic persons not violently insane or afflicted with a contagious disease who are committed by the probate or juvenile courts. The Connecticut State Hospital, the Norwich State Hospital, the Fairfield State Hospital, and the State Farm for Inebriates provide care and treatment for insane persons committed by the probate or juvenile courts.

Adult Delinquents.—The State Prison, the State Reformatory, the State Farm for Women, and the State Prison for Women provide for the confinement and training of adult delinquents. The Board of Pardons has jurisdiction over the granting of commutations, releases, and pardons.

---

[1] The Public Welfare Council advises and assists the Commissioner of Welfare in the administration of his duties. It may inspect almshouses and other institutions caring for dependents and take the necessary action to correct abuses found to exist. The Commissioner of Welfare is empowered to cooperate with the Federal Government and the several States in the promotion of activities in the field of public welfare and to administer any money appropriated by the Federal Government for such purposes.

[2] See discussion of care of dependent and neglected children, above, for other powers of the Commissioner of Welfare and the Public Welfare Council in relation to children.

CONNECTICUT PUBLIC WELFARE AGENCIES
Statutory and Constitutional Organization

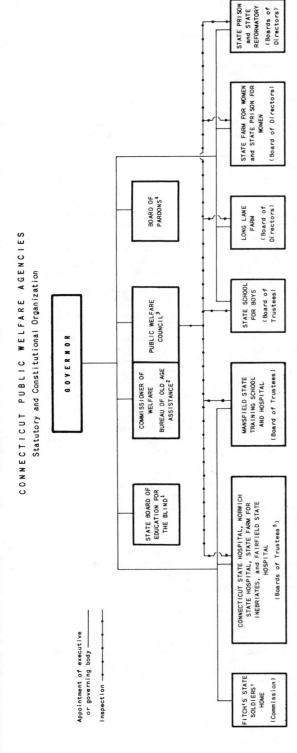

Appointment of executive
or governing body ————————

Inspection ·–·–·–·–·–·–·

[1] Composed of the Governor, the chief Justice of the Supreme Court, and 3 members appointed by the Governor.

[2] The Commissioner of Welfare is in charge of the bureau and appoints necessary personnel for the bureau.

[3] The Public Welfare Council advises and assists the Commissioner of Welfare.

[4] Composed of the Governor, the judge of the Supreme Court of Errors, and 4 others appointed by the Governor.

[5] 1 board of trustees serves both the Norwich State Hospital and the State Farm for Inebriates.

[6] Town selectmen are ex officio overseers of the poor. In Manchester they appoint a board of public welfare commissioners.

[7] Appointed by the General Assembly. Assists the Commissioner of Welfare in the administration of aid to dependent children in their own homes.

SUMMARY OF STATUTORY PROVISIONS FOR PUBLIC WELFARE
DELAWARE

Relief and Public Assistance.—General relief and old age assistance are administered by the State Old Age Welfare Commission. Indigent poor may be cared for in the State Welfare Home. Aid to dependent children in their own homes is administered by the State Mothers' Pension Commission. [1]

Cases involving dependent and neglected children come within the jurisdiction of juvenile courts. All such children are wards of the State, and the State Board of Charities is responsible for their placement and supervision. The State board is authorized to allot funds to certain child-caring agencies and it may establish homes and other agencies or contract with any approved agency or home for the care of dependent or neglected minors. Any person or social agent conducting or supporting a home for children and all institutions supported in whole or in part by public funds, receiving and caring for dependent, neglected, or delinquent minors, are subject to investigation by the State Board of Charities. The board is empowered to license persons or associations operating children's boarding homes. The Children's Bureau of Delaware is established to provide for the enforcement of laws for protection of children, to render services to children in their own homes, to provide for those in need of special care, to cooperate with other child-caring organizations, and to accept children committed to its care. The Detention Home for Juveniles receives children committed to it by juvenile courts.

Juvenile Delinquents.—Juvenile courts have jurisdiction in cases involving delinquent children. The court may allow the child to remain at home, commit it to the care of a probation officer, or place it in a family home. Delinquent boys may be committed to the Ferris Industrial School. Delinquent white girls may be committed to the State Industrial School for Girls, and delinquent colored girls may be committed to the State Industrial School for Colored Girls. Delinquent children may also be committed to the Detention Home for Juveniles or to the House of Refuge in Philadelphia, Pa. [2]

Services to the Blind.—The State Commission for the Blind has general supervision and control of the education, training, and welfare of blind persons.

Insane and Mental Defectives.—The State Home for the Feeble-minded provides care and treatment for feeble-minded persons committed by the court of general sessions of the county or juvenile court of the city of Wilmington, or admitted under agreement between the commission for the State Home for the Feeble-minded and the parents, guardian, or custodians of a feeble-minded person. The State Hospital at Farnhurst receives a person upon certification of insanity by two physicians to the superintendent of the hospital. The board of trustees of the hospital may summons a jury of six persons to determine a person's sanity. A person so committed may appeal to the chancellor of the State, who must provide a hearing before a jury.

Adult Delinquents.—The Newcastle County Workhouse, the Kent County Jail and Workhouse, and the Sussex County Jail and Workhouse provide for confinement and training of adult delinquents. The Commission on Prison Industries has charge of occupational training of prisoners and sale of prison products. The Governor may remit fines and forfeitures and grant pardons and reprieves, and commutations of sentences except in cases of impeachment, but he may not grant a pardon or reprieve for more than 6 months or commute a sentence without the written recommendation of a majority of the Board of Pardons. The State Board of Parole has charge of the parole of prisoners and the supervision of persons on parole.

Education of the Blind.—The State Commission for the Blind may recommend to the Governor that a blind child be placed in an institution for the instruction and training of blind persons.

Maternal and Child Health.—The State Board of Charities licenses maternity wards in general hospitals.

---

[1] The State Old Age Welfare Commission and the State Mothers' Pension Commission must cooperate with the Federal Government in the administration of old age assistance and aid to dependent children in their own homes, respectively.

[2] See discussion of care of dependent and neglected children, above, for powers of the Children's Bureau of Delaware and the State Board of Charities in relation to children.

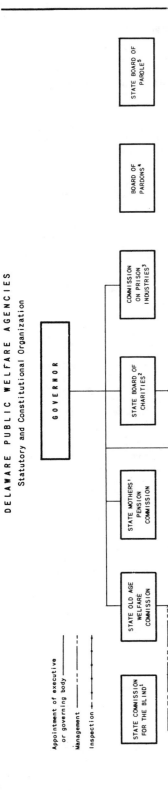

DELAWARE PUBLIC WELFARE AGENCIES

Statutory and Constitutional Organization

Appointment of executive
or governing body ──────────

Management ── ── ──

Inspection ─•─•─•─

[1] Appointed by the superior court judges of the State.

[2] The Governor is an ex officio member.

[3] Composed of 6 members appointed by the Governor, and the chairman of the board of trustees of each penal institution in the State producing or capable of producing commodities, or some agency selected by the respective boards.

[4] Composed of the chancellor, the lieutenant governor, the secretary of state, the State treasurer, and the auditor of accounts.

[5] Appointed by the judges of the Supreme Court.

[6] Composed of the Governor, the State treasurer, the president of the State Board of Charities, the judge of the juvenile court, and 5 persons appointed by the judge of the juvenile court.

[7] A State-aided child welfare agency.

[8] Appointed by the judges of the superior court and the court of general sessions of the State.

[9] Appointed by the levy court of the county.

SUMMARY OF STATUTORY PROVISIONS FOR PUBLIC WELFARE
FLORIDA

Relief and Public Assistance.—General relief is administered by boards of county commissioners, county boards of charity or county welfare boards where established, and city and town councils. The State Welfare Board may accept such duties as are delegated to it by any county or municipal agency. The State board may establish and operate almshouses, public homes, farms, schools, and hospitals for the indigent.

Old age assistance is administered by the State Welfare Board[1] through district boards of social welfare. There are two programs for aid to dependent children in their own homes. One is administered by boards of county commissioners and the other by the State Welfare Board through district boards of social welfare. Two programs for blind assistance are similarly administered.

Cases involving dependent and neglected children come within the jurisdiction of juvenile courts. The State Welfare Board, with the consent of the parents or a guardian, may place a child in a public or private home or institution or in a foster home. The State board may delegate activities to the district boards to be performed under its supervision. All child welfare institutions or agencies must meet with the standards and regulations for proper treatment and supervision prescribed by the State board for the care of dependent children away from their homes. Associations, institutions, or persons receiving or desiring to receive dependent, neglected, or delinquent children must also meet standards required by the juvenile courts. The juvenile courts cooperate with the State Welfare Board in the board's administration of provisions for the care of dependent, neglected and morally defective, and physically handicapped children.

Provisions for veterans' pensions are administered by boards of county commissioners under the supervision of the State Board of Pensions.[2] Care of veterans in the Old Confederate Soldiers' and Sailors' Home is administered by the board of managers of the home, under the supervision of the Board of Commissioners of State Institutions.

Juvenile Delinquents.—Juvenile courts have jurisdiction in cases involving delinquent children. The court may commit a juvenile delinquent to a probation officer, allow it to remain in its own home, or order it placed in a family home. The child may also be committed to a private child-caring institution or association or to an institution incorporated under laws of the State or provided by a city, county, or the State for care of delinquent children, including the State Industrial School for Boys and the State Industrial School for Girls. A child committed to an institution is subject to the control of the county judge. A child under 18 years of age sentenced to the State Prison may have its sentence commuted by the State Board of Pardons to detention in one of the industrial schools. County boards of visitors appointed by the juvenile courts must visit persons, societies, associations, and institutions, except State institutions, receiving delinquent children; they manage any detention home that may be established by the board of county commissioners.[3]

Insane and Mental Defectives.—The State Hospital for the Indigent Insane provides care and treatment for insane persons committed by the judges of the county or circuit courts. The State Farm Colony for Epileptics and Feeble-minded is an asylum for the care, protection, training, segregation, and employment of the feeble-minded and epileptics. Commitments to the colony are made by county judges, subject to acceptance by the Board of Commissioners of State Institutions. Juvenile courts must cooperate with the State Welfare Board in the board's administration of provisions for the care of mentally defective children.

Adult Delinquents.—The State Prison and State Prison Farm provide for confinement and training of adult delinquents. The State Board of Pardons may remit fines and forfeitures, commute punishment, and grant pardons except in cases of treason and impeachment.

---

[1] The State Welfare Board must cooperate with, and is authorized to act as agent of, the Federal Government in public welfare matters of mutual concern.

[2] Need is not specified as a condition of eligibility for veterans' pensions or for care in the Old Confederate Soldiers' and Sailors' Home.

[3] See discussion of care of dependent and neglected children, above, for powers of the State Welfare Board in relation to children.

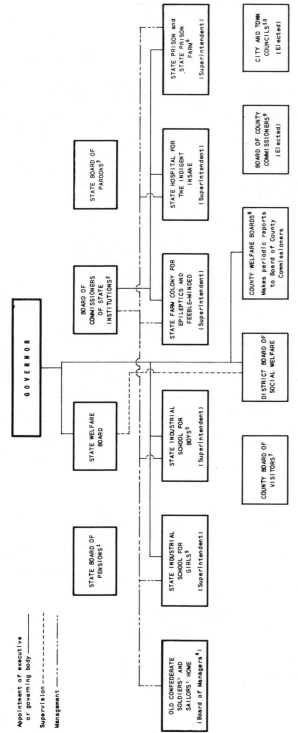

FLORIDA PUBLIC WELFARE AGENCIES
Statutory and Constitutional Organization

Appointment of executive
or governing body ————————
Supervision ——————————————
Management ———— —— ——

GOVERNOR

STATE BOARD OF PENSIONS[1]

STATE WELFARE BOARD

BOARD OF COMMISSIONERS OF STATE INSTITUTIONS[2]

STATE BOARD OF PARDONS[3]

OLD CONFEDERATE SOLDIERS' AND SAILORS' HOME[4]
(Board of Managers[4])

STATE INDUSTRIAL SCHOOL FOR GIRLS[5]
(Superintendent)

STATE INDUSTRIAL SCHOOL FOR BOYS[5]
(Superintendent)

STATE FARM COLONY FOR EPILEPTICS AND FEEBLE-MINDED[2]
(Superintendent)

STATE HOSPITAL FOR THE INDIGENT INSANE
(Superintendent)

STATE PRISON and STATE PRISON FARM[6]
(Superintendent)

COUNTY BOARD OF VISITORS[7]

DISTRICT BOARD OF SOCIAL WELFARE

COUNTY WELFARE BOARDS[8]
Makes periodic reports to Board of County Commissioners

BOARD OF COUNTY COMMISSIONERS[9]
(Elected)

CITY AND TOWN COUNCILS[10]
(Elected)

[1] Composed of the Governor, the comptroller, and the treasurer of the State.

[2] Composed of the Governor and the following administrative officers of the executive department: the secretary of state, the attorney general, the comptroller, the treasurer, the superintendent of public instruction, and the commissioner of agriculture.

[3] Composed of the Governor, the secretary of state, the comptroller, the attorney general, and the commissioner of agriculture.

[4] Composed of the president of the United Daughters of the Confederacy, the State commander of United Confederate Veterans, the State commander of Sons of Confederate Veterans, the comptroller of the State, and a 5th person appointed by the Governor upon nomination of the other 4.

[5] The Board of Commissioners of State Institutions may delegate to the State Welfare Board the supervision and control of the school, provided that the State Welfare Board acts under control of the Board of Commissioners of State Institutions.

[6] The commissioner of agriculture acts as an executive for the management of the State Prison and State Prison Farm. The Board of Commissioners of State Institutions, of which the commissioner of agriculture is a member, elects the superintendent.

[7] Appointed by the judge of the juvenile court.

[8] Appointed in counties with a population of over 155,000.

[9] The State Board of Pensions supervises the administration of veterans' pensions by the board of county commissioners. The board of county commissioners in a county with a population of 9,700 to 10,500 may appoint a county board of charity to administer general relief.

[10] May administer general relief.

SUMMARY OF STATUTORY PROVISIONS FOR PUBLIC WELFARE
GEORGIA

Relief and Public Assistance.—General relief, old age assistance, aid to dependent children in their own homes, and blind assistance are administered by the county or district departments of public welfare under the supervision of the State Department of Public Welfare.[1]

Cases involving dependent and neglected children come within the jurisdiction of the juvenile courts which may appoint advisory boards to cooperate with the courts in matters affecting dependent, neglected, and delinquent children. The advisory boards must visit all institutions, societies, or associations receiving children. The State Department of Public Welfare licenses and supervises all private and local child-caring agencies and institutions. It must cooperate with the Federal Government, county officials, juvenile courts, and child-caring agencies and institutions in developing services for the protection and care of homeless, dependent, and neglected children and children in danger of becoming delinquent. The county or district departments of public welfare must administer the care and treatment of dependent, neglected, delinquent, and handicapped children and pass upon all applications for admission to or discharge from county institutions. The Georgia Industrial Home (a private institution) receives dependent and neglected children committed to it by juvenile courts.

Direct relief to veterans is administered by county directors of public welfare under the supervision of the State Department of Public Welfare. Veterans' pensions are administered by the State Department of Public Welfare assisted by county directors of public welfare. Care of veterans in the Confederate Soldiers' Home is administered by the State Department of Public Welfare. County directors of public welfare assist the State department in the determination of eligibility of applicants for admission to the home.[2]

Juvenile Delinquents.—Juvenile courts have jurisdiction in cases involving delinquent children. The court may place a child in the care of a probation officer, allow it to remain in its own home, place it in a family home, or commit it to the State Training School for Boys, the State Training School for Girls, or to any other training school for the correction, reformation, or protection of children. It may also allow proceedings to be undertaken against the child under laws governing the commission of crimes.[3]

Services to the Blind.—The State Department of Public Welfare must initiate or cooperate with other agencies in developing measures for the prevention of blindness, the restoration of eyesight, and the vocational adjustment of blind persons. The State department must foster employment in regular industries, independent business, sheltered workshops, or home industry of the adult blind and their instruction in their homes. The State Factory for the Blind furnishes employment and a home for such blind workers who desire it.

Insane and Mental Defectives.—The State Department of Public Welfare must administer or supervise all mental hygiene work and all noninstitutional care for the mentally ill or feeble-minded. The Milledgeville State Hospital provides care and treatment for the insane, epileptics, idiots, and demented inebriates committed by the courts of ordinary. The State Training School for Mental Defectives provides care and treatment for defective persons who are unable to care for themselves. Persons may be committed by the court of ordinary or admitted by a voluntary application made to the superintendent of the school.

Adult Delinquents.—The State Prison Commission provides for the confinement and training of adult delinquents in prison farms and camps. This commission as the the State Board of Pardons investigates all applications for executive clemency

---

[1]The State Department of Public Welfare inspects county, municipal, and private charitable institutions and agencies. It also must cooperate with the Federal Government and act as its agent in welfare matters of mutual concern.

[2]Need is not specified as a condition of eligibility for veterans' pensions or care in the Confederate Soldiers' Home.

[3]See discussion of care of dependent and neglected children, above, for powers of advisory boards of juvenile courts, the State department, and county or district departments of public welfare in relation to children. The State Children's Code Commission studies existing laws of Georgia and other States affecting child welfare and drafts child welfare laws to be presented to the Legislature.

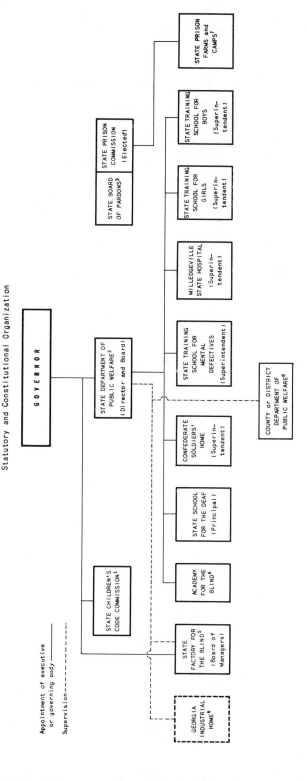

GEORGIA PUBLIC WELFARE AGENCIES

Statutory and Constitutional Organization

Appointment of executive
or governing body ——————————
Supervision ———————————————

GOVERNOR

STATE CHILDREN'S CODE COMMISSION[1]

STATE DEPARTMENT OF PUBLIC WELFARE[2]
(Director and Board)

STATE BOARD OF PARDONS[3]

STATE PRISON COMMISSION
(Elected[7])

GEORGIA INDUSTRIAL HOME[4]

STATE FACTORY FOR THE BLIND[5]
(Board of Managers)

ACADEMY FOR THE BLIND[6]

STATE SCHOOL FOR THE DEAF
(Principal)

CONFEDERATE SOLDIERS' HOME
(Superintendent)

STATE TRAINING SCHOOL FOR MENTAL DEFECTIVES
(Superintendent)

MILLEDGEVILLE STATE HOSPITAL
(Superintendent)

STATE TRAINING SCHOOL FOR GIRLS
(Superintendent)

STATE TRAINING SCHOOL FOR BOYS
(Superintendent)

STATE PRISON FARMS and CAMPS[7]

COUNTY or DISTRICT DEPARTMENT OF PUBLIC WELFARE[8]

[1] Composed of a superior court judge, a member of the House of Representatives, a State senator, and a representative from each of the following: Federation of Women's Clubs, State Council of Social Agencies, State Board of Health, State Department of Public welfare, State Federation of Labor, State Department of Education, and State League of Women Voters.

[2] The department may designate private institutions as State institutions, contract with them for activities deemed necessary, and supervise and cooperate with such institutions.

[3] Members of the State Prison Commission constitute the State Board of Pardons.

[4] A State-aided institution. The president of the Senate and the speaker of the House of Representatives appoint a visiting committee, consisting of 6 members from the House and 3 from the Senate, to inspect this and similar institutions.

[5] The factory is managed by a board of 7 members appointed by the Governor. The State treasurer, the State superintendent of schools, the director of public welfare, the state supervisor of purchases, and the State supervisor of vocational rehabilitation are ex officio members.

[6] The State Department of Public Welfare appoints necessary officers.

[7] The State Prison Commission appoints necessary wardens and guards of farms and camps, the number of which is not specified by statute. The State Department of Public welfare cooperates in supervision of all correctional activities, including operation of all penal and correctional institutions of the state.

[8] Appointed by the board of county commissioners or the constituted fiscal or financial agent of each county with the approval of the State Department of Public welfare.

and makes recommendations to the Governor. The board also has full power to establish rules and regulations for paroling prisoners. The State Department of Public Welfare must cooperate in the supervision of all correctional activities including the operation of all penal and correctional institutions of the State, the administration of paroles, the supervision of probation services, the segregation of first offenders, and the inspection of local jails.

Crippled Children.—The State Department of Public Welfare is designated as the agency to supervise the administration of a program of services for children who are crippled or who are suffering from conditions which lead to crippling. The purpose of such a program is to develop, extend, and improve services for locating such children and providing them with facilities for diagnosis, medical and surgical care, corrective services, hospitalization, and aftercare. The State department may delegate this authority to an appropriate State, county, or municipal department or agency and may cooperate with institutions and agencies caring for crippled children.

Education of the Deaf, Dumb, and Blind.—The Academy for the Blind and the State School for the Deaf provide education for the blind and deaf youths, respectively.

SUMMARY OF STATUTORY PROVISIONS FOR PUBLIC WELFARE
IDAHO

Relief and Public Assistance.—General relief is administered by the boards of county commissioners or county welfare commissions, under the supervision of the State Department of Public Assistance. Old age assistance, aid to dependent children in their own homes, and blind assistance are administered by county welfare commissions under the supervision of the State Department of Public Assistance.[1]

Cases involving dependent and neglected children come within the jurisdiction of the probate courts. County welfare commissions, under the supervision of the State Department of Public Assistance, are empowered to provide services for the protection and care of dependent, neglected, and delinquent children and to cooperate with other State departments and agencies, with the probate courts, and with any public or private agencies or organizations providing such services.[2] The Children's Home Finding and Aid Society of North Idaho, and the Children's Home Finding and Aid Society of Idaho are child-caring agencies receiving State aid. State aid is also given to the Salvation Army for its child welfare activities.

Direct relief to veterans is administered by the State Veterans' Welfare Commission. Care of veterans in the State Soldiers' Home is administered by the commandant of the home.[3]

Juvenile Delinquents.—Probate courts have jurisdiction in cases involving delinquent children. The court may allow a child to remain in its own home, place it in a family home, or commit it to the State Industrial Training School or other State child-caring institution or to a county child-caring institution. The Board of State Prison Commissioners may place any child under the age of 15 years, sentenced to the State Prison, in a school of correction, either within or outside of the State.[4]

Services to the Blind.—The State Department of Public Welfare has power either by itself or in cooperation with other agencies to develop measures for the prevention of blindness, the restoration of eyesight, and the vocational adjustment of blind persons.

Insane and Mental Defectives.—The State Hospital North and the State Hospital South provide care and treatment for insane persons, and the State School and Colony provides care and treatment for feeble-minded and epileptic persons committed by magistrates of the counties. Provisions for the sterilization of inmates are administered by the State Board of Eugenics. County welfare commissions have power to furnish services for protection and care of mentally defective children and to cooperate with the probate courts, the State Department of Public Assistance, and other State departments and agencies, and any public or private agencies or organizations providing such services.

Adult Delinquents.—The State Prison provides for confinement and training of adult delinquents. The Board of State Prison Commissioners, in conjunction with the State Board of Education, must prepare courses of study for prisoners. Provisions for sterilization of prisoners are administered by the State Board of Eugenics. The State Board of Pardons has power to remit fines and forfeitures and to grant commutations and pardons in all cases except treason or impeachment. It may parole prisoners upon recommendation of the warden of the prison. The Governor may grant respites or reprieves in all cases except treason or impeachment, but such respites or reprieves may not extend beyond the next session of the State Board of Pardons, when they must be passed upon by the board. The Governor may, in cases of treason, suspend the execution of sentence until it is acted upon by the legislature.

---

[1]The State Department of Public Assistance has power to cooperate with the Federal Government in matters of public welfare, authorized by the Federal Social Security Act or other acts of Congress, and in the administration of Federal funds granted to aid in the functions of the department.

[2]County welfare commissions have the same power in relation to physically defective children.

[3]*Need* is not specified as a condition of eligibility for care in the State Soldiers' Home.

[4]See discussion of care of dependent and neglected children, above, for powers of the State Department of Public Welfare and county welfare commissions in relation to children.

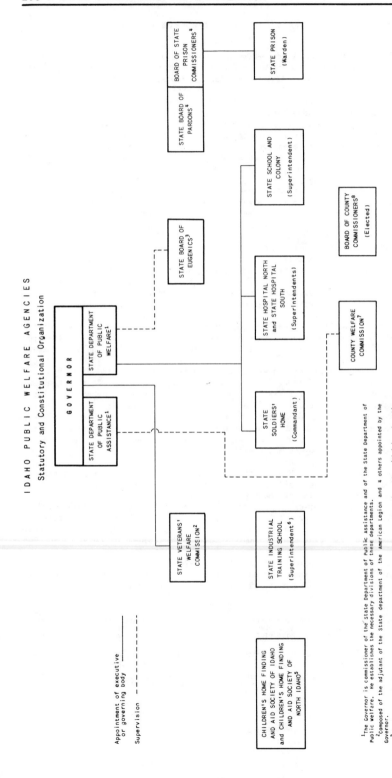

IDAHO PUBLIC WELFARE AGENCIES

Statutory and Constitutional Organization

Appointment of executive
or governing body ─────────

Supervision ─ ─ ─ ─ ─ ─ ─

[1] The Governor is commissioner of the State Department of Public Assistance and of the State Department of Public Welfare. He establishes the necessary divisions of these departments.

[2] Composed of the adjutant of the State department of the American Legion and 4 others appointed by the Governor.

[3] Composed of the State public health advisor of the State Department of Public welfare (division of public health), the warden of the State prison, the superintendent of the State Hospital North, the State Hospital South, the State School and Colony, and the State Industrial Training School.

[4] Composed of the Governor, the secretary of state, and the attorney general.

[5] These institutions receive State aid.

[6] Appointed by the State Board of Education.

[7] The County welfare commission is appointed as follows: 1 member is appointed by the board of county commissioners, and 3 others are appointed by the State department and the board of county commissioners, jointly.

[8] Poor relief is administered by the board of county commissioners under the supervision of the State Department of Public Assistance.

SUMMARY OF STATUTORY PROVISIONS FOR PUBLIC WELFARE
ILLINOIS

Relief and Public Assistance.—General relief is administered by the overseer of the poor or similar officer of the respective city, town, village, or precinct, subject to rules and regulations prescribed by the city council, board of trustees, board of town auditors, board of county commissioners, or supervisors. However, in counties with a population over 500,000 (Cook County) general relief is administered by the county bureau of public welfare under the supervision of the State Department of Public Welfare. The State Emergency Relief Commission must determine, on the basis of county requisitions, the allotments of State funds made for general relief purposes. The State Department of Public Welfare must inspect and investigate outdoor poor relief and almshouses.

Old age assistance is administered by the county departments of public welfare and in counties with a population over 500,000 by the county bureau of public welfare under the supervision of the State Department of Public Welfare. Aid to dependent children in their own homes is administered by the juvenile courts according to standards of administration set by the State Department of Public Welfare.[1] Blind assistance is administered by the boards of county commissioners or supervisors.[1]

The juvenile, circuit, or county courts have jurisdiction in cases involving dependent and neglected children.[1] The county boards of visitation must visit annually all institutions to which children are committed by the juvenile courts, and report to the courts and to the State Department of Public Welfare the condition of the children cared for in such institutions. The State Soldiers' and Sailors' Children's School receives dependent and neglected children whose fathers or mothers served in the Army, Navy, or Marine Corps of the United States. Children may also be confined in poor farms. The State Department of Public Welfare is empowered to license home-finding associations and orphanages. The department must investigate and visit almshouses and family homes and examine all associations which propose caring for dependent, neglected, or delinquent children.

Direct relief for veterans is administered by the commander, quartermaster, or relief committee of the local veterans' organization, where existent, in conjunction with the overseer of the poor or the county board of commissioners or supervisors. If no such organization exists in a town, a local relief committee administers such aid in conjunction with the overseer of the poor. Care in the State Soldiers' and Sailors' Home, the State Soldiers' Widows' Home, and the State Home for the Rehabilitation of World War Veterans is administered by the State Department of Public Welfare through the superintendent or managing officer of the respective institutions. Admission to the State Home for the Rehabilitation of World War Veterans is upon voluntary application to the managing officer or by court commitment.

Juvenile Delinquents.—The juvenile, circuit, or county courts have jurisdiction of cases involving delinquent children. The court may appoint some suitable person or probation officer as guardian of the child and permit the child to remain in its own home, order it placed in some suitable family home, or commit it to some training school, industrial school, or to any institution or association incorporated under the laws of the State to care for dependent and delinquent children. The St. Charles School for Boys and the State Training School for Girls at Geneva receive delinquent children committed by the courts.[2]

Services to the Blind.—The Department of Public Welfare must direct the rehabilitation of every physically handicapped person residing in the State. The department must visit the adult blind in their homes to instruct them in industrial

---

[1] In counties of 500,000 or more population (Cook County) all powers, functions, and duties included in the term *Social Service Functions*, are consolidated in the county bureau of public welfare. Included are those functions relating to: dependent children where, in cases of pure dependency, the action of a court of record is not invoked; deaf and blind children; blind adults.

[2] See discussion of care of dependent and neglected children, above, for applicable powers and duties of the State Department of Public Welfare and county boards of visitation.

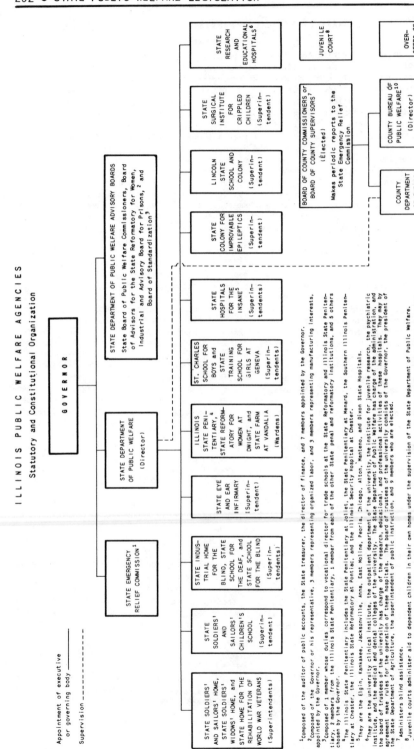

ILLINOIS PUBLIC WELFARE AGENCIES

Statutory and Constitutional Organization

pursuits and develop occupations. The department must employ the necessary teachers and assistants.[3]

Insane and Mental Defectives.—The Elgin, Kankakee, Jacksonville, Anna, East Moline, Peoria, Chicago, Alton, Manteno, and Dixon State Hospitals care for insane persons. The Lincoln State School and Colony cares for feeble-minded persons. The State Colony for Improvable Epileptics cares for persons suffering from epilepsy or other mental disease. Commitments to these institutions are made by the county courts and in some instances by voluntary agreement.

Adult Delinquents.—The Illinois State Penitentiary, State Reformatory for Women at Dwight, and the State Farm at Vandalia provide confinement and training for adult delinquents. Insane delinquents are cared for in the psychiatric division of the Illinois State Penitentiary. The board of parole, in the State Department of Public Welfare, exercises jurisdiction over the granting of paroles and is charged with supervision and aftercare of paroled persons.

Crippled Children.—The State Surgical Institute for Crippled Children receives children upon commitment by the county courts. The State commission for physically handicapped children promotes special classes, special instruction, vocational guidance, training, placement, and medical diagnosis and treatment of all physically handicapped children, including those crippled or deformed.[3]

Deaf, Dumb, and Blind.—The State School for the Blind and the State School for the Deaf provide education for the deaf, dumb, and blind and promote the intellectual, moral, and physical culture of these persons to fit them for earning their own livelihood and for future usefulness in society.[3] The State Industrial Home for the Blind is maintained for the purpose of promoting the welfare of the blind by teaching them trades and affording them a home and such employment as best tends to make them self-supporting and consequently independent. The State Eye and Ear Infirmary provides board and medical and surgical treatment for indigent persons afflicted with diseases of the eye and ear.

---

[3]The State commission for physically handicapped children coordinates the activities of the State Departments of Public Welfare, Public Instruction, and Public Health as such relate to all handicapped children including those crippled or deformed, blind, or deaf. The commission must promote vocational guidance, training, placement, etc.; must promote special classes and instruction; must stimulate and coordinate all private and public efforts relative to the care, treatment, education, and social service of the foregoing classes.

SUMMARY OF STATUTORY PROVISIONS FOR PUBLIC WELFARE
INDIANA

Relief and Public Assistance.—General relief is administered by township over-seers of the poor. The Governor's Commission on Unemployment Relief coordinates and assists the several agencies of the State engaged in the relief of the unem-ployed and investigates the administration of relief by township overseers. Old age assistance is administered by county or district departments of public welfare under the supervision of the division of public assistance of the State Department of Public Welfare.[1]

Aid to dependent children in their own homes and foster care of destitute chil-dren who do not need to be declared public wards are administered by county or district departments of public welfare. The division of public assistance of the State department supervises aid to dependent children, and the children's division of that department supervises the care of destitute children.

Blind assistance is administered by the State department, through its division of public assistance, assisted by county or district departments of public welfare.

Cases involving dependent and neglected children come within the jurisdiction of juvenile courts. The State Department of Public Welfare, children's division, administers or supervises all public child welfare services. The division licenses and must inspect private child-caring agencies and supervises and inspects local public child-caring agencies, institutions, and boarding homes. It must also supervise the care of dependent and neglected children placed in family homes or institutions. The county or district departments of public welfare under the supervision of the State Department of Public Welfare, children's division, ad-minister care and treatment of dependent and neglected children and may, with the permission of the juvenile court, commit a child to an orphan asylum or, under order of the court, may indenture a child as an apprentice. Dependent and neglected children may be made wards of the board of county commissioners which represents children placed in institutions, homes, or agencies. Dependent and neglected boys may be committed to the State Boys' School.

Orphans and children of veterans and nurses who served in wars may be admitted to the State Soldiers' and Sailors' Children's Home, upon application to the board of trustees of the home by a parent or guardian. Care of veterans in the State Soldiers' Home is administered by the board of trustees of the home.

Juvenile Delinquents.—Juvenile courts have jurisdiction in cases involving de-linquent children. The court may allow a child to remain at home, place it in a private home, make it a ward of the county or a probation officer, or commit it to the State Boys' School or State Girls' School, or to any other State penal or reformatory institution authorized to receive children. The court may, when health or conditions require, cause the child to be placed in a public hospital or insti-tution for treatment or special care. Administration of probation by the juvenile court is supervised by the State Probation Commission.[2]

Services to the Blind.—The State Board of Industrial Aid for the Blind must maintain a register of the blind, describing conditions, causes of blindness, and capacity for education and industrial training of each blind person in the State. The board must act as a bureau of information and industrial aid to assist the blind to find employment and to market their products. It may establish and main-tain both schools for industrial training of adult blind and workshops for their employment; it may also pay wages and distribute products of the blind. The board may promote visits among the blind in their homes and cooperate with the State library in circulation of books to the blind. The board must investigate causes of blindness and cooperate with the State board of health in adopting and enforcing preventive measures.

---

[1] The State department, division of medical care, must supervise the operation of all agencies caring for dependent, mentally or physically handicapped, or aged adults, and approve the incor-poration of charitable agencies. The State Department of Public Welfare is designated as the State agency to cooperate with the Federal Government in the administration of the Federal Social Security Act, and to act as agent of the Federal Government in the administration of Federal funds for public welfare and in all welfare matters of mutual concern.

[2] See discussion of care of dependent and neglected children, above, for powers of the State department and county or district departments of public welfare, and boards of county commissioners in relation to children.

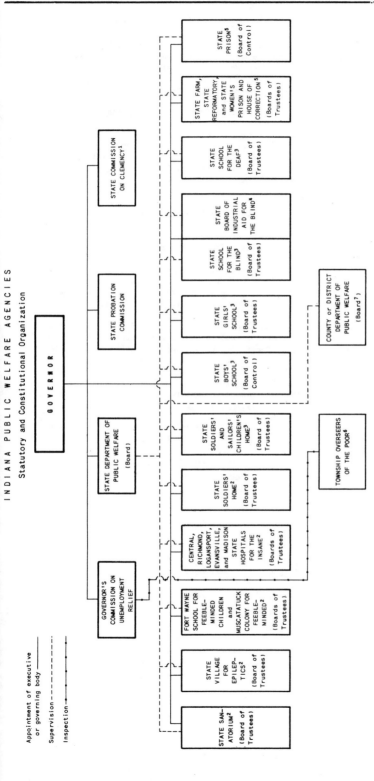

INDIANA PUBLIC WELFARE AGENCIES

Statutory and Constitutional Organization

Appointment of executive or governing body ——————

Supervision ——————————

Inspection ——•——•——•——

GOVERNOR

GOVERNOR'S COMMISSION ON UNEMPLOYMENT RELIEF

STATE DEPARTMENT OF PUBLIC WELFARE (Board)

STATE PROBATION COMMISSION

STATE COMMISSION ON CLEMENCY[1]

STATE SANATORIUM[2] (Board of Trustees)

STATE VILLAGE FOR EPILEPTICS[2] (Board of Trustees)

FORT WAYNE SCHOOL FOR FEEBLE-MINDED CHILDREN and MUSCATATUCK COLONY FOR FEEBLE-MINDED[2] (Boards of Trustees)

CENTRAL, RICHMOND, LOGANSPORT, EVANSVILLE, and MADISON STATE HOSPITALS FOR THE INSANE[2] (Boards of Trustees)

STATE SOLDIERS' HOME[2] (Board of Trustees)

STATE SOLDIERS' AND SAILORS' CHILDREN'S HOME[3] (Board of Trustees)

STATE BOYS' SCHOOL[3] (Board of Control)

STATE GIRLS' SCHOOL[3] (Board of Trustees)

STATE SCHOOL FOR THE BLIND[3] (Board of Trustees)

STATE BOARD OF INDUSTRIAL AID FOR THE BLIND[4]

STATE SCHOOL FOR THE DEAF[3] (Board of Trustees)

STATE FARM, STATE REFORMATORY, and STATE WOMEN'S PRISON AND HOUSE OF CORRECTION[5] (Boards of Trustees)

STATE PRISON[5] (Board of Control)

COUNTY or DISTRICT DEPARTMENT OF PUBLIC WELFARE[7] (Board)

TOWNSHIP OVERSEERS OF THE POOR[6]

[1] Composed of the Governor's secretary of penal affairs, 1 member of the board of control of the State Prison, and 1 member of the board of trustees of the State Reformatory, appointed by the Governor.

[2] The division of medical care of the State Department of Public Welfare has the immediate supervision of this institution.

[3] The children's division of the State Department of Public Welfare has the immediate supervision of this institution.

[4] Composed of the board of trustees of the State School for the Blind, under the immediate supervision of the division of public assistance of the State Department of Public Welfare.

[5] The division of corrections of the State Department of Public Welfare has the immediate supervision of this institution.

[6] Township trustees are ex officio overseers of the poor.

[7] Appointed by the judge of the circuit court.

Insane and Mental Defectives.—Care and treatment of insane persons committed by circuit or superior courts are provided in the Central, Richmond, Logansport, Evansville, and Madison State Hospitals for the Insane. The Fort Wayne School for Feeble-minded Children with both a custodial and an educational department provides care and treatment of children and women committed by circuit courts. The Muscatatuck Colony for Feeble-minded and the State Village for Epileptics provide care and treatment for feeble-minded and epileptic persons, respectively, committed by circuit courts.

Adult Delinquents.—The division of corrections of the State Department of Public Welfare must supervise all correctional activities, including paroles, inspection of local jails, and the recommendation of clemency to the State Commission on Clemency. The State Commission on Clemency must examine petitions to the Governor for pardon or parole, other than temporary parole. The State Probation Commission supervises administration of juvenile and adult probation in all courts of the State. The State Prison, the State Farm, the State Reformatory, and the State Women's Prison and House of Correction provide for confinement and training of adult delinquents.

Crippled Children.—The State Department of Public Welfare must administer services to crippled children, including services for locating crippled children and providing medical, surgical, corrective, and other care, and facilities for diagnosis, hospitalization, and aftercare for children who are crippled or who are suffering from conditions which lead to crippling. Such children may be placed in a hospital approved by the State department or in the James Whitcomb Riley Hospital for Children.[3] Children may be admitted to this hospital upon commitment by any circuit, criminal, or juvenile court, or by application of the State Department of Public Welfare upon recommendation of the county or district board of public welfare.

Vocational Rehabilitation.—The State Department of Public Welfare must cooperate with county departments of public welfare and the children's bureau of the United States Department of Labor together with other State agencies charged with the administration of State laws for vocational rehabilitation of physically handicapped children.

Education of the Deaf, Dumb, and Blind.—The State School for the Blind and the State School for the Deaf provide academic and industrial instruction of blind, and deaf and dumb children, respectively. Applications for admission are made to the boards of trustees.

Tuberculars.—The State Sanatorium provides care and treatment for tuberculars admitted upon application to the board of trustees of the sanatorium.

---

[3] The James Whitcomb Riley Hospital is controlled by the board of trustees of the State university.

SUMMARY OF STATUTORY PROVISIONS FOR PUBLIC WELFARE
IOWA

Relief and Public Assistance.—General relief is administered by the county boards of supervisors or township trustees as overseers of the poor. The State Emergency Relief Administration allocates State funds to counties. Old age assistance and blind assistance are administered by the State Department of Social Welfare assisted by the county boards of social welfare. The juvenile courts administer aid to dependent children in their own homes.

Cases involving dependent and neglected children come within the jurisdiction of juvenile courts. The State Department of Social Welfare through the subdivision of child welfare supervises all public child welfare services and all private child-caring agencies and institutions. County boards of supervisors must appoint suitable persons to care for destitute orphans; they supervise and govern county homes admitting children. The State Juvenile Home and the State Soldiers' Orphans' Home care for dependent and neglected children.

Direct relief to veterans is administered by county soldiers' relief commissions. Veterans and their wives or widows are admitted to the State Soldiers' Home by the State Board of Control of State Institutions upon the certification of residence by the county board of supervisors.

Juvenile Delinquents.—The juvenile court has jurisdiction over delinquent children. The court may continue the proceedings from time to time and commit the child to the care and custody of a probation official or other suitable person. It may commit the child to a family home, allow it to remain in its own home, or commit it to any institution in the State, incorporated and maintained for the purpose of caring for such children; or it may cause the child to be placed in a public or State hospital for treatment or special care, or in a private hospital which will receive it. The court may also commit delinquent children to the State Juvenile Home, the State Training School for Boys, or the State Training School for Girls.[1]

Services to the Blind.—The State Commission for the Blind has the following duties: to act as a bureau of information and industrial aid for the blind; to assist the blind in finding employment; to maintain a complete register of the blind; to teach them trades; and to give such assistance as may be necessary or advisable to help the adult blind market their products. The commission may establish workshops for the employment of the blind.

Insane and Mental Defectives.—The Cherokee, Clarinda, Independence, and Mount Pleasant State Hospitals for the Insane provide care and treatment for insane persons, and the State Hospital and Colony for Epileptics and Feeble-minded provides care and treatment for epileptic and feeble-minded persons. The county commissions of insanity have jurisdiction over all applications for commitment to these institutions. The State Institution for Feeble-minded Children provides training, instruction, care, and support for feeble-minded children voluntarily admitted upon application of the parents, guardian, or county attorney or upon commitment by the courts. The State Psychopathic Hospital cares for persons suffering from some abnormal mental condition that can probably be remedied by observation, by medical or surgical treatment, and by hospital care.[2] Recommendations for sterilization may be made by the State Board of Eugenics. An appeal from such recommendation may be made to the district court.

Adult Delinquents.—The State Penitentiary, Men's Reformatory, and the Women's Reformatory provide confinement and training for adult delinquents. The State Board of Parole, on recommendation of the trial judge and prosecuting attorney, may parole, after sentence and before commitment, prisoners who have not been previously convicted of a felony or sentenced for a term of life imprisonment. The State Board of Parole may parole prisoners after commitment, provided they are not serving a life term or under sentence of death and are not infected with a communicable venereal disease.

Care of Tuberculars.—The State Sanatorium provides care and treatment for residents of the State afflicted with pulmonary tuberculosis.

---

[1]See discussion of care of dependent and neglected children, above, for powers of the State Department of Social Welfare in relation to children.

[2]The State Psychopathic Hospital is controlled and managed by the State Board of Education.

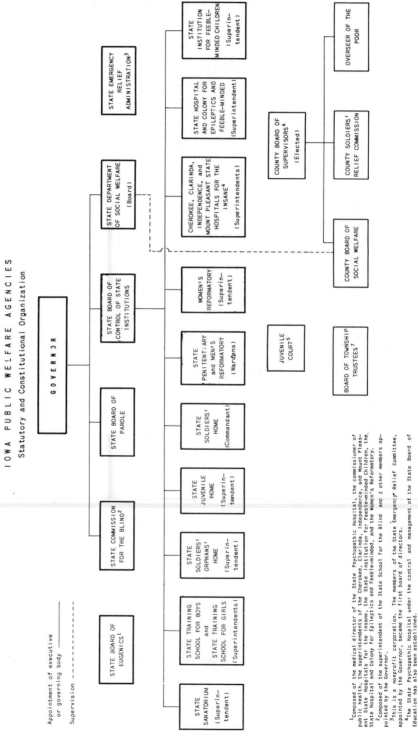

IOWA PUBLIC WELFARE AGENCIES
Statutory and Constitutional Organization

1Composed of the medical director of the State Psychopathic Hospital, the commissioner of public health, the superintendents of the Cherokee, Clarinda, Independence, and Mount Pleasant State Hospitals for the Insane, the State Institution for Feeble-Minded Children, the State Hospital and Colony for Epileptics and Feeble-Minded, and the Women's Reformatory.

2Composed of the superintendent of the State School for the Blind and 2 other members appointed by the Governor.

3This is a nonprofit corporation. The members of the State Emergency Relief Committee, appointed by the Governor, became the first board of directors.

4The State Psychopathic Hospital under the control and management of the State Board of Education has also been established.

5Administers aid to dependent children in their own homes.

6May administer general relief.

7Township trustees are subject to general rules of the county board of supervisors in providing general relief.

SUMMARY OF STATUTORY PROVISIONS FOR PUBLIC WELFARE
KANSAS

Relief and Public Assistance.—General relief, old age assistance, aid to dependent children in their own homes, and blind assistance are administered by the county boards of social welfare under the supervision of the State Board of Social Welfare.[1]

Cases involving dependent and neglected children come within the jurisdiction of juvenile courts. The State Board of Social Welfare must develop a child welfare service program and administer or supervise child welfare activities, including those undertaken by private agencies and all activities of the county boards of social welfare. The board is also empowered to license child-caring agencies. The county boards of social welfare may find suitable homes for dependent children referred to them by the courts and supervise children so placed. The county boards supervise county parental homes caring for dependent, neglected, or delinquent children. The State Board of Administration controls the State Orphans' Home which receives dependent and neglected children and has power of visitation, inspection, and supervision over all child-caring institutions and associations.

Veteran relief is administered by the county boards of social welfare under supervision of the State Board of Social Welfare. Care in the State Soldiers' Home and Mother Bickerdyke Annex is administered by the board of managers of the home.

Juvenile Delinquents.—The juvenile courts have jurisdiction of cases involving delinquent children. The court may commit such children to the State Industrial School for Boys, the State Industrial School for Girls, or to any suitable institution, or allow them to remain at home subject to the control of a probation officer, or may authorize such children to be boarded out in a family home. The county boards of social welfare may find suitable homes for delinquent children referred to them by the courts and supervise children so placed.[2]

Services to the Blind.—The State Board of Social Welfare must initiate or cooperate with other agencies in developing programs for prevention of blindness, restoration of eyesight, and vocational rehabilitation of blind persons. It may also create a department for the blind within the State board. The State Institution for the Education of the Blind conducts a summer school from June 1 to September 1 for the educational instruction and vocational training of adult blind persons.

Insane and Mental Defectives.—The county probate courts have jurisdiction in cases involving insane and other defective persons. The probate judge must apply for the admission of an insane person to a State hospital for the insane and all applications for admission to any of the institutions under the State Board of Administration must be made to the board. The Topeka, Osawatomie, and Larned State Hospitals care for insane persons. The State Training School cares for feeble-minded, idiotic, and imbecile youths. The State Hospital for Epileptics provides care and treatment for epileptics.[3]

Adult Delinquents.—The State Penitentiary, State Industrial Reformatory, and State Industrial Farm for Women provide for confinement and training of adult delinquents. The State Prison Board fixes the conditions for the parole or release of prisoners.

Crippled Children.—The State Orphans' Home cares for crippled children.[4]

Deaf, Dumb, and Blind.—The State Institution for the Education of the Deaf and the State Institution for the Education of the Blind provide education for deaf and blind youths, respectively.

Tuberculars.—The State Sanatorium for Tuberculosis provides care and treatment for citizens of the State suffering from tuberculosis.

[1] The State Board of Social Welfare must cooperate with the Federal Government in any program providing Federal financial assistance in the field of social welfare.

[2] See discussion of care of dependent and neglected children, above, for powers of the State Board of Social Welfare in relation to children.

[3] Courts exercising criminal jurisdiction may commit insane and epileptic persons to the State Asylum for the Dangerous Insane located at the State Penitentiary.

[4] The State university hospital provides care and treatment for crippled children. The State Crippled Children's Commission, appointed by the Governor, must cooperate with the State Departments of Agriculture, Education, and Health and with all other persons and agencies interested in the discovery, care, and education of crippled children. The commission has power to approve or disapprove hospitals and homes providing services to crippled children.

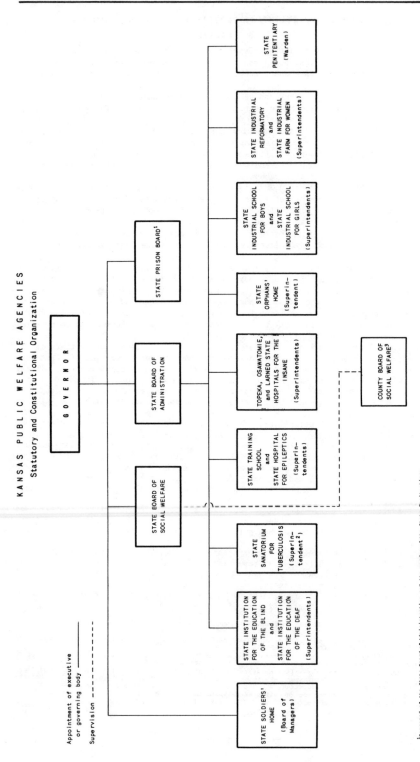

KANSAS PUBLIC WELFARE AGENCIES
Statutory and Constitutional Organization

Appointment of executive or governing body ————
Supervision — — — — — — —

GOVERNOR

STATE BOARD OF SOCIAL WELFARE

STATE BOARD OF ADMINISTRATION

STATE PRISON BOARD[1]

STATE SOLDIERS' HOME (Board of Managers)

STATE INSTITUTION FOR THE EDUCATION OF THE BLIND and STATE INSTITUTION FOR THE EDUCATION OF THE DEAF (Superintendents)

STATE SANATORIUM FOR TUBERCULOSIS (Superintendent[2])

STATE TRAINING SCHOOL and STATE HOSPITAL FOR EPILEPTICS (Superintendents)

TOPEKA, OSAWATOMIE, and LARNED STATE HOSPITALS FOR THE INSANE (Superintendents)

STATE ORPHANS' HOME (Superintendent)

STATE INDUSTRIAL SCHOOL FOR BOYS and STATE INDUSTRIAL SCHOOL FOR GIRLS (Superintendents)

STATE INDUSTRIAL REFORMATORY and STATE INDUSTRIAL FARM FOR WOMEN (Superintendents)

STATE PENITENTIARY (Warden)

COUNTY BOARD OF SOCIAL WELFARE[3]

[1]Composed of the State Board of Administration and the warden of the State Penitentiary.
[2]The superintendent is appointed by the State Board of Administration with the advice and recommendation of an advisory commission selected by the Governor.
[3]The board of county commissioners constitutes the county board of social welfare.

SUMMARY OF STATUTORY PROVISIONS FOR PUBLIC WELFARE
KENTUCKY

Relief and Public Assistance.—General relief and blind assistance are administered by the county courts under the supervision of the State Department of Welfare.[1] Old age assistance is administered by the State Department of Welfare. Aid to dependent children in their own homes is administered by county children's bureaus or by county welfare departments, if established, under the supervision of the division of child welfare in the State Department of Welfare.

Cases involving dependent and neglected children come within the jurisdiction of the juvenile courts. The State Department of Welfare is empowered to administer and supervise all child-caring activities including the inspection of all public and private child-caring agencies; the department is empowered to license child-caring agencies and must supervise the work and methods of all institutions, associations, or societies receiving State aid. The department may provide care for such children as may be committed to it. The county children's bureaus must perform such child welfare activities as may be requested by the division of child welfare in the State Department of Welfare or by the county fiscal court or county judge. They must obtain for dependent, neglected, delinquent, and defective children the benefits of the laws relating to child welfare. The Louisville and Jefferson County Children's Home receives dependent and neglected children committed to it by juvenile courts. Private State-aided agencies receiving and placing children include the Children's Home Society for White Children and the Children's Home Society for Colored Children.

Confederate pensions are administered by the division of Confederate pensions in the State Military Department, assisted by the county judges. The State Department of Welfare is empowered to contract for the care of Confederate veterans.

Juvenile Delinquents.—Juvenile courts have jurisdiction in cases involving delinquent children. The court may allow proceedings against the child under the criminal law and transfer the case to the court exercising such jurisdiction, or it may allow the child to remain in its own home, subject to visitation of a probation officer, or commit it to any State, county, or city institution caring for delinquent children. The House of Reform for Boys, the House of Reform for Girls, and the Louisville and Jefferson County Children's Home provide care and training for delinquent children.[2]

Services to the Blind.—The State School for the Blind must direct vocational education, training, and employment of adult blind.

Insane and Mental Defectives.—The Eastern, Western, and Central State Hospitals for the Insane and the State Feeble-minded Institute provide care and treatment for insane, feeble-minded, and epileptic persons committed by the circuit courts. Drug addicts, upon agreement to remain 6 months or longer, may be voluntarily admitted to any of the State institutions caring for persons of unsound mind.

Adult Delinquents.—The State Penitentiary and the State Reformatory provide for the confinement, labor, and training of adult delinquents. The State Department of Welfare receives and considers all applications for paroles and has the power of refusal. Paroles may not be granted, however, without the approval of the Governor.

---

[1] The State Department of Welfare is empowered to administer and supervise all forms of public assistance, organize and supervise county welfare departments, and assist other departments, agencies, and institutions of the State and Federal Governments. It must act as agent of the Federal Government in welfare matters of mutual concern and in the administration of Federal grants for welfare purposes.

[2] See discussion of care of dependent and neglected children, above, for powers and duties of the State Department of Welfare, and the county children's bureaus in relation to children.

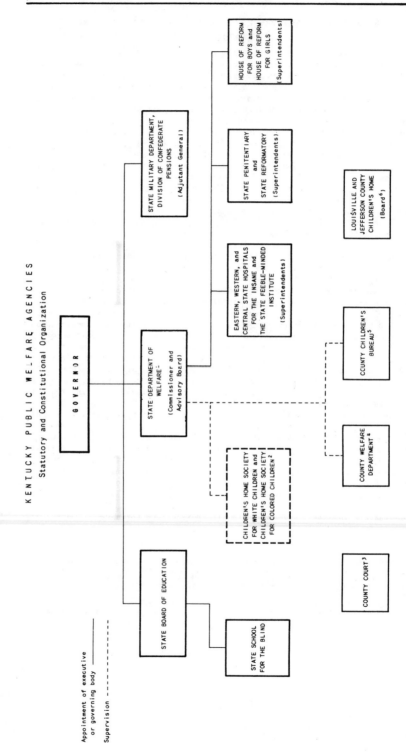

KENTUCKY PUBLIC WELFARE AGENCIES
Statutory and Constitutional Organization

Appointment of executive
or governing body —————

Supervision – – – – – – – – –

GOVERNOR

STATE BOARD OF EDUCATION

STATE DEPARTMENT OF WELFARE[1]
(Commissioner and Advisory Board)

STATE MILITARY DEPARTMENT, DIVISION OF CONFEDERATE PENSIONS
(Adjutant General)

STATE SCHOOL FOR THE BLIND

CHILDREN'S HOME SOCIETY FOR WHITE CHILDREN and CHILDREN'S HOME SOCIETY FOR COLORED CHILDREN[2]

EASTERN, WESTERN, and CENTRAL STATE HOSPITALS FOR THE INSANE and THE STATE FEEBLE-MINDED INSTITUTE
(Superintendents)

STATE PENITENTIARY and STATE REFORMATORY
(Superintendents)

HOUSE OF REFORM FOR BOYS and HOUSE OF REFORM FOR GIRLS
(Superintendents)

LOUISVILLE AND JEFFERSON COUNTY CHILDREN'S HOME
(Board[6])

COUNTY COURT[3]

COUNTY WELFARE DEPARTMENT[4]

COUNTY CHILDREN'S BUREAU[5]

[1] The State Department of Welfare consists of the following divisions: division of public assistance, division of child welfare, division of hospitals and mental hygiene, division of corrections, and the laboratory of criminal identification and statistics.

[2] State-aided private institutions.

[3] Administers general relief and blind assistance under the supervision of the State Department of Welfare.

[4] The State Department of Welfare may organize and supervise county welfare departments.

[5] Appointment of bureau in following manner: the county judge and county superintendent of schools submit a list of 9 persons to the division of child welfare of the State Department of Welfare, which recommends 3 persons who are appointed by the judge and the superintendent.

SUMMARY OF STATUTORY PROVISIONS FOR PUBLIC WELFARE
LOUISIANA

Relief and Public Assistance.—General relief, old age assistance, aid to dependent children in their own homes, and blind assistance are administered by the State Department of Public Welfare through the parish departments of public welfare.[1] The State Hospital Board must provide care and treatment for indigent sick persons in public and private hospitals and other institutions, and it must also provide treatment after hospitalization. The Northeast Louisiana Charity Hospital, the Shreveport Charity Hospital, the New Orleans Charity Hospital, and the Baton Rouge Charity Hospital have been established for the treatment of indigent persons.

Cases involving dependent and neglected children come within the jurisdiction of the juvenile courts which report to the State Board of Charities and Corrections concerning the disposition of such children. The parish departments of public welfare, under the supervision of the State Department of Public Welfare, administer care and treatment to dependent, neglected, delinquent, and handicapped children. The State Board of Charities and Corrections has supervisory and visitorial powers over all State, local, and private institutions of a charitable or penal nature. The Industrial School for Girls provides care for dependent and neglected girls.

Veterans' pensions are administered by the State Department of Public Welfare. Care of veterans in the State Soldiers' Home is administered by the board of directors of the home.[2]

Juvenile Delinquents.—Juvenile courts have jurisdiction in cases involving delinquent children. Delinquent boys may be committed to the State Training Institute and delinquent girls, to the State Industrial School for Girls.[3]

Services to the Blind.—The State Board for the Blind must maintain a register of the blind describing the condition, cause of blindness, and capacity for education and industrial training of each blind person. The board acts as a bureau of information and industrial aid for the blind in order to assist in finding employment, to teach trades, and to assist in marketing products. It must give home instruction, and it may provide vocational training, establish workshops, and pay wages for work therein. It must make inquiries concerning the causes of blindness to ascertain what proportion of such cases is preventable, and it must cooperate with other agencies in the adoption and enforcement of preventive measures.

Insane and Mental Defectives.—The East Louisiana State Hospital and the Central Louisiana State Hospital provide care and treatment for insane persons committed by district courts. The State Colony and Training School for Feeble-minded provides care and treatment for feeble-minded persons committed by district or parish courts or admitted upon proper application.

Adult Delinquents.—The State Penitentiary provides for confinement and training of adult delinquents. The State Board of Parole has charge of the parole of prisoners. The Governor has power to grant reprieves and may, except in cases of impeachment or treason, upon recommendation of the lieutenant governor, the attorney general, and the presiding judge of the court before which the conviction was obtained, or any two of them, commute sentences and remit fines and forfeitures.

---

[1]The State Department of Public Welfare must cooperate with and act as the agent of the Federal Government in public welfare matters of mutual concern.

[2]Need is not specified as a condition of eligibility for veterans' pensions or care in the State Soldiers' Home.

[3]See discussion of care of dependent and neglected children, above, for powers of the State Board of Charities and Corrections in relation to children.

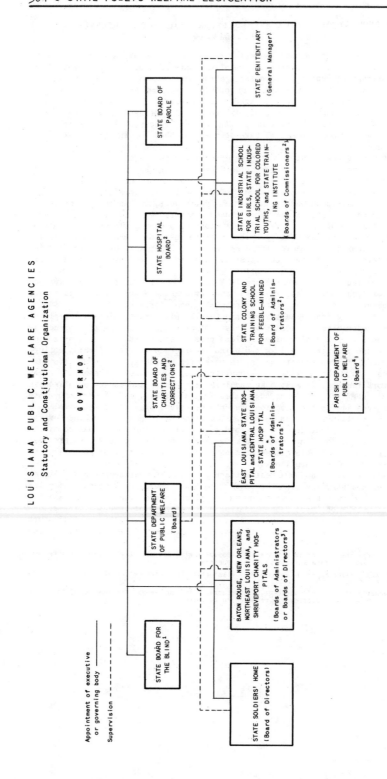

LOUISIANA PUBLIC WELFARE AGENCIES
Statutory and Constitutional Organization

Appointment of executive
or governing body ——————
Supervision - - - - - - - - - -

GOVERNOR

STATE BOARD FOR THE BLIND[1]

STATE DEPARTMENT OF PUBLIC WELFARE (Board)[1]

STATE BOARD OF CHARITIES AND CORRECTIONS[2]

STATE HOSPITAL BOARD[2]

STATE BOARD OF PAROLE

STATE PENITENTIARY (General Manager)

STATE SOLDIERS' HOME (Board of Directors)

BATON ROUGE, NEW ORLEANS, NORTHEAST LOUISIANA, and SHREVEPORT CHARITY HOSPITALS (Boards of Administrators or Boards of Directors[3])

EAST LOUISIANA STATE HOSPITAL and CENTRAL LOUISIANA STATE HOSPITAL (Boards of Administrators[2])

STATE COLONY AND TRAINING SCHOOL FOR FEEBLE-MINDED (Board of Administrators[2])

STATE INDUSTRIAL SCHOOL FOR GIRLS, STATE INDUSTRIAL SCHOOL FOR COLORED YOUTHS, and STATE TRAINING INSTITUTE (Boards of Commissioners[2])

PARISH DEPARTMENT OF PUBLIC WELFARE (Board[4])

[1] The superintendent of the State School for the Blind is a member.
[2] The board is composed of the members of the State Board of Public Welfare.
[3] The governor is a member of the board of administrators of the New Orleans Charity Hospital. The board of administrators of the Baton Rouge Charity Hospital consists of the Governor, the mayor of Baton Rouge, the president of the police jury of East Baton Rouge, and 3 others appointed by the Governor.
[4] Appointed by the parish board of commissioners or the parish police jury from a list submitted by the State Department of Public Welfare. In the parish of New Orleans the board is appointed by the commission council of New Orleans from a list submitted by the State department.

SUMMARY OF STATUTORY PROVISIONS FOR PUBLIC WELFARE
MAINE

Relief and Public Assistance.—General relief is administered by city, town, or plantation overseers of the poor. The State Department of Health and Welfare must investigate and inspect all systems of public charity and public institutions. Old age assistance is administered by the old age assistance commission in the State Department of Health and Welfare. Aid to dependent children in their own homes is administered by the State Department of Health and Welfare assisted by municipal boards of child welfare. Blind assistance is administered by the State Department of Health and Welfare.

Cases involving dependent and neglected children come within the jurisdiction of probate courts and municipal courts. The State Department of Health and Welfare may provide care for such children. It must also investigate the condition and management of all institutions and agencies receiving public support, and it is empowered to license child-caring agencies.[1] The State Military and Naval Children's Home provides care and education for poor and neglected children of the State with preference being given to children of soldiers and sailors.

Direct relief to veterans is administered by the overseers of the poor and pensions by the State Department of Health and Welfare.

Juvenile Delinquents.—Probate courts of cities or municipal courts of towns or cities have jurisdiction in cases involving delinquent children. The court may place such a child in the custody of a probation officer, or an agent of the State Department of Health and Welfare. The court may also commit such a child to the State School for Boys or the State School for Girls.[2]

Insane and Mental Defectives.—The Bangor State Hospital and Augusta State Hospital provide care and treatment for insane persons committed by the municipal officers who constitute a board of examiners. The Pownal State School provides care and training for idiots and feeble-minded persons committed by the probate judges who may also commit insane persons to the State hospitals. Sterilization of any insane or feeble-minded person may be ordered by the commissioner of the State Department of Health and Welfare.

Adult Delinquents.—The State Prison, the State Reformatory for Men, and the State Reformatory for Women provide for the confinement and training of delinquent adults. The State parole board has authority to grant or revoke paroles. The State Department of Health and Welfare must establish standards and procedures for parole and supervise the parole of inmates of State penal and correctional institutions.

Crippled Children.—The State Department of Health and Welfare, through its bureau of health, is authorized to administer and supervise a program of services for children who are crippled or who are suffering from conditions which lead to crippling.[3]

Education of the Deaf, Dumb, and Blind.—The State School for the Deaf is devoted to the education and instruction of deaf and dumb children. With the consent of the parents or guardians, the State Department of Health and Welfare may admit any deaf and dumb child who is a resident of the State. The department licenses and supervises State-aided institutions for defectives. The Maine Institution for the Blind receives State aid from the bureau of social welfare of the State Department of Health and Welfare.[4]

Tuberculars.—The Central, Northern, and Western State Sanatoriums for Treatment of Tuberculosis admit residents of the State suffering from tuberculosis

---

[1] The State Department of Health and Welfare through its bureau of social welfare is authorized to cooperate with the Federal Government in establishing, extending, and strengthening child welfare services for the protection and care of homeless, dependent, and neglected children, and children in danger of becoming delinquent.

[2] See discussion of care of dependent and neglected children, above, for powers of the State Department of Health and Welfare in relation to children.

[3] The purpose of the program is to develop, extend, and improve services for locating such children, to provide for medical, surgical, corrective, and other services and care, and to provide facilities for diagnosis, hospitalization, and aftercare.

[4] The Governor may also provide for the education of blind children either within or without the State.

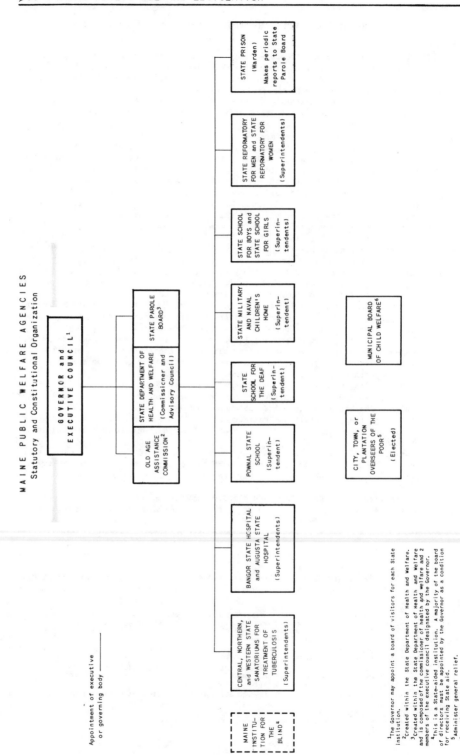

MAINE PUBLIC WELFARE AGENCIES
Statutory and Constitutional Organization

Appointment of executive
or governing body ——————

GOVERNOR and
EXECUTIVE COUNCIL[1]

OLD AGE
ASSISTANCE
COMMISSION[2]

STATE DEPARTMENT OF
HEALTH AND WELFARE
(Commissioner and
Advisory Council)

STATE PAROLE
BOARD[3]

MAINE
INSTITU-
TION FOR
THE
BLIND[4]

CENTRAL, NORTHERN,
and WESTERN STATE
SANATORIUMS FOR
TREATMENT OF
TUBERCULOSIS
(Superintendents)

BANGOR STATE HOSPITAL
and AUGUSTA STATE
HOSPITAL
(Superintendents)

POWNAL STATE
SCHOOL
(Superin-
tendent)

STATE
SCHOOL FOR
THE DEAF
(Superin-
tendent)

STATE MILITARY
AND NAVAL
CHILDREN'S
HOME
(Superin-
tendent)

STATE SCHOOL
FOR BOYS and
STATE SCHOOL
FOR GIRLS
(Superin-
tendents)

STATE REFORMATORY
FOR MEN and STATE
REFORMATORY FOR
WOMEN
(Superintendents)

STATE PRISON
(Warden)
Makes periodic
reports to State
Parole Board

CITY, TOWN, or
PLANTATION
OVERSEERS OF THE
POOR[5]
(Elected)

MUNICIPAL BOARD
OF CHILD WELFARE[6]

[1] The Governor may appoint a board of visitors for each State institution.

[2] Created within the State Department of Health and Welfare.

[3] Created within the State Department of Health and Welfare and is composed of the commissioner of health and welfare and 2 members of the executive council designated by the Governor.

[4] This is a State-aided institution. A majority of the board of directors must be appointed by the Governor as a condition for receiving State aid.

[5] Administer general relief.

[6] Composed of the overseers of the poor, ex officio, unless a city, a town, or a plantation provides for a special board.

according to the diagnosis of any regular practicing physician in the State, or of the superintendent of any one of the sanatoriums.

Maternal and Child Health Services.—The department, through its division of health, is authorized to administer a program to extend and improve its services for promoting the health of mothers and children, especially in rural areas and in areas suffering from severe economic distress.

SUMMARY OF STATUTORY PROVISIONS FOR PUBLIC WELFARE
MARYLAND

Relief and Public Assistance.—General relief,[1] old age assistance, aid to dependent children in their own homes, and blind assistance are administered by the county welfare boards, and in Baltimore City by the department of welfare, under the supervision of the Board of State Aid and Charities. Where county welfare boards have not been established, another agency may be designated by the Board of State Aid and Charities.[2]

Cases involving dependent and neglected children come within the jurisdiction of county juvenile courts, and in Baltimore City within the jurisdiction of the magistrate of juvenile causes. The Board of State Aid and Charities must establish rules and regulations for child-caring agencies and institutions which it is empowered to license, visit, and inspect. Care of all dependent, neglected, and delinquent children is administered by county welfare boards and in Baltimore City by the department of welfare under the supervision of the Board of State Aid and Charities. The county trustees of the poor or the county commissioners in counties where no county welfare board exists must place all poor children in their charge in some educational institution or home for children. The Training School for Boys and the Montrose School for Girls care for dependent or neglected children.

Veteran relief is administered by the State Veterans' Commission through the State service officer.

Juvenile Delinquents.—The juvenile courts and the magistrate of juvenile causes in Baltimore City have jurisdiction in cases involving delinquent children. A child may be allowed to remain at home subject to the supervision of a probation officer, or it may be committed to some agency or to some suitable institution organized for the care of children. The Training School for Boys, the Montrose School for Girls, and the State Training School for Colored Girls are State institutions established for the care and training of delinquent children. The St. Mary's Industrial School for Boys, the House of Reformation for Colored Boys, the House of the Good Shepherd, and the House of the Good Shepherd for Colored Girls are State-aided private institutions established for the same purpose.[3]

Services to the Blind.—All blind adults with sufficient ability and of good character are entitled to the benefits of the Workshop for the Blind.

Insane and Mental Defectives.—The State Board of Mental Hygiene has the power to investigate and examine all public or private institutions authorized by law to care for insane persons. The Spring Grove, Eastern Shore, Springfield, and Crownsville (Negro) State Hospitals for the Insane provide care and treatment for insane State residents committed by the circuit courts. The Rosewood State Training School must receive and care for all idiots, imbeciles, and feeble-minded persons whom the board of visitors of the school may deem proper subjects. The school is divided into two departments, one educational and the other custodial.

Adult Delinquents.—The State Penitentiary and the State House of Corrections provide for confinement and training of adult delinquents. The parole commissioner has power of visitation over all institutions caring for juvenile or adult delinquents and must investigate the advisability of making recommendations to the Governor for conditional pardons. The commissioner must supervise all persons paroled and all persons placed under suspended sentence.

---

[1]In the absence of State funds, general relief is administered by the trustees of the poor, justices of the peace, boards of county commissioners, or agents designated by them depending upon the law applicable in particular counties.

[2]The Board of State Aid and Charities is charged with the investigation, study, and consideration of the whole system of public and private charitable institutions, organizations, and agencies. It must cooperate with the Federal Government in matters of mutual concern pertaining to assistance to dependent children, the needy aged, and the needy blind. The board may accept any and all allotments of Federal funds and take advantage of any Federal economic act.

[3]See discussion of care of dependent and neglected children, above, for powers of the Board of State Aid and Charities, county welfare boards, department of welfare in Baltimore City, county commissioners, or county trustees of the poor, in relation to children.

MARYLAND PUBLIC WELFARE AGENCIES
Statutory and Constitutional Organization

Appointment of executive
or governing body ─────────
Supervision ─ ─ ─ ─ ─ ─ ─

GOVERNOR

STATE BOARD OF MENTAL HYGIENE

STATE VETERANS' COMMISSION

BOARD OF STATE AID AND CHARITIES

PAROLE COMMISSIONER

DEPARTMENT OF PUBLIC WELFARE
(Board and Director)

WORKSHOP FOR THE BLIND
(Board of Directors[1])

SPRINGFIELD STATE HOSPITAL FOR THE INSANE
(Board of Managers[2])
Makes periodic reports to Director of Department of Public Welfare

EASTERN SHORE STATE HOSPITAL FOR THE INSANE
(Board of Managers[3])
Makes periodic reports to Director of Department of Public Welfare

SPRING GROVE STATE HOSPITAL FOR THE INSANE
(Board of Managers)
Makes periodic reports to Director of Department of Public Welfare

CROWNSVILLE STATE HOSPITAL FOR INSANE NEGROES
(Board of Managers[2])
Makes periodic reports to Director of Public Welfare

ROSEWOOD STATE TRAINING SCHOOL
(Board of Visitors)
Makes periodic reports to Director of Department of Public Welfare

TRAINING SCHOOL FOR BOYS
(Board of Managers[3])

MONTROSE SCHOOL FOR GIRLS and STATE TRAINING SCHOOL FOR COLORED GIRLS
(Boards of Managers)

STATE PENITENTIARY and STATE HOUSE OF CORRECTIONS
(Wardens)

ST. MARY'S INDUSTRIAL SCHOOL FOR BOYS[4] and HOUSE OF REFORMATION FOR COLORED BOYS[5]

HOUSE OF THE GOOD SHEPHERD and HOUSE OF THE GOOD SHEPHERD FOR COLORED GIRLS[6]

COUNTY WELFARE BOARD[8]

DEPARTMENT OF WELFARE OF BALTIMORE CITY
(Director[7])

[1] This is a State-aided institution. 3 members are appointed by the Governor and 2 others elected by the board of directors of the Maryland School for the Blind.

[2] Composed of the Governor, the State treasurer, the comptroller of the treasury, and 6 members appointed by the Governor.

[3] Composed of the Governor, the State treasurer, the comptroller of the treasury, and 9 members appointed by the Governor.

[4] This is a State-aided institution. The Governor and the mayor of Baltimore City appoint 5 persons every 2 years to represent the State and city on the board of trustees.

[5] This is a State-aided institution. The board of managers is composed of 2 members appointed by the mayor and city council of Baltimore, 2 members appointed by the Governor, and 12 members elected by the members of the association for the House of Reformation for Colored Boys.

[6] These are State-aided institutions.

[7] Appointed by the mayor with the consent of the city council. An advisory welfare committee is also appointed to assist the director.

[8] Appointed by the board of county commissioners.

SUMMARY OF STATUTORY PROVISIONS FOR PUBLIC WELFARE
MASSACHUSETTS

Relief and Public Assistance.—General relief is administered by the local boards of public welfare.[1] The State Infirmary provides care for sick indigents who are not insane or infected with a contagious disease. Old age assistance and aid to dependent children in their own homes are administered by the local boards of public welfare under the supervision of the State Department of Public Welfare. Blind assistance is administered by the State director of the division of the blind in the State Department of Education.[2]

Cases involving dependent and neglected children come within the jurisdiction of the juvenile courts. The local boards of public welfare and the State Department of Public Welfare may receive children and provide suitable care for them.[3] They must regularly visit all children placed in homes or institutions. The State department is empowered to license all child-caring agencies.

Veteran relief is administered by the town selectmen or city aldermen under the supervision of the Commissioner of State Aid and Pensions.[4] Care in the State Soldiers' Home is administered by the board of trustees of the home, under the supervision of the Governor and council.

Juvenile Delinquents.—Juvenile courts have jurisdiction in cases involving delinquent children. The court may place such a child in the care of a probation officer or, with the consent of the State Department of Public Welfare, in the care of a reputable person, or commit the child to any institution, except a jail or house of correction, to which it might be committed upon a conviction for violation of the law. The Lyman School for Boys, the Industrial School for Boys, and the Industrial School for Girls receive and care for delinquent children.[5]

Services to the Blind.—The director of the division of the blind in the State Department of Education must perform the following functions: establish a bureau to aid the blind in finding employment and developing home industries; maintain a register of the blind describing their condition, the causes of blindness, and their capacity for education and industrial training; establish and equip industrial training schools and workshops for the training and employment of blind persons; and provide temporary support for workmen or pupils received in the schools and workshops. The director may provide instruction at home, furnish materials and tools, and assist in the marketing of products. He may also register cases of persons, whose eyesight is seriously defective, who are likely to become blind, and he may take such measures, in cooperation with other authorities, for the prevention of blindness or conservation of eyesight as he may deem advisable.

Insane and Mental Defectives.—The State Department of Mental Diseases has general supervision of all public and private institutions for the insane, feeble-minded, epileptics, and persons addicted to the intemperate use of narcotics or stimulants. The following institutions provide care and treatment for insane or feeble-minded persons: Belchertown State School, Boston Psychopathic Hospital, Boston State Hospital, Danvers State Hospital, Foxborough State Hospital, Gardner State Hospital, Grafton State Hospital, Walter E. Fernald State School, Medfield State Hospital, Metropolitan State Hospital, Monson State Hospital, Northampton State Hospital, Taunton State Hospital, Westborough State Hospital, Worcester State Hospital, Wrentham State School, and Norfolk State Hospital.

Persons may be admitted on court commitment, or if mentally competent to make application, may apply for admission to the trustees, superintendent, or manager of any of these institutions. The Walter E. Fernald State School, the Belchertown State School, and the Wrentham State School must maintain departments for the instruction and education of feeble-minded persons who are of school age.

---

[1] Local boards of public welfare must report all cases of nonresidents to the State Department of Public Welfare which in turn must examine such cases and order such aid as it deems expedient.

[2] The State Departments of Public Welfare, Public Health, and Education must cooperate with the appropriate Federal authorities in the administration of the Social Security Act.

[3] In Boston the institutions department is vested with the powers and duties conferred upon the local boards of public welfare with respect to children's aid.

[4] In Boston veteran relief is administered by the soldiers' relief commissioner.

[5] See discussion of care of dependent and neglected children, above, for powers of the State and local departments of public welfare in relation to children.

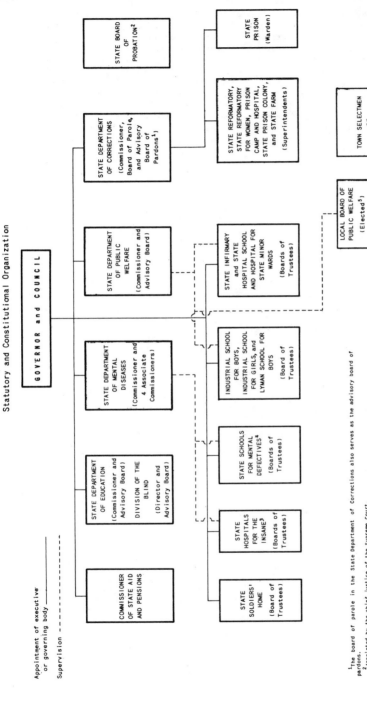

MASSACHUSETTS PUBLIC WELFARE AGENCIES

Statutory and Constitutional Organization

Appointment of executive or governing body ———————

Supervision – – – – – – – – – – – – –

GOVERNOR and COUNCIL

COMMISSIONER OF STATE AID AND PENSIONS

STATE DEPARTMENT OF EDUCATION (Commissioner and Advisory Board)
DIVISION OF THE BLIND[3] (Director and Advisory Board)

STATE DEPARTMENT OF MENTAL DISEASES (Commissioner and 4 Associate Commissioners)

STATE DEPARTMENT OF PUBLIC WELFARE (Commissioner and Advisory Board)

STATE DEPARTMENT OF CORRECTIONS (Commissioner, Board of Parole, and Advisory Board of Pardons[1])

STATE BOARD OF PROBATION[2]

STATE SOLDIERS' HOME (Board of Trustees)

STATE HOSPITALS FOR THE INSANE[3] (Boards of Trustees)

STATE SCHOOLS FOR MENTAL DEFECTIVES[4] (Boards of Trustees)

INDUSTRIAL SCHOOL FOR BOYS, INDUSTRIAL SCHOOL FOR GIRLS, and LYMAN SCHOOL FOR BOYS (Board of Trustees)

STATE INFIRMARY and STATE HOSPITAL AND HOSPITAL FOR STATE MINOR WARDS (Boards of Trustees)

STATE REFORMATORY, STATE REFORMATORY FOR WOMEN, PRISON CAMP AND HOSPITAL, STATE PRISON COLONY, and STATE FARM (Superintendents)

STATE PRISON (Warden)

TOWN SELECTMEN or CITY COUNCIL[6]

LOCAL BOARD OF PUBLIC WELFARE (Elected[5]) Makes periodic reports to State Department of Public Welfare

[1] The board of parole in the State Department of Corrections also serves as the advisory board of pardons.

[2] Appointed by the chief justice of the Supreme Court.

[3] They are the Boston Psychopathic Hospital, Boston State Hospital, Danvers State Hospital, Foxborough State Hospital, Gardner State Hospital, Grafton State Hospital, Medfield State Hospital, Metropolitan State Hospital, Monson State Hospital, Northampton State Hospital, Taunton State Hospital, Westborough State Hospital, Worcester State Hospital, and Norfolk State Hospital.

[4] They are the Belchertown State School, Walter E. Fernald State School, and Wrentham State School.

[5] The town selectmen act as the board of public welfare in towns which have not authorized the election of such a board.

[6] The administration of veteran relief by town or city officials is supervised by the commissioner of State Aid and Pensions.

Adult Delinquents.—The State Prison, the State Reformatory, the State Reformatory for Women, the Prison Camp and Hospital, the State Prison Colony, and the State Farm provide for the confinement and training of adult delinquents. The State board of parole may grant permits for prisoners to be at liberty and when acting as the State advisory board of pardons must consider all petitions for pardon or commutation of sentence referred to it by the Governor. The State Board of Probation must supervise and promote the coordination of all probation work.

Crippled Children.—The State Hospital School and Hospital for State Minor Wards provide education and care for crippled and deformed children admitted upon application of the child's guardian to the board of trustees of the institution.

Maternal and Child Health.—The State Department of Public Welfare may grant licenses to maintain boarding houses for infants, and it has supervision over all maternity hospitals licensed by it.

SUMMARY OF STATUTORY PROVISIONS FOR PUBLIC WELFARE
MICHIGAN

Relief and Public Assistance.—State funds for general relief are administered by the State Emergency Welfare Relief Commission with the advice of county welfare relief commissions. In those counties wherein the distinction between township, city, or county poor is not abolished local funds for general relief are administered by the supervisors of the city or town, by the director of the poor in fourth-class cities, and by the county superintendents of the poor. Where the distinction is abolished local funds are administered by county superintendents of the poor. Old age assistance is administered by the State old age assistance bureau of the State Welfare Department assisted by the county welfare agents and the county old age assistance boards. Mothers' pensions are administered by the county probate courts (juvenile division) while aid to dependent children in their own homes and blind assistance are administered by the State Emergency Welfare Relief Commission through county welfare relief commissions.

Cases involving dependent and neglected children come within the jurisdiction of the county probate courts (juvenile division). The State Welfare Commission may make all necessary rules and regulations to protect the interests of minor children. The commission is empowered to license all persons, societies, associations, organizations, and corporations receiving, maintaining, or placing out children, and may revoke any license granted by it. The commission may visit all licensed child-caring agencies. County welfare agents must act as agents of the State Welfare Commission and the probate courts. They must visit at least once a year all children in homes and report their findings to the commission. The State Children's Institute receives children committed to it by the county probate courts (juvenile division). The State Child Guidance Institute makes inquiries into the causes of child delinquency, improves methods of treatment in cases of delinquent, neglected, and defective children, and coordinates the work of public and private agencies in examining and caring for children under 21 years of age referred to it for examination by the probate court (juvenile division).

Direct relief to veterans is administered by the county soldiers' and sailors' relief commission. Care in the State Soldiers' Home and in the Dormitory for Ex-nurses and Veterans' Dependents is administered by a board of managers.

Juvenile Delinquents.—The county probate courts (juvenile division) have jurisdiction in cases involving delinquent children. The court may place a child on probation under the care of its parents, guardians, or friends. It may also commit a child to the State Girls' Training School, the State Boys' Vocational School, or to any State or public institution authorized by law to receive such children. The court may, in certain instances, transfer the case to the criminal court.[1] The bureau of probation within the State Department of Corrections must cooperate in the prevention and treatment of juvenile delinquency.

Services to the Blind.—The State institute commission of the State Welfare Department must afford opportunities to indigent blind persons for such instruction and training as will fit them to earn, in whole or in part, their own support. The State Employment Institution for the Blind provides assistance, treatment, employment, and instruction for the blind.

Insane and Mental Defectives.—The Kalamazoo, Pontiac, Traverse City, Newberry, Ionia, and Ypsilanti State Hospitals provide curative and scientific treatment for insane persons. The State Farm Colony for Epileptics cares for epileptic persons exclusive of the insane and the idiotic. The Lapeer State Home and Training School and the Mt. Pleasant State Home and Training School provide care for feeble-minded persons. Feeble-minded children receive care and treatment at the State Children's Village. The State Psychopathic Hospital at the State University Hospital provides for the observation and treatment of those persons afflicted with an abnormal mental condition. All commitments are made by the probate courts of the county. Persons may also be admitted by voluntary agreement in some cases.

---

[1] See discussion of care of dependent and neglected children, above, for powers of the State Welfare Commission and the county welfare agent in relation to children.

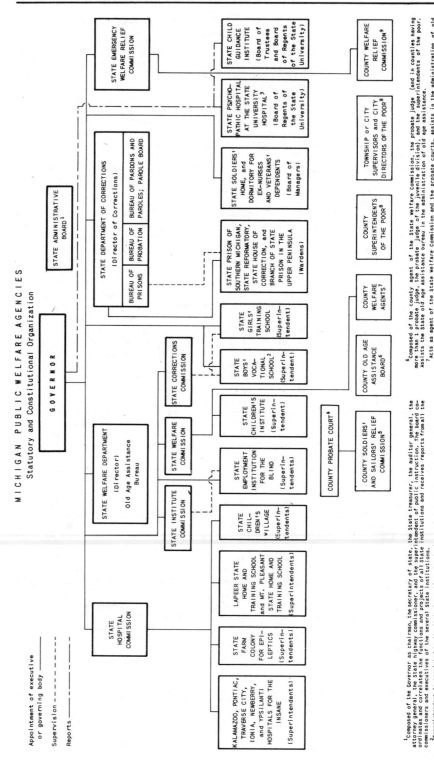

MICHIGAN PUBLIC WELFARE AGENCIES
Statutory and Constitutional Organization

Appointment of executive
or governing body ————————
Supervision ————————
Reports ————————

[1] Composed of the Governor as chairman, the secretary of state, the State treasurer, the auditor general, the attorney general, the State highway commissioner, and the superintendent of public instruction. The board coordinates and correlates the functions and projects of all State institutions and receives reports from all the commissioners and executives of the several State institutions.

[2] Superintendent is appointed by the State Corrections Commission subject to the approval of the Governor.

[3] The State Psychopathic Hospital, as part of the State University Hospital, has been established and is under the control of the board of regents of the State university, which board consists of 8 elective members.

[4] Administers mothers' pension law.

[5] Administers direct relief to veterans.

[6] Composed of the county agent of the State Welfare Commission, the probate judge (and in counties having more than 1 probate judge, the probate judge of the juvenile division), and the superintendents of the poor. Assists the State old age assistance bureau in the administration of old age assistance.

[7] Acts as agent of the State Welfare Commission and the probate courts. Assists in the administration of old age assistance.

[8] Appointed by the county board of supervisors and administers local funds for general relief.

[9] Advises the State Emergency Welfare Relief Commission in the distribution of State funds for general relief and assists it in the administration of State plans providing for blind assistance and aid to dependent chil-

Adult Delinquents.—The State Prison of Southern Michigan, the State House of Correction and branch of State Prison in the Upper Peninsula, and the State Reformatory provide for the confinement and training of adult delinquents.

The bureau of probation within the State Department of Corrections exercises general supervision over adult probation in the State and local courts.

The bureau of pardons and paroles within the State Department of Corrections supervises or investigates prisoners released or eligible to be released and aids parolees in securing employment. The parole board within the bureau investigates each eligible prisoner and determines exclusively on its own initiative whether paroles are to be granted.

SUMMARY OF STATUTORY PROVISIONS FOR PUBLIC WELFARE
MINNESOTA

Relief and Public Assistance.—In counties operating under the county system, whereby the poor are chargeable to the county, general relief is administered by the county commissioners as supervisors of the poor (or by agents appointed by them including the overseers of the poor) or in some counties by boards of poor commissioners. In counties operating under the town system, whereby the poor are chargeable to their respective political subdivision, the town boards, city council, and village council, acting as overseers of the poor, are responsible for the administration of general relief. State funds made available for general relief are administered by county or city welfare boards under the supervision of the State Executive Council. County welfare boards may cooperate with boards of county commissioners, city, village, or borough councils, town boards, or other local authorities charged with the administration of relief to the poor, upon request of such authorities.[1]

Old age assistance and aid to dependent children in their own homes are administered by the county welfare boards under the supervision of the State Board of Control.[2] Blind assistance is administered by the State Board of Control.

Cases involving dependent and neglected children come within the jurisdiction of juvenile courts. The State Board of Control must cooperate with juvenile courts in promoting the enforcement of all laws for the protection of dependent, neglected, and illegitimate children and receive children committed to it; the board assumes guardianship of these children or children committed to institutions under its management. The board manages all State child-caring institutions, must cooperate with all public or private child-caring agencies, and is empowered to license all private children's homes. County or city welfare boards are charged with the administration of all child welfare activities and must perform such duties as may be required by the State Board of Control to enforce all laws for the protection of children. The State Public School for Dependent Children receives and cares for dependent or neglected children.

The State Soldiers' Home board administers direct relief to veterans and care in the State Soldiers' Home.[3] Veterans' pensions are administered by the State adjutant general.[4]

Juvenile Delinquents.—Juvenile courts have jurisdiction in cases involving delinquent children. A child may be allowed to remain in its own home or may be placed in a family home, subject to the visitation and supervision of a probation officer. The court may also commit such a child to any institution caring for delinquent children. The State Training School for Boys receives delinquent boys and the State Home School for Girls receives delinquent girls.[5]

Services to the Blind.—The State Board of Control is empowered to aid the blind by home instruction and training. It may assist them in securing tools, appliances, and supplies, and it may aid in marketing the products of their labors. The board may care for and relieve those not capable of self-support and utilize any other practicable method for alleviating their condition.

Insane and Mental Defectives.—Insane, as well as inebriate, feeble-minded, and epileptic persons are cared for in the Anoka, Hastings, Willmar, Fergus Falls, Rochester, St. Peter, and Moose Lake State Hospitals for the Insane. Detention hospitals are also maintained in connection with the State hospitals. The State School for Feeble-minded cares for feeble-minded children, and the State Colony

---

[1] In counties containing a city of the first class—i.e., with population over 50,000—operating under a home rule charter, the boards of county commissioners are the county welfare boards. The poor and hospital commission of any county, where established, constitutes the county welfare board.

[2] The State Board of Control has authority to accept the provisions of the Federal Social Security Act.

[3] The State Soldiers' Home welfare agent, appointed by the State Board of Control, may grant assistance, where other adequate aid is not available, to the dependent family of a veteran who is receiving hospitalization. The State Executive Council may also extend direct relief to disabled veterans of all wars through such agencies as it may designate.

[4] *Need* is not specified as a condition of eligibility for veterans' pensions.

[5] See discussion of care of dependent and neglected children, above, for the powers and duties of the State Board of Control and the county or city welfare boards in relation to children.

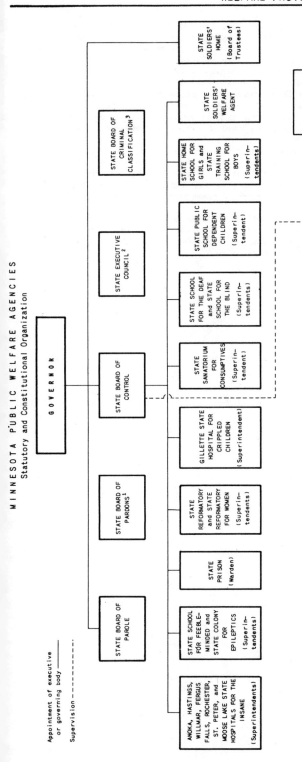

MINNESOTA PUBLIC WELFARE AGENCIES
Statutory and Constitutional Organization

Appointment of executive
or governing body ―――――
Supervision ―――――――――

[Chart hierarchy:]

GOVERNOR

STATE BOARD OF PAROLE

STATE BOARD OF PARDONS[1]

STATE EXECUTIVE COUNCIL[2]

STATE BOARD OF CRIMINAL CLASSIFICATION[3]

STATE SOLDIERS' HOME (Board of Trustees)

STATE BOARD OF CONTROL

ANOKA, HASTINGS, WILLMAR, FERGUS FALLS, ROCHESTER, ST. PETER, and MOOSE LAKE STATE HOSPITALS FOR THE INSANE (Superintendents)

STATE SCHOOL FOR FEEBLE-MINDED and STATE COLONY FOR EPILEPTICS (Superintendents)

STATE PRISON (Warden)

STATE REFORMATORY and STATE REFORMATORY FOR WOMEN (Superintendents)

GILLETTE STATE HOSPITAL FOR CRIPPLED CHILDREN (Superintendent)

STATE SANATORIUM FOR CONSUMPTIVES (Superintendent)

STATE SCHOOL FOR THE DEAF and STATE SCHOOL FOR THE BLIND (Superintendents)

STATE PUBLIC SCHOOL FOR DEPENDENT CHILDREN (Superintendent)

STATE HOME SCHOOL FOR GIRLS and STATE TRAINING SCHOOL FOR BOYS (Superintendents)

STATE SOLDIERS' WELFARE AGENT

BOARD OF COUNTY COMMISSIONERS[4] (Elected)

OVERSEER OF THE POOR[8]

BOARD OF POOR COMMISSIONERS[6] [7]

COUNTY or CITY WELFARE BOARD[5] [6]

TOWN BOARDS and CITY and VILLAGE COUNCILS[4]

[1] Composed of the Governor, the chief justice of the Supreme Court, and the attorney general.

[2] Composed of the Governor, the attorney general, the State auditor, the State treasurer, and the secretary of state.

[3] Composed of the chairman of the State Board of Parole and the 2 members of the State Board of Control with longest continuous service.

[4] May administer local funds for general relief.

[5] Except in counties containing a city of the 1st class and counties having a poor and hospital commission, 3 members are appointed by the board of county commissioners and 2 members are appointed by the State Board of Control from a list submitted by the board of county commissioners. In a county containing a city of the 1st class which operates under a home rule charter and has a board of public welfare for the city, the board of county commissioners is the county welfare board. If a city contains taxable property with an assessed valuation of more than 95 percent of the assessed valuation of all property in the county, the city board of public welfare is the county welfare board. In any county having a population of more than 200,000, an assessed valuation of more than $250,000,000, and an area of over 5,000 square miles, the board of poor commissioners is continued as the county welfare board. In any county having a poor and hospital commission, such commission is the county welfare board.

[6]

[7] Administration of State funds for general relief is supervised by the State Executive Council.

[8] Appointed in counties having a population of over 75,000 and an area of over 5,000 square miles by chairman of the board of county commissioners, with the approval of district court judges.

Appointment is optional with the board of county commissioners.

for Epileptics cares for epileptic persons. Persons may be committed to these institutions by the county courts or admitted by voluntary agreement. The State Board of Control must cooperate with the juvenile courts in promoting the enforcement of all laws for the protection of defective children.

Adult Delinquents.—The State Board of Criminal Classification must study and classify all prisoners and determine to which institution they shall be assigned. The State Prison and the State Reformatories for Men and Women, respectively, provide for confinement and training of adult delinquents. The State Board of Parole grants paroles and final discharges, and it exercises supervision over paroled and discharged convicts. The State Board of Pardons is empowered to grant reprieves, commutations, and pardons.

Crippled Children.—The State Board of Control must cooperate with the juvenile courts in promoting the enforcement of all laws for the protection of defective children. It appoints the superintendent of the Gillette State Hospital for Crippled Children which provides care and treatment for indigent children who are crippled and deformed or who are suffering from disease from which they are likely to become crippled or deformed.

Deaf, Dumb, and Blind.—The State School for the Deaf and the State School for the Blind provide education for the deaf and dumb, and the blind, respectively.

Tuberculars.—The State Sanatorium for Consumptives provides care for tuberculars not cared for in a county tuberculosis sanatorium.

SUMMARY OF STATUTORY PROVISIONS FOR PUBLIC WELFARE
MISSISSIPPI

Relief and Public Assistance.—General relief is administered by the county boards of supervisors.[1] Old age assistance and blind assistance are administered by the county welfare agent and the county boards of public welfare under the supervision of the State Department of Public Welfare. Chancery courts are charged with the administration of aid to dependent children in their own homes. They may appoint local citizens' boards for this purpose or delegate the duty to any public or private child welfare agency.

Cases involving dependent or neglected children come within the jurisdiction of the chancery courts, which may commit children to the State Industrial and Training School. County boards of supervisors are authorized to bind out or apprentice children or commit them to orphan asylums or child-caring organizations.

State Board of Public Welfare must administer or supervise all public child welfare services; must inspect all private child-caring agencies, institutions, and boarding homes; supervise the care of dependent and neglected children in foster homes or in institutions, especially children placed for adoption or those of illegitimate birth. The board must supervise the importation of children. County departments of public welfare may assume responsibility for the care and support of dependent children needing public care away from their homes, and may place such children in proper institutions or private homes, and may cooperate with public or private authorities in the placing of such children in proper institutions or suitable private homes. The necessary maintenance is to be provided for children in need of care in foster homes, under circumstances which do not require that such children become wards of the court, from public funds made available for welfare services.

Veterans' pensions are administered by county boards of inquiry under the supervision of the State Pension Commissioner.[2] Care in the Jefferson Davis Beauvoir Soldiers' Home is administered by the board of directors of the home.

Juvenile Delinquents.—Chancery courts have jurisdiction in cases involving delinquent children. The court may remand the case to the circuit court or may commit such a child to the care and control of a probation officer. It may also permit a child to be placed in a suitable home or family home, or commit it to the State Industrial and Training School.[3]

Services to the Blind.—The State Commission for the Blind must maintain a bureau of information to assist the blind in finding employment, developing home industries, and marketing their products. It may establish workshops and furnish materials, tools, and books for the purpose of rehabilitating blind persons. It may maintain a register of persons whose eyesight is seriously defective and who are likely to become blind. It may also, in cooperation with other authorities, take such measures as it may deem advisable for the prevention of blindness or conservation of eyesight.

Insane and Mental Defectives.—The State Insane Hospitals at Whitfield and Jackson and the East Mississippi State Hospital at Meridian provide care and treatment for insane residents of the State committed by the chancery courts. The Ellisville State School for the Feeble-minded provides care and treatment for feeble-minded residents of the State committed by the chancery courts. The county boards of supervisors must temporarily provide for persons alleged to be insane pending investigation and for persons who cannot be admitted to the above institutions. Idiots, fools, and known incurables may not be admitted to the above institutions but must be cared for in the county home.

Adult Delinquents.—The State Penitentiary provides for the confinement and training of adult delinquents. The Governor has the power to grant reprieves and pardons, except in the case of impeachment or treason.

[1] The Mississippi State Charity Hospitals at Jackson and Vicksburg, the South Mississippi Charity Hospital at Laurel, the Natchez Charity Hospital at Natchez, and the Matty Hersee Hospital at Meridian provide medical and surgical treatment for the poor and needy citizens of the State.

[2] *Need* is not specified as a condition of eligibility for either veterans' pensions or for care in the Jefferson Davis Beauvoir Soldiers' Home.

[3] See discussion of care of dependent and neglected children, above, for powers and duties of the State Department of Public Welfare and county departments of public welfare in relation to children.

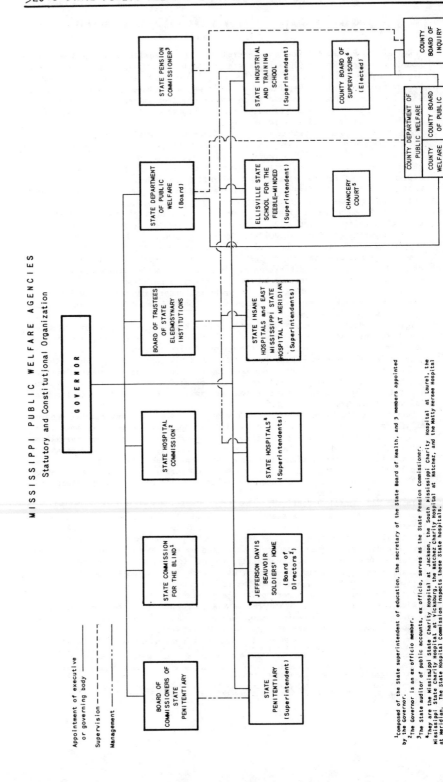

MISSISSIPPI PUBLIC WELFARE AGENCIES

Statutory and Constitutional Organization

Appointment of executive or governing body ──────

Supervision ── ── ──

Management ── ─ ── ─

GOVERNOR

BOARD OF COMMISSIONERS OF STATE PENITENTIARY

STATE COMMISSION FOR THE BLIND[1]

STATE HOSPITAL COMMISSION[2]

STATE PENSION COMMISSIONER[3]

BOARD OF TRUSTEES OF STATE ELEEMOSYNARY INSTITUTIONS

STATE DEPARTMENT OF PUBLIC WELFARE (Board)

STATE INDUSTRIAL AND TRAINING SCHOOL (Superintendent)

COUNTY BOARD OF SUPERVISORS[6] (Elected)

COUNTY BOARD OF INQUIRY

JEFFERSON DAVIS BEAUVOIR SOLDIERS' HOME (Board of Directors[2])

STATE PENITENTIARY (Superintendent)

STATE HOSPITALS[4] (Superintendents)

STATE INSANE HOSPITALS and EAST MISSISSIPPI STATE HOSPITAL AT MERIDIAN (Superintendents)

ELLISVILLE STATE SCHOOL FOR THE FEEBLE-MINDED (Superintendent)

CHANCERY COURT[5]

COUNTY DEPARTMENT OF PUBLIC WELFARE

COUNTY WELFARE AGENT

COUNTY BOARD OF PUBLIC WELFARE

[1] Composed of the State superintendent of education, the secretary of the State Board of Health, and 3 members appointed by the Governor.

[2] The Governor is an ex officio member.

[3] The State auditor of public accounts, ex officio, serves as the State Pension Commissioner.

[4] They are the Mississippi State Charity Hospital at Jackson, the South Mississippi Charity Hospital at Laurel, the Mississippi State Charity Hospital at Vicksburg, the Natchez Charity Hospital at Natchez, and the Matty Hersee Hospital at Meridian. The State Hospital Commission inspects these State hospitals.

[5] Administers aid to dependent children in their own homes.

[6] Administers general relief.

SUMMARY OF STATUTORY PROVISIONS FOR PUBLIC WELFARE
MISSOURI

Relief and Public Assistance.—State funds for general relief are administered by the State Social Security Commission with the advice of the county social security commission. General relief financed exclusively from local funds is administered by the county courts or by city boards of social welfare where established. Old age assistance and aid to dependent children in their own homes are administered by the State Social Security Commission with the advice of the county social security commission.[1] Blind assistance is administered by the State Commission for the Blind which may be assisted by county or city probate judges.

Cases involving dependent and neglected children come within the jurisdiction of juvenile courts. The State Social Security Commission administers or supervises all child welfare activities including the operation of State institutions for children which includes the State Home for Children. It must license and supervise all child-caring agencies and institutions, except those conducted by well-known religious orders, and it must supervise juvenile probation under the direction of the juvenile courts. The St. Louis Board of Children's Guardians is empowered to receive children committed by the juvenile courts for care, treatment, and placement. County boards of visitors (appointed by circuit courts) must regularly visit all county and municipal institutions or corrective institutions receiving county or municipal funds.

Veteran relief, in the form of care in the Confederate Soldiers' Home and the State Federal Soldiers' Home, is administered by the board of trustees of each home.

Juvenile Delinquents.—Juvenile courts have jurisdiction in cases involving delinquent children. The court may allow a child to remain in its own home or place it in a family home subject to the supervision of a probation officer, or it may commit the child to the State Training School for Boys, the State Industrial Home for Girls, the State Industrial Home for Negro Girls, or to any State or county institution caring for children.[2]

Services to the Blind.—The State Commission for the Blind must perform the following duties: maintain a register of blind persons in the State for the purpose of securing employment; maintain shops and workrooms for the employment of blind persons; provide a means for the sale of products; and procure materials and tools to furnish aid to blind persons engaged in home industries. It must also adopt such measures as it deems expedient for the prevention and cure of blindness.

Insane and Mental Defectives.—There are four State hospitals providing care and treatment for insane persons committed by county courts or received by voluntary agreement. The State School for Feeble-minded and Epileptics provides care and treatment for feeble-minded and epileptic persons, upon a written request accompanied by the certificate of the county court and supported by the opinion of two physicians.

Adult Delinquents.—The State Penitentiary and the Intermediate Reformatory for Young Men provide for the confinement and training of adult delinquents. The State Board of Probation and Parole must select prisoners to be recommended to the Governor and make recommendations for parole, commutation of sentence, or pardon. The board must investigate and make recommendations upon the merits of all applications for executive clemency. It also supervises all persons paroled or released under conditional pardons.

Tuberculars.—The State Sanatorium provides treatment for tuberculous citizens of the State who may apply to the county court for admission. Citizens of St. Louis make application to the city comptroller for admission to the sanatorium.

---

[1] The State Social Security Commission must cooperate with the Federal Government in public welfare matters of mutual concern.

[2] See discussion of care of dependent and neglected children, above, for powers of the State Social Security Commission, the city board of children's guardians of St. Louis, and the county boards of visitors in relation to children.

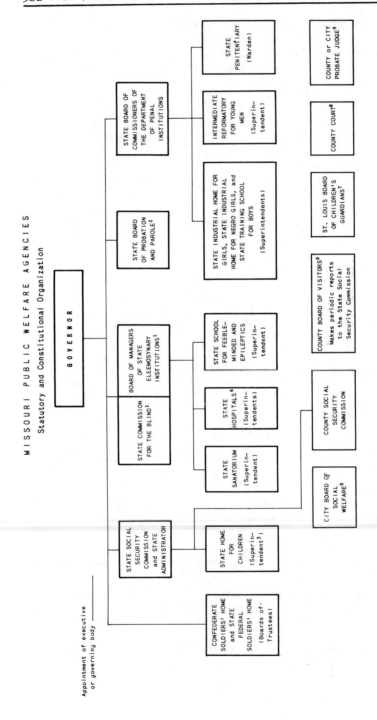

MISSOURI PUBLIC WELFARE AGENCIES
Statutory and Constitutional Organization

Appointment of executive or governing body ———

[1] The Board of Managers of State Eleemosynary institutions also serves as the State Commission for the Blind.

[2] Composed of the lieutenant governor and 2 other members appointed by the Governor.

[3] Director of children's bureau of the State Social Security Commission is the superintendent, ex officio.

[4] State Hospitals for the insane have been established.

[5] Established in first-class cities. Composed of the mayor and 6 other members, 3 of whom are appointed by the mayor and 3 by the county court.

[6] Composed of 6 persons appointed by the circuit court of the county.

[7] Appointed by the mayor.

[8] Administers local general relief program.

SUMMARY OF STATUTORY PROVISIONS FOR PUBLIC WELFARE
MONTANA

Relief and Public Assistance.—General relief, old age assistance, aid to dependent children in their own homes, and blind assistance are administered by county departments of public welfare under supervision of the State Department of Public Welfare.[1] The State Department of Public Welfare also supervises private institutions providing care for needy, indigent, handicapped, or dependent adults.

Cases involving dependent and neglected children come within the jurisdiction of district courts. County juvenile improvement committees appointed by the district courts assist the courts in their work with juveniles. The State Department of Public Welfare must administer or supervise all child welfare activities except those administered by the State Board of Health and make provision for establishing, extending, and strengthening child welfare services for the protection and care of homeless, dependent, and neglected children, and children in danger of becoming delinquent, including those in public and private institutions. Under this authority it may license and must supervise private and local child-caring agencies. The State Department of Public Welfare must supervise the care of dependent, neglected, and delinquent children in foster family homes and in institutions, and enforce laws pertaining to children. County departments of public welfare administer these child welfare services locally under supervision of the State department. County juvenile improvement committees perform such duties as the juvenile courts may designate and supervise detention homes where established. The State Orphans' Home receives and cares for dependent and neglected children who are physically and mentally fit. The State Vocational School for Girls receives and cares for neglected girls who are physically and mentally fit.

Care of veterans in the State Soldiers' Home is administered by the board of managers of the home. The Veterans' State Welfare Commission provides assistance to World War veterans in securing employment, education, training, and comfort.

Juvenile Delinquents.—District courts have jurisdiction in cases involving delinquent children. Such children may be left in their own homes, placed under supervision of a probation officer, placed in a family home, or committed to a State or private institution or a county detention home.[2] The State Industrial School receives delinquent children of sound mind and body. Delinquent girls, if mentally and physically fit, may be committed to the State Vocational School for Girls.

Services to the Blind.—The State Department of Public Welfare must develop and cooperate with other State agencies in developing services to the blind, including prevention of blindness, location of blind persons, medical services for eye conditions, and vocational guidance and training.

Insane and Mental Defectives.—The State Insane Asylum and the Hospital for Inebriates provide care and treatment for insane persons and inebriates, respectively, committed by district courts. The chairman of the board of county commissioners may commit insane persons to the State Insane Asylum, with the approval of the district court. The State Training School provides for detention and training of epileptic and feeble-minded minors and adults. Minors capable of mental, moral, or physical training, may be committed to the school by the district courts and may be retained by the executive board after they become 21 years of age if they are mentally unfit for release. The State Board of Eugenics has charge of sterilizations.[3] The State Department of Public Welfare must use available funds for cases where special medical or material assistance is necessary to rehabilitate subnormal children, and it must supervise agencies and institutions caring for mentally handicapped children and adults.

Adult Delinquents.—The State Prison provides for confinement and training of adult delinquents. The Governor has power to grant pardons and commutations and

---

[1] The State Department of Public Welfare must cooperate with and act as agent of the Federal Government in public welfare matters of mutual concern.

[2] See discussion of care of dependent and neglected children, above, for powers of the State Department of Public Welfare and county departments of public welfare in relation to children.

[3] The State Board of Eugenics consists of the chief physician of each institution for mentally deficient persons, the president of the State medical association, a female member of the State medical association, and the secretary of the State Board of Health.

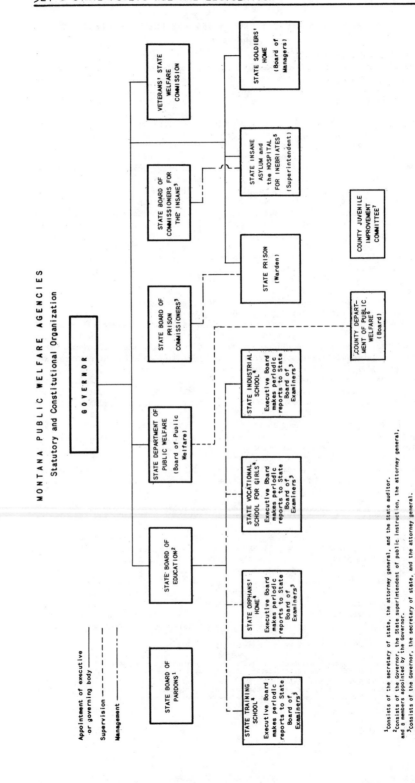

MONTANA PUBLIC WELFARE AGENCIES
Statutory and Constitutional Organization

Appointment of executive
or governing body
Supervision
Management

GOVERNOR

STATE BOARD OF PARDONS[1]

STATE BOARD OF EDUCATION[2]

STATE DEPARTMENT OF PUBLIC WELFARE
(Board of Public Welfare)

STATE BOARD OF PRISON COMMISSIONERS[3]

STATE BOARD OF COMMISSIONERS FOR THE INSANE[3]

VETERANS' STATE WELFARE COMMISSION

STATE TRAINING SCHOOL[4]
Executive Board makes periodic reports to State Board of Examiners[3]

STATE ORPHANS' HOME[4]
Executive Board makes periodic reports to State Board of Examiners[3]

STATE VOCATIONAL SCHOOL FOR GIRLS[4]
Executive Board makes periodic reports to State Board of Examiners[3]

STATE INDUSTRIAL SCHOOL[4]
Executive Board makes periodic reports to State Board of Examiners[3]

STATE PRISON
(Warden)

STATE INSANE ASYLUM and the HOSPITAL FOR INEBRIATES[5]
(Superintendent)

STATE SOLDIERS' HOME
(Board of Managers)

COUNTY DEPART- MENT OF PUBLIC WELFARE[6]
(Board)

COUNTY JUVENILE IMPROVEMENT COMMITTEE[7]

[1]Consists of the secretary of state, the attorney general, and the State auditor.
[2]Consists of the Governor, the State superintendent of public instruction, the attorney general, and 8 members appointed by the Governor.
[3]Consists of the Governor, the secretary of state, and the attorney general.
[4]The executive board of each institution consists of 2 members appointed by the Governor with the consent of the State Board of Education. The superintendent of the institution is an ex officio member. The State Board of Education appoints the superintendent for each institution.
[5]The officers of the State Insane Asylum constitute the officers of the Hospital for Inebriates.
[6]Board of county commissioners is ex officio the county welfare board.
[7]Appointed by the district judge.

to remit fines and forfeitures subject to approval of the State Board of Pardons.

Crippled Children.—The State Department of Public Welfare must make provisions to extend and improve services for locating crippled children, for medical, surgical, corrective, and other services, and for facilities for diagnosis, hospitalization, and aftercare of children who are crippled or who are suffering from conditions which lead to crippling.

Education of the Deaf, Dumb, and Blind.—The State School for the Deaf and Blind provides education for deaf, dumb, and blind children. Applications for admission are made to the State Board of Education.

Maternal and Child Health.—The State Department of Public Welfare licenses and inspects maternity homes.

SUMMARY OF STATUTORY PROVISIONS FOR PUBLIC WELFARE
NEBRASKA

Relief and Public Assistance.—General relief is administered by county boards of commissioners or supervisors, or by county boards of public welfare. Old age assistance and blind assistance are administered by county assistance committees under the supervision of the State Board of Control. Aid to dependent children in their own homes is administered by juvenile courts except for a supplementary program which is administered by county assistance committees under the supervision of the State Board of Control.

Cases involving dependent and neglected children come within the jurisdiction of juvenile courts. The State Board of Control supervises the administration of all child welfare activities and must promote the enforcement of laws for the protection of dependent, neglected, and delinquent children and must cooperate with all public and private child welfare agencies.[1] The board has the care and custody of all children committed to it by the juvenile courts and may place such children in homes or institutions. The county assistance committee acting as the county child welfare boards under the supervision of the State Board of Control may assume charge of and provide for destitute children who cannot be cared for in their own homes and children committed to them by the juvenile courts. The committee must cooperate with all public and private institutions, organizations, and agencies concerned with the care, support, education, and general welfare of children in the county. The State School for Dependent Children receives and cares for dependent and neglected children.

Veteran relief is administered by the county soldiers' relief commission. Veterans are admitted to the State Soldiers' and Sailors' Home upon application to the boards of county commissioners with the final approval of the State Board of Control.

Juvenile Delinquents.—Juvenile courts have jurisdiction in cases involving delinquent children. Such children may be allowed to remain in their own homes subject to the visitation of the probation officers. They may be committed to some suitable institution, association or individual, or to the State Industrial School for Girls or the State Industrial School for Boys. The county assistance committees, acting as the child welfare boards, must investigate complaints involving delinquent children, bring such cases before the juvenile courts, and receive any delinquents discharged to their care by the courts.[2]

Services to the Blind.—The State Board of Control must maintain a register of the blind in the State describing condition and cause of blindness and their capacity for educational and industrial training. It must assist blind persons to find remunerative employment, market their wares, and obtain tools and materials needed in their work. It must also provide suitable and practicable home teaching for those who are unable to attend the State School for the Blind, and must collect information relating to the cause, prevention, and cure of blindness.

Insane and Mental Defectives.—Boards of county commissioners of insanity pass upon all applications for the care of persons alleged to be insane. Upon determination of insanity they may authorize a hospital for the insane to receive such persons. In the event that such arrangements cannot be made, the commissioners must see that the persons are suitably provided for. The Norfolk, Hastings, Lincoln, and Genoa State Hospitals are maintained for the reception and treatment of insane persons. The county boards also constitute the subcommissions of the State Commission for the Control of Feeble-minded Persons; and they may apprehend, examine, commit, establish guardianships for, transfer, and maintain custody of any feeble-minded person within their respective counties, under the rules and regulations of the State commission. Feeble-minded persons may receive care and treatment in the State Institution for the Feeble-minded.

---

[1] The State Board of Control through the director of assistance and the director of health must cooperate with the Children's Bureau of the Department of Labor of the United States to develop plans for child welfare services.

[2] See discussion of care of dependent and neglected children, above, for powers of the State Board of Control in relation to children.

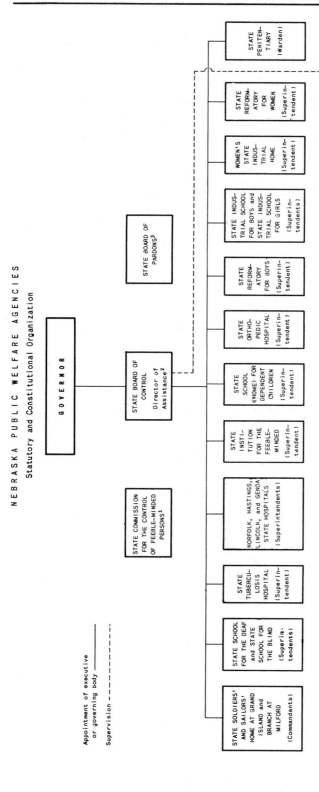

NEBRASKA PUBLIC WELFARE AGENCIES
Statutory and Constitutional Organization

Appointment of executive
or governing body ——————
Supervision — — — — — — —

GOVERNOR

STATE BOARD OF PARDONS[3]

STATE BOARD OF CONTROL
Director of Assistance[2]

STATE COMMISSION FOR THE CONTROL OF FEEBLE-MINDED PERSONS[1]

STATE PENITENTIARY (Warden)

STATE REFORMATORY FOR WOMEN (Superintendent)

WOMEN'S STATE INDUSTRIAL HOME (Superintendent)

STATE INDUSTRIAL SCHOOL FOR BOYS and STATE INDUSTRIAL SCHOOL FOR GIRLS (Superintendents)

STATE REFORMATORY FOR BOYS (Superintendent)

STATE ORTHOPEDIC HOSPITAL (Superintendent)

STATE SCHOOL (HOME) FOR DEPENDENT CHILDREN (Superintendent)

STATE INSTITUTION FOR THE FEEBLE-MINDED (Superintendent)

NORFOLK, HASTINGS, LINCOLN, and GENOA STATE HOSPITALS (Superintendents)

STATE TUBERCULOSIS HOSPITAL (Superintendent)

STATE SCHOOL FOR THE DEAF and STATE SCHOOL FOR THE BLIND (Superintendents)

STATE SOLDIERS' AND SAILORS' HOME AT GRAND ISLAND and BRANCH AT MILFORD (Commandants)

COUNTY ASSISTANCE COMMITTEE[7]

COUNTY SOLDIERS' RELIEF COMMISSION[6]

COUNTY BOARD OF PUBLIC WELFARE[5]

JUVENILE COURT[4]

[1] Composed of the chairman of the State Board of Control, the superintendent of the State Institution for the Feeble-minded, and the attorney general.

[2] The director of assistance is executive secretary of the State Board of Control.

[3] Composed of the Governor, the attorney general, and the secretary of state.

[4] Administers original program for aid to dependent children in their own homes.

[5] Appointed jointly by the county commissioners and the county judge. Establishment is optional.

[6] Composed of 3 persons appointed by the county board of commissioners or supervisors.

[7] Composed of the board of county commissioners or supervisors, the county treasurer, and, where established, the county board of public welfare.

Adult Delinquents.—The State Penitentiary, the State Reformatory for Women, the Women's State Industrial Home, and the State Reformatory for Boys provide for confinement and training of adult delinquents. The State Board of Pardons has the power to grant commutations, pardons, and paroles.

Crippled Children.—The State Board of Control, through the director of assistance, must expend State assistance funds allotted for crippled children to supplement other State, county, municipal, and private funds. Such funds must be used to extend and improve services for locating physically handicapped and crippled children, and for providing facilities for diagnosis, medical, surgical, corrective, and other services and care, hospitalization, and aftercare for children who are physically handicapped or crippled, or who are suffering from conditions which lead to crippling. The State Orthopedic Hospital provides care for crippled, ruptured, and deformed children.

Education of the Deaf, Dumb, and Blind.—The State School for the Deaf and the State School for the Blind provide for the education of deaf, dumb, and blind youths who cannot acquire an education in the common schools of the State.

Tuberculars.—The State Tuberculosis Hospital is maintained primarily for indigent tuberculous patients. Other tuberculous patients may be admitted under such rules and regulations as may be prescribed by the State Board of Control.

SUMMARY OF STATUTORY PROVISIONS FOR PUBLIC WELFARE
NEVADA

Relief and Public Assistance.—General relief, old age assistance, aid to dependent children in their own homes, and blind assistance are administered by boards of county commissioners under the supervision of the State Welfare Department.[1]

Cases involving dependent and neglected children come within the jurisdiction of the juvenile departments of the district courts. The State Welfare Department must supervise all child welfare services and provide supervisory or advisory services to county governments. The department is empowered to license child-caring agencies. Boards of county commissioners must apprentice minors who become county charges. The State School of Industry and the State Orphans' Home receive dependent and neglected children. County probation committees may be required to investigate any child-caring society, association, or corporation when requested by the courts, and exercise control over the internal affairs of any detention home established by the board of county commissioners. The State Board of Relief, Work Planning, and Pension Control must encourage the activities of county probation committees; and county boards of relief, work planning, and pension control, when established, must cooperate with the county probation committees in family welfare work.

Juvenile Delinquents.—Juvenile departments of district courts have jurisdiction in cases involving delinquent children. The court may allow a child to remain in its own home, appoint a guardian and order the child placed in a family home, or commit the child to an institution incorporated by Nevada or any other State, or provided by the State or any county, city, town, or village. The State School of Industry receives juvenile delinquents.[2]

Insane and Mental Defectives.—The State Hospital for Mental Diseases provides care and treatment for insane persons, idiots, and adult feeble-minded persons committed by district court judges or, in their absence, by county clerks. Feeble-minded minors may also be committed to this institution for temporary care until provision can be made for them in another State. The board of county commissioners must provide care, education, and support for feeble-minded children of their respective counties.

Adult Delinquents.—The State Prison provides for confinement and training of adult delinquents. The State Board of Parole Commissioners has charge of paroles, remission of fines and forfeitures, pardons, and commutations.

---

[1] The State Welfare Department must cooperate with the Federal Government in public welfare matters and administer or supervise the administration of Federal funds for public welfare. The State Board of Relief, Work Planning, and Pension Control, which is also the State Welfare Department, must cooperate with the Federal emergency relief administrator of the State and officers of the Federal Government empowered to administer Federal relief (either work or direct), and it has the power to make available to the several counties funds supplied to the board by the State and Federal governments for relief of destitution and the purchase of supplies to be used for relief projects. County boards of relief, work planning, and pension control, where established, must assist the State board, make investigations, and report to the county and municipal authorities concerning the questions of dependency and the distribution of relief funds.

[2] See discussion of care of dependent and neglected children, above, for powers of the State Board of Relief, Work Planning, and Pension Control; county boards of relief, work planning, and pension control; county probation committees; and boards of county commissioners in relation to children.

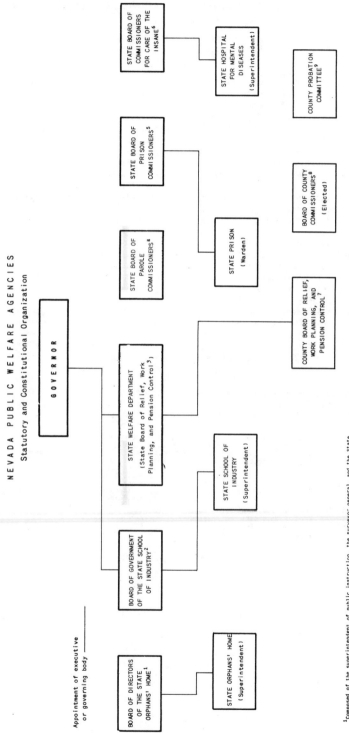

NEVADA PUBLIC WELFARE AGENCIES
Statutory and Constitutional Organization

GOVERNOR

Appointment of executive or governing body ——————

BOARD OF DIRECTORS OF THE STATE ORPHANS' HOME[1]

STATE ORPHANS' HOME (Superintendent)

BOARD OF GOVERNMENT OF THE STATE SCHOOL OF INDUSTRY[2]

STATE SCHOOL OF INDUSTRY (Superintendent)

STATE WELFARE DEPARTMENT (State Board of Relief, Work Planning, and Pension Control[3])

COUNTY BOARD OF RELIEF, WORK PLANNING, AND PENSION CONTROL[7]

STATE BOARD OF PAROLE COMMISSIONERS[4]

STATE PRISON (Warden)

BOARD OF COUNTY COMMISSIONERS[8] (Elected)

STATE BOARD OF PRISON COMMISSIONERS[5]

STATE BOARD OF COMMISSIONERS FOR CARE OF THE INSANE[6]

STATE HOSPITAL FOR MENTAL DISEASES (Superintendent)

COUNTY PROBATION COMMITTEE[9]

[1] Composed of the superintendent of public instruction, the surveyor general, and the State treasurer.

[2] Governor is an ex officio member.

[3] Designated as the board of the State Welfare Department.

[4] Composed of the Governor, the justices of the Supreme Court, and the attorney general.

[5] Composed of the Governor, the secretary of state, and the attorney general.

[6] Composed of the Governor, the State comptroller, and the State treasurer.

[7] Appointment is optional with the State Board of Relief, Work Planning, and Pension Control.

[8] General relief, old age assistance, blind assistance, and aid to dependent children in their own homes are administered by the board of county commissioners under the supervision of the State Welfare Department.

[9] Appointed by the judge or judges of the district court.

SUMMARY OF STATUTORY PROVISIONS FOR PUBLIC WELFARE
NEW HAMPSHIRE

Relief and Public Assistance.—General relief is administered by town overseers of the poor in all cases except those for which no town or person is responsible. Relief for such cases is administered by boards of county commissioners. Old age assistance, blind assistance, and aid to dependent children in their own homes are administered by the State Department of Public Welfare.[1] In the administration of these welfare activities the commissioner of public welfare, in the State Department of Public Welfare, must consult with the officials of the counties or towns required to contribute to the cost before determining eligibility of applicants.

Cases involving dependent and neglected children come within the jurisdiction of the juvenile courts. Neglected children may be committed by the juvenile courts to the care of the State Department of Public Welfare. The department must develop a State program for child welfare, and supervise the administration of such program by local officials or administer such child welfare activities directly. The department is empowered to license and must supervise all private institutions and boarding homes providing services or care to dependent, neglected, delinquent, or defective children. Local officials must find homes for children and contract for their support.

Veteran relief is administered in counties by the boards of county commissioners and in towns by the overseers of the poor. Care of veterans in the State Soldiers' Home is administered by the board of managers of the home.

Juvenile Delinquents.—Juvenile courts have jurisdiction in cases involving delinquent children and may order necessary care or custody, place them on probation, or commit them to the State Industrial School.[2]

Services to the Deaf and Blind.—The State Department of Public Welfare must develop a program for, or cooperate with other agencies in providing, services to the blind. These services include the locating of blind persons, medical services for eye conditions, vocational guidance and training for the blind, placement of blind persons in employment, instruction of the adult blind in their homes, other services to blind persons, and a program for the prevention of blindness.[3] The department must develop plans to provide assistance to the deaf.

Insane and Mental Defectives.—The State Hospital for the Insane provides care and treatment for insane persons committed by probate judges or admitted upon proper application to the superintendent of the institution. The Laconia State School for the Feeble-minded provides care and treatment for feeble-minded persons who are committed by probate judges. Insane or feeble-minded children coming within the jurisdiction of a juvenile court may be committed to an appropriate institution.[3]

Adult Delinquents.—The State Prison provides for confinement and training of adult delinquents. The State Probation Department provides psychiatric and psychological services. Probation officers of the department make investigations for courts upon request, perform services assigned by the State board of probation or any court, and supervise persons paroled from any institution, at the request of the institution. They also supervise, at the request of the court, persons placed on probation. The State Board of Parole makes recommendation to the Governor and council for parole of convicts and has custody of paroled convicts.

Medical Care.—The State Department of Public Welfare must develop and administer a plan for providing medical or other remedial care in cooperation with State health authorities and county and local officials. The department must develop a plan to provide assistance to tuberculous persons.

---

[1] The department must cooperate with the Federal Government in carrying out the purposes of the Federal Social Security Act and in other matters of mutual concern pertaining to public welfare, child welfare services, and public assistance.

[2] See discussion of care of dependent and neglected children, above, for other powers and duties of the State Department of Public Welfare in relation to children.

[3] The department must supervise all private agencies and institutions providing care to aged, blind, feeble-minded, and other dependent persons.

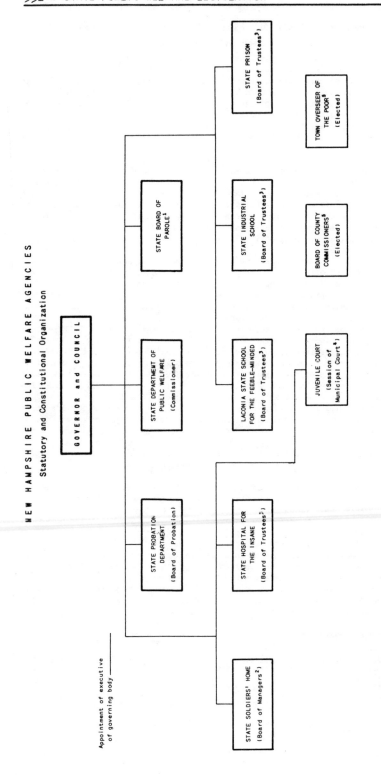

NEW HAMPSHIRE PUBLIC WELFARE AGENCIES

Statutory and Constitutional Organization

Appointment of executive
of governing body —————

GOVERNOR and COUNCIL

STATE SOLDIERS' HOME
(Board of Managers[2])

STATE PROBATION
DEPARTMENT
(Board of Probation)

STATE DEPARTMENT OF
PUBLIC WELFARE
(Commissioner[)]

STATE BOARD OF
PAROLE[1]

STATE PRISON
(Board of Trustees[3])

STATE HOSPITAL FOR
THE INSANE
(Board of Trustees[5])

LACONIA STATE SCHOOL
FOR THE FEEBLE-MINDED
(Board of Trustees[3])

STATE INDUSTRIAL
SCHOOL
(Board of Trustees[3])

TOWN OVERSEER OF
THE POOR[5]
(Elected)

JUVENILE COURT
(Session of
Municipal Court[4])

BOARD OF COUNTY
COMMISSIONERS[5]
(Elected)

[1] Composed of the board of trustees of the State Prison.

[2] Composed of the Governor, commanders of the Grand Army of the Republic, the United Spanish War Veterans, and the Veterans of Foreign Wars, the adjutant of the American Legion for New Hampshire, and 5 additional members appointed by the Governor with the advice of the council.

[3] The Governor and 1 member of the council appointed by him serve as ex officio members of the boards of trustees.

[4] Has jurisdiction over neglected and delinquent children.

[5] Administers general relief and veteran relief.

SUMMARY OF STATUTORY PROVISIONS FOR PUBLIC WELFARE
NEW JERSEY

Relief and Public Assistance.—General relief is administered by overseers of the poor, county welfare boards, or local assistance boards.[1] The State Financial Assistance Commission apportions State and Federal funds for relief and public assistance. The Board of Control of the State Department of Institutions and Agencies is empowered to inspect all county and city institutions for the poor and must inspect all institutions or organizations which receive State funds.

Old age assistance is administered by county welfare boards under the supervision of the division of old age assistance of the State Department of Institutions and Agencies.[2] Aid to dependent children in their own homes is administered by county welfare boards assisted by the State Board of Children's Guardians. Appeals may be taken to the State Department of Institutions and Agencies. Blind assistance is administered jointly by county welfare boards and the commissioner of institutions and agencies with the State Commission for the Amelioration of the Condition of the Blind serving in an advisory capacity.

Cases involving dependent and neglected children come within the jurisdiction of the juvenile and domestic relations courts. The State Department of Institutions and Agencies may cooperate with the county welfare boards in developing services for care of dependent and neglected children and children in danger of becoming delinquent. The Board of Control of the State Department of Institutions and Agencies has power to visit all institutions or agencies where children are placed and to inspect private agencies caring for dependent children; it must inspect all institutions or organizations which receive State funds. The State Board of Children's Guardians has care and supervision of children adjudged public charges and must place children in homes or, for temporary care, in child-caring institutions. It has general supervision over all dependent and neglected children who are public charges, including those in county institutions.

Veterans' pensions are administered by the State Adjutant General.[3] Care in the State Memorial Home for Disabled Soldiers and the State Memorial Home for Disabled Soldiers, Sailors, Marines, and Their Wives and Widows is administered by the boards of managers of the homes; judges of the courts of common pleas certify eligibility of applicants. The board of managers of the State Memorial Home for Disabled Soldiers may grant relief to persons as outpatients.

Juvenile Delinquents.—Juvenile courts have jurisdiction in cases involving delinquent children. The court may commit a child to a probation officer, State or county institution, or to the State Board of Children's Guardians. Boys may be committed to the State Home for Boys, and girls to the State Home for Girls.[4]

Services to the Blind.—The State Commission for the Amelioration of the Condition of the Blind must maintain a register of the blind in the State; may study causes of blindness and cooperate with other agencies for prevention of blindness; and may make loans to the blind of capital and equipment for productive activity.[5]

---

[1] In counties operating under the county system whereby the poor are chargeable to the county, general relief is administered by county welfare boards. In counties operating under the local system whereby the poor are chargeable to the townships, towns, boroughs, and cities, general relief is administered by the overseers of the poor for the respective political subdivision. Local assistance boards must be appointed in all municipalities (including counties). To administer general relief financed from State funds the county boards of chosen freeholders in counties operating under the local system may establish a county welfare house which is controlled by the county welfare board and the county superintendent of welfare. The superintendent has general jurisdiction of the poor throughout the county or that portion of the county which maintains a welfare house. He has the authority and power of an overseer of the poor in municipalities which have no such duly constituted officer and which consent to his acting in this capacity. However, county welfare boards in such instances have the power to designate some other officer as overseer of the poor.

[2] The State Department of Institutions and Agencies is authorized to cooperate with the Federal Government in public welfare matters of mutual concern.

[3] *Need* is not specified as a condition of eligibility for veterans' pensions.

[4] See discussion of care of dependent and neglected children, above, for powers of the State Board of Children's Guardians, State Department of Institutions and Agencies, and county welfare boards in relation to children.

[5] The commission may also provide instruction of indigent deaf, dumb, blind, feeble-minded, or partially blind persons. The State Board of Institutions and Agencies has power to inspect private institutions and noninstitutional agencies for care of blind, deaf, and dumb persons.

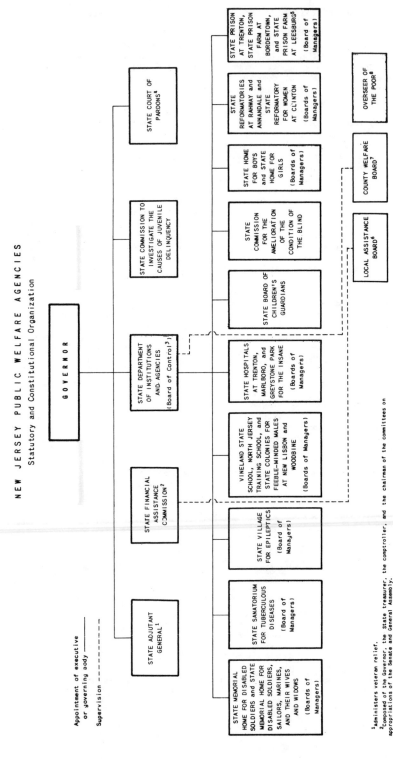

NEW JERSEY PUBLIC WELFARE AGENCIES
Statutory and Constitutional Organization

Appointment of executive
or governing body ————————
Supervision ————————

[1] Administers veteran relief.
[2] Composed of the Governor, the State treasurer, the comptroller, and the chairman of the committees on appropriations of the Senate and General Assembly.
[3] The Governor is an ex officio member.
[4] Composed of the Governor, the Chancellor, and 6 judges of the court of errors and appeals.
[5] These 3 institutions constitute the State prison system.
[6] Must be established by the chief executive of municipality with the consent of the governing body to administer State funds for general relief.
[7] Appointed by the county board of chosen freeholders.
[8] Appointed by the governing body of the municipality.

Insane and Mental Defectives.—The State Department of Institutions and Agencies controls State institutions for insane and mentally defective persons. The Board of Control of the State Department of Institutions and Agencies has power to inspect county insane hospitals, private institutions, and noninstitutional agencies for care of the insane, epileptic, and feeble-minded; it must inspect institutions and organizations which receive State funds. Care and treatment for the insane are provided in the State Hospitals at Trenton, Marlboro, and Greystone Park. The Vineland State School provides care and treatment for mentally defective women and children. Feeble-minded women are cared for in the North Jersey Training School, and mentally defective males and defective delinquent males are cared for in the State Colonies for Feeble-minded Males at New Lisbon and Woodbine. Epileptic persons are cared for in the State Village for Epileptics. Commitments to all these institutions are made by courts of common pleas.

Adult Delinquents.—The State Department of Institutions and Agencies has control of the State prison system, and the Board of Control of the State Department of Institutions and Agencies has power to inspect county and city correctional institutions and places of detention. The State Prison at Trenton, State Prison Farms at Bordentown and Leesburg, the State Reformatories at Rahway and Annandale (for men), and the State Reformatory for Women at Clinton provide for confinement and training of adult delinquents. Subject to the procedure prescribed by the Board of Control of the State Department of Institutions and Agencies, the boards of managers of correctional institutions have charge of paroles. The State Court of Pardons may remit fines and forfeitures, grant paroles, commute sentences, and grant pardons except in cases of impeachment.

Tuberculars.—The State Sanatorium for Tuberculous Diseases provides care and treatment for tuberculous persons committed by courts of common pleas. The State Department of Institutions and Agencies has power to inspect county tuberculosis hospitals.

SUMMARY OF STATUTORY PROVISIONS FOR PUBLIC WELFARE
NEW MEXICO

Relief and Public Assistance.—Local funds for general relief are administered by boards of county commissioners, city councils, or other governing boards of cities, towns, or villages. State funds for general relief, old age assistance, aid to dependent children in their own homes, and blind assistance are administered by the State Department of Public Welfare assisted by local boards of public welfare.[1] The State department must inspect and require reports from all private institutions, boarding homes, and agencies providing assistance, care, or other direct services to the aged, blind, and other dependent persons.[2]

District courts have jurisdiction in cases involving dependent and neglected children. The Orphans' Home and Industrial School provides care for such children. The State Department of Public Welfare must administer and supervise all child welfare activities, and it must inspect and require reports from all private institutions, boarding homes, and agencies providing assistance, care, or other direct services to dependent, neglected, and delinquent children.

Juvenile Delinquents.—Juvenile courts have jurisdiction in cases involving delinquent children who are wards of the court. Delinquent boys may be committed to the State Industrial School, and delinquent girls may be committed to the State Girls' Welfare Home.[3]

Services to the Blind.—The State Department of Public Welfare must initiate, or cooperate with other agencies in developing, measures for the prevention of blindness, restoration of eyesight, and vocational adjustment of blind persons.

Insane and Mental Defectives.—The State Insane Asylum and State Home and Training School for Mental Defectives provide care and treatment for insane persons and mental defectives, respectively. Commitments to these institutions are made by district courts. Care and service to mentally defective children are administered or supervised by the State Department of Public Welfare. The State Department must also inspect and require reports from all private institutions, boarding homes, and agencies providing assistance, care, or other direct services to the feeble-minded.

Adult Delinquents.—The State Penitentiary provides for confinement and training of adult delinquents. The State Prison Board adopts regulations for prisoners, including regulations for paroles.

Crippled Children.—The State Department of Public Welfare must administer services for crippled children, including extension and improvement of services for locating children who are crippled or who are suffering from conditions which lead to crippling. It must provide corrective and other services, care, and facilities for diagnosis, hospitalization, and aftercare for such children. The department supervises those services not administered directly by it, and must inspect and require reports from all private institutions, boarding homes, and agencies providing assistance, care, or other direct services to crippled children.

Vocational Rehabilitation.—The State Department of Public Welfare must cooperate with health and welfare groups and any State agency charged with the administration of laws providing for vocational rehabilitation of physically handicapped persons.

[1] The State department may, in its discretion, establish local boards of public welfare and may allow such boards to determine whether or not assistance shall be granted and the amount thereof.

[2] The State Department of Public Welfare must cooperate with and act as the agent of the Federal Government in public welfare matters of mutual concern. It must develop plans in cooperation with other public and private agencies for the prevention as well as treatment of conditions giving rise to public welfare problems. For names of State-aided institutions, see organizational chart.

[3] See discussion of care of dependent and neglected children, above, for powers of the State Department of Public Welfare in relation to children.

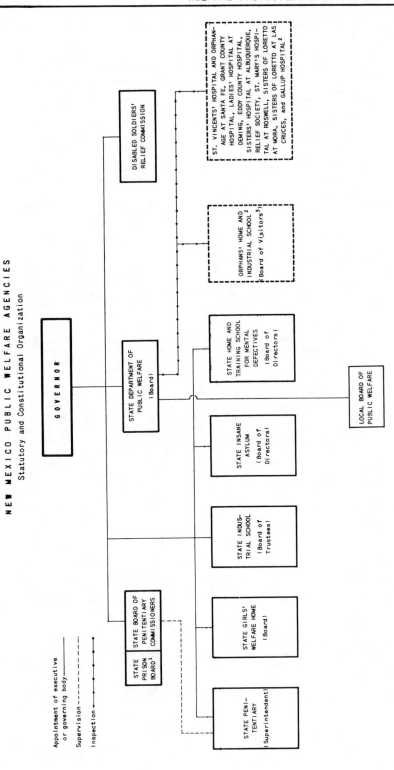

NEW MEXICO PUBLIC WELFARE AGENCIES
Statutory and Constitutional Organization

Appointment of executive
or governing body ─────────
Supervision ─ ─ ─ ─ ─ ─ ─ ─
Inspection ●─●─●─●─●─●

GOVERNOR

DISABLED SOLDIERS' RELIEF COMMISSION

ST. VINCENTS' HOSPITAL AND ORPHANAGE AT SANTA FE, GRANT COUNTY HOSPITAL, LADIES' HOSPITAL AT DEMING, EDDY COUNTY HOSPITAL, SISTERS' HOSPITAL AT ALBUQUERQUE, RELIEF SOCIETY, ST. MARY'S HOSPITAL AT ROSWELL, SISTERS OF LORETTO AT MORA, SISTERS OF LORETTO AT LAS CRUCES, and GALLUP HOSPITAL[2]

ORPHANS' HOME AND INDUSTRIAL SCHOOL[2] (Board of Visitors[3])

STATE DEPARTMENT OF PUBLIC WELFARE (Board)

STATE HOME AND TRAINING SCHOOL FOR MENTAL DEFECTIVES (Board of Directors)

STATE INSANE ASYLUM (Board of Directors)

STATE INDUSTRIAL SCHOOL (Board of Trustees)

STATE GIRLS' WELFARE HOME (Board)

STATE BOARD OF PENITENTIARY COMMISSIONERS

STATE PRISON BOARD[1]

STATE PENITENTIARY (Superintendent)

LOCAL BOARD OF PUBLIC WELFARE

[1]Consists of the State Board of Penitentiary Commissioners and the superintendent of the penitentiary.

[2]These institutions are State-aided.

[3]Consists of the archbishop of the State, the Governor, the attorney general, and the chief justice of the Supreme Court.

SUMMARY OF STATUTORY PROVISIONS FOR PUBLIC WELFARE
NEW YORK

Relief and Public Assistance.—General relief, old age assistance, and blind assistance are administered by the local public welfare officials of the public welfare districts,[1] under the supervision of the State Department of Social Welfare. Aid to dependent children in their own homes is administered by the city and county boards of child welfare, where they exist, or by the local public welfare officials.

Cases involving dependent and neglected children come within the jurisdiction of the children's courts. All children boarded, placed out, or committed by court order are subject to the visitation and supervision of the State Department of Social Welfare which must also visit, investigate, and supervise all child-caring institutions, city and county boards of child welfare, and commissioners of public welfare. Local public welfare officials are responsible for the welfare of children in need of public care, support, and protection not inconsistent with the jurisdiction of the children's court, and exclusive of the children under the care of the local boards of child welfare. They must cooperate with the children's courts, boards of child welfare, and other governmental and private agencies. They must also administer relief and care to children directly or through an authorized agency, administer and supervise relief to families with destitute children in order to prevent separation, and investigate and institute cases involving neglected children before the children's court. The Thomas Indian School provides care, training, and education for orphan, destitute, or neglected Indian children.

Pensions in the form of a cash allowance for veterans having a service-connected disability of at least 10 percent and in need are administered by the veteran relief commissioner of the State bureau for the relief of sick and disabled New York veterans in the division of military and naval affairs of the executive department under the supervision of the State Adjutant General. Other pensions in the form of annuities for permanent disability because of loss of sight are administered by the State Adjutant General. Direct relief is administered by the relief committees of various veteran organizations.[2] Admissions to the State Women's Relief Corps Home are determined by the board of visitors of the home, and care therein is supervised by the State Board of Social Welfare.

Juvenile Delinquents.—The children's courts have jurisdiction in cases involving delinquent children. Such children may be placed on probation, remain at home or in the home of a relative or other fit person or agency, or they may be committed to a suitable institution or discharged to the custody of the commissioner of public welfare or other officer, board, or department authorized to receive children. All children boarded out, placed, or committed by a court order are subject to the visitation and supervision of the State Department of Social Welfare. Public welfare officials must bring cases involving delinquent children before the children's court and receive delinquent children discharged to their care by such court. The State Training School for Girls, the State Training School for Boys, and the State Agricultural and Industrial School provide care and training for children committed to them by the children's court.

Services to the Blind.—The State commission for the blind, under the supervision and control of the State Board of Social Welfare, must maintain a register describing the condition, causes of blindness, capacity for education, and industrial training of each blind person in the State. The commission must maintain one or more bureaus of information and may establish training schools and workshops to aid the blind in finding employment and teach them trades and occupations.

---

[1]For the purpose of administration of public relief, the cities of New York, Kingston, Oswego, Poughkeepsie, and the town and city of Newburgh each constitute a city public welfare district. Further, the territory of each county and the territory of each county exclusive of one of the above cities constitute a county public welfare district. The city of Auburn may elect to become a city public welfare district. In the administration of old age assistance, the territory of each public welfare district constitutes an old age assistance district. The Buffalo Board of Social Welfare is responsible for the administration of general relief and veteran relief in the city of Buffalo.

[2]Civil War nurses are eligible to receive relief from the State Department of Social Welfare or the State Department of the National Association of Civil War Army Nurses upon application to a local public welfare official.

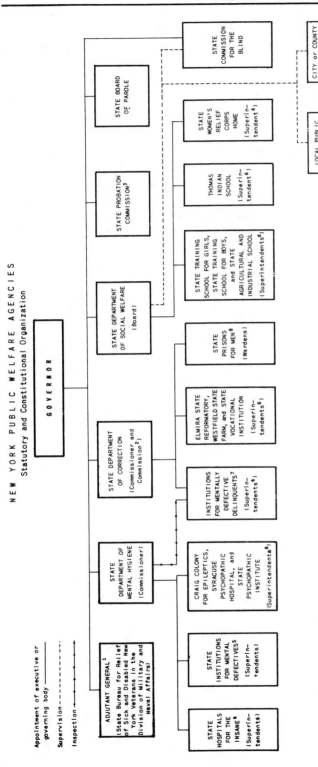

N E W   Y O R K   P U B L I C   W E L F A R E   A G E N C I E S
Statutory and Constitutional Organization

Appointment of executive or governing body ——————
Supervision ———————————
Inspection ⊷⊷⊷⊷⊷⊷⊷⊷⊷⊷

GOVERNOR

ADJUTANT GENERAL[1]
(State Bureau for Relief of Sick and Disabled New York Veterans in the Division of Military and Naval Affairs)

STATE DEPARTMENT OF MENTAL HYGIENE
(Commissioner)

STATE DEPARTMENT OF CORRECTION
(Commissioner and Commission[2])

STATE DEPARTMENT OF SOCIAL WELFARE
(Board)

STATE PROBATION COMMISSION[3]

STATE BOARD OF PAROLE

STATE COMMISSION FOR THE BLIND

STATE HOSPITALS FOR THE INSANE[4]
(Superin-tendents)

STATE INSTITUTIONS FOR MENTAL DEFECTIVES[5]
(Superin-tendents)

CRAIG COLONY FOR EPILEPTICS, SYRACUSE PSYCHOPATHIC HOSPITAL, and STATE PSYCHOPATHIC INSTITUTE
(Superintendents[6])

INSTITUTIONS FOR MENTALLY DEFECTIVE DELINQUENTS[7]
(Superin-tendents[6])

ELMIRA STATE REFORMATORY, WESTFIELD STATE FARM, and STATE VOCATIONAL INSTITUTION
(Superin-tendents[6])

STATE PRISONS FOR MEN[8]
(Wardens)

STATE TRAINING SCHOOL FOR GIRLS, STATE TRAINING SCHOOL FOR BOYS, and STATE AGRICULTURAL AND INDUSTRIAL SCHOOL
(Superintendents[6])

THOMAS INDIAN SCHOOL
(Superin-tendent[6])

STATE WOMEN'S RELIEF CORPS HOME
(Superin-tendent[6])

LOCAL PUBLIC WELFARE OFFICIALS[9]

CITY or COUNTY BOARD OF CHILD WELFARE[10]

[1] The Adjutant General must appoint with the approval of the governor a veterans' relief commissioner in each assembly district, who must extend relief to all qualified persons. The Adjutant general may at any time remove these officials.

[2] The commission investigates and acts in an advisory capacity.

[3] Composed of the state commissioner of corrections, the director of probation in the State Department of Correction, 4 members appointed by the Governor, and 1 member elected by the others.

[4] These are the Binghamton State Hospital, Brooklyn State Hospital, Buffalo State Hospital, Central Islip State Hospital, Creedmoor State Hospital, Gowanda State Homeopathic Hospital, Harlem Valley State Hospital, Hudson River State Hospital, Kings Park State Hospital, Manhattan State Hospital, Marcy State Hospital, Middletown State Homeopathic Hospital, Pilgrim State Hospital, Rochester State Hospital, Rockland State Hospital, St. Lawrence State Hospital, Utica State Hospital, and Willard State Hospital. Each institution has a board of visitors appointed by the Governor.

[5] These are the Letchworth Village, Newark State School, Rome State School, Syracuse State School, and Wassaic State School. Each institution has a board of visitors appointed by the Governor.

[6] Each institution has a board of visitors appointed by the Governor.

[7] These are the Albion State Training School, Dannemora State Hospital, Matteawan State Hospital, the institution for Male Defective Delinquents at Napanoch, and Woodbourne Institution for Defective Delinquents.

[8] These are Attica Prison, Auburn Prison, Clinton Prison, Great Meadow Prison, Sing Sing Prison, and Wallkill Prison.

[9] The term public welfare official includes county commissioner of public welfare, city commissioner of public welfare, town public welfare officer, or city public welfare officer. Such officials are appointed or elected according to the law applicable to the particular county or city.

[10] A county board is appointed by the county judge, and the county commissioner of public welfare is a member, ex officio. A city board is appointed by the mayor.

It may also assist blind persons to become self-supporting by furnishing materials and machinery, and may assist them in the sale and distribution of their products.

Insane and Mental Defectives.—The State Department of Mental Hygiene has jurisdiction, supervision, and control of all State institutions for insane, mentally deficient, and epileptic persons.[3] Patients are admitted to institutions upon court commitment or upon voluntary application. The children's courts have jurisdiction in cases involving defective children, and local public welfare officials must administer care to such children.[4]

Adult Delinquents.—The commissioner of the Department of Correction is charged with the supervision, management, and control of the State institutions for adult delinquents. Six State prisons,[5] the Elmira State Reformatory, the Westfield State Farm, and the State Vocational Institution provide for the confinement and training of adult delinquents. The Albion State Training School, the Institution for Male Defective Delinquents, the Matteawan State Hospital, the Dannemora State Hospital, and the Woodbourne Institution for Defective Delinquents provide for confinement, care, treatment, and training of mentally deficient adult delinquents. The director of probation in the State Department of Correction exercises general supervision over the administration of probation with the advice of the State Probation Commission. The State Board of Parole administers provisions relating to parole and supervises all persons so released.

[3] See organizational chart for institutions caring for these persons.

[4] The children's court and the public welfare officials have similar duties in relation to physically handicapped children.

[5] See organizational chart.

SUMMARY OF STATUTORY PROVISIONS FOR PUBLIC WELFARE
NORTH CAROLINA

Relief and Public Assistance.—General relief is administered by boards of county commissioners through county superintendents of public welfare.[1] Old age assistance and aid to dependent children in their own homes are administered by county boards of charities and public welfare under the supervision of the State Board of Charities and Public Welfare.[2] Boards of county commissioners, subject to review by the State Board of Allotments and Appeal, may review and change decisions of the county boards of charities and public welfare. Blind assistance is administered by boards of county commissioners under the supervision of the State Commission for the Blind.

Cases involving dependent and neglected children come within the jurisdiction of juvenile courts. The State Board of Charities and Public Welfare must promote the welfare of dependent and delinquent children and provide for the placement and supervision of such children. The board licenses and must inspect private agencies and institutions for children and must investigate and supervise such institutions together with all other charitable institutions in the State. The county superintendent of public welfare is the agent of the State board for any work done by the State board within the county. He has supervision of the care of all dependent, neglected, and delinquent children in the respective counties. Homes and hospitals for indigent orphan children may be established and maintained by boards of county commissioners with the approval of the State Board of Charities and Public Welfare.

Veterans' pensions are administered by the State Board of Pensions; county pension boards certify the eligibility of applicants. The county commissioners may increase the amount of the pensions to Confederate veterans, within the county, above the amount paid by the State.[3] Care in the Confederate Soldiers' Home and the Confederate Women's Home is administered by the boards of directors of the homes.

Juvenile Delinquents.—Juvenile courts have jurisdiction in cases involving delinquent children. The courts may place the child on probation, commit it to the custody of a relative or other person, or commit it to the custody of the State Board of Charities and Public Welfare to be placed in an institution, society, association, or in a family home.[4] The Eastern Carolina Industrial Training School for Boys, the Stonewall Jackson Manual Training and Industrial School, and the Morrison Training School receive and care for juvenile delinquents.

Services to the Blind.—The State Commission for the Blind must maintain a register describing the condition, causes of blindness, and capacity for education and industrial training of each blind person. It must maintain one or more bureaus of information and industrial aid for the purpose of finding employment and teaching trades and occupations which may be followed in the home. It may furnish materials and equipment, establish one or more training schools and workshops for employment, pay wages and all necessary expenses during the training period, provide for the sale and distribution of products of the blind, and promote visits among the blind in their homes. The commission must investigate causes of blindness and take measures for the prevention of blindness.[5]

Insane and Mental Defectives.—The State Board of Charities and Public Welfare is responsible for the promotion of the welfare of insane and mentally defective

---

[1] The State Board of Charities and Public Welfare and the commissioner are authorized to designate the city of Rocky Mount as a welfare district, and to administer to the needy in that district through an officer appointed by the city manager subject to the approval of the State board and to be known as the city welfare officer. The city welfare officer must perform within the district all duties of county superintendents of welfare.

[2] The State Board of Charities and Public Welfare must investigate and supervise all charitable institutions in the State, and it must cooperate with the Federal Government in public welfare matters of mutual concern.

[3] Need is not specified as a condition of eligibility for veterans' pensions.

[4] See discussion of care of dependent and neglected children, above, for powers of the State Board of Charities and Public Welfare in relation to children.

[5] Similar provisions have been made for deaf persons. The State Bureau of Labor for the Deaf must ascertain what trades and occupations are most suitable for the deaf, study methods of education for promoting general welfare of the deaf, and aid them to secure employment.

NORTH CAROLINA PUBLIC WELFARE AGENCIES

Statutory and Constitutional Organization

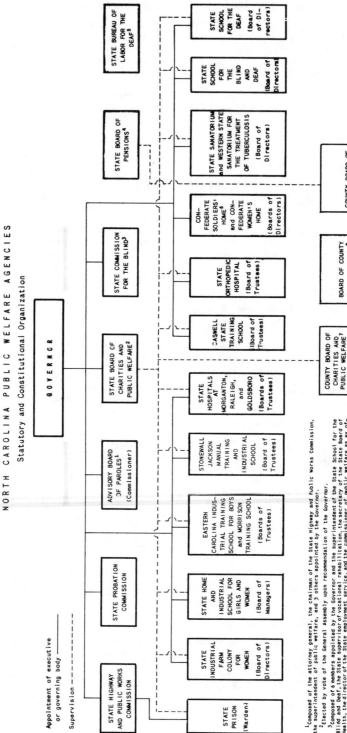

Appointment of executive or governing body ————
Supervision - - - - - - -

GOVERNOR

STATE BUREAU OF LABOR FOR THE DEAF[5]

STATE SCHOOL FOR THE DEAF (Board of Directors)

STATE SCHOOL FOR THE BLIND AND DEAF (Board of Directors)

STATE BOARD OF PENSIONS[4]

STATE SANATORIUM and WESTERN STATE SANATORIUM FOR THE TREATMENT OF TUBERCULOSIS (Board of Directors)

COUNTY BOARD OF PENSIONS[9]

STATE COMMISSION FOR THE BLIND[3]

CONFEDERATE SOLDIERS' HOME[6] and CONFEDERATE WOMEN'S HOME (Boards of Directors)

STATE ORTHOPEDIC HOSPITAL (Board of Trustees)

BOARD OF COUNTY COMMISSIONERS[8] (Elected)

STATE BOARD OF CHARITIES AND PUBLIC WELFARE[2]

CASWELL STATE TRAINING SCHOOL (Board of Trustees)

COUNTY BOARD OF CHARITIES AND PUBLIC WELFARE[7] Makes periodic reports to Board of County Commissioners

ADVISORY BOARD OF PAROLES[1] (Commissioner)

STATE HOSPITALS AT MORGANTON, RALEIGH, and GOLDSBORO (Boards of Trustees)

STATE PROBATION COMMISSION

STONEWALL JACKSON MANUAL TRAINING AND INDUSTRIAL SCHOOL (Board of Trustees)

EASTERN CAROLINA INDUSTRIAL TRAINING SCHOOL FOR BOYS and MORRISON TRAINING SCHOOL (Boards of Trustees)

STATE HOME AND INDUSTRIAL SCHOOL FOR GIRLS AND WOMEN (Board of Managers)

STATE HIGHWAY AND PUBLIC WORKS COMMISSION

STATE INDUSTRIAL FARM COLONY FOR WOMEN (Board of Directors)

STATE PRISON (Warden)

[1] Composed of the attorney general, the chairman of the State Highway and Public Works Commission, the superintendent of public welfare, and 3 others appointed by the Governor.

[2] Elected by vote of the General Assembly upon recommendation of the Governor.

[3] Composed of 6 members appointed by the Governor and the superintendent of the State School for the Blind and Deaf, the State Supervisor of vocational rehabilitation, the secretary of the State Board of Health, the director of the State employment service, and the commissioner of public welfare as ex officio members.

[4] Composed of the Governor, the attorney general, and the State auditor.

[5] The commissioner of the bureau is appointed by the commissioner of labor and printing.

[6] The board of directors of the Confederate Soldiers' Home consists of 7 members, 3 elected by the Soldiers' Home Association and 4 appointed by the Governor.

[7] 1 member is appointed by the board of county commissioners, 1 by the State Board of Charities and Public Welfare, and the 3d is selected by the first 2 members. The county superintendent of public welfare, who is the executive of the county board of charities and public welfare, is appointed by the board of county commissioners and the county board of charities and public welfare, jointly.

[8] The administration of blind assistance by the board of county commissioners is supervised by the State Commission for the Blind, and the board's participation in the administration of old age assistance and aid to dependent children in their own homes is supervised by the State Board of Charities and Public Welfare.

[9] Composed of the clerk of the superior court and 3 members appointed by the State auditor.

persons. The State Hospital at Morganton provides care and treatment for insane white persons. The State Hospital at Raleigh provides care and treatment for insane and epileptic Indians and white persons. The State Hospital at Goldsboro provides care and treatment for Negro insane and feeble-minded. Commitments to these institutions are made by the clerks of superior courts. The Caswell State Training School provides care and treatment for feeble-minded and mentally defective persons admitted upon applications approved by the local welfare officer, the judge of the juvenile court or the clerk of the court, and the board of trustees of the school. The county superintendent of public welfare may petition for the sterilization of any feeble-minded, epileptic, or mentally deficient person on parole from a State institution, or at the request of a superintendent of an institution he may make a similar petition in relation to inmates of the institution.

Adult Delinquents.—The State Board of Charities and Public Welfare must investigate and supervise all penal institutions in the State. The State Prison, State Industrial Farm Colony for Women, and the State Home and Industrial School for Girls and Women provide for confinement and training of adult delinquents. The State Highway and Public Works Commission establishes and controls all prison camps; and it has charge of employment of prisoners. The Advisory Board of Paroles assists the Governor in granting pardons, paroles, reprieves, and commutations. The State Probation Commission must supervise administration of probation except in cases under jurisdiction of the juvenile courts; and it must cooperate with the courts. The commission is authorized to cooperate with county superintendents of public welfare and the State Board of Charities and Public Welfare.

Crippled Children.—The State Orthopedic Hospital provides care and treatment for crippled children.

Education of the Deaf, Dumb, and Blind.—The State School for the Blind and the Deaf provides education and care for blind white children and for deaf and blind colored children. Application for admission is made to the board of directors of the school. The State School for the Deaf provides education and care for deaf white children admitted upon application to the board of directors of the school.

Tuberculars.—The State Sanatorium for the Treatment of Tuberculosis and the Western State Sanatorium for the Treatment of Tuberculosis provide care and treatment for patients admitted by the board of directors of these institutions.

Maternal and Child Health.—The State Board of Charities and Public Welfare must inspect and make reports on maternity homes.

SUMMARY OF STATUTORY PROVISIONS FOR PUBLIC WELFARE
NORTH DAKOTA

Relief and Public Assistance.—General relief is administered by county welfare boards under the supervision of the State Public Welfare Board. Old age assistance, aid to dependent children in their own homes, and blind assistance are administered by the State Public Welfare Board assisted by the county welfare boards.[1]

Cases involving dependent and neglected children come within the jurisdiction of juvenile courts. It is the power and duty of the State Public Welfare Board to promote the welfare of dependent, neglected, and delinquent children and to provide for the placement and supervision of dependent, neglected, and delinquent children subject to the control of any court having jurisdiction of the case.[2] The State board is also empowered to license child-caring agencies. County welfare boards under the supervision of the State Public Welfare Board must cooperate with all licensed private agencies and must coordinate all public and private activities in behalf of children. County boards of visitors and children's guardians, where established, must visit child-caring institutions, societies, associations, and persons receiving children. Boards of county commissioners may bind out poor children and see that they are properly cared for.

Veterans' pensions are administered by the State adjutant general and the Governor; and care in the State Soldiers' Home is administered by the board of trustees of the home.[3]

Juvenile Delinquents.—Juvenile courts have jurisdiction in cases involving delinquent children. The court may allow a child to remain at home; appoint a guardian and order the child placed in a family home; or it may commit the child to an association, an incorporated institution for delinquent children, to the State Training School, or to a local public institution for delinquent children. It may permit proceedings against the child in accordance with laws governing the commission of crimes. When the health of the child requires, the court may place it in a public hospital or institution.[4]

Services to the Blind.—The State Public Welfare Board must develop or cooperate with other agencies in developing measures for the prevention of blindness, the restoration of eyesight, and the vocational adjustment of blind persons. Employment and instruction for the blind is provided in the State Blind Asylum.

Insane and Mental Defectives.—The State Hospital for the Insane and the Grafton State School provide care and treatment for the insane and for the feeble-minded, idiotic, and epileptic, respectively. Commitments are by boards of county commissioners of insanity. A board of county commissioners of insanity may, in conjunction with the juvenile court, commit any feeble-minded dependent, neglected, or delinquent child to the Grafton State School. Sterilization of inmates is the responsibility of the board of examiners of each institution.[5]

Adult Delinquents.—The State Penitentiary provides for confinement and training of adult delinquents. The board of examiners of the institution determines whether an inmate should be sterilized. The Governor, in conjunction with the State Board of Reprieves, Commutations, and Pardons may remit fines and forfeitures, and may grant reprieves, commutations, and pardons except in cases of treason and impeachment. The State Board of Pardons must pass upon applications for discharge or parole of all persons sentenced under the indeterminate sentence law.

---

[1]The State Public Welfare Board must act as the agent of the State in any social welfare activity initiated by the Federal Government and must cooperate with the Federal Government in public welfare matters of mutual concern.

[2]The State Board of Administration has similar powers and duties in relation to children. In order to receive benefits under the Federal Social Security Act, the State Board of Administration and the State Public Welfare Board agreed to consolidate the activities of the children's bureau of the State Board of Administration with those of the newly organized division of child welfare of the State Public Welfare Board by employing one supervisor to administer both agencies.

[3]*Need* is not specified as a condition of eligibility for veterans' pensions or care in the State Soldiers' Home.

[4]See discussion of care of dependent and neglected children, above, for powers of the county boards of visitors and children's guardians, State Public Welfare Board, and State Board of Administration in relation to children.

[5]The board of examiners for each institution consists of the chief medical officers of the institution, the secretary of the State Board of Health, and a physician appointed by the State Board of Administration.

NORTH DAKOTA PUBLIC WELFARE AGENCIES
Statutory and Constitutional Organization

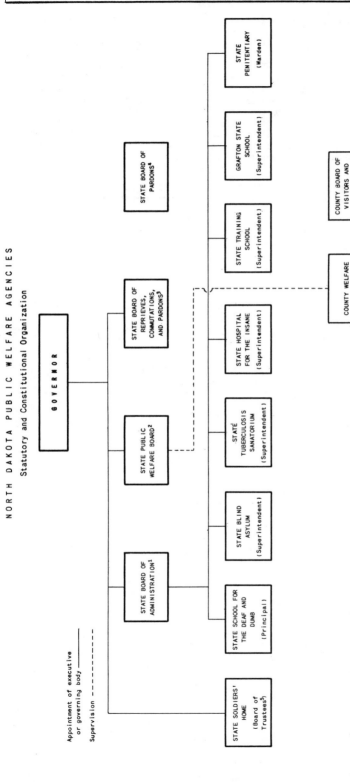

Appointment of executive
or governing body ——————

Supervision — — — — —

[1]Composed of the superintendent of public instruction, the commissioner of labor, and 3 members appointed by the Governor.

[2]Appointed by the Governor, the attorney general, and the commissioner of agriculture and labor.

[3]Composed of the Governor, the attorney general, the chief justice of the Supreme Court, and 2 members appointed by the Governor.

[4]Composed of the warden of the State Penitentiary, the prison physician, the chaplain, and 1 other person appointed by the State Board of Administration.

[5]Composed of 5 members, 4 of whom are appointed by the Governor and the 5th by the department commander of the Grand Army of the Republic.

[6]Not less than 3 nor more than 7 members may be county commissioners. Other members are appointed by county commissioners with consent of the State Public Welfare Board.

[7]Establishment optional with district judge.

GOVERNOR

STATE BOARD OF ADMINISTRATION[1]

STATE PUBLIC WELFARE BOARD[2]

STATE BOARD OF REPRIEVES, COMMUTATIONS, AND PARDONS[3]

STATE BOARD OF PARDONS[4]

STATE SOLDIERS' HOME
(Board of Trustees[5])

STATE SCHOOL FOR THE DEAF AND DUMB
(Principal)

STATE BLIND ASYLUM
(Superintendent)

STATE TUBERCULOSIS SANATORIUM
(Superintendent)

STATE HOSPITAL FOR THE INSANE
(Superintendent)

STATE TRAINING SCHOOL
(Superintendent)

GRAFTON STATE SCHOOL
(Superintendent)

STATE PENITENTIARY
(Warden)

COUNTY WELFARE BOARD[6]

COUNTY BOARD OF VISITORS AND CHILDREN'S GUARDIANS[7]

Crippled Children.—The State Public Welfare Board must secure surgical and hospital care for crippled children committed to it by the county courts and administer services to crippled children under provisions of the Federal Social Security Act.[6]

Education of the Deaf and Dumb.—The State School for the Deaf and Dumb provides education for children of suitable age and capacity. The Governor may arrange with the States of South Dakota or Minnesota for the education of blind children.

Tuberculars.—The Tuberculosis Sanatorium provides care and treatment for tubercular persons admitted upon the approval of the superintendent of the Tuberculosis Sanatorium and the State Board of Administration.

Public Health Service and Maternal and Child Health.—The State Public Welfare Board must administer, allocate, and distribute State and Federal funds available for public health service and maternal and child health.

---

[6]These provisions include services for locating crippled children, providing medical, surgical, corrective, and other care, and facilities for diagnosis, hospitalization, and aftercare for children who are crippled or who are suffering from conditions which lead to crippling.

SUMMARY OF STATUTORY PROVISIONS FOR PUBLIC WELFARE
OHIO

Relief and Public Assistance.—General relief is administered by boards of county commissioners, township trustees, or city directors of public safety. The State Relief Director must examine the conduct and method of local relief administration and the State auditor is empowered to make outside investigation of relief recipients. Old age assistance is administered by the division of aid for the aged of the State Department of Public Welfare. Aid to dependent children in their own homes is administered by juvenile court judges or other board or agency designated by charter or local law, under the supervision of the division of public assistance of the State Department of Public Welfare. Blind assistance is administered by boards of county commissioners under the supervision of the commission for the blind within the Department of Public Welfare.[1]

Cases involving dependent and neglected children come within the jurisdiction of juvenile courts or courts of common pleas and probate courts where there are no juvenile courts. The State Department of Public Welfare, through the division of public assistance, licenses child-caring and child-placing agencies and must investigate the care given by all public and private institutions and agencies. It must seek family homes for the wards of the department and maintain a bureau of juvenile research. Boards of trustees of county children's homes or county child welfare boards, where established by boards of county commissioners with the approval of the director of the State Department of Public Welfare, must receive children for care and treatment and locate homes for such children. The probation department of the juvenile court supervises children placed in private homes. The State Soldiers' and Sailors' Orphans' Home provides care for children of indigent soldiers, sailors, marines, and nurses. Such children are admitted upon application to the trustees of the home.

Direct relief to veterans is administered by county soldiers' relief commissions which appoint township or ward soldiers' relief committees to assist them. Veterans are admitted to the State Soldiers' and Sailors' Home and the Madison Home for veterans upon application to the State Department of Public Welfare.

Juvenile Delinquents.—Cases involving delinquent children come within the jurisdiction of the juvenile courts. The court may commit a child to a county children's home, private home, State or county institution, training or industrial school, a child-caring association approved by the State Department of Public Welfare, or to the State Department of Public Welfare. The court may order a child placed in a public or private hospital or institution for special care if the health or condition of the child requires it. Boards of county visitors[2] represent the interests of a child when proceedings have been instituted for its commitment to the Boys' State Industrial School or the Girls' State Industrial Home or to institutions receiving juvenile delinquents.

Services to the Blind.—The commission for the blind within the State Department of Public Welfare must act as a bureau of information and industrial aid to assist the blind in finding employment and to teach trades. The commission must maintain a register of the blind, describing condition and causes of blindness and capacity for training of each blind person in the State. It must also investigate causes of blindness and cooperate with the State Board of Health in developing and enforcing preventive measures. It may establish and maintain industrial training schools and workshops, provide for support of the blind during training, pay wages, and handle the sale of their products.

Insane and Mental Defectives.—Commitments to the State Hospitals for the Insane, the State Institutions for Feeble-minded, and the State Hospital for Epileptics are made by probate judges. Voluntary applications for admission to these institutions are made to the superintendents and are regulated by the division of mental diseases in the State Department of Public Welfare. The State Department of

---

[1] The State Department of Public Welfare is designated as the State agency to cooperate with the Federal Government in the administration of the Federal Social Security Act.

[2] Boards of county visitors (appointed by probate judge) must investigate all public and private charitable and correctional institutions supported in whole or in part by county or municipal taxation or under county or municipal control.

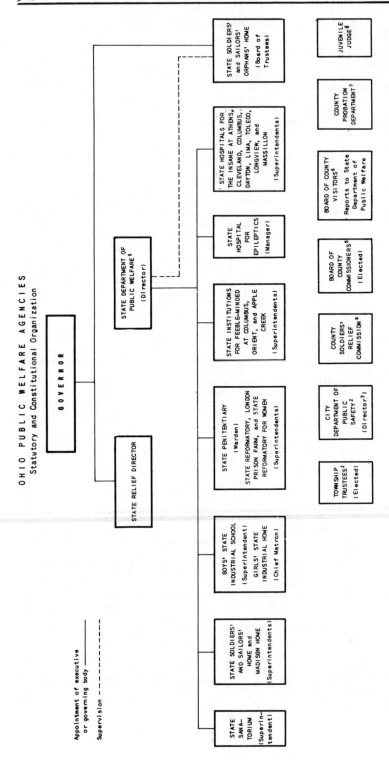

OHIO PUBLIC WELFARE AGENCIES
Statutory and Constitutional Organization

Appointment of executive
or governing body ——————
Supervision – – – – – – –

[1] The department includes the following divisions: division of public assistance, division of aid for the aged, division of charities, commission for the blind, bureau of juvenile research, board of parole, bureau of criminal identification and investigation, and division of mental diseases which includes a bureau of mental hygiene. The commissioner of mental diseases and an advisory council division of mental diseases are appointed by the Governor. The director of public welfare is an executive officer of the commission for the blind which consists of the superintendent of the State School for the Blind (controlled by the State department of Education) and 5 members appointed by the Governor.

[2] May administer general relief.

[3] Appointed by the mayor.

[4] Appointed by the judge of the court of common pleas. The county soldiers' relief commission must appoint township or ward soldiers' relief committees.

[5] Administration of aid to the blind assistance by boards of county commissioners is supervised by the commission for the blind in the State department of Public Welfare. The board of county commissioners, with the approval of the division of charities of the State Department of Public Welfare, may appoint a county child welfare board.

[6] Appointed by the probate judge.

[7] May be established by the judge or judges of the court of common pleas with concurrence of the board of county commissioners.

[8] Administration of aid to dependent children in their own homes by the juvenile judge is supervised by the division of public assistance of the State department of Public Welfare.

Public Welfare must act as a lunacy commission to determine the mental condition of any person committed to any hospital or county jail and may remove such person to the proper institution. The division of mental diseases has general supervision of institutions maintained by public funds for the mentally ill and licenses private hospitals for such patients. The bureau of mental hygiene, within the division of mental diseases, must investigate causes and methods of prevention of mental illness.

Adult Delinquents.—The State Penitentiary, the State Reformatory, the London Prison Farm, and the State Reformatory for Women provide for confinement and training of adult delinquents. The division of public assistance of the State Department of Public Welfare and boards of county visitors must investigate county and municipal jails and workhouses. The board of parole, in the State Department of Public Welfare, has power to parole, pardon, release, and grant commutations and reprieves. County probation departments, when established, supervise, according to rules of the board of parole, persons on parole or persons conditionally pardoned from penal, reformatory, or correctional institutions, if so requested by the State Department of Public Welfare. The State department must supervise probation and parole officers throughout the State, and endeavor to secure the enforcement of probation and parole laws.

Crippled Children.—The State Department of Public Welfare, through the division of public assistance, must locate crippled children and children who are suffering from conditions which lead to crippling and provide them with services including facilities for diagnosis, medical, surgical, and corrective care, hospitalization, and aftercare. The department must arrange for the treatment and education of crippled children committed to it by juvenile courts.

Tuberculars.—The State Sanatorium provides care for tuberculous residents of the State. Admissions and discharges of patients are governed by rules of the State Department of Health, subject to approval of the State Department of Public Welfare.

SUMMARY OF STATUTORY PROVISIONS FOR PUBLIC WELFARE
OKLAHOMA

Relief and Public Assistance.—General relief financed by State funds is administered by the State Board of Public Welfare through such agencies as it may establish.[1] General relief financed by State and county funds is administered by the the board of county commissioners and the county health officer acting as the county welfare board under the supervision of the State Board of Public Welfare. The State board may appoint a representative to act in the place of the county welfare board. Indoor relief, financed by county funds alone, is administered by boards of county commissioners acting as overseers of the poor.[2] Old age assistance, aid to dependent children in their own homes, and blind assistance are administered by the State Public Welfare Commission[3] assisted by county assistance boards.

Cases involving dependent and neglected children come within the jurisdiction of juvenile courts. The State Public Welfare Commission is authorized to establish a division for the protection and care of homeless dependent and neglected children and children in danger of becoming delinquent and to provide adequate child welfare services. The State Commissioner of Charities and Corrections is empowered to license child-caring agencies and must inspect and examine all private agencies and State and local institutions. Boards of county commissioners may establish county homes for children. The State Board of Public Affairs may contract for the care of children in child-caring institutions not State owned or operated. The board may appoint officers to cooperate with all public and private child-caring agencies, and to find homes in institutions for children and supervise such homes. The Whitaker State Orphan Home, the West Oklahoma Home for White Children, and the Institute for Colored Deaf, Blind, and Orphans receive and care for children.

Veterans' pensions are administered by the State Commissioner of Pensions assisted by the county judges. Care of veterans in the Confederate Soldiers' Home and Union Soldiers' Home is administered by the board of trustees of each home, under the supervision of the State Commissioner of Charities and Corrections. The State Soldiers' Relief Commission must provide emergency temporary and permanent relief for honorably discharged, disabled, and diseased ex-service persons of the World War and other wars of the United States.

Juvenile Delinquents.—Juvenile courts have jurisdiction in cases involving delinquent children. The court may commit a child to the custody of a probation officer or other person, or to an accredited association caring for dependent and neglected children; allow the child to remain at home; or place it in a family home. It may also commit children to the State Training School for White Boys, State Industrial School for White Girls, State Training School for Colored Boys, State Training School for Colored Girls, or to any institution incorporated under State laws that may care for delinquent children or that may be provided by the city or county for care of delinquent children. Care in State institutions is supervised by the board of managers for children's institutions. Juvenile courts must report to the State Commissioner of Charities and Corrections regarding cases of delinquent children.[4]

Services to the Blind.—The State Commission for the Adult Blind must obtain information concerning the adult blind in the State, find employment for them, and perform such other duties as may tend to make them more efficient.

Insane and Mental Defectives.—The State Lunacy Commission has general supervision of policy of the State hospitals for the insane. The Central, Eastern,

[1] The State Board of Public Welfare is authorized to cooperate with Federal agencies in order to procure Federal funds for general relief.

[2] The State Commissioner of Charities and Corrections has the power to investigate the entire system of public charities and corrections and to examine the management of all almshouses, prisons, jails, reform and industrial schools, hospitals, infirmaries, dispensaries, orphanages, and all public and private retreats and asylums which receive State, county, or city funds. The commissioner must inspect and license private hospitals, infirmaries, dispensaries, retreats, rescue homes, orphanages, and foundling institutions.

[3] The State Public Welfare Commission has the authority to cooperate with the Federal Government in order to secure the benefits of the Federal Social Security Act.

[4] See discussion of care of dependent and neglected children, above, for powers of the State Public Welfare Commission and the State Commissioner of Charities and Corrections in relation to children.

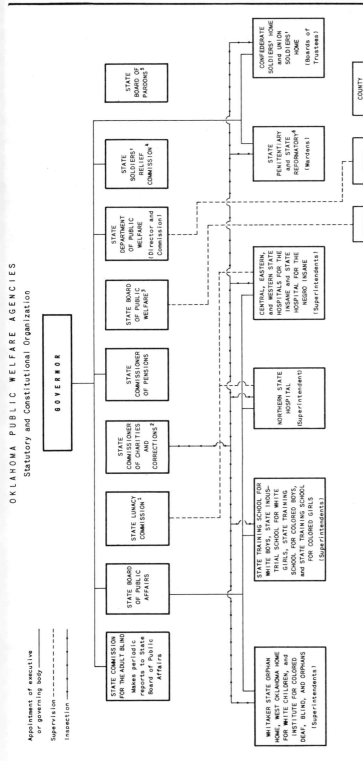

OKLAHOMA PUBLIC WELFARE AGENCIES
Statutory and Constitutional Organization

and Western State Hospitals for the Insane and the State Hospital for the Negro Insane provide care and treatment for insane persons committed by county courts. The Northern State Hospital provides care and treatment for epileptic and feeble-minded persons committed by county courts. The State Commissioner of Charities and Corrections represents before the court having jurisdiction defective minors who are inmates of public institutions.

Adult Delinquents.—The State Penitentiary and the State Reformatory provide for confinement and training of adult delinquents. Applications for pardons, paroles, and commutations of sentences must be passed upon by the State Board of Pardons.

SUMMARY OF STATUTORY PROVISIONS FOR PUBLIC WELFARE
OREGON

Relief and Public Assistance.—There are two programs for the administration of general relief. Institutional care is administered by county courts or boards of county commissioners without supervision; direct relief is administered by county relief committees under the supervision of the State Relief Committee. Old age assistance is administered by the State Relief Committee assisted by the county relief committees. Aid to dependent children in their own homes and blind assistance are administered by the county relief committees under supervision of the State Relief Committee. The State Commission for the Blind and Prevention of Blindness must cooperate with the State Relief Committee in the administration of blind assistance and, upon request, make investigations and recommendations to the committee regarding medical service for restoration of sight and employability of the applicant.

Cases involving dependent and neglected children come within the jurisdiction of juvenile courts. The State Relief Committee administers child welfare services and is authorized to cooperate with any agencies in the State providing protection and care of dependent or neglected children or children in danger of becoming delinquent.[1] County relief committees are charged with the administration of all assistance and relief to children within their respective counties under the control and supervision of the State Relief Committee. The State Child Welfare Commission licenses and must inspect and supervise all child-caring agencies in the State, and it must report abuses to the State Board of Control. The commission may also require reports from juvenile courts on children placed out under court order. County boards of visitors appointed by juvenile courts must inspect all institutions to which commitments are made.

Direct relief to veterans is administered by the county relief committee and commander or captain of the post or camp representing the war in which the veterans were engaged, in cooperation with the county courts. Where there is no post or camp, direct relief is administered by the county judge or, in counties of 100,000 population or more, by an officer appointed by the board of county commissioners.

Juvenile Delinquents.—Juvenile courts have jurisdiction in cases involving delinquent children. The court may commit a child to the care of a probation officer, cause it to be placed in a family home or a county or city institution, or commit the child to the State Training School (for boys) or to the State Industrial School (for girls).[2]

Services to the Blind.—The State Commission for the Blind and Prevention of Blindness must maintain a register of the blind, describing the condition, cause of blindness, and capacity for education and industrial training of each blind person. It must maintain a bureau for the prevention of blindness, one or more bureaus for vocational aid, and may establish one or more training schools and workshops for employment of blind persons. It is empowered to pay employees suitable wages and to devise means for the sale and distribution of their products. The commission may also pay necessary expenses for blind persons during their training in any suitable occupation and provide home teaching, materials, tools, and social service. It may provide medical and surgical treatment. The Oregon Blind Trade School provides vocational training to adult blind.

Insane and Mental Defectives.—The State Hospital and the Eastern State Hospital provide care and treatment for insane persons and the Fairview Home for Feeble-minded cares for and trains feeble-minded, idiotic, or epileptic persons. Commitments to these institutions are made by the county or circuit judges. Provisions for the sterilization of insane, feeble-minded, and epileptic persons are administered by the State Board of Eugenics.[3]

---

[1] The State Relief Committee is authorized to accept and disburse Federal funds for public welfare.

[2] See discussion of care of dependent and neglected children, above, for powers of the State Child Welfare Commission, State Board of Control, State Relief Committee, and county boards of visitors in relation to children.

[3] The State Board of Eugenics is composed of the superintendents of the two hospitals for the insane, the superintendent of the penitentiary, and members of the State Board of Health.

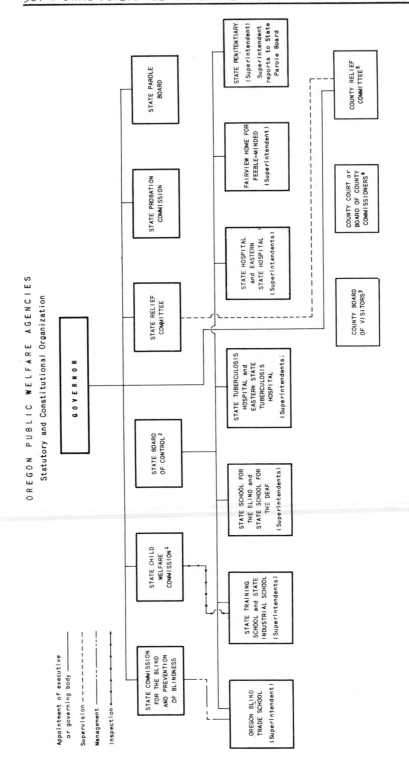

OREGON PUBLIC WELFARE AGENCIES
Statutory and Constitutional Organization

Appointment of executive or governing body ——————
Supervision – – – – – –
Management ——— " ———
Inspection ●——●——●

GOVERNOR

STATE COMMISSION FOR THE BLIND AND PREVENTION OF BLINDNESS

STATE CHILD WELFARE COMMISSION[1]

STATE BOARD OF CONTROL[2]

STATE RELIEF COMMITTEE

STATE PROBATION COMMISSION

STATE PAROLE BOARD

OREGON BLIND TRADE SCHOOL (Superintendent)

STATE TRAINING SCHOOL and STATE INDUSTRIAL SCHOOL (Superintendents)

STATE SCHOOL FOR THE BLIND and STATE SCHOOL FOR THE DEAF (Superintendents)

STATE TUBERCULOSIS HOSPITAL and EASTERN STATE TUBERCULOSIS HOSPITAL (Superintendents)

STATE HOSPITAL and EASTERN STATE HOSPITAL (Superintendents)

FAIRVIEW HOME FOR FEEBLE-MINDED (Superintendent)

STATE PENITENTIARY (Superintendent) Superintendent reports to State Parole Board

COUNTY BOARD OF VISITORS[3]

COUNTY COURT or BOARD OF COUNTY COMMISSIONERS[4]

COUNTY RELIEF COMMITTEE[5]

[1] member appointed by the president of the State university, 1 appointed by the president of the State medical association, and the 3 remaining members appointed by the Governor.

[2] Composed of the Governor, the secretary of state, and the State treasurer, ex officio.

[3] appointed by the county judge.

[4] Administers local general relief program.

[5] The Governor appoints 4 of the 7 members. The others are members of the board of county commissioners or of the county court.

Adult Delinquents.—The State Penitentiary provides for confinement and training of adult delinquents. Paroles may be granted by the Governor upon his own motion or upon recommendation of the State Parole Board. The State Probation Commission is charged with the administration of probation. Provisions for sterilization are administered by the State Board of Eugenics.

Crippled Children.—The State Relief Committee administers the program of services to children who are crippled or who are suffering from conditions which lead to crippling. The committee must supervise the administration of those services that it does not administer directly, and it is authorized to cooperate with other health and welfare groups administering laws providing for vocational rehabilitation of physically handicapped children.

Education of the Deaf, Dumb, and Blind.—The State School for the Blind and the State School for the Deaf provide education for all blind and deaf children, respectively. Appropriations for readers for blind students attending State institutions of higher learning must be distributed under supervision of the State Commission for the Blind and Prevention of Blindness.

Tuberculars.—The State Tuberculosis Hospital and the Eastern State Tuberculosis Hospital admit patients upon application to the superintendent of the proper institution. An application must be accompanied by a certification of residence by the county or circuit judge of the county.

SUMMARY OF STATUTORY PROVISIONS FOR PUBLIC WELFARE
PENNSYLVANIA

Relief and Public Assistance.—General relief, old age assistance, aid to dependent children in their own homes, and blind assistance are administered by county boards of assistance under the supervision of the State Department of Public Assistance.[1]

Juvenile courts have jurisdiction in cases involving dependent and neglected children. The State Department of Welfare has supervision over all children's institutions and boarding homes licensed by it, and may provide for the placing of children. The Thaddeus Stevens Industrial School and the State Soldiers' Orphans' School receive and care for dependent and neglected children. The local authorities of county and city institution districts under the supervision of the State Department of Welfare must place all dependent children committed to their care in foster homes or institutions. County commissioners may establish and maintain homes and schools for dependent and neglected children.

Relief to veterans is administered by the State adjutant general. Veterans' pensions are administered by the State Department of Military Affairs.[2] The State veterans' commission acts in an advisory capacity to the State Department of Military Affairs and the adjutant general. Care of veterans in the State Soldiers' and Sailors' Home is administered by the board of trustees of the home under the supervision of the State Department of Military Affairs.

Juvenile Delinquents.—Juvenile courts have jurisdiction in cases involving delinquent children, except in cases where a child is charged with murder. The court may allow a child to remain in its own home, place it in a family home, or commit it to a city, State, or county child-caring institution, incorporated association or society, or to an industrial or training school. Delinquent boys may be committed to the State Industrial School, while both delinquent boys and delinquent girls may be committed to the State Training School.[3]

Services to the Blind.—The State Council for the Blind must formulate a general program for the prevention of blindness and the improvement of the conditions of the blind. It must make recommendations to public or private agencies concerned with the blind and cooperate with such agencies in matters concerning their education, welfare, and placement. It must also supply information to other agencies concerning the mental and physical condition of blind persons. The boards of county commissioners in county institution districts and city departments of public welfare in city institution districts under the supervision of the State Department of Welfare may provide employment for the blind.

Insane and Mental Defectives.—The following State hospitals provide for the care and treatment of the insane: Homeopathic State Hospital for the Insane at Allentown, State Hospital for the Insane at Danville, State Hospital for the Criminal Insane at Farview, Harrisburg State Hospital, State Hospital for Insane of Southeastern District at Norristown, Western State Hospital for the Insane at Torrance, State Hospital for the Insane at Warren, and the State Asylum for Chronic Insane of Pennsylvania at South Mountain. The Laurelton State Village for Feeble-minded Women, the Pennhurst State School for Feeble-minded and Epileptics, the Polk State School for Feeble-minded, and the Selinsgrove State Colony for Epileptics provide for the care and treatment of feeble-minded and epileptic persons.[4] The Dixmont Hospital and the Elwyn Training School are State-aided institutions which provide care and treatment for mental defectives. Persons are admitted to these institutions by voluntary application, application of a friend or relative, order of court of common pleas or other court of record, by commitment upon physician's certificate, or upon an inquiry of a commission which finds that the person is mentally ill. The State Department of Welfare supervises all places

---

[1] The department must cooperate with agencies of the United States Government in matters of mutual concern.

[2] Need is not specified as a condition of eligibility for veterans' pensions.

[3] See discussion of care of dependent and neglected children, above, for the powers of the State Department of Welfare in relation to children.

[4] Selinsgrove State Colony for Epileptics also receives and cares for insane persons.

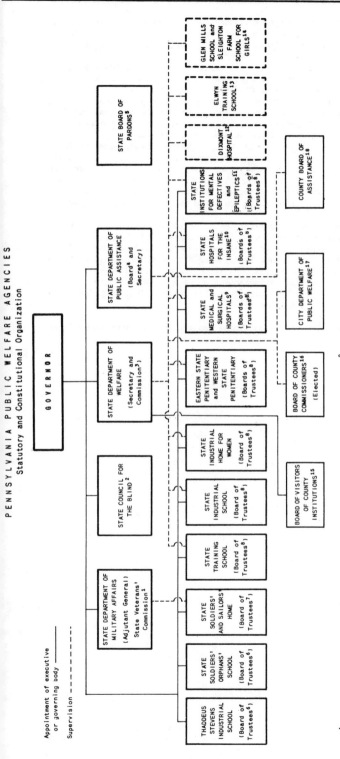

PENNSYLVANIA PUBLIC WELFARE AGENCIES
Statutory and Constitutional Organization

Appointment of executive or governing body ————
Supervision – – – – – – –

GOVERNOR

THADDEUS STEVENS INDUSTRIAL SCHOOL (Board of Trustees[6])

STATE SOLDIERS' ORPHANS' SCHOOL (Board of Trustees[6])

STATE DEPARTMENT OF MILITARY AFFAIRS (Adjutant General) State Veterans' Commission[1]

STATE SOLDIERS' AND SAILORS' HOME (Board of Trustees[7])

STATE TRAINING SCHOOL (Board of Trustees[8])

STATE COUNCIL FOR THE BLIND[2]

STATE INDUSTRIAL SCHOOL (Board of Trustees[8])

STATE INDUSTRIAL HOME FOR WOMEN (Board of Trustees[8])

BOARD OF VISITORS OF COUNTY INSTITUTIONS[15]

STATE DEPARTMENT OF WELFARE (Secretary and Commission[3])

EASTERN STATE PENITENTIARY and WESTERN STATE PENITENTIARY (Boards of Trustees[8])

BOARD OF COUNTY COMMISSIONERS[16] (Elected)

STATE DEPARTMENT OF PUBLIC ASSISTANCE (Board[4] and Secretary)

STATE MEDICAL and SURGICAL HOSPITALS[9] (Boards of Trustees[8])

STATE HOSPITALS FOR THE INSANE[10] (Boards of Trustees[8])

STATE INSTITUTIONS FOR MENTAL DEFECTIVES and EPILEPTICS[11] (Boards of Trustees[8])

CITY DEPARTMENT OF PUBLIC WELFARE[17]

COUNTY BOARD OF ASSISTANCE[18]

STATE BOARD OF PARDONS[5]

DIXMONT HOSPITAL[12]

ELWYN TRAINING SCHOOL[13]

GLEN MILLS SCHOOL and SLEIGHTON FARM SCHOOL FOR GIRLS[14]

[1] Composed of the adjutant general and 5 members appointed by the Governor. Constitutes an advisory commission within the State Department of Military Affairs.

[2] Composed of the secretary of welfare as the executive officer, the superintendent of public instruction, the secretary of labor and industry, and 4 members appointed by the Governor. Constitutes a departmental administrative board within the State Department of Welfare.

[3] The State welfare commission is an advisory body.

[4] Composed of the state treasurer, the auditor general, and 7 members appointed by the Governor.

[5] Composed of the lieutenant governor, the secretary of the commonwealth, the attorney general, and the secretary of internal affairs. Constitutes a departmental administrative board within the State Department of Justice.

[6] Constitutes a departmental administrative board within the State Department of Public Instruction, with the superintendent of public instruction as an ex officio member.

[7] Constitutes a departmental administrative board within the State Department of Military Affairs, with the adjutant general as an ex officio member.

[8] Constitutes a departmental administrative board within the State Department of Welfare, with the secretary of welfare as an ex officio member.

[9] These are the Ashland, Blossburg, Connellsville, Philipsburg, Hazleton, Locust Mountain, Nanticoke, Coaldale, Scranton, and Shamokin State Hospitals.

[10] These are the Homeopathic State Hospital for the Insane at Allentown, State Hospital for the Insane at Danville, State Hospital for the Criminal Insane at Farview, Harrisburg State Hospital, State Hospital for the Insane of Southeastern District at Norristown, Western State Hospital for the Insane at Torrance, State Hospital for the Insane at Warren, State Asylum for Chronic Insane of Pennsylvania at South Mountain.

[11] These are the Laureldon State Village for Feeble-minded Women, Pennhurst State School for Feeble-minded and Epileptics, Polk State School for Feeble-minded, and Selinsgrove State Colony for Epileptics.

[12] State-aided hospital for the insane.

[13] State-aided hospital for mental defectives.

[14] State-aided correctional institutions.

[15] Appointment of board is optional.

[16] The governing body of the county institution district.

[17] The governing body of the city institution district.

[18] Appointment by the Governor with the consent of two-thirds of the State Senate.

of detention of the insane and mentally unsound persons, and must enforce regulations on all matters relative to such persons. Requisitions for State funds for care of the insane in county or private institutions must be approved by the State Department of Welfare.

Adult Delinquents.—The Eastern State Penitentiary, the Western State Penitentiary, the State Industrial Home for Women, and the State Industrial School provide for the confinement and training of adult delinquents. Except in cases of impeachment, the State Board of Pardons is empowered to hear applications for, and to make recommendations to the Governor upon, the remission of fines and forfeitures, the granting of reprieves, commutations of sentence, and pardons. The board supervises prisoners paroled from the above institutions.

Crippled Children.—Juvenile courts may commit dependent and neglected children who are crippled to a home for crippled children, an orthopedic hospital, the State Hospital for Crippled Children,[5] or some other institution. All such homes and institutions except the State Hospital for Crippled Children are under the supervision of the State Department of Welfare, and requisitions for State funds for the care of crippled children in homes or hospitals must be approved by that department.

State Owned Medical and Surgical Hospitals.—The following State hospitals which are under the supervision and direction of the State Department of Welfare provide treatment for sick and injured persons: Ashland State Hospital, Blossburg State Hospital, Connellsville State Hospital, Philipsburg State Hospital, Hazleton State Hospital, Locust Mountain State Hospital, Nanticoke State Hospital, Coaldale State Hospital, Scranton State Hospital, and Shamokin State Hospital. Indigent injured persons must be given precedence in admission to the Ashland, Blossburg, Connellsville, and Philipsburg State Hospitals.

---

[5]The State Hospital for Crippled Children is under the jurisdiction of the State Department of Health.

SUMMARY OF STATUTORY PROVISIONS FOR PUBLIC WELFARE
RHODE ISLAND

Relief and Public Assistance.—General relief is administered by the local directors of public welfare or by local work relief bureaus under the supervision of the State Unemployment Relief Commission.[1] Old age assistance is administered by the Bureau of Old Age Security[2] of the Division of Social Security in the State Department of Public Welfare. Aid to dependent children in their own homes is administered by the Bureau of Aid to Dependent Children of the Division of Social Security in the State Department of Public Welfare, assisted by local directors of public welfare or local boards of aid to dependent children.[3] Blind assistance is administered by the State Department of Public Welfare.[3]

Cases involving dependent and neglected children come within the jurisdiction of juvenile courts. The State Department of Public Welfare must promote the enforcement of all laws for the protection of dependent and neglected children. It must cooperate with the courts and all public and private child welfare agencies, and is empowered to license child-caring agencies. The Bureau of Children's Care of the Division of Social Security in the State Department of Public Welfare may receive and place dependent, neglected, and vagrant children in foster homes or private institutions. All organizations caring for children must report annually to the State department. The State Home and School under the control of the State Department of Public Welfare receives and cares for dependent and neglected children.

Direct relief granted to veterans by cities and towns is administered by town councils or boards of aldermen. Direct relief granted to veterans by the State is administered by the Division of Soldiers' and Sailors' Relief in the State Department of Public Welfare. Care of veterans in the State Soldiers' Home is administered by the commandant of the home under the supervision of the Division of Soldiers' and Sailors' Relief in the State Department of Public Welfare.

Juvenile Delinquents.—Juvenile courts have jurisdiction in cases involving delinquent children. The court may parole a child to the care of a probation officer, parent, or custodian; or it may commit it to the Sockanosset School for Boys or the Oaklawn School for Girls.[4] The State Department of Public Welfare must promote the enforcement of all laws for the protection of delinquent children, and the Director of Public Welfare may, at the request of a parent or guardian, admit a child to one of the above institutions.

Services to the Blind.—The Division of Rehabilitation of Crippled and Blind in the State Department of Education administers provisions for the rehabilitation of the blind. The division may provide for the instruction of the adult blind in their homes. The supervisor of the Bureau for the Blind, in the division, must keep a register of the blind describing their condition, causes of blindness, and capacity for educational and industrial training. He must maintain a placement service for trained applicants and determine fitness of blind applicants for work. He has charge of home teaching, workshops, and salesrooms for the sale of products of the blind, and he must cooperate with the State Board of Vocational Training. The State Department of Public Welfare must cooperate with the Bureau for the Blind in the Department of Education, and with other agencies in measures for the prevention of blindness, restoration of sight, and vocational adjustment of blind persons.

Insane and Mental Defectives.—The State Director of Public Welfare may designate the indigent and insane persons who shall be beneficiaries of State aid. The State Hospital for Mental Diseases cares for both voluntary patients who are mentally ill or drug addicts and patients committed as insane by district courts or the Supreme Court. The State Department of Public Welfare promotes enforcement of all laws for the protection of defective children. The Director of the State

---

[1] Indoor relief or care by contract with private families is administered by local officials without State supervision. The State Infirmary receives persons who have no legal settlement in a town or who are sent at the expense of the town.

[2] The bureau may make such rules and regulations as are necessary to conform to Federal legislation concerning the protection, welfare, and assistance of aged persons.

[3] The State Department of Public Welfare must cooperate with the Federal Social Security Board.

[4] See discussion of care of dependent and neglected children, above, for powers and duties of the State Department of Public Welfare relating to children.

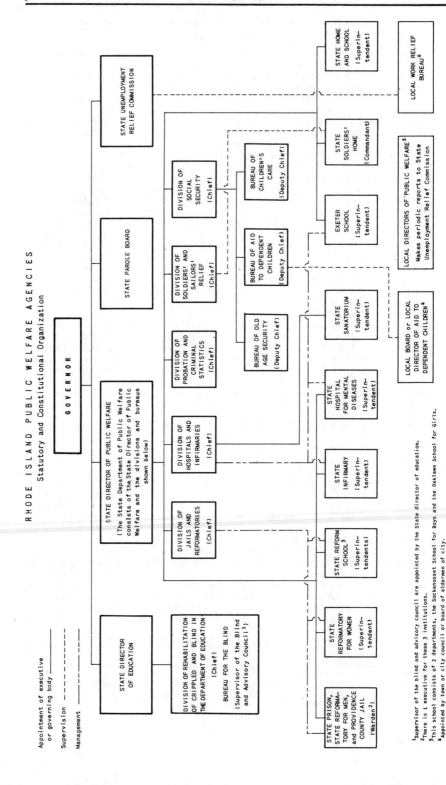

RHODE ISLAND PUBLIC WELFARE AGENCIES
Statutory and Constitutional Organization

[1] Supervisor of the blind and advisory council are appointed by the State director of education.

[2] There is 1 executive for these 3 institutions.

[3] This school consists of 2 departments, the Sockanosset School for Boys and the Oaklawn School for Girls.

[4] Appointed by town or city council or board of aldermen of city.

[5] 1 or more elected in each town.

[6] Consists of the public works or highway commissioner, the town treasurer, and 1 other qualified elector of the town. If both the local work relief bureau and the local director of public welfare are designated by the town council to administer work relief and home relief, the local Director serves as executive of-

Department of Education makes recommendations to the Governor for the selection of imbecile children as beneficiaries of State aid. The Exeter School provides education and custodial care for feeble-minded children and adults who are admitted upon application to the State Department of Public Welfare or committed to the School by district or juvenile courts.

Adult Delinquents.—The State Prison, State Reformatory for Men, State Reformatory for Women, and Providence County Jail provide for the confinement and training of adult delinquents. The State Parole Board has charge of paroles from these institutions. The State Department of Public Welfare may parole certain persons in county jails and persons in State institutions under its control who are not under the jurisdiction of the State Parole Board. The Division of Probation and Criminal Statistics supervises and controls all persons who are placed on probation by the courts or who are on parole from penal and correctional institutions. It must gather criminal statistics and make them available to the various officers of the State.

Crippled Children.—The State Department of Public Welfare must provide the State Department of Public Health with lists of crippled children in State institutions and otherwise cooperate with it in the care of crippled children.

Tuberculars.—The State Sanatorium cares for tuberculars with a legal residence in a city or town who are admitted at the request of local directors of public welfare and at the expense of the city or town. Indigent patients who have no legal settlement in a city or town are cared for at the expense of the State. Patients of the sanatorium are admitted upon application to the superintendent.

SUMMARY OF STATUTORY PROVISIONS FOR PUBLIC WELFARE
SOUTH CAROLINA

Relief and Public Assistance.—General relief provided from county funds is administered by boards of county commissioners.[1] General relief provided from State funds, old age assistance, aid to dependent children in their own homes, and blind assistance are administered by the State Department of Public Welfare[2] through the county departments of public welfare.[3]

Cases involving dependent and neglected children come within the jurisdiction of juvenile courts. County advisory boards to juvenile courts must visit public and private institutions to which children are committed and cooperate with the courts for the welfare of children. These boards control and manage the county detention homes. Boards of county commissioners may bind out children. The State Department of Public Welfare is empowered to cooperate with the Federal Government in the administration of child welfare services for the protection and care of dependent and neglected children and children in danger of becoming delinquent.[4] County departments of public welfare, under the supervision of the State Department of Public Welfare, must promote the enforcement of laws for the protection of children and for general child welfare. The State Children's Bureau may place out in family homes for adoption destitute, neglected, and delinquent children committed to its care. Care of children in the John de la Howe Industrial School is administered by a board of trustees.

Veterans' pensions are administered by county boards of honor.[5] Care in the State Confederate Home is administered by the commission for the home, under the supervision of the State Department of Public Welfare.

Juvenile Delinquents.—Juvenile courts have jurisdiction in cases involving delinquent children. The court may place the children on probation or commit them to the custody of a relative or other person, to the custody of the State Department of Public Welfare for placement in a family home, to an institution maintained by the State or any subdivision thereof, or to a private institution or association authorized to care for children. The State Industrial School for White Boys, the State Industrial School for White Girls, and the State Reformatory for Negro Boys care for juvenile delinquents. The case of a child 14 years of age or over charged with a felony may be transferred to the circuit court.[6]

Services to the Blind.—The State Department of Public Welfare must cause to be maintained a register of the blind in the State, describing the condition, cause of blindness, and capacity for education and industrial training of each blind person. It may develop, or cooperate with other agencies in developing, measures for prevention of blindness, the restoration of eyesight, and vocational adjustment of blind persons. The State advisory council for the blind, under direction of the State Department of Public Welfare, must inquire into the causes of blindness, inaugurate and cooperate in preventive measures, provide treatment for restoration of eyesight, aid the blind in finding employment, teach trades and occupations, and assist in disposing of products made in home industries.

Insane and Mental Defectives.—The State Hospital provides care and treatment for insane persons admitted upon application to the superintendent or committed

---

[1]Relief from county funds is administered in Darlington County by a county commission of public welfare appointed by the county board of directors. The commission may be abolished at any time in order to conform to State or Federal legislation and to obtain State and/or Federal funds.

[2]The State Department of Public Welfare has authority to investigate all public and private charitable institutions and agencies. Charitable organizations must be approved by the State Department of Public Welfare before they may be incorporated. It is also authorized to act as the agent of the State, and to cooperate with any Federal agency for the purpose of carrying out matters of mutual concern and to administer any Federal funds granted the State in the furtherance of duties of the department.

[3]In Charleston County the county welfare board administers relief and public assistance financed from State funds under the supervision of the State department.

[4]The State department is authorized to investigate public or private institutions and agencies concerned with the care, custody, or training of persons or dealing with the problems of delinquency, dependency, or defectiveness.

[5]Need is not specified as a condition of eligibility for veterans' pensions.

[6]See discussion of care of dependent and neglected children, above, for powers of the State Children's Bureau, the State Department of Public Welfare, county departments of public welfare, and county advisory boards to juvenile courts in relation to children.

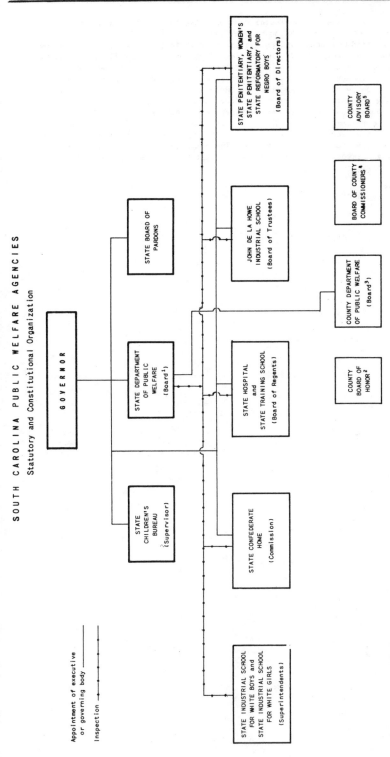

SOUTH CAROLINA PUBLIC WELFARE AGENCIES
Statutory and Constitutional Organization

Appointment of executive
or governing body

Inspection

GOVERNOR

STATE CHILDREN'S BUREAU
(Supervisor)

STATE DEPARTMENT OF PUBLIC WELFARE
(Board[1])

STATE BOARD OF PARDONS

STATE INDUSTRIAL SCHOOL FOR WHITE BOYS and STATE INDUSTRIAL SCHOOL FOR WHITE GIRLS
(Superintendents)

STATE CONFEDERATE HOME
(Commission)

STATE HOSPITAL and STATE TRAINING SCHOOL
(Board of Regents)

JOHN DE LA HOWE INDUSTRIAL SCHOOL
(Board of Trustees)

STATE PENITENTIARY, WOMEN'S STATE PENITENTIARY, and STATE REFORMATORY FOR NEGRO BOYS
(Board of Directors)

COUNTY BOARD OF HONOR[2]

COUNTY DEPARTMENT OF PUBLIC WELFARE
(Board[3])

BOARD OF COUNTY COMMISSIONERS[4]

COUNTY ADVISORY BOARD[5]

[1] Elected by the general Assembly. The board appoints an advisory council of public welfare and an advisory council for the blind.

[2] Composed of Confederate veterans elected by the county.

[3] The Charleston County welfare board is appointed by a majority (including the Senator) of the Charleston County legislative delegation.

[4] Appointed by the Governor in some counties and elected in other counties.

[5] Appointed by juvenile court judge.

by probate judges. The State Training School provides care and treatment for feeble-minded persons admitted upon application to the board of regents of the school or committed by probate judges. Public or private institutions and agencies concerned with the care, custody, or training of persons or the handling of problems of defectiveness, are subject to investigation by the State Department of Public Welfare. Juvenile courts have jurisdiction of children under 16 years of age who are insane or feeble-minded. The State Children's Bureau must place in institutions defective and otherwise handicapped children committed to its care.

Adult Delinquents.—The State Penitentiary and the Women's State Penitentiary provide for confinement and training of adult delinquents. The State Board of Pardons must make recommendations on petitions for pardons or commutations of sentences referred to it by the Governor. The State Department of Public Welfare has authority to investigate public or private institutions and agencies concerned with the problems of delinquency.

SUMMARY OF STATUTORY PROVISIONS FOR PUBLIC WELFARE
SOUTH DAKOTA

Relief and Public Assistance.—General relief is administered by boards of county commissioners assisted by township boards or governing bodies of towns or cities. Old age assistance, aid to dependent children in their own homes, and blind assistance are administered by the State Department of Social Security.[1]

Cases involving dependent and neglected children come within the jurisdiction of the juvenile courts. The division of child welfare in the State Department of Social Security must secure the enforcement of all laws relative to the welfare of children, and it must develop satisfactory standards of care in public and private child-caring organizations. All public and private institutions and homes in the State which receive and care for children are subject to the visitation, inspection, and supervision of the State Board of Charities and Corrections. The county child welfare boards must perform such duties as may be required of them by the State Department of Social Security through the division of child welfare, and they must act in a general advisory capacity to county and municipal authorities relative to all social questions.

Relief to veterans and to their wives or widows is provided in the State Soldiers' Home. The county judges make all commitments to the home. The State board of managers of the State Soldiers' Home is empowered to grant direct relief to Civil War veterans and to their wives or widows.

Juvenile Delinquents.—Juvenile courts have jurisdiction in cases involving delinquent children. The court may allow a delinquent child to remain in its own home subject to the visitation of a probation officer or commit it to a child-caring institution or association, such as the State Training School. The State parole officer is charged with the duty of securing homes and employment for all persons paroled from the State Training School. In his supervision of all such persons, he may obtain the assistance of the county child welfare boards and probation officers.[2]

Services to the Blind.—The State Department of Social Security must develop, or cooperate with other agencies that are developing, measures for the prevention of blindness, the restoration of eyesight, and the vocational adjustment of blind persons.

Insane and Mental Defectives.—The Yankton State Hospital provides care and treatment for the insane and the State School and Home for Feeble-minded provides care, treatment, and education for imbecile, feeble-minded, and epileptic persons. County boards of commissioners of the insane, which constitute subcommissions of the State Commission for the Control of the Feeble-minded, must investigate cases involving the insane or feeble-minded, and they may make commitments to appropriate institutions. The State commission has authority in all matters pertaining to the care, supervision, and control of feeble-minded persons not confined in the State School and Home for Feeble-minded and determines conditions under which such persons may remain outside this institution. Inspection of all private homes or institutions providing mental treatment of children or adults must be made by the State Board of Charities and Corrections. This board, together with the superintendent of the State School and Home for Feeble-minded, must investigate and examine all cases of sterilization of inmates of the home and may order the necessary operations to be performed. Appeal from such orders is allowed to the State Commission for Control of the Feeble-minded, and then to the circuit court. Standards for care of mentally handicapped children by public agencies and private organizations must be developed by the division of child welfare in the State Department of Social Security which must also promote the enforcement of laws relative to the welfare of such children.

---

[1]The department must cooperate with the Federal Government in such a reasonable manner necessary to qualify for Federal aid for assistance to the needy aged, assistance to the needy blind, aid to dependent children, and child welfare services.

[2]See discussion of care of dependent and neglected children, above, for powers and duties of the State Board of Charities and Corrections, the county child welfare boards, and the division of child welfare in the State Department of Social Security in relation to children.

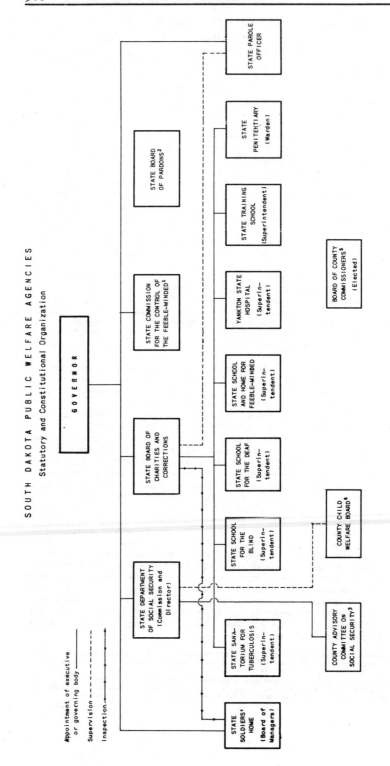

SOUTH DAKOTA PUBLIC WELFARE AGENCIES
Statutory and Constitutional Organization

GOVERNOR

Appointment of executive
or governing body ─────────
Supervision ─ ─ ─ ─ ─ ─ ─ ─
Inspection ─•─•─•─•─•─•─

STATE DEPARTMENT OF SOCIAL SECURITY (Commission and Director)

STATE BOARD OF CHARITIES AND CORRECTIONS

STATE COMMISSION FOR THE CONTROL OF THE FEEBLE-MINDED[1]

STATE BOARD OF PARDONS[2]

STATE SOLDIERS' HOME (Board of Managers)

STATE SANA-TORIUM FOR TUBERCULOSIS (Superin-tendent)

STATE SCHOOL FOR THE BLIND (Superin-tendent)

STATE SCHOOL FOR THE DEAF (Superin-tendent)

STATE SCHOOL AND HOME FOR FEEBLE-MINDED (Superin-tendent)

YANKTON STATE HOSPITAL (Superin-tendent)

STATE TRAINING SCHOOL (Superintendent)

STATE PENITENTIARY (Warden)

STATE PAROLE OFFICER

COUNTY ADVISORY COMMITTEE ON SOCIAL SECURITY[3]

COUNTY CHILD WELFARE BOARD[4]

BOARD OF COUNTY COMMISSIONERS[5] (Elected)

[1] Composed of the superintendent of the State School and Home for Feeble-minded and 2 members appointed by the Governor.
[2] Composed of the presiding judge of the Supreme Court, the secretary of state, and the attorney general.
[3] Appointment is optional.
[4] Composed of the county superintendent of schools, the county superintendent of health, the county judge, and 2 members appointed by the State Department of Social Security, division of child welfare.
[5] Administers general relief.

Adult Delinquents.—The State Penitentiary provides for the confinement and training of adult delinquents. The State Board of Pardons is empowered to establish rules and regulations governing applications for pardons, commutations of sentences, and remissions of fines. The State parole officer under the supervision, direction, and control of the State Board of Charities and Corrections must assist in enforcing provisions for paroles, pardons, and indeterminate and suspended sentences. He must also supervise all persons paroled or discharged, attempt to secure homes and employment for them, and aid in their reformation. The Governor, upon recommendation of the warden of the penitentiary and the State Board of Charities and Corrections, may parole certain convicts. The Governor may also remit fines and forfeitures, and grant reprieves, commutations, and pardons, except in cases of impeachment. In case of life imprisonment the recommendation of the State Board of Pardons is required.

Education of the Deaf, Dumb, and Blind.—The State School for the Deaf and the State School for the Blind provide education for deaf and blind youths of the State. The State Board of Charities and Corrections may provide care for dependent blind infants. It must inspect private agencies or institutions providing for the physical treatment of children or adults.

Tuberculars.—The State Sanatorium for Tuberculosis provides care and treatment for residents of the State suffering from tuberculosis. Application is made to the superintendent, and county residence is certified by the county judge.

Maternal and Child Health.—The division of child welfare in the State Department of Social Security must secure the enforcement of laws for the protection of unmarried mothers and unmarried pregnant women so as to protect the health, well-being, and general interests of the child. It must further the development of local public services for children through consultation and demonstration services.

SUMMARY OF STATUTORY PROVISIONS FOR PUBLIC WELFARE
TENNESSEE

Relief and Public Assistance.—General relief is administered by county courts. Old age assistance, aid to dependent children in their own homes, and blind assistance are administered by the Department of Institutions and Public Welfare[1] through regional directors who act jointly with county judges or chairmen of the county court. Juvenile court judges having jurisdiction coextensive with the geographical limitations of the respective county also act with the regional directors, county judges, or chairmen of the county courts in furnishing aid to dependent children in their own homes.

Cases involving dependent and neglected children come within the jurisdiction of the juvenile courts which may appoint boards to visit all agencies receiving such children. The Department of Institutions and Public Welfare must administer or supervise all child welfare services including the licensing and inspection of private child-caring agencies and the supervision and inspection of local child-caring agencies, institutions, and boarding homes. It must supervise the care of dependent and neglected children in foster homes and institutions. Regional directors of public welfare must perform, in their respective regions, such duties as may be prescribed by the commissioner of the Department of Institutions and Public Welfare. The Tennessee Industrial School receives and cares for dependent and neglected children. The county courts are empowered to bind out as apprentices orphans and children of persons unable to provide for their support, and they may establish institutions for neglected children.

Veteran relief in the form of pensions is administered by the State Board of Pension Examiners.[2] Admissions to the Confederate Soldiers' Home are determined by the Department of Institutions and Public Welfare.

Juvenile Delinquents.—Juvenile courts have jurisdiction in cases involving delinquent children. The court may commit any such child to the Tennessee Industrial School, the State Training and Agricultural School for Boys, the State Training and Agricultural School for Colored Boys, the State Vocational School for Girls, or the State Vocational School for Colored Girls. Counties, cities, and towns are empowered to establish local reformatories.[3]

Services to the Blind.—The commissioner of the State Department of Education must maintain a register of the blind in the State, describing the condition, causes of blindness, and capacity for education and industrial training of each blind person. He must act as a bureau of information and industrial aid to assist the blind to find employment and to develop home industries. He must also establish and maintain one or more schools for industrial training and workshops, pay employees wages, and devise means for the sale of products. The commissioner may provide temporary board and lodging for workmen or pupils received at any industrial school or workshop, devise means to facilitate the circulation of books, and promote visits among the aged or helpless blind in their homes.

Insane and Mental Defectives.—The Central, Eastern, and Western State Hospitals provide care and treatment for insane persons committed by county judges, chairmen of county courts, and probate judges or courts. The State Hospital for the Criminally Insane cares for insane criminals committed by judges of criminal courts and those transferred from other institutions upon certification of insanity by the superintendent and physician of the institution from which they are transferred. The State Home and School for Feeble-minded Persons cares for persons admitted upon application of parents or guardians to the commissioner of the Department of Institutions and Public Welfare or the superintendent of the home, or committed by the judges of the chancery, circuit, county, or probate courts.

---

[1]The department must administer or supervise all functions established, or to be established, pursuant to the provisions of the Federal Social Security Act, with the exception of unemployment compensation, maternal and child health, public health, vocational rehabilitation, and crippled children's services. The department must cooperate with the Federal Social Security Board and with any other Federal agency in any reasonable manner necessary to qualify for Federal aid except as heretofore mentioned.

[2]Need is not specified as a condition of eligibility for veterans' pensions.

[3]See discussion of care of dependent and neglected children, above, for powers and duties of the Department of Institutions and Public Welfare and the regional directors of public welfare in relation to children.

TENNESSEE PUBLIC WELFARE AGENCIES

Statutory and Constitutional Organization

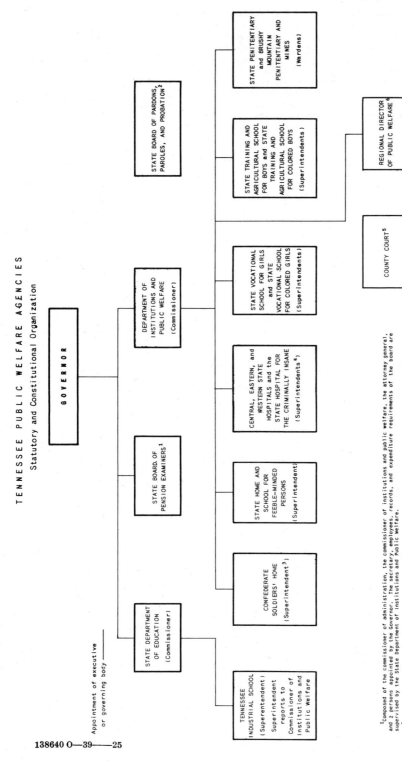

Appointment of executive
or governing body ————

GOVERNOR

STATE DEPARTMENT OF EDUCATION
(Commissioner)

TENNESSEE INDUSTRIAL SCHOOL
(Superintendent)
Superintendent reports to
Commissioner of Institutions and Public Welfare

STATE BOARD OF PENSION EXAMINERS[1]

CONFEDERATE SOLDIERS' HOME
(Superintendent[3])

DEPARTMENT OF INSTITUTIONS AND PUBLIC WELFARE
(Commissioner)

STATE HOME AND SCHOOL FOR FEEBLE-MINDED PERSONS
(Superintendent)

CENTRAL, EASTERN, and WESTERN STATE HOSPITALS and the STATE HOSPITAL FOR THE CRIMINALLY INSANE
(Superintendents[4])

STATE VOCATIONAL SCHOOL FOR GIRLS and STATE VOCATIONAL SCHOOL FOR COLORED GIRLS
(Superintendents)

STATE TRAINING AND AGRICULTURAL SCHOOL FOR BOYS and STATE TRAINING AND AGRICULTURAL SCHOOL FOR COLORED BOYS
(Superintendents)

STATE BOARD OF PARDONS, PAROLES, AND PROBATION[2]

STATE PENITENTIARY and BRUSHY MOUNTAIN PENITENTIARY AND MINES
(Wardens)

COUNTY COURT[5]

REGIONAL DIRECTOR OF PUBLIC WELFARE[6]

[1] Composed of the commissioner of administration, the commissioner of institutions and public welfare, the attorney general, and 2 persons appointed by the Governor. The secretary, employees, records, and expenditure requirements of the board are supervised by the State Department of Institutions and Public Welfare.

[2] The commissioner of institutions and public welfare is ex officio chairman; the secretary and the director are appointed by the commissioner of institutions with the approval of the Governor.

[3] The Governor appoints an advisory committee to cooperate in the management of the home.

[4] The superintendent of the Central State Hospital is also the superintendent of the State Hospital for the Criminally Insane.

[5] Administers general relief and acts jointly with the regional director of public welfare in determining eligibility for old age assistance, aid to dependent children in their own homes, and blind assistance.

[6] A region may include 1 or more counties.

Adult Delinquents.—The State Penitentiary and the Brushy Mountain Penitentiary and Mines provide for the confinement and training of adult delinquents. The State Board of Pardons, Paroles, and Probation must advise and make recommendations to the Governor with respect to pardons. It must, upon request of the Governor, make investigations and report upon the circumstances, records, and the social, physical, and mental conditions of prisoners under consideration by the Governor for pardon, commutation of sentence, or restoration of citizenship. The board must study cases of all persons eligible for parole to determine their fitness for parole. Persons who are paroled are subject to the supervision of agents of the board. Regional directors of public welfare must visit all penal and correctional institutions within their respective regions.

SUMMARY OF STATUTORY PROVISIONS FOR PUBLIC WELFARE
TEXAS

Relief and Public Assistance.—State programs for general relief, blind assistance, and aid to dependent children in their own homes are administered by the State Board of Control, division of public welfare,[1] through local agencies which it designates. Local programs for general relief and aid to dependent children, administered by county commissioners' courts, are also provided for. Old age assistance is administered by the State Old Age Assistance Commission through local agencies which it designates.

Cases involving dependent and neglected children come within the jurisdiction of the juvenile courts. The county juvenile board, composed of the judges of the several district and criminal district courts and in some instances the county judges, may recommend the type of care to be given children adjudged to be dependent and neglected. All commitments to State charitable and reformatory institutions by juvenile courts must be approved by the division of public welfare of the State Board of Control. The division must promote general child welfare services and the enforcement of all laws for the protection of children. It also licenses and must inspect all agencies caring for dependent, neglected, defective, and illegitimate children. The county commissioners' courts may appoint child welfare boards to perform such duties as the commissioners or State Board of Control may require. Such courts may establish detention homes and schools for dependent and delinquent children. The State Orphans' Home, the Waco State Home, the State Colored Orphans' Home, and the State Deaf, Dumb, and Blind Asylum for Colored Youths and Colored Orphans receive and care for dependent and neglected children.

State pensions to veterans are administered by county judges. The State Board of Control must pass upon all applications for admission to the State Confederate Home and the State Confederate Woman's Home.

Juvenile Delinquents.—Juvenile courts have jurisdiction in cases involving delinquent children. County juvenile boards may recommend the type of care to be given delinquent children. Commitment may be made to the State Girls' Training School, or the State Juvenile Training School, and must be approved by the State Board of Control, division of public welfare. The State board must promote the enforcement of all laws for the protection of delinquent children. It also licenses and inspects all agencies and must visit State supported institutions caring for such children.

Services to the Blind.—The State Commission for the Blind must maintain a bureau of information to aid the blind in finding employment, to develop home industries, and to market products of the blind. The commission may furnish materials, establish workshops, provide vocational guidance, and take measures in cooperation with other agencies for prevention of blindness.

Insane and Mental Defectives.—Care and treatment of insane, epileptic, and feeble-minded persons committed by county courts are provided by the Wichita Falls, Terrell, Rusk, San Antonio, and Austin State Hospitals. The Austin State School and the Abilene State Hospital provide care and treatment for feeble-minded and epileptic persons, respectively, committed by county courts. The State Board of Control cooperates with local boards of education and the State Department of Public Instruction for improvement of the mental and physical condition of children who present problems in development.

Adult Delinquents.—The State Penitentiary, work camps, and farms provide for confinement, employment, and training of adult delinquents. The State Board of Pardons and Paroles must make rules and regulations regarding paroles, and it supervises persons on parole. Application for parole may be made to the State Board of Pardons and Paroles, or the board may consider the parole of a prisoner on its own initiative or at the request of the Governor. The board has no power to parole except by and through the Governor in the exercise of his powers of executive clemency. It must investigate applications for pardon by the Governor.

---

[1] The State Board of Control, through the division of public welfare, is authorized to cooperate with the Federal Social Security Board and with the Children's Bureau of the United States Department of Labor for the distribution of Federal funds.

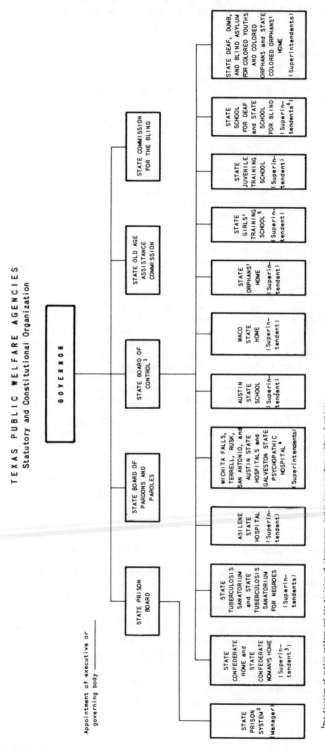

TEXAS PUBLIC WELFARE AGENCIES
Statutory and Constitutional Organization

Appointment of executive or governing body —————

[1]The division of public welfare and the division of eleemosynary institutions perform welfare functions. Local units of administration may be set up in counties or districts and local boards of public welfare may be established to serve in an advisory capacity to such local units.

[2]Includes penitentiary, work camps, and farms.

[3]The superintendent of the State Confederate Woman's Home is appointed with the approval of the Governor.

[4]The Dallas State Hospital, consisting of the Dallas State Psychopathic Hospital and the State Cancer and Pellagra Hospital, has been provided by statute but has not been established.

[5]A State Colored Girls' Training School has been provided by statute but has not been established.

[6]The advisory board of the State School for the Blind consists of the Governor, the lieutenant governor, and the attorney general.

[7]Composed of the judges of the several district and criminal courts, together with the county judge of any county having a population of over 100,000.

[8]Appointment is optional and if established performs duties required by the commissioners' court or State Board of Control. These Boards must be dissolved when local boards of public welfare are established. See footnote 1, above.

Crippled Children.—The State Board of Control, through the division of public welfare, is empowered to develop plans necessary to provide services specified in the Social Security Act.[2]

Education of the Deaf, Dumb, and Blind.—The State School for the Blind, the State School for the Deaf, and the State Deaf, Dumb, and Blind Asylum for Colored Youths receive children upon application.

Tuberculars.—The State Tuberculosis Sanatorium and the State Tuberculosis Sanatorium for Negroes provide care and treatment for tuberculous persons admitted upon application through the county judge to the State health officer.

---

[2]These services include provisions for locating crippled children and facilities for treatment, hospitalization, and aftercare.

SUMMARY OF STATUTORY PROVISIONS FOR PUBLIC WELFARE

UTAH

Relief and Public Assistance.—General relief,[1] old age assistance, aid to dependent children in their own homes, and blind assistance are administered by county or district departments of public welfare under the supervision of the State Department of Public Welfare.[2]

Cases involving dependent and neglected children come within the jurisdiction of juvenile courts. The Juvenile Court and Probation Commission has general control of juvenile courts and probation officers of the courts. The State Department of Public Welfare must promote the enforcement of laws excepting laws whose administration is expressly vested in some other State department for the protection of dependent, neglected, delinquent, and illegitimate children. To this end it must cooperate with juvenile courts and licensed public or private child welfare agencies and institutions.[3] The county or district departments of public welfare, under the supervision of the State Department of Public Welfare, must administer care for dependent, neglected, or delinquent children. All children's aid societies or institutions, except the State Industrial School, must make annual reports to the Juvenile Court and Probation Commission, and are subject to visitation, inspection, and supervision by the boards of county commissioners.

Veterans' pensions are administered by the attorney general of the State and the department commander of the Grand Army of the Republic.

Juvenile Delinquents.—Juvenile courts have jurisdiction in cases involving delinquent children. A case of felony may be transferred to the district court. The court may allow a child to remain in its own home or commit it to the custody of a relative or other person, or to any State private child-caring institution or agency. The State Industrial School, which is governed by a board of trustees, receives juvenile delinquents.[4]

Services to the Blind.—The board of trustees of the State School for the Deaf and State School for the Blind has general supervision of adult blind and must maintain a register of the blind in the State. The board may establish and maintain homes and workshops, furnish materials and tools, aid in marketing products, and provide a circulating library for the blind of the State.

Insane and Mental Defectives.—The State Department of Public Welfare must promote the enforcement of laws for the protection of mentally defective children. Feeble-minded children and adults are committed by district courts to the State Training School which provides instruction in the case of children. All insane persons in the State, whether or not in the State Hospital, are under the supervision of the board of trustees of the hospital. The hospital cares for insane persons committed by the district courts, voluntary patients, and feeble-minded and epileptics for whom applications for admission are made to the superintendent of the hospital and approved by the board of trustees. Judges of district courts must have cognizance of all applications for admission, and boards of county commissioners must authorize the expense of voluntary patients who are indigent.

Adult Delinquents.—The State Prison provides for confinement and training of adult delinquents. The State Board of Pardons may grant paroles and reductions of sentences. The Governor also may grant respites and reprieves, except in cases of treason or impeachment, but such respites and reprieves may not extend beyond the next session of the State Board of Pardons, at which time the board may continue or terminate the respite or reprieve, or pardon the offense.

Crippled Children.—The State Department of Public Welfare must make available and use, either directly or wherever appropriate through the State Board of Health,

---

[1] Hospitals or poorhouses maintained by the county receive persons only upon an order of the board of county commissioners.

[2] The State Department of Public Welfare must cooperate with the Federal Government in public welfare matters of mutual concern.

[3] The following State-aided societies care for children: Neighborhood House, Children's Service Society, and Children's Aid Society.

[4] See discussion of care of dependent and neglected children, above, for powers of the State Department of Public Welfare and the Juvenile Court and Probation Commission in relation to delinquent children.

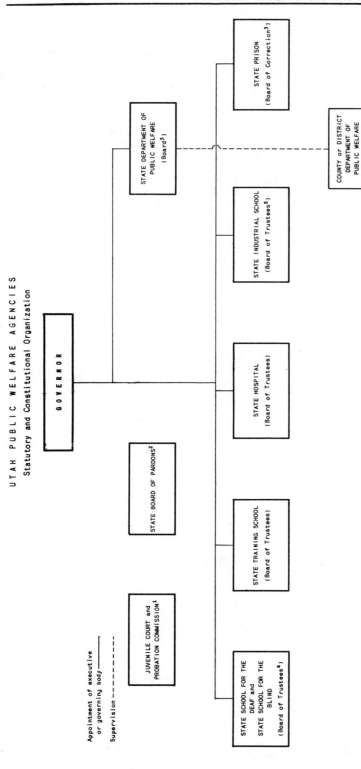

UTAH PUBLIC WELFARE AGENCIES
Statutory and Constitutional Organization

Appointment of executive
or governing body ———————
Supervision — — — — — — — —

GOVERNOR

JUVENILE COURT and PROBATION COMMISSION[1]

STATE SCHOOL FOR THE DEAF and STATE SCHOOL FOR THE BLIND (Board of Trustees[4])

STATE BOARD OF PARDONS[2]

STATE TRAINING SCHOOL (Board of Trustees)

STATE HOSPITAL (Board of Trustees)

STATE DEPARTMENT OF PUBLIC WELFARE (Board[3])

STATE INDUSTRIAL SCHOOL (Board of Trustees[5])

STATE PRISON (Board of Correction[3])

COUNTY or DISTRICT DEPARTMENT OF PUBLIC WELFARE (Board[6])

[1] Composed of the Governor, the attorney general, and the State superintendent of public instruction.
[2] Composed of the Governor, the attorney general, and 6 justices of the Supreme Court.
[3] The Governor is an ex officio member.
[4] Composed of the attorney general and 5 members appointed by the Governor.
[5] Composed of the attorney general, the State superintendent of public instruction, and 5 members appointed by the Governor.
[6] Appointed by the board of county commissioners. 1 member must be a county commissioner of the county or of 1 of the counties constituting the district if 2 or more counties unite to form a district.

State Board of Education, or other organization, such State funds as may be required to obtain Federal funds for aid to crippled children.

Education of the Deaf, Dumb, and Blind.—The State Department of Public Welfare must make available to recipients of blind assistance suitable opportunities for educational or vocational advancement offered by any State institution, public or private. If a person refuses to accept such a privilege, his allowance may be discontinued or reduced. The State School for the Deaf and the State School for the Blind provide education for deaf and dumb, and blind children, respectively, admitted under rules of the board of trustees of the schools.

Public Health.—The State Department of Public Welfare must make available and use, either directly or wherever appropriate through the State Board of Health, State Board of Education, or other organization, such State funds as may be required to secure Federal funds for public health, public health nursing, and maternal and child health.

Aid to Handicapped Persons and Vocational Rehabilitation.—The State Department of Public Welfare must administer or supervise aid to handicapped persons. The department must make available and use, either directly or wherever appropriate through the State Board of Health, State Board of Education, or other organization, such State funds as may be required to secure Federal funds made available for vocational rehabilitation.

SUMMARY OF STATUTORY PROVISIONS FOR PUBLIC WELFARE
VERMONT

Relief and Public Assistance.—General relief is administered by overseers of the poor in organized towns and supervisors in unorganized towns and gores. The State Department of Public Welfare must investigate the administration of general relief and the condition of almshouses. Blind assistance and aid to dependent children in their own homes are administered by the State Department of Public Welfare, and old age assistance is administered by the State Old Age Assistance Commission assisted by locally designated officials.[1]

Cases involving dependent and neglected children come within the jurisdiction of the juvenile courts which are assisted in their investigations by the commissioner of public welfare acting as the State probation officer.[2] The State Department of Public Welfare supervises and controls such children as it may take under its care or those committed to its care by the courts. The department must place such children in homes or institutions and supervise the care given therein. All child-caring institutions soliciting public support are subject to the visitation of the department. The department administers care given to children in the Kinstead Home. The overseers of the poor must report all cases of dependent, neglected, or delinquent children to the commissioner of public welfare.

Direct relief to veterans is administered by the State Board to Aid Indigent Veterans, assisted by town or city officials. Care in the State Soldiers' Home is administered by the board of trustees of the home.[3]

Juvenile Delinquents.—Juvenile courts have jurisdiction in cases involving delinquent children. Such children may be allowed to remain in their own homes or may be placed in a family home. The court may also commit the child to the State Department of Public Welfare, to a citizen who will care for the child without charge, to an association, to the Weeks School, or other institution.[4]

Services to the Blind.—The State Department of Public Welfare may maintain a register of the blind describing the condition, causes of blindness, and the capacity for training of each blind person. It may also act as a bureau of information and industrial aid for the blind, circulate books, furnish materials and tools for home industries, assist in marketing products and finding employment for blind persons, and contribute to the support of blind residents receiving instruction in industrial institutions outside the State.

Insane and Mental Defectives.—The commissioner of public welfare through the State Board of Supervisors of the Insane supervises the care of the insane, including the licensing of private institutions for the insane and inebriates. Commitments are made upon certification of two physicians; appeal upon commitment may be taken to the probate court whose decision is final. Insane persons receive care and treatment in the Brattleboro Retreat, by contract with the commissioner of public welfare, and in the State Hospital for the Insane. Mentally deficient and feeble-minded persons who are beneficiaries of State aid may be placed in the Austine Institution at Brattleboro by the commissioner of public welfare. Idiotic and feeble-minded children may be cared for in institutions selected by the commissioner, either within or outside the State. The Brandon State School is one such institution to which idiotic and feeble-minded children are admitted in the following order of preference: (1) those committed from the Weeks School by the certificate of the commissioner and two physicians; (2) dependent children committed by probate courts; (3) those for whom application is made to the probate court

---

[1] The State Department of Public Welfare is authorized to cooperate with the Federal Social Security Board and the United States Children's Bureau, and to comply with the provisions of the Federal Social Security Act in order to obtain funds available for child welfare services, aid to dependent children, and assistance to the blind. The State Old Age Assistance Commission is authorized to cooperate with the Federal Social Security Board as may be required in order to obtain Federal grants for old age assistance.

[2] The commissioner of public welfare serves ex officio as the State probation officer, the commissioner of deaf, blind, idiotic, feeble-minded, or epileptic children of indigent parents, the commissioner of indigent tuberculous persons and indigent children predisposed to tuberculosis, and the commissioner of tuberculosis hospitals.

[3] Need is not specified as a condition of eligibility for admission to the State Soldiers' Home.

[4] See discussion of care of dependent and neglected children, above, for care and supervision by the State Department of Public Welfare.

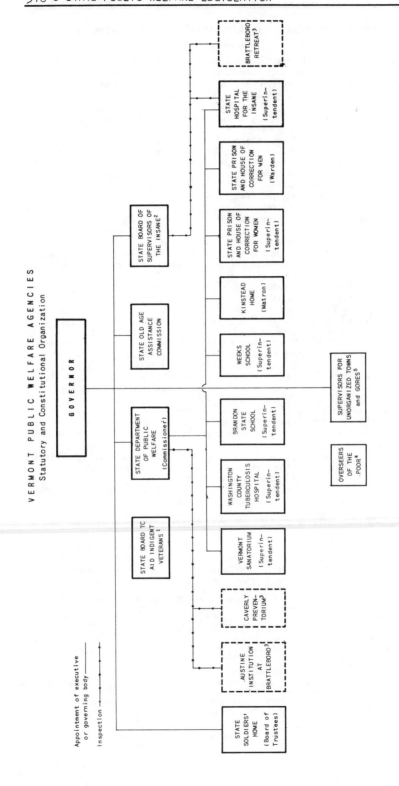

VERMONT PUBLIC WELFARE AGENCIES
Statutory and Constitutional Organization

Appointment of executive
or governing body _____
Inspection •—•—•—•

[1] Composed of 3 trustees of the State Soldiers' Home elected by the
board of trustees of the home.

[2] The commissioner of public welfare through the State Board of
Supervisors of the insane exercises all the powers and duties of the
board.

[3] This is a State-aided institution.

[4] Appointed by selectmen of the town. The State commissioner of
public welfare must investigate the administration of general relief.

[5] The State commissioner of public welfare must investigate the administration of general relief.

and who may be received upon the payment of a fee determined by the commissioner. Women, if insane or mentally defective, may also be committed to the Brandon School with the approval of the Governor. Sterilization of mental defectives and insane persons is under the control of the commissioner of public welfare.

Adult Delinquents.—The State Prison and House of Correction for Men and the State Prison and House of Correction for Women provide for confinement and training of adult male and female delinquents. The commissioner of public welfare may inspect county jails and report to the Governor thereon. The commissioner has general supervision of administration of laws relating to probation, and of persons placed on probation or persons paroled by the Governor.

Crippled Children.—The State Department of Public Welfare may provide medical and surgical treatment for indigent physically defective or crippled children.

Deaf, Dumb, and Blind.—The commissioner of public welfare may provide instruction for blind, deaf, and dumb children and for blind adults in such schools as he may designate, within or outside the State.[5] The deaf and dumb may be sent to the Austine Institution at Brattleboro.

Tuberculars.—The commissioner of public welfare must designate indigent tuberculous persons who have been investigated and approved by selectmen of towns or mayors of cities to receive treatment at the Vermont Sanatorium, Washington County Tuberculosis Hospital, Caverly Preventorium, or similar institutions.

---

[5]The board of listers in each town must certify to the commissioner of public welfare the names of epileptic, idiotic, feeble-minded, deaf, dumb, and blind persons in the town and specify whether such persons are subjects for State charity.

SUMMARY OF STATUTORY PROVISIONS FOR PUBLIC WELFARE
VIRGINIA

Relief and Public Assistance.—General relief, aid to dependent children in their own homes, and old age assistance are administered by county or city boards of public welfare, under the supervision of the State Board of Public Welfare. Blind assistance is administered by county and city boards of public welfare, under the supervision of the State Commission for the Blind.

Cases involving dependent and neglected children come within the jurisdiction of the juvenile and domestic relations courts where established. Otherwise, the county circuit courts or the city corporation or hustings courts have jurisdiction in such cases. The State Board of Public Welfare is authorized to create a children's bureau to have general supervision of the welfare of dependent, neglected, and delinquent children. The board may receive court commitments of children and make arrangements for their care. The board is empowered to license child-caring agencies and must regularly inspect all public and private institutions and agencies. County and city boards of public welfare must cooperate with the juvenile and domestic relations courts. The superintendent of public welfare, under the direction of the State board, has supervision of dependent children placed for care within the county or city by the State Board of Public Welfare.[1]

Direct relief to veterans is administered by the county circuit court or city corporation or hustings court, in cooperation with the county or city boards of pension commissioners. Confederate veterans' pensions are administered by the State comptroller in cooperation with the county circuit courts or city hustings or corporation courts. Care in the Confederate Soldiers' Home (Robert E. Lee Camp No. 1) is administered by the board of visitors of the home.

Juvenile Delinquents.—Juvenile and domestic relations courts where established, county circuit courts, or city corporation or hustings courts have jurisdiction in cases involving delinquent children. Courts may commit such children to the State Board of Public Welfare or any agency approved by it except that delinquent children who are to be placed in a State institution must be committed to the Board of Public Welfare. The State Home and Industrial School for Girls, the State Industrial School for Boys, the State Industrial School for Colored Girls, and the State Manual Labor School for Colored Boys receive juvenile delinquents.

Services to the Blind.—The State Commission for the Blind is authorized to act as a bureau of information and industrial aid to assist blind persons in finding employment and to teach them home industries. It must maintain a register of the blind describing the condition, causes of blindness, and capacity for training of each blind person. It must also make inquiries concerning the causes of blindness and cooperate with the State Board of Health in the development of preventive measures. It may establish and maintain schools for industrial training and workshops for the employment of suitable blind persons, pay wages, and distribute products of the blind.

Insane and Mental Defectives.—Insane and inebriate white persons may be committed to the Eastern, Western, or Southwestern State Hospitals for Insane. The Central State Hospital for Colored Insane receives insane and inebriate colored persons. Feeble-minded and epileptic white persons may be committed to the State Colony for Epileptics and the Feeble-minded, and feeble-minded and epileptic colored persons are committed to a special department of the Central State Hospital for Colored Insane. Persons are committed to these institutions by the judge of the circuit or corporation court or any justice of the peace and two physicians acting as a commission. Voluntary patients may be admitted by superintendents under regulation of the State Hospital Board. The children's bureau of the State Board of Public Welfare has general supervision of the welfare of mentally defective children.

Adult Delinquents.—The State Prison Board of the prison system is charged with the government and control of the State parole system. The State Penitentiary, The State Penitentiary Farm, the State Farm for Defective Misdemeanants, and the State Industrial Farm for Women provide for confinement, work, and training of adult delinquents.

---

[1]The superintendent of public welfare must act as agent of the State board in relation to any activity of the State board in the county or city.

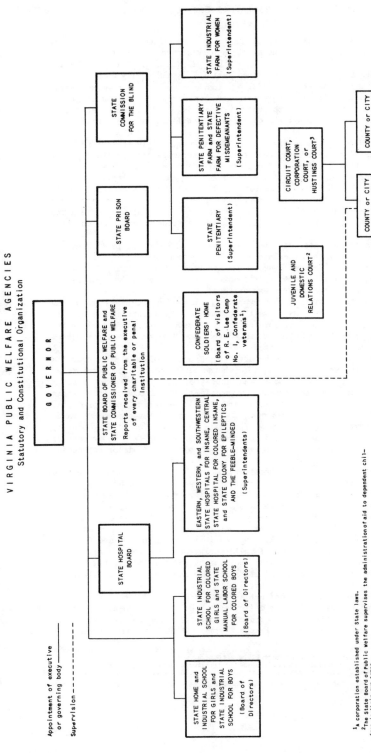

VIRGINIA PUBLIC WELFARE AGENCIES
Statutory and Constitutional Organization

Appointment of executive
or governing body ─────────
Supervision ─ ─ ─ ─ ─ ─ ─ ─

GOVERNOR

STATE HOSPITAL BOARD

STATE BOARD OF PUBLIC WELFARE and STATE COMMISSIONER OF PUBLIC WELFARE
Reports received from the executive of every charitable or penal institution

STATE PRISON BOARD

STATE COMMISSION FOR THE BLIND

STATE HOME and INDUSTRIAL SCHOOL FOR GIRLS and STATE INDUSTRIAL SCHOOL FOR COLORED BOYS
(Board of Directors)

STATE INDUSTRIAL SCHOOL FOR COLORED GIRLS and STATE MANUAL LABOR SCHOOL FOR COLORED BOYS
(Board of Directors)

EASTERN, WESTERN, and SOUTHWESTERN STATE HOSPITALS FOR INSANE, CENTRAL STATE HOSPITAL FOR COLORED INSANE, and STATE COLONY FOR EPILEPTICS AND THE FEEBLE-MINDED
(Superintendents)

CONFEDERATE SOLDIERS' HOME
(Board of visitors of R. E. Lee Camp No. 1, Confederate veterans[1])

STATE PENITENTIARY
(Superintendent)

STATE PENITENTIARY FARM and STATE FARM FOR DEFECTIVE MISDEMEANANTS
(Superintendent)

STATE INDUSTRIAL FARM FOR WOMEN
(Superintendent)

JUVENILE AND DOMESTIC RELATIONS COURT[2]

CIRCUIT COURT, CORPORATION COURT, or HUSTINGS COURT[3]

COUNTY or CITY BOARD OF PUBLIC WELFARE[4]
(Superintendent)

COUNTY or CITY BOARD OF PENSION COMMISSIONERS

[1] A corporation established under State laws.

[2] The State Board of Public Welfare supervises the administration of aid to dependent children in their own homes.

[3] Administers direct relief to veterans and assists in the administration of veterans' pensions.

[4] In cities of the first class the officer in charge of the division or department of public welfare constitutes the local board of public welfare. In each second class city the local board is composed of 3 members appointed by the judge of the corporation court, or in the absence of such court by the judge of the circuit court having jurisdiction within the city. In counties the board is composed of 3 members appointed by the judge of the circuit court. At the discretion of the appointing judge, 1 member of the local board may be a member of the county board of supervisors or a member of the city council or other governing body. In a county which has adopted a county executive, county manager, or executive manager form of government, the members of the board of public welfare are appointed by the board of county supervisors. However, in counties operating under the county manager form of government such boards may be appointed by the county manager, board of county supervisors, or other governing body.

SUMMARY OF STATUTORY PROVISIONS FOR PUBLIC WELFARE
WASHINGTON

Relief and Public Assistance.—General relief is administered by the county administrator of public assistance under the supervision of the State Department of Social Security acting through the division of public assistance. Old age assistance is administered by the State Department of Social Security acting through the division of old age assistance assisted by the boards of county commissioners. Aid to dependent children in their own homes and blind assistance are administered by the boards of county commissioners under the supervision of the State Department of Social Security acting through the division for children and the division for the blind, respectively.[1]

Cases involving dependent and neglected children come within the jurisdiction of juvenile courts. The State Department of Social Security through the division for children must supervise all child welfare services; pass upon the suitability of proposed child-caring agencies and institutions; inspect, supervise, and provide rules and regulations for the operation of all child-caring agencies. County boards of commissioners must administer child welfare services in their respective counties and act as agents of the State in this regard. They must, in cooperation with the State Department of Social Security, appoint advisory committees on child welfare.

Care of veterans in the State Veterans' Home and in the State Soldiers' Home and Colony is administered by the superintendent of the home under the supervision of the State Department of Finance, Budget, and Business. County funds for direct relief to veterans are administered by the commander of the military post representing the war in which the veteran was engaged.

Juvenile Delinquents.—Juvenile courts have jurisdiction in cases involving delinquent children. The court may commit a child to an institution, training or industrial school, to the care of some citizen or association, or may allow the child to remain at home.[2] The State Training School for Boys and the State School for Girls receive and care for delinquent children.

Services to the Blind.—The State Department of Social Security through its division for the blind and in cooperation with the division of vocational rehabilitation of the State Board of Vocational Education may provide aid to adult blind persons by finding them employment, instructing them in trades or occupations to be followed in their homes, and assisting them in marketing their products. It may provide training schools, workshops, materials and maintenance during training, home visitation, and home teaching. The State Department of Social Security through the division for the blind in cooperation with the State Department of Health must provide services for the prevention of blindness and for corrective treatment.

Insane and Mental Defectives.—The Northern, Eastern, and Western State Hospitals for Insane provide care and treatment for insane persons, and the State Narcotic Farm Colony cares for drug addicts committed by superior courts. Persons who are feeble-minded, idiotic, epileptic, or who are so physically defective as to prevent their education in common schools are admitted to the State Custodial School; persons who are so mentally defective as to be unfit for such education are admitted to the Western State Custodial School. Applications for admission are filed by parents or guardians, superintendents of child-caring institutions, county school superintendents, boards of county commissioners, or by juvenile courts under orders of commitment. The Institutional Board of Health may authorize the sterilization of inmates of these institutions.

Adult Delinquents.—The State Penitentiary and the State Reformatory provide for confinement and training of adult delinquents. Delinquent women are sent to the penitentiary. The Institutional Board of Health may authorize the sterilization of inmates. The State Board of Prison, Terms and Paroles determines the

---

[1] The State Department of Social Security, acting through its several divisions, is authorized to cooperate with the Federal Government in welfare matters of mutual concern. The department, through the division of unemployment compensation and the division of employment service is charged with the administration of unemployment compensation and of the State employment service.

[2] See discussion of care of dependent and neglected children, above, for powers of the State Department of Social Security in relation to children.

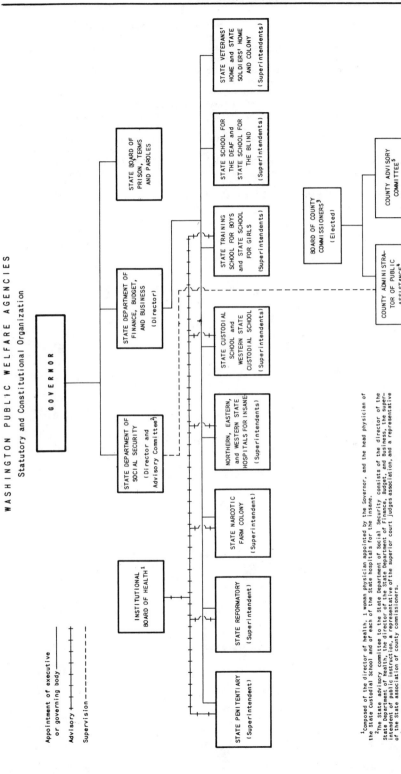

WASHINGTON PUBLIC WELFARE AGENCIES
Statutory and Constitutional Organization

GOVERNOR

Appointment of executive
or governing body ─────────
Advisory ──┼──┼──┼──
Supervision ──────────

INSTITUTIONAL
BOARD OF HEALTH[1]

STATE DEPARTMENT OF
SOCIAL SECURITY
(Director and
Advisory Committee[2])

STATE DEPARTMENT OF
FINANCE, BUDGET,
AND BUSINESS
(Director)

STATE BOARD OF
PRISON, TERMS
AND PAROLES

STATE PENITENTIARY
(Superintendent)

STATE REFORMATORY
(Superintendent)

STATE NARCOTIC
FARM COLONY
(Superintendent)

NORTHERN, EASTERN,
and WESTERN STATE
HOSPITALS FOR INSANE
(Superintendents)

STATE CUSTODIAL
SCHOOL and
WESTERN STATE
CUSTODIAL SCHOOL
(Superintendents)

STATE TRAINING
SCHOOL FOR BOYS
and STATE SCHOOL
FOR GIRLS
(Superintendents)

STATE SCHOOL FOR
THE DEAF and
STATE SCHOOL FOR
THE BLIND
(Superintendents)

STATE VETERANS'
HOME and STATE
SOLDIERS' HOME
AND COLONY
(Superintendents)

BOARD OF COUNTY
COMMISSIONERS[3]
(Elected)

COUNTY ADMINISTRA-
TOR OF PUBLIC
ASSISTANCE[4]

COUNTY ADVISORY
COMMITTEE[5]

[1]Composed of the director of health, 1 woman physician appointed by the Governor, and the head physician of
the State Custodial School and of each of the State hospitals for the insane.

[2]The State advisory committee to the State Department of Social Security consists of the director of the
State Department of Social Security, the director of the State Department of Finance, Budget, and Business, the superintendent of public instruction, a representative of the superior court judges association, and a representative
of the State association of county commissioners.

[3]The responsibility for the administration of aid to dependent children and blind assistance is placed upon
the board of county commissioners under the supervision of the State Department of Social Security.

[4]The administrator must be certified as eligible by the State Department of Social Security.

[5]The committee is appointed by the board of county commissioners in cooperation with the State Department of
Social Security.

length of sentence of each convicted person within the maximum penalty provided by law or fixed by the court, grants reductions of terms and paroles, supervises persons paroled or under suspended sentences or conditional pardons, and makes recommendations to the Governor for pardons.

Crippled Children.—The State Department of Social Security, through its division for children, may administer a program of services for crippled children or children suffering from conditions which lead to crippling. The program includes services for locating such children, medical, surgical, and corrective services, and facilities for diagnosis, hospitalization, and aftercare. It may supervise the administration of those services which are not administered directly by it, and cooperate with medical, health, and welfare groups and any agency administering provisions for vocational rehabilitation of physically handicapped children.

Deaf, Dumb, and Blind.—The State School for the Deaf and the State School for the Blind provide education for deaf, mute, and blind persons. The county school superintendent must report names of such persons to the board of county commissioners, director of the State Department of Finance, Budget, and Business, and the superintendents of the two schools.

SUMMARY OF STATUTORY PROVISIONS FOR PUBLIC WELFARE
WEST VIRGINIA

Relief and Public Assistance.—General relief is administered by county public assistance councils under the supervision of the State Department of Public Assistance. The management and operation of county infirmaries or institutions providing relief is vested in the respective county courts. Such management and operation may, by written consent, be transferred to the county public assistance councils. Old age assistance,[1] aid to dependent children in their own homes, and blind assistance are administered by the State Department of Public Assistance[2] assisted by county public assistance councils.

Cases involving dependent and neglected children come within the jurisdiction of juvenile courts. The State Department of Public Assistance receives children committed by the courts, and supervises children's institutions and organizations receiving children for the purpose of care, training, or placing them in other institutions or in private homes. State child-caring institutions, which include the State Children's Home and the State Colored Children's Home, are supervised by the State Board of Control. County public assistance councils must cooperate with the State Department of Public Assistance and private and charitable organizations in the county. County courts may establish and maintain county detention homes.

Juvenile Delinquents.—Juvenile courts have jurisdiction in cases involving delinquent children. The court may order a child placed under the supervision of a probation officer, permit proceedings to be undertaken against the child in accordance with the laws of the State governing the commission of crimes or violation of municipal ordinances, or commit the child to an industrial or correctional institution. Such institutions include the State Industrial School for Boys, the State Industrial School for Colored Boys, the State Industrial Home for Girls, and the State Industrial Home for Colored Girls. Children are paroled from these institutions to the State Department of Public Assistance.[3]

Insane and Mental Defectives.—The Weston, Spencer, and Huntington State Hospitals (for white persons), and the Lakin State Hospital (for colored persons) provide care and treatment for insane persons committed by county mental hygiene commissions. Voluntary patients are admitted to these institutions upon application to the State Board of Control. The State Training School cares for feeble-minded persons committed by county mental hygiene commissions.[4] The State Board of Control licenses and investigates private hospitals caring for the insane or mental defectives, and may require the State Department of Public Assistance to investigate children who are mentally defective. The State Board of Education makes rules relating to the education of the feeble-minded.

Adult Delinquents.—The State Penitentiary provides for confinement and training of adult delinquents. The Governor is authorized to issue paroles.

Crippled Children.—The State Department of Public Assistance, with the cooperation of county public assistance councils, must locate crippled children requiring treatment and administer the program for care, treatment, education, hospitalization, and aftercare. The Welch, McKendree, and Fairmont Emergency Hospitals receive deformed, crippled, or otherwise defective children for surgical or orthopedic treatment.[5] The State Department of Education makes rules relating to the education of physically disabled or crippled children of school age.

Physical Rehabilitation.—The State Department of Public Assistance must administer the adult physical rehabilitation program and provide surgical and medical treatment, and hospitalization. It must supervise the treatment of physically

---

[1] The State Home for Aged and Infirm Colored Men and Women receives colored persons who are aged and infirm, without means of support.

[2] The State Department of Public Assistance must cooperate with the Federal Government in public welfare matters of mutual concern.

[3] See discussion of care of dependent and neglected children, above, for powers of the State Department of Public Assistance and county public assistance councils in relation to children.

[4] The county mental hygiene commission consists of the president of the county court, the prosecuting attorney, and the clerk of the court.

[5] The hospitals also admit other persons in need of hospitalization, giving preference to persons accidentally injured in the State.

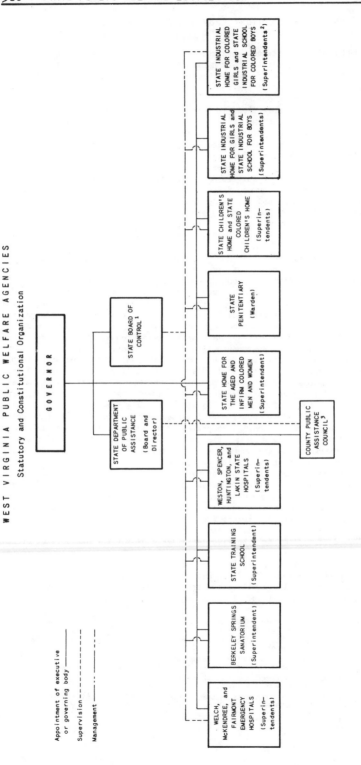

WEST VIRGINIA PUBLIC WELFARE AGENCIES
Statutory and Constitutional Organization

[1] In addition to the management of the institutions shown, the State Board of Control has control of the business and fiscal affairs of the Hopemont, Pinecrest, and Denmar Sanatoria for tuberculars, of the State Schools for the (white) Deaf and Blind, and of the State School for the Colored Deaf and Blind.

[2] The State and Negro Boards of Education, sitting as 1 body, supervise and control the educational affairs of these institutions.

[3] Appointed by the Governor from a list submitted by the State Department of Public Assistance.

handicapped persons and cooperate with governmental, public, and private institutions and agencies engaged in activities related to or connected with the physical rehabilitation of adults.

Note.—The Berkeley Springs Sanatorium provides treatment to persons suffering from diseases benefited by the spring water.

The director of the State Bureau of Negro Welfare and Statistics must study economic and social conditions of the Negroes of the State, promote the welfare of the race, and encourage harmonious relations between the white and Negro races.

SUMMARY OF STATUTORY PROVISIONS FOR PUBLIC WELFARE
WISCONSIN

Relief and Public Assistance.—Every town, village, and city is charged with the relief and support of all poor and indigent persons having settlement therein. Counties are responsible for those not having settlement in a town, village, or city. The county board of supervisors may abolish the distinction between town, village, city, and county poor, in which case the county must relieve and support all poor and indigent persons. The board of supervisors may also return the support of such persons to the towns, villages, and cities. In counties having established a county home or hospital, the following provisions apply: if the population is less than 250,000, the county board of trustees has charge of all indoor and outdoor relief, or the county board of supervisors may employ some competent person to have charge of outdoor relief; if the population is 250,000 or more, the manager of county institutions has charge of all relief. In counties which have not established a county home or hospital, county boards of trustees have charge of all relief, or the county boards of supervisors may otherwise provide for the support and maintenance of the poor. State relief funds are administered in accordance with rules and regulations adopted by the Industrial Commission or other agency designated by the Governor to administer relief, except that standards of eligibility must be determined by individual local units.[1] The State Board of Control has supervision over all county and municipal institutions.

In counties of 500,000 or more the county board of supervisors may establish county departments of public welfare, and in counties of less than 500,000 the county board of supervisors may establish county pension departments. These departments administer old age assistance, blind assistance, and aid to dependent children in their own homes. Where such agencies are not in existence, the following provisions apply: the county court administers old age assistance and acting as a juvenile court administers aid to dependent children; the county board of supervisors administers blind assistance subject to an appeal by applicant to the county court in case of denial of aid. The pension department of the Industrial Commission supervises the administration of old age assistance, aid to dependent children in their own homes, and blind assistance.[2]

County courts acting as juvenile courts have jurisdiction in cases involving dependent and neglected children. The State Board of Control acting through its juvenile department must promote the enforcement of all laws for the protection of defective, illegitimate, dependent, or delinquent children, exclusive of the administration of laws vested in some other State agency. The board must cooperate with all public and private agencies and institutions and is empowered to license child-caring agencies and institutions. The board must supervise all local institutions, all child welfare agencies, and the placement of children in foster homes. The county boards of supervisors may establish agencies necessary for the protection of dependent, neglected, and defective children. They must make provision for the temporary detention of children in detention homes. Care of children in the State Public School is administered by the State Board of Control. County boards of visitation must investigate child welfare agencies and report concerning them to the county courts and the State Board of Control.

Temporary aid to veterans is furnished by village trustees, town boards, or common councils, or by the county board of trustees if the veteran has no legal residence in the town, city, or village within the respective county. Direct relief to veterans is administered by the county soldiers' relief commission. Care of veterans in the Grand Army Home for Veterans is administered by the adjutant general in conjunction with the board of managers of the home.[3] The Soldiers'

---

[1]The public welfare department of the Industrial Commission is empowered to cooperate with the Federal Government in relation to grants to the State of Federal funds and commodities for relief purposes, and in connection with the various employment and rehabilitation programs conducted by the Federal Government.

[2]The pension department of the Industrial Commission is directed to cooperate with the Federal Government in order that the State may obtain Federal grants for old age assistance, aid to dependent children, and blind assistance.

[3]*Need* is not specified as a condition of eligibility for admission to the Grand Army Home for Veterans.

WISCONSIN PUBLIC WELFARE AGENCIES

Statutory and Constitutional Organization

Appointment of executive
or governing body ——————
Supervision — — — — — —

GOVERNOR

SOLDIERS' REHABILITATION BOARD[1]

STATE BOARD OF CONTROL

STATE DEPARTMENT OF CORRECTIONS
Board and Director

STATE DEPARTMENT OF MENTAL HYGIENE
Board and Director

INDUSTRIAL COMMISSION
PUBLIC WELFARE DEPARTMENT[2] | PENSION DEPARTMENT[3]

GRAND ARMY HOME FOR VETERANS[4]
(Board of Managers)

STATE PUBLIC SCHOOL[5]
(Superintendent)

STATE SCHOOL FOR THE DEAF
(Superintendent)

STATE SCHOOL FOR THE BLIND
(Superintendent)

STATE TUBERCULOSIS SANATORIUM, NORTHERN STATE TUBERCULOSIS SANATORIUM, and STATE TUBERCULOSIS CAMP
(Superintendents)

STATE WORKSHOP FOR THE BLIND[7]

STATE FIELD AGENCY FOR ADULT BLIND[7]

STATE INDUSTRIAL SCHOOL FOR BOYS and STATE INDUSTRIAL SCHOOL FOR GIRLS
(Superintendents)

CENTRAL STATE HOSPITAL FOR INSANE
(Superintendent)

STATE PRISON
(Warden)

STATE REFORMATORY and STATE INDUSTRIAL HOME FOR WOMEN
(Superintendents)

NORTHERN STATE COLONY AND TRAINING SCHOOL and SOUTHERN STATE COLONY AND TRAINING SCHOOL
(Superintendents)

MENDOTA and WINNEBAGO HOSPITALS FOR THE INSANE[6]
(Superintendents)

COUNTY SOLDIERS' RELIEF COMMISSION[9]
Reports to the County Board of Supervisors

BOARD OF TRUSTEES OF COUNTY INSTITUTIONS[10]

COUNTY SUPERINTENDENT OF OUTDOOR RELIEF[11]

COUNTY DEPARTMENT OF PUBLIC WELFARE[12]

COUNTY PENSION DEPARTMENT[13]

COUNTY BOARD OF VISITATION[14]

TOWN BOARDS, VILLAGE TRUSTEES, and CITY COMMON COUNCILS[8]

[1] Composed of the secretary of the State Board of Health, the director of the Wisconsin Psychiatric Institute, the adjutant general, the State commander of the American Legion, the State commander of the Disabled American Veterans of the World War, the State commander of Foreign Wars, and a member of the medical department of the University of Wisconsin appointed by the Governor.

[2] Created within the Industrial Commission by executive order.

[3] Created within the Industrial Commission by statute. Consists of a member of the Industrial Commission selected by the commission, the director of the budget, and the supervisor of pensions who as the administrator of the department is selected by the Industrial Commission in accordance with civil service laws.

[4] Composed of the adjutant general, the State surgeon, the chief quartermaster, the departmental commander of the G.A.R., and 4 members appointed by the Governor. The adjutant general, with the approval of the board of managers in matters of general policy, operates the home.

[5] The State Department of Public Instruction inspects the educational work of the school and assists the State Board of Control in developing physical, vocational, and moral training of children.

[6] The State Psychiatric Institute is also established by the board of regents of the State university as part of the university.

[7] Established by the State Board of Control.

[8] May administer general relief.

[9] Appointed by the county judge.

[10] In counties of less than 250,000 population the county board of supervisors appoints a board of trustees for each county institution; in counties of 250,000 or more the county board of supervisors appoints 1 board of trustees of county institutions, with 1 manager in charge of the superintendents of the individual institutions and of the department of outdoor relief.

[11] Appointment by county board of supervisors is optional.

[12] May be established by the county board of supervisors in counties of 500,000 or more.

[13] May be established by the county board of supervisors in counties of less than 500,000.

[14] Appointment by the juvenile court is optional.

Rehabilitation Board provides for the treatment and hospitalization of physically incapacitated veterans.

Juvenile Delinquents.—County courts acting as juvenile courts have jurisdiction in cases involving delinquent children. The State Industrial School for Boys and the State Industrial School for Girls receive delinquent children. The State Board of Control may transfer children from other institutions to the State Public School.[4]

Services to the Blind.—The State Workshop for the Blind provides materials and tools for employment and instruction of adult blind. The State Field Agency for Adult Blind must maintain a register of the blind in the State describing causes of blindness, and conditions and capacity for training of each blind person; visit the blind in their homes and provide home instruction; cooperate with the State Board of Health for prevention of blindness; establish an employment agency for the blind, industrial schools and workshops for training and employment of the blind, and a trade bureau for supplying raw materials at cost to the blind; and devise means for the sale and distribution of their products.

Insane and Mental Defectives.—The Mendota and Winnebago State Hospitals for the Insane and the State Psychiatric Institute provide care and treatment for insane persons committed by county and district courts. The Central State Hospital for the Insane is for criminally insane persons. The State Department of Mental Hygiene may sit as a commission in lunacy to determine the sanity of any person committed to any hospital or asylum for the insane. The State department must inspect all institutions in the State where insane persons are confined and has control of transfers between institutions and the State Psychiatric Institute. It must also make provision for care of drug addicts. The Northern State Colony and Training School and the Southern State Colony and Training School care for and train mentally deficient and epileptic persons committed by county and district courts. The State Department of Mental Hygiene has charge of sterilizations. The State department promotes the enforcement of all laws for the protection of mentally defective children.

Adult Delinquents.—The State Prison, State Reformatory, and State Industrial Home for Women provide for confinement and training of adult delinquents. The State Department of Corrections supervises all county and municipal penal institutions and has charge of sterilizations. The State department, with approval of the Governor, may parole prisoners of the State Prison or House of Correction in Milwaukee County. The Governor has power to grant reprieves, pardons, and commutations for all offenses except treason (he may suspend execution of sentence after conviction) and cases of impeachment.

Crippled Children.—Juvenile courts may commit crippled children to the State Public School, and the State Board of Control may transfer such children to some other appropriate hospital. County courts may commit such children to the State Orthopedic Hospital for Children.

Deaf, Dumb, and Blind.—The State School for the Blind and the State School for the Deaf provide education for deaf and blind children, respectively.

Tuberculars.—The State Tuberculosis Sanatorium, the Northern State Tuberculosis Sanatorium, and the State Tuberculosis Camp care for tuberculous persons admitted under regulations of the State Board of Control.

---

[4]See discussion of care of dependent and neglected children, above, for powers and duties of various agencies relating to delinquent children.

SUMMARY OF STATUTORY PROVISIONS FOR PUBLIC WELFARE
WYOMING

Relief and Public Assistance.—General relief is administered by county departments of public welfare under the supervision of the State Department of Public Welfare. Old age assistance, aid to dependent children in their own homes, and blind assistance are administered by the State Department of Public Welfare assisted by county departments of public welfare.[1]

Cases involving dependent and neglected children come within the jurisdiction of district courts. County departments of public welfare, under the supervision of the State Department of Public Welfare, provide care for needy children in private families when they cannot be cared for in their own homes and render such assistance as is needed. The State Board of Charities and Reform[2] has supervision and control of the State Children's Home which provides care for dependent and neglected children. The State board also has jurisdiction over all orphan and dependent children not otherwise provided for and must make application to the district court for appointment as guardian of a child coming under its control. All public and private child-caring agencies or institutions in the State must report annually to the State Board of Charities and Reform.

Care of veterans is provided in the State Soldiers' and Sailors' Home. Applications for admission are made to the State Board of Charities and Reform.

Juvenile Delinquents.—District courts have jurisdiction in cases involving delinquent children. The court may commit a child to a child-caring agency or institution in the State, or, under arrangements made by the State Board of Charities and Reform, to a house of refuge or industrial school of any State. The State Board of Charities and Reform has jurisdiction over all delinquent girls not otherwise provided for. Delinquent girls may be committed to the Girls' School and any juvenile delinquent may be committed to the Industrial Institute.

Services to the Blind.—The field agent of the State Board of Education must maintain personal contact with blind adults and children, provide instruction in reading and trades, and arrange for purchase of books, tools, and other equipment necessary for instruction to enable such persons to become useful citizens.[3] The State Department of Public Welfare must initiate, or cooperate with other agencies in developing, measures for prevention of blindness, restoration of eyesight, and vocational adjustment of blind persons.

Insane and Mental Defectives.—The State Hospital provides care and treatment for insane persons committed by district courts. Unless relatives demand a jury, the county lunacy commission (appointed by the court) sits in lieu of a jury. The State Training School provides care and treatment for feeble-minded or epileptic persons who are committed by district courts; minors may be admitted upon the voluntary application of parent or guardian and the payment of maintenance.

Adult Delinquents.—The State Penitentiary provides for confinement and training of adult delinquents. The State Commission on Prison Labor directs prison industries and training of prisoners. The State Board of Pardons must investigate applications for clemency and make recommendations to the Governor.

Education of the Deaf, Dumb, and Blind.—The State Board of Education has general supervision of the deaf and blind and must provide for their education (see paragraph "Services to the Blind"). The State Board of Charities and Reform has jurisdiction over all deaf, dumb, and blind persons not otherwise provided for.

Tuberculars.—The State Tuberculosis Sanatorium provides for the segregation, assistance, medical care, and surgical treatment of all citizens of the State who become afflicted with tuberculosis.

---

[1] The State Department of Public Welfare must cooperate with and act as the agent of the Federal Government in public welfare matters of mutual concern.

[2] The State Board of Charities and Reform has control of the General Hospital, Hot Springs State Park, and Saratoga Hot Springs, although primarily they have health rather than welfare functions.

[3] The field agent must also perform these services for deaf and dumb persons.

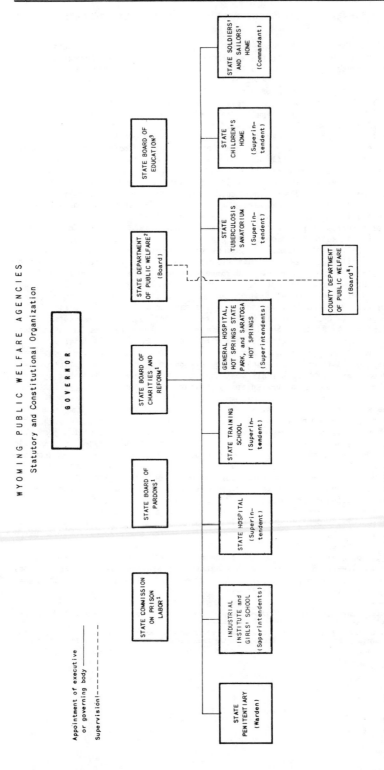

WYOMING PUBLIC WELFARE AGENCIES
Statutory and Constitutional Organization

GOVERNOR

Appointment of executive
or governing body ————————
Supervision ———————————

STATE COMMISSION ON PRISON LABOR[1]

STATE BOARD OF PARDONS[1]

STATE BOARD OF CHARITIES AND REFORM[1]

STATE DEPARTMENT OF PUBLIC WELFARE[2]
(Board)

STATE BOARD OF EDUCATION[3]

STATE PENITENTIARY
(Warden)

INDUSTRIAL INSTITUTE and GIRLS' SCHOOL
(Superintendents)

STATE HOSPITAL
(Superintendent)

STATE TRAINING SCHOOL
(Superintendent)

GENERAL HOSPITAL, HOT SPRINGS STATE PARK, and SARATOGA HOT SPRINGS
(Superintendents)

STATE TUBERCULOSIS SANATORIUM
(Superintendent)

STATE CHILDREN'S HOME
(Superintendent)

STATE SOLDIERS' AND SAILORS' HOME
(Commandant)

COUNTY DEPARTMENT OF PUBLIC WELFARE
(Board[4])

[1] Composed of the Governor, the secretary of state, the State auditor, the State treasurer, and the State superintendent of public instruction. The State Commission on Prison Labor also includes the warden of the State Penitentiary.

[2] Composed of the Governor, the secretary of state, the State auditor, the State treasurer, and the State superintendent of public instruction.

[3] Appointed by the State superintendent of public instruction, with the approval of the Governor; the superintendent is an ex officio member.

[4] Composed of 5 members: the superintendent of schools of the largest city or town in the county, 2 members appointed by the board of county commissioners, 1 appointed by the district judge of the district in which the county is located, and 1 appointed by the State Department of Public Welfare.

SUMMARY OF STATUTORY PROVISIONS FOR PUBLIC WELFARE
ALASKA

Relief and Public Assistance.—General relief is administered by the Territorial Department of Public Welfare, and care in the Pioneers' Home is administered by the board of trustees of the home. Old age assistance and aid to dependent children in their own homes are administered by the Territorial Department of Public Welfare.[1]

Cases involving dependent and neglected children come within the jurisdiction of the United States Commissioners. The Territorial Department of Public Welfare has jurisdiction of juveniles in the Territory, and it may provide for the keeping of records of all juveniles and for the payment of bills in connection with their care or commitment. The boards of children's guardians act as the legal guardians of children committed to their control. The boards may commit such children to the care and custody of some person, association, or institution, and may pay for their care and maintenance. They may also bind out or apprentice children or give them in adoption. All persons, institutions, or associations caring for children are subject to the visitation, inspection, and supervision of the boards which must furnish the department with copies of all commitments made and report to the department semiannually concerning their operations.

Juvenile Delinquents.—The United States Commissioners exercise jurisdiction over cases involving delinquent children. They may commit such children to a reform school, an orphan asylum, a charitable institution, or to the board of children's guardians in the judicial district.[2]

Insane and Mental Defectives.—The United States Commissioners, serving ex officio as probate judges, may adjudge persons to be insane and commit them to an asylum or sanitarium.[3]

Adult Delinquents.—Adult delinquents are confined in city jails and in Federal jails in the Territory. However, persons committed for long terms are sent to Federal penitentiaries located in the various States.

---

[1]The Territorial Department of Public Welfare is vested with the entire superintendence of needy persons. It must cooperate with the Federal Government in matters of mutual concern pertaining to old age assistance, aid to dependent children, blind assistance, and other forms of public assistance. It must also cooperate with the Federal Government in establishing, extending, and strengthening services for the protection and care of homeless, dependent, and neglected children, and children in danger of becoming delinquent.

[2]See discussion of care of dependent and neglected children, above, for powers of the boards of children's guardians and the Territorial Department of Public Welfare in relation to delinquent children.

[3]There are no asylums in the Territory. Insane persons are committed to the Sanitarium Company, Portland, Oreg.

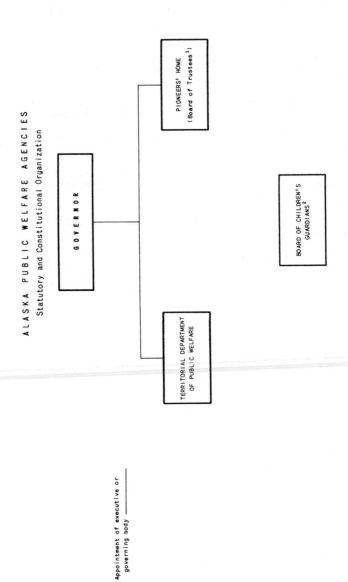

ALASKA PUBLIC WELFARE AGENCIES
Statutory and Constitutional Organization

GOVERNOR

TERRITORIAL DEPARTMENT OF PUBLIC WELFARE

PIONEERS' HOME (Board of Trustees[1])

BOARD OF CHILDREN'S GUARDIANS[2]

Appointment of executive or governing body ⎯⎯⎯

[1] The Governor is an ex officio member.
[2] Established in each judicial district and composed of the district judge, the United States Marshal, and 1 woman appointed by the Territorial Department of Public Welfare.

SUMMARY OF STATUTORY PROVISIONS FOR PUBLIC WELFARE
DISTRICT OF COLUMBIA

Relief and Public Assistance.—General relief, including care in the Municipal Lodging House and Home for the Aged and Infirm, and aid to dependent children in their own homes are administered by the Board of Public Welfare. Old age assistance and blind assistance are administered by the Commissioners of the District of Columbia, through such agent or agency as they may designate.[1] The Commissioners have designated the Board of Public Welfare to administer these programs.

Cases involving dependent and neglected children come within the jurisdiction of the juvenile court. The court may commit a child to the care of the Board of Public Welfare, to the National Training School for Boys, or to the National Training School for Girls. The Board of Public Welfare must exercise legal guardianship, care, and supervision over all dependent, neglected, or delinquent children committed to it by the juvenile court. The board may bind out or apprentice any such children, make provision for their care and treatment in private homes or in public or private institutions, or give them in adoption to foster parents. The board may place white boys and girls in the Industrial Home School and colored boys in the Industrial Home School for Colored Children. The Commissioners of the District of Columbia must aid the Washington Humane Society in the enforcement of all laws relating to or affecting the protection of children.

Juvenile Delinquents.—The juvenile court has jurisdiction in cases involving delinquent children, and it may defer sentence and parole the child to the care of a probation officer, subject to further proceedings. The court may also commit delinquent children to the Board of Public Welfare, the National Training School for Girls, or the National Training School for Boys.[2]

Services to the Blind.—Aid and services to the blind are administered by the Board of Public Welfare.

Insane and Mental Defectives.—St. Elizabeth's Hospital receives persons legally adjudged insane by the District Court of the United States for the District of Columbia. The Commissioners of the District of Columbia may place persons in the hospital for a period not exceeding 30 days pending adjudication or pending return to their place of residence. Admission is also possible by voluntary agreement. The District Training School receives feeble-minded persons under 45 years of age committed by the District Court. Commitments of children to these institutions are made by the juvenile court in cooperation with the children's bureau of the Board of Public Welfare. Gallinger Municipal Hospital—psychopathic division—receives for observation persons alleged to be insane or feeble-minded.

Adult Delinquents.—The Reformatory, Workhouse, and Washington Asylum and Jail provide for confinement and training of adult delinquents. The Board of Indeterminate Sentence and Parole may authorize the release of a prisoner on parole upon such terms and conditions as it may prescribe.

Tuberculars.—The Tuberculosis Hospital provides care and treatment for adult tuberculars, and the Children's Tuberculosis Sanatorium provides care and treatment for tuberculous children.

---

[1] The board of commissioners, or their designated agencies, are authorized and directed to cooperate with the Social Security Board of the United States Government.

[2] See discussion of care of dependent and neglected children, above. The Board of Public Welfare has the same powers in relation to delinquent children as in relation to dependent and neglected children.

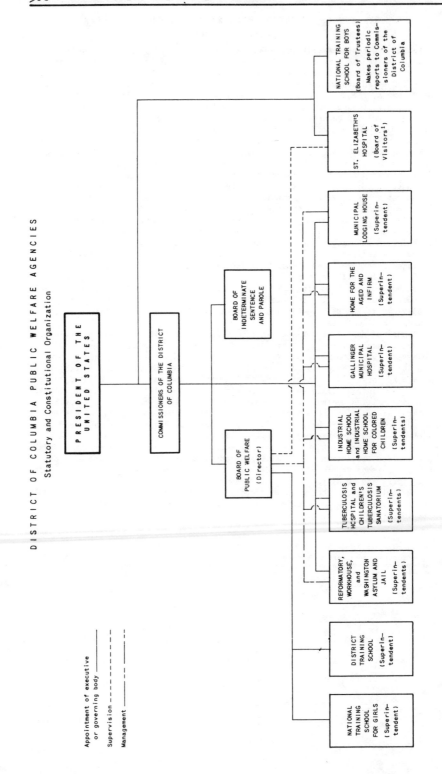

DISTRICT OF COLUMBIA PUBLIC WELFARE AGENCIES
Statutory and Constitutional Organization

Appointment of executive
or governing body ————
Supervision ———— — — — —
Management ———— — — —

PRESIDENT OF THE
UNITED STATES

COMMISSIONERS OF THE DISTRICT
OF COLUMBIA

BOARD OF
PUBLIC WELFARE
(Director)

BOARD OF
INDETERMINATE
SENTENCE
AND PAROLE

NATIONAL TRAINING
SCHOOL
FOR GIRLS
(Superin-
tendent)

DISTRICT
TRAINING
SCHOOL
(Superin-
tendent)

REFORMATORY,
WORKHOUSE,
and
WASHINGTON
ASYLUM AND
JAIL
(Superin-
tendents)

TUBERCULOSIS
HOSPITAL and
CHILDREN'S
TUBERCULOSIS
SANATORIUM
(Superin-
tendents)

INDUSTRIAL
HOME SCHOOL
and INDUSTRIAL
HOME SCHOOL
FOR COLORED
CHILDREN
(Superin-
tendents)

GALLINGER
MUNICIPAL
HOSPITAL
(Superin-
tendent)

HOME FOR THE
AGED AND
INFIRM
(Superin-
tendent)

MUNICIPAL
LODGING HOUSE
(Superin-
tendent)

ST. ELIZABETH'S
HOSPITAL
(Board of
Visitors[1])

NATIONAL TRAINING
SCHOOL FOR BOYS
(Board of Trustees)
Makes periodic
reports to Commis-
sioners of the
District of
Columbia

[1]The superintendent is appointed by the Secretary of the Interior.

SUMMARY OF STATUTORY PROVISIONS FOR PUBLIC WELFARE
HAWAII

Relief and Public Assistance.—General relief, old age and blind assistance, and aid to dependent children in their own homes are administered by the county public welfare commissions under the supervision of the Territorial Board of Public Welfare.[1]

Cases involving dependent and neglected children come within the jurisdiction of juvenile courts. The Territorial Board of Public Welfare must administer child welfare activities and must cooperate with public or private authorities in placing children in institutions or homes. It must set standards for organizations or institutions caring for children. The county public welfare commissions, under the supervision of the Territorial Board of Public Welfare, must cooperate with the board in carrying out the child welfare program.

Juvenile Delinquents.—The juvenile courts have jurisdiction of cases involving delinquent children. They may place such children on probation in the care and custody of a probation officer or such other person as the judge may designate, or commit them to some industrial and reformatory school. Children subversive to the order and discipline of such institutions may be sentenced by the court to imprisonment in some public jail. The judge may, when the health of the child requires, place it in a public hospital or institution for treatment. The Waialee Training School for Boys and the Kawailoa Training School for Girls receive delinquent children committed by the courts or by voluntary agreement with their parents or guardians.[2]

Services to the Blind.—The Territorial Board of Public Welfare must maintain a register of the blind, describing the conditions, causes of blindness, capacity for education, and industrial training of blind persons with recommendations for rehabilitation and relief. The board must maintain one or more agencies for employment information and industrial aid in order to assist the blind in finding employment and to provide instruction in trades and occupations which may be followed at home. It must also assist the sale of products of home industries. The board may aid individual blind persons to become self-supporting by furnishing materials, machinery, and other facilities. It must investigate the causes of blindness and cooperate with other agencies in developing measures for the prevention of blindness and the restoration of eyesight.

Insane and Mental Defectives.—The district magistrates or circuit judges hear complaints alleging persons to be insane and may order such persons committed to a suitable hospital. Appeals on behalf of persons adjudged insane may be made to the commissioners of insanity who may parole or release such persons from hospitals. The Territorial Hospital for the Insane provides care and treatment for insane persons and persons suffering from mental diseases. The Waimano Home for the Feeble-minded provides care and treatment for feeble-minded persons committed by courts or admitted by voluntary agreement with their parents or guardians.

Adult Delinquents.—The Territorial Board of Prison Directors governs, controls, and supervises all territorial prisons and prison camps. The board must consider and advise the Governor upon all applications for pardons which he refers to it and may, with his approval, provide for the parole of prisoners. Local boards of prison inspectors supervise the government and discipline of county jails. They must consider and advise the Governor upon all applications for pardons referred to them, and they must perform all acts and duties required of them by the Territorial Board of Prison Directors.

---

[1] The Territorial Board of Public Welfare must cooperate with the Federal Government in carrying out the purposes of the Social Security Act.

[2] See discussion of care of dependent and neglected children, above, for powers and duties of the Territorial Board of Public Welfare of the county public welfare commissions in relation to children.

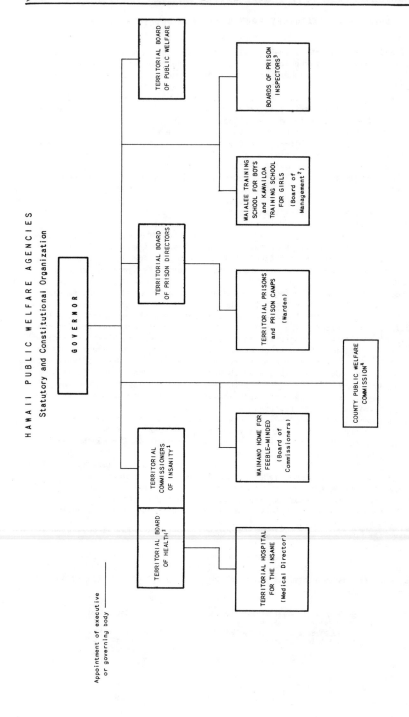

HAWAII PUBLIC WELFARE AGENCIES
Statutory and Constitutional Organization

GOVERNOR

TERRITORIAL BOARD OF HEALTH[1]

TERRITORIAL COMMISSIONERS OF INSANITY[1]

TERRITORIAL BOARD OF PRISON DIRECTORS

TERRITORIAL BOARD OF PUBLIC WELFARE

TERRITORIAL HOSPITAL FOR THE INSANE (Medical Director)

WAIMANO HOME FOR FEEBLE-MINDED (Board of Commissioners)

COUNTY PUBLIC WELFARE COMMISSION[4]

TERRITORIAL PRISONS and PRISON CAMPS (Warden)

WAIALEE TRAINING SCHOOL FOR BOYS and KAWAILOA TRAINING SCHOOL FOR GIRLS (Board of Management[2])

BOARDS OF PRISON INSPECTORS[3]

Appointment of executive or governing body ———

[1]Members of the Territorial Board of Health constitute the Territorial Commissioners of insanity. The attorney general is an ex officio member.

[2]The judge of the juvenile court of the first judicial circuit may act as a member ex officio.

[3]Appointed for each judicial circuit.

[4]The judges of the juvenile courts are ex officio members.